A Frequency Dictionary of Spanish

A Frequency Dictionary of Spanish is an invaluable tool for all learners of Spanish, providing a list of the 5,000 most frequently used words in the language. Based on a 20-million word corpus which is evenly divided between spoken, fiction and non-fiction texts from both Spain and Latin America, the dictionary provides the user with a detailed frequency-based list plus alphabetical and part of speech indexes.

All entries in the rank frequency list feature the English equivalent, a sample sentence plus an indication of major register variation. The dictionary also contains 30 thematically organized lists of frequently used words on a variety of topics.

A Frequency Dictionary of Spanish aims to enable students of all levels to maximize their study of Spanish vocabulary in an efficient and engaging way.

Mark Davies is Associate Professor at the Department of Linguistics, Brigham Young University at Provo in Utah.

Routledge Frequency Dictionaries

General Editors:
Anthony McEnery
Paul Rayson

Consultant Editors:
Michael Barlow
Asmah Haji Omar
Geoffrey Leech
Barbara Lewandowska-Tomaszczyk
Josef Schmied
Andrew Wilson

Other books in the series:

A Frequency Dictionary of German: Core vocabulary for learners
hbk 0–415–31632–4
pbk 0–415–31633–2

Coming soon:
A Frequency Dictionary of Polish

A Frequency Dictionary of Spanish

Core vocabulary for learners

Mark Davies

Routledge
Taylor & Francis Group

NEW YORK AND LONDON

First published 2006
by Routledge
270 Madison Ave, New York, NY 10016

Simultaneously published in the UK
by Routledge
2 Park Square, Milton Park, Abingdon, Oxon OX14 4RN

Routledge is an imprint of the Taylor & Francis Group

Typeset in Parisine by Keystroke, Jacaranda Lodge, Wolverhampton
Printed and bound in Great Britain by TJ International Ltd, Padstow, Cornwall

British Library Cataloguing-in-Publication Data
A catalogue record for this book is available from the British Library

Library of Congress Cataloging-in-Publication Data
Davies, Mark, 1963 Apr. 22 –
    A frequency dictionary of modern Spanish/Mark Davies.
       p. cm. — (Routledge frequency dictionaries)
    Includes bibliographical references and index.
    1. Spanish language—Word frequency—Dictionaries. I. Title. II. Series.
    PC4691.D38 2005
    463'.21—dc22

ISBN10: 0–415–33428–4 (hbk)
ISBN10: 0–415–33429–2 (pbk)
ISBN13: 9–78–0–415–33428–0 (hbk)
ISBN13: 9–78–0–415–33429–7 (pbk)

Contents

Thematic vocabulary lists

Series preface

There is a growing consensus that frequency information has a role to play in language learning. Data derived from corpora allows the frequency of individual words and phrases in a language to be determined. That information may then be incorporated into language learning. In this series, the frequency of words in large corpora is presented to learners to allow them to use frequency as a guide in their learning. In providing such a resource, we are both bringing students closer to real language (as opposed to textbook language, which often distorts the frequencies of features in a language, see Ljung 1990) and providing the possibility for students to use frequency as a guide for vocabulary learning. In addition we are providing information on differences between frequencies in spoken and written language as well as, from time to time, frequencies specific to certain genres.

Why should one do this? Nation (1990) has shown that the 4,000–5,000 most frequent words account for up to 95 percent of a written text and the 1,000 most frequent words account for 85 percent of speech. While Nation's results were for English, they do at least present the possibility that, by allowing frequency to be a general guide to vocabulary learning, one task facing learners – to acquire a lexicon which will serve them well on most occasions most of the time – could be achieved quite easily. While frequency alone may never act as the sole guide for a learner, it is nonetheless a very good guide, and one which may produce rapid results. In short, it seems rational to prioritize learning the words one is likely to hear and use most often. That is the philosophy behind this series of dictionaries.

The information in these dictionaries is presented in a number of formats to allow users to access the data in different ways. So, for example, if you would prefer not to simply drill down through the word frequency list, but would rather focus on verbs, the part of speech index will allow you to focus on just the most frequent verbs. Given that verbs typically account for 20 percent of all words in a language, this may be a good strategy. Also, a focus on function words may be equally rewarding – 60 percent of speech in English is composed of a mere 50 function words.

We also hope that the series provides information of use to the language teacher. The idea that frequency information may have a role to play in syllabus design is not new (see, for example, Sinclair and Renouf 1988). However, to date it has been difficult for those teaching languages other than English to use frequency information in syllabus design because of a lack of data. While English has long been well provided with such data, there has been a relative paucity of such material for other languages. This series aims to provide such information so that the benefits of the use of frequency information in syllabus design can be explored for languages other than English.

We are not claiming, of course, that frequency information should be used slavishly. It would be a pity if teachers and students failed to notice important generalizations across the lexis presented in these dictionaries. So, for example, where one pronoun is more frequent than another, it would be problematic if a student felt they had learned all pronouns when they had learned only the most frequent pronoun. Our response to such issues in this series is to provide indexes to the data from a number of perspectives. So, for example, a student working down the frequency list who encounters a pronoun can switch to the part of speech list to see what other pronouns there are in the dictionary and what their frequencies are. In short, by using the lists in combination a student or teacher should be able to focus on specific words and groups of words. Such a use of the data presented here is to be encouraged.

Tony McEnery and Paul Rayson
Lancaster, 2005

References

Ljung, M. A. (1990)
A Study of TEFL Vocabulary, Stockholm: Almqvist & Wiksell International.

Nation, I. S. P. (1990)
Teaching and learning vocabulary, Boston: Heinle and Heinle.

Sinclair, J. M. and Renouf, A. (1988)
"A lexical syllabus for language learning," in R. Carter and M. McCarthy (eds.) *Vocabulary and Language Teaching*, London: Longman, pp. 140–158.

Acknowledgments

I am indebted to Douglas Biber, James Jones, and Nicole Tracy from Northern Arizona University, who helped with the part of speech tagging and lemmatization of the 20 million word corpus. I am also grateful to a number of graduate students from both Illinois State University and Brigham Young University who helped with this project. From ISU I would particularly like to thank Alysse Rasmussen, Bradley Alexander, Amanda Pflum, Erin Miller, and Ardythe Woerley. From BYU I would like to thank Rossana Quiroz, Hermán Jara, Cecilia Tocaimaza, Gabriela Poletti, Stephen Mouritsen, Ben Stull, Curtis Snyder, David Staley, and Rebecca Cottrell. Finally, I am very grateful to Kathy, Spencer, Joseph, and Adam, who were so supportive as this book was being written, and to whom this book is dedicated.

Abbreviations

Meaning		Example
art	article	1 **el, la** *art* the
adj	adjective	888 **oscuro** *adj* dark, obscure
adv	adverb	587 **apenas** *adv* hardly, barely
conj	conjunction	117 **aunque** *conj* although, even though
f	feminine	33 **la** *pron* [3rd person] (obj-f)
+ fam	familiar	136 **te** *pron* you (obj/+fam)
– fam	formal	269 **usted** *pron* you (subj/–fam)
interj	interjection	2337 **ay** *interj* oh no!, oh my!
m	masculine	21 **lo** *pron* [3rd person] (obj-m)
n	neuter	110 **esto** *pron* this (n)
nc	noun – common	1019 **estudiante** *nc* student
nf	noun – feminine	116 **casa** *nf* house
nf (el)	noun – feminine (with *el*)	194 **agua** *nf (el)* water
nm	noun – masculine	253 **libro** *nm* book
nmf	noun – masc/fem (different meanings)	4857 **cometa** *nmf* comet (m), kite (f)
nm/f	noun – masc/fem (masc form given)	538 **autor** *nm/f* author
num	number	823 **doce** *num* twelve
obj	object	136 **te** *pron* you (obj/+fam)
dir obj	direct object	33 **la** *pron* [3rd person] (dir obj-f)
indir obj	indirect object	19 **le** *pron* [3rd person] (indir obj)
pl	plural	4193 **lente** *nmf* lens [pl] glasses
prep	preposition	48 **sobre** *prep* on top of, over, about
pron	pronoun	191 **nosotros** *pron* we (subj)
sg	singular	814 **tú** *pron* you (subj-sg/+fam)
subj	subject	52 **yo** *pron* I (subj)
v	verb	710 **sentar** *v* to sit (down), seat
//	separates speakers in sample phrase	2172 ¿fue algo premeditado? // No; fue espontáneo.

Introduction

The value of a frequency dictionary of Spanish

What is the value of a frequency dictionary for language teachers and learners? Why not simply rely on the vocabulary lists in a course textbook? The short answer is that although a typical textbook provides some thematically-related vocabulary in each chapter (foods, illnesses, transportation, clothing, etc.), there is almost never any indication of which of these words the student is most likely to encounter in actual conversation or texts. In fact, sometimes the words are so infrequent in actual texts that the student may never encounter them again in the "real world", outside of the test for that particular chapter.

While the situation for the classroom learner is sometimes bleak with regards to vocabulary acquisition, it can be equally as frustrating for independent learners. These individuals may pick up a work of fiction or a newspaper and begin to work through the text word for word, as they look up unfamiliar words in a dictionary. Yet there is often the uncomfortable suspicion on the part of such learners that their time could be maximized if they could simply begin with the most common words in Spanish, and work progressively through the list.

Finally, frequency dictionaries can be a valuable tool for language teachers. It is often the case that students enter into an intermediate language course with deficiencies in terms of their vocabulary. In these cases, the teacher often feels frustrated, because there does not seem to be any systematic way to bring less advanced students up to speed. With a frequency dictionary, however, the teacher could assign remedial students to work through the list and fill in gaps in their vocabulary, and they would know that the students are using their time in the most effective way possible.

What is in this dictionary?

This frequency dictionary is designed to meet the needs of a wide range of language students and teachers, as well as those who are interested in the computational processing of Spanish. The main index contains the 5,000 most common words in Spanish, starting with such basic words as *el* and *de*, and quickly progressing through to more intermediate and advanced words. Because the dictionary is based on the actual frequency of words in a large 20 million word corpus (collection of texts) of many different types of Spanish texts (fiction, non-fiction, and actual conversations), the user can feel comfortable that these are words that one is very likely to subsequently encounter in the "real world".

In addition to providing a listing of the most frequent 5,000 words, the entries provide other information that should be of great use to the language learner. Each entry also shows the part of speech (noun, verb, etc.), a simple definition of the word in English, and an actual example of the word in context, taken from the 100 million word Corpus del Español (www.corpusdelespanol.org). Finally, the entries show whether the word is more common in spoken, fiction, or non-fiction texts, so that the learner acquires greater precision in knowing exactly when and where to use the word.

Aside from the main frequency listing, there are also indexes that sort the entries by alphabetical order and part of speech. The alphabetical index can be of great value to students who for example want to look up a word from a short story or newspaper article, and see how common the word is in general. The part of speech indexes could be of benefit to students who want to focus selectively on verbs, nouns, or some other part of speech. Finally, there are a number of thematically-related lists and lists related to common grammatical problems for beginning and intermediate students, all of which should enhance the learning experience. The expectation, then, is that this frequency dictionary will significantly maximize the efforts of a wide range of students and teachers who are involved in the acquisition of Spanish vocabulary.

Previous frequency dictionaries of Spanish

There have been a number of other frequency dictionaries and lists for Spanish (Buchanan 1927, Eaton 1940, Rodríguez Bou 1952, García Hoz 1953, Juilland and Chang-Rodríguez 1964, Alameda and Cuetos 1995, Sebastián, Carreiras, and Cuetos 2000), but all of these suffer from significant limitations. First, all of these frequency dictionaries are based exclusively on written Spanish, and contain no data from the spoken register. Second, five of the dictionaries (Buchanan 1927, Eaton 1940, Rodríguez Bou 1952, García Hoz 1953, Juilland and Chang-Rodríguez 1964) are based on texts from the 1950s or earlier, and are now quite outdated. Third, the two dictionaries that have been produced in the last ten years both suffer from other important limitations. Alameda and Cuetos (1995) only lists exact forms (e.g. *digo, dices, dijeran*) rather than lemma (e.g. *decir*), and very few of the written texts that it uses are from outside of Spain. The other recent dictionary – Sebastián, Carreiras, and Cuetos (2000) – exists only in electronic form and is extremely hard to acquire, especially outside of Spain.

Among the dictionaries just mentioned, most researchers recognize Chang-Rodríguez (1964) as the most complete frequency dictionary of Spanish to date. Yet because of its methodological limitations, its list of words is somewhat problematic. As mentioned, all of the texts are from nearly fifty years ago (or before), they are nearly all from Spain, and they are all from written texts. In addition, due to limitations in data collection of more than forty years ago, the corpus is quite small (less than a million words), and is limited just to written texts – spoken Spanish is not represented at all in the wordlist.

Because of the limitations just mentioned, the vocabulary in Chang-Rodríguez is highly skewed. For example, the word *poeta* is word number 309 in the frequency list, with other cases like *lector* (453), *gloria* (566), *héroe* (601), *marqués* (653), *dama* (696), and *príncipe* (737). This skewing is not limited just to nouns, but also includes what would in a normal corpus be much lower frequency verbs, like *acudir* (498), *figurar* (503), *podar* (1932) and *malograr* (2842), and the adjectives *bello* (612), *fecundo* (2376), and *galán* (2557).

On the other hand, there are a number of what we would expect to be highly frequent words that are not in their list. For example, its list of the top 5,000 words of Spanish does not include the following words (the numbers in parenthesis show their placement in our list):

- nouns: oportunidad 626, equipo 737, película 827, control 889, televisión 1079, rama 1161, acceso 1316, marca 1371, tratamiento 1419, experto 1453, paciente 1512, parque 1763
- verbs: enfrentar 914, recuperar 967, identificar 988, controlar 1071, transmitir 1203, grabar 1449, distribuir 1504, fallar 1666, investigar 1752, quebrar 2376, apretar 2405, fumar 2472
- adjectives: capaz 412, extraño 552, temprano 1201, listo 1457, ocupado 1612, probable 1842, latino 1864, sucio 1995, japonés 2171, básico 2296, moreno 2304, feo 2382, cruel 2453

Thus, while Chang-Rodríguez (1964) was quite an achievement for its time, it seems clear that forty years later it is time for a new frequency dictionary of Spanish, which is based on the more advanced data collection techniques that are now available.

The corpus

In order to have an accurate listing of the top 5,000 words in Spanish, the first step is to create a robust and representative corpus of Spanish. In terms of robustness, our 20,000,000 word corpus is more than twenty times larger than the corpus used in Chang-Rodríguez (1964). The texts were taken in large part from the 1900s portion of the Corpus del Español (www.corpusdelespanol.org), which contains 100 million words of text from the 1200s – 1900s, and which I had previously created with a grant from the US National Endowment for the Humanities from 2001 – 2002.

In terms of being representative, the corpus contains a much wider collection of registers and text types than that of any previous frequency dictionary of Spanish. As we see in Table 1, two-thirds of the corpus comes from the written register, while a full one-third (6,750,000 words) comes from spoken Spanish.

Approximately one half of the spoken corpus comes from transcriptions of natural speech, including 2,300,000 words in the *Habla Culta* corpus of conversations with speakers from eleven different countries, and 1,000,000 words from the *Corpus Oral de Referencia*, which contains transcripts of

Table 1 Composition of 20 million word Modern Spanish corpus

	No. of words	Spain	No. of words	Latin America
Spoken	1.00	España Oral[1]	2.00	Habla Culta (ten countries)
	0.35	Habla Culta (Madrid, Sevilla)		
3.35	1.35		2.00	
Transcripts/ Plays	1.00	Transcripts/Interviews (congresses, press conferences, other)	1.00	Transcripts/Interviews (congresses, press conferences, other)
	0.27	Interviews in the newspaper *ABC*		
	0.40	Plays	0.73	Plays
3.40	1.67		1.73	
Literature	0.06	Novels (BV[2])	1.60	Novels (BV[2])
	0.00	Short stories (BV[2])	0.87	Short stories (BV[2])
	0.19	Three novels (BYU[3])	1.11	Twelve novels (BYU[3])
	2.17	Mostly novels, from LEXESP[4]	0.18	Four novels from Argentina[5]
			0.20	Three novels from Chile[6]
6.38	2.42		3.96	
Texts	1.05	Newspaper *ABC*	3.00	Newspapers from six different countries
	0.15	Essays in LEXESP[4]	0.07	Cartas ("letters") from Argentina[5]
	2.00	Encarta encyclopedia	0.30	Humanistic texts (e.g. philosophy, history from Argentina[5])
			0.30	Humanistic texts (e.g. philosophy, history from Chile[6])
6.87	3.20		3.67	
Total	8.64		11.36	

Sources:

1 *Corpus oral de referencia de la lengua española contemporánea* (http://elvira.lllf.uam.es/docs_es/corpus/corpus.html)

2 The *Biblioteca Virtual* (http://www.cervantesvirtual.com)

3 Fifteen recent novels, acquired in electronic form from the Humanities Research Center, Brigham Young University

4 *Léxico informatizado del español* (http://www.edicionsub.com/coleccion.asp ?coleccion=90)

5 From the *Corpus lingüístico de referencia de la lengua española en Argentina* (http://www.lllf.uam.es/~fmarcos/informes/corpus/coarginl.html)

6 From the *Corpus lingüístico de referencia de la lengua española en Chile* (http://www.lllf.uam.es/~fmarcos/informes/corpus/cochile.html)

conversations, lectures, sermons, sports broadcasts, and many other types of spoken Spanish. The written corpus is divided in half between literature and non-literary texts, including newspaper articles, essays, encyclopedias, letters, and humanistic texts. In addition to a having a good selection of different genres, this corpus is the first to have a good balance of texts from both Latin America and Spain – approximately 43 percent of the texts come from Spain, while 57 percent come from Latin America. In terms of the time period represented, virtually all of the texts are from 1970–2000, with the clear majority being from the 1990s.

Annotating the data from the corpus

In order to create a useful and accurate listing of the top 5,000 words in Spanish, the entire 20 million words of text needs to first be tagged and lemmatized.

Tagging means that we assign a part of speech to each word in the corpus. In order to do this, we created a lexicon of Spanish, which contained more than 400,000 separate word forms, with their part of speech and lemma (where lemma refers to the "base word" or "dictionary headword" to which each individual form belongs). For example, the following are five word forms from the 400,000 word lexicon:

Word form / lemma / part of speech (pos)

---

lápices / lápiz / noun_masc_pl
tengo / tener / verb_present_1pers_sg
francesa / francés / adjective_fem_sg

pronto / pronto / adverb
doscientas / doscientos / number_fem_pl

In cases where there is just one lexicon entry for a given word form, then that form is easy to annotate (e.g. *tengo* = tener / verb_present). For many other word forms, however, a given word form has to have more than one entry in the lexicon. For example, *trabajo* "(the) work, I work" can either be [lemma = trabajo, pos = noun_masc_sg] or [lemma = trabajar, pos = verb_present_ 1pers_sg]. Another example would be *limpia* "clean, 3sg cleans", which can be either [lemma = limpio, pos = adjective_fem_sg] or [lemma = limpiar, pos = verb_present_3pers_sg]. Such is the case for thousands of different word forms. In these cases, we used rules to tag the text. For example, in the case of *trabajo*, the tagger uses the preceding definite article [*el*] to tag [*el trabajo*] as [lemma = trabajo, pos = noun_masc_sg], whereas it would use the preceding subject pronoun [*yo*] to tag [*yo trabajo*] as [lemma = trabajar, pos=verb_present_1pers_sg].

In many other cases, it is even more difficult than using simply rules to disambiguate the different lemma and parts of speech of a given word form, and in these cases we have used probabilistic information. For example, one of the most difficult classes of words to tag are past participles (e.g. *dicho, controlado, apagado*). The "rule-based" component of the tagger looks for a preceding form of haber "to have" and identifies the word as the form of a verb; for example *he* [*escrito*] "I have written" is [lemma = escribir, pos = verb_pp_masc_sg]. In a case like [*periódico escrito*], however, *escrito* can either be a past participle of the verb *escribir* (leí el periódico escrito ayer "I read the newspaper (that was) written yesterday") or it can have a more adjective-like sense ("the *written*

newspaper, as opposed to the electronic newspaper"). In cases such as these, we looked at the total number of cases where the past participle was preceded in the corpus by *ser* (which suggests a passive / verbal reading) or by *estar* (which suggests a resultative / adjectival reading). If the cases with *ser* were more common with this particular past participle, then ambiguous cases like [N + Past Part] (*periódico escrito*) would be marked as passive/verb. The fact that all of the data was stored in a relational database made this type of probabilistic tagging and lemmatization much easier to carry out than may have been possible with linear, word-by-word annotation.

In terms of the actual process used to annotate the corpus, the following are the steps that we followed. First, I created the 400,000 word lexicon, as discussed above. Second, the entire corpus was tagged using rule-based procedures. This was carried out at Northern Arizona University under the direction of Professor Douglas Biber and with the substantial involvement of James Jones and Nicole Tracy, and was part of a separate grant that we had received from the US National Science Foundation to analyze syntactic variation in Spanish. Finally, I input this preliminary tagged and lemmatized information into a MS SQL Server database, where I cleaned up the rule-based annotation and carried out many probabilistically-based re-annotations of the data, as described above. This entire process took more than two years, and was carried out from 2002–2004.

We have not carried out formal tests to determine the accuracy of the part of speech tagging and lemmatization, but we have examined the annotation in detail at many different stages of the project. After the preliminary tagging, we determined which word forms belonged to two or more lemma that were within the 20,000 most frequent lemma in the corpus (i.e. *limpia* or *trabajo*, as mentioned above). For each one of these forms, we examined the collocations (words to the left and right) to make sure that we had annotated these forms correctly, and made any necessary adjustments. Later we went through each of the 6,000 most frequent lemma, and again looked for any form for any of these lemma that also appeared as a member of another lemma, and again checked the collocations and made the appropriate adjustments. Finally, we continually compared our list to that in Chang-Rodríguez, and carefully examined all of the forms of any word that was in our list but was not in Chang-Rodríguez, or any word that was in their list but was not in our top 5,000 words. While the tagging is not perfect, we feel confident that it is quite accurate.

Organizing and categorizing the data

Even after annotating the corpus for part of speech and lemma – as described in the previous section – there remained a number of difficult decisions regarding how the lemma should be grouped together. In most cases, we have followed the parts of speech from Chang-Rodríguez (1964). In some cases, however, we have conflated categories that Chang-Rodríguez kept distinct. The three primary areas of difference are the following:

Noun/adjective

In many cases there is only minor syntactic and semantic difference between nouns and adjectives in Spanish, as in the case of *ella es católica* "she is (a) Catholic". This holds true not only for religions and nationalities (*él es ruso / italiano* "he is (a) Russian / (an) Italian"), but also cases like *los ricos no ayudan a los pobres* "the rich don't help the poor" or *los últimos recibieron más que los primeros* "the ones who came last got more than those who came early". In most cases, these were assigned a final part of speech of [adjective], and learners can easily apply this information to these cases where there is a more nominal sense.

Past participle

It is often very hard to disambiguate between the [passive / verbal] and [adjectival / resultative] senses of the past participle, as shown above with the example of *periódico escrito*. One solution would be to simply include all past participles as part of the verbal lemma, so that *organizado* is listed with *organizar*, *descrito* is listed with *describir*, etc. Yet there are other cases where the past participle has a clearly adjectival sense, as in *los niños cansados* "the tired children", *un libro pesado* "a heavy book", or *unos casos complicados* "some complicated cases".

Our approach has been to manually check each of the adjective entries in the dictionary, which have the form of a past participle. When the majority of the occurrences of this initially-tagged form have a strongly agentive reading, then that past participle would be re-assigned to the verbal lemma.

Determiner/pronoun/adjective/adverb

Many frequency lists and dictionaries create fine-grained distinctions between these categories, which may be of minimal use to language learners. For example, some frequency lists and dictionaries distinguish between determiner and adjective. Yet it is probably impossible to say where the category [determiner] ends and [adjective] starts, as in cases like *varios, algunos, cuyos* "several, some, whose". As a result, we follow the lead of Chang-Rodríguez, and assign all determiners (except the articles *el* and *la*) to the category [adjective].

Yet we also depart from Chang-Rodríguez on a number of points, primarily with regards to the categorization of pronouns, adjectives, and adverbs. For example, they distinguish between the adjectival use of *temprano* = "early" (*fue un verano temprano* "it was an early summer") and the adverbial use (*el verano llegó temprano* "summer arrived early"). While they list the word twice in the dictionary, we assume that a learner can easily apply the meaning to both cases, and simply list it once under [adjective]. Similarly, Chang-Rodríguez distinguishes between the adjectival use of *todo* = "all/every" (*están todos los hombres* "all the men are here") and the putative pronominal use (*están todos* "everyone is here"), whereas we list *todo* just once – again as an [adjective]. In fact, with an atomistic division of part of speech categories, the same word can theoretically span three different parts of speech – noun, adjective, and adverb – and the question is whether to list them all separately in the dictionary. For example, Chang-Rodríguez lists *menos* "less/least" three times in the dictionary – as noun (*había menos de lo que queríamos* "there was less than we wanted"), adjective (*había menos dinero del que queríamos* "there was less money than we wanted"), and adverb (*cobraron menos que nosotros* "they charged less than us"). In our dictionary, we assume that the learner can easily apply the one meaning to the three contexts, and we accordingly conflate the three uses to the [adjective] category. Finally, we group together the masculine and feminine forms of the definite article (*el/la*), as both we and Chang-Rodríguez have done for all other determiners (*ese/esa, otro/otra*, etc.).

Finally, we should note that there is one category of words with which we separate more lemma than is typically done in other frequency dictionaries. Other dictionaries will often include all of the forms of a pronoun under the masculine / singular / subjective case form of the pronoun. For example, Chang-Rodríguez group together under the one entry yo "I" the following pronouns: *me* "me", *nos* "us", *nosotros* "we", *le/les* "to 3sg/3pl", and even *se* (the "reflexive marker" in Spanish). Because they are morphologically distinct, forms would not be readily recognized as forms that are related to *yo*, we include them (and similar pronouns) as their own entries.

Range, frequency, and weighting

At this point each of the 20 million words of text had been assigned to a lemma and part of speech, and with some lemma these categories were conflated, as discussed in the previous section. The final step was to determine exactly which of these words would be included in the final list of 5,000 words. One approach would be to simply use frequency counts. For example, all lemma that occur 240 times or more in the corpus would be included in the dictionary.

Imagine, however, a case where a particular scientific term was used repeatedly in eight encyclopedia entries and six newspaper articles (for a total of fourteen segments in the 5000+ segment non-fiction corpus), but did not appear in any works of fiction or in any of the spoken texts. Alternatively, suppose that a given word is spread throughout an entire register (spoken, fiction, non-fiction), but that it is still limited almost exclusively to that register. Should the word still be included in the frequency dictionary? The argument could be made that we should look at more than just raw frequency counts in cases like this, and that we ought to include some measure of how well the word is "spread across" all of the registers in the entire corpus.

As a clear example of the contrast between "frequency" and "range", consider the following table. The words to the left have a "range" of at least 80, meaning that the word appears at least once in 80 or more of the 100 blocks in the corpus (each block has 200,000 words, which is 1/100th of the 20 million words in the corpus). The words to the right, on the other hand, have more limited range, and occur in less than 30 of the 100 blocks in the corpus. Most would easily agree that the words shown at the left would be more useful in a frequency dictionary, because they represent a wide range of texts and text types in the corpus.

	Wide range					Narrow range			
freq	Spanish	POS	English	range	range	Spanish	POS	English	freq
236	demostración	nf	demonstration	88	29	radicalismo	n	radicalism	233
247	desconfianza	nf	mistrust	82	29	sodio	n	sodium	210
233	mención	nf	mention	82	25	autonómico	adj	self-governed	248
237	innecesario	adj	unnecessary	81	24	graso	adj	fatty	238
248	aceptable	adj	acceptable	80	20	serbio	adj	Serbian	223
232	recepción	nf	reception	79	20	electromagnético	adj	electromagnetic	221
239	décimo	adj	tenth	79	16	champiñón	n	mushroom	207
247	molesto	adj	bothered	78	16	aminoácido	n	amino acid	234
231	complicación	nf	complication	77	16	neutron	n	neutron	216
214	cuidadoso	adj	careful	74	15	dirigencia	n	leadership	204

A second issue deals with the relative weights assigned to the three main registers – spoken, fiction, and non-fiction. Is one register more "important" in terms of how well it represents what we perceive to be the most "useful" variety of Spanish? Consider first

the following table. The words to the left occur in at least 95 percent of all of the blocks of text from the spoken part of the corpus but in less than 60 percent of the blocks from the non-fiction portion, while those to the right have wide range in non-fiction texts (at least 96 percent) but relatively poor range in spoken texts (less than 45 percent). It seemed fairly uncontroversial that the "spoken" list at the left represents more basic vocabulary, and so we would argue that a higher weight should be given to words that occur more in the spoken register than in the non-fiction register.

+ Range in spoken					+ Range in non-fiction				
Spanish	POS	English	oral	non-f	Spanish	POS	English	oral	non-f
trescientos	num	three hundred	1.00	0.58	adopción	n	adoption	0.28	0.97
ti	pron	(prep+) you	1.00	0.58	incremento	nm	increment	0.32	0.97
mañana	adv	tomorrow	1.00	0.66	incorporación	nf	incorporation	0.36	1.00
poquito	adj	a little bit	0.96	0.34	asentar	v	to establish	0.36	0.97
lunes	nm	Monday	0.96	0.53	prolongado	adj	prolonged	0.40	0.97
últimamente	adv	lately	0.96	0.58	reemplazar	v	to replace	0.40	0.97
montón	nm	(a) lot	0.96	0.58	magnitud	nf	magnitude	0.44	0.97
sábado	nm	Saturday	0.96	0.61	expansión	nf	expansion	0.44	0.97
contento	adj	happy	0.96	0.63	incrementar	v	to increment	0.44	0.97
señora	nf	Ms	0.96	0.66	modalidad	nf	modality	0.44	0.97

How does the spoken register compare to the fiction register? Again, the words to the left have good range in spoken texts but more limited range in fiction, whereas the opposite is true for the words to the right. It is interesting that there are more words referring to "concrete" concepts in the fiction, which probably relates to the fact that fiction includes more description than conversation, since everything has to be spelled out explicitly. Assuming that we favor these concrete/descriptive words more, we might then give a slightly higher weighting to the fiction sub-corpus.

+ Range in spoken					+ Range in fiction				
Spanish	POS	English	oral	fict	Spanish	POS	English	oral	fict
trescientos	num	three hundred	1.00	0.69	arrugado	adj	wrinkled	0.16	0.97
evolución	nf	evolution	1.00	0.72	asombro	nm	amazed	0.24	0.97
cifra	nf	figure	1.00	0.77	maldito	adj	damn	0.32	0.97
eliminar	v	eliminate	1.00	0.79	chupar	v	to suck	0.36	0.97
determinado	adj	certain	1.00	0.82	inesperado	adj	unexpected	0.36	0.97
horario	nm	schedule	1.00	0.82	puño	nm	fist	0.40	0.97
prácticamente	adv	practically	1.00	0.85	pañuelo	nm	handkerchief	0.40	0.97
plantear	v	to propound	1.00	0.87	uña	nf	fingernail	0.40	0.97
absolutamente	adv	absolutely	1.00	0.87	rubio	adj	blonde	0.40	0.97
setenta	num	seventy	1.00	0.87	hervir	v	to boil	0.40	0.97

The final calculation

After looking at the issue of range, frequency, and the weights for different registers, we created the following formula:

$$x = 2*(RaO2/10) + 13*(RaO1/25) + 20*(RaF/39) + 15*(RaNF/38) + 2*(FrO2/12600) +$$

$$13*(FrO1/32400) + 20*(FrF/56600) + 15*(FrNF/41300)$$

where:

$RaO2$, $FrO2$ = range, raw frequency in "non-core" spoken texts

RaO1, FrO1 = range, raw frequency in "core" spoken texts

RaF, FrF = range, raw frequency in fiction texts

RaNF, FrNF = range, raw frequency in fiction texts

(Note: We have divided the spoken texts into "core" and "non-core" texts. The non-core spoken texts are those texts that may have been subsequently modified and may reflect written characteristics to some degree, such as those from press conferences, political speeches, and governmental transcripts. We view these as being less valuable (and thus they have a much lower weighting) than the "core" texts, which represent all other spoken texts. Note also that due to rounding up at a previous stage, the range values add up to 102: 10+25+39+38. In the final calculation, we subtract 2 from the total.)

As a concrete example, let's take the word *alojar* "to host or accommodate". This word occurs in the following number of blocks of text: 0 in O2 ("non-core" spoken), 9 in O1 ("core" spoken), 30 in F (fiction) and 24 in NF (non-fiction). In each case, the actual range is divided by the total number of text blocks for that register – 10 for O2, 25 for O1, 39 for F, and 38 for NF. Thus, if the word appears in every block of a given register, it will have a value of [1.00]; otherwise, it represents a percentage of all blocks. The values [2, 13, 20, 15] refer to the weighting given to each register. The values for the two spoken sub-corpora combined have a weighting of 15 percent, while it is 20 percent for fiction and 15 percent for non-fiction. We perform similar calculations for the raw frequency in each register. The weighting between the different registers is the same, but this time we divide by a given number [12,600, 32,400, 56,000, 413,000], which represents the raw frequency of the tenth most common word in the corpus in each of those registers. (In fact, to account for the large numbers, we actually use log values for all of these raw frequency numbers.) In the case of *alojar*, the raw frequency values in the four registers are [0, 20, 94, 65]. Therefore, after inserting the actual data for *alojar* into the formula, we obtain the following (remember that we will log values for each number that is followed by [^{L}] in the bottom line):

$$45.47 = 2*(0/10) + 13*(9/25) + 20*(30/39) +$$
$$15*(24/38) + 2*(0^L/12,600^L) +$$
$$13*(20^L/32,400^L) + 20*(94^L/56,600^L) +$$
$$15*(65^L/41,300^L)$$

It is this figure of [45.47] for *alojar* that represents its score, and determines whether the word is included in the dictionary. We simply take the top 5,000 scores, and these words are those that are included here.

While the actual formula may seem complicated, hopefully the general criteria for the inclusion of a word in the dictionary are somewhat easier to understand. First, weighting is given to all three registers – spoken, fiction, and non-fiction – and it is unlikely that a word will be included if it is common in only one of these three registers. Second, equal weighting (50 percent / 50 percent) is given to both range and raw frequency. In other words, a word must not only occur many times in the corpus; it must also be "spread out" well throughout the entire corpus. Third, there is a slight weighting advantage given to the fiction register, although the final weighting is still relatively equal – 30 percent spoken, 40 percent fiction, 30 percent non-fiction.

The main frequency index

Chapter 2 contains the main index in this dictionary – a rank-ordered listing of the top five thousand words (lemma) in Spanish, starting with the most frequent word (the definite article *el*) and progressing through to *cueva* "cave", which is number 5,000. The following information is given for each entry:

> rank frequency (1, 2, 3, . . .), headword, part of speech, English equivalent, sample sentence, range count, raw frequency total, indication of major register variation

As a concrete example, let us look at the entry for *bruja* "witch":

> **4305 bruja** *nf* witch, hag
> • había una leyenda de una bruja que se montaba en una escoba
> 61-251 +f -nf

This entry shows that word number 4305 in our rank order list is [bruja], which is a feminine noun [nf] that can be translated as [witch, hag] in English. We then see an actual sentence or phrase that shows the word in context. The two following numbers show that the word occurs in sixty-one of the 100 equally-sized blocks from the corpus (i.e. the range count), and that this lemma occurs 251 times in the corpus. Finally, the [+f -nf] indicates that the word is much more common in the fiction register than would otherwise be expected, while it is less common than would otherwise be expected in the non-fiction register.

Let us briefly add some additional notes to the explanation just given.

The part of speech

Remember that some categories have been conflated, such as noun/adjective with religions and nationalities (*católico, americano*), or adjective/pronoun (*todos*). With nouns, there are several different markings for gender. Most nouns are either *nm* (masculine; *año, libro*) or *nf* (feminine; *tierra, situación*). Nouns that are feminine but are preceded by the articles 'el' and 'un' are marked *nf (el)*: *agua, alma*, while nouns that have the same form for masculine or feminine are marked *nc* (*joven, artista*). In most cases, professions are marked *nm/f* (*autor, director*), which means that only the masculine form appears in the dictionary, but the frequency statistics have been grouped together with a possible feminine form (*autora, directora*). Finally, a few nouns have both masculine and feminine forms (nmf), but these have different meanings (*cometa* = comet (m), kite (f); *radio* = radio set (m), radio "means of communication" (f)).

English equivalent

Only the most basic translations for the word are given. This is not a bilingual dictionary, which lists all possible meanings of a given word, and intermediate to advanced users will certainly want to consult such a dictionary for additional meanings. Also note that high frequency phrases in which a given word occurs are not given, except when the vast majority of all occurrences of that word occur within such a phrase. There are a handful of such words in the dictionary, and they are marked as such (e.g. 180 *sin* [*embargo*], 333 *a* [*medida*] *que*, 347 *a* [*través*], 1679 *no* [*obstante*], 1944 *a* [*menudo*], etc.). Finally, in most cases we have not given the special senses that the word acquires when used pronominally (i.e. with *se*), although this is noted in a handful of cases where a very high percentage of the occurrences are with *se*, as in *rendirse* "to give in" or *colarse* "to slip in".

Phrase in context

All of these phrases and sentences come from the Corpus del Español (www.corpusdelespanol.org). The goal has been to choose phrases whose meaning

reflects well the basic meaning of the word with the minimal number of words, and this has been more possible in some cases than in others. With "invented" sentences it would have certainly been possible to have concise sentences that express the core meaning very clearly, but this would have been at the expense of less authentic examples. Finally, in some cases the original sentence has been shortened by taking out some words whose absence does not affect the basic meaning of the phrase as a whole.

Register variation

The symbols [+o -o +f -f +nf -nf] show that the word in question has a high (+) or low (-) score (a combination of frequency and range) in the indicated register (oral, fiction, non-fiction). These symbols appear only when the word is in the top 8–9 percent or the bottom 8–9 percent of the words in that register, in terms of its relative frequency to the other two registers. Remember that there are some words that are marked [+o] that may not be as common in regular conversations as they are in our oral corpus. This is due to the fact that we have many press conferences, political speeches, and interviews with politicians in our oral corpus, although we have tried to compensate for this by giving these corpora a lower weighting (see the final calculation on pp. 7–8).

Thematic vocabulary ("call-out boxes")

Placed throughout the main frequency-based index are approximately thirty "call-out boxes", which serve to display in one list a number of thematically-related words. These include lists of words related to the body, food, family, weather, professions, nationalities, colors, emotions, verbs of movement and communication, and several other semantic domains. In addition, however, we have focused on several topics in Spanish grammar that are often difficult for beginning and intermediate students. For example, there are lists that show the most common diminutives, superlatives, and derivational suffixes to form nouns, the most common verbs and adjectives that take the subjunctive, which verbs most often take the "reflexive marker" *se*, which verbs most often occur almost exclusively in the imperfect and preterit, and which adjectives occur almost exclusively with the two copular verbs *ser* and *estar*. Finally, there are even more advanced lists that compare the use of nouns, verbs, adjectives, and adverbs across registers, and show which words are used primarily in spoken, fiction, and non-fiction texts. Related to this is a list showing which are the most frequent words that have entered the language in the past 100–200 years.

Alphabetical and part of speech indexes

Chapter 3 contains an alphabetical listing of all words listed in Chapter 2. Each entry includes the following information: 1) lemma 2) part of speech 3) a basic English translation, and 4) rank order frequency. Chapter 4 contains "part of speech" listings of the 5,000 words in Chapters 2 and 3. Within each of the categories (noun, verb, adjective, etc.) the lemma are listed in order of descending frequency. Because each entry is linked to the other two indexes via the rank frequency number, each of the entries in this index contains only the rank frequency and lemma.

References

The following are the frequency dictionaries of Spanish mentioned previously. They are listed in order of publication.

Buchanan, M.A. (1927)
A Graded Spanish Word Book. Toronto: University of Toronto Press.

Eaton, H. (1940)
An English – French – German – Spanish Word Frequency Dictionary, New York: Dover Publications.

Rodríguez Bou, L. (1952)
Recuento de Vocabulario Español, Rió Piedras: Universidad de Puerto Rico.

García Hoz, V. (1953)
Vocabulario Usual, Vocabulario Común y Vocabulario Fundamental, Madrid: CSIC.

Juilland, A. and Chang-Rodríguez, E. (1964)
Frequency Dictionary of Spanish Words, The Hague: Mouton.

Alameda, J.R. and Cuetos, F. (1995)
Diccionario de Frecuencias de las Unidades Lingüísticas del Castellano, Oviedo: Universidad de Oviedo.

Sebastián, N., Martí, M.A., Carreiras, M.F. and Cuetos, F. (2000)
LEXESP, Léxico Informatizado del Español, Barcelona: Ediciones de la Universitat de Barcelona. (CD-ROM only).

Frequency index

Format of entries

1 **el, la** *art* the
• esa mujer era la mujer que yo quería ser
100 | 2037803

2 **de** *prep* of, from
• el hijo de un hermano mío
100 | 1319834

3 **que** *conj* that, which
• dice que no
100 | 662653

4 **y** *conj* and
• él y ella sabían leer y escribir
100 | 562162

5 **a** *prep* to, at
• se fue a la cama
100 | 529899

6 **en** *prep* in, on
• no está en la casa
100 | 507233

7 **un** *art* a, an
• era un hombre simpático
100 | 434022

8 **ser** *v* to be (norm)
• es nuevo, es bueno
100 | 374194 +o

9 **se** *pron* ["reflexive" marker]
• la abuela se acostó tranquila
100 | 329012

10 **no** *adv* no
• no hay modo de negar nada
100 | 257365 +o

11 **haber** *v* to have (+Ved)
• no ha dicho nada
100 | 196962

12 **por** *prep* by, for, through
• así fue por mucho tiempo
100 | 190975

13 **con** *prep* with
• hay un hombre con ella
100 | 184597

14 **su** *adj* his/her/their/your (–fam)
• ¿quién era? ¿Su hermana? ¿Su amiga?
100 | 187810

15 **para** *prep* for, to, in order to
• ¡tengo una sorpresa sensacional para ti!
100 | 126061

16 **como** *conj* like, as
• ser compositor en España es como ser torero en Finlandia
100 | 106840

17 **estar** *v* to be (location, change from norm)
• él está en el trabajo
100 | 106429 +o

18 **tener** *v* to have
• estaba seguro de tener buena memoria
100 | 106642 +o

19 **le** *pron* [3rd person] (indir obj)
• nunca le dijo la verdad
100 | 98211

20 **lo** *art* the (+ n)
• lo mejor es estudiar mucho
100 | 91035

21 **lo** *pron* [3rd person] (dir obj-m)
• lo compré en la tienda
100 | 92519

22 **todo** *adj* all, every
• todos los hombres son iguales
100 | 88057

23 **pero** *conj* but, yet, except
• no significa nada para mí, pero no puedo olvidarla
100 | 82435 +o

24 **más** *adj* more
• él necesitaba más dinero
100 | 92352

25 **hacer** *v* to do, make
• he podido hacer lo que me gusta
100 | 81619

26 **o** *conj* or
• sí esperaba uno o dos muertos
100 | 82444

27 **poder** *v* to be able to; can
• ¡se hace lo que se puede!
100 | 76738

28 **decir** *v* to tell, say
• parece que dice la verdad
100 | 79343 +o

29 este *adj* this (m) [esta (f)]
- y entendía estas cosas muy bien
100 | 80544

30 ir *v* to go
- me habían invitado a ir a su casa
100 | 70352 +o

31 otro *adj* other, another
- ¿por qué no podía ser otra cosa?
100 | 61726

32 ese *adj* that (m) [esa (f)]
- ¿dónde viven esas mujeres?
100 | 60989 +o

33 la *pron* [3rd person] (dir obj-f)
- la puso en su bolsillo
100 | 55523

34 si *conj* if, whether
- si quiere cazar, vamos a cazar
100 | 53608

35 me *pron* me (obj)
- ¿cuando me va a llamar?
97 | 95577 +o

36 ya *adv* already, still
- su marido ya ha dicho todo
100 | 46778 +o

37 ver *v* to see
- había que subir para ver las ruinas
100 | 45854 +o

38 porque *conj* because
- lo vendo sólo porque tengo un apuro muy grande
100 | 44500 +o

39 dar *v* to give
- me dio esta carta para Ud.
100 | 40233

40 cuando *conj* when
- aquella es de mis nietos, cuando eran bebés
100 | 39726

41 él *pron* he, [ellos] them (m)
- él es bastante simpático
100 | 38597

42 muy *adv* very, really
- está muy contento con mi trabajo
100 | 39558 +o

43 sin *prep* without
- se habían quedado sin dinero
100 | 40432

44 vez *nf* time (specific occurrence)
- es la primera vez que estoy junto al mar
100 | 35286

45 mucho *adj* much, many, a lot (adv)
- por lo visto tienen mucho dinero
100 | 36391 +o

46 saber *v* to know (a fact), find out
- ellos lo saben y lo reconocen
100 | 37092 +o

47 qué *pron* what?, which?, how (+ adj)!
- no sé qué voy a hacer
100 | 42000 +o

48 sobre *prep* on top of, over, about
- dejó el papel sobre la mesa y se fue
100 | 35038

49 mi *adj* my
- mi casa es su casa
99 | 45636 +o

50 alguno *adj* some, someone (pron)
- habló algunas palabras con el agente de negocios
100 | 30485

51 mismo *adj* same
- pronunciando el mismo discurso en siete idiomas
100 | 29569

52 yo *pron* I (subj)
- ¡Yo soy el padre!
98 | 54635 +o

53 también *adv* also
- y también van a estar los otros
100 | 33348

54 hasta *prep* until, up to, even (adv)
- toda la noche, hasta las tres de la mañana
100 | 29506

55 año *nm* year
- no lo supo hasta casi un año después
100 | 33053

56 dos *num* two
- de allí salieron dos hermanas solteras
100 | 27733

57 querer *v* to want, love
- quiero que este proceso salga con limpieza
100 | 28696 +o

58 entre *prep* between, among
- la cosa es entre tú y yo
100 | 30756

59 así *adv* like that
- la vida es así
100 | 24832

60 primero *adj* first
- las primeras palabras que nos enseñan a leer y escribir
100 | 26553

61 desde *prep* from, since
- lo había pensado desde el primer momento
100 | 25288

62 grande *adj* large, great, big
- lo ha mirado a los grandes ojos negros
100 | 25963

63 eso *pron* that (n)
- y eso no es todo
99 | 31636 +o

64 ni *conj* not even, neither, nor
- pero ni eso me tranquilizó
100 | 24261

65 nos *pron* us (obj)
- nos vio en la calle
99 | 26349 +o

66 llegar *v* to arrive
- como para llegar hasta el fondo de las almas
100 | 22878

67 pasar *v* to pass, spend (time)
- tras la ventana lo veo pasar una y otra vez
100 | 22466

68 tiempo *nm* time (general), weather
- he estado mucho tiempo con ella
100 | 22432

69 ella *pron* she, [ellas] them (f)
- ella es muy estudiosa
100 | 24770

70 sí *adv* yes
- quiero una respuesta concreta: sí o no
100 | 33828 +o

71 día *nm* day
- cada día hay más problemas
100 | 24715

72 uno *num* one
- hay uno que ya lo está haciendo
100 | 21407 +o

73 bien *adv* well
- y entonces hice bien en quedarme
100 | 21589 +o

74 poco *adj* little, few, a little bit (adv)
- trabajó poco tiempo con él
100 | 20986

75 deber *v* should, ought to; to owe
- te debes calmar, le aconsejó T.
100 | 22232

76 entonces *adv* so, then
- vamos entonces a cambiarlo
100 | 23548 +o

77 poner *v* to put (on), get (+adj)
- puso el cuchillo en manos de M.
100 | 20330

78 cosa *nf* thing
- estoy ya interesado en otra cosa
100 | 23943 +o

79 tanto *adj* so much, so many
- no podía creer que haya tanta gente junta
100 | 20531

80 hombre *nm* man, mankind, husband
- yo soy un hombre de pocas necesidades
100 | 20292

81 parecer *v* to seem, look like
- parecía dormir, tan inmóvil estaba
100 | 19964

82 nuestro *adj* our
- no servía para nuestro país porque somos diferentes
100 | 20666

83 tan *adv* such, as, too, so
- en esa mujer está todo; y por eso es tan maravillosa
100 | 19002

84 donde *conj* where
- yo sé donde está la llave
100 | 18852

85 ahora *adv* now
- lo importante ahora es contarte lo que le pasó
100 | 21030 +o

86 parte *nf* part, portion
- el arte es una parte tan importante de la cultura
100 | 20319

87 después *adv* after
- vamos a dar un paseo después de comer
100 | 20229

88 vida *nf* life
- ha dedicado toda la vida a la música
100 | 18045

89 quedar *v* to remain, stay
- el aire empezó a quedarse quieto
100 | 18152

90 siempre *adv* always, forever
- siempre ha sido así
100 | 17689

91 creer *v* to believe, think
- creo en la justicia de Dios
100 | 21257 +o

92 hablar *v* to speak, talk
- algunos hablan el idioma romaní
100 | 19006 +o

93 llevar *v* to take, carry
- colgado al hombro llevaba un bolso
100 | 17062

94 dejar *v* to let, leave
- ella no dejó que yo lo olvidara
100 | 18185

95 nada *pron* nothing, (not) at all
- no hay nada que hacer
100 | 19365 +o

96 cada *adj* each, every
- de aprender cada día un poco más
100 | 17155

97 seguir *v* to follow, keep on
- el calor sofocante que sigue al mediodía
100 | 16104

98 menos *adj* less, fewer
- no vale más ni menos que la anterior
100 | 15527

99 nuevo *adj* new
- marcaba el comienzo de una nueva vida para mí
100 | 17381

100 encontrar *v* to find
- encontró un lugar apropiado para instalar la sucursal
100 | 15556

101 algo *pron* something, somewhat
- tengo algo que decirte
100 | 15600

102 sólo *adv* only, just
- no siempre vestía ropa de mujer; sólo en carnaval
100 | 19753

103 pues *conj* then, well then
- pues venga usted cuando quiera
100 | 20246 +o

104 llamar *v* to call, name
- el juez se llamaba Pedro Barreda
100 | 14694

Animals (animal 497) top 50 words

caballo 780-M horse	**oveja** 3556-F sheep	**cabra** 4912-F goat
perro 939-M dog	**paloma** 3700-F dove	**elefante** 4945-M elephant
gato 1412-M cat	**ratón** 3856-M mouse	**águila** 5027-M eagle
pájaro 1824-M bird	**gallo** 3872-M rooster	**mosquito** 5206-M mosquito
ave 2207-M bird	**mariposa** 3883-F butterfly	**sapo** 5386-M toad
vaca 2234-F cow	**lobo** 3898-M wolf	**pajarito** 5849-M little bird
toro 2331-M bull	**serpiente** 4150-F snake	**rana** 6137-F frog
ganado 2425-M livestock	**conejo** 4316-M rabbit	**tortuga** 6179-F turtle
pez 2426-M fish	**hormiga** 4553-F ant	**zorro** 6434-M fox
león 2756-M lion	**oso** 4555-M bear	**víbora** 6576-F viper
mosca 2956-F fly	**gusano** 4559-M worm	**murciélago** 6586-M bat
gallina 3023-F hen	**tigre** 4582-M tiger	**grillo** 6613-M cricket
cerdo 3200-M pig	**burro** 4610-M donkey	**cisne** 6641-M swan
pollo 3231-M chicken	**araña** 4717-F spider	**ballena** 7360-F whale
mono 3471-M monkey	**abeja** 4741-F bee	**cuervo** 7556-M raven
rata 3497-F rat	**buey** 4772-M ox	**gaviota** 7978-F seagull
insecto 3542-M insect	**pato** 4786-M duck	

105 **venir** v to come
• unos afirman que el jazz viene de África
100 | 15979 +o

106 **pensar** v to think
• trataba de pensar de dónde podría sacar el dinero
100 | 15616

/ 107 **aquel** adj that (over there)
• unos veinte millones de pesetas (de aquella época)
100 | 17351

∨ 108 **momento** nm moment, time
• estaba pasando uno de los peores momentos de mi vida
100 | 14918

109 **sino** conj but, except, rather
• no somos nosotros el centro sino ella
100 | 14175

, 110 **esto** pron this (n)
• quiero esto o aquello
100 | 15165 +o

111 **salir** v to leave, go out
• para que le abriese la reja para salir al bosque
100 | 14339

112 **volver** v to return, to V again
• los habitantes afectados puedan volver a sus casas
100 | 15275

113 **forma** nf form, shape, way
• necesito estar en buena forma física
100 | 16077

114 **antes** adv before
• quería verla antes de salir
100 | 13259

115 **bueno** adj good
• si estaba de buen humor, nos besábamos sin ruido
100 | 13138 +o

116 **casa** nf house
• hoy la gente vive en la calle; no vive en su casa
100 | 16408

117 **aunque** conj although, even though
• aunque hay problemas, muchos se pueden evitar
100 | 13916

118 **mundo** nm world
• no se parecía a ninguna ciudad del mundo
100 | 13168

' 119 **tres** num three
• tres direcciones: diagonal, horizontal y vertical
100 | 12786

120 **tal** adj such (a)
• bien sabía que tal cosa era imposible
100 | 12514

121 **mejor** adj best, better (adv)
• yo, al fin y al cabo, soy el mejor amigo
100 | 12456

122 **tomar** v to take, drink
• mi padre tomó un sorbo de agua y continuó hablando
100 | 12645

123 cierto *adj* certain, sure, true
- no sé si esto es cierto o no
100 | 12363

124 conocer *v* to know (someone or place)
- ella conoce muy bien a Nicolás
100 | 12264

125 hacia *prep* toward, towards
- sus sentimientos hacia él son todavía tan firmes
100 | 13446

126 cómo *adv* how?
- mamá, ¿cómo puedo vivir?
100 | 13888 +o

127 mujer *nf* woman, wife
- su mamá es una mujer muy enferma y no puede trabajar
100 | 14797

128 vivir *v* to live
- vamos a Buenos Aires, a vivir en la miseria
100 | 11519

129 aquí *adv* here
- ¡Aquí hay dos también!
100 | 14442 +o

130 caso *nm* case, occasion
- luego, en este caso está plenamente justificada
100 | 12852

131 sentir *v* to feel, regret
- lloraba de sentirse tan depravado
100 | 13150

132 luego *adv* later, afterwards
- luego va con su esposa y la contagia
100 | 11115

133 país *nm* country
- de todos los países de las Américas
100 | 15588

134 tratar *v* to try, treat, deal with
- eso es precisamente lo que tratamos de evitar
100 | 10988

135 lugar *nm* place, position
- es el lugar más lindo de la costa
100 | 11214

136 te *pron* you (obj/+fam)
- ¿no te han hablado?
94 | 29887 +o-nf

137 persona *nf* person
- era una persona de mucho talento
100 | 11178 +o

138 mayor *adj* larger, older, main
- yo trabajé la mayor parte del tiempo
100 | 12208

139 último *adj* last, final
- se opuso al viaje hasta el último momento
100 | 12186

140 propio *adj* own, proper, typical
- le doy dinero de mi propio bolsillo
100 | 11518

141 quien *pron* who, whom
- ahora o, quién sabe, nunca
100 | 11212

142 mirar *v* to look, watch
- y los ojos mirando al infinito
100 | 15461 +o

143 hora *nf* hour, time (specific)
- deben celebrarse a primera hora de la tarde
100 | 9911

144 ninguno *adj* no, none, nobody (pron)
- ninguno de mis cuatro varones se ha graduado de nada
100 | 10089

145 trabajo *nm* work, job, effort
- pasó su vida entera dedicado a su trabajo
100 | 9842

146 casi *adv* almost, nearly
- estamos casi siempre solos
100 | 10865

147 punto *nm* point, dot, period
- desde mi punto de vista son las más significativas
100 | 10359

148 durante *adv* during, for (time)
- durante una semana traté de no verla
100 | 12196

149 cualquier *adj* any, anyone (pron)
- en cualquier caso, necesitamos soledad
100 | 9453

150 mano *nf* hand
- se pueden contar con los dedos de una mano
100 | 13309

151 nunca *adv* never, ever
- se aprecia ahora más que nunca la libertad
100 | 10700

152 manera *nf* way, manner
- lo hizo de manera muy informal
100 | 9598

153 cual *pron* which, who, whom
- el pañuelo con el cual me limpié
100 | 9802

154 mientras *conj* while, whereas, as long as
- nos miró mientras comía un gran trozo de pan
100 | 10386

155 contar *v* to tell, count
- me contó una larga y estúpida historia
100 | 8534

156 fin *nm* end
- se habrá terminado la humanidad y ése será el fin de la Historia
100 | 9451

157 tipo *nm* type, kind
- reconozco tu oposición a este tipo de ideología
100 | 10144 +o

158 gente *nf* people
- la gente tiene miedo de perder su identidad
99 | 11206 +o

159 además *adv* also, as well, besides
- además de español, ¿hablas algún otro idioma?
100 | 9917 +o

17

160 solo *adj* lonely, alone
- se sentía solo, espantosamente solo
100 | 8784

161 empezar *v* to begin, start
- lentamente su auto empieza a avanzar
100 | 9291

162 ejemplo *nm* example
- hay otras, por ejemplo las guerras
100 | 10799 +o

163 esperar *v* to wait, hope (for), expect
- los astrónomos llevaban siglos esperando a que sucediera
100 | 9062

164 hoy *adv* today, nowadays
- ayer estuvo aquí; hoy puede estar allá
100 | 9119 +o

165 lado *nm* side
- está situada al lado derecho
100 | 8293

166 hijo *nm* son, [pl] children
- cada padre espera que su hijo sea más que él
100 | 8856

167 allí *adv* there, over there
- allí están, junto a la playa
100 | 9806

168 éste *pron* this one (m), [ésta (f)]
- ¿qué esperabas de un lugar como éste?
100 | 9298

169 problema *nm* problem
- para resolver un problema tan sencillo
100 | 11485 +o

170 cuenta *nf* bill, account
- sería bueno sacar la cuenta y calcular gastos
100 | 7822

171 medio *nm* means, middle; pormedio: through
- por medio de la música, se conocen los sentimientos
100 | 8234

172 contra *prep* against, opposite
- hermanos contra hermanos y padres contra hijos
100 | 9607

173 buscar *v* to look for
- decidí volver a la calle y buscar un empleo
100 | 7882

174 dentro *adv* inside
- ¿o algo quedó dentro del pozo tapiado?
100 | 7575

175 largo *adj* long
- tenía el pelo largo a la altura de los pechos
100 | 8397

176 palabra *nf* word
- jamás dijo una palabra en inglés
100 | 8640

177 existir *v* to exist
- ¿puede existir alguien que sea perfecto?
100 | 8521

178 niño *nm* child, little boy
- he tenido suerte desde que era niño
100 | 9124

179 entrar *v* to enter
- ¡este maldito no puede entrar en nuestra casa!
100 | 8291

180 embargo *nm* sin embargo: nevertheless
- el concierto tendrá, sin embargo, un significado especial
100 | 8145

181 único *adj* only, unique, sole
- era el único hijo varón de la familia
100 | 8058

182 padre *nm* father
- ¿es el padre de mi futuro hijo?
100 | 10518

183 trabajar *v* to work
- comenzaban a trabajar de camareros
100 | 7728 +o

184 pequeño *adj* little, small, young
- a pesar de su pequeño tamaño estaba llena de detalles
100 | 8092

185 alto *adj* tall, high
- desde lo alto de los Alpes
100 | 7742

186 cambio *nm* change
- podía requerir un cambio de actitud
100 | 8059

187 escribir *v* to write
- mi padre escribe unas cartas tan cortas
100 | 7771

188 cuatro *num* four
- tienen cuatro patas y cuernos
100 | 6880

189 ahí *adv* there
- está ahí en la mesa de luz
100 | 9514 +o

190 perder *v* to lose, miss
- el golpe me hizo perder el equilibrio
100 | 7788

191 nosotros *pron* we (subj)
- jamás lo hemos hecho nosotros
97 | 10697 +o

192 historia *nf* history, story
- los períodos más diversos de la historia del arte
100 | 7080

193 idea *nf* idea
- podemos renunciar a la idea de la igualdad
100 | 6877

194 agua *nf* (el) water
- Déme usted un vaso de agua, que tengo mucha sed
100 | 8456

195 producir *v* to produce, cause
- nunca llegó a producirse el tercer y prometido ataque
100 | 9422

196 noche *nf* night, evening
- trabaja por la mañana, por la tarde, y por la noche
99 | 10350

197 ciudad *nf* city
- quieren estar en la ciudad y no salir al campo
100 | 7690

198 modo *nm* way, manner
- hay diferencia entre el modo de hablar y el de escribir
100 | 7254

199 nombre *nm* name, noun
- Susana no es mi nombre verdadero
100 | 7132

200 ocurrir *v* to happen, occur
- el miedo a lo que pudiera ocurrir me inmovilizó
100 | 6547

201 familia *nf* family
- la familia es la unidad social más significativa
100 | 6410

202 realidad *nf* reality, actuality
- le habló a Rosabel, que en realidad se llamaba María
100 | 7157

203 entender *v* to understand
- todavía no entiendo demasiado bien lo que pasó
100 | 7233 +o

204 pedir *v* to ask for, request
- me atreví a pedirle que me diera clases
100 | 6653

205 recibir *v* to receive
- Pavlov recibe el Premio Nobel por sus estudios
100 | 6574

206 obra *nf* work, book, deed
- la primera obra literaria de Dante fue La Vida Nueva
100 | 7601

207 importante *adj* important
- el momento más importante de la ceremonia
100 | 9472 +o

208 medio *adj* half, middle
- la noche sorprendió a los viajeros a medio camino
100 | 7011

209 verdad *nf* truth
- ¡diga la verdad! ¡Todo le acusa!
99 | 8795 +o

210 mes *nm* month
- tendrá lugar el próximo mes de noviembre
100 | 6312

211 todavía *adv* still, yet
- los animales que todavía están vivos
99 | 7382 +o

212 razón *nf* reason; tener razón: to be right
- es verdad, tienes razón; ella no es de San Juan
100 | 6161

213 cuanto *adj* en cuanto a: in terms of, regarding
- hoy hay más apatía en cuanto a estas cuestiones
100 | 6057

214 bajo *prep* under, underneath
- hacía dos o tres grados bajo cero
100 | 7606

215 recordar *v* to remember, remind
- prefiero no recordar esa época de mi vida
100 | 6684

216 grupo *nm* group
- ¿cuál será su papel en ese grupo de trabajo?
100 | 7948

217 mil *num* thousand
- unos mil años han pasado desde entonces
100 | 6044 +o

218 humano *adj* human
- somos seres humanos, y gente normal
100 | 6939

219 terminar *v* to finish, end
- cuelga sin terminar la conversación
100 | 6340

220 permitir *v* to allow, permit
- no se me permitió jugar allí por varios días
100 | 7481

221 aparecer *v* to appear
- detrás suyo, Teresa apareció por la puerta de la cocina
100 | 5938

222 conseguir *v* to get, acquire, obtain
- vas a robar, para conseguir plata
100 | 6030

223 comenzar *v* to begin, start
- a los veintidós años comenzó a aprender castellano
100 | 6796

224 varios *adj* several, various
- está constituida por varios dialectos
100 | 6683

225 posible *adj* possible
- trató de hacer el menor ruido posible para no despertarla
100 | 6732

226 servir *v* to serve
- destapa la botella y sirve unas copas
100 | 5438

227 general *adj* general
- es decir, algo equivalente a los genes en sentido general
100 | 7443

228 sacar *v* to take out
- la Lechuza sacó un revólver y mató a este muchacho
100 | 5715

229 necesitar *v* to need
- vas a necesitar un trabajo nuevo
100 | 5415

230 relación *nf* relationship, relation
- he tenido una relación muy estrecha con los compositores
100 | 6886

231 cinco *num* five
- gozo de tener los cinco sentidos
100 | 5384 +o

232 cuerpo *nm* body
- el cuerpo humano se compone de millones de células
100 | 7615

233 nadie *pron* nobody, anybody
- nadie sabe nada
99 | 8513

234 mantener *v* to keep, maintain
- Luis cruzó los brazos y se mantuvo sereno
100 | 6267

235 hecho *nm* fact, happening
- le gustó el hecho de que yo estuviese allí
100 | 5914

236 ante *prep* before, in the presence of
- qué hacer y cómo actuar ante estas circunstancias
100 | 7560

237 principio *nm* beginning, principle
- tiene fiebre al principio de la enfermedad
100 | 6238

238 resultar *v* to result, turn out
- todo con gran precisión; el viaje resultó perfecto
100 | 6170

239 igual *adj* equal, same (as)
- los indios son seres humanos iguales que nosotros
100 | 5712

240 señor *nm* sir, Mr, lord
- ¿puedo pagar con dólares? Sí señor
98 | 10029 +o

241 pueblo *nm* people, village
- el libro no representa al pueblo portugués
99 | 7138

242 tarde *nf* afternoon, evening
- eran las dos de la tarde y yo estaba sin comer nada
100 | 6459

243 segundo *adj* second
- en la segunda mitad del siglo
100 | 6397

244 leer *v* to read
- prefiero leer a los autores de moda
100 | 5834

245 caer *v* to fall
- no quiero caer en mi tumba siendo joven
100 | 6441

246 cambiar *v* to change
- no van a cambiar las relaciones de poder
100 | 5595

247 ojo *nm* eye
- los grandes ojos verdes la miraban con ternura
100 | 10717

248 calle *nf* street
- llegó a la esquina de la calle La Merced y la Huancavelica
100 | 6253

249 presentar *v* to introduce, present
- P. me presentó con gravedad a una chica virgen
100 | 6406

250 blanco *adj* white
- esta foto es en blanco y negro
100 | 5666

251 crear *v* to create
- lo que A. creaba con las manos era un don sobrenatural
100 | 5645

252 abrir *v* to open
- todos quieren abrir la puerta para ir a jugar
100 | 6350

253 libro *nm* book
- ¿está usted escribiendo un libro sobre la política?
100 | 6068

254 distinto *adj* distinct, different
- abrirían las puertas a un futuro distinto para mí
100 | 6225

255 fuerza *nf* strength, force, power
- hay artistas excepcionales, con una fuerza increíble
100 | 6449

256 luz *nf* light
- desaparece la luz hasta el oscuro
100 | 6164

257 según *prep* according to
- según su experiencia, ésa era la pista correcta
100 | 6851

258 santo *nm* saint (m)
- todos iban detrás del Santo Patrono con rezos y cánticos
100 | 6218

259 claro *adj* clear
- esto constituye un claro precedente
100 | 5745 +o

260 frente *nmf* al frente: facing; frente a: across from
- lo Uno frente a lo Otro, el Bien frente al Mal
100 | 7457

261 considerar *v* to consider
- no podía considerar la primera hipótesis con seriedad
100 | 6737

262 amigo *nm* friend
- ¿No tienes un amigo a quien me podrías presentar?
99 | 6059

263 oír *v* to hear
- no se oía ningún sonido
99 | 7750 +o

264 cuyo *adj* whose
- el oxígeno, cuyo número atómico es 8
100 | 6789

265 sentido *nm* sense, feeling
- una cantante-actriz en el sentido actual del término
100 | 6465

266 acabar *v* acabar de V: to have just Ved; finish
• la que ahora se acaba de traducir al castellano
99 | 6343

267 paso *nm* step, pace
• sí, la escritura fue un paso decisivo
100 | 6144

268 situación *nf* situation
• ¿cómo es la situación allí actualmente?
100 | 6220

269 usted *pron* you (subj/–fam)
• los tiene usted, señor alcalde
89 | 19531 +o -nf

270 bastante *adj* rather, fairly, quite a bit (adv)
• estoy bastante satisfecho con mi vida
100 | 4928 +o

271 convertir *v* to convert, change, become
• el café llegó a convertirse en la bebida más popular de Cuba
100 | 6423

272 gracia *nf* (pl) thank you; grace, favor
• bueno, gracias por tu tiempo, ¿eh?
99 | 5477 +o

273 siglo *nm* century, age
• los poetas más populares del siglo XX
100 | 9253

274 dios *nm* god, divinity
• ahora sé que hay un Dios en los cielos
100 | 6080

275 malo *adj* bad
• éste se lamentó de su mala suerte
100 | 5025

276 tierra *nf* earth, land, ground
• la tierra daba el maíz, el trigo y el arroz
100 | 6225

277 papel *nm* paper, role, part
• el poco papel que tenemos lo dedicamos a libros
100 | 4628

278 madre *nf* mother
• ahora está casada, es madre de familia
100 | 7522

279 tampoco *adv* neither, nor, either
• porque yo no la conozco y él tampoco la conoce
100 | 4869

280 social *adj* social
• no me gusta la vida social, no voy a ninguna parte
100 | 8196 +o

281 viejo *adj* old, aged
• el viejo tiene como ochenta años, y está loco
100 | 7526

282 aún *adv* still, yet
• se está muriendo; aún está en coma
100 | 6532

283 tema *nm* theme, subject, topic
• entre ellos pues está el tema de la ecología
100 | 5942 +o

284 político *adj* political
• nos afiliamos a un partido político
100 | 10182

285 español *adj* Spanish
• la lengua española de hoy es el castellano
98 | 7083

286 ganar *v* to win, earn
• a los diez años ganó el Premio Nobel
99 | 4846

287 formar *v* to form
• sus componentes se marchaban para formar sus propios grupos
100 | 5834

288 clase *nf* kind, class, order
• ¿qué otra clase de música le interesa?
100 | 5182

289 traer *v* to bring, carry
• sí, me trae un zumo de naranjas, por favor
100 | 5009

290 partir *v* to divide, leave; a partir de: starting
• a partir de los cuatro minutos la tarifa es estable
100 | 5078

291 dinero *nm* money
• ¿hay mucho dinero?, ¿es muy rico?
100 | 4145

292 quién *pron* who?, whom?
• ¿quién es el padre de su hijo?
99 | 6080 +o

293 morir *v* to die
• la pobre murió de pulmonía meses después
99 | 6027

294 incluso *adv* including, even (adv)
• e incluso puede detectar cuando hay errores
100 | 5455 +o

295 campo *nm* field, country
• mi campo principal es la enfermedad coronaria
100 | 5280

296 aceptar *v* to accept
• A. estuvo indecisa en aceptar su petición de matrimonio
100 | 4315

297 quizás *adv* perhaps, maybe
• quizás sí, pero de otra forma
99 | 5349

298 cabeza *nf* head (part of body)
• planteaba muchas preguntas en mi cabeza
100 | 6831

299 realizar *v* to fulfill, carry out
• el viaje se realizó en noviembre
100 | 6698

300 ciento *num* hundred
• se pueda confiar ciento por ciento
100 | 4389 +o

301 mal *adv* badly
• mucha gente habla mal de él
100 | 4489

Body (cuerpo 232 humano) top 60 words

mano 150-F hand	**cuello** 1920-M neck	**bigote** 4182-M mustache
ojo 247-M eye	**hombro** 1927-M shoulder	**hígado** 4203-M liver
cabeza 298-F head	**nariz** 2119-F nose	**ceja** 4227-F eyebrow
cara 356-F face	**rodilla** 2208-F knee	**cadera** 4279-F hip
pie 386-M foot	**oreja** 2407-F ear	**riñón** 4292-M kidney
lengua 596-F tongue	**estómago** 2636-M stomach	**codo** 4412-M elbow
sangre 613-F blood	**nervio** 2744-M nerve	**mejilla** 4528-F cheek
brazo 620-M arm	**labio** 2759-M lip	**entrañas** 4681-F bowels
boca 635-F mouth	**cabello** 2920-M hair	**cráneo** 4750-M skull
corazón 649-M heart	**músculo** 3029-M muscle	**muslo** 4807-M thigh
pelo 1056-M hair	**garganta** 3090-F throat	**tobillo** 5113-M ankle
pierna 1201-F leg	**uña** 3106-F fingernail, toenail	**arteria** 5551-F artery
dedo 1248-M finger, toe	**cintura** 3323-F waist	**mandíbula** 5649-F jaw
espalda 1499-F back	**pulmón** 3420-M lung	**nuca** 5704-F nape of neck
pecho 1649-M chest	**vientre** 3434-M womb	**nalga** 6396-F buttocks
hueso 1695-M bone	**barba** 3451-F beard	**pupila** 6476-F pupil
cerebro 1734-M brain	**vena** 3512-F vein	**intestino** 6682-M intestine
seno 1776-M bosom	**puño** 3563-M fist	**retina** 6712-F retina
diente 1859-M tooth	**esqueleto** 4121-M skeleton	**pulgar** 6732-M thumb
		pestaña 7018-F eyelash

302 orden *nmf* order; sequence (m), religious order (f)
- hay que poner todo en orden de prioridad
100 | 4837

303 don *nm* courtesy title (m), Mr, gift
- ¿cómo era don Manuel?
96 | 8262

304 semana *nf* week
- no todos los días, pero varios días de la semana
100 | 3960

305 suponer *v* to suppose, assume
- era absurdo suponer que la guerrilla cambiara sus planes
100 | 4114

306 comprender *v* to understand
- los había leído todos, sin comprender mucho
100 | 4510

307 final *nmf* al final: finally, in the end
- pero al final, el resultado es la perfección
100 | 4770

308 interés *nm* interest
- usted, de verdad, sí tiene interés en este tema
100 | 5016

309 siguiente *adj* following, next
- al día siguiente se levantó más decidido que nunca
100 | 4055

310 vista *nf* view, sight
- era un territorio fértil con una hermosa vista hacia la cordillera
100 | 4420

311 lograr *v* to achieve, get, manage
- un director no puede lograr buenos resultados sin ayuda
100 | 5387

312 demás *adj* the rest, others
- serán la envidia de los demás colegas latinoamericanos
100 | 4602

313 acuerdo *nm* accord; de acuerdo: in agreement
- estoy de acuerdo con esa interpretación
100 | 5570 +o

314 difícil *adj* difficult, hard
- es duro, difícil tomar una decisión como ésta
100 | 4285 +o

315 número *nm* number
- ella escribía su número telefónico en un papelito
100 | 5235

316 explicar *v* to explain
- ¿podría explicar los detalles de este análisis?
100 | 4782

317 negro *adj* black
- la existencia de un agujero negro en la galaxia M87
- 99 | 5448

318 fondo *nm* bottom, end
- ese es el sistema, y en el fondo funciona
- 100 | 4752

319 camino *nm* road, route, path
- es un camino muy largo el que nos queda por recorrer
- 100 | 4937

320 voz *nf* voice
- un hombre de voz vibrante y rica empezó a cantar
- 100 | 6853

321 estudio *nm* study, learning
- he colaborado en un estudio de epidemiología descriptiva
- 100 | 5155 +o

322 necesario *adj* necessary
- ahora es necesario dirigir más oraciones a Dios
- 100 | 4662

323 preguntar *v* to ask (a question)
- les voy a preguntar si quieren comer
- 96 | 7208

324 allá *adv* there, over there
- miren allá, cerca del puente
- 100 | 5605

325 tocar *v* to touch, play (instrument)
- se acercó hasta tocar su rodilla con la mía
- 100 | 4556 +o

326 valor *nm* value, worth
- hay que descubrir el valor artístico de la obra de arte
- 100 | 4350

327 reconocer *v* to recognize, admit
- no pudo reconocer quién era
- 100 | 4435

328 estudiar *v* to study
- Adam quiere estudiar teología y ser sacerdote
- 100 | 4668 +o

329 alcanzar *v* to reach, catch up with
- la economía tiene posibilidades de alcanzar la prosperidad
- 100 | 4803

330 nacer *v* to be born
- Picasso nació en Málaga en 1881
- 100 | 3914

331 dirigir *v* to direct, manage
- usted dirigió la Orquesta Nacional en 1954
- 100 | 4076

332 correr *v* to run
- ahorita corre tres kilómetros y medio
- 100 | 4808

333 medida *nf* measure; a medida que: to the extent
- el artista crece a medida que madura
- 100 | 4501

334 menor *adj* younger, youngest
- E. era el menor de los hermanos
- 100 | 3960

335 demasiado *adj* too much, too many
- esta casa es demasiado grande para una persona
- 100 | 4760

336 solamente *adv* only
- la opinión es solamente una hipótesis
- 100 | 3666 +o

337 bueno *adv* well...
- bueno, ¿y ahora qué hacemos?
- 94 | 14521 +o -nf

338 utilizar *v* to use, utilize
- sería una buena idea utilizar colores pálidos
- 100 | 6268

339 centro *nm* center, middle, downtown
- no necesitan estar solos en el centro del escenario
- 100 | 4332

340 necesidad *nf* necessity, need
- sentía la necesidad de ser comprendido
- 100 | 3714

341 condición *nf* condition
- afecta a la condición física de todos los órganos
- 100 | 4828

342 pagar *v* to pay
- estamos tratando de pagar esta deuda
- 100 | 4130

343 ello *pron* it (subj-n)
- ¿qué se perdía con ello?
- 99 | 4804

344 falta *nf* lack, shortage
- sería una locura, una falta de ese sentido de la realidad
- 100 | 3789

345 ayudar *v* to help
- espero ganar dinero para ayudar a mi pobre madre
- 100 | 3482

346 diez *num* ten
- a mí me bastaban los diez mandamientos
- 100 | 3740 +o

347 través *adv* a través: across, over, through
- los sentimientos que han llegado a mí a través de la música
- 100 | 5326

348 antiguo *adj* old, ancient, former
- es una de las obras más antiguas – fines del siglo XIII
- 100 | 4673

349 tu *adj* your (sg/+fam)
- ésta es tu casa y ésta es tu cama
- 91 | 10913 +o -nf

350 edad *nf* age
- se acercaba a la edad de encontrar un hombre con quien casarse
- 100 | 3870

351 estado *nm* state, condition, status
- hay un estado de incertidumbre que flota en el ambiente
100 | 5287

352 ser *nm* being
- se puede ser un ser humano perfecto y un bárbaro en cultura
100 | 4601

353 gustar *v* to be pleasing to
- ¡no me gusta que te acaricie!
94 | 8103 +o

354 puerta *nf* door
- ¿por dónde estará la puerta de salida?
98 | 6136

355 jugar *v* to play (sport/game)
- puede jugar a la pelota
100 | 4053

356 cara *nf* face, expression
- aparece la cara del hombre con sus bigotes de cepillo
98 | 5568

357 mí *pron* me (obj prep)
- el regalo era para mí
91 | 11031 +o -nf

358 época *nf* time, age, period
- en la época romana se utilizaba más el bronce
100 | 5007

359 color *nm* color
- coincide con los colores primarios: rojo, azul y amarillo
100 | 4156

360 escuchar *v* to listen to
- tuvo oportunidad de escuchar comentarios de viajeros
99 | 5008

361 experiencia *nf* experience
- tengo experiencia de la vida y del amor
100 | 3568

362 movimiento *nm* movement
- estaba encabezando un movimiento de subversión
100 | 5542

363 cumplir *v* to fulfill
- necesita algo más para cumplir su trabajo
99 | 4150

364 especial *adj* special
- siento también una especial predilección por Stravinski
100 | 3971

365 diferente *adj* different, separate
- en un entorno urbano el reto, en cambio, es diferente
99 | 5066

366 pesar *nm* sorrow; a pesar de: in spite of
- comprendí su decisión a pesar de que me entristeciera mucho
100 | 4024

367 posibilidad *nf* possibility
- debes considerar la posibilidad de dar en adopción a tu bebé
100 | 4177

368 ofrecer *v* to offer, present
- el Hotel D. ofrece su menú en francés
100 | 3730

369 descubrir *v* to discover
- otro policía descubrió un paquete en el suelo
100 | 4206

370 anterior *adj* previous, preceding
- en términos de dólares, el anterior fue un año sobresaliente
100 | 3585

371 juego *nm* game, play, sport
- he escrito algunos libros de juego y diversión
100 | 3689

372 levantar *v* to raise, lift
- de pronto se levantó y fue hasta su biblioteca
100 | 4984

373 pobre *adj* poor
- el pobre, va a tener que trabajar
100 | 3823

374 aire *nm* air, wind, appearance
- el helicóptero puede estacionarse en el aire
100 | 4675

375 seis *num* six
- cinco por seis son treinta
100 | 3509 +o

376 intentar *v* to try, attempt
- ¿somos tan tontos como para intentar repetir la historia?
100 | 4110

377 guerra *nf* war, warfare
- qué pronto se olvida a las víctimas de una guerra
99 | 6108

378 junto *adv* together with, next to
- trabajábamos juntos en el Congreso
100 | 4182

379 resultado *nm* result, outcome
- fue el resultado de muchas acciones que parecían inútiles
100 | 4244

380 usar *v* to use
- mi teléfono no funciona y quisiera usar el tuyo
100 | 3537

381 decidir *v* to decide
- ¿cómo decidió usted ser director de orquesta?
99 | 3924

382 repetir *v* to repeat
- no voy a repetir este pecado más en la vida
100 | 3210

383 olvidar *v* to forget
- no he podido olvidar aquella noche de tu despedida
98 | 4224

384 ley *nf* law, bill, rule
- el casamiento civil es una ley de este país
100 | 5722

385 aspecto *nm* aspect, appearance
- uno de los aspectos más controvertidos del modernismo
100 | 4016

386 pie *nm* foot, base
• está enfermo y tiene un pie en el cementerio
100 | 5048

387 valer *v* to be worth, cost
• ¡estas joyas tienen que valer muchos millones!
100 | 3341 +o

388 especie *nf* kind, sort, species
• el único que llegó a ser una especie de monstruo fui yo
100 | 4268

389 comer *v* to eat
• te comiste todo el queso
100 | 4300

390 servicio *nm* service, helpfulness
• es un servicio público que beneficia al individuo
100 | 3835

391 cerca *adv* close, near
• nos sentábamos cerca del fuego
100 | 3770

392 mostrar *v* to show
• con un dedo me mostró un agujerito negro
99 | 4184

393 actividad *nf* activity, action
• pienso que el arte es una actividad mental
100 | 4482

394 tercero *adj* third
• en uno de los primeros años de la tercera década del siglo
100 | 3390

395 cuál *pron* which?
• primero dime cuál es tu nombre
100 | 3957 +o

396 pronto *adv* soon, quick
• pronto lo tuvieron todo hecho
100 | 4791

397 ocupar *v* to occupy, use
• volvió a ocupar su lugar
100 | 3307

398 cuestión *nf* question, matter
• creo que es una cuestión de sinceridad
100 | 3881 +o

399 duda *nf* doubt
• no existía duda alguna en que era hijo mío
100 | 3805

400 diferencia *nf* difference
• ¿sabés la diferencia entre el contador y el matemático?
100 | 3768

401 mañana *nf* morning, tomorrow
• sí, todo el día está allá, desde la mañana hasta la tarde
98 | 4513 +o

402 mover *v* to move, incite
• después de mover a uno y otro lado la cabeza
100 | 3772

403 continuar *v* to continue
• da la orden para continuar la marcha
100 | 3856

404 cantidad *nf* quantity, amount
• todo esto genera una cantidad de datos formidables
100 | 3677

405 acción *nf* action, act, deed
• esta acción legal pretendía acelerar la liberalización económica
100 | 4397

406 suceder *v* to happen
• ¿qué pasa?, ¿sucedió algo malo?, ¿algún problema?
100 | 3509

407 fijar *v* to set, fix, [se] notice
• lo primero que hizo fue fijar fecha definitiva
100 | 2929 +o

408 sociedad *nf* society
• creaban una sociedad multicultural que vivía en paz
100 | 5484

409 referir *v* to refer (to)
• me voy a referir a los dos últimos puntos
100 | 3354

410 acercar *v* to come near
• él me miró, se acercó, me besó
100 | 3543

411 capaz *adj* capable, able
• ¿es usted capaz de describir su propia carrera?
100 | 3258

412 bajo *adj* short, low
• las puertas de madera son bajas y rudas
100 | 3245

413 libre *adj* free, vacant
• estaré más tranquilo y con más tiempo libre
100 | 3652

414 natural *adj* natural
• decidió que su conducta era natural y sincera
100 | 3821

415 dedicar *v* to dedicate, devote
• cuando se quedó sola se dedicó más horas a escribir
100 | 3324 +o

416 realmente *adv* really, actually, in fact
• ¿antes de nacer nosotros existía realmente el mundo?
99 | 3824 +o

417 peso *nm* peso (money), weight, load
• por lo menos son quince mil pesos por mes
100 | 3063

418 efecto *nm* effect
• para estudiar el efecto del Sol sobre la emisión de rayos X
99 | 4282

419 objeto *nm* object, thing
• será objeto de estudio para las predicciones meteorológicas
100 | 3605

420 verdadero *adj* true, real
• cuyo verdadero nombre no conoció nadie
100 | 3063

421 dónde *adv* where?
- ¿Dónde está escrito esto en la historia?
98 | 4145 +o

422 aprender *v* to learn
- no hay manera de aprender el otro lenguaje
100 | 2995

423 amor *nm* love
- ¡por el amor más grande del mundo; el amor de Dios!
97 | 5049

424 muerte *nf* death
- sólo la muerte no tiene remedio, Juan
98 | 5332

425 partido *nm* party, group, (sports) match
- fue consejero de un candidato del partido conservador
98 | 7030 +o

426 económico *adj* economic
- es necesario tener progreso económico
99 | 6548 +o

427 derecho *nm* right, justice, law
- los catalanes tienen el derecho a usar los dos idiomas que son suyos
99 | 5731

428 poder *nm* power
- le dio el poder de manejar la economía mundial
100 | 5191

429 importancia *nf* importance
- ¿qué proyectos de importancia tiene en su agenda?
100 | 2956

430 sistema *nm* system
- están situados a 4 mil años luz del sistema solar
99 | 8160

431 viaje *nm* travel, trip
- le suceden todo tipo de aventuras durante su viaje
99 | 2921

432 suelo *nm* ground, floor
- durmió en el suelo sobre varias mantas
100 | 3575

433 respecto *nm* respect, con respecto a: with regards to
- los grupos varían con respecto al número que lo componen
100 | 3435

434 conocimiento *nm* knowledge
- desplegó un conocimiento variado de los costumbres del país
100 | 3390

435 libertad *nf* freedom, liberty
- les falta la libertad, el hábito de pensar libremente
100 | 4137

436 encima *adv* above, on top, in addition
- nos pueden elevar por encima de nuestra realidad
100 | 3167

437 comprar *v* to buy
- me iba a comprar un televisor
98 | 3444 +o

438 común *adj* common
- el talento no es una cosa muy común
100 | 3470

439 abierto *adj* open, unlocked
- dormía con un ojo abierto
100 | 3144

440 próximo *adj* next
- pasará el próximo semestre enseñando literatura
100 | 3279

441 atención *nf* attention
- llaman mucho la atención y causan un gran impacto
100 | 2778

442 joven *adj* young
- ¿qué novedad le puede aportar una cantante joven como usted?
100 | 3136

443 subir *v* to go up
- el sistema de subir y bajar verticalmente
100 | 3661

444 esfuerzo *nm* effort, endeavor
- no ha sido vano su esfuerzo
100 | 3180

445 pasado *adj* past, last
- las cosechas serían buenas, pero no tanto como el año pasado
100 | 3296

446 evitar *v* to avoid, prevent
- actuó rápido para evitar su segura humillación
100 | 3110

447 resto *nm* rest, remainder, leftover
- en el Perú y Japón sí, pero no en el resto del mundo
100 | 3279

448 interesar *v* to interest
- no le interesa conocer el mundo
100 | 2539 +o

449 zona *nf* area, zone
- conquistó la zona alemana de Samoa en agosto de 1914
100 | 4364

450 miedo *nm* fear
- yo no tengo miedo de morir
100 | 3458

451 fuera *adv* out, outside, away
- hace como diez años que está fuera del Paraguay
100 | 2504

452 proceso *nm* process, procedure
- el proceso de gestación de la criatura no fue normal
100 | 6038

453 vivo *adj* alive, bright
- el país está musicalmente vivo y palpitante
100 | 3024

Food (comida 873) top 70 words

General terms:

alimento 1143-M food, nourishment

alimentación 2989-F feeding, food

plato 1836-M plate, dish

bebida 2828-F drink, beverage

cena 2971-F dinner

almuerzo 3104-M lunch

desayuno 3157-M breakfast

ingrediente 4708-M ingredient

banquete 4734-M banquet, feast

Specific foods/drinks:

agua 194-F water

carne 787-F meat

vino 917-M wine

(café) 1250-M coffee, café

leche 1334-F milk

pan 1392-M bread

fruta 1701-F fruit

huevo 1900-M egg

azúcar 2033-MF sugar

té 2145-M tea

(alcohol) 2421-M alcohol

pescado 2584-M fish

sal 2608-F salt

(papa) 2669-F potato (also Pope)

manzana 2853-F apple

naranja 2950-F orange

postre 2985-M dessert

miel 2990-F honey

dulce 3100-M candy

arroz 3130-M rice

cerveza 3134-F beer, ale

queso 3182-M cheese

grasa 3275-F grease, fat, lard

maíz 3314-M corn, maize

harina 3614-F flour

uva 3682-F grape

jugo 3712-M juice

pasta 3771-F pasta, dough

chocolate 3776-M chocolate

sopa 3795-F soup

mate 3865-M mate

tomate 3920-M tomato

trigo 3961-M wheat

verdura 4480-F vegetable

whisky 4571-M whisky

crema 4598-F cream

caldo 4637-M broth, soup

torta 4715-F cake

caramelo 4762-M caramel, piece of candy

coco 4929-M coconut

cebolla 5051-F onion

manteca 5521-F butter, lard

jamón 5614-M ham

helado 5668-M ice cream

pastel 5687-M cake

plátano 5726-M banana

limón 5970-M lemon

galleta 6051-F cookie

nuez 6067F nut

patata 6293-F potato

pavo 6426-M turkey

pera 6445-F pear

cereal 6521-M cereal

ensalada 6551-F salad

tortilla 6851-F tortilla

piña 7341-F pineapple

ajo 7486-M garlic;

zanahoria 7602-F carrot

mantequilla 7825-F butter, margarine

---

454 **cerrar** v to close
- lo mejor era cerrar los ojos y dormir
100 | 3099

455 **echar** v to throw, cast
- me echó de la casa y me fui
98 | 3867

456 **responder** v to answer, respond
- el Gobierno respondió por escrito a este diputado
99 | 3270

457 **sufrir** v to suffer, undergo
- sufrió la eterna tragedia del grande
100 | 3220

458 **completo** adj complete
- tienes mi apoyo completo
100 | 2437

459 **minuto** nm minute
- antes del partido se va a guardar un minuto de silencio
98 | 3163

460 **contrario** adj contrary, opposite
- al principio nadie se alarmó; al contrario, se alegraron
100 | 3242

461 **mesa** nf table, board
- la mesa estaba puesta para la cena
99 | 3588

462 **real** adj royal, real, authentic
- fuimos a la biblioteca del palacio real de Madrid
100 | 3671

463 ocasión *nf* opportunity, occasion
• no se puede perder esta ocasión porque es la
última
100 | 3093

464 importar *v* to matter, import
• no le importa nada de nada
99 | 2936

465 público *adj* public
• el 4 de marzo da su último concierto
público
99 | 5459

466 obtener *v* to obtain
• se hace la guerra para obtener la paz
100 | 4029

467 programa *nm* program, plan
• van a aprender mucho de este programa
escolar
99 | 4161 +o

468 favor *nm* favor, benefit
• están a favor de los serbios
100 | 3182

469 lejos *adv* far (away, off)
• ese sitio estaba lejos del pueblo
100 | 3024

470 siete *num* seven
• aprobó el cursillo "Cómo ser feliz en siete
días"
100 | 2592 +o

471 enorme *adj* enormous, vast
• hay una enorme cantidad de cuadros muy
significativos
100 | 3074

472 respuesta *nf* answer, reply
• la única respuesta fue el silencio
100 | 3232

473 línea *nf* line, course
• la línea del horizonte que separa el cielo del
mar
100 | 3677

474 espacio *nm* space, room
• ya no quedaba espacio para nadie alrededor
del tranvía
99 | 3313

475 nivel *nm* level
• el nivel del mar empezaba a aumentar
98 | 5116 +o

476 gobierno *nm* government
• el feudalismo fue la forma de gobierno
98 | 6630

477 cabo *nm* end, bit; llevar a cabo: to carry out
• llevó a cabo un importante trabajo
científico
99 | 3080

478 observar *v* to observe
• en los que se pueden observar bajo
microscopio
99 | 3512

479 indicar *v* to indicate
• el Conductor le indica el lugar que debe
ocupar
100 | 2608

480 alguien *pron* somebody, someone,
anyone
• alguien vino a preguntar por usted
96 | 3978 +o

481 pregunta *nf* question
• cada pregunta abría un mar de respuestas
98 | 3270 +o

482 claro *adv* of course, clearly
• ¡Claro! Así está mucho mejor
93 | 7500 +o -nf

483 atrás *adv* back, behind, ago
• se olvidaba de mirar hacia atrás o hacia los
lados
100 | 2787

484 imagen *nf* image, picture
• es un intento evidente de dañar mi imagen
pública
100 | 3803

485 carrera *nf* career, course, race
• su carrera como «jazzman» profesional
empezó en Cannes
99 | 3038

486 imaginar *v* to imagine
• me imagino que Uds. tienen la misma
situación
99 | 3170 +o

487 soler *v* to be accustomed to
• en las noches cálidas la familia suele reunirse
en el patio
99 | 3713

488 ambos *adj* both
• se extendían a ambos lados de la carretera
98 | 4054

489 profundo *adj* deep, profound
• el mejor y más profundo conocimiento del
poeta
100 | 2707

490 detener *v* to stop, detain
• su pupila se detenía sobre el papel
100 | 3559

491 desarrollar *v* to develop
• tratando de desarrollar un . . . nuevo sistema
electrónico
100 | 3855

492 ocho *num* eight
• entre las siete y media, ocho de la mañana
100 | 2443 +o

493 señalar *v* to point (out), signal
• nos hizo señas y señaló hacia adelante
100 | 3347

494 elegir *v* to choose, elect
• los caminos son muchos y hay que elegir el
mejor
100 | 2853

495 figura *nf* figure
• descubrió en el ruidoso grupo la figura de su
padre
100 | 3004

496 principal *adj* main, principal
• ¿cuál es el problema principal?
100 | 4056

497 animal *nm* animal
- ¿es hombre, animal o cosa?
96 | 4248

498 base *nf* base, basis
- la mitología griega es la base de la literatura
100 | 3505

499 preparar *v* to prepare
- todos los ingredientes para preparar un plato notable
100 | 2320

500 proponer *v* to propose
- le voy a proponer que nos casemos
100 | 2769

501 demostrar *v* to show, demonstrate
- todos me escuchaban inmóviles, sin demostrar la menor sorpresa
100 | 2927

502 significar *v* to mean
- la paloma azul debía significar la libertad
100 | 2792

503 posición *nf* position
- -Vi que mi posición en aquel momento era inútil
100 | 3302

504 motivo *nm* motive, cause
- revelan el motivo de la construcción de las pirámides
100 | 2431

505 prueba *nf* proof, trial, test
- fue prueba de fidelidad y confianza conyugal
100 | 2628

506 política *nf* politics, policy
- se lanzan a un frenético debate sobre política
100 | 4678

507 nacional *adj* national
- le dieron el premio nacional de poesía
99 | 4894

508 lleno *adj* full, filled
- joven y lleno de esperanzas por una vida mejor
100 | 3055

509 reunir *v* to gather, meet, collect
- le permitieron reunir una fortuna de proporciones grotescas
100 | 2237

510 faltar *v* to be lacking
- me falta una persona a quien comunicar mis impresiones
98 | 3028

511 supuesto *adj* supposed; por supuesto: of course
- no entendí, por supuesto, nada, ni una palabra
99 | 2960 +o

512 acompañar *v* to accompany
- deberá acompañar a la novia a la iglesia
100 | 2830

513 dato *nm* data, fact
- tenemos grandes bases de datos de secuencias de proteínas
100 | 2622

514 fácil *adj* easy
- no es fácil explicar con precisión lo que sucedió
100 | 2609

515 desear *v* to want, desire, wish for
- dijo que deseaba venir a México
100 | 2711

516 adelante *adv* forward, further
- el gobierno sigue adelante con el proyecto
100 | 2528

517 empresa *nf* firm, company, venture
- operaba con una empresa constructora del Reino Unido
100 | 3168

518 asunto *nm* matter, issue, affair
- se ha creado una gran polémica sobre el asunto
98 | 3064

519 presencia *nf* presence, appearance
- un ruido que advirtió a los ladrones de su presencia en la casa
100 | 3014

520 suyo *pron* his, hers, yours (- fam), theirs
- señor, lo que es mío, es suyo
99 | 3143

521 cultura *nf* culture
- fue una primitiva cultura indoeuropea
100 | 3930

522 serie *nf* series
- en la combustión intervienen una serie de factores
100 | 3407

523 millón *num* million, fortune
- le ha proporcionado un cheque de un millón de pesetas
98 | 5951 +o

524 enseñar *v* to teach, show
- ¿qué objeto tiene enseñar química en Secundaria?
100 | 2384 +o

525 construir *v* to construct, build
- la robótica tiende a construir modelos diminutos
99 | 2767

526 vender *v* to sell
- tuvieron que vender el maíz para comprar el lienzo
99 | 2484

527 representar *v* to represent
- representa uno de los aspectos más desconocidos
100 | 3312

528 desaparecer *v* to disappear, vanish
- se hizo desaparecer en la oscuridad
100 | 2509

529 mandar *v* to send, order
- la primera carta que Rita nos mandó de Francia
99 | 2833

530 carácter *nm* personality, nature
- es un hombre de carácter apacible, reflexivo y afectuoso
100 | 3054

531 mayoría *nf* majority
- la mayoría de los cánceres humanos no tienen un origen vírico
99 | 4075

532 escuela *nf* school
- dicta clases en la Escuela de Medicina de esa Universidad
100 | 3098

533 rojo *adj* red
- su boca, muy roja, apenas se movió
100 | 3121

534 tras *prep* after, behind
- A. había retornado a su tierra tras años de lucha
97 | 5106

535 superior *adj* superior, upper
- una cantidad de dinero superior a su sueldo anual
100 | 2898

536 andar *v* to walk, function
- casi nadie andaba por las calles
95 | 4203 +o

537 corto *adj* short, brief
- su único día libre, era el día más corto de la semana
100 | 1995

538 autor *nm/f* writer, author
- cuando un autor escribe un mal libro, se cierra o se tira a la papelera
100 | 2835

539 hermano *nm* brother, [pl] siblings
- éramos tres hermanos, dos hermanos mayores y yo
98 | 3309

540 conocido *adj* known, well-known
- Velázquez fue también un pintor muy conocido en Sevilla
100 | 2643

541 preferir *v* to prefer
- en realidad prefiero una buena hamburguesa con una coca cola
100 | 2304

542 asegurar *v* to assure, secure, insure
- podía asegurar que él sería la próxima víctima
99 | 2899

543 función *nf* function, meeting
- ¿qué función tienen las Academias en este sentido?
99 | 3669

544 arriba *adv* up, above
- desde arriba yo veía a mis dos hijas
98 | 2574

545 serio *adj* serious
- esa muchacha tiene un problema serio
100 | 2307

546 causa *nf* cause
- la barrera puede romperse a intervalos por causa de las mareas
100 | 2967

547 suficiente *adj* sufficient, enough
- no tuvo el tiempo suficiente para ejecutar sus proyectos
100 | 2407

548 grave *adj* serious, solemn
- hay momentos de crisis grave en el mundo
100 | 2318

549 decisión *nf* decision
- es difícil tomar una decisión como ésta
100 | 2865

550 música *nf* music
- la gente se detenía siempre a escuchar la música que tocaban
97 | 4350

551 extraño *adj* strange, foreign
- tenían un extraño color de azúcar quemada
100 | 2927

552 crecer *v* to grow, increase
- nació y creció el muchacho en La Huerta
99 | 2911

553 surgir *v* to appear, spring (forth)
- veía surgir la sombra terrible
100 | 2916

554 tú *pron* you (subj-sg/+fam)
- ¡qué clase de hombre eres tú!
90 | 9403 +o -nf

555 expresión *nf* expression
- Johnny cambió su sonrisa por una expresión concentrada
100 | 2473

556 alrededor *adv* about, around, round
- entraron alrededor de las ocho de la mañana
100 | 2164

557 matar *v* to kill
- el gato sirve para matar a los ratones
98 | 3175

558 entregar *v* to deliver
- entregó el paquete a las criaturas
99 | 2323

559 río *nm* river
- recorriendo el río Amazonas y atravesando los Andes
99 | 3192

560 seguridad *nf* security, safety
- unas dudas sobre la calidad y seguridad de los medicamentos
100 | 2239

561 término *nm* term (language), end
- se centra en el significado literal del término descrito
100 | 3294

562 colocar *v* to place, position
- vuelve a colocar las rosas dentro del jarrón
100 | 2270

563 metro *nm* meter, subway
- produce kilogramos de vegetales por metro cuadrado
99 | 2305

564 médico *nm/f* doctor
- el médico le toma la muestra al paciente
100 | 2492

565 establecer *v* to establish
- de ser posible establecer ese tipo de contacto personal
99 | 3832

566 guardar *v* to keep, save
- lo voy a guardar debajo de mi colchón
100 | 2528

567 arte *nm* art, skill
- la creación de un museo de arte moderno y contemporáneo
99 | 3581

568 iniciar *v* to initiate, start
- el curso se inició en enero
99 | 3250

569 bajar *v* to come down, let down
- el Dow Jones de Wall Street bajó 52 puntos en un día
98 | 3029

570 consecuencia *nf* consequence
- la obstrucción se produce como consecuencia de la aparición de grasas
99 | 2787

571 notar *v* to notice
- volví a notar esos extraños ruidos en el callejón
98 | 2303

572 acto *nm* act, action
- ser culto es, para mí, un acto voluntario
100 | 2689

573 meter *v* to put (into)
- lo desnudó, lo metió en la cama
93 | 4445 +o -nf

574 absoluto *adj* absolute
- mantiene el control absoluto de los oyentes
100 | 2323

575 pena *nf* trouble; valer la pena: be of worth
- ésa es una cosa que sí vale la pena recordarla
98 | 2309 +o

576 actuar *v* to act
- esa manera de actuar es producto de la desesperación
99 | 2729

577 segundo *nm* second
- ahí, ahí sí, espérame un segundo
100 | 1978

578 altura *nf* height, altitude
- a siete mil metros de altura hay que usar oxígeno
100 | 2096

579 deseo *nm* desire, wish
- tienen gran entusiasmo y deseo de participar activamente
100 | 2355

580 precisamente *adv* precisely
- el problema no era precisamente el cuidado de la rosa
96 | 2947 +o

581 joven *nc* teenager, young person
- está dirigido a los jóvenes entre 16 y 20 años
100 | 2768

582 veinte *num* twenty
- mide tres metros veinte centímetros
99 | 2172 +o

583 sueño *nm* dream, sleep
- tenía sueño de ser estrella de cine
100 | 3508

584 pretender *v* to attempt
- no sale siempre lo que uno pretende
100 | 2357

585 tarea *nf* task, job
- les ayuda a hacer una tarea dentro del hogar
100 | 1964

586 carta *nf* letter, (playing) card
- comienza a escribir de nuevo y a leer la carta
97 | 2718

587 apenas *adv* hardly, barely
- apenas quedaban menos de 75.000 soldados
100 | 3760

588 propiedad *nf* property
- cedería la propiedad a un grupo de entidades financieras
98 | 3085

589 producto *nm* product
- el arte es, en parte muy grande, producto de su época
100 | 3425

590 personal *adj* personal
- según mi propia experiencia personal como tal
100 | 2401

591 simplemente *adv* simply, just
- me visitan simplemente por ser familia
100 | 2188 +o

592 imposible *adj* impossible
- estaba muy oscuro y era imposible verla
100 | 2138

593 gusto *nm* pleasure, taste, preference
- mi personal gusto artístico no es nada conservador
99 | 2056

594 ayuda *nf* help, aid
- para que las personas afectadas puedan recibir la ayuda que necesitan
100 | 2041

595 acordar *v* to remember, remind
- hoy ya nadie se acuerda de los antiguos soldados
98 | 3023 +o

596 lengua *nf* language, tongue, strip (of land)
- Góngora es uno de los máximos poetas de la lengua castellana
99 | 2706

597 cortar *v* to cut
- salió al jardín y cortó el tallo más largo de su rosal
100 | 2116

598 plan *nm* plan
- nos explicó que tenía preparado un plan infalible
99 | 2611

599 corresponder *v* to correspond with
- introduce un número que corresponde a su tarjeta
100 | 2364

600 vuelta *nf* return, turn
- ¿y el viaje de ida y vuelta en barco?
100 | 2385

601 romper *v* to break
- no quería romper la unidad de la familia
100 | 2201

602 siquiera *adv* even (if)
- ni siquiera ha preguntado mi nombre
98 | 3288

603 adquirir *v* to acquire, get
- por unas cuantas pesetas es posible adquirir un par de tarjetas
100 | 2224

604 proyecto *nm* project, plan
- esta última fase del proyecto no llegó a ser realizada
99 | 3021

605 memoria *nf* memory
- habla pausadamente, buscando en la memoria la palabra exacta
99 | 2426

606 origen *nm* origin, cause
- las mesas redondas de origen griego surgieron en el período helenístico
100 | 2835

607 elemento *nm* element
- era un elemento esencial en la estilística culta
98 | 3668

608 inglés *adj* English
- y no tardó en dominar la lengua inglesa
96 | 2989

609 mercado *nm* market
- se fue al mercado a comprar verduras
100 | 2828

610 curso *nm* course, direction
- después hice el curso de literatura contemporánea
99 | 2485 +o

611 lanzar *v* to throw, launch
- giró para lanzar una mirada de reproche
100 | 2580

612 aprovechar *v* to take advantage of
- yo quiero aprovechar esta oportunidad
100 | 1830

613 sangre *nf* blood
- la sangre empezaba a fluir de la herida
99 | 3106

614 interior *nm* interior, inside
- comían en el interior y otros al aire libre
100 | 2088

615 duro *adj* hard
- reflejaba la dura realidad de la posguerra italiana
99 | 2126

616 apoyar *v* to support, lean on
- los municipios deben apoyar la educación
99 | 2592

617 negar *v* to deny, refuse
- no puedo negar esta evidencia
99 | 2316

618 avanzar *v* to advance, progress
- una procesión que avanza por la avenida
100 | 2362

619 uso *nm* use
- nunca recuperaré el uso de la mano derecha
99 | 2803

Clothing (ropa 1285) words # 1 – 7500

General terms:

prenda 2939-F piece of clothing

(talla) 4330-F size (of clothing), stature

Specific pieces/parts of clothing:

traje 1710-M suit

zapato 1932-M shoe

vestido 2220-M dress

camisa 2443-F shirt

pantalón 2489-M pants

bota 2735-F boot

botón 2865-M button

sombrero 2899-M hat

abrigo 2996-M overcoat

falda 3143-F skirt

corbata 3238-F tie

manga 3266-F sleeve

guante 3392-M glove

pañuelo 3900-M handkerchief, shawl

manto 3904-M cloak

cinturón 3922-M belt

chaqueta 4372-F jacket

camiseta 4427-F T-shirt

blusa 5254-F blouse

zapatilla 5610-F sneakers

chaleco 5810-M vest

sostén 6321-M bra

gorro 6705-M cap

delantal 7417-M apron

620 brazo *nm* arm
- nos tomamos de la mano y del brazo mientras caminábamos
99 | 3950

621 profesor *nm/f* professor, teacher
- fue profesor de física teórica en la universidad
97 | 2906

622 resolver *v* to resolve, settle, work out
- tenemos que resolver el conflicto
100 | 2485

623 futuro *nm* future
- en la actualidad, y más aún en el futuro
100 | 2193

624 oportunidad *nf* opportunity, chance
- ahora teníamos la oportunidad de aprovechar nuestra experiencia
100 | 2364

625 mitad *nf* half, middle
- es un libro sobre la primera mitad del siglo
100 | 2159

626 costar *v* to cost, be hard
- la pensión les costaba más o menos seis mil pesos
99 | 2039

627 rico *adj* rich, tasty
- no quiero ser rica; quiero ser famosa
99 | 2259

628 recuerdo *nm* memory, keepsake
- es la memoria, el recuerdo de la experiencia vivida
100 | 2851

629 total *adj* total, entire
- el número total de asistentes sería de treinta personas
100 | 2272

630 exigir *v* to demand
- ya no exige sangre como los dioses paganos
100 | 2089

631 abajo *adv* down, below, downward
- ¿se podría echar abajo la alianza opositora?
99 | 2267

632 opinión *nf* opinion, view
- ¿cuál es su opinión sobre el gobierno español?
100 | 2891

633 aumentar *v* to increase
- el primer objetivo es aumentar el número de visitantes
99 | 2540

634 recoger *v* to pick up
- se inclinó hacia la derecha para recoger una maleta
99 | 2417

635 boca *nf* mouth, entrance, opening
- cállese la boca, hijo, que estamos estudiando
98 | 3688

636 dirección *nf* direction, address
- luego desearíamos navegar en dirección a otras estrellas
100 | 2240

637 puro *adj* pure, clean
- se llenaba los pulmones con el aire puro
100 | 2282

638 abandonar *v* to abandon, leave (a place)
- cuánto nos dolerá abandonar este lugar que tanto amamos
100 | 2679

639 pieza *nf* piece, part
- el huarache es una pieza de pan cortado por la mitad
99 | 2301

640 profesional *adj* professional
- creo que era un salvavidas profesional, pagado
99 | 2346 +o

641 imponer *v* to impose, enforce
- a menudo trataba de imponer su voluntad
100 | 2523

642 obligar *v* to obligate, force
- me obligó a terminar una novela
100 | 2164

643 físico *adj* physical
- su trabajo requería un gran esfuerzo físico
100 | 2343

644 actitud *nf* attitude
- hay que tener siempre una actitud de metódico escepticismo
99 | 2599

645 mar *nmf* sea
- sobre todo en la región costera del mar Rojo
97 | 3385

646 francés *adj* French
- era una auténtica madame francesa
96 | 4221

647 entrada *nf* entrance, admission ticket
- llegamos nada más que hasta la entrada de la casa
100 | 1743

648 contacto *nm* contact
- nos mantendremos en contacto por vía telefónica
100 | 1942

649 corazón *nm* heart, core
- el amor llena tu corazón
98 | 3090

650 aplicar *v* to apply
- lo amarró a un árbol y le aplicó una feroz paliza
100 | 2249

651 capital *nmf* capital; city (f), money (m)
- Praga es la capital de la República Checa
100 | 2824

652 rápido *adj* quick, fast
- vamos a buscar una solución lo más rápido posible
100 | 2208

653 título *nm* title, heading
- esa novela tiene también otro título
100 | 2072

654 pertenecer *v* to belong
- un 30 por ciento confiesa pertenecer a otras religiones
100 | 2006

655 cuarto *nm* room, chamber
- dormía en un cuarto donde estaba la cama de ella
100 | 2377

656 material *nm* material, element
- la aplicación de los materiales superconductores de alta temperatura
100 | 2174

657 golpe *nm* hit, strike, punch
- se murió por un golpe recibido en el cráneo
100 | 2489

658 disponer *v* to have means, dispose
- el enemigo dispone de tropas y armas
100 | 2212

659 comunicación *nf* communication
- la falta de comunicación es nuestra principal limitación
100 | 2303 +o

660 expresar *v* to express
- ya expresó su opinión contraria
99 | 2277

661 simple *adj* simple, mere, simple-minded
- al principio papá lo veía como un simple juego
100 | 2370

662 totalmente *adv* totally, completely
- el departamento estaba totalmente desnudo
99 | 2005 +o

663 provocar *v* to cause, provoke
- la brisa provoca una blanca lluvia de flores
100 | 2873

664 normal *adj* normal, usual, regular
- los altibajos son algo normal de la vida diaria
99 | 1972 +o

665 defender *v* to defend, protect
- debemos defender nuestros derechos
100 | 2410

666 enfermedad *nf* illness, sickness
- Diría aún que el rock es una enfermedad de los jóvenes
100 | 2627

667 bien *nm* goods, property, benefit
- el número de bienes que pueda poseer en un momento dado
100 | 2382

668 materia *nf* matter, subject
- en materia musical, la tecnología ha sufrido un receso
98 | 3039

669 quitar *v* to remove, take away
- sin problemas quita la sábana que cubre la cara de uno
97 | 2290

670 conservar *v* to conserve, preserve
- una señora que conserva recuerdos de su padre
100 | 2100

671 moderno *adj* modern
- he escrito sobre el arte moderno
100 | 3005

672 sitio *nm* place, space
- de ocupar el sitio que me correspondía en la casa
97 | 2307 +o

673 depender *v* to depend on
- no me gusta depender de otra gente
99 | 2389

674 naturaleza *nf* nature, character
- su naturaleza racional encierra un espíritu poético
100 | 2806

675 capacidad *nf* capacity
- tenía una gran capacidad para entender los tiempos nuevos
99 | 2909

676 actual *adj* current
- ¿la gente del actual Gobierno lo sabe?
99 | 3049

677 marcar *v* to mark, note, dial
- vemos así la estrella Polar, que marca el norte mejor que una brújula
100 | 2211

678 distancia *nf* distance
- ¿qué puedo decir a miles de kilómetros de distancia?
99 | 2314

679 pleno *adj* complete, full
- el tiempo es un ladrón experto que roba a pleno día
100 | 1880

680 cerrado *adj* closed
- las cámaras de TV de circuito cerrado
100 | 1626

681 compartir *v* to share
- espero que compartas tu jubilación conmigo
99 | 1919

682 información *nf* information
- trató de obtener información más precisa
98 | 3111

683 ambiente *nm* environment, atmosphere
- un ambiente silencioso le ayudó para concentrarse
100 | 2039

684 especialmente *adv* especially
- no era especialmente devota del amor en cautiverio
99 | 2349

685 desarrollo *nm* development
- dicen que ya hay planes de desarrollo urbano
97 | 4574 +o

686 sol *nm* sun
- se levanta antes del sol y no hay luz eléctrica
97 | 3367

687 muerto *adj* dead
- viven sobre materia orgánica muerta o en descomposición
99 | 2741

688 consistir v to consist of
- la carga suele consistir de materias primas
100 | 2079

689 constituir v to constitute, consist of
- los miembros que pueden constituir un sector competitivo
97 | 3992

690 dispuesto adj willing, ready
- estaba dispuesto a hacer cualquier sacrificio por la Patria
100 | 1940

691 cubrir v to cover
- se cubre el rostro con un pañuelo
100 | 1990

692 funcionar v to work, function
- un sistema hidráulico que funcionaba mediante estanques de agua
100 | 1824

693 compañero nm companion, classmate
- fue compañero mío de universidad, muy buen amigo
97 | 2263 +o

694 salida nf exit, escape, outcome
- quizá por miedo a meterse en un callejón sin salida
99 | 1859

695 caber v to fit (into)
- no van a caber las cosas en la casa
99 | 1816

696 conciencia nf conscience, consciousness
- se dormía en paz con su conciencia y con Dios
99 | 2216

697 atender v to serve, attend to
- los médicos se alternarían para atender a los pacientes
100 | 1608

698 enfermo adj ill, sick
- el cayó enfermo de tuberculosis
98 | 2119

699 insistir v to insist on
- el gobierno no debería insistir en este tipo de intervenciones
99 | 2067

700 costumbre nf habit, custom, usage
- tampoco faltaban, como era costumbre, las faltas de respeto
99 | 2028

701 detrás adv behind
- pueden estar detrás de ese árbol
99 | 2252

702 paz nf peace
- de inmediato que se siente en un ambiente de paz y armonía
99 | 2335

703 noticia nf news
- ¿qué noticias tienen de la isla de Mallorca?
99 | 2093

704 circunstancia nf circumstance
- tuvimos que enfrentar una circunstancia económica difícil
100 | 1942

705 dolor nm pain, ache, sorrow
- se levantó quejándose de un dolor de espalda
99 | 2382

706 privado adj private
- los sectores público y privado han reducido sus obligaciones
100 | 2353

707 estilo nm style
- la casa era de estilo antiguo, con una gran galería al frente
98 | 2907

708 precio nm price, cost, value
- ¡lleven tres al precio de uno!
97 | 4011

709 popular adj popular
- ¿se trata de música popular o culta?
100 | 2222

710 sentar v to sit (down), seat
- los niños pasaban a sentarse en un escritorio
99 | 2541

711 planta nf plant, floor
- ninguna planta capaz de dar frutos puede crecer sobre esta tierra
99 | 2451

712 personaje nm character (e.g. movie)
- es difícil comprenderlo porque era un personaje muy complicado
98 | 2518

713 famoso adj famous, well-known
- es un hombre que ya es famoso precisamente por esas hazañas
99 | 1912

714 éxito nm success
- tiene mucho éxito con sus piezas teatrales
100 | 2257

715 hija nf daughter
- es hija de padres divorciados
96 | 3141

716 merecer v to deserve, be worthy (of)
- un interesante artista viajero que merece la pena conocer
99 | 1474

717 edificio nm building
- era un colegio estilo colonial el edificio
99 | 1872

718 autoridad nf authority
- la autoridad no se impone, se gana con el respeto
99 | 2972

719 piedra nf stone, rock
- se había obtenido obsidiana (piedra volcánica)
100 | 2488

720 incluir v to include
- el Partido no incluye ni excluye a nadie
98 | 3126

721 conjunto nm group, set
- para mí fue el conjunto de cosas el que no me gustó
99 | 2383

722 treinta *num* thirty
- van a venir unas treinta personas
99 | 2078 +o

723 cuánto *adj* how much?
- ¿Cuánto tiempo querías? ¿Una eternidad?
93 | 3009 +o

724 inmediato *adj* immediate
- anunció que regresaría de inmediato al aeropuerto
100 | 1782

725 suerte *nf* luck, fortune
- yo también estuve en esa guerra, aunque tuve la suerte de sobrevivir
97 | 2504

726 cruzar *v* to cross
- dudó un momento sin cruzar la calle
99 | 2642

727 tender *v* to tend to, lay out
- la historia tendía a ser endiabladamente repetitiva
100 | 1755

728 finalmente *adv* finally, at last
- la casa fue finalmente demolida
98 | 2136

729 junto *adj* together
- desde hace varios años trabaja junto con el profesor
99 | 1908

730 anunciar *v* to announce, advertise
- le oí anunciar la llegada de su invitado
100 | 1881

731 espíritu *nm* spirit, ghost
- son, en cambio, una muestra del mismo espíritu de intolerancia
100 | 2190

732 miembro *nm* member, limb
- es el miembro más destacado del grupo
98 | 2795

733 directo *adj* direct, straight
- entramos y fui directo al dormitorio
100 | 2004

734 despertar *v* to wake (up), arouse
- se volvió a dormir y se despertó de nuevo
100 | 2375

735 recurso *nm* resource, recourse, means
- tienen todas nuestras técnicas y recursos a su disposición
100 | 2861

736 pared *nf* (interior) wall
- en la pared se ve colgada una pintura
98 | 2419

737 equipo *nm* team, equipment, outfit
- volvió a Madrid para formar un equipo de trabajo
97 | 3576

738 error *nm* error, mistake
- en fin, hay la posibilidad de corregir el error
100 | 1697

739 preciso *adj* precise, necessary
- en el preciso instante en que la puerta resonó contra la pared
100 | 1614

740 diverso *adj* different, several, diverse
- las cortezas de árboles de diversas especies
98 | 2800

741 dificultad *nf* difficulty, obstacle
- nos encontramos en dificultades con esta nación
100 | 1706

742 comentar *v* to comment on
- buscamos el manuscrito para comentar algunos pasajes
98 | 2148

743 publicar *v* to publish
- voy a publicar otro libro con el resto
99 | 2192

744 familiar *adj* familiar, of the family
- por tradición, el negocio familiar pasa a los hijos
100 | 1489

745 voluntad *nf* will, willpower, intention
- donde hay una voluntad hay un camino
99 | 2220

746 reunión *nf* meeting, reunion
- vamos a tener una reunión con él el próximo lunes
100 | 2180

747 modelo *nc* model, pattern
- ¿alguna vez has sido modelo de un pintor?
100 | 2553

748 cargar *v* to load (up), carry
- cargó en su mochila todo lo necesario y partió
100 | 1779

749 fecha *nf* date, day
- lo celebro inmortalizando esta fecha en mi diario
100 | 1767

750 participar *v* to participate
- me quería meter en eso, participar y trabajar en todo eso
98 | 2385

751 impedir *v* to prevent, hinder
- nadie puede impedir este suceso
100 | 1950

752 propósito *nm* intention, purpose
- estamos totalmente de acuerdo con el propósito de la iniciativa
100 | 1717

753 salvar *v* to save, rescue
- la amaba porque le había salvado la vida
100 | 1592

754 cuidado *nm* care, carefulness
- mira, tú tienes que tener cuidado con tu forma de expresarte
100 | 1350

755 puesto *nm* job, place, position
- me ofrecieron un puesto como redactora para la América Latina
100 | 1476

Transportation (transporte 1657) words # 1 – 7500

General terms:	Types of transportation:	
calle 248-F street	**(metro)** 563-M meter, subway	**bicicleta** 3955-F bicycle
camino 319-M road, route, path	**coche** 1131-M car	**buque** 3974-M ship, vessel
carretera 1818-F highway, road	**barco** 1164-M boat, ship	**tranvía** 4502-M tram, streetcar
avenida 2876-F freeway, motorway	**tren** 1220-M train	**autobús** 4676-M bus
autopista 4523-F freeway, motorway	**avión** 1283-M airplane	**cohete** 4937-M rocket
	vehículo 1446-M vehicle, car	**vagón** 5174-M carriage, wagon
callejón 5268-M alley	**automóvil** 1578-M automobile	**helicóptero** 6101-M helicopter
puerto 1364-M port, harbor	**carro** 1871-M car, cart	**ómnibus** 6766-M bus
vuelo 1665-M flight	**auto** 2259-M auto	**camioneta** 6807-F small truck, station wagon
(tráfico) 2188-M traffic, trade	**camión** 2503-M truck, van	**moto** 6979-F motorcycle
paseo 2209-M walk, ride	**ferrocarril** 2537-M railway	**subterráneo** 7042-M Underground
tránsito 2792-M traffic, transit	**nave** 2542-F spacecraft, ship	
aeropuerto 2993-M airport	**taxi** 3402-M taxi	**barca** 7252-F (small) boat
chofer 5719-M driver	**bote** 3840-M boat, container	**lancha** 7444-F boat, barge

756 grado *nm* degree, grade
• las discusiones llegaban a un grado de violencia
99 | 2139

757 escapar *v* to escape
• sentí deseos de salir corriendo, escapar de aquella casa
99 | 2028

758 lucha *nf* fight, struggle, wrestle
• la lucha contra el desempleo es la principal prioridad
99 | 2250

759 tirar *v* to throw, pull
• el público se puso furioso y nos tiró tomates
97 | 2440

760 entero *adj* entire, whole, complete
• son conocidos en el mundo entero
99 | 1765

761 jefe *nm/f* leader, boss, manager
• es el jefe de una nueva tribu de guerreros
99 | 2232

762 interesante *adj* interesting
• te quieren contar cosas interesantes que te diviertan
98 | 2038 +o

763 amplio *adj* wide, ample, broad
• se encontraba en el amplio y fresco corredor de una vivienda
98 | 2220

764 contestar *v* to answer, reply
• no puede contestar esta pregunta
96 | 2428

765 periódico *nm* newspaper, periodical
• su padre bajó el periódico que leía
100 | 1863

766 preocupar *v* to worry
• cada día le preocupa más la suerte del muchacho
98 | 1964 +o

767 prestar *v* to lend
• creo que te podré prestar unos mil soles
100 | 1351

768 par *nmf* pair, couple (m); a la par: at same time
• acaba de comprar un par de zapatos
99 | 1909

769 público *nm* public, audience
• lo que me motiva es el contacto con el público
100 | 1900

770 pesar *v* to weigh
• el diamante pesaba sin cortar 60,25 quilates
100 | 2082

771 final *adj* final
• lo que cuenta es el resultado final
100 | 1572

772 calidad *nf* quality
• para mejorar la calidad de vida de los mexicanos
99 | 1970

773 exponer *v* to expound, expose
• el marido trató de exponer su verdadera situación económica
100 | 1454

774 civil *adj* civil
- hay que respetar el código civil
98 | 2305

775 ciencia *nf* science, knowledge
- han sostenido que incluso la ciencia no es tan racional como se supone
98 | 2566

776 tamaño *nm* size, dimension
- volvió con un paquetón de papas fritas de tamaño gigante
99 | 1750

777 mas *conj* but, however
- es posible mas lo dudo
95 | 2046

778 doctor *nm/f* doctor
- su salud decayó y el doctor le recomendó una vida más tranquila
96 | 2442

779 cuadro *nm* painting, picture
- observó el cuadro colgado en la pared de enfrente
99 | 2079

780 caballo *nm* horse
- montaban a caballo y jugaban polo
97 | 2668

781 responsabilidad *nf* responsibility
- con la libertad viene la responsabilidad
98 | 1933 +o

782 cincuenta *num* fifty
- entre los cuarenta y los cincuenta años
99 | 1706 +o

783 interno *adj* internal
- la estructura sufría «un colapso interno»
99 | 3042

784 detalle *nm* detail
- conoce en detalle los horrores de la dictadura
99 | 1611

785 marcha *nf* march, progress
- se pone en marcha un mecanismo enloquecido
98 | 2032

786 nueve *num* nine
- las nueve vidas del gato
99 | 1655 +o

787 carne *nf* meat, flesh
- me gusta la carne de conejo
96 | 2231

788 jamás *adv* never
- ¡Jamás he visto cosa más grandiosa y sensacional!
97 | 2487

789 pensamiento *nm* thought, thinking
- un pensamiento extraño nació en mi mente
99 | 2423

790 viajar *v* to travel
- le gustaba viajar en tren
99 | 1468

791 cargo *nm* position, charge, fee
- ¿desde cuando ocupa usted el cargo de Director Musical?
98 | 2033

792 separar *v* to separate
- sonrió sin separar los labios
100 | 1606

793 santa *nf* saint (f)
- el 30 de agosto es también la fiesta de Santa Rosa de Lima
98 | 1845

794 construcción *nf* construction
- suelen instalarse durante la construcción del edificio
100 | 1930

795 juicio *nm* judgment
- no sabemos cuál será el juicio de la crítica sobre tus escritos
100 | 1629

796 terreno *nm* ground, earth, terrain
- éste es un terreno muy árido
99 | 1797

797 piso *nm* floor, story
- había una escalera hasta el tercer piso
97 | 1925

798 compañía *nf* company
- la compañía de teléfonos fue un monopolio de Estado
98 | 1914

799 regresar *v* to return (to a place)
- luego de catorce días regresó a su casa
98 | 2561

800 texto *nm* text
- es un libro de texto en ciencias
98 | 2065

801 fuente *nf* source; fountain
- la fuente de su inspiración hay que buscarla en Eurípides
100 | 2365

802 presente *nm* present
- no viven en el futuro ni en el pasado, ¡viven en el presente!
100 | 1307

803 definitivo *adj* definitive, conclusive
- ese adiós fue definitivo porque nunca volví a hablar con ella
99 | 1681

804 revista *nf* magazine, journal
- publica una revista en la que colabora regularmente
98 | 1502

805 esperanza *nf* hope
- yo creo que hay que tener fe, esperanza y caridad
98 | 1821

806 máquina *nf* machine
- una máquina que convierte la energía mecánica en eléctrica
98 | 1879

807 contemplar *v* to contemplate
- R. la contempló en silencio, compadecido
99 | 1922

808 recorrer *v* to travel, cover (distance)
- su trabajo le permitió viajar y recorrer el mundo
100 | 1795

809 frase *nf* phrase
- bastaría una sola palabra o una frase para decirlo
97 | 1589

810 perfecto *adj* perfect
- queríamos encontrar el sitio perfecto
98 | 1584

811 sala *nf* room, hall
- me conduce hasta la puerta de la sala que da acceso a la galería
97 | 1834

812 durar *v* to last
- esta suerte no te va a durar toda la vida
100 | 1348

813 instrumento *nm* instrument
- el músico probó su instrumento disparando algunas notas
100 | 1721

814 aquello *pron* that over there (n)
- aquello era un palacio
96 | 2184

815 defensa *nf* defense, plea
- para luchar hasta la muerte en defensa de la patria amenazada
100 | 1793

816 director *nm/f* director, manager, principal
- ejerce este control el director de cada departamento
97 | 2180 +o

817 retirar *v* to take away, retire
- retiró su nombre de la contienda por la presidencia
98 | 1647

818 explicación *nf* explanation
- el mito es una explicación imaginativa del mundo y del hombre
100 | 1464

819 artículo *nm* article, product, item
- no podía concentrarse en el artículo que estaba escribiendo
100 | 2147

820 debajo *adv* underneath, below
- buscan algo debajo de una mesa
98 | 1583

821 permanecer *v* to stay, remain
- estoy condenado a permanecer aquí
97 | 2573

822 asistir *v* to attend
- llegó marzo y los chicos no pudieron asistir a clases
100 | 1270

823 doce *num* twelve
- la iglesia de los Doce Apóstoles
99 | 1528 +o

824 radio *nmf* radio; set (m), communication (f)
- fue transmitido en cadena nacional por la radio y la televisión
97 | 1803

825 organizar *v* to organize
- quisiera organizar un grupo de teatro
100 | 1453

826 película *nf* movie, film
- en la misma zona donde se había rodado la película «West Side Story»
94 | 2852

827 elección *nf* election, choice
- este año tendremos elección de 10 gobernadores
99 | 3018

828 visita *nf* visit, visitor, guest
- tras una visita a la ciudad de San Francisco
100 | 1736

829 contener *v* to contain
- una dieta que no contiene las cosas que te llevan a la obesidad
96 | 2367

830 apoyo *nm* support, backing
- cuando necesité ayuda, ella volvió para darme su apoyo
99 | 1988

831 presidente *nm* president
- el Presidente es la máxima autoridad del país
95 | 3904

832 arma *nf* (el) weapon
- después de decir esto, sacó un arma y disparó
99 | 2174

833 árbol *nm* tree
- las ramas del árbol, que dan sombra
96 | 2381

834 visitar *v* to visit
- me gustaría visitar Los Ángeles
99 | 1598

835 informar *v* to inform
- pero alguien le informó que ya se había ido
98 | 1530

836 encuentro *nm* meeting, game, skirmish
- acepté el encuentro en el café habitual
98 | 1733

837 parecido *adj* similar
- el resultado daba algo parecido a la locura
99 | 1384

838 corriente *nf* current, flow
- la corriente eléctrica fluye por uno de los electrodos
100 | 1656

839 lectura *nf* reading
- orientaba mi afición por las letras con la lectura de los clásicos
100 | 1359

840 existencia *nf* existence, life
- él ignoraba la existencia de los otros
98 | 2352

841 lenguaje *nm* language, speech
- dueño de un lenguaje basado en el habla popular
100 | 2051

842 enviar *v* to send
- para enviarle dinero a Pancho
97 | 1690

843 aun *adv* even (though), still
- era popular, aun sin publicar sus principales obras
- 98 | 2189

844 destino *nm* destination, destiny
- para abordar su vuelo con destino a Estados Unidos
- 99 | 1818

845 educación *nf* education
- y nada contribuye más a ellas que la educación y la cultura
- 98 | 2441 +o

846 cuidar *v* to take care of
- debía cuidar la virginidad de la hija
- 99 | 1463

847 intervenir *v* to intervene
- en espera del momento apropiado para intervenir
- 100 | 1312

848 operación *nf* operation
- con el objetivo de elaborar una operación de rescate
- 99 | 1844

849 raro *adj* strange, rare, scarce
- no sé; me suena raro lo que dicen ustedes
- 99 | 1729

850 perfectamente *adv* perfectly
- con un aspecto perfectamente sereno
- 97 | 1343 +o

851 extender *v* to extend, spread
- ella extiende sobre la mesita un mapa astral
- 97 | 2356

852 comprobar *v* to verify, prove
- tuvo oportunidad de comprobar la cruda realidad
- 99 | 1526

853 nota *nf* note, grade
- la «españolada» tiene siempre una nota de carácter despectivo
- 98 | 1702

854 particular *adj* particular, peculiar
- una forma particular de vestirse y de caminar
- 99 | 1410

855 ése *pron* that one (m), [ésa (f)]
- ése es el único que no está aquí
- 93 | 2537 +o

856 militar *adj* military
- las autoridades civiles y militares harán respetar esta decisión
- 98 | 2702

857 dormir *v* to sleep
- esta cama es para dormir la siesta en verano
- 93 | 3617

858 unido *adj* united
- tenemos un candidato fuerte, tenemos un Partido unido
- 100 | 2001

859 discutir *v* to argue, discuss
- parecía discutir con un interlocutor invisible
- 99 | 1457

860 extraordinario *adj* extraordinary, exceptional
- yo creo que tiene un talento extraordinario como director
- 99 | 1385

861 teatro *nm* theater, drama
- amalgamaban las bellas artes, la literatura, el teatro y la música
- 95 | 2735

862 enfrentar *v* to confront, face
- prefieren huir a enfrentarse con los soldados
- 100 | 1722

863 recién *adv* recently, just
- amigos que recién habían tenido un hijo
- 98 | 1793

864 negocio *nm* business, transaction
- a base de negocios ilícitos acumuló una fortuna importante
- 98 | 1634

865 letra *nf* letter, handwriting, lyrics
- la letra es un jeroglífico
- 98 | 1632

866 peor *adv* worse
- cada día que pasa veo peor y escribo menos
- 94 | 1764 +o

867 sentimiento *nm* feeling, sentiment
- se molesta, hay en ella un sentimiento de frustración
- 99 | 1913

868 conducir *v* to lead, drive
- el mismo camino que nos condujo a ese lugar
- 99 | 1997

869 completamente *adv* completely
- me olvidé completamente de mí misma
- 100 | 1286

870 firmar *v* to sign
- acabamos de firmar una carta de protesta
- 99 | 1460

871 solución *nf* solution, answer
- no encontraría la solución a mis problemas
- 98 | 2171

872 mío *pron* mine
- mozo, otro café igual al mío
- 89 | 3943 +o -nf

873 comida *nf* food, meal
- en los restaurantes no se servía comida antes de las ocho
- 97 | 1739

874 impresión *nf* impression, printing
- me da la impresión de que no quiere enterarse
- 99 | 1555

875 plano *nm* plane, map, level
- A., en el plano sentimental, se mueve muy seguro de dos cosas
- 100 | 1427

876 intención *nf* intention
- comunicó a los dueños su intención de comprarles el piso
- 100 | 1420

877 ritmo *nm* rhythm
- es un ritmo de vida y un sistema de vida muy distinto
100 | 1719

878 verde *adj* green
- los vegetales de hoja verde, como las espinacas y la col
97 | 2092

879 exacto *adj* exact, faithful, true
- en ese momento, en ese exacto momento, no antes ni después
100 | 1187

880 respetar *v* to respect
- hay que respetar a las personas mayores
99 | 1364

881 banco *nm* (financial) bank, bench
- el Banco de México garantiza una parte del crédito
97 | 1681

882 inmediatamente *adv* immediately
- pensé inmediatamente en ti
100 | 1196

883 sostener *v* to support, hold up
- subimos a la plataforma que sostenía la cama
98 | 2203

884 piel *nf* skin, hide, fur
- tenía la piel muy sucia; me desnudé y lo llevé al baño
95 | 2406

885 delante *adv* (in) front (of), ahead
- el caballo marchaba delante y a la derecha
97 | 1681

886 religioso *adj* religious
- un sentimiento religioso que expresa admiración
99 | 2313

887 advertir *v* to notice, warn
- una compañera le advirtió que aquello era una falsificación
98 | 2118

888 oscuro *adj* dark, obscure
- estás en el punto más oscuro del bosque
96 | 2292

889 control *nm* control
- y esto, sin ese control, se ha vuelto salvaje
97 | 2570

890 investigación *nf* investigation
- están dedicados a la investigación financiera y de propiedades
96 | 2723 +o

891 transformar *v* to transform, change
- la política básica fue transformar China en una sociedad socialista
99 | 1638

892 conversación *nf* conversation
- quería continuar la conversación sobre la pintura y el arte
97 | 1785

893 verano *nm* summer
- esperan el calor del verano que cada día parecía más lejano
97 | 1608

894 respeto *nm* respect, regard
- hasta ese momento sentía un respeto muy grande hacia él
99 | 1650

895 norte *nm* north
- creo que en el norte y el centro del país se ha logrado eso
98 | 2237

896 mediante *prep* by means of
- se salvó mediante el remedio ése
98 | 2678

897 cuarto *adj* fourth
- un veinticinco por ciento, la cuarta parte, está cubierta de bosques
100 | 1140

898 tradición *nf* tradition
- deberías ser fiel a la tradición religiosa
99 | 2046

899 bastar *v* to be sufficient
- una sola lección le bastó para conocerlo todo
97 | 1855

900 población *nf* population
- hay una población de 75 mil personas
96 | 3580

901 pareja *nf* couple, pair
- una pareja de enamorados se besa
98 | 1670

902 pasado *nm* past
- Ud. sólo piensa en el pasado. // Si, pero es tan lindo recordar
99 | 1697

903 diario *nm* newspaper
- las noticias que lee en el diario acerca de lo que pasa en Inglaterra
98 | 1564

904 azul *adj* blue
- y los colores básicos: azul, amarillo, verde y rojo
95 | 2291

905 mencionar *v* to mention, cite
- se deben mencionar algunos detalles más
98 | 1711

906 generación *nf* generation
- está criando la nueva generación de hijos
100 | 1578

907 frío *adj* cold
- las temperaturas son aún más frías durante el invierno
98 | 2000

908 visión *nf* vision
- teníamos sobre todo una misma visión de la vida
99 | 1590

909 concreto *aj* concrete, real
- de buscar una solución al problema concreto de las minas
99 | 1767

910 plantear *v* to propose, present
- quisiéramos aquí plantear la cuestión
96 | 2247 +o

Family (familia 201-F) words # 1 – 10,000

hijo 166-M son (plural=children)	**papá** 2281-M dad	**sobrina** 5071-F niece
padre 182-M father	**mamá** 2286-F mom	**cuñado** 5239-M brother in law
madre 278-F mother	**pariente** 2297-MF relative	**hermanito** 6113-M little brother
hermano 539-M brother (plural=siblings)	**abuela** 2408-F grandmother	**nieta** 6141-F granddaughter
hija 715-F daughter	**viuda** 2488-F widow	**bisabuela** 6510-F great grandmother
esposa 951-F wife	**nieto** 2615-M grandchild	
marido 1032-M husband	**esposo** 2676-M husband, spouse	**suegra** 6816-F mother in law
hermana 1256-F sister	**novia** 2726-F girlfriend, bride	**suegro** 6952-M father in law
abuelo 1740-M grandfather (plural=grandparents)	**novio** 2730-M boyfriend, groom	**yerno** 8467-M son in law
tío 1755-M uncle	**prima** 3283-F female cousin	**cuñada** 9651-F sister in law
primo 1860-M cousin	**sobrino** 3593-M nephew	**viudo** 9657-M widower
tía 2199-F aunt	**padrino** 4732-M godparent	**nuera** 9926-F daughter in law

911 probar *v* to test, prove, try
- metió la mano adentro para probar la temperatura
99 | 1303

912 derecho *adj* right, straight
- ¿dónde está? // Derecho por el corredor, a la derecha
100 | 1385

913 peligro *nm* danger, menace
- ante el peligro de la muerte, Douglas recordó toda su vida
99 | 1610

914 oro *nm* gold
- no faltan los lingotes, barras y monedas de oro y plata
95 | 2157

915 justo *adv* just
- está colocada en el medio - justo frente a la silla
98 | 1296

916 manejar *v* to drive, handle
- quiero manejar un auto
100 | 1214

917 vino *nm* wine
- para acompañar un plato así, tiene que ser vino tinto
97 | 1783

918 unir *v* to unite, join (together)
- lo que Dios ha unido no lo separe el hombre
98 | 1720

919 caminar *v* to walk
- sólo debía caminar dos cuadras para llegar a la terminal
97 | 2699

920 coincidir *v* to coincide, agree
- se entienden, a pesar de no coincidir siempre en sus opiniones
99 | 1268

921 etapa *nf* stage, period
- entró en la etapa final de su enfermedad
98 | 1862

922 sencillo *adj* simple, plain, easy
- ¿es más difícil o más sencillo que antes?
98 | 1331

923 silencio *nm* silence
- Castro guarda silencio en cuanto al número de encarcelados
94 | 3596

924 salvo *adv* except (for), but
- todo ha envejecido salvo esa mirada
99 | 1223

925 llenar *v* to fill
- un espacio se puede llenar con muchos elementos bonitos
98 | 1793

926 dominar *v* to dominate, master
- dominaba tres lenguas: el griego, el latín, y el osco
99 | 1638

927 determinado *adj* determined, fixed
- se levantó con aire determinado para marcharse
95 | 2786 +o -f

928 artista *nc* artist, performer
- el artista pintó también retablos de madera de gran formato
96 | 1692

929 medir *v* to measure
- la Colonia Güell mide precisamente 44 metros de alto
99 | 1326

930 labor *nf* labor, work, task
- se habla mucho de su labor en el terreno del psicoanálisis
99 | 1215

931 perdido *adj* lost
- no todo estaba perdido y era posible conseguir un empleo
100 | 1639

932 cielo *nm* sky, heaven, ceiling
- cree ver en el cielo una nube negra
94 | 2642

933 práctica *nf* practice, skill
- necesitas poner en práctica tus ideas
99 | 1879

934 límite *nm* limit
- habían llegado al límite de su paciencia
99 | 1562

935 masa *nf* mass, dough, bulk, crowd
- para determinar la masa atómica de diversos elementos
99 | 1984

936 directamente *adv* directly, straight away
- se metió directamente en la pelea
99 | 1393

937 atravesar *v* to cross
- para llegar al monte tenía que atravesar la pista caminando
100 | 1224

938 formación *nf* formation, education
- ¿cuál ha sido su formación académica?
98 | 2083

939 perro *nm* dog
- el gato, el perro y los pollos fueron domesticados muy pronto
96 | 2139

940 izquierda *nf* left
- los miró de arriba abajo y de izquierda a derecha
98 | 1400

941 destacar *v* to emphasize, stand out
- quisiera destacar los puntos siguientes
98 | 1930

942 cercano *adj* near
- su lugar de trabajo se encontraba cercano a la residencia
100 | 1309

943 cuarenta *num* forty
- era una mujer de unos cuarenta años
97 | 1534 +o

944 pronunciar *v* to pronounce
- su manera de pronunciar el castellano
99 | 1036

945 distinguir *v* to distinguish
- el desdichado no distingue entre lo cierto y lo ilusorio
98 | 1529

946 energía *nf* energy, power
- no encontró ni las palabras ni la energía para hacerlo
98 | 2641

947 confianza *nf* confidence, trust
- hay una gran confianza entre los alumnos y la profesora
99 | 1317

948 adecuado *adj* adequate, suitable
- buscó el lugar adecuado donde plantar su nido
97 | 1819

949 introducir *v* to introduce, bring in
- ahorita se pueden introducir las nuevas tecnologías
99 | 1769

950 flor *nf* flower
- el clavel y las rosas, tulipán y ¿cuál era la otra flor?
93 | 2226

951 esposa *nf* wife
- la delicada solicitud de Elena, su esposa y compañera permanente
96 | 1523

952 comunicar *v* to communicate
- la novela sirve más bien para comunicar ideas
100 | 1124

953 italiano *adj* Italian
- tantas ciudades italianas que son casi como un museo
98 | 1966

954 invitar *v* to invite
- le voy a invitar con un café caliente
95 | 1614 +o

955 responsable *adj* responsible
- siempre me sentí responsable de nuestra separación
99 | 1599

956 feliz *adj* happy, fortunate
- con un aplausito cortés, y una sonrisita feliz
92 | 2076 +o

957 revolución *nf* revolution
- los progresos en la ciencia y la revolución de las comunicaciones
97 | 1333

958 instalar *v* to install
- trataba de instalar un columpio para los niños
98 | 1432

959 tardar *v* to delay, take long
- el tren se tardó doce horas en llegar a Roma
98 | 1212

960 mejorar *v* to improve, get better
- no va a mejorar, R. suspiró con aire de resignación
98 | 1399 +o

961 maestro *nm* teacher (m), master
- en términos académicos, soy maestro de Humanismo en la Universidad
97 | 1472

962 emplear *v* to employ
- el pintor necesita emplear sus talentos en sus obras
98 | 1749

963 alemán *adj* German
- la firma de electricidad alemana AEG, en Berlín
96 | 2904

964 convenir *v* to be agreeable, be convenient
- no conviene que me vean en un consultorio de esos
97 | 1182

965 recuperar *v* to recuperate, recover
- pareció recuperar parte de sus menguadas fuerzas
98 | 1480

966 fenómeno *nm* phenomenon
- el muchacho debe de ser un fenómeno para recuperarse tan pronto
99 | 2002

967 presión *nf* pressure
- está ejerciendo mucha presión para que no lo publiquemos
100 | 1716

968 dado *adj* given
- todos ellos, en un momento dado, fueron rivales
99 | 1217

969 alumno *nm* student, pupil
- yo fui muy buen alumno en la matemática
96 | 1799 +o

970 teoría *nf* theory
- un artículo acerca de la fusión nuclear o la Teoría de la Relatividad
97 | 3145

971 probablemente *adv* probably
- probablemente después de misa se viene a cocinar
99 | 1261

972 tono *nm* tone
- habla de forma pausada y en tono bajo
97 | 1804

973 salud *nf* health
- ayudan a elevar el nivel de salud a través de la alimentación
98 | 1582

974 definir *v* to define
- la suma de los actos que define una vida
97 | 1845

975 superar *v* to overcome, surpass
- el sistema inmunológico supera a la bacteria
98 | 1656

976 señora *nf* Mrs., lady, madam
- Señora Shoemaker, ¿cuándo descubrió este cometa?
88 | 4183 +o -nf

977 exactamente *adv* exactly
- quedan exactamente dos segundos y seis décimas
96 | 1626 +o

978 afirmar *v* to assert, affirm
- afirmó que E. pertenecía a una horrible clase de hombre
97 | 2574

979 diario *adj* daily
- no es como . . . cualquier cosa de la vida diaria
100 | 1048

980 histórico *adj* historical
- el único manuscrito histórico con miniaturas del mundo bizantino
96 | 2314

981 debido *adj* debido a: due to
- una infección intestinal, debido a la falta de higiene
96 | 2056

982 vía *nf* por vía: by means; road, way
- esa información que ha venido a esta Cámara por vía periodística
98 | 1741

983 interpretar *v* to interpret
- la expresión en su rostro era difícil de interpretar
100 | 1273

984 alma *nf* (el) soul
- en el fondo de su alma se encendió una llamarada de rebelión
94 | 2484

985 admitir *v* to admit
- ella no quería admitir su culpabilidad
99 | 1311

986 identificar *v* to identify
- permitió identificar con precisión las causas de la contaminación
100 | 1207

987 madera *nf* wood
- se exporta madera de pino del sur de Brasil
97 | 1953

988 fiesta *nf* party, feast
- ¿le gustaría celebrar su fiesta de cumpleaños?
93 | 1813

989 calor *nm* heat, warmth
- era verano, el piso todavía estaba caliente; hacía calor
95 | 1966

990 mínimo *adj* minimum
- son alumnas que no tienen el mínimo interés por aprender
100 | 1283

991 afectar *v* to affect
- los déficits fiscales sí pueden afectar la economía
95 | 2503

992 hogar *nm* home, hearth
- el niño tiene derecho a un hogar y a un padre, a un apellido
100 | 1192

993 mente *nf* mind
- tenía una mente analítica y científica
98 | 1435

994 seguramente *adv* surely, securely
- se sentó a mi lado, seguramente para darme confianza
96 | 1523 +o

995 preocupación *nf* worry, concern
- su rostro expresaba preocupación y tristeza
100 | 1177

996 reducir *v* to reduce
- el importe del maíz se reducía a cero
98 | 1936

997 concepto *nm* concept
- hoy tenemos un concepto muy museístico de la obra de arte
95 | 2185

998 montar *v* to ride, mount, assemble
- vieron que yo montaba bien a caballo
97 | 1282

999 teléfono *nm* phone, telephone
- la llamo por teléfono y me dice que recibió el mensaje
94 | 1676

1000 hoja *nf* sheet, leaf
- se da tiempo para escribir en una hoja de papel
97 | 1781

1001 parar *v* to stop (moving)
- me parece que se le paró el reloj
95 | 1510 +o

1002 doble *adj* double
- como personaje solitario investido de doble personalidad
100 | 1093

1003 devolver *v* to return, give back
- la respuesta pareció devolverle a su hermano el buen humor
98 | 1179

1004 ejercer *v* to practice, exercise
- viene al pueblo con intenciones de ejercer su profesión
99 | 1633

1005 poseer *v* to possess, own
- el libro posee una calidad estética notable
96 | 2134

1006 proteger *v* to protect
- la ley protege cuidadosamente al menor
99 | 1532

1007 causar *v* to cause, bring about
- el fuego causó severos daños en el área
98 | 1362

1008 rápidamente *adv* rapidly, quickly
- el bombero baja rápidamente por la escalera
100 | 1175

1009 determinar *v* to determine, decide
- nadie más que ella determinó el destino de la familia
98 | 1921

1010 fuerte *adj* strong
- lo vio tan fuerte, bien alimentado, limpio, hermoso
100 | 1218

1011 escritor *nm/f* writer
- de la pluma del escritor nacen los libros
93 | 2279

1012 intento *nm* attempt, try
- al segundo intento tampoco pudo
100 | 1315

1013 cobrar *v* to charge (money)
- parece que le quería cobrar una cuenta vieja
98 | 1349

1014 regla *nf* rule, ruler, regulation
- no creo que sea la excepción de la regla
98 | 1471

1015 dividir *v* to divide
- voy a dividir el cuadro en diez partes iguales
100 | 1529

1016 riesgo *nm* risk
- lo preocupante para mí es el riesgo de que nos descubran
98 | 1765

1017 policía *nc* police, police force, police officer
- el policía dirige el tráfico, que no pase nadie
92 | 2134

1018 inventar *v* to invent, make up
- los periodistas tienen que inventar malas noticias
97 | 1221

1019 estudiante *nc* student
- era suficiente para una estudiante de cuarto curso
96 | 1819

1020 plaza *nf* square, marketplace
- una muchedumbre en la plaza principal bailaba
95 | 1821

1021 limitar *v* to limit
- la terapia ambiental se limita a los pacientes hospitalizados
99 | 1430

1022 llamada *nf* call, knock
- el teléfono sonaba y sonaba, y la llamada no tenía respuesta
96 | 1434

1023 sensación *nf* sensation, feeling
- la nostalgia me da una sensación de juventud
96 | 1737

1024 enemigo *nm* enemy
- el enemigo de mi enemigo es mi amigo
98 | 1690

1025 unidad *nf* unit, unity
- las hermanas no quieren romper la unidad de la familia
96 | 2361

1026 luchar *v* to fight, wrestle
- habían dedicado su existencia a luchar contra el libertinaje
98 | 1308

1027 idioma *nm* (specific) language
- habla en un idioma extraño
96 | 1297

1028 raíz *nf* root
- hay cosas que se deben cortar de raíz, antes de que produzcan males
99 | 1329

1029 compromiso *nm* compromise, engagement
- hicieron todos un compromiso de unidad en el Partido
100 | 1224

1030 comentario *nm* remark, comment
- me gustaría hacer un comentario sobre cuál es el resultado final
98 | 1174

1031 carga *nf* load, charge, cargo
- muchos cuadros tienen mucha carga emocional en sus imágenes
97 | 1461

1032 marido *nm* husband
- para que encontrase un marido para su hija
92 | 2447

1033 quince *num* fifteen
- yo tenía quince años
97 | 1379 +o

1034 constante *adj* constant
- hay un constante movimiento, el yin y el yang
99 | 1406

1035 derecha *nf* right, right hand
- se dirige a la puerta de la derecha de salida a la calle
99 | 1326

1036 extremo *nm* edge, border, end
- cuando el pistón se encuentra en el extremo izquierdo del cilindro
99 | 1280

1037 individuo *nm* individual, person
- no forman un colectivo – son todos individuos
97 | 2062

1038 contenido *nm* contents, content
- le llena la boca a la fuerza hasta vaciar el contenido del plato
97 | 1718

1039 semejante *adj* similar, such, alike
- es una situación muy semejante a la española, ¿no?
99 | 1514

1040 obligación *nf* obligation
- moralmente, mi obligación es proteger al niño
98 | 1370

1041 corte *nmf* court (f), cut (m)
- en audiencia especial por el pleno de la Corte Suprema de Justicia
98 | 1262

1042 extranjero *adj* foreign, alien
- una nueva invasión española o extranjera de cualquier origen
98 | 1193

1043 total *nm* (sum) total
- el Estado tiene un total de 2.00 kilómetros de autopistas de peaje
99 | 1073

1044 acudir *v* to attend, go to, frequent
- B. dejó la caja y acudió a recibirlos
98 | 1353

1045 daño *nm* harm, injury, damage
- no había tenido la intención de hacerle daño a nadie;
99 | 1072

1046 tarde *adv* late
- llegó tarde a clase porque el despertador no sonó
95 | 1445

1047 mensaje *nm* message
- cree que la visión del sueño fue un mensaje divino
97 | 1285

1048 analizar *v* to analyze
- no tenía tiempo de analizar sus actos
99 | 1458

Materials (material 656-M) words # 1 – 7500

(papel) 277-M paper, role, part	**lana** 3060-F wool	**mármol** 4199-M marble
piedra 719-F stone, rock	**acero** 3064-M steel	**alambre** 4255-M wire
oro 914-M gold	**cemento** 3098-M cement	**cera** 4593-F wax
madera 987-F wood	**seda** 3271-F silk	**encaje** 4850-M lace
plata 1281-F silver	**plomo** 3386-M lead	**diamante** 4984-M diamond
hierro 1716-M iron	**cartón** 3393-M cardboard	**porcelana** 5229-F porcelain
tela 1719-F cloth, fabric	**bronce** 3413-M bronze	**aluminio** 5341-M aluminum
(cristal) 2026-M crystal, window	**petróleo** 3427-M oil	**cerámica** 5777-F ceramic
metal 2075-M metal	**paja** 3483-F straw, hay	**arcilla** 5878-F clay
vidrio 2112-M glass	**cobre** 3503-M copper	**granito** 6212-M granite
barro 2894-M clay	**algodón** 3613-M cotton	**marfil** 6677-M ivory
plástico 2947-M plastic	**goma** 3677-F rubber	**adobe** 7308-M adobe
ladrillo 3056-M brick	**carbón** 3909-M coal	**yeso** 7357-M plaster
	perla 4172-F pearl	

1049 lista *nf* list, roster, roll
• me dio una lista de personas a quienes yo
  podía enviar mi libro
  97 | 1141

1050 región *nf* region
• existen en la región comprendida entre 0 y
  25 grados de latitud
  98 | 2880

1051 evidente *adj* evident, obvious
• es evidente que no va a ayudarme
  97 | 1295

1052 niña *nf* child, young girl
• comenzó a llorar como una niña pequeña
  91 | 2842 +o -nf

1053 culpa *nf* blame, fault
• oígame, que yo no tengo la culpa si he
  perdido la documentación
  95 | 1598

1054 encargar *v* to entrust, [se] take charge of
• ¿quién se va a encargar de este proyecto?
  99 | 1012

1055 discusión *nf* discussion, argument
• entraríamos en una discusión final sobre
  el particular
  99 | 1092

1056 pelo *nm* hair
• era rubio y flaco, de pelo corto
  95 | 2130

1057 destinar *v* to assign, appoint
• me ocuparé de destinar un lugar para
  pensar
  99 | 1246

1058 comparar *v* to compare
• es posible comparar la forma oral y
  escrita
  99 | 1081

1059 celebrar *v* to celebrate
• fuimos a celebrar nuestra liberación
  95 | 1910

1060 fe *nf* faith
• le hubiera abrumado sin la fe y la esperanza
  en Dios
  97 | 1278

1061 fijo *adj* fixed, steady
• no hay nada fijo ni decidido en este interior
  100 | 1063

1062 central *adj* central
• tenemos que ir al punto central ahora
  mismo
  97 | 1857

1063 referencia *nf* reference, allusion
• en su cuaderno no hay ninguna referencia a
  su pecado
  98 | 1300

1064 sur *nm* south
• es una isla que queda al sur del continente
  97 | 2102

1065 gesto *nm* gesture
• no pude hablar y le hice un gesto afirmativo
  con la cabeza
  97 | 2255

1066 perspectiva *nf* perspective
• ésta es una buena reforma desde la
  perspectiva del mercado oficial
  99 | 1276

1067 preparado *adj* prepared
• no estaba preparado para la sorpresa de esa
  noche
  99 | 1053

1068 sonar *v* to sound, ring
• ¿escuchaste sonar las campanas?
  95 | 1818

1069 manifestar *v* to express, show
• tampoco le manifestó sus dudas acerca de la
  combatividad
  97 | 1496

1070 controlar *v* to control
• hay que controlar eso; que no resulte excesivo
  97 | 1845

1071 saltar *v* to jump, leap, hop
• saltó por la ventanita y echó a correr
  96 | 1512

1072 acaso *adv* by chance, maybe
• no te acuso de nada. ¿Acaso te sientes
  culpable?
  94 | 1817

1073 colegio *nm* (high) school, college
• no no, yo tengo una educación del colegio
  religioso
  92 | 2137 +o

1074 inmenso *adj* immense, vast, huge
• busqué esconderme entre unas inmensas
  rocas
  99 | 1359

1075 venta *nf* sale
• para que tengan otro mercado para la venta
  de sus productos
  98 | 1014

1076 documento *nm* document
• le pidieron el documento de identidad
  99 | 1397

1077 citar *v* to cite, quote
• sabe lo que dice; citó datos y fuentes
  97 | 1317

1078 televisión *nf* TV, television
• habrá transmisiones de televisión y radio
  93 | 2231 +o

1079 chico *nm* boy
• mostró la estatura de un chico de seis a siete
  años
  91 | 2303

1080 novela *nf* novel
• estaba leyendo una novela de terror
  91 | 2527

1081 requerir *v* to require
• se requiere un mínimo de dos para consolidar
  los postulados
  97 | 1772

1082 moral *adj* moral
• tengo la convicción de que la música posee
  un gran poder moral
  98 | 1409

1083 alcance *nm* reach, scope
- su teoría está fuera del alcance intelectual normal
100 | 982

1084 curioso *adj* curious, strange
- lo curioso era que también hablaban en yiddish
95 | 1362

1085 crisis *nf* crisis
- después tuvo un ataque de ansiedad, pero la crisis no fue tan severa
96 | 2222

1086 fundamental *adj* fundamental
- es un paso fundamental en el proceso
95 | 2370 +o

1087 incorporar *v* to incorporate, include
- hay que incorporar más fruta en la dieta
97 | 1411

1088 presente *adj* present, current
- es el primer semestre del presente año
99 | 1114

1089 máximo *adj* maximum
- esto sería lo máximo que se podría lograr
98 | 1468

1090 literatura *nf* literature
- es un libro de la literatura sudamericana
94 | 1989

1091 batalla *nf* battle
- dedicándose en primer lugar a una batalla legal para obtener su DNI
99 | 1422

1092 europeo *adj* European
- como proyección de lo europeo sobre América Latina
94 | 2743

1093 dueño *nm* owner, landlord (m)
- un señor que era el dueño y señor de la pequeña empresa
98 | 1181

1094 perseguir *v* to persecute, pursue, chase
- la angustia me va a perseguir un tiempo sin fin
99 | 1019

1095 vecino *nm* neighbor
- si el vecino pone una tienda, yo pongo otra enfrente
97 | 1255

1096 sector *nm* sector, area, section
- se trasladó a otro sector de la ciudad
93 | 3164

1097 pintura *nf* painting, paint
- una selección de obras maestras de la pintura y la escultura española
97 | 1683

1098 accidente *nm* accident, irregularity
- un hilo de sangre en la boca después del horrible accidente
100 | 908

1099 oficial *adj* official, authorized
- el guaraní es el idioma oficial de Paraguay
98 | 1708

1100 procurar *v* to try, seek
- el juez procuraba hacer algo sin lograrlo
99 | 1059

1101 numeroso *adj* numerous
- era un ejército numeroso y bien armado
97 | 1888

1102 influencia *nf* influence
- es evidente que Berta tiene una influencia positiva en mamá
98 | 2259

1103 intelectual *adj* intellectual
- importantes en el desarrollo del pensamiento intelectual
97 | 1496

1104 empleado *nm* employee
- con peligro para los empleados que allí trabajaban
99 | 1167

1105 casar *v* to marry
- se casó a los quince años con el dueño de una peluquería
90 | 2023 +o

1106 prácticamente *adv* practically
- la Seguridad Social estaba prácticamente en quiebra
96 | 1704 +o

1107 moneda *nf* coins, currency
- tendría una moneda - de veinte centavos, nada más
97 | 1408

1108 facilidad *nf* ease, facility
- es un hombre inteligente con una gran facilidad de expresión
98 | 838

1109 matrimonio *nm* marriage, married couple
- nosotros tuvimos cinco hijos en el matrimonio
95 | 1502

1110 escaso *adj* scarce, very little
- el gobierno ha ofrecido el escaso incremento del 2%
96 | 1338

1111 iglesia *nf* church
- yo me voy a la iglesia, a rezar por mi alma
92 | 1908

1112 ayer *adv* yesterday
- ayer se levantó temprano
89 | 2887 +o

1113 oficina *nf* office
- trabajo en la oficina de capacitación
96 | 1213 +o

1114 cristiano *adj* Christian
- el mandamiento cristiano de sepultar a los muertos
95 | 1633

1115 institución *nf* institution
- han hecho variar de modo considerable la institución del matrimonio
97 | 1953

1116 someter *v* to subject
- te vamos a someter a una prueba de resistencia
98 | 1585

1117 fundar *v* to found, base
- su intención de fundar una colonia penitenciaria
97 | 1554

1118 seguro *adj* safe, sure, secure
- uno se siente muy seguro con un jefe así
99 | 1113

1119 intenso *adj* intense, acute
- estaban poseídos por un sueño muy intenso de independencia
99 | 1209

1120 frío *nm* cold
- porque en diciembre hacía frío y había que vestirse de lana
96 | 1399

1121 domingo *nm* Sunday
- asistía a la Iglesia los domingos
92 | 1535 +o

1122 reacción *nf* reaction
- me llama para despedirse, mi reacción inmediata le sorprende
98 | 1695

1123 elevar *v* to elevate, raise
- trataban de elevar su voz sobre los demás
99 | 972

1124 cantar *v* to sing
- comenzó a cantar con una voz muy dulce
92 | 2012

1125 acontecimiento *nm* event, happening
- el día de la comida fue acontecimiento memorable
98 | 1155

1126 costa *nf* coast
- un parque nacional que hay en la costa del Pacífico hacia el sur
98 | 1670

1127 peligroso *adj* dangerous
- era peligroso caminar en la oscuridad
98 | 1168

1128 lento *adj* slow
- hubo de sufrir con paciencia el correr lento de las horas
98 | 1225

1129 método *nm* method
- me impresiona mucho su método científico de investigación
96 | 2541

1130 comunidad *nf* community
- mi nombre únicamente circula entre la comunidad médica nacional
94 | 2334 +o

1131 coche *nm* car, carriage
- ¿no podemos venir ni en el coche ni en el tren?
93 | 1962

1132 asumir *v* to assume, take on
- el papá asumió la responsabilidad
96 | 1517

1133 aclarar *v* to clarify, clear up
- hay que aclarar una cosa poco clara
98 | 999

1134 arrastrar *v* to drag, pull
- el abuelo arrastró su sillón hasta la ventana
98 | 1489

1135 página *nf* page
- cojo el periódico y leo primero las páginas deportivas
95 | 1412

1136 declarar *v* to declare, testify
- ¿tiene que declarar algo sobre el crimen?
97 | 1500

1137 frecuencia *nf* frequency
- se ha citado con mucha frecuencia en varias ocasiones
97 | 1583

1138 conclusión *nf* conclusion, end
- la reflexión terminaba en una conclusión poco optimista
98 | 1257

1139 escena *nf* scene, stage, setting
- aparece en la escena artística en 1960
96 | 1479

1140 falso *adj* false
- hay preguntas de verdadero o falso
98 | 1140

1141 estructura *nf* structure
- está sustentada por una estructura reticular de tubos de acero
93 | 3236 +o f

1142 beneficio *nm* benefit, profit
- nos agrupamos para luchar en beneficio de todos
97 | 1110

1143 alimento *nm* food, nourishment
- el arroz es un tipo de alimento básico
96 | 1788

1144 tranquilo *adj* calm, tranquil, relaxed
- si me dejaran tranquilo y en paz
92 | 1623 +o

1145 velocidad *nf* speed, velocity
- no hay mayor velocidad que la de la luz
96 | 1904

1146 barrio *nm* neighborhood, district
- en mi barrio vivía gente de países distintos
91 | 1773

1147 nombrar *v* to name, appoint
- fue nombrado dictador en el 82 a.C
98 | 1004

1148 análisis *nm* analysis
- al lado de excelentes análisis se han colocado caprichosas aproximaciones
98 | 1759

1149 confundir *v* to confuse
- ahora la geografía se me confunde en la memoria
98 | 1006

1150 frontera *nf* border, frontier
- la frontera entre la Argentina y el Paraguay era el Río Paraguay
99 | 1178

1151 describir *v* to describe
- no te voy a describir la escena
98 | 1461

1152 lejano *adj* distant
- un sonido lejano, intermitente, cruel, nada más, oí
97 | 1341

1153 breve *adj* brief, short
- les ruego que no pronuncien discursos, por breves que sean
99 | 1323

1154 temor *nm* fear
- el temor paralizó sus miembros por un instante
99 | 1252

1155 calcular *v* to calculate, figure out
- lo ha pensado bien y ha calculado cada palabra
100 | 986

1156 conformar *v* to conform
- O. no se conformó fácilmente con la ausencia de L.
98 | 904

1157 ataque *nm* attack, raid
- durante el ataque, Mussolini se encontraba en Verona con Hitler
96 | 1523

1158 pintar *v* to paint
- un trabajo para pintar varias casas
95 | 1089

1159 cine *nm* cinema, US movie theater
- la foto, el cine y la televisión iban a barrer al libro
93 | 1896

1160 rama *nf* branch, bough, limb
- el mono saltó de la rama y lo espantó
96 | 1212

1161 repartir *v* to divide, deliver, distribute
- son nueve panes a repartir entre diez hombres
99 | 852

1162 comienzo *nm* start, beginning
- y esto es el comienzo de todo lo que vino después
93 | 1806

1163 exterior *adj* exterior, outside
- lo de adentro no se amolda a la realidad exterior
99 | 1415

1164 barco *nm* boat, ship
- me sentí perdido en medio de aquel barco y de aquel océano
93 | 1841

1165 partida *nf* game, match, departure
- juega una partida de ajedrez con la muerte
99 | 1120

1166 hallar *v* to find (out)
- tratan de hallar en el cosmos la antimateria perdida
94 | 2156

1167 ordenar *v* to put in order, organize
- arrugó la frente como para ordenar sus pensamientos
98 | 1455

1168 aparato *nm* apparatus, device
- un sismómetro es un aparato que simplemente detecta las ondas
97 | 1218

1169 convencer *v* to convince, persuade
- nadie los va a convencer de lo contrario
98 | 1083

1170 médico *adj* medical
- de niveles de ejercicio, revisiones médicas o dietas
99 | 1307

1171 extranjero *nm* foreigner
- conoce a los extranjeros de distintos países
97 | 1104

1172 cámara *nf* camera, chamber
- la escena fue grabada por la cámara de seguridad del banco
96 | 1361

1173 creación *nf* creation
- para permitir la creación de 26.000 puestos escolares nuevos
99 | 1576

1174 rodear *v* to surround
- consiguieron rodear a las tropas británicas
96 | 1234

1175 ajeno *adj* not belonging to, detached
- estás en el mundo, pero ajeno al mundo
96 | 1146

1176 reflejar *v* to reflect
- los términos se debían modificar para reflejar los cambios
98 | 1348

1177 gana *nf* desire
- si tengo ganas de trabajar, lo puedo hacer en tres horas
90 | 1829 +o -nf

1178 seco *adj* dry, arid
- el río está seco y no circula
93 | 1615

1179 quinto *adj* fifth
- el mes, el quinto de ese año, o sea mayo
97 | 1003

1180 moda *nf* fashion, form
- es una costumbre nueva, una moda nueva
95 | 1181

1181 absolutamente *adv* absolutely, completely
- tu poder general es absolutamente válido
95 | 1375 +o

1182 rechazar *v* to reject
- es libre para aceptar o rechazar la propuesta
97 | 1334

1183 contribuir *v* to contribute
- estaría dispuesto a contribuir en tan digna obra
97 | 1288

1184 ruido *nm* noise
- sólo oigo el ruido del tráfico
94 | 1752

1185 cama *nf* bed (furniture)
- no podía dormir en esa cama pequeña
90 | 2973

1186 infantil *adj* of children, childlike, infantile
- tenía un rostro infantil, lleno de luz, mejillas sonrosadas
96 | 1066

1187 técnica *nf* technique, skill
- la técnica de microdiálisis utiliza sondas
95 | 2385 +o -f

1188 consejo *nm* advice, council, counsel
- hay que tener paciencia, fue el consejo de la comadre
99 | 917

1189 internacional *adj* international
- gozan hoy día de un gran prestigio internacional
94 | 2687

1190 violencia *nf* violence
- los cadáveres mostraban signos de violencia, heridas de bala
96 | 1534

1191 original *adj* original
- vamos a seguir con el plan original
100 | 1073

1192 sonido *nm* sound
- vuelve a escucharse el sonido del avión
90 | 1619

1193 vencer *v* to overcome, conquer
- puedes ayudarnos a vencer la miseria y el miedo
97 | 1350

1194 estrella *nf* star
- la estrella más cercana es Alpha Centauri
92 | 2287

1195 útil *adj* useful
- todo era útil, que todo servía para algo
100 | 913

1196 alejar *v* to move away
- se alejó de ella, dio unos pasos, se sintió solo
97 | 1560

1197 mirada *nf* gaze, look
- refleja una mirada límpida, inocente y sorprendida
91 | 3054

1198 tremendo *adj* tremendous, dreadful, huge
- el no tener donde vivir es un problema tremendo
97 | 931 +o

1199 cuándo *adv* when?
- ¿Cuándo vuelven? – preguntó
94 | 1298 +o

1200 temprano *adj* early
- demasiado temprano para dar un diagnóstico definitivo
99 | 1035

1201 pierna *nf* leg
- tenían las piernas y el cuerpo adaptados para caminar erguidos
92 | 2354

1202 transmitir *v* to transmit, broadcast
- los conciertos que transmite en directo Radio 2
97 | 1072

1203 marchar *v* to go, leave, march
- recogió la cartera y se marchó a toda prisa
93 | 1585

1204 hambre *nf* (el) hunger, starvation
- a veces cuando tengo hambre, como demasiado
96 | 1312

1205 placer *nm* pleasure
- Es siempre un gran placer caminar junto a ti
94 | 1430

1206 profesión *nf* profession, occupation
- ejerció la profesión de abogado
98 | 1006

1207 destruir *v* to destroy, ruin
- el equipo militar piensa destruir a este enemigo
100 | 1174

1208 separado *adj* separate
- de verse lejos de sus hijos, separado de ellos quizá para siempre
99 | 855

1209 opinar *v* to think, be of the opinion
- no quisiera opinar ni entrar en una controversia
99 | 1018 +o

1210 objetivo *nm* objective
- con el objetivo de reducir los riesgos para la salud
93 | 2071

1211 honor *nm* honor, honesty
- tengo el honor de presentar ante la Cámara el proyecto de ley
97 | 1001

1212 montaña *nf* mountain
- el alpinista consideraba el desafío de la montaña severa
95 | 1220

1213 cometer *v* to commit
- después de cometer el horrendo crimen el asesino se entregó
97 | 950

1214 lógico *adj* logical
- todo había sido tan natural, tan lógico
95 | 1156 +o

1215 instante *nm* instant, moment
- ¡rápido! Cada instante malgastado, perdimos dinero
92 | 2014

Time (tiempo 68-M) (also weather)

General terms:

vez 44-F time (specific occurrence)

tiempo 68-M time (general)

momento 108-M moment

fecha 749-F date, day

rato 1478-M while, moment

horario 2095-M schedule, timetable

fase 2310-M phase, stage

calendario 3656-M calendar

Relative time:

pasado 902-M past

presente 802-M present

futuro 623-M future

Units of time (small to large)

segundo 577-M second

minuto 459-M minute

hora 143-F hour

día 71-M day

semana 304-F week

mes 210-M month

temporada 1887-F season

año 55-M year

década 2127-F decade

generación 906-F generation

etapa 921-F stage, period

siglo 273-M century

época 358-F age, period

Parts of the day (morning to night)

alba 5369-M dawn

madrugada 2241-F dawn, daybreak

mañana 401-F morning, tomorrow

mediodía 2618-M noon, midday

tarde 242-F afternoon, evening;

crepúsculo 6469-M dusk, twilight

atardecer 4186-M evening, dusk

noche 196-F night

medianoche 5790-F midnight

víspera 3541-F eve

Days of week (in order)

lunes 2187-M Monday

martes 3490-M Tuesday

miércoles 3431-M Wednesday

jueves 2606-M Thursday

viernes 2483-M Friday

sábado 1816-M Saturday

domingo 1121-M Sunday

Months (in order)

enero 1449-M January

febrero 1722-M February

marzo 2002-M March

abril 1922-M April

mayo 1422-M May

junio 2349-M June

julio 1559-M July

agosto 1244-M August

septiembre 2574-M September

octubre 1688-M October

noviembre 2148-M November

diciembre 1341-M December

Seasons

primavera 2325-F spring

verano 893-M summer

otoño 3357-M autumn

invierno 1340-M winter

1216 viento *nm* wind, scent
- un viento de huracán amenaza arrancar el techo
90 | 2389

1217 lluvia *nf* rain
- el Cairo recibe sólo 26 mm de precipitaciones de lluvia al año
96 | 1686

1218 ejército *nm* army
- le impidió seguir la ofensiva contra el ejército iraquí hasta el final
95 | 1596

1219 trasladar *v* to move, transfer
- debido a su salud, se traslada a vivir en Viña
97 | 975

1220 tren *nm* train, convoy
- el tren vuelve a parar en otra estación
94 | 1248

1221 concluir *v* to conclude, finish
- no tuvo tiempo de concluir su propio pensamiento
95 | 1336

1222 círculo *nm* circle, club
- la proporción entre el diámetro y la circunferencia de un círculo
96 | 1075

1223 auténtico *adj* authentic
- que parece un auténtico dinosaurio en pleno siglo XX
95 | 1177 +o

1224 hermoso *adj* beautiful, lovely
- ese pájaro se caracteriza por su sonido muy hermoso
93 | 1834

1225 oponer *v* to oppose
- nuestro grupo se opone a este proyecto
100 | 938

1226 ventaja *nf* advantage, benefit
- cada uno tiene su ventaja y su desventaja
98 | 1200

1227 figurar *v* to appear, represent, figure (in)
- mi nombre no figuraba en ningún diccionario de autores
97 | 847

1228 terrible *adj* terrible
- me daba miedo hablar de algo tan terrible como la guerra
94 | 1387

1229 isla *nf* island
- el hogar es como una isla de decencia en el mar de la perdición
94 | 1757

1230 torno *nm* en torno a: about, regarding
- todo lo que está ocurriendo en torno a la reforma del impuesto
95 | 1528

1231 sentado *adj* seated
- el juez estaba sentado detrás de un escritorio
94 | 1949

1232 amistad *nf* friendship
- un hombre muy profundo, fiel a la amistad y al amor
95 | 1032

1233 concentrar *v* to concentrate
- la actualidad mediática concentra sus focos sobre este libro
98 | 969

1234 correcto *adj* correct, suitable
- ¡cuidado!, que no es correcto besar a extraños
97 | 906

1235 mañana *adv* tomorrow
- ¿Entonces mañana va a comer otra vez…?
88 | 1778 +o -nf

1236 cadena *nf* chain
- para interrumpir la fotosíntesis y romper la cadena alimenticia
97 | 1370

1237 político *nm/f* politician
- la reelección como el político más popular
97 | 1248

1238 rey *nm* king
- como nuestro amigo y admirado Rey Juan Carlos y la Reina Sofía
92 | 1833

1239 permanente *adj* permanent
- vivían en permanente lucha con las ratas
96 | 1370

1240 ánimo *nm* zest, spirit, heart
- con ese deseo, con ese ánimo, con ese vehemente sentir de las gentes
97 | 1068

1241 trato *nm* treatment, manner, agreement
- exigente pero cortés en el trato con los músicos
99 | 744

1242 ejercicio *nm* exercise, practice
- no puedo intervenir en el ejercicio de sus funciones
95 | 1453

1243 organización *nf* organization
- el estado es una forma de organización social
95 | 2564

1244 agosto *nm* August
- tengo que comer el 24 de agosto con el nuevo ministro
98 | 1052

1245 secretario *nm/f* secretary
- así lo indicó el secretario general en una Comisión
94 | 1317

1246 norteamericano *adj* North American
- escucharon el discurso del presidente norteamericano
95 | 1619

1247 ignorar *v* to be unaware
- no puedo ignorar el heroísmo del pueblo paraguayo
98 | 1047

1248 dedo *nm* finger, toe, digit
- el juez golpeaba con la yema de los dedos sobre los papeles
91 | 2580

1249 gasto *nm* expense, expenditure
- me daría también una suma mensual para mis gastos menores
96 | 1439

1250 café *nm* coffee, café
- ¿qué tomas tú? // Café, café negro doble
92 | 1593

1251 diálogo *nm* dialogue, conversation
- en el primer acto, hay un diálogo entre Don José y Zúñiga
96 | 1151 +o

1252 dudar *v* to (have) doubt
- yo dudo de que el Gobierno tenga la capacidad
97 | 991

1253 comercial *adj* commercial, shopping
- está empleado en una firma comercial importante
94 | 1773

1254 discurso *nm* lecture, discourse, talk
- en 1988 pronunció el discurso: «Chopín en España»
96 | 1348

1255 obligado *adj* obliged, required
- no me siento obligado ni responsable
99 | 1035

1256 hermana *nf* sister
- fue mi papá, fue mi hermana, fueron mis hijos, fue mi suegra
93 | 1947

1257 descansar *v* to rest
- sin descansar tuvimos que correr a Chorrillos
99 | 897

1258 caja *nf* bank, box, safe
- ¿para qué queremos nosotros el dinero en la Caja de Ahorros?
94 | 1161

1259 juez *nc* judge
- no habrá en España un juez que sea capaz de condenarle
95 | 1421

1260 particular *nm* particular, detail, individual
- hablo en particular de los antiguos regímenes comunistas
97 | 967

1261 americano *adj* American
- ¿viste las series americanas que dan por televisión?
95 | 1533 +o

1262 poeta *nc* poet
- muchos vieron en Whitman al «poeta de América»
91 | 1698

1263 interior *adj* interior, inside
- que sirve de pórtico de entrada al extenso espacio interior
97 | 1259

1264 sorpresa *nf* surprise
- quiero darle una sorpresa; la emoción será doble
94 | 1271

1265 ventana *nf* window
- cubre la ventana con la cortina
93 | 2483

1266 característica *nf* characteristic, aspect
- hay una característica que hace única a la pintura
96 | 1854

1267 adoptar *v* to adopt
- ¿estaría con tiempo de adoptar otra postura?
97 | 1584

1268 arrancar *v* to start (machine), uproot
- abordó su auto, arrancó el motor diesel
97 | 1106

1269 disfrutar *v* to enjoy
- disfruta de los mínimos placeres de esa vida
96 | 959

1270 práctico *adj* practical, skillful
- esperar años hasta ver los resultados prácticos de sus hallazgos
99 | 1004

1271 suma *nf* sum, amount, summary
- rehusa gastar tal suma de dinero
96 | 1029

1272 molestar *v* to bother, disturb, upset
- esto me molestó de verdad, pero traté de dominar mi desagrado
94 | 1117 +o

1273 excelente *adj* excellent
- se obtienen excelentes resultados en pocos días
99 | 822

1274 volumen *nm* volume
- aporta un volumen de agua de 34 millones de litros por segundo
98 | 1046

1275 estación *nf* station, season
- ella descendía en la estación del metro Pino Suárez
98 | 1241

1276 atrever *v* to dare
- esperó resignado, sin atreverse a salir
92 | 1383

1277 cultural *adj* cultural
- por la supremacía económica, cultural, lingüística sobre los otros
90 | 2791 +o -f

1278 complejo *adj* complex, complicated
- ¡quién podrá saber cuán complejo es el corazón humano!
99 | 1298

1279 argumento *nm* argument, plot
- ha escrito relatos breves con su argumento muy bien determinado
97 | 997

1280 categoría *nf* category
- la física entra en la misma categoría que la biología y la sociología
96 | 1021

1281 plata *nf* silver, money
- ornamentados con perlas e hilos de oro y plata
91 | 1653

1282 conflicto *nm* conflict
- el conflicto árabe-israelí tiene raíces profundamente religiosas
95 | 2008

1283 avión *nm* plane, airplane, aircraft
- se presentó un incidente en un avión de la British Airways
93 | 1478

1284 débil *adj* weak
- una ampolleta eléctrica echaba una débil luz sobre nosotros
98 | 928

1285 ropa *nf* clothes, clothing
- está vestida de ropa deportiva
93 | 2025

1286 examen *nm* examination, exam
- yo tuve un examen de matemáticas en la Preparatoria
98 | 948

1287 habitante *nm* inhabitant
- soy parte de esta ciudad, soy su habitante
97 | 1510

1288 acerca *adv* about, concerning
- escribió un cuento acerca de un muchacho
94 | 1276

1289 ceder *v* to give way, yield
- necesitaremos ceder mucho para llegar a un acuerdo
99 | 860

1290 justicia *nf* justice, fairness
- el castigo es cosa de la justicia
94 | 1314

1291 independiente *adj* independent, self-sufficient
• eso se llama ser independiente y no «el nene de mamá»
97 | 1316

1292 criterio *nm* criterion
• se puede tener criterio para saber lo que es bueno y lo que es malo
97 | 1345

1293 atraer *v* to attract
• queremos atraer la atención de los hombres
98 | 900

1294 convencido *adj* convinced, persuaded
• estoy convencido de que no estoy solo
98 | 891

1295 plazo *nm* deadline, installment
• nos dio una hora de plazo, y se sentó a esperar tranquilamente
95 | 1509

1296 pendiente *adj* aware of, pending
• ha estado pendiente de lo que estaba ocurriendo en cada momento
97 | 936

1297 kilómetro *nm* kilometer
• ¿sabes cuánto es un kilómetro de distancia?
95 | 1264

1298 hospital *nm* hospital
• jefe del Servicio de Infecciosos del hospital Clínico de Barcelona
93 | 1368 +o

1299 satisfacción *nf* satisfaction
• te recogemos con satisfacción y con orgullo
95 | 809 +o

1300 futuro *adj* future
• dará sus frutos en algún tiempo futuro
97 | 1051

1301 acumular *v* to accumulate, amass
• deseosos de acumular una fortuna para el hijo
97 | 884

1302 desconocido *adj* unknown
• salí sin mapa con rumbo desconocido
98 | 1210

1303 practicar *v* to practice
• para practicar otros deportes de montaña y de aventura
98 | 998

1304 gozar *v* to enjoy
• gozaban de un privilegio político
99 | 980

1305 muchísimo *adj* great many, great amount
• ¡ahora vas a poder ganar muchísimo dinero!
91 | 1614 +o

1306 sesenta *num* sixty
• contó no treinta sino sesenta segundos
96 | 1031 +o

1307 silla *nf* chair, seat
• me senté en una silla baja junto al fuego
95 | 1478

1308 justificar *v* to justify, excuse
• no quiero justificar ninguna acción criminal
98 | 979

1309 tradicional *adj* traditional
• vivía en una familia tradicional
94 | 1456

1310 soportar *v* to endure, stand (something)
• ya no puedo soportar estos disgustos
96 | 1164

1311 juventud *nf* youth
• un recorrido biológico por la infancia, la pubertad y la juventud
93 | 1205

1312 resistir *v* to resist, endure
• soy fuerte y puedo resistir mucho
98 | 1087

1313 aparte *adv* apart, aside, separately
• no pertenezco a nadie aparte de mi propia realidad
97 | 810 +o

1314 triste *adj* sad, unhappy
• era sujeto silencioso y triste que vivía aislado
92 | 1538

1315 acceso *nm* access, entry
• prohibían el acceso de los niños a la extensa sala
96 | 990

1316 marco *nm* frame, mark, setting
• se componía de grandes espejos de marco dorado
97 | 1045

1317 vestir *v* to wear, dress
• vistió el abrigo de cordero, se enrolló la bufanda
94 | 1309

1318 prensa *nf* press
• editores, distribuidores y vendedores de prensa y revistas
95 | 1362 +o

1319 excepción *nf* exception
• me pregunto si soy la excepción a la regla
99 | 972

1320 sorprender *v* to surprise
• abrió la puerta de golpe como para sorprender a quien estuviera
93 | 1314

1321 ausencia *nf* absence
• basta para determinar la presencia o ausencia de cierto elemento
95 | 1196

1322 proceder *v* to proceed, start
• vamos a proceder como una nación distinta
95 | 1326

1323 condenar *v* to convict, condemn
• le condenó a morir en aquellos horrorosos días de la guerra
95 | 1081

1324 sombra *nf* shade, shadow
• tomó la siesta a la sombra de los árboles
93 | 2553

1325 **similar** *adj* similar
• algo similar le ocurría al resto de la familia
95 | 1727

1326 **consumir** *v* to consume, take in
• no debía consumir más sal de lo conveniente
96 | 853

1327 **sugerir** *v* to suggest, hint at
• su intención era sugerir unas ideas
97 | 947

1328 **activo** *adj* active
• hubo un activo ir y venir de hombres
95 | 1433

1329 **clásico** *adj* classic
• los mejores ejemplos del período clásico se encuentran en Tikal
94 | 1852

1330 **profundidad** *nf* depth, profundity
• tiene por lo menos, un metro de profundidad
98 | 870

1331 **conceder** *v* to grant, concede
• la eficacia suficiente para conceder lo deseado
97 | 893

1332 **reciente** *adj* recent
• en España es ésta una moda relativamente reciente
98 | 1270

1333 **eléctrico** *adj* electric
• es la base del motor eléctrico y el transformador
97 | 1369

1334 **leche** *nf* milk
• estimula la formación de leche en las glándulas mamarias maduras
92 | 1398

1335 **consideración** *nf* consideration, regard
• que someteremos a la consideración del Consejo Político
98 | 945

1336 **componer** *v* to compose, be part of
• objetos que van a componer un pequeño museo recordatorio
97 | 975

1337 **premio** *nm* prize, reward
• Pavlov recibe el Premio Nobel por sus estudios sobre la fisiología
93 | 925

1338 **bello** *adj* beautiful, fine
• se hospedaba en esa bella mansión de una familia inglesa
91 | 1516

1339 **nacimiento** *nm* birth, origin
• la Navidad, que se conmemora el nacimiento de Jesucristo en Belén
98 | 919

1340 invierno *nm* winter
- en invierno la gente suele tener miedo, el frío es tremendo
95 | 1004

1341 diciembre *nm* December
- se apagó un mediodía de diciembre, diez días antes de Navidad
95 | 1159

1342 brillante *adj* brilliant, shiny, sparkling
- dejando entrever un sol brillante y frío
96 | 1223

1343 comportamiento *nm* behavior, conduct
- el hipotálamo participa en la regulación del comportamiento sexual
94 | 1516

1344 crítica *nf* criticism, critique
- resentimiento que expresó en las críticas sobre su conducta
96 | 1280 +o

1345 femenino *adj* feminine, female
- el pequeño y femenino corazón de nuestra hija
95 | 1088

1346 fuego *nm* fire, gunfire
- me quema el fuego que prendí
94 | 1947

1347 tendencia *nf* tendency, style
- existe una fuerte tendencia a descargar esta responsabilidad
94 | 1626

1348 fino *adj* fine, delicate
- caía un fino polvillo
94 | 1154

1349 norma *nf* standard, pattern, norm
- se cumplen las leyes como norma invariable
93 | 1547

1350 inferior *adj* lower, inferior
- bajó a la parte inferior del puente
96 | 1192

1351 arreglar *v* to fix, arrange
- el hombre arregló las cosas por las buenas
91 | 1235 +o -nf

1352 rueda *nf* wheel
- no incluía jeeps, remolques, ni vehículos de ruedas
95 | 893

1353 puente *nm* bridge
- pasa un puente sobre el abismo
96 | 928

1354 animar *v* to cheer up
- sonríe tratando de animar un tanto la situación
96 | 826

1355 rasgo *nm* feature, trait
- es el primer rasgo saliente de la actitud hispánica
97 | 1093

1356 positivo *adj* positive
- clasificamos en sí y no, en positivo y negativo
93 | 1436 +o -f

1357 cuento *nm* story, tale
- le gustaría reproducirlo en cuentos y novelas
90 | 1619

1358 definitivamente *adv* definitely, finally
- ¿Visión? ¿Delirio? No; definitivamente no
97 | 837

1359 signo *nm* sign, mark, symbol
- su signo del Zodíaco coincide con el signo afortunado
96 | 1190

1360 señal *nf* sign, mark, token
- ¿tiene alguna señal particular en el cuerpo? // Una cicatriz
92 | 1328

1361 apuntar *v* to point, note, aim
- cuando el barco apunta hacia el viento, pierde velocidad
93 | 1101

1362 campaña *nf* campaign
- fueron expresadas en una nueva campaña de reforma ideológica
93 | 2230

1363 liberar *v* to free, liberate
- tomar las armas y liberar al país
98 | 1071

1364 puerto *nm* port, harbor
- el puerto que sirve para tráfico oceánico
95 | 1416

1365 profundamente *adv* profoundly, deeply
- procuro estudiar más profundamente la realidad
99 | 617

1366 aventura *nf* adventure
- era una historia de heroísmo y muerte, de acción y aventura
94 | 1005

1367 pesado *adj* heavy, boring, tiresome
- el silencio se hizo igual de pesado que el aire
96 | 1124

1368 complicado *adj* complicated, complex
- algo más se presentía, más hondo y complicado
99 | 746

1369 añadir *v* to add
- hay que añadir los ingredientes según la receta
90 | 1607

1370 marca *nf* mark, brand, trademark
- se quitó el chaleco y le mostró la marca en el brazo
98 | 812

1371 girar *v* to rotate, revolve
- hacía girar el sombrero en la cabeza
92 | 1251

1372 ilusión *nf* illusion, hope, dream
- fue ilusión todo ese romance
96 | 1071

1373 os *pron* you (obj-pl/+fam)
- os he visto a los dos en esa tienda
87 | 2154

1374 compra *nf* shopping, buy, purchase
- salimos mi mamacita y yo a hacer compras al Centro
94 | 781

1375 inteligencia *nf* intelligence
- no tiene su inteligencia ni su intención, pero sí más conocimientos
97 | 959

1376 volar *v* to fly
- volaba con piloto automático
93 | 1141

1377 loco *adj* crazy, insane
- estos hijos de diablo van a volverme loco
89 | 2060 -nf

1378 virtud *nf* virtue, quality
- es una gran virtud ser disciplinado
96 | 1107

1379 remedio *nm* alternative, cure, solution
- al final no tuvieron más remedio que ceder
94 | 938

1380 delicado *adj* delicate
- la fabricación de vidrio es un proceso delicado y exigente
97 | 758

1381 facilitar *v* to facilitate
- el objetivo era facilitar el desarrollo social y económico
97 | 989

1382 territorio *nm* territory
- la Amazonia ocupa un territorio de 6.000.000 kilómetros cuadrados
93 | 2204

1383 facultad *nf* faculty, ability
- es mucho más fácil enseñar en la Facultad de Educación
95 | 936

1384 solicitar *v* to solicit, request
- era su esposa, quería solicitar el divorcio
94 | 1052

1385 fotografía *nf* photograph
- me gustó mucho el paisaje, y entonces decidí sacar la fotografía
96 | 1187

1386 techo *nm* roof
- es una casa clásica campesina, con techo de tejas
96 | 1141

1387 temer *v* to fear
- empecé a temer que una bomba atómica iba a caer
94 | 1388

1388 conducta *nf* conduct, behavior
- no encontraba en su conducta algo que mereciese un golpe tan brutal
97 | 1401

1389 violento *adj* violent
- los incesantes ataques que anuncian cada vez más violentos
98 | 878

1390 aquél *pron* that one over there (m)
- ¿y cuál es su coche? - Aquél
95 | 1062

1391 salto *nm* jump, hop, skip
- al dar un salto maravilloso, me quebré la pierna
93 | 1252

1392 pan *nm* bread
- ni hay agua ni hay peces ni pan para darle de comer
94 | 1132

1393 atacar *v* to attack
- nos atacó con igual o mayor violencia
96 | 1014

1394 sano *adj* healthy, wholesome
- era un animal sano, fuerte y hermoso
96 | 739

1395 pegar *v* to hit, stick (on)
- empezaron a tirarme cosas; uno me pegó y yo me defendí
89 | 1860 +o -nf

1396 juzgar *v* to judge
- me juzgó siempre loca y no sé si también mala pecadora
97 | 866

1397 limpio *adj* clean
- procuraba mantener limpio el uniforme, que era blanco
94 | 900

1398 disposición *nf* disposal, disposition
- tendrá a su disposición todas las armas legales apropiadas
95 | 1113

1399 posterior *adj* rear, backside
- las subieron al asiento posterior del automóvil
95 | 1580

1400 general *nm* general
- aumentó rápidamente entre los generales del Ejército Imperial
93 | 1148

1401 disciplina *nf* discipline, subject
- imponía la disciplina escolar
97 | 933

1402 relacionado *adj* related, regarding
- es un lugar relacionado con nuestra historia
94 | 1182

1403 habitual *adj* usual, habitual, customary
- se llevó de maravilla, lo que no era habitual en todos los cantantes
92 | 1138

1404 personal *nm* personnel, staff, staffing
- el personal que trabaja ahí no lo ve de la misma manera
97 | 773

1405 interrumpir *v* to interrupt
- suspiro en silencio para no interrumpir la concentración
96 | 986

1406 columna *nf* column, spine
- la longitud de la columna de mercurio en un termómetro
98 | 1012

1407 verdaderamente *adv* truly
- le saca el empleo a los que verdaderamente necesitan
94 | 1056 +o

1408 fabricar *v* to manufacture
- contrató a gente para fabricar y vender el producto
94 | 890

1409 únicamente *adv* only
- me dedico únicamente a mi arte
96 | 934

1410 nervioso *adj* nervous, uptight
- el pobre anciano estaba temblando, nervioso
90 | 1547

1411 indio *nm* Indian
- me da miedo de que hagan como los españoles con los indios en América
92 | 1597

1412 gato *nm* cat
- Esto es ya el juego del gato y el ratón
95 | 1104

1413 margen *nmf* edge, margin, border, brink
- los hippies, que llevan una vida un poco al margen de la sociedad
95 | 920

1414 material *adj* material
- lo invisible está más allá de lo material
96 | 1009

1415 resistencia *nf* resistance, opposition
- fue combatido por la resistencia popular
98 | 1120

1416 consciente *adj* conscious, aware
- el pueblo está muy consciente de sus traidoras acciones
97 | 874

1417 pérdida *nf* loss
- destruyen las células, dando lugar a pérdida de memoria y demencia
97 | 1169

1418 tratamiento *nm* treatment, processing
- se utiliza para el tratamiento de pacientes que sufren hipertensión
95 | 1509

1419 entrevista *nf* interview, meeting
- en la segunda entrevista no se puede decir «nunca»
94 | 938

1420 espectáculo *nm* spectacle, show
- el teatro no es sólo espectáculo, sino también cultura
93 | 1093

1421 personalidad *nf* personality, celebrity
- un hombre que les fascina con su personalidad enigmática
94 | 1135

1422 mayo *nm* May
- estoy hablando del mes de mayo de 1996
94 | 1201

1423 confiar *v* to trust, confide
- me contó que confía en Dios y lee la Biblia
96 | 894

1424 operar *v* to operate
- la economía china operó bajo un tipo de sistema feudal
95 | 875

1425 representación *nf* representation
- reemplazado por una representación objetiva de los objetos
95 | 1213

1426 régimen *nm* regime, diet
- no pensaría eso mismo del régimen de Franco, del franquismo
93 | 1802

1427 punta *nf* tip, point
- empieza a saltar en la punta de los pies
92 | 1285

1428 vital *adj* vital, lively, essential
- eso era de vital importancia
96 | 744

1429 alegría *nf* joy, happiness
- S. sentía la alegría de vivir, bajo un cielo sin nubes
91 | 1289

1430 basar *v* to base on, base upon
- voy a basar el argumento en hechos concretos
93 | 1873

1431 igualmente *adv* equally
- era igualmente cariñosa con ella y con los niños
97 | 751

1432 misión *nf* mission, task
- él es cura y su misión es decir misa, bautizar a los muchachos, casar
96 | 951

1433 estimar *v* to estimate, hold in esteem
- el problema es el de estimar resultados válidos
95 | 890

1434 cotidiano *adj* daily
- era de lo más natural y cotidiano
96 | 860

1435 confirmar *v* to confirm
- los investigadores tratan de confirmar si es verdad
96 | 935

1436 empleo *nm* work, job, occupation
- o buscar empleo en el registro de ofertas de trabajo
95 | 1010

1437 previo *adj* previous
- los cambiaron sin previo aviso
96 | 1178

1438 participación *nf* participation, involvement
- pero debemos tener una mayor participación cívica
96 | 1390

1439 integrar *v* to integrate, fit in
- el teólogo buscaba integrar la religión y la ciencia
92 | 1488

1440 período *nm* period, time
- estamos en un período histórico especial
90 | 1769 +o

1441 busca *nf* search, hunt
- están a la busca de nuevos mercados
96 | 888

1442 superficie *nf* surface, area
- las ondas sísmicas que se generen en la superficie de Júpiter
91 | 2050

1443 aprobar *v* to pass (test), approve
- estudian mucho para aprobar los exámenes
94 | 1359 +o

1444 chino *adj* Chinese
- una escaramuza entre las tropas japonesas y chinas
94 | 1286

1445 pasión *nf* passion, desire
- se necesita mucha pasión para ser pintor
95 | 1060

1446 vehículo *nm* vehicle, car
- bajaron del vehículo cuando el conductor estacionó
96 | 1039

1447 inteligente *adj* intelligent
- era muy inteligente y lo había comprendido todo
95 | 806

1448 grabar *v* to record, engrave
- en un sismógrafo para grabar movimientos verticales
96 | 894

1449 enero *nm* January
- ¿te acuerdas que se daba en enero y luego en julio?
95 | 1087

1450 capítulo *nm* chapter
- este capítulo debe leerse cuidadosamente
95 | 987

1451 fracaso *nm* failure, collapse
- la realidad ha demostrado el fracaso del comunismo
97 | 899

1452 experto *nm* expert
- pronto se convirtió en un experto en armas y explosivos
94 | 888

1453 inquietud *nf* restlessness, anxiety
- tiene la intranquilidad e inquietud de niño
96 | 715

1454 nuevamente *adv* anew, again
- empezaron nuevamente las peleas con ella
93 | 1031

1455 once *num* eleven
- eran las once menos cuarto
92 | 908

1456 listo *aj* ready, clever, smart
- en la mesa estaba listo mi desayuno
93 | 773 +o

1457 equivocar *v* to be wrong
- y me equivoqué; jamás volví a ver mi dinero
94 | 843 +o

1458 organismo *nm* organization, organism, (human) body
- ¿han recibido alguna ayuda de un organismo privado?
93 | 2197 -f

1459 canción *nf* song
- sonarán el himno nacional y la canción catalana «Els Segadors»
90 | 1162

1460 religión *nf* religion
- existía otra religión aparte de la que nosotros profesábamos
94 | 1341

1461 correspondiente *adj* corresponding
- acompaña a la denuncia el correspondiente diagnóstico médico
94 | 915

1462 departamento *nm* department, apartment
- la noticia se filtró del departamento central de policía
90 | 1110

1463 generalmente *adv* generally, usually
- a las diez y media generalmente el movimiento comenzaba
94 | 1218

1464 periodista *nc* journalist
- ¿cuál es su profesión? // Periodista // ¿Dónde escribe?
91 | 1340

1465 seguido *adj* in a row, successive
- no pude dormir durante dos días seguidos
98 | 551

1466 llorar *v* to cry
- lloraba; se enjugó los ojos con la servilleta
85 | 2632 -nf

1467 griego *adj* Greek
- un gran poeta griego de la antigüedad
93 | 1528

1468 interpretación *nf* interpretation, interpreting
- de desarrollar su propia interpretación sobre lo que habían estudiado
96 | 1103

1469 maestro *adj* master
- esperaba poder escribir por fin su obra maestra
94 | 746

1470 barato *adj* inexpensive
- todo era muy barato y la gente vivía con más comodidades
95 | 715 +o

1471 proyectar *v* to project
- usa una lente para proyectar la imagen negativa
96 | 746

1472 belleza *nf* beauty
- se da cuenta de la belleza natural que tiene Colombia
93 | 1205

1473 universidad *nf* university, college
- Nebrija busca refugio en la Universidad de Alcalá
90 | 1921 +o -f

Natural features and plants top 60 words

General terms:

tierra 276-F earth, land, ground

campo 295-M field, country

(naturaleza) 674-F nature, character

ambiente 683-M environment, atmosphere

terreno 796-M earth, ground, terrain

paisaje 1508-M landscape

Specific features:

río 559-M river

mar 645-MF sea

sol 686-M sun

árbol 833-M tree

cielo 932-M sky, heaven

flor 950-F flower

estrella 1194-F star

montaña 1212-F mountain

isla 1229-F island

bosque 1506-M forest

arena 1635-F sand

valle 1663-M valley

playa 1713-F beach

canal 1804-M canal

jardín 1837-M garden

monte 1844-M mountain

rosa 1978-F rose

orilla 2096-F edge, shore

selva 2138-F forest, jungle

horizonte 2140-M horizon

onda 2160-F wave, ripple

luna 2394-F moon

ola 2406-F wave, billow

desierto 2431-M desert

lago 2680-M lake

grano 2748-M grain, kernel

hierba 2850-F herb, grass, weed

laguna 2961-F lagoon

cauce 3075-M bed, ditch

cerro 3187-M hill

(cañón) 3229-M canyon (also cannon)

(sierra) 3390-F mountain range, saw

paja 3483-F straw, thatching

cumbre 3523-F summit, top

océano 3646-M ocean

vegetación 3837-F vegetation

pasto 3870-M grass, pasture

colina 4003-F hill, slope

pino 4157-M pine (tree)

llanura 4196-F plain, prairie

arroyo 4218-M brook, stream

(cima) 4291-F summit, peak

cordillera 4432-F mountain range

bahía 4770-F bay

latitud 4771-F latitude

vegetal 4921-M plant

volcán 4981-M volcano

cueva 5000-F cave

pantano 5024-M swamp

vertiente 5057-F slope, mountainside

cascada 6251-F waterfall

estrecho 6404-M strait

catarata 6531-F waterfall

golfo 6987-M gulf

prado 7287-M meadow

península 7354-F peninsula

meseta 7483-F plateau

1474 riqueza *nf* riches, wealth
- las viejas glorias de España, la riqueza de su imperio del siglo XVI
- 95 | 970

1475 notable *adj* outstanding, noteworthy
- este libro posee una calidad estética notable
- 95 | 1090

1476 beber *v* to drink
- a comer un trozo y a beber un vaso de leche
- 88 | 1648

1477 claramente *adv* clearly
- hemos entendido claramente su mensaje
- 96 | 868

1478 rato *nm* moment, while, time
- cuando hacía buen tiempo, se paseaba un rato sola por el parque
- 88 | 2251 -nf

1479 encargado *adj* in charge of
- ¿quien está encargado de velar por su imperio?
- 95 | 683

1480 técnico *adj* technical
- director artístico y director técnico
- 94 | 1518 +o -f

1481 ciego *adj* blind
- ha tenido una fe ciega en aquella criatura
- 94 | 946

1482 individual *adj* individual
- su misión era solitaria, su problema individual
- 94 | 1249

1483 apreciar *v* to appreciate
- yo pude apreciar sus méritos
- 95 | 850

1484 experimentar *v* to experience, experiment
- experimentó un amor remozado, vibrante e impulsivo
- 95 | 884

1485 justamente *adv* just, exactly
- es justamente porque me tienen confianza
- 90 | 897 +o

1486 amar *v* to love
- cuánto amaba a ese muchachito hermoso
88 | 1638

1487 equilibrio *nm* balance
- hay que encontrar el equilibrio entre el contenido y la forma
95 | 1055

1488 universal *adj* universal
- crearon una declaración universal de los derechos humanos
95 | 1107

1489 ah *interj* oh
- ah, bueno . . . ¿Ya movieron los materiales?
81 | 5347 +o -nf

1490 fruto *nm* fruit, result
- este fármaco es fruto de dieciocho años de trabajo
96 | 831

1491 representante *nc* representative
- se nombró un representante gubernamental para buscar la paz
93 | 1248

1492 robar *v* to rob, steal
- robar diez pesos era pecado mortal
91 | 975 +o

1493 reír *v* to laugh (at)
- se rió, como si hubiera dicho algo muy chistoso
83 | 2836 -nf

1494 literario *adj* literary
- hay una dualidad entre el inglés literario y el inglés oral
89 | 1581

1495 exceso *nm* excess
- comencé a sentirme sumamente enfermo por el exceso de trabajo
97 | 724

1496 capa *nf* layer, coat
- la capa de ozono que protege la vida de la radiación ultravioleta
93 | 1075

1497 defecto *nm* defect
- el Telescopio Espacial Hubble (HST) tiene un defecto de fabricación
96 | 608

1498 fábrica *nf* factory, manufacture
- en la fábrica se producen cosas de plástico
93 | 763

1499 espalda *nf* back (body)
- ofendido, me dio la espalda
91 | 1945

1500 mezclar *v* to mix
- en sus ojos se mezclaban la alegría y la preocupación
97 | 703

1501 género *nm* sort, gender, genre
- te estoy comprendiendo bien sin ningún género de dudas
95 | 1169

1502 continuo *adj* continuous
- durante cinco años continuos lo conocí
95 | 1072

1503 distribuir *v* to distribute, deliver
- esa carta se distribuye a todos los demás
97 | 630

1504 economía *nf* economy, economics, thriftiness
- para gastar en obras públicas y reactivar la economía
93 | 2505 +o -f

1505 apartar *v* to move away, separate
- se apartó del rebaño para seguir su propio camino
95 | 1138

1506 bosque *nm* forest
- se dirigió al pequeño bosque de pinos fronterizo a la casa
91 | 1295

1507 reclamar *v* to demand, require
- «Por favor, déme diez relojes», reclama una mujer
94 | 900

1508 paisaje *nm* landscape
- un paisaje extraño: una montaña, un río y árboles con flores
92 | 1104

1509 quemar *v* to burn
- me propongo cortar mucha leña y quemar mucho carbón
92 | 983

1510 llamado *nm* call, calling
- esto es como un llamado de Dios para ejecutar acciones solidarias
96 | 875

1511 paciente *nc* patient
- no todos los pacientes experimentan dolor torácico
91 | 2009

1512 elevado *adj* elevated, high, lofty
- existía un elevado índice de pobreza y analfabetismo
97 | 1093

1513 obedecer *v* to obey
- voy a obedecer a mi padre; voy a cumplir con su deseo
98 | 785

1514 tensión *nf* tension, stress, strain
- nada me parecía serio, a pesar de la tensión y el anormal silencio
97 | 959

1515 establecido *adj* established
- era la única de las colonias establecidas que elegía diputados
96 | 970

1516 local *adj* local
- cuando podíamos rivalizar con la producción local
94 | 1527

1517 satisfacer *v* to satisfy
- satisfacía su ego que ella le sacara las botas
97 | 607

1518 concebir *v* to conceive, understand
- concibió el plan para alcanzar su propósito
97 | 726

1519 ministro *nm/f* (government) secretary, minister
- el Ministro de Hacienda dice que no hay mucho que negociar
90 | 2084

1520 impulso *nm* impulse, momentum
- lo que realmente me dio el impulso fue una cosa muy curiosa
96 | 1138

1521 reaccionar *v* to react
- el agua reacciona con los minerales
97 | 642

1522 comercio *nm* commerce, trade
- ¿cómo se pasa del monopolio al comercio libre?
94 | 1435

1523 naturalmente *adv* naturally
- los paraguayos somos naturalmente músicos
89 | 1206 +o

1524 acusar *v* to accuse
- no puedo mentir para acusar a mis amigos
94 | 835

1525 espera *nf* wait
- estamos en espera de soluciones que vendrán el próximo año
91 | 1024

1526 gastar *v* to spend (money)
- tuvo que gastar todo lo que tenía para alquilar las flechitas
94 | 863

1527 reserva *nf* reservation, reserve
- abandonando toda reserva, le puso delante la realidad desnuda
95 | 933

1528 regalar *v* to give (as a gift)
- a mi tía nunca le gustó regalar dinero
90 | 979 +o -nf

1529 competencia *nf* competition, contest
- hay una competencia bastante fuerte entre ambos
95 | 1659

1530 quejar *v* to complain
- se quejaba de dolencias de viejo
92 | 763 +o

1531 penetrar *v* to penetrate, come in
- por la ventana abierta penetra el aire fresco
95 | 840

1532 vacío *adj* empty, vacant
- tarea cumplida, noche vacía
93 | 1169

1533 aislado *adj* isolated
- estaba solo, aislado en medio del gran silencio
96 | 738

1534 rendir *v* [se] to give in; to render
- habría caído de rodillas para rendir tributo a la obra
96 | 629

1535 observación *nf* observation
- siempre al día en la observación de la política contemporánea
95 | 985

1536 registrar *v* to register, record
- se dedicaron a registrar y a conservar la herencia folclórica
94 | 1214

1537 limpiar *v* to clean
- le limpian los labios con las servilletas
94 | 761

1538 vacío *nm* emptiness, void
- el salto en el vacío, es generalmente un salto hacia la muerte
95 | 940

1539 atribuir *v* to attribute
- de no saber a qué atribuir semejante aire optimista
96 | 802

1540 cifra *nf* figure, number, amount
- han triplicado la cifra de exportación
93 | 1108 +o -f

1541 ocultar *v* to hide
- cubría el rostro para ocultar sus ojos
95 | 1057

1542 escala *nf* scale, ladder, rank
- iniciador de luchas políticas de escala nacional
94 | 1056

1543 enterar *v* to find out [se]
- me quiero enterar cómo van sus problemas
89 | 1308 +o -nf

1544 procedimiento *nm* procedure, proceedings
- hemos establecido un procedimiento para negociar
93 | 1400

1545 ajustar *v* to adjust, tighten
- ajusta un botón de la chaqueta
97 | 611

1546 fórmula *nf* formula
- plantean la siguiente fórmula matemática: $z = x - (x/y) * y$
92 | 1012

1547 ámbito *nm* sphere, space
- en el ámbito nacional hay una gobernabilidad garantizada
94 | 1254

1548 informe *nm* report
- ya he leído el informe escrito
93 | 1149

1549 dimensión *nf* dimension, size
- el arte ha introducido una dimensión más humana en la vida moderna
94 | 949

1550 cliente *nc* client, customer
- hablábamos de los negocios, de los clientes, y de las ventas
90 | 859

1551 manifestación *nf* protest, manifestation
- la policía acabará de disolver esa manifestación en la plaza
94 | 1041

1552 aspirar *v* to aspire, want
- todo el mundo aspiraba a ello y quería conseguirlo en dos días
97 | 728

1553 pico *nm* y pico: and a bit; beak, peak
- a través de estos cuarenta y pico años
97 | 661

1554 sensibilidad *nf* sensitivity
- la sensibilidad estética es inherente a la naturaleza humana
98 | 594

1555 recurrir *v* to resort to
- no saben recurrir a su propia iniciativa
95 | 803

1556 múltiple *adj* multiple, many
- la pintura es infinita, múltiple, cambiante
96 | 758

1557 regreso *nm* return
- tomamos el tren de regreso en la tarde
94 | 932

1558 temperatura *nf* temperature
- su temperatura crítica es de 28 grados Kelvin
93 | 1793

1559 julio *nm* July
- que vamos a tener el cuatro de julio, el día de la independencia
93 | 1252

1560 poderoso *adj* powerful
- organizó un poderoso ejército de 300.000 hombres
96 | 1100

1561 digno *adj* worthy
- es digno de toda consideración
95 | 790

1562 bomba *nf* bomb, explosion, pump
- con el lanzamiento de la primera bomba atómica sobre Hiroshima
94 | 822

1563 órgano *nm* organ
- el corazón es un órgano que sirve para enviar sangre a los pulmones
94 | 1298

1564 inútil *adj* useless
- yo trataba de calmarlas pero era inútil
92 | 1139

1565 avance *nm* advance, progress
- explicó cómo eso significaba un avance para la civilización
94 | 1369

1566 humanidad *nf* humanity, mankind
- voy a educar a la humanidad por medio de la música
94 | 898

1567 firma *nf* company, signature, signing
- afirma que hay contactos con la firma Sony
94 | 816

1568 soldado *nm/f* soldier
- vestido con el uniforme de soldado de la Guerra del Pacífico
91 | 1502

1569 sólido *adj* solid, strong
- no tenía ningún argumento sólido para contestarle
98 | 717

1570 firme *adj* firm, steady
- tenemos la firme convicción de reconocer errores
97 | 932

1571 extremo *adj* extreme
- nada poseían salvo la extrema pobreza
95 | 831

1572 conforme *adj* in agreement
- como artista no estoy conforme con la sociedad
95 | 690

1573 esencial *adj* essential
- ni me parece esencial ni lo considero un requisito previo
94 | 1113

1574 huir *v* to flee, run away
- huyó hacia la calle como alma en pena
92 | 1284

1575 percibir *v* to perceive, notice
- pudo percibir la dulzura de su aroma
92 | 1084

1576 clima *nm* climate
- el clima era tropical, húmedo, con vegetación abundante
94 | 1090

1577 emoción *nf* emotion, excitement
- fueron momentos de gran tensión, de gran emoción
92 | 1223

1578 automóvil *nm* automobile
- era un automóvil Chevrolet último modelo de la década del 50
93 | 976

1579 transcurrir *v* to occur, take place
- ¿cuántos días podrían transcurrir para que lleguen?
95 | 862

1580 mal *nm* evil
- reflejaba la eterna lucha entre el bien y el mal
94 | 712

1581 recomendar *v* to recommend
- me recomendó que leyera las instrucciones
95 | 542

1582 habilidad *nf* ability, skill, talent
- no tengo habilidad para tocar el jazz
94 | 616

1583 identidad *nf* identity
- ellos sufrieron de una quiebra de la identidad nacional
93 | 958

1584 desgracia *nf* misfortune, bad luck
- se emborracha y condena a su familia a la desgracia económica
94 | 852

1585 corregir *v* to correct, rectify
- vamos a corregir algunos errores
95 | 712

1586 amarillo *adj* yellow
- los colores cálidos (rojo, amarillo y anaranjado)
92 | 1245

1587 consultar *v* to consult
- vio al gobernador consultar su reloj
94 | 610

1588 deber *nm* duty, obligation
- todos tenemos el deber de alimentar esa luz de esperanza
95 | 908

1589 cola *nf* line, queue, tail
- yo era la primera de la larga cola de carros
92 | 842

1590 padecer *v* to suffer
- un riesgo elevado de padecer enfermedades coronarias
93 | 813

1591 progreso *nm* progress
- está haciendo un gran progreso en la lucha contra el narcotráfico
95 | 907

1592 elaborar *v* to make, develop
- hice fuego y logré elaborar un café pasable
91 | 1353

1593 soñar *v* to dream
- yo soñaba con ser piloto
89 | 1235

1594 muestra *nf* proof, sample, sign
- en pocas semanas empezó a dar muestras de restablecimiento
91 | 1088

1595 acostumbrado *adj* accustomed
- ya estoy acostumbrado al calor y al frío
92 | 708

1596 hábito *nm* habit
- era un hábito que se repetía invariablemente en cada ocasión
95 | 637

1597 gritar *v* to shout
- ¡tápate la cabeza! - gritó una voz a mi lado
87 | 2232

1598 artístico *adj* artistic
- París se convirtió en el centro artístico de Europa
92 | 1253

1599 mecanismo *nm* mechanism
- que establezcamos un mecanismo para decidir la reforma del Estado
93 | 1494

1600 vivienda *nf* housing, dwelling
- la distancia de la vivienda a los centros de trabajo
93 | 1007

1601 ocupado *adj* busy, occupied
- pensando que estaría muy ocupado trabajando para los tres
97 | 639

1602 área *nf* (el) area, zone
- encerrando un área circular de unos treinta metros de diámetro
90 | 2327 +o -f

1603 traducir *v* to translate
- la posibilidad de traducir una lengua con toda exactitud
96 | 722

1604 efectivamente *adv* in fact, actually, indeed
- veremos si efectivamente se justifica la ayuda
88 | 1189 +o

1605 interesado *adj* (self-) interested
- tú estabas muy interesada en las ruinas de Tiahuanacu
96 | 583

1606 mezcla *nf* mixture, blend
- ella era una mezcla de amor, de sadomasoquismo, de promiscuidad
95 | 902

1607 excesivo *adj* excessive
- el coche corría a excesiva velocidad
97 | 657

1608 sumar *v* to add up, amount to
- los diputados sumaron 64 votos en favor
94 | 822

1609 alimentar *v* to feed, support
- la lejanía y la nostalgia alimentan la imaginación
95 | 869

1610 habitación *nf* room, bedroom, habitat
- tocaban la puerta de la habitación 222 del Hotel Diamante
88 | 1782

1611 instrucción *nf* instruction
- fue sometido a una intensa instrucción militar
96 | 821

1612 eliminar *v* to eliminate, exclude
- la ventilación elimina los olores y sabores
93 | 974

1613 versión *nf* version, account
- presentó en Londres la versión inglesa de sus crónicas
94 | 984

1614 lujo *nm* luxury
- no podía permitirse el lujo de comprometerlo
93 | 724

1615 intervención *nf* intervention
- le prometió su intervención ante cualquier emergencia
93 | 1409

1616 llegada *nf* arrival
- para celebrar el V Centenario de la llegada de Colón a América
94 | 949

1617 alrededor *nm* surrounding area, vicinity
- entró y dio una mirada a su alrededor
95 | 837

1618 testigo *nm* witness
- soy testigo directo de tal falsedad
93 | 746

1619 dominio *nm* power, control
- intentaría extender su dominio e influencia
91 | 1451

1620 raza *nf* race, lineage
- fue el primer presidente de raza negra de la República de Sudáfrica
94 | 869

Weather

Nouns:

calor 989-M heat

frío 1120-M cold

viento 1216-M wind

lluvia 1217-F rain

temperature 1558-F temperature

clima 1576-M climate

nube 1961-F cloud

atmósfera 2003-F atmosphere

(rayo) 2197-M lightning

nieve 2423-F snow

fresco 2679-M cool

humedad 2777-F humidity

tormenta 2841-F storm

terremoto 4100-M earthquake

niebla 4274-F fog

inundación 4902-F flood

temporal 5043-M storm, gale

torrente 5178-M torrent, flood

brisa 5493-F breeze

tempestad 5873-F (thunder) storm

precipitación 5962-F precipitation

trueno 6182-M thunder

relámpago 6206-M lightning

neblina 6764-F fog

huracán 7407-M hurricane

rocío 7639-M dew

llovizna 8118-F drizzle, sprinkle

bochorno 8979-M sultry weather

nevada 9139-F snowfall

vendaval 11272-M gale, tempest

granizo 12037-M hail

escarcha 12985-F frost

Adjectives:

fresco 2124 cool

despejado 5643 clear

templado 5857 mild

nublado 7104 cloudy

soleado 8216 sunny

Verbs:

llover 2053 to rain

despejar 4573 to clear up

nevar 9500 to snow

lloviznar 23011 to sprinkle

1621 **renunciar** v to give up, renounce
- no debemos renunciar a esa idea excelente
94 | 816

1622 **descubrimiento** nm discovery
- el descubrimiento de otro quark, el «charm quark»
95 | 1032

1623 **vacaciones** nf vacation
- iba a pasar vacaciones en Viña del Mar
90 | 660 +o

1624 **provincia** nf province, region
- nació en la provincia de Badajoz y se formó en la escuela sevillana
88 | 1896 +o -f

1625 **saber** nm knowledge
- el saber de los geógrafos griegos se difundió por Europa
96 | 644

1626 **argentino** adj Argentine
- no se puede hablar del dialecto argentino, sino del dialecto porteño
87 | 2046

1627 **cómodo** adj comfortable, convenient
- no es cómodo, es molesto
96 | 559

1628 **acostumbrar** v to be accustomed to
- no me puedo acostumbrar a este clima
94 | 793

1629 **fácilmente** adv easily
- los misterios no pueden explicarse fácilmente
95 | 553

1630 **claridad** nf clearness, clarity
- mi mirada borrosa no me permite ver con claridad
95 | 839

1631 **negativo** adj negative, pessimistic
- otro aspecto negativo es la libertad controlada
94 | 834

1632 **revisar** v to check, revise, inspect
- el médico revisó el vendaje de las manos
97 | 632

1633 **carecer** v to be without
- una experiencia difícil, por carecer de ayuda
94 | 1052

1634 **científico** adj scientific
- pronunciamientos de sociedades científicas, de grupos de expertos
91 | 1870 -f

1635 **arena** nf sand
- los pies descalzos juegan con la arena limpia y granulosa del arroyo
96 | 921

1636 **postura** nf posture, position, attitude
- parecía preocupado y trataba de adoptar una postura natural
92 | 945

1637 **salón** nm hall, room
- en el salón social hay eventos culturales, hay asambleas
89 | 1137

1638 **escenario** nm stage, setting, scene
- eso crea una mayor familiaridad entre escenario y audiencia
91 | 1062

1639 armado *adj* armed
- el conflicto armado de 1994 trajo para nosotros dos impactos
93 | 823

1640 largo *nm* a lo largo: throughout; length
- los peces crecen a lo largo de sus vidas
95 | 670

1641 prometer *v* to promise
- prometió que mañana cumpliría con su deber
91 | 1055

1642 contento *adj* happy, content
- estoy contento, verdaderamente feliz de estar de nuevo con usted
87 | 1128 +o -nf

1643 hotel *nm* hotel
- pasamos tres días en un hotel de primera clase
88 | 1171 +o

1644 oficio *nm* job, occupation, function
- nuestro oficio es remover las ruinas y recolectar trastos
93 | 821

1645 descender *v* to descend
- descendió de la cabina y empezó a cruzar la pista
93 | 949

1646 cubierto *adj* covered
- las piernas delgadas y fuertes, cubiertas con media de seda
91 | 1370

1647 fila *nf* line, row, file
- extendió de un extremo a otro una inmensa fila de peregrinos
93 | 849

1648 patrón *nm* employer, landlord, patron saint
- tu jefe o patrón tiene cada día una cara más espantosa
91 | 1152

1649 pecho *nm* chest, breast
- él la reclinó sobre su pecho
88 | 1895

1650 tienda *nf* shop, store, tent
- la tienda que me gustaba mucho por la variedad de muebles
91 | 894

1651 típico *adj* typical
- una de esas típicas leyendas chilenas
94 | 829

1652 protección *nf* protection
- no hay protección contra esa enfermedad fatal
94 | 944

1653 funcionario *nm* civil servant
- es un burócrata, un funcionario estatal
92 | 1166

1654 reproducir *v* to reproduce, repeat
- cada una de estas láminas reproduce un color
96 | 639

1655 constar *v* to consist of, comprise
- el observatorio consta de cuatro telescopios
95 | 626

1656 crítico *adj* critical
- sus observaciones críticas podían llegar a ser cáusticas
95 | 889

1657 transporte *nm* transportation, transport
- Iberia ha detentado el monopolio del transporte aéreo español
95 | 953

1658 red *nf* network, net, system
- se hace pública y pasa a ser difundida por toda la red
91 | 1212

1659 caída *nf* fall, drop, falling
- puede durar tres meses pero la caída de Sadam es una caída inevitable
93 | 976

1660 castellano *adj* Castilian, Spanish
- en edición bilingüe: castellano e inglés
89 | 852

1661 asociar *v* to associate with
- a veces, la Naturaleza se asocia con los malvados
94 | 1012

1662 desconocer *v* to not know, not recognize
- todavía se desconoce la identidad del cuerpo
96 | 657

1663 valle *nm* valley
- las aguas que discurren a lo largo de un valle
92 | 1046

1664 fallar *v* to fail, miss
- una cosa que no falla es infalible
94 | 534

1665 vuelo *nm* flight
- el pájaro detuvo su vuelo en medio del aire
91 | 1006

1666 vecino *adj* nearby, neighboring
- nos encontraremos en la posada vecina
95 | 701

1667 sexo *nm* sex
- se puede diagnosticar el sexo del feto antes del parto
90 | 1142

1668 iniciativa *nf* initiative
- estaba dispuesto a no tomar ninguna iniciativa
95 | 1063

1669 increíble *adj* incredible, unbelievable
- tenía una elocuencia increíble; podía hacerlo reír o llorar
93 | 851

1670 concentración *nf* concentration, gathering
- la visita de Leah no perturbó en absoluto mi concentración
96 | 920

1671 grito *nm* cry, shout, scream
- la madre pega un grito de triunfo
88 | 1870

1672 esencia *nf* essence
- para penetrar la esencia de la música, para trascender el sonido
99 | 672

1673 cocina *nf* kitchen
- entra a la cocina y se prepara un té
  86 | 1415

1674 mental *adj* mental
- la actividad mental que expresa una aguda realidad psíquica
  95 | 894

1675 reflejo *nm* reflection
- no he mirado mi reflejo en un espejo hace media docena de años
  93 | 1094

1676 definición *nf* definition
- la definición del diccionario generalmente parece banal
  94 | 810 +o

1677 preocupado *adj* worried, concerned
- el Conde estaba preocupado y necesitaba tomar una decisión
  93 | 583

1678 perdonar *v* to forgive, excuse
- «Perdone que le despierte», Doctor
  86 | 1094 +o -nf

1679 obstante *adj* no + obstante: nevertheless
- no obstante, parece haber indicios de una reducción reciente
  89 | 1618

1680 abogado *nm/f* lawyer
- porque si soy abogado, naturalmente tengo que conocer las leyes
  88 | 1228 +o

1681 agradecer *v* to thank for
- le agradezco muchísimo su presencia aquí
  87 | 952 -nf

1682 admirar *v* to admire
- para quedarse en el parque y admirar los desteñidos colores
  92 | 778

1683 sesión *nf* session, meeting
- he convocado esta sesión extraordinaria para estudiar el problema
  93 | 727

1684 íntimo *adj* close, intimate
- ese hombre era tu íntimo amigo
  90 | 827

1685 reloj *nm* clock, watch
- el reloj de la torre daba las doce
  91 | 1119

1686 estrecho *adj* narrow
- para caminar por serenas y estrechas calles secundarias
  96 | 857

1687 muchacho *nm* boy
- en aquella época yo era un muchacho de doce años
  84 | 2494 +o -nf

1688 octubre *nm* October
- la primera tierra que pisó Cristóbal Colón el 12 de octubre de 1492
  93 | 1027

1689 exposición *nf* exhibition, display
- habrá una exposición internacional en el Museo de Arte Moderno
  91 | 921

1690 ingreso *nm* entrance, admission, income
- todas las niñas dan su examen de ingreso a la universidad
  92 | 1671

1691 revelar *v* to reveal, disclose
- el efecto de revelar el contraste entre filosofías
  91 | 1205

1692 dibujo *nm* drawing, sketch
- la de Van Gogh es un dibujo hecho con pluma de caña y tinta sepia
  92 | 808

1693 frecuente *adj* frequent
- es muy frecuente ahora el divorcio por cosas sin importancia
  96 | 694

1694 inevitable *adj* inevitable, unavoidable
- de hecho, los cambios serán cada vez más inevitables
  97 | 618

1695 hueso *nm* bone
- sólo piel y hueso emergían de aquel cuerpo
  90 | 1163

1696 ligero *adj* light (in weight), slight
- se siente ligero, ingrávido y, de pronto, otra vez pesado
  93 | 914

1697 militar *nm* soldier, military person
- bueno el aeropuerto estaba protegido por los militares
  93 | 959

1698 motor *nm* engine, motor
- M. encendió el motor y antes de arrancar aceleró varias veces
  94 | 1030

1699 oposición *nf* opposition
- abogaba por una ceremonia simple, en oposición a la Iglesia católica
  91 | 1545

1700 patio *nm* courtyard, playground, yard
- en el centro del patio hay un árbol y a sus lados unos asientos de piedra
  88 | 1653

1701 fruta *nf* fruit
- además de frutas como piña, sandía, naranja, papaya y plátano
  90 | 783

1702 ideal *nm* ideal, goal
- es necesario planificar la familia para realizar los ideales de vida humana
  94 | 623

1703 izquierdo *adj* left (opposite of right)
- el lado izquierdo simboliza la muerte
  90 | 783

1704 ti *pron* you (obj prep-sg/+fam)
- no, la carta no es para ti
  83 | 1886 +o -nf

1705 actor *nm* actor
- había logrado un notable éxito como dramaturgo y actor teatral
88 | 1199

1706 confusión *nf* confusion
- la confusión y el desorden eran los síntomas característicos
97 | 566

1707 bonito *adj* pretty, nice
- ¡qué vestido tan bonito! ¡Qué elegante era el sombrero!
86 | 1692 +o -nf

1708 agregar *v* to add, gather
- nadie era capaz de agregar nada a lo dicho
90 | 1562

1709 corriente *adj* current, common
- José es el nombre más popular o corriente
92 | 678

1710 traje *nm* suit, dress, costume
- vestido con mi traje marinero, la gorra en una mano
86 | 1211

1711 exigencia *nf* requirement, demand
- el gobierno abolió la exigencia del visado para entrar en el país
95 | 665

1712 víctima *nf* victim, casualty
- ¡mi única hija ha sido víctima de este maníaco sexual!
91 | 1132

1713 playa *nf* beach, seaside
- estamos sentados en la playa y a lo lejos van pasando los barcos
89 | 963

1714 trabajador *nm/f* worker, laborer
- un 20 de los trabajadores andaluces se dedican al comercio
91 | 1183

1715 primario *adj* primary
- la producción del sector primario continúa siendo muy importante
95 | 971

1716 hierro *nm* iron
- construyeron un puente moderno de hierro
90 | 1276

1717 ideal *adj* ideal
- hay dos procesos: uno el proceso ideal y otro el proceso real
94 | 616

1718 completar *v* to complete
- voy a completar mi carrera con un curso de filosofía
95 | 690

1719 tela *nf* cloth, fabric
- no había tela para los uniformes porque se acabó el algodón
93 | 783

1720 ancho *adj* wide
- la tierra era grande, ancha, muy grande, sí, sí
96 | 942

1721 producción *nf* production
- podían controlar la producción del oro de sus minas
87 | 3421 +o -f

1722 febrero *nm* February
- creo que viene otra vez en enero o en febrero
92 | 917

1723 símbolo *nm* symbol
- el árbol era el símbolo de nuestro amor
94 | 788

1724 agradable *adj* nice, pleasant
- sin duda no era un personaje agradable ni sensible
91 | 723 +o

1725 medicina *nf* medicine
- ¿por qué no se toma su medicina, señor? Se sentirá mucho mejor
94 | 938

1726 combatir *v* to fight against
- es necesario evitar y combatir al materialismo
94 | 617

1727 búsqueda *nf* search
- no es búsqueda porque ya se ha encontrado
90 | 923

1728 colectivo *adj* collective, joint
- para lograr la promoción colectiva y no la individual
94 | 881

1729 tranquilidad *nf* tranquility, peace
- hay tranquilidad; hay sensación de que las cosas funcionan bien
93 | 566 +o

1730 espejo *nm* mirror, reflection
- vio al mozo aquel reflejado en el espejo del ropero
89 | 1475

1731 secreto *adj* secret
- estoy hablando de cosas que no son secretas, sino publiquísimas
94 | 944

1732 comprensión *nf* understanding
- asintió con un ademán de comprensión y entendimiento
96 | 612

1733 incapaz *adj* incapable
- es haragán, incapaz de moverse por nada
95 | 739

1734 cerebro *nm* brain
- ¿qué se sabe sobre la neuroanatomía del cerebro humano?
89 | 1167

1735 satisfecho *adj* satisfied
- estoy muy satisfecho con el resultado
92 | 739

1736 reducido *adj* reduced, limited
- fue después de eso que quedé así, idiota, reducido, inútil, maldito
93 | 713

1737 tiro *nm* throw, shot
- se puede marcar un gol directamente con un tiro libre
89 | 959

Professions (profesión 1206-F) top words # 1 – 5000

autor 538-M/F writer

medico 564-M/F doctor

profesor 621-M/F professor, teacher

jefe 761-M/F boss, manager

doctor 778-M/F doctor

director 816-M/F director, manager

artista 928-C artist

maestro 961-M teacher (m)

escritor 1011-M/F writer

policía 1017-C police officer

estudiante 1019-C student

dueño 1093-M owner, landlord (m)

empleado 1104-M/F employee

político 1237-M/F politician

secretario 1245-M/F secretary

juez 1259-M/F judge

poeta 1262-C poet

periodista 1464-C journalist

ministro 1519-M/F minister, secretary

soldado 1568-M/F soldier

abogado 1680-M/F lawyer

militar 1697-M/F soldier, military person

actor 1705-M actor

trabajador 1714-M/F worker, laborer

ingeniero 1761-M/F engineer

oficial 1781-C official

agente 1806-C agent

guardia 1842-C guard

especialista 1886-C specialist

sacerdote 1974-M priest

cura 2103-M priest

pintor 2218-M/F painter

obrero 2243-M/F laborer

vendedor 2266-M/F salesperson

capitán 2370-C captain

comerciante 2442-C merchant

músico 2518-M/F musician

corredor 2591-M/F broker

filósofo 2653-M/F philosopher

científico 2745-M/F scientist

amo 2787-M master, boss (m)

arquitecto 2808-M/F architect

ayudante 2901-C helper, assistant

investigador 2981-M/F researcher

técnico 2982-M/F technician

conductor 3016-M/F driver, conductor

enfermero 3122-M/F nurse

cantante 3147-C singer

historiador 3159-M/F historian

cazador 3376-M/F hunter

pastor 3474-M/F shepherd

administrador 3527-M/F administrator, manager

monja 3548-F nun

dueña 3557-F landlady, owner (f)

pescador 3824-M/F fisherman

físico 3868-M/F physicist

maestra 3966-F teacher (f)

embajador 3987-M/F ambassador

cocinero 4023-M/F cook

fotógrafo 4027-M/F photographer

consejero 4089-M/F advisor, counselor

piloto 4249-M/F pilot, driver

portero 4315-M/F porter, doorkeeper

comisario 4332-M/F commissioner, delegate

senador 4386-M/F senator

gobernante 4396-C ruler, leader

asesor 4466-M/F adviser, consultant

novelista 4468-C novelist

bailarín 4508-M/F dancer

inspector 4521-M/F inspector

economista 4544-C economist

servidumbre 4602-F servitude, staff of servants

psicólogo 4604-M/F psychologist

actriz 4606-F actress

fiscal 4612-C district attorney, prosecutor

editor 4651-M/F editor, publisher

cirujano 4698-M/F surgeon

intérprete 4716-C performer, interpreter

diplomático 4722-M/F diplomat

sargento 4727-M/F sergeant

jinete 4789-M/F rider, horseman

agricultor 4794-M/F farmer

guerrero 4885-M/F warrior, soldier

marinero 4949-M/F sailor

1738 aportar v to provide, contribute
• ellos son los que quieren aportar recursos
91 | 974 +o

1739 derivar v to derive, come (from)
• con el vocabulario que se deriva del capitalismo
91 | 1233

1740 abuelo nm grandfather
• entonces sería, pues, mi abuelo, mi papá y mi hermano
85 | 1515 -nf

1741 prohibir v to prohibit, forbid
• el prohibir fumar es un debate público
94 | 600

1742 proporcionar v to supply
- es necesario proporcionar alimento a la cría
  89 | 1319

1743 maravilloso adj wonderful, marvelous
- era un hombre maravilloso, encantador, una mente abierta
  88 | 841 +o

1744 saludar v to greet, say hello
- «Buenas noches», saludó E.
  89 | 1213

1745 relacionar v to relate
- cada órgano se relaciona al otro
  96 | 610

1746 declaración nf declaration, statement
- lee una declaración oficial para descartar dudas
  91 | 1334

1747 relativo adj relative
- no de forma absoluta, sino como un índice relativo
  91 | 1404 -f

1748 sujeto nm subject, individual
- el hombre es el sujeto de los beneficios de la economía
  92 | 985

1749 investigar v to investigate
- me propuse investigar la menor anormalidad
  93 | 836

1750 ubicar v to find, locate
- no le costó mucho trabajo ubicar su dirección
  92 | 912

1751 enseñanza nf teaching, instruction
- dedicó su vida a la enseñanza y dirección de su colegio
  90 | 1194 +o -f

1752 musical adj musical
- es un sonido mecánico, pero también musical
  89 | 1169

1753 permiso nm permission, permit
- V. me dio permiso para hacer ciertos recortes
  94 | 656

1754 evolución nf evolution, development
- hablan de Darwin y de varias teorías sobre la evolución de la especie
  91 | 1446 +o -f

1755 tío nm uncle, guy
- a otra pradera, donde vivían sus tíos y sus primas
  82 | 2352 +o -nf

1756 moral nf morals, ethics
- es un compendio de la doctrina y la moral de la Iglesia católica
  93 | 676

1757 redondo adj round
- una luna inmensa, redonda, amarilla, brillaba en el cielo
  91 | 755

1758 modificar v to modify
- y modificó radicalmente su actitud
  91 | 1116

1759 sujeto adj fastened, subject to
- dos horcas que quedan sujetas a un techo no visible
  94 | 548

1760 parque nm park
- el primer parque nacional fue el Parque Nacional Yellowstone
  93 | 854

1761 ingeniero nm/f engineer
- James Watt, el ingeniero escocés, perfeccionó el motor a vapor
  92 | 811 +o

1762 lavar v to wash
- primero iría a lavar toda la ropa
  88 | 931

1763 borde nm edge
- se sientan en el borde de la cama
  93 | 1075

1764 invadir v to invade, overcome
- decidieron no invadir otros territorios
  95 | 794

1765 entusiasmo nm enthusiasm
- me llenó de alegría, entusiasmo y deseos de trabajar
  93 | 780

1766 evidentemente adv evidently, obviously
- quienes evidentemente no eran médicos, aunque habían fingido serlo
  88 | 1014 +o

1767 independencia nf independence
- para festejar el cumpleaños de la Independencia de la Patria
  91 | 1093

1768 mentira nf lie
- para verificar qué había de verdad y de mentira en esos juegos
  87 | 950 +o -nf

1769 exclusivamente adv exclusively
- la economía no depende exclusivamente del trabajo
  93 | 806 +o

1770 sueldo nm salary, pay
- me pagó mi sueldo y me despidió
  90 | 652 +o

1771 desplazar v to replace, move, shift
- en la ventana, la claridad desplaza a las sombras
  93 | 828

1772 comparación nf comparison
- se ha hecho una comparación entre Calderón y Shakespeare
  95 | 604

1773 setenta num seventy
- en mayo, cumpliré los setenta años
  91 | 700 +o

1774 romano adj Roman
- la regulación de la lengua latina en el Imperio romano
  90 | 1486

1775 sagrado adj sacred
- sino el rito sagrado de un mito inmemorial
  91 | 754

1776 seno *nm* breast, bosom, cavity
- ¿por qué a los hombres les gustarán tanto los senos de las mujeres?
93 | 814

1777 adelantar *v* to move forward
- vamos a tener que adelantar la fecha
94 | 677

1778 canto *nm* singing, chant
- mezclaban canto y baile español en coreografías muy simples
92 | 809

1779 potencia *nf* power, potential
- tienen miles de proyectiles estratégicos, son una potencia nuclear
91 | 1183

1780 examinar *v* to examine, inspect
- tras examinar la joya con una lupa
91 | 673

1781 oficial *nc* official, officer
- la autoridad de los oficiales romanos para castigar a los delincuentes
92 | 1030

1782 fortuna *nf* fortune, fate
- a los seis meses, su fortuna pasaba de quinientos mil pesos
92 | 795

1783 crimen *nm* crime, murder
- luchamos contra la delincuencia y el crimen
94 | 641

1784 suave *adj* soft, gentle, mild
- se sentía un viento suave de otoño
92 | 997

1785 opuesto *adj* opposite, contrary
- huía hacia la orilla opuesta
94 | 739

1786 sustituir *v* to substitute, replace
- sustituyó a los militares por agentes de la policía
91 | 985

1787 ciudadano *nm* citizen
- ¿quiénes serán los ciudadanos de la Europa de la próxima generación?
87 | 1958

1788 implicar *v* to implicate, imply
- se calló para no implicarse a si mismo
92 | 1218

1789 baño *nm* bathroom, bath, swim
- se metió al baño para ducharse
86 | 1114

1790 sabio *adj* wise, learned
- las desgracias le hacen a uno sabio e inteligente
95 | 759

1791 ingresar *v* to join, deposit, admit
- debía ingresar a la milicia o a la iglesia
93 | 679

1792 respirar *v* to breathe
- un pulmón inmenso respira en la noche
91 | 899

1793 caliente *adj* hot, warm, spirited
- quieren comer un poco de comida caliente
87 | 1006

1794 reconocimiento *nm* recognition, acknowledgment
- suponen reconocimiento de méritos musicales
93 | 815

1795 exterior *nm* exterior, outside
- en el exterior de los extremos del tubo se sitúan dos espejos
91 | 828

1796 sexual *adj* sexual
- cuyo primer mandamiento era la abstinencia sexual
87 | 1190

1797 respectivo *adj* respective
- debe cada uno hacer en su respectivo trabajo
95 | 665

1798 situado *adj* situated, located
- la casa del cura estaba situada cerca de la iglesia
90 | 1259

1799 crédito *nm* credit, reputation
- pero se le puede pagar con la tarjeta de crédito
92 | 1128

1800 alternativa *nf* alternative
- a todos no les queda otra alternativa que buscar la solución política
91 | 823

1801 rodeado *adj* surrounded
- en la sala estaba rodeado de libros
93 | 806

1802 esconder *v* to hide, conceal
- buscó el pecho de su madre para esconder la cara
91 | 994

1803 cuando *adv* when
- aquella es de mis nietos, cuando eran bebes todavía
87 | 951 +o -nf

1804 canal *nm* channel, canal
- estamos en contra de privatizar el canal de televisión
92 | 982

1805 suficientemente *adv* enough
- no eran suficientemente cómodos para ella
94 | 555

1806 agente *nc* agent
- había sido en sus buenos años agente especial de la Gestapo
91 | 1001

1807 pago *nm* payment
- se habían retrasado en el pago del alquiler
93 | 861

1808 filosofía *nf* philosophy
- «De todos modos tenemos que morir» era la filosofía del hombre
92 | 1213

1809 alterar *v* to alter, modify
- no tenemos derecho a alterar el plan del Creador
94 | 679

1810 lector *nm* reader, lecturer
- no me interesa como lector ese tipo de literatura
87 | 1199

1811 emitir *v* to emit, give (off)
- R. lo siguió sin emitir una palabra
92 | 874

1812 magnífico *adj* magnificent, splendid
- dije que era bueno y hasta magnífico
90 | 696 +o

1813 triunfo *nm* triumph, victory
- para nosotros el poder no será un triunfo sino un sacrificio
90 | 1238

1814 inclinar *v* to bow, tilt, incline
- M. inclinó ligeramente la cabeza con el debido respeto
91 | 850

1815 campesino *adj* rural
- la dramática situación de las familias mineras y campesinas
89 | 1284

1816 sábado *nm* Saturday
- porque ya no tenía descanso los sábados y los domingos
86 | 899 +o -nf

1817 amiga *nf* friend (f)
- había venido al hospital a visitar a una amiga enferma
82 | 1464 +o -nf

1818 carretera *nf* highway, road
- hay 3.39.644 km de carreteras, de los que el 46% está pavimentado
86 | 938 +o

1819 desprender *v* to detach, release, remove
- estira la ropa, se desprende de ella, queda desnuda
96 | 742

1820 efectivo *adj* effective
- ¿cuál es el tratamiento más efectivo a aplicar?
94 | 959

1821 victoria *nf* victory, triumph
- una importante victoria sobre una poderosa fuerza militar
90 | 1151

1822 circular *v* to circulate, go around, flow
- el líquido que circula en el interior de estos ventrículos
95 | 593

1823 pelear *v* to fight, struggle
- fueron a pelear y a dar su vida
91 | 746

1824 pájaro *nm* bird
- parece un pájaro volando en el cielo
89 | 1153

1825 biblioteca *nf* library
- este manuscrito está en la Biblioteca Nacional
90 | 781

1826 reflexión *nf* reflection
- será motivo de profunda reflexión y análisis
90 | 912

1827 aplicado *adj* applied
- la distinción entre ciencia básica y aplicada no existe
94 | 608

1828 aconsejar *v* to advise, counsel
- le aconsejó que conservara la calma y leyera un libro
92 | 492

1829 vocación *nf* vocation, calling
- pero su vocación no era de maestro, ni de obrero, ni de técnico
89 | 709

1830 casado *adj* married
- soy un hombre casado y padre de familia
89 | 860 +o

1831 continente *nm* continent
- el continente africano ha tenido muchos cambios climáticos
93 | 864

1832 severo *adj* severe
- era un hombre fuerte, de carácter firme y severo
94 | 700

1833 tabla *nf* chart, board, table, plank
- memorizar la tabla de los elementos era inútil
92 | 678

1834 justo *adj* fair, just
- ganar una causa justa que nos beneficia a todos
92 | 673

1835 ensayo *nm* essay, rehearsal
- desea escribir un ensayo sobre la República Argentina
90 | 688

1836 plato *nm* plate, dish
- te daban un plato lleno de papas fritas
85 | 934

1837 jardín *nm* garden
- salgo al jardín a mirar mis plantas
85 | 1446

1838 imaginación *nf* imagination, fantasy
- creí que era mi imaginación y no presté mucha atención
92 | 962

1839 precioso *adj* beautiful, precious
- un lugar precioso, lleno de jardines con flores
87 | 863 +o

1840 probable *adj* probable
- es probable que se la abandone por completo
93 | 747

1841 poesía *nf* poetry, poem
- se define la poesía sanjuanista como poesía «profana y erótica»
86 | 1228

1842 guardia *nc* guard, watch, lookout
- era jefe militar de la Guardia Pretoriana
89 | 1057

1843 privilegio *nm* privilege
- por años he tenido el privilegio de ser su confidente
94 | 701

1844 monte *nm* mountain
- El Titanic es el monte Everest para las tecnologías de imagen
90 | 1020

1845 conmigo *pron* with me
- dime que no estás enfadado conmigo
82 | 1668 +o -nf

1846 arrojar *v* to throw, fling
- arrojó el vaso de mezcal al piso
93 | 945

1847 precisión *nf* precision
- no recuerdo con precisión cuánto duró aquel programa
94 | 702

1848 sacrificio *nm* sacrifice
- nos cuesta hacer un sacrificio para construir una nueva iglesia
93 | 690

1849 criticar *v* to criticize
- podíamos criticar todo lo que no nos guste
93 | 681 +o

1850 hundir *v* to sink, submerge
- tuvo ganas de hundir la cabeza bajo el agua
89 | 966

1851 hilo *nm* thread, yarn, wire
- la manipulación del hilo de seda fue un proceso secreto
92 | 871

1852 entendido *adj* understood
- nos confundió el código mal entendido
94 | 458 +o

1853 aparentemente *adv* apparently
- pasó una pareja aparentemente feliz
94 | 527

1854 aparición *nf* appearance, apparition
- sistemas que contribuyen a la aparición de la enfermedad
90 | 1077

1855 poema *nm* poem
- le escribe un poema diario a su novia
85 | 1099

1856 avanzado *adj* advanced
- tenía el solicitante un cáncer muy avanzado
92 | 631

1857 curiosidad *nf* curiosity, quaintness
- la curiosidad de saber hasta qué punto podía ser verdad
92 | 880

1858 afuera *adv* outside
- vamos a salir afuera un rato
87 | 1189 -nf

1859 diente *nm* tooth, cog
- la Biblia dice «ojo por ojo y diente por diente»
85 | 1465

1860 primo *nm* cousin
- porque eran las mamás, los papás, los tíos, los primos
89 | 865

1861 encerrar *v* to shut (in)
- definían espacios para encerrar sus caballos
92 | 708

1862 latino *adj* Latin
- congregaciones latinas y congregaciones americanas
88 | 924

1863 apariencia *nf* appearance, aspect
- miraban fijamente, sin apariencia de sorpresa
94 | 766

1864 novedad *nf* latest news, newness
- ¿qué novedades ha habido durante mi ausencia?
92 | 566

1865 espiritual *adj* spiritual
- la vida espiritual puede ser una fuente de paz interior
93 | 739

1866 limitado *adj* limited
- tienen aplicaciones limitadas, debido a su pobre resistencia
94 | 760

1867 castigo *nm* punishment, penalty
- van a recibir castigo por sus actos tan malos
92 | 645

1868 constantemente *adv* constantly
- como araña que cambia constantemente de rincón
92 | 515

1869 denominar *v* to call, name
- lo que algo se denomina ahora «movilidad social»
87 | 2167 -f

1870 vestido *adj* dressed
- no voy a ponerme desnuda delante de la gente que está vestida
85 | 1195

1871 carro *nm* car, cart
- lo encierran con carro y todo en garajes alumbrados
90 | 785

1872 eterno *adj* eternal
- en la tumba que visitaba dormían el sueño eterno dos hombres
90 | 870

1873 aumento *nm* increase, rise
- el hielo se puede fundir por aumento de temperatura
91 | 1497

1874 pobreza *nf* poverty, lack, scarcity
- la pobreza y la desigualdad son problemas antiguas
93 | 654

1875 impulsar *v* to push, promote, drive
- se incorpora para impulsar la canoa apoyándose en las vigas
93 | 742

1876 caro *adj* expensive, difficult, dear
- trescientos pesos es muy caro . . ., mi marido no tiene dinero
91 | 573 +o

1877 empujar *v* to push, shove
- empujó con una mano el portón de madera
92 | 934

1878 dólar *nm* dollar
- 156 pesetas equivalían a un dólar estadounidense en 1999
87 | 1570 +o

1879 inicial *adj* initial
- la violenta expansión inicial del legendario big bang
92 | 892

1880 local *nm* place, quarters
- yo edifiqué un local especial para ese colegio
92 | 662

1881 dictar *v* to dictate, announce
- la imparcialidad del tribunal sabrá dictar el veredicto más justo
96 | 567

1882 dulce *adj* sweet
- «Bienvenidos al hogar, dulce hogar»
87 | 873

1883 chocar *v* to crash into, collide with
- oigo el ruido de la bola al chocar contra la pared
94 | 440

1884 industria *nf* industry, factory
- esa industria está muy desarrollada en el país
90 | 1702

1885 caballero *nm* gentleman, knight
- es buena costumbre que los caballeros les den la acera a las damas
87 | 980

1886 especialista *nc* specialist
- especialistas en botánica, climatización, ingeniería metálica

90 | 810

1887 temporada *nf* season, period, time
- pronto llega la temporada turística
91 | 839

1888 divino *adj* divine
- consúltalo con la Divina Providencia
91 | 773

1889 humor *nm* mood, humor
- permaneció silencioso sin conseguir apreciar su sentido de humor
87 | 788

1890 borrar *v* to erase
- es casi como borrar lo que se ha escrito con tinta
86 | 747

1891 nación *nf* nation
- la entrada de nuestro país en el grupo de naciones europeas
89 | 1610

1892 felicidad *nf* happiness
- yo creo que la felicidad viene de dentro, no viene de fuera, ¿no?
85 | 974

1893 amante *nc* lover
- también podría ser su amante y amarla todos los días
89 | 765

1894 alejado *adj* remote, distant, aloof
- viajar a algún lugar alejado, aislado de las computadoras y la red
95 | 477

1895 aguantar *v* to endure, put up with
- fue muy duro y papá tuvo que aguantar muchas cosas
85 | 978 -nf

1896 coger *v* to hold, take, catch
- volvió a coger su silla y a sentarse
79 | 1817 +o -nf

1897 cálculo *nm* calculation, calculus
- además, ya hizo su aritmética y su cálculo de costos
92 | 606

1898 composición *nf* composition, make-up, essay
- para conocer la composición de las estructuras de DNA
92 | 994

1899 rapidez *nf* speed, velocity
- una cortina metálica se deslizó con gran rapidez y tremendo ruido
94 | 491

1900 huevo *nm* egg
- entierran los huevos en nidos que construyen en la tierra
86 | 933

1901 elemental *adj* elemental, basic
- nada más que el material escolar, que era muy elemental.
93 | 617

1902 crecimiento *nm* growth, increase
- ha experimentado el crecimiento más rápido en Europa
89 | 1975

1903 clave *nf* key
- teclea una clave secreta, que elige el mismo usuario
93 | 568

1904 golpear *v* to hit, strike
- golpeó la puerta con tanta fuerza que saltaron las bisagras
88 | 1215

1905 tragedia *nf* tragedy
- evitemos una tragedia humana de enormes proporciones
91 | 716

1906 colección *nf* collection
- conserva una colección de periódicos del siglo XIX
89 | 726

1907 chica *nf* girl, female
- es una chica joven de catorce años
80 | 1666 -nf

Creating nouns

The main suffixes that Spanish uses to form nouns (especially abstract nouns) are similar to those in English. The following lists show the most common words for each suffix. We provide the ten most frequent cognates with English, followed (when available) by words whose meaning is less obvious, with their English equivalent.

-ción/sión:
[COGNATES]

relación 230-F

situación 268-F

condición 341-F

cuestión 398-F

acción 405-F

atención 441-F

ocasión 463-F

posición 503-F

función 543-F

decisión 549-F

-or (agent)
[COGNATES]

autor 538-M writer

profesor 621-M teacher

doctor 778-M doctor

director 816-M director

escritor 1011-M writer

actor 1705-M actor

trabajador 1714-M worker

lector 1810-M reader

pintor 2218-M painter

vendedor 2266-M salesperson

(not agent)

señor 240-M Mr.

valor 326-M courage

color 359-M color

amor 423-M love

favor 468-M favor

interior 614-M inside

dolor 705-M pain

-ista (category of person):
[COGNATES]

artista 928-MF

especialista 1886-MF

protagonista 2536-MF

turista 3177-MF

novelista 4468-MF

economista 4544-MF

cronista 6201-MF

dentista 6775-MF

taxista 6779-MF

(not person)

vista 310-F view

revista 804-F magazine

lista 1049-F list

entrevista 1419-F interview

pista 2065-F track

conquista 2650-F conquest

autopista 4523-F freeway, motorway

-ía (more abstract)
[COGNATES]

mayoría 531-F

compañía 798-F

energía 946-F

teoría 970-F

categoría 1280F

economía 1504-F

filosofía 1808-F

poesía 1841-F

fantasía 2050-F

garantía 2106-F

(more concrete)

día 71-M day

vía 982-F road, way

policía 1017-MF police

fotografía 1385-F photograph

alegría 1429-F joy

tía 2199-F aunt

guía 2318-MF guide

-ura
[COGNATES]

figura 495-F

cultura 521-F

literatura 1090-F

estructura 1141-F

aventura 1366-F

temperatura 1558-F

postura 1636-F

criatura 2235-F

ruptura 2457-F

arquitectura 2516-F

(less obvious)

altura 578-F height

lectura 839-F reading

pintura 1097-F painting

cura 2103-FM priest

escritura 2432-F writing

locura 2441-F insanity

basura 2594-F garbage

-dad
[COGNATES]

realidad 202-F

necesidad 340-F

posibilidad 367-F

actividad 393-F

cantidad 404-F

sociedad 408-F

seguridad 560-F

propiedad 588-F

oportunidad 624-F

enfermedad 666-F

(less obvious)

ciudad 197-F city

verdad 209-F truth

edad 350-F age

-ismo
[COGNATES]

organismo 1458-M

mecanismo 1599-M

abismo 3612-M

realismo 3780-M

optimismo 3864-M

turismo 4012-M

periodismo 4652-M

comunismo 4775-M

socialismo 5077-M

capitalismo 5161-M

(less obvious)

espejismo 6183-M mirage

1908 prestigio *nm* prestige
- la Real Academia era un centro de prestigio social
93 | 636

1909 ascender *v* to ascend, be promoted
- ascender o descender a otros niveles sociales
94 | 614

1910 sección *nf* section, cut
- dedicó una página entera en la sección de deportes
92 | 724

1911 complicar *v* to complicate, make difficult
- el trabajo se complicaba por las inadecuadas herramientas que disponía
94 | 340

1912 anciano *adj* elderly, aged
- conservaba sus encantos, en realidad no se sentía anciana
86 | 1211

1913 fiel *adj* faithful, loyal
- mi papá es muy fiel a mi mamá
92 | 738

1914 roto *adj* broken, torn
- el pedazo de vidrio roto que alguna vez fue espejo
91 | 754

1915 bolsa *nf* bag, purse, stock exchange
- le extendía a su amiga la bolsa con hielos y la botella
88 | 822

1916 cinta *nf* tape, ribbon, film, strip
- apaga el televisor y saca la cinta de vídeo
86 | 700

1917 engañar *v* to trick, deceive
- sólo como ilusión, para engañar al estómago
89 | 709

1918 elegante *adj* elegant, smart, stylish
- una casa muy elegante, rodeada de un gran parque
91 | 667

1919 agotar *v* to exhaust, wear out, run out
- el tiempo se agota, y la muerte lo cerca sin remedio
95 | 514

1920 cuello *nm* neck, collar
- una almohada en la que tú reposas tu cuello cuando te acuestas
85 | 1414

1921 continuación *nf* continuation, follow-up
- la continuación de la música clásica es la música moderna
92 | 679

1922 abril *nm* April
- eso fue el diez de abril como a la una de la tarde
87 | 1092

1923 precisar *v* to do exactly, specify
- entendía sus intenciones sin precisar palabras
92 | 616

1924 actuación *nf* performance, acting
- celebró una actuación pública en el teatro Victoria del Paralelo
90 | 1024 +o -f

1925 factor *nm* factor, cause, influence
- ¿la caza controlada puede ser un factor de equilibrio de fauna?
86 | 1996 +o -f

1926 esquina *nf* corner
- desapareció en la esquina sin mirar atrás
87 | 1168

1927 hombro *nm* shoulder
- un chico camina con una mochila al hombro
85 | 1698

1928 infancia *nf* infancy, childhood
- prefiero no hablar de mi infancia ni de los años de orfandad
90 | 797

1929 suspender *v* to suspend, hang, fail
- tuvieron que suspender las transmisiones de radio
94 | 608

1930 descanso *nm* rest, interval, break
- hacen un pequeño descanso después de haber leído veinticuatro hojas
90 | 562

1931 ampliar *v* to enlarge, increase, expand
- era el momento de ampliar el negocio, buscar nuevos mercados
91 | 711

1932 zapato *nm* shoe
- todas las clases sociales llevaban sandalias o zapatos de madera
88 | 1185

1933 parecer *nm* opinion, looks
- y, lo que – a mi parecer – es más importante
91 | 762

1934 familiar *nm* relative
- a que me regalen sus fortunas, y las de sus familiares y parientes
91 | 572

1935 mérito *nm* worth, merit
- tuvo un gran mérito histórico, eso es indiscutible
92 | 575

1936 cultivar *v* to cultivate, produce
- ¿cómo pueden cultivar si no tienen tierra?
92 | 633

1937 oportuno *adj* opportune, timely
- en momento oportuno emprendieron el cruce
93 | 463

1938 explotar *v* to explode, exploit
- explotó una bomba en un mercado en Jerusalén
93 | 514

1939 significativo *adj* significant, meaningful
- fue un proyecto muy famoso y muy significativo
89 | 1098

1940 despedir *v* to say goodbye (to), dismiss
• se despidió de cada uno, y despúes fue a su casa
87 | 1129

1941 suelto *adj* loose
• se me cayó el diente suelto
89 | 715

1942 muro *nm* (outer) wall, rampart
• ya se cayó el muro de Berlín; Gorbachov vende Pizza Hut en la Plaza Roja
90 | 897

1943 colaborar *v* to collaborate, work together
• colabora con sus empleadores en pequeños detalles
93 | 549

1944 menudo *adv* a menudo: often
• es que ella padece muy a menudo de dolores de cabeza
89 | 1129

1945 invertir *v* to invest
• ¿en qué debo invertir el dinero?
93 | 598

1946 montón *nm* lot of, heap, pile
• se casó y tiene un montón de hijos
83 | 862 +o -nf

1947 revolucionario *adj* revolutionary
• era un ciudadano militante del partido revolucionario
90 | 1058

1948 disco *nm* disc, disk, record
• este «tesoro informativo», en un solo disco compacto de lectura óptica
86 | 800

1949 indispensable *adj* indispensable, essential
• es indispensable para crear un mercado líquido y eficiente
93 | 557

1950 demanda *nf* petition, request, demand
• se puede responder a la demanda de incrementar el gasto social
90 | 1254

1951 mundial *adj* worldwide
• París era el centro mundial de las bellas letras
90 | 1511 -f

1952 mueble *nm* (piece of) furniture
• puro mueble roto, sillas sin sus patas
87 | 802

1953 desastre *nm* disaster
• soy un desastre, no estoy capacitada para opinar de nada
94 | 538

1954 secreto *nm* secret
• ¿cuál es el secreto de la longevidad de su voz?
89 | 1124

1955 oriental *adj* eastern, oriental
• su interés por la filosofía oriental y el misticismo
91 | 1051

1956 regular *adj* regular
• de forma regular – es decir, una estructura métrica
91 | 661

1957 angustia *nf* anguish, distress
• el público se dispersa con sentimientos de angustia bajo los paraguas
85 | 1020

1958 provenir *v* to come from, be from
• nacer sin madre es como provenir de un laboratorio
93 | 669

1959 forzar *v* to force
• un ladrón que trató de forzar la puerta de su casa
95 | 530

1960 doméstico *adj* domestic
• la mujer que contrataron para las tareas domésticas
91 | 675

1961 nube *nf* cloud
• una nube ocultó el sol
85 | 1106

1962 criar *v* to bring up, rear
• quiero criar a mi hija pese a que estoy soltera
90 | 560

1963 miseria *nf* misery, wretchedness
• hay que resolver el hambre y la miseria
89 | 700

1964 personalmente *adv* personally
• yo voy a estar controlándolo personalmente
88 | 520 +o

1965 peor *adj* worse, worst
• ese desastre era el peor del año
90 | 590

1966 significado *nm* meaning
• ¿qué significado tiene? ¿Qué importancia le da usted a esto?
89 | 821

1967 fama *nf* reputation, fame
• la señorita Raquel tenía fama de ser una mujer dura
91 | 575

1968 palacio *nm* palace
• la familia que vivió en aquel palacio tenía que ser riquísima
87 | 792

1969 oído *nm* hearing, ear
• cosas que ella conocía sólo por el tacto, el oído o el olfato
85 | 1145

1970 conveniente *adj* convenient
• en el momento oportuno y en el lugar conveniente
92 | 580 +o

1971 polvo *nm* dust, powder
• con la mano limpió el polvo de uno de los cristales
88 | 1112

1972 confesar *v* to confess, admit
• F. nunca me confesó si era cierto o no
85 | 1034

1973 mecánico *adj* mechanical
• fue un acto mecánico y repetido
92 | 550

1974 sacerdote *nm* priest
- un consagrado sacerdote organizó el viaje del Papa
86 | 828

1975 lentamente *adv* slowly
- avanzó muy lentamente escalera arriba
89 | 934

1976 eficaz *adj* effective
- no es una medicina eficaz para las enfermedades
90 | 830

1977 lección *nf* lesson
- le enseñaba una lección de cómo vivir y cómo sobrevivir
89 | 562

1978 rosa *nf* rose
- llené un vaso con agua y con la rosa
85 | 899

1979 nocturno *adj* nocturnal, evening
- la oscuridad del mar nocturno ciega los ojos
91 | 615

1980 posiblemente *adv* possibly
- en este aspecto, posiblemente no haya tantas diferencias
89 | 700 +o

1981 doblar *v* to bend, turn
- tienes que doblar la esquina que sigue
89 | 775

1982 disminuir *v* to decrease, diminish
- debemos combatir la pobreza y disminuir la desigualdad
90 | 985

1983 averiguar *v* to investigate, find out
- llamamos a su casa para averiguar qué se había hecho de él
90 | 553

1984 sospechar *v* to suspect, suppose
- pensó o sospechó que el ladrón era también un hombre
92 | 699

1985 pasear *v* to go for a walk, ride
- me gustaba pasear por ese lugar abierto
84 | 988

1986 olor *nm* smell, odor, fragrance
- sentí que el olor de café venía de la cocina
84 | 1798

1987 radical *adj* radical
- he sido radical en mis ideas y actitudes
91 | 1007

1988 decidido *adj* determined, resolute
- lo nuestro es hermoso y estoy decidido a luchar por él
91 | 576

1989 contrato *nm* contract, agreement
- en marzo firmó un contrato con esta casa discográfica
90 | 776

1990 presentación *nf* presentation, introduction
- es autor teatral tan conocido que no necesita presentación
91 | 549

1991 cárcel *nf* jail, prison
- la cárcel es para los ladrones
86 | 772

1992 división *nf* division
- es un criterio de especialización y de división del trabajo
90 | 963 +o -f

1993 revés *nm* al revés: backwards, upside down, inside out
- ¿qué le parece si hacemos las cosas al revés?
90 | 544 +o

1994 sucio *adj* dirty, filthy, underhanded
- éste no era un sucio crimen de amor y celos
86 | 1011

1995 depositar *v* to deposit, place, store
- va al banco a depositar unos miles de pesos
91 | 509

1996 captar *v* to capture, attract
- como si quisiera captar y retener los latidos del corazón
91 | 544

1997 cualidad *nf* quality, attribute
- su obra posee una cualidad extática, casi religiosa
92 | 541

1998 empeñar *v* [se] to insist on
- un oficial de policía que se empeñaba en prender al chino
89 | 580

1999 sobrevivir *v* to survive, outlive
- la capacidad de las personas para sobrevivir a las tragedias
88 | 845

2000 índice *nm* index, forefinger
- un país pequeño, pobre, con un índice de desarrollo humano bajísimo
91 | 746

2001 salvaje *adj* wild, savage, uncultivated
- ésos son salvajes y ésos son animales domésticos
89 | 633

2002 marzo *nm* March
- esto ocurrió desde principios de marzo o un poco después
90 | 1088

2003 atmósfera *nf* atmosphere, environment
- tiene la atmósfera mística de un templo
88 | 1005

2004 planeta *nm* planet
- Marte es el planeta más próximo con una superficie visible
87 | 1152

2005 industrial *adj* industrial
- es siempre una economía industrial o comercial
87 | 1829 +o -f

2006 orgullo *nm* pride
- siente el orgullo de ser hija de un pueblo inmortal
91 | 738

2007 jornada *nf* (working) day, shift
- entró en casa después de una jornada laboral especialmente agotadora
  86 | 730

2008 desnudo *adj* nude, naked
- dibujaba la silueta del cuerpo desnudo
  86 | 1316

2009 querido *adj* dear, beloved
- nuestra querida patria, la hermosa isla de Cuba
  85 | 777 -nf

2010 absurdo *adj* absurd
- pertenecen a otra época: extraña, absurda y romántica
  90 | 668

2011 dramático *adj* dramatic
- el final de la comedia fue dramático
  91 | 672

2012 palo *nm* stick, pole
- tres palos de duraluminio de 32,5 metros de longitud
  88 | 756

2013 diseño *nm* design
- se emplearon diseños geométricos en blanco y negro
  91 | 945 -f

2014 liberal *adj* liberal
- fue más salvaje que el liberal o comunista
  85 | 1412

2015 lógica *nf* logic
- mi manera de ser tiende a la razón, a la lógica, al pensamiento
  90 | 661

2016 herencia *nf* inheritance, legacy
- ese carácter era una herencia de su bisabuela nórdica
  92 | 583

2017 legal *adj* legal
- al pueblo una norma legal para empresarios y obreros
  91 | 987

2018 artificial *adj* artificial
- los fotógrafos usan luz artificial para iluminar las escenas
  92 | 654

2019 deporte *nm* sport
- el béisbol, ya un deporte olímpico, se juega en muchos países
  87 | 1141 +o

2020 reina *nf* queen
- sentada como la reina en su trono
  91 | 631

Diminutives ("small – ") and superlatives ("very – ")

Diminutives express the idea of smallness or endearment (for example *gato/gatito* cat/kitty), and are formed by adding the suffix - (c)*ito* (or - *ico* and - *illo* in some dialects). Superlatives express the idea of "very/really X" (for example *alto/altísimo* tall/really tall), and are formed by adding the suffix - *ísimo*. Both take the normal endings for number and gender. The English translations in the following lists show the meaning of the base form.

Diminutives:

[noun]:

señorita 2622-F Miss

casita 3849-F house

muchachito 5143-M boy

hijito 5236-M son

pobrecito 5451-M unfortunate person

pajarito 5849-M bird

animalito 5854-M animal

hermanito 6113-M brother

mesita 6456-F table

cosita 6465-F thing

viejito 6690-M old person

perrito 7002-M dog

carrito 8211-M car, cart

mujercita 8347-F woman

abuelita 8461-F grandmother

señorito 9271-M Mr.

cajita 9547-F box

angelito 9732-MF angel

hombrecito 9745-M man

[adjective]:

poquito 2463 few, little

pequeñito 4566 small

chiquito 5769 small

bajito 6083 short

igualito 7906 same

[adverb]:

ahorita 9586 now

despacito 24385 slow

Superlatives:

muchísimo 1305 many

altísimo 3478 tall

larguísimo 4609 long

mismísimo 4901 same

bellísimo 5150 beautiful

importantísimo 5549 important

gravísimo 6743 serious

riquísimo 6801 rich

santísimo 7777 holy

rarísimo 8325 strange

clarísimo 9512 clear

amplísimo 10461 wide

antiquísimo 11183 old

grandísimo 13156 large

buenísimo 13717 good

fortísimo 13953 strong

malísimo 14034 bad

rapidísimo 14144 fast

brevísimo 14171 brief

valiosísimo 15008 courageous

2021 bandera *nf* flag
- la bandera de la región está compuesta por tres franjas horizontales
- 90 | 679

2022 influir *v* to (have) influence
- impotente para poder influir de una manera positiva
- 89 | 893 +o -f

2023 maravilla *nf* wonder, marvel
- ¡ay, qué cosa tan bonita! ¡Qué maravilla!
- 88 | 539

2024 modesto *adj* modest, humble
- como si eso fuese poco; modesta, carente de estilo
- 91 | 556

2025 banda *nf* (musical) band, sash
- toco el clarinete y la guitarra en la banda del pueblo
- 89 | 900

2026 cristal *nm* glass, crystal, window
- se rompió el cristal de la ventana
- 85 | 1165

2027 objetivo *adj* objective, impartial
- representación de la realidad se volvía objetiva, y mecánica
- 90 | 848

2028 anécdota *nf* anecdote
- ¿tienes algún recuerdo especial o anécdota de tu vida universitaria?
- 90 | 454 +o

2029 universitario *adj* university
- fue profesor universitario de física teórica
- 85 | 868 +o

2030 sensible *adj* sensitive, sentient
- su alma primitiva, sensible a todas las emociones del amor
- 91 | 585

2031 leyenda *nf* legend
- en la leyenda griega, Prometeo trajo el fuego a la tierra
- 90 | 570

2032 muerto *nm* dead person
- acá todos descansan, los vivos y los muertos
- 85 | 875

2033 azúcar *nm* sugar
- le echaban un poquito de azúcar y era muy refrescante
- 87 | 739

2034 multiplicar *v* to multiply
- el ruido del disparo se multiplica millones de veces
- 92 | 455

2035 inclinación *nf* slope, incline, tendency
- controla la inclinación de la carrocería en las curvas
- 94 | 429

2036 formal *adj* formal, polite
- que se construyera una sala formal para las visitas
- 90 | 766

2037 doler *v* to hurt
- me están empezando a doler las heridas otra vez
- 85 | 935 +o -nf

2038 primitivo *adj* primitive
- se sitúan estéticamente entre lo primitivo y lo refinado
- 90 | 858

2039 oculto *adj* hidden, occult
- muy esotérico; como ciencias ocultas
- 90 | 659

2040 rostro *nm* face, countenance
- su rostro nunca parece cambiar de expresión
- 83 | 2757

2041 separación *nf* separation
- no hay separación de poderes, es una monarquía absoluta
- 93 | 531

2042 eco *nm* echo, response
- ¡bumbumbumbumbum! Es el eco de las montañas
- 91 | 615

2043 definido *adj* definite
- tenía la sensación de andar hacia algo definido y concreto
- 93 | 586

2044 favorecer *v* to favor, help
- la relajación favorece tu capacidad de concentración
- 90 | 850

2045 cita *nf* appointment, date, quotation
- nos gustaría tener una cita con usted
- 88 | 600

2046 actualidad *nf* present (time)
- ni siquiera en la actualidad son muchos los que conocen el tema
- 88 | 1257 +o -f

2047 externo *adj* external, outward
- el cambio fue sólo externo, por dentro seguía igual
- 86 | 1554 -f

2048 escoger *v* to choose
- resignamos a escoger entre ser buenas o ser malas
- 90 | 558

2049 colgar *v* to hang (up)
- le colgó al cuello el relicario para la buena suerte
- 86 | 1087

2050 fantasía *nf* fantasy, fancy
- empieza a confundir la fantasía con la realidad
- 89 | 731

2051 promesa *nf* promise
- necesitamos cumplir la promesa nuestra que hicimos
- 87 | 652

2052 pata *nf* leg, paw
- casi la golpea con una de las patas de la mesa
- 86 | 851

2053 llover _v_ to rain
- siempre llueve en Londres, todo el mundo lo sabe
88 | 734 -nf

2054 foto _nf_ photo, picture
- las fotos mostraban un dormitorio pintado de azul
82 | 1060

2055 administración _nf_ administration
- ¿qué tipo de administración harán los representantes del Gobernador?
87 | 1042 +o -f

2056 absorber _v_ to absorb, soak up
- incapaz aún de absorber la magnitud de su fracaso
92 | 577

2057 civilización _nf_ civilization
- la armonía espiritual que perseguía la civilización de Teotihuacán
89 | 845

2058 organizado _adj_ organized
- es un estudiante disciplinado y organizado
92 | 714

2059 ocupación _nf_ occupation, use
- ¿cual es tu ocupación actual? // Soy profesora
92 | 591

2060 mero _adj_ mere
- aquellas palabras no eran un mero sermón de púlpito
91 | 692

2061 asiento _nm_ seat, chair
- le ofreció el asiento a una persona vieja
86 | 861

2062 compuesto _adj_ composite, mixed
- ambas entidades, protón y neutrón, están compuestas de quarks
89 | 937

2063 imitar _v_ to imitate, copy, mimic
- Goethe se propuso imitar la libertad estilística de Shakespeare
90 | 539

2064 solitario _adj_ solitary, lonely
- gente solitaria que daría lo que fuera por tener a alguien
89 | 886

2065 pista _nf_ clue, track, trace
- dará una pista definitiva para resolver esta cuestión
88 | 852

2066 testimonio _nm_ testimony, evidence
- no tengo más testimonio que el rumor de la calle
89 | 585

2067 regalo _nm_ gift, present
- fue regalo de mi esposa en mi cumpleaños
86 | 717

2068 educar _v_ to educate
- se tiene que educar, se tiene que preparar
88 | 517 +o

2069 comprometer _v_ to compromise
- no quería comprometer su carrera abogando por un preso político
92 | 548

2070 aproximar _v_ to come near, closer
- se aproximó al mostrador e hizo su pedido
90 | 639

2071 bailar _v_ to dance
- aprendían a bailar el charlestón con el profesor
82 | 1175

2072 inspirar _v_ to inspire, inhale
- era capaz de inspirar y alentar una ambición de grandeza
89 | 821

2073 contradicción _nf_ contradiction
- su verdadero carácter estaba en contradicción con su conducta
92 | 488

2074 agarrar _v_ to grasp, catch
- de meter la mano para agarrar un gallo
83 | 1002 -nf

2075 metal _nm_ metal
- algunos metales se vuelven superconductores
86 | 962

2076 aceite _nm_ oil
- los ponen a cocer y los sirven con aceite de oliva
88 | 787

2077 prolongar _v_ to extend, prolong
- el paisaje que se prolonga hasta el horizonte
91 | 686

2078 código _nm_ code
- cada célula contiene un código genético íntegro
91 | 605

2079 estricto _adj_ strict, rigorous
- la expresión es justa en su sentido más estricto
93 | 577

2080 doloroso _adj_ painful
- como parecía ser un tema doloroso para él, no le pregunté nunca
88 | 522

2081 unión _nf_ union
- con abrazos y besos emocionados sellaron la unión de ambas familias
89 | 750

2082 extensión _nf_ extension, area, expanse
- lo que equivale a doce veces la extensión de España
90 | 953

2083 duro _nm_ duro (money)
- estoy pensando poner un negocio y cobrar a diez duros la entrada ¿no?
87 | 515

2084 adentro _adv_ inside
- allí adentro estaba uno de los salones de té
85 | 1154 -nf

2085 idéntico *adj* identical
- los impactos eran siete, de idéntico tamaño los agujeros
89 | 622

2086 previsto *adj* foreseen, planned
- ¿tiene previsto algún plan de consulta?
89 | 739

2087 adaptar *v* to adapt
- y que él adaptó a los tiempos actuales
89 | 647 +o -f

2088 varón *nm* male, man
- ¿su bebé fue niña o varón?
86 | 747

2089 situar *v* to situate, place, locate
- este punto se puede situar en el centro
89 | 912

2090 característico *adj* characteristic
- un tipo de cáncer muy específico, característico de estas edades
92 | 895

2091 evidencia *nf* evidence, certainty
- no existe ninguna evidencia de la realidad material de ese mundo
88 | 730

2092 dignidad *nf* dignity
- se gana con el respeto y la seguridad de la dignidad humana
89 | 633

2093 escándalo *nm* scandal
- el divorcio sería un escándalo enorme
90 | 666

2094 colega *nc* colleague
- hablando animadamente con colegas de su edad
89 | 545

2095 horario *nm* schedule, timetable
- depende de los horarios del vuelo
87 | 513 +o

2096 orilla *nf* shore, edge
- fue a pasar sus vacaciones a la orilla del mar
89 | 797

2097 curar *v* to cure
- la mayoría de los milagros eran para curar a los enfermos
87 | 542

2098 copia *nf* copy
- me ha dicho que soy una copia exacta de mi padre
91 | 465

2099 huella *nf* trace, track, footstep
- voy a borrar toda huella de tu nombre en esta casa
88 | 710

2100 desempeñar *v* to carry out, fulfill
- tengo tan arduas tareas que desempeñar en el manejo de la casa
91 | 694

2101 ejemplar *nm* copy, issue
- un ejemplar de la cuarta edición de «Los Caprichos» de Goya
89 | 489

2102 extraer *v* to extract, take out
- extrajo el tapón y por el agujero introdujo un objeto
89 | 736

2103 cura *nmf* priest (m), cure (f)
- en cambio - dijo - los curas y la iglesia son amigos de los ricos
82 | 1141

2104 apagar *v* to turn off, extinguish
- ¿puedes apagar la música de la radio?
86 | 830

2105 prever *v* to foresee, anticipate, forecast
- no podíamos prever cuál sería nuestro destino
91 | 551

2106 garantía *nf* guarantee, warranty
- hay que hacerlo con absoluta garantía de los derechos fundamentales
90 | 724

2107 vaso *nm* (drinking) glass, vase
- entonces levanta el vaso y brinda con el licenciado
84 | 1058

2108 perfil *nm* profile, outline
- en las figuras ópticas se puede ver una copa o el perfil de una cara
90 | 647

2109 proporción *nf* proportion
- no tiene población en proporción a su territorio
90 | 815

2110 expulsar *v* to expel, throw out
- los ingleses expulsaron a los portugueses de Ormuz en 1622
92 | 501

2111 ceremonia *nf* ceremony
- jamás olvidaría el de su ceremonia de graduación
87 | 737

2112 vidrio *nm* glass, pane
- los primeros objetos de vidrio se fabricaron en Oriente Próximo
83 | 1159

2113 ruta *nf* route
- cada cual tomó su ruta y llegó al destino
90 | 691

2114 anuncio *nm* advertisement, announcement
- después de un anuncio de nuestro sponsor magnánimo
86 | 714

2115 trece *num* thirteen
- once, doce, trece . . . ¡Este reloj está loco de remate!
89 | 484 +o

2116 soledad *nf* loneliness, solitude
- la soledad me asusta: quiero estar entre hombres y mujeres
82 | 1261

2117 tesis *nf* thesis, exposition
- sobre la tesis de que los bogotanos no se bañan
89 | 763 +o

2118 rincón *nm* corner, nook
- lo encontraron, ebrio e inconsciente, en un rincón oscuro de la plaza
87 | 899

2119 nariz *nf* nose
- toma el aire por tu nariz y tu boca
84 | 1257

2120 ochenta *num* eighty
- en la década de los ochenta
89 | 578

2121 bolsillo *nm* pocket
- sacó una libretita del bolsillo de su chaqueta
85 | 995 -nf

2122 exhibir *v* to exhibit, show off
- ningún proceso puede exhibir una gama tan amplia de aplicaciones
90 | 529

2123 asociación *nf* association
- pertenezco a una asociación o a una cofradía
89 | 788 -f

2124 fresco *adj* cool, healthy, fresh
- una brisa fresca, que luego se convirtió en vendaval
88 | 805

2125 mando *nm* command, authority
- vamos a darte el mando de todos esos para defender la paz
89 | 790

2126 sabor *nm* taste, flavor, sensation
- al despertar, tiene cierto sabor amargo en los labios
85 | 684

2127 década *nf* decade
- el láser fue desarrollado en las décadas de 1950 y 1960
84 | 2819 -f +nf

2128 preparación *nf* preparation, training
- nuevas perspectivas en la preparación de vacunas contra el sida
90 | 758 -f

2129 tapar *v* to cover, wrap
- no gritó porque P. le había tapado la boca con la mano
87 | 609

2130 acceder *v* to consent, agree, accede
- decidí acceder a su invitación y fui hacia él
88 | 616

2131 atractivo *adj* attractive
- haciendo más interesantes sus clases, más atractivas, más vivas
93 | 424

2132 afecto *nm* affection, fondness
- pasó a su lado y la miró con afecto y le sonrió
90 | 482

2133 encender *v* to turn on
- había que encender las luces del comedor
84 | 1240

2134 protesta *nf* objection, protest
- había una protesta en contra de ese concepto
89 | 637

2135 patria *nf* native land, fatherland
- ha regresado a la patria de la niñez
88 | 635

2136 consumo *nm* consumption
- una manera de vivir que se juzgaba por su consumo de cigarros puros . . .
87 | 1162 +o -f

2137 católico *adj* Catholic
- en oposición a la Iglesia católica y al luteranismo
86 | 1078

2138 selva *nf* forest, jungle
- sobre el tapizado verde de la selva tropical, con tucanes y guacamayos
89 | 619

2139 deuda *nf* debt
- me fui a ganar este dinero para que pague su deuda
88 | 845

2140 horizonte *nm* horizon
- a lo lejos, la línea del horizonte que separa el cielo del mar
88 | 813

2141 disparar *v* to shoot (at)
- los sargentos que me enseñan a disparar una pistola
85 | 678

2142 masculino *adj* masculine, manly, male
- están basadas en los órganos sexuales femenino y masculino
89 | 570

2143 talento *nm* talent, skill
- de mi abuela heredé el talento artístico
87 | 578

2144 gas *nm* gas
- los productores de carbón, gas natural, petróleo y energía nuclear
87 | 1128

2145 té *nm* tea
- un código de salud que les prohibe consumir té, café, alcohol y tabaco
83 | 666

2146 gloria *nf* glory, fame
- un gran compositor obtiene la gloria en vida
85 | 673

2147 cansado *adj* tired, tiresome
- estoy cansado y quiero dormir
82 | 929 +o -nf

2148 noviembre *nm* November
- la época de primavera y verano, o sea, desde el mes de noviembre a marzo
87 | 944

2149 candidato *nm* candidate
- Tony Blair venció a John Major, candidato del Partido Conservador
87 | 2201

2150 llave *nf* key, faucet, wrench
- saqué la llave y abrí la puerta
84 | 883

2151 inconveniente *nm* inconvenience, drawback
- las ciudades grandes tenían ya el inconveniente de separar a las familias
92 | 390

2152 afán *nm* eagerness, zeal, effort
- lo que no me parece bien es este afán de consumismo
90 | 511

2153 atar *v* to tie (up)
- pasaron una cuerda que ataron al armazón del carro
88 | 545

2154 etcétera *n* etcetera
- aproveché para comprar hierba, azúcar, whisky, etcétera, en el almacén
80 | 1363 +o -f

2155 comisión *nf* commission, committee
- el general acaba de confiarme una comisión difícil
88 | 831

2156 desesperado *adj* desperate, hopeless
- estaba desesperado por el hambre y la humillación
86 | 683

2157 generar *v* to generate
- la esperanza de generar nuevos modos de pensamiento
81 | 1794 -f

2158 posesión *nf* possession
- están en posesión de armas ilegales
90 | 625

2159 dama *nf* lady, dame
- vieron a una dama muy elegante desde un balcón
82 | 885

2160 onda *nf* wave, ripple
- el agujero negro emite grandes cantidades de ondas de rayos X
85 | 1284

2161 botella *nf* bottle, flask
- pedí una botella de agua mineral
82 | 920

2162 torre *nf* tower
- en un altillo idílico, con vista de la torre Eiffel
88 | 539

2163 abarcar *v* to encompass, comprise
- cierto sonido creció hasta abarcar la totalidad de la tarde
90 | 620

2164 combinación *nf* combination
- yo creo que es una combinación de las dos cosas ¿no?
90 | 608

2165 cadáver *nm* corpse, body
- alejándome del lugar, donde quedó el cadáver de la víctima
85 | 883

2166 paquete *nm* package, packet
- saca un paquete de cleenex y se limpia la mancha
84 | 686

2167 apellido *nm* last name
- ¿Qué ha pasado con su apellido, Pérez, que antes utilizaba?
87 | 601

2168 caído *adj* fallen
- aparecés vos como un ángel caído del cielo
90 | 640

2169 japonés *adj* Japanese
- una grabadora ultramoderna, diminuta, japonesa
85 | 989

2170 brindar *v* to offer
- perderán los privilegios que les brindaba el antiguo sistema
90 | 545

2171 conferencia *nf* conference, lecture
- lo anunciamos en una gran conferencia de prensa, ¿eh?
86 | 657 +o

2172 espontáneo *adj* spontaneous
- ¿fue algo premeditado? // No; fue espontáneo
91 | 436

2173 propuesta *nf* proposal, proposition
- ustedes hacen una propuesta que favorece a los minusválidos
83 | 1722 -f

2174 intensidad *nf* intensity, force
- va a defendernos con la misma intensidad a todos
89 | 778

2175 explosión *nf* explosion
- una explosión de gas hizo saltar los vidrios
88 | 560

2176 urbano *adj* urban, city, urbane
- el hombre ha empezado a vivir en grandes núcleos urbanos
85 | 1057

2177 odio *nm* hatred
- no me mueve el odio sino el amor
89 | 635

2178 valioso *adj* valuable, precious
- M. le entregó el valioso rosario de oro
88 | 499

2179 universo *nm* universe
- aún el universo entero, con sus miles de galaxias
88 | 878

2180 agudo *adj* sharp, acute
- tiene un agudo espíritu crítico, no soporta el desorden
87 | 705

2181 milagro *nm* miracle
- escapó de milagro a cuatro tiros de revólver
84 | 769

2182 entrega *nf* delivery
- la entrega de la cosa es el cumplimiento del contrato
89 | 479

2183 repente *adv* de + repente: suddenly
- de repente nos tiramos al agua
80 | 999 +o -nf

2184 solucionar *v* to solve, settle
- decidió solucionar el problema de una manera muy inteligente
89 | 485 +o

2185 mapa *nm* map
- levantó el mapa de casi toda la superficie del planeta
85 | 575

2186 héroe *nm* hero
- describe las hazañas de un héroe de la cultura escandinava, Beowulf
85 | 691

2187 lunes *nm* Monday
- dijo que volvería el lunes o martes de la semana próxima
80 | 684 +o -nf

2188 tráfico *nm* traffic, trade
- él está preso por tráfico de autos robados
86 | 573

2189 terror *nm* terror, horror
- sufren del terror a la muerte y a la soledad
86 | 652

2190 casualidad *nf* chance, coincidence
- por suerte, por casualidad, de pronto encontré a mis padres
86 | 468 +o

2191 tonto *adj* stupid, dumb
- siempre me pareció algo tonto y sin sentido
82 | 894 -nf

2192 risa *nf* laugh, chuckle
- es una risa larga, continuada, alegre y contagiosa
80 | 1388 -nf

2193 cuerda *nf* cord, rope
- el hombre se echó la cuerda al cuello
85 | 784

2194 consulta *nf* consultation, advice
- en previa consulta con los otros miembros del tribunal
87 | 631 +o

2195 edición *nf* edition, publication
- un libro que en su primera edición sólo tenía unas cincuenta páginas
84 | 629

2196 acomodar *v* to be/make comfortable
- ella se acomodó entre los almohadones y leyó
89 | 588

2197 rayo *nm* ray, beam, lightning
- los primeros rayos de sol iluminaron la moqueta
85 | 1053

2198 cuadrado *adj* square
- noventa y tres litros por metro cuadrado
88 | 500

2199 tía *nf* aunt
- mi prima y mi tía Julia eran inseparables
76 | 1933 +o -nf

2200 adulto *nm* adult, grown-up
- el 5 por 100 de los adultos padece una enfermedad depresiva
90 | 545

2201 voto *nm* vote
- estableció el voto universal, directo y secreto para todos
80 | 1710 +o

2202 calma *nf* calm, lull
- entretanto, necesitas calma y paciencia
90 | 586

2203 sorprendente *adj* surprising, astonishing
- muestra la sorprendente generosidad del zar
90 | 498

2204 favorable *adj* favorable, suitable
- es necesario mantener un clima favorable para la inversión
88 | 636

2205 oferta *nf* offer, bid, supply
- es una oferta tentadora, yo le aconsejo que la acepte
85 | 849

2206 vergüenza *nf* embarrassment
- sentían vergüenza de cantar en voz alta enfrente de los demás
82 | 843 -nf

2207 ave *nm* bird
- creo que estos huevos son de ave
84 | 891

2208 rodilla *nf* knee
- estaba así de rodillas para mirar lo de abajo
82 | 1107

2209 paseo *nm* walk, ride
- lo tomamos como un paseo por la plaza del pueblo
83 | 764

2210 variar *v* to change, vary
- el hecho de variar de actividad y de salir de la rutina
87 | 893 -f

2211 culpable *adj* guilty
- culpables o inocentes, hemos sido castigados por un destino ciego
86 | 622

2212 normalmente *adv* normally
- sí, normalmente es un tipo bastante práctico
84 | 908 +o -f

2213 secundario *adj* secondary
- en las escuelas primarias y secundarias
88 | 660 -f

2214 registro *nm* register, record
- no se hizo registro de donde fueron enterrados
87 | 659

2215 infinito *adj* infinite
- que nuestro Santo Padre, cuya bondad es infinita, os conceda la fe
84 | 704

2216 válido *adj* valid
- una iniciativa válida, meditada, y bien hecha
89 | 535 -f

2217 gordo *adj* fat, thick
- yo no sé cómo estoy gorda porque no como nada
84 | 882 -nf

2218 pintor *nm/f* painter
- el pintor practica también el arte plástico
84 | 913

Nouns – differences across registers

The following lists show the nouns that occur with a much higher frequency than would be expected in either the spoken, fiction, or non-fiction registers. In each case, the word is in the top 10 percent of words for that register, in terms of its relative frequency to the other two registers.

Spoken	Fiction	Non-fiction
cosa 78-F thing	**sonrisa** 2755-F smile	**década** 2128-F decade
persona 137-F person	**labio** 2760-M lip	**inversión** 2459-F investment
tipo 157-M type	**cuaderno** 3221-M notebook	**componente** 2657-M component
gente 158-F people	**prisa** 3254-F hurry	
ejemplo 162-M example	**lástima** 3295-F pity	**variación** 2704-F variation
problema 169-M problem	**beso** 3323-M kiss	**tecnología** 2932-F technology
verdad 209-F truth	**cintura** 3324-F waist	**porcentaje** 3016-M percentage
señor 240-M sir	**costado** 3357-M side, flank	**manifiesto** 3112-M poner de manifiesto: to show
gracia 272-F (pl) thank you	**dormitorio** 3383-M bedroom	**transición** 3140-F transition
tema 283-M theme	**vientre** 3435-M womb	**continuidad** 3196-F continuity
acuerdo 313-M agreement	**toque** 3449-M touch	**trayectoria** 3216-F trajectory
estudio 321-M study	**barba** 3452-F beard	**secuencia** 3242-F sequence
cuestión 398-F question	**aliento** 3455-M breath	**estabilidad** 3252-F stability
mañana 401-F morning	**brillo** 3464-M shine	**conexión** 3303-F connection
partido 425-M party	**pesadilla** 3480-F nightmare	**salario** 3308-M salary
programa 467-M program	**seña** 3534-F sign, mark	**autonomía** 3318-F autonomy
nivel 475-M level	**escritorio** 3540-M desk	**pauta** 3326-F guideline
pregunta 481-F question	**ceniza** 3547-F ash	**duración** 3337-F duration
millón 523-M million	**dueña** 3558-F landlady	**apertura** 3369-F opening
pena 575-F valer la p.: have worth	**puño** 3564-M fist	**permanencia** 3430-F permanence
curso 610-M course	**sillón** 3605-M armchair	**logro** 3434-M achievement
comunicación 659-F communi- cation	**cortina** 3631-F curtain	**mandato** 3444-M mandate
sitio 672-M place, space	**disgusto** 3661-M disgust	**centenar** 3481-M hundred
desarrollo 685-M development	**lecho** 3733-M (river) bed	**concesión** 3487-F concession
compañero 693-M companion	**pistola** 3746-F pistol	**utilización** 3492-F utilization
		defensor 3500-M defender

Comments

Notice how the words from fiction tend to focus on concrete things and emotions, while the words from non-fiction deal more with abstract concepts. The words from the spoken register contain some of the most common nouns in Spanish, but also contain more specific words. This reflects the fact that there were many interviews on cultural, scientific, and political topics in the oral portion of the corpus.

2219 delito *nm* crime, offense
- se está acusando a mi clienta de un delito muy grave
84 | 834 +o

2220 vestido *nm* dress
- lucía un vestido blanco como de novia
81 | 1046 -nf

2221 relato *nm* tale, story
- la historia surgió como un relato natural, objetivo
85 | 1047

2222 baile *nm* dance, ball
- ¿te gusta el canto y el baile flamenco?
83 | 839

2223 misterio *nm* mystery
- cosas hay que no llegan a saberse: es un mundo de misterio
83 | 838

2224 otorgar *v* to give, grant, award
- su jefe le prometió otorgar un aumento salarial
90 | 797

2225 ciclo *nm* cycle
- ahora, todo el ciclo iba a comenzar de nuevo
88 | 919

2226 principalmente *adv* principally, mainly
- esto es lo que principalmente nos ha preocupado
86 | 851

2227 cesar *v* to cease, stop
- llenaba sin cesar vasos de cerveza
90 | 696

2228 síntoma *nm* symptom
- los celos eran síntoma de amor
87 | 585

2229 amenaza *nf* threat
- me acostumbraron a obedecer bajo la amenaza de terribles castigos
88 | 829

2230 acá *adv* here, around here
- estuve por acá el sábado pasado
80 | 1588 +o -nf

2231 recorrido *nm* journey, itinerary, route
- a todo el recorrido que hace uno por esa carretera
90 | 444

2232 concepción *nf* conception
- presupone una concepción de la realidad no como algo ya dado
86 | 1091 -f

2233 tristeza *nf* sadness
- las víctimas se sumergen en una tristeza infinita
86 | 850

2234 vaca *nf* cow
- ¿qué productos se sacan de la leche de las vacas?
83 | 608

2235 criatura *nf* creature, child
- ¿cómo iba a andar esa criatura sin papá?
85 | 728

2236 creencia *nf* belief
- la semana santa estimula la creencia en Jesús
90 | 690

2237 desagradable *adj* unpleasant
- dejó en su piel un desagradable olor a grasa y humo
87 | 429

2238 núcleo *nm* nucleus, core
- la iglesia se convirtió en núcleo espiritual de sus vidas
87 | 1170 -f

2239 amenazar *v* to threaten
- agarró su revólver para amenazar al ladrón
89 | 646

2240 perdón *nm* forgiveness, pardon
- hizo la señal de la cruz y pidió perdón por sus pecados
81 | 806 +o -nf

2241 madrugada *nf* dawn, daybreak
- estudiaron toda la noche hasta la madrugada
84 | 780

2242 agresivo *adj* aggressive
- se pone muy agresivo y no reconoce a nadie
91 | 418

2243 obrero *nm/f* worker, laborer
- la selección de los obreros para determinados trabajos
86 | 653

2244 parado *adj* stopped, standing
- vio a varios pájaros parados en una rama
85 | 603

2245 callar *v* to be/make quiet
- me costó mucho trabajo callarme, pero lo hice, no dije nada 78 | 1118 -nf

2246 cariño *nm* love, affection
- un santo cuya vida simboliza el amor, el cariño y la generosidad
82 | 695 +o -nf

2247 vigilar *v* to watch over, guard
- debíamos tomar precauciones porque la policía nos vigilaba
88 | 496

2248 ángel *nm* angel
- ¡y tan bueno que era!, porque era un ángel de bondad
84 | 1062

2249 rigor *nm* harshness, rigor
- se les aplica el rigor de la ley
89 | 483

2250 orientar *v* guide, show the way
- tuve que orientar a un joven sobre un lugar específico
89 | 440

2251 contraste *nm* contrast
- el contraste entre ambas hermanas era profundo y visible
88 | 536

2252 turno *nm* turn, shift; en turno a: around
- grita con fervor cuando le toca el turno de decir su frase
85 | 683

2253 exclusivo *adj* exclusive
- recordó un centro "privado", casi exclusivo para nosotros
91 | 539

2254 portar *v* to behave [se], carry
- el que se portó como un tonto fue el general B.
90 | 437

2255 reino *nm* kingdom, reign
- el legado pasó al reino de León y, finalmente, a la Corona de Castilla
86 | 979

2256 aproximadamente *adv* approximately
- los tres tenían aproximadamente la misma edad
83 | 1021 +o -f

2257 prohibido *adj* prohibited
- estas actividades están prohibidas en las reservas
90 | 524

2258 funcionamiento *nm* functioning, operation
- sabemos el correcto funcionamiento del sistema
87 | 689

2259 auto *nm* auto, car
- sale más caro irse en auto que en bus
81 | 1059

2260 ala *nf* (el) wing, flank
- a este pájaro habrá que cortarle las alas
84 | 853

2261 debate *nm* debate
- se ha agudizado el debate sobre la efectividad de las investigaciones
83 | 1441 +o -f

2262 grueso *adj* thick
- se ve la enorme cadena, gruesa y pesada
86 | 866

2263 aplicación *nf* application
- no hay una aplicación práctica de la teoría
86 | 1132 -f

2264 laboratorio *nm* laboratory
- en un laboratorio donde procesaba los vídeos
83 | 871

2265 urgente *adj* urgent
- dígame, ¿qué era eso tan urgente que tenía que contarme?
88 | 424

2266 vendedor *nm/f* salesperson
- es el vendedor de pescado que va de casa en casa
85 | 511

2267 copa *nf* cup, glass, top (tree)
- logró el subcampeonato en la Copa del Mundo en 1974
81 | 983

2268 avisar *v* to inform, announce
- tu padre ya me avisó que llegaba hoy
85 | 551

2269 renovar *v* to renew, renovate
- trataban de dormir un poco para renovar sus fuerzas
92 | 412

2270 tratado *nm* treaty, treatise
- el congreso no ratificó el tratado de límites
84 | 1285 -f

2271 democrático *adj* democratic
- un Gobierno democrático, defensor de las libertades cívicas
83 | 1749 -f

2272 soltar *v* to release, loosen, let out
- y tomándose el trago, soltó una risa amarga
84 | 1049

2273 abordar *v* to board, get in/on
- tomados de la mano, fueron a abordar el coche
88 | 553

2274 castigar *v* to punish
- Dios nos castiga por tantos pecados cometidos
87 | 538

2275 rechazo *nm* rejection, refusal
- me da pena el rechazo de mis padres
91 | 480

2276 totalidad *nf* whole, totality
- un incendio destruyó en su totalidad el convento
89 | 664

2277 fracasar *v* to fail, to be unsuccessful
- la Armada fracasó
92 | 422

2278 catorce *num* fourteen
- ¿cómo es posible trabajar catorce horas al día?
83 | 592 +o

2279 calificar *v* to grade, rate, qualify
- para hacer una evaluación y calificar el resultado del debate
88 | 628

2280 juntar *v* to bring together
- nos reunimos para juntar la plata para comprar la lotería
81 | 696 -nf

2281 papá *nm* dad
- en realidad su papá es trujillano y su madre de Lima
73 | 2357 +o -nf

2282 necesariamente *adv* necessarily
- no implica necesariamente un deterioro mental, al menos severo
89 | 597 +o -f

2283 considerable *adj* considerable
- era una mujer de considerable posición social
87 | 574

2284 cero *num* zero, naught, nil
- el cero absoluto se sitúa alrededor de -273 grados centígrados
84 | 628 +o

2285 ejecutar *v* to execute, carry out
- practica para ejecutar con perfección su obra
88 | 516

2286 mamá *nf* mom
- la casa es de mamá y ella prácticamente mantenía la casa
71 | 2743 +o -nf

2287 vela *nf* candle, sail, vigil
- llevaba un candelabro con una sola vela
84 | 795

2288 protestar *v* to protest, object
- con tono exaltado se había puesto a protestar violentamente
87 | 511

2289 establecimiento *nm* establishment
- el establecimiento de conexiones nerviosas entre las células
86 | 602

2290 gris *adj* gray, gloomy
- una larga nube gris, franja de humo flotante e inmóvil
84 | 1086

2291 matiz *nm* shade, tint, nuance
- no sólo blancas sino de matices de colores imprecisos
88 | 431

2292 impresionar *v* to impress
- a mí no me impresionó tanto la escena de la crucifixión
88 | 458

2293 meta *nf* goal, aim, purpose
- mi última meta es llegar a ser intérprete
88 | 467

2294 comportar *v* to behave
- se comportaba como si fuese dueña de casa
88 | 490

2295 básico *adj* basic, essential
- el salario no alcanzaba para cubrir las necesidades básicas
83 | 1651 +o -f

2296 comodidad *nf* comfort, convenience
- ni el dinero ni las comodidades dan la felicidad a una persona
88 | 347

2297 pariente *nc* relative
- no tenía amigo ni pariente en quien confiar
85 | 704

2298 abandonado *adj* abandoned
- se puede permitir que nos dejen aquí, abandonados, sin poder salir?
86 | 519

2299 distribución *nf* distribution
- quiere controlar personalmente la distribución de sus libros
88 | 778 -f

2300 invitación *nf* invitation
- en vez de desaprobación, era invitación a comer más
90 | 456

2301 destrucción *nf* destruction
- la contaminación será inevitable, y la destrucción de la naturaleza
90 | 566

2302 indígena *adj* indigenous, native
- hija de padres campesinos, con ancestro indígena
85 | 911

2303 moreno *adj* dark, brown
- ni rubio ni moreno, ni tan alto ni tan bajo
85 | 486

2304 alegre *adj* happy, lively, cheerful
- era muy simpática, muy, muy divertida, muy alegre
85 | 783

2305 opción *nf* option, choice
- siempre y cuando haya opción a otros y la gente pueda elegir
85 | 618

2306 extenso *adj* extensive, large
- se trata de un proceso largo y extenso y profundo
89 | 576

2307 ruso *adj* Russian
- el pueblo ruso tiene que seguir haciendo cola para comprar pan
79 | 1346

2308 máximo *nm* maximum
- ¿cuál es el mínimo y cuál es el máximo?
87 | 594 -f

2309 tarjeta *nf* card
- le pagaremos con tarjeta de crédito
82 | 555 +o

2310 fase *nf* phase, stage
- la primera fase de la lucha finalizó en junio
84 | 1185 -f

2311 veinticinco *num* twenty-five
- ¡Veinticinco años y no sabe lo que es el amor!
85 | 515 +o -nf

2312 tropa *nf* troops, forces
- el soldado era de la tropa revolucionaria
81 | 1173

2313 remoto *adj* remote, far-off
- fui confinado a un remoto curato de la campaña
88 | 606

2314 socio *nm* member, partner
- se ha hecho socio del Club de Solteros
87 | 462

2315 comunista *adj* Communist
- el partido comunista de la ex Unión Soviética
81 | 1391

2316 abundante *adj* abundant, plentiful
- la zona húmeda cuenta con abundante vegetación
87 | 627

2317 dibujar *v* to draw, sketch
- no sé dibujar ni una mesa
87 | 527

2318 guía *nc* guide, leader
- ha viajado dos veces a ese país como guía de un tour
88 | 447

2319 judío *adj* Jewish
- arrojan luz sobre la historia judía, y la lengua hebrea
81 | 1255

2320 impresionante *adj* impressive, astonishing
• un libro impresionante, por la grandeza épica de algunos relatos
87 | 461

2321 hielo *nm* ice
• todo esto ya es agua y nieve, el hielo se está fundiendo
82 | 677

2322 gobernar *v* to govern
• gobernar no es solamente administrar un Estado
87 | 820

2323 occidental *adj* occidental, western
• fue la primera visita de un artista occidental a la China posterior de Mao
85 | 1765 -f

2324 deshacer *v* to undo, destroy, take apart
• cuesta mucho deshacer una decisión mal tomada
89 | 516

2325 primavera *nf* spring, spring-like
• en la primavera el clima es templado
84 | 634

2326 mutuo *adj* mutual
• el propósito del matrimonio es el amor mutuo y la procreación
91 | 399

2327 simpatía *nf* sympathy, affinity
• nos mirábamos con simpatía porque los dos nos entendíamos
86 | 464

2328 reconstruir *v* to reconstruct
• trataba de reconstruir qué había pasado con él
92 | 373

2329 centímetro *nm* centimeter
• un metro de profundidad y sesenta centímetros de ancho
83 | 561

2330 pantalla *nf* screen, monitor
• de pronto se ilumina la pantalla con números
82 | 631

2331 toro *nm* bull
• las corridas de toros son una parte importante de la tradición
82 | 735

2332 denunciar *v* to denounce
• querían denunciar sus atrocidades
82 | 651

2333 cultivo *nm* cultivation, crop
• el cultivo de plantas originó también la destrucción de la vegetación
86 | 1097

2334 horror *nm* horror, atrocity
• también me ha hecho recordar escenas de horror y destrucción
84 | 596

2335 bienestar *nm* wellbeing, welfare
• su existencia dependía la salud y el bienestar de mucha gente
89 | 455

2336 paciencia *nf* patience
• necesitamos tener paciencia y esperar
83 | 611

2337 ay *interj* oh no!, oh my!
• ¡Ay, por Dios!
76 | 1584 +o -nf

2338 romántico *adj* romantic
• algo de ese mundo perdido y romántico
83 | 658

2339 convicción *nf* conviction
• lo malo era que lo decía sin convicción alguna
86 | 637

2340 plenamente *adv* fully
• y en esto coincidía plenamente con su amigo
89 | 388

2341 uniforme *nm* uniform
• vestía el uniforme de Capitán General
87 | 618

2342 media *nf* average; a medias: halfways
• he leído a medias, porque no he terminado de leerla
85 | 554

2343 mínimo *nm* minimum
• la educación no está dando el mínimo de conocimientos que se supone
91 | 425

2344 doscientos *num* two hundred
• dentro de doscientos años no quedarán vestigios
87 | 376 +o

2345 garantizar *v* to guarantee
• el nuevo gobierno garantiza su seguridad personal
87 | 807

2346 compañera *nf* female companion
• lo iba traduciendo a una compañera de viaje que estaba a su lado
84 | 578 +o -nf

2347 pintado *adj* painted
• todo estaba pintado del color anaranjado
85 | 694

2348 combinar *v* to combine
• el alucine del peyote se combina con el fanatismo religioso
89 | 659

2349 junio *nm* June
• bueno, el mes de junio estuve un poco fastidiado
83 | 1101 -f

2350 drama *nm* drama
• ¿te gusta la comedia o el drama?
87 | 577

2351 distante *adj* distant, far, remote
• que siempre recuerda de su pasado distante cuando era niño
89 | 404

2352 sencillamente *adv* simply
• la leo y la leo porque sencillamente me gusta
82 | 655 +o

Colors (color 359) top 50 words # 1 – 8000

blanco 250 white

negro 317 black

rojo 533 red

verde 878 green

azul 904 blue

amarillo 1586 yellow

gris 2290 gray

(dorado) 2696 golden, gold-plated

rubio 3269 blonde

(celeste) 4026 sky-blue, heavenly

rosado 4461 pink

marrón 4951 brown

violeta 5654 violet

plateado 5927 silver

morado 6279 purple

castaño 8010 brown (hair)

anaranjado 8225 orange

Comments

Psychologists and linguists have noted that the more basic color distinctions (light/dark; white/black) and the primary colors (red, yellow, and blue) are lexicalized more frequently in languages of the world than secondary colors like orange or purple. The frequency data for these color terms in Spanish shows the same tendency.

2353 **equivocado** *adj* mistaken, wrong
• usted estaba equivocado; pensaba en tal cosa y era esta otra
89 | 434

2354 **doble** *nm* double
• se gastará el doble de lo que se tiene que gastar
88 | 410

2355 **episodio** *nm* episode, incident
• yo les contaré un episodio de mi propia vida
87 | 598

2356 **divertir** *v* to amuse, entertain
• la primera función del teatro es entretener y divertir
83 | 670 -nf

2357 **afirmación** *nf* statement, assertion
• no acepto la afirmación de que somos el único país comunista
89 | 659

2358 **conquistar** *v* to conquer, win (over)
• Mangu Kan logró conquistar casi toda China
88 | 560

2359 **bar** *nm* (snack) bar, café
• se acomodó en el bar y encendió su primer cigarrillo
78 | 813 -nf

2360 **fantástico** *adj* fantastic, unreal
• el mundo imaginario y fantástico soñado por Mozart
85 | 479

2361 **liberación** *nf* liberation
• tras la liberación de del territorio de la dominación alemana
91 | 471

2362 **actualmente** *adv* now, at present
• su hija vive actualmente en Dinamarca
82 | 1209 +o -f

2363 **envolver** *v* to wrap
• ciertos embalsamadores egipcios llegaron a envolver a las momias
85 | 667

2364 **estancia** *nf* stay, stance, ranch
• ¿qué ha aprendido de su estancia en esta ciudad?
84 | 601

2365 **emprender** *v* to undertake, embark on
• ¿qué le costaba emprender un viaje a Europa?
88 | 621

2366 **anticipar** *v* to anticipate, advance
• anticipó horas difíciles si sigue lloviendo
88 | 453

2367 **humilde** *adj* humble, modest
• no corresponde a una gran mansión, sino a una humilde casa
87 | 516

2368 **variedad** *nf* variety
• se podía sembrar y cosechar gran copia y variedad de frutos
86 | 996

2369 **desarrollado** *adj* developed, grown
• las serpientes tienen el sistema nervioso bien desarrollado
86 | 828 -f

2370 **capitán** *nm* captain, chief
• este capitán era comandante de la flota
80 | 998

2371 **droga** *nf* drug
• las drogas adictivas como la nicotina y la cocaína
82 | 851 +o

2372 **específico** *adj* specific
• aquél era el remedio específico para el vicio de comer tierra
84 | 1258 +o -f

2373 taller *nm* workshop, shop
- trabaja en un taller de automóviles
83 | 593

2374 desorden *nm* disorder, mess
- estuvo en un estado casi permanente de guerra y desorden
90 | 468

2375 quebrar *v* to break, bend, weaken
- la voz de la autoridad quebró el silencio: -¡Alto!
87 | 453

2376 encerrado *adj* locked (up)
- desgraciadamente, no salgo, estoy encerrada aquí en casa
84 | 519

2377 esclavo *nm* slave
- no se sentía libre sino esclavo de una fuerza interior
83 | 605

2378 injusto *adj* unfair, unjust
- nos parece injusto y equivocado
87 | 403

2379 sucesivo *adj* successive, following
- podría ser; en forma sucesiva; sucede mucho
88 | 617

2380 sumamente *adv* extremely, highly
- tu esposo es un hombre sumamente ocupado
84 | 590 +o

2381 feo *adj* ugly, nasty, rude
- sólo hombres feos y mujeres atractivas
81 | 681 -nf

2382 equilibrar *v* to balance
- para equilibrar la oferta y la demanda
89 | 402

2383 asomar *v* to appear, show, stick (out)
- la jovencita se asomaba detrás de los visillos de la sala
81 | 1028

2384 optar *v* to choose, opt for
- a pesar de todo, optó por lo peor
89 | 526

2385 manejo *nm* handling, management
- el manejo de los recursos institucionales y humanos
89 | 459

2386 lágrima *nf* tear, teardrop
- tenía lágrimas en los ojos
80 | 1107

2387 colaboración *nf* collaboration
- los cursos se dan en colaboración con las comunidades autónomas
87 | 606 -f

2388 orgulloso *adj* proud, arrogant
- era orgulloso como un pavo real
86 | 508

2389 ángulo *nm* angle
- un ángulo de 45 grados con respecto a la superficie
84 | 567

2390 impacto *nm* impact
- M. sintió el impacto de ver matar a un hombre
89 | 561

2391 urgencia *nf* urgency
- para hacerlo ahora, sin ese sentimiento de urgencia o de emergencia
87 | 497

2392 excepcional *adj* exceptional, unusual
- los enormes trastornos que ocasionó tan excepcional actividad solar
89 | 436

2393 creador *nm* creator
- Dios es el creador de todas las cosas
85 | 608

2394 luna *nf* moon
- las distancias de la Tierra al Sol y de la Tierra a la Luna
83 | 1165

2395 instalación *nf* installation, facilities
- existe un proyecto de instalación de videocámaras
87 | 638 -f

2396 homenaje *nm* homage, tribute
- rindió homenaje a la patria
87 | 412

2397 ruina *nf* ruin, collapse
- los grandes abatimientos precursores de ruina y de catástrofe
86 | 487

2398 generoso *adj* generous
- se ve generoso porque le da más que recibe
84 | 546

2399 académico *adj* academic
- obtuvo su título académico en la Escuela de Bellas Artes
84 | 646

2400 azar *nm* random, chance, hazard
- no hemos dejado nada al azar, nada que pudiese comprometer la vida del niño
85 | 508

2401 estallar *v* to break out, explode, start
- los soldados se prepararon mucho antes de estallar la guerra
84 | 770

2402 copiar *v* to copy
- las imágenes se hacían difíciles de copiar o dibujar
87 | 359

2403 inaugurar *v* to inaugurate, start
- llegó el momento de inaugurar la nueva iglesia
89 | 382

2404 apretar *v* to squeeze, tighten, compress
- E. apretó la niña contra el pecho y comenzó a rezar
81 | 975

2405 razonable *adj* reasonable
- usted es un hombre razonable, así uno se puede entender
88 | 434

2406 ola *nf* wave, billow
- el sonido era un poco como las olas del mar
- 85 | 539

2407 oreja *nf* ear
- aprendí a escuchar, a abrir mis orejas como flores
- 82 | 877

2408 abuela *nf* grandmother
- entonces la madre llora, y llora la abuela, y llora la nieta
- 76 | 1373 -nf

2409 amable *adj* kind, nice, friendly
- con una amplia, amable sonrisa y cálidas palabras de felicitación
- 80 | 638 +o -nf

2410 doña *nf* courtesy title (f), Mrs.
- todos conocían bien a su madre, doña Blanca Vergara
- 72 | 1787 -nf

2411 rígido *adj* rigid, stiff, firm
- siempre ha seguido un rígido vegetarianismo
- 88 | 498

2412 arco *nm* arch, arc, bow
- me conduje bajo el arco de la puerta principal
- 84 | 682

2413 oriente *nm* East
- Fernando de Magallanes buscaba una ruta al Oriente
- 82 | 774

2414 rumbo *nm* direction, course, bearing
- ¿y por qué no marcharse rumbo a América?
- 84 | 749

2415 ejecución *nf* performance, execution
- para eliminar los obstáculos que impidieran la ejecución de este plan
- 87 | 495

2416 mentir *v* to (tell a) lie
- está obligado a mentir o a callar la verdad de cosas terribles
- 83 | 618

2417 ordenado *adj* organized, clean
- me convierte en un ser meticuloso, ordenado, responsable, eficiente
- 90 | 375

2418 contratar *v* to hire, contract
- tuvo que contratar a otra empleada
- 89 | 376

2419 caos *nm* chaos
- el desarrollo mundial hoy es un caos, una anarquía
- 91 | 301

2420 colonia *nf* colony, cologne
- la lucha por la independencia de las colonias de España
- 84 | 754

2421 alcohol *nm* alcohol
- lo que matan más que la heroína que es el tabaco y el alcohol
- 81 | 689

2422 apropiado *adj* appropriate
- el sitio no es apropiado para un encuentro amoroso
- 87 | 474

2423 nieve *nf* snow
- la nieve seguía cayendo suave
- 82 | 524

2424 multitud *nf* multitude
- somos una multitud de gentes honradas
- 87 | 619

2425 ganado *nm* livestock, cattle
- es más económico criar y engordar el ganado en la Argentina
- 86 | 486

2426 pez *nm* (alive) fish
- en las costas de Maine, pescaban el pez espada
- 83 | 694

2427 líder *nc* leader
- tú eres el líder de los trabajadores y sólo a ti te hacen caso
- 85 | 1002 -f

2428 resuelto *adj* resolved, determined
- esto sí es oportunismo, lo hacen cuando ya está resuelto
- 87 | 396

2429 club *nm* club, society
- vamos al club, cada cual está con su grupo de amigos
- 78 | 809 +o

2430 posteriormente *adv* afterwards
- vamos a ver qué pasó, posteriormente, con el teatro literario
- 82 | 953 +o -f

2431 desierto *nm* desert
- la arena lo devora todo en el desierto
- 84 | 615

2432 escritura *nf* writing, scripture
- ejerce una escritura apenas legible
- 81 | 679

2433 árabe *adj* Arab
- en la encrucijada de tres mundos: el árabe, el judío y el cristiano
- 82 | 756

2434 danza *nf* dance
- algunas máscaras bailan una danza macabra
- 82 | 779

2435 concierto *nm* concert, concerto
- tenía que proponer e imponer un concierto para guitarra y orquesta
- 80 | 658 +o

2436 partidario *nm* supporter, partisan
- yo no soy partidario de los noviazgos largos
- 87 | 620

2437 templo *nm* temple, church
- el saqueo de Jerusalén y la destrucción del Templo en el año 68
- 81 | 768

2438 líquido *nm* liquid
- limpiaron el líquido con la toalla
- 82 | 737

2439 debilidad *nf* weakness
- está dedicada al estudio del mal, de la debilidad, y del sufrimiento
87 | 464

2440 ambición *nf* ambition
- era capaz de inspirar y alentar una ambición de grandeza
87 | 398

2441 locura *nf* madness, insanity
- ¡todo a la vez! Pero, ¡qué locura!
83 | 677

2442 comerciante *nc* merchant, businessman
- soy comerciante, vendo cortes de telas
85 | 376

2443 camisa *nf* shirt
- no usábamos traje, nada más que camisa y pantalón
80 | 925 -nf

2444 pluma *nf* pen, feather
- toma la pluma y escribe en el libro de visitas
83 | 632

2445 pelota *nf* ball
- ¿qué crees tú del juego de pelota, de nuestro béisbol?
78 | 787

2446 pasaje *nm* fare, passage, lane
- le venden a uno el pasaje por kilómetros
79 | 615

2447 limpieza *nf* cleanliness, purity
- lo que hay que hacer es la limpieza y que esté limpio el pueblo
86 | 359

2448 admiración *nf* admiration
- secretamente, sentía una mezcla de envidia y de admiración por A.
87 | 444

2449 fantasma *nm* ghost, phantom
- se vuelve transparente, como fantasmas que se escurren
81 | 635

2450 transformación *nf* transformation
- la transformación es esencialmente un cambio de una forma de sociedad
85 | 812 -f

2451 caza *nf* hunting (game)
- de las vigas cuelgan animales de caza: aves y liebres
82 | 616

2452 retener *v* to keep, retain
- los padres prefieren retener en casa a sus hijos
89 | 464

2453 cruel *adj* cruel, harsh
- una mala persona; cruel con las mujeres
84 | 528

2454 prender *v* to turn on, apprehend
- no veía nada y no quería prender la linterna
82 | 691 -nf

2455 almacén *nm* warehouse, store
- fue hasta el almacén a buscar alguna cosa que faltaba
83 | 545

2456 expectativa *nf* expectation, hope, prospect
- pueden crear falsas expectativas en los pacientes
86 | 470

2457 ruptura *nf* break-up, rupture
- hasta la ruptura de la Unión Soviética en 1991
88 | 613

2458 inversión *nf* investment, outlay
- su construcción supone una gran inversión de tiempo y energía
81 | 2018 -f +nf

2459 visible *adj* visible
- Capella es la estrella más visible de esta formación
83 | 609

2460 herida *nf* wound, injury
- el hombre sufrió una herida de cuchillo
84 | 659

2461 hipótesis *nf* hypothesis
- es una hipótesis que probablemente no sea verificable
85 | 811

2462 formular *v* to formulate
- se ha decidido a formular la pregunta en voz alta
86 | 616

2463 poquito *adj* little bit
- precisamente a la diez o un poquito más tarde
75 | 1184 +o -nf

2464 variado *adj* varied, mixed
- hay muchas personas en muy variadas actividades
86 | 511

2465 giro *nm* turn, draft, expression
- el helicóptero se eleva mediante el giro de un rotor en el eje vertical
86 | 354

2466 esquema *nm* outline, diagram, plan
- no hay ninguna decisión porque todavía no hay un esquema de privatización
86 | 720 -f

2467 mito *nm* myth
- el mito es una explicación imaginativa y fantástica del hombre
83 | 770

2468 oscuridad *nf* darkness
- brillaron en la oscuridad como luces de desafío
83 | 1101 -o

2469 pensión *nf* boarding house
- vivía en una pensión con actrices y bohemios
83 | 520

2470 desaparición *nf* disappearance
- notaban mi desaparición y mi regreso
88 | 441

2471 repetido *adj* repeated
- hablé con él en repetidas ocasiones
88 | 381

2472 fumar *v* to smoke
- en vez de fumar, masca el tabaco
79 | 964 -nf

2473 envuelto *adj* wrapped
- la abrió y sacó el objeto envuelto en papel
83 | 763

2474 especializar *v* to specialize, major in
- bueno, uno se especializa en letras o en biología o matemáticas
84 | 824 -f

2475 últimamente *adv* lately, recently
- últimamente el frío de la noche nos ha matado
82 | 444 +o -nf

2476 caracterizar *v* to characterize, portray
- el egoísmo innato que caracteriza a la raza humana
84 | 1004 -f

2477 paralelo *adj* parallel
- donde las líneas paralelas se representan como convergentes
86 | 476

2478 ordinario *adj* vulgar, ordinary
- pero qué ordinario, ¿cómo es que le dice eso a una mujer?
89 | 445

2479 designar *v* to designate
- se designa con el nombre de mixed border
87 | 508

2480 bloque *nm* block
- la integración de sus miembros en un bloque económico regional
86 | 565

2481 cierre *nm* zipper, closing
- hasta que el cierre de la mochila revienta y vuela el contenido
87 | 378

2482 broma *nf* joke
- puede ser una cruel broma de mis compañeros de niñez
79 | 651 -nf

2483 viernes *nm* Friday
- trabajé toda la semana y el viernes cambié un mísero cheque en el banco
79 | 641 +o -nf

2484 creciente *adj* growing, increasing
- con una tendencia todavía claramente creciente
84 | 880 -o

2485 tumba *nf* tomb, grave
- la viuda se sentó al borde de la tumba
84 | 675

2486 competir *v* to compete
- sabe que tiene que competir con calidad y variedad
87 | 552 -f

2487 despacho *nm* office, study
- ayer entró el expediente de divorcio en el despacho del juez
80 | 776

2488 viuda *nf* widow
- ella es la viuda del hombre desaparecido
82 | 537

2489 pantalón *nm* pants, trousers
- hoy he ido con pantalones cortos, a jugar al tenis
77 | 996 -nf

2490 intercambio *nm* exchange, interchange
- un club internacional de intercambio de postales antiguas
86 | 528

2491 mancha *nf* stain, spot
- es una mancha que no sale con el detergente
81 | 665

2492 retrato *nm* portrait, photograph
- las facetas de la pintura goyesca: el retrato, y el arte religioso
82 | 787

2493 lata *nf* (tin) can
- es que al abrir la lata de sopa Campbells
78 | 541 -nf

2494 combate *nm* combat, battle, fight
- los Habsburgo españoles abandonaron el combate contra el turco
84 | 730

2495 instancia *nf* instance
- pero en última instancia, lo que te llena, lo que te llena
85 | 580

2496 secar *v* to dry
- se secó el sudor de la frente con un pañuelo
83 | 561

2497 roca *nf* rock
- se trata de una roca de basalto olivino, de unas 25 toneladas
77 | 832

2498 herramienta *nf* tool
- la brújula magnética sirve como una herramienta direccional
85 | 501

2499 anónimo *adj* anonymous
- me siento anónimo; siempre soy un desconocido
86 | 386

2500 panorama *nm* panorama, landscape
- cuando tenía ante la vista un magnífico panorama de ilusiones
87 | 504

2501 trágico *adj* tragic
- luego fue el trágico accidente del helicóptero
83 | 464

2502 imprimir *v* to print
- imprimió una copia, la empaquetó y se la mandó a su editor
87 | 348

2503 camión *nm* truck, van, tanker
- viajamos de México hasta Chicago en camión
80 | 795

2504 olvido *nm* forgetfulness, omission
- no podrán actuar sobre la memoria ni el olvido
85 | 537

Opposites: frequent pairs

más 24 more	**menos** 98 less	**largo** 175 long	**corto** 537 short
primero 60 first	**último** 139 last	**alto** 185 tall	**bajo** 412 low
grande 62 large	**pequeño** 184 small	**blanco** 250 white	**negro** 317 black
mucho 45 many	**poco** 74 few	**verdadero** 420 true	**falso** 1140 false
nuevo 99 new	**viejo** 281 old	**abierto** 439 open	**cerrado** 680 closed
bueno 115 good	**malo** 275 bad	**lleno** 508 full	**vacío** 1532 empty
mejor 121 better	**peor** 1965 worse	**fácil** 514 easy	**difícil** 314 difficult
mayor 138 older	**menor** 334 younger	**rico** 627 rich	**pobre** 373 poor
posible 225 possible	**imposible** 592 impossible		

Comments

In nearly every case, the positive term (*más, largo, lleno*) is more common than the "negative" term (*menos, corto, vacío*). The two exceptions are *difícil/fácil* and *pobre/rico*.

2505 estrategia *nf* strategy
- hay que desarrollar una estrategia de alianzas y de pactos
- 85 | 951

2506 muchacha *nf* girl
- yo era una muchacha de diecinueve años, nada más
- 73 | 1572 -nf

2507 conversar *v* to converse, talk
- iban a tomar el té y a conversar de libros
- 77 | 831 -nf

2508 propaganda *nf* advertising, propaganda
- una fuerte campaña de propaganda ideológica
- 86 | 414 +o

2509 lamentar *v* to regret
- lamentaba la muerte de mi gran amigo
- 83 | 531 -nf

2510 misa *nf* (religious) mass
- me lo pongo para la misa del domingo
- 79 | 656

2511 alzar *v* to lift, raise
- alzó la cara y tuvo una mirada de pálido desprecio
- 80 | 1186 -o

2512 inicio *nm* beginning, start
- es el inicio de una nueva etapa en nuestra vida musical
- 83 | 927

2513 fútbol *nm* soccer
- y las actividades deportivas, como el fútbol
- 77 | 1047

2514 esfera *nf* sphere, globe
- en el año 966 Polonia entró en la esfera de la cultura cristiana
- 85 | 520

2515 iluminar *v* to illuminate, light up
- un rayo de sol poniente vino a iluminar el viejo crucifijo
- 85 | 490

2516 arquitectura *nf* architecture
- alquiló un lugar, con una arquitectura verdaderamente fascinante
- 79 | 990

2517 especialidad *nf* specialty, specialized field
- le preguntan sobre su especialidad y profesión
- 85 | 517 +o -f

2518 músico *nm/f* musician
- una marcha de Souza, el músico favorito del pueblo americano
- 80 | 641

2519 relativamente *adv* relatively
- esta distinción es relativamente reciente; no es anterior al siglo XIX
- 85 | 696 -f

2520 eh *interj* eh
- te interesa la palabra, ¿eh?
- 67 | 15797 +o -nf

2521 eje *nm* axis, shaft, crux
- atraviesan el eje de rotación de la Tierra
- 85 | 602

2522 guiar *v* to guide, lead, steer
- es tratar de guiar nuestro destino hacia lugares más cuerdos
- 87 | 318

2523 efectuar *v* to carry out, cause to happen
- no se atrevía a efectuar ningún movimiento
- 84 | 742

2524 abandono *nm* abandonment, desertion
- delitos como abandonos, explotación de niños, y malos tratos
- 84 | 431

2525 museo *nm* museum
- se construyó un museo de arte moderno
80 | 662

2526 propietario *nm* owner
- el propietario de la joyería ha sufrido un robo
82 | 781

2527 trozo *nm* piece, chunk
- le corta en pedacitos un trozo de carne y para que los coma
83 | 748

2528 riguroso *adj* rigorous, severe
- hacer una dieta rigurosa y escasa de grasas
88 | 387

2529 armonía *nf* harmony
- el busca su armonía espiritual en la naturaleza
87 | 485

2530 pacto *nm* pact, agreement
- para establecer un pacto de no agresión entre ambos estados
83 | 596

2531 calentar *v* to warm, heat
- mucho se van a calentar, junto a la chimenea apagada
80 | 512

2532 atento *adj* attentive, polite
- caminaba con fatiga, demasiado vigilante para estar atento
84 | 471

2533 selección *nf* selection, choice
- la selección musical es excelente, pasan temas suaves
83 | 925 +o -f

2534 proseguir *v* to continue, carry on
- permanecí un rato más para proseguir la conversación
86 | 515

2535 incómodo *adj* uncomfortable
- incluso estar alojando en saco de dormir, incómodo
85 | 349

2536 protagonista *nc* protagonist, main character
- era la cruel protagonista de su propia historia
82 | 637

2537 ferrocarril *nm* railway
- puentes y túneles, vías de ferrocarril, caminos, carreteras
86 | 502

2538 inocente *adj* innocent, naïve
- sé que parece muy inocente y muy pura
80 | 630

2539 fatal *adj* fateful, deadly, awful
- la fatal decisión de poner fin a su existencia
83 | 395

2540 intimidad *nf* private life, intimacy
- le gusta la soledad y guardada celosamente la intimidad
82 | 558

2541 enfrente *adv* in front (of)
- estamos en un parque enfrente de la escuela
83 | 455

2542 nave *nf* spacecraft, ship
- la nave espacial Apolo, en su misión a la Luna
79 | 801

2543 oración *nf* prayer
- rezando la oración milagrosa con que impetraba piedad a la Virgen
80 | 549

2544 cansancio *nm* tiredness, weariness
- cuando el sol ya se pierde y el cansancio me pone a dormir
85 | 551

2545 noble *adj* noble
- la vida no es noble, ni buena, ni sagrada
84 | 440

2546 escondido *adj* hidden
- como estaban escondidos, no pudimos verlos
79 | 660 -nf

2547 tejido *nm* fabric, tissue
- en lana de colores sobre un tejido de fondo de lino
81 | 862

2548 trampa *nf* trick, trap; hacer trampa: to cheat
- sino a la vida natural, normal, es decir, a no hacer trampa
84 | 531

2549 hondo *adj* deep
- hay algo muy hondo que se conmueve con la música
80 | 628

2550 descripción *nf* description
- ¿podría hacer una descripción del pueblecito ese?
84 | 602

2551 pecado *nm* sin
- ¿de manera que nada del pecado de la fornicación, eh? - dije con sorna
79 | 538

2552 cansar *v* to tire, annoy
- se fue porque se cansó de don Juan, ya no lo aguantaba
79 | 478 -nf

2553 divertido *adj* funny, amusing
- ahí tengo una foto muy divertida donde yo estaba toreando
80 | 509 -nf

2554 injusticia *nf* injustice
- como un hombre ante la adversidad, contra la injusticia y la tiranía
86 | 349

2555 heredar *v* to inherit
- mi madre heredó la casa de su padre
86 | 352

2556 librar *v* to liberate, set free
- les asignaba la sagrada misión de librar al pueblo
84 | 435

2557 adiós *nm* goodbye
- ¡Adiós, hasta luego, Marisa!
79 | 584

2558 brillar *v* to shine, twinkle, be outstanding
- esperaba ver brillar ese diamante lujoso
81 | 762

2559 rescatar *v* to rescue, save
- para rescatar a una menor secuestrada
85 | 445

2560 tabaco *nm* tobacco, cigarette, cigar
- suelo fumar mi pipa con tabaco barato
77 | 610

2561 juvenil *adj* young, juvenile
- su mente juvenil no estaba preparada para asimilar tantos axiomas
83 | 433

2562 ausente *adj* absent
- el cuerpo vacío; mi cabeza vacía; el corazón ausente
86 | 445

2563 suceso *nm* event, incident
- el suceso le había ocurrido poco antes de caer enfermo
84 | 638

2564 extrañar *v* to miss, long for
- me iba a extrañar porque se había acostumbrado a mis visitas
86 | 373

2565 asustar *v* to frighten, scare
- le gritó sólo para asustar a su hermanito
77 | 658 +o -nf

2566 mediado *adj* mid, middle
- más o menos a mediados de abril volví del trabajo
84 | 718 -f

2567 antecedente *nm* antecedent
- puede considerarse como un antecedente de las guías actuales
84 | 461

2568 barrera *nf* barrier, obstacle
- apareció una barrera que impidió el paso
87 | 443

2569 estético *adj* esthetic
- ¿tiene usted un credo estético como director?
84 | 561

2570 anotar *v* to annotate, jot, note
- y anotar en el primer papel en blanco que encontró
82 | 451

2571 tribunal *nm* court
- este es el tribunal que nos va a juzgar
83 | 630

2572 bravo *adj* fierce, angry
- el león no es tan bravo como lo pintan
81 | 474

2573 invasión *nf* invasion
- en la guerra de la Independencia contra la invasión napoleónica
84 | 588

2574 septiembre *nm* September
- antes de empezar en septiembre las clases
81 | 848 +o -f

2575 dependencia *nf* dependence, dependency
- la dependencia económica de estos países con respecto a la URSS
84 | 525

2576 democracia *nf* democracy
- buscan la democracia y una auténtica representatividad
76 | 1741 -f

2577 sutil *adj* subtle
- ella es capaz de percibir una sutil diferencia entre ambos sonidos
84 | 424

2578 maduro *adj* mature, ripe
- la persona ya madura la comprende mejor que el joven
84 | 406

2579 mezclado *adj* mixed
- porque iba mezclada con algo confusamente siniestro y oscuro
86 | 347

2580 remontar *v* to go back to (time)
- su origen se remonta al principio de los siglos
87 | 404

2581 limitación *nf* limitation
- un hombre con grandes sueños pero obvias limitaciones
84 | 596 -f

2582 lindo *adj* pretty, nice, lovely
- es un lindo regalo, creo yo
72 | 1293 +o -nf

2583 invitado *nm* guest
- servir a los invitados es el deber de toda dueña de casa
79 | 479

2584 pescado *nm* fish
- una especie de sopa de pescado con muchos mariscos
79 | 454

2585 continuamente *adv* continuously
- que su nombre inmortal vibre continuamente en nuestros labios
85 | 325

2586 obvio *adj* obvious
- era obvio que I. no iba a matarme
86 | 419

2587 estrictamente *adv* strictly
- de modo que, ya ve usted, no éramos estrictamente musulmanes
87 | 362

2588 obstáculo *nm* obstacle
- había logrado vencer el único obstáculo que me separaba del evento
88 | 490

2589 aspiración *nf* ambition, aspiration
- su mayor aspiración es que se logre resolver la situación
87 | 419

2590 simpático *adj* nice, likeable, friendly
- era muy simpática, muy divertida, muy alegre
79 | 490 -nf

2591 corredor *nm/f* broker, corridor, runner
- el empleo más detestable del orbe: corredor de propiedades
74 | 1092

2592 exquisito *adj* exquisite, superb
- este perfume era exquisito y su frasco también inolvidable
84 | 313

2593 resumen *nm* summary
- concedió una larga entrevista; éste es un resumen de la conversación
83 | 336

2594 basura *nf* garbage, rubbish
- se dedica a recoger basura en la playa
82 | 400

2595 escalera *nf* stairs, ladder
- bajaban por la escalera del segundo piso
75 | 980 -nf

2596 gravedad *nf* seriousness, gravity
- con mucha cautela, por la extrema gravedad de las circunstancias
86 | 612

2597 fundamento *nm* foundation, ground
- intentó un entusiasmo que no sentía, algo sin fundamento firme
83 | 540

2598 sustancia *nf* substance, essence
- o la defensa inmunológica contra sustancias extrañas al organismo
80 | 1270

2599 convocar *v* to convene, summon
- convocó a una conferencia en el salón de baile
81 | 672

2600 harto *adj* fed up with
- estoy harto de los sermones de René
81 | 495 -nf

2601 derrota *nf* defeat, loss
- le infligió una derrota a su enemigo
82 | 801

2602 sospecha *nf* suspicion
- vivió con la sospecha de que alguien lo observaba
83 | 524

2603 exagerado *adj* exaggerated
- porque 4 contra 40 mil es un poco exagerado
88 | 275

2604 huelga *nf* strike, protest
- se puso en huelga de hambre durante diez días
81 | 717

2605 abuso *nm* abuse, misuse
- esto era inhumano, un evidente abuso de autoridad
87 | 396

2606 jueves *nm* Thursday
- aquí el jueves es el día de moda, el domingo no se trabaja
78 | 515 +o -nf

2607 arreglo *nm* arrangement
- tienen un arreglo entre ellos; documentos firmados tienen
83 | 320

2608 sal *nf* salt
- le echo la sal, ajo, cebolla, pimienta, y el orégano
82 | 483

2609 dosis *nf* dose
- se le han aplicado dos dosis de morfina para el dolor de la gangrena
85 | 408

2610 acento *nm* accent, stress
- canta en español pero con acento inglés
82 | 423

2611 aviso *nm* warning
- sin previo aviso de algún trueno o relámpago, comenzó a llover
84 | 362

2612 lazo *nm* bow, knot, tie, lasso
- para desanudar el lazo que me estrangula
85 | 429

2613 conservador *adj* conservative
- yo antes era liberal y me he convertido en conservador
82 | 832 -f

2614 entorno *nm* environment, surroundings
- sumamente susceptible a las influencias del entorno musical
80 | 665

2615 nieto *nm* grandchild
- R. es el nieto del abuelo
80 | 501 -nf

2616 príncipe *nm* prince
- el heredero es su hijo mayor, Carlos, príncipe de Gales
81 | 550

2617 imprescindible *adj* essential, indispensable
- es absolutamente imprescindible contar con el transporte marítimo
81 | 467

2618 mediodía *nm* noon, midday
- deban celebrarse a mediodía o a primera hora de la tarde
81 | 567 -nf

2619 gota *nf* drop
- el médico dijo que no me quedaba una gota de sangre en el cuerpo
78 | 618

2620 cajón *nm* drawer
- tuvo gran dificultad en poner la llave en el cajón del escritorio
81 | 579

2621 generalizar *v* to generalize, popularize
- en 1915, Einstein generalizó su hipótesis
85 | 540 +o -f

2622 señorita *nf* young woman
- quedó viuda muy joven, o sea, prácticamente una señorita solterona
73 | 845 +o -nf

2623 preferencia *nf* preference
- yo tenía preferencia por los criminales y no por las víctimas
86 | 396

2624 habitar *v* to inhabit
- la casa donde habita una mujer es un hogar
82 | 534

2625 pozo *nm* well, shaft
- se encontraba un pozo de donde los monjes recogían agua
84 | 497

2626 rumor *nm* rumor, murmur
- más rumores no confirmados e información caótica
80 | 742

2627 armar *v* to arm, put together
- se armaban con cañones en el castillo
79 | 575 -nf

2628 concurso *nm* competition, gathering
- el cuento ganó un primer premio en un concurso latinoamericano
82 | 466

2629 tesoro *nm* treasure, thesaurus
- las mil llaves de oro de las estrellas, como un tesoro intocable . . .
81 | 429

2630 presupuesto *nm* budget
- hay un presupuesto de doscientos millones anuales para el edificio
80 | 911 +o -f

2631 rural *adj* rural, country
- ha cambiado de una población rural a una población urbana
82 | 634 +o -f

2632 vigilancia *nf* surveillance, vigilance
- su casa quedaría sin vigilancia y era seguro que alguien entraría
84 | 351

2633 supremo *adj* supreme
- el Ser Supremo que nos ha creado y dado un alma
84 | 574

2634 confuso *adj* confused, mixed up
- estaba demasiado confuso para tomar una decisión
85 | 490

2635 presa *nf* dam, prisoner (f)
- se forma una pequeña presa; también se pueden formar lagos
86 | 504

2636 estómago *nm* stomach
- comenzó a sentir unos fuertes dolores en el estómago y a vomitar
80 | 631

2637 anular *v* to annul, cancel
- en apelar a las autoridades eclesiásticas para anular su matrimonio
88 | 348

2638 decisivo *adj* decisive, conclusive
- jugó un papel decisivo en la ejecución de la revolución
83 | 648

2639 bola *nf* ball, sphere
- como si la pelota fuera una bola de cristal
80 | 612

2640 determinación *nf* determination
- ella lo rechazó con una determinación inflexible
85 | 436

2641 reforma *nf* reform, improvement
- para llevar a cabo la reforma agraria
79 | 1735 +o -f

2642 bruto *adj* brutal, coarse, clumsy
- es un bestia, un bestia bruto
85 | 391

2643 verso *nm* verse, poem
- escribió el último verso del último poema de su último libro
76 | 697

2644 requisito *nm* prerequisite, requirement
- ¿qué es necesario hacer?, ¿qué requisitos? // Bueno, cinco años de estudio
86 | 468

2645 adolescente *nc* adolescent
- se llevó a cabo con aquellos jóvenes, adolescentes, niñas y varones
78 | 616

2646 sentimental *adj* sentimental
- soy una tonta sentimental en respecto al amor
81 | 390

2647 herido *adj* wounded, injured
- tenía el corazón herido, y se estaba muriendo
83 | 494

2648 kilo *nm* kilogram
- ahora no como, estoy veinticinco kilos debajo de mi peso
75 | 488

2649 alargar *v* to enlarge, elongate
- luego el embrión humano comienza a alargarse
83 | 436

2650 conquista *nf* conquest
- se buscaba unificar ambos imperios e intentar la conquista de Europa
82 | 654

2651 luminoso *adj* bright, luminous
- un cielo luminoso y claro
82 | 576

2652 particularmente *adv* particularly, personally
- los problemas eran particularmente los de su época
80 | 579

2653 filósofo *nm* philosopher
- Hegel (1770-1813), filósofo alemán, máximo representante del idealismo
81 | 838

2654 genio *nm* genius, disposition
- no poseemos la brillante palabra, el genio poético
83 | 445

2655 sucesión *nf* succession, series
- la historia de Italia es una sucesión de caídas de reyes sin importancia
86 | 452

2656 componente *nm* component, ingredient
- los quarks son los componentes fundamentales de la materia
82 | 921 -f +nf

2657 transparente *adj* transparent, clear
- todo esto es público y transparente
81 | 513

2658 sufrimiento *nm* suffering
- había llevado mucho dolor y sufrimiento y muerte
82 | 570

2659 aparente *adj* apparent
- no hay ningún tipo de cambio aparente o visible
84 | 496

2660 entidad *nf* entity
- el comienzo de nuestro país como entidad autónoma
80 | 940 -f

2661 saludo *nm* greeting
- Saludos, Juanjo. // Muy buenos días, José Luis
77 | 490 -nf

2662 estimular *v* to stimulate, encourage
- yo no escribo para estimular la imaginación de nadie
85 | 581

2663 certeza *nf* certainty
- no sabía con certeza cuánto tiempo estuvo perdida
87 | 474

2664 depósito *nm* deposit, sediment
- él lo utilizaba como depósito para guardar los libros viejos
80 | 592

2665 húmedo *adj* humid, damp
- bajé las ventanillas y entró un aire húmedo
76 | 924

2666 pasillo *nm* hall, corridor
- nos encontrábamos en un pasillo estrecho, de unos quince metros
78 | 794

2667 pisar *v* to step on
- un día pisó los bordes del vasto misterio forestal
81 | 542

2668 solidaridad *nf* solidarity, togetherness
- una armonía basada en la solidaridad de los hombres
82 | 457

2669 papa *nmf* Pope (m), potato (f)
- el papa Juan Pablo II presidió la ceremonia en la basílica
78 | 685

2670 geografía *nf* geography
- desconocen la geografía y las costumbres de los países donde viven
84 | 335

2671 leve *adj* slight, trifling, light
- ¡no se pierda usted ni el más leve susurro!
82 | 574

2672 juguete *nm* toy
- cuando era chico, el único juguete que tenía era un camión de madera
80 | 368 -nf

2673 violar *v* to violate, trespass, rape
- un espectro que viola la serenidad interminable de las dunas
86 | 364

2674 chiste *nm* joke, funny story
- festejaban cada chiste a las carcajadas
76 | 462 +o -nf

2675 aprendizaje *nm* learning, apprenticeship
- de participación activa del niño en el aprendizaje de la ciencia
82 | 694

2676 esposo *nm* husband, spouse
- no dijiste nada de que habías estado casada ni de tu esposo muerto
79 | 640 -nf

2677 boda *nf* marriage, wedding
- celebramos la boda con mi mujer, en la iglesia
77 | 581

2678 realista *adj* realistic
- «El extranjero» no es ni realista ni fantástico
84 | 515

2679 fresco *nm* freshness, coolness
- me gusta oír los pájaros, sentir el fresco de la mañana
82 | 406

2680 lago *nm* lake
- Thoreau construyó una cabaña al lado del lago de Walden
79 | 639

2681 enriquecer *v* to enrich
- quedan algunos para enriquecer colecciones muy valiosas
85 | 375

2682 prestado *adj* borrowed, lent
- he tenido que pedir dinero prestado para poder dártelo a ti
88 | 230

2683 orientación *nf* orientation, direction
- echó en una mochila sus instrumentos de orientación y sus mapas
84 | 534 +o -f

2684 madurez *nf* maturity, ripeness
- para suponer que madurez implica aceptar responsabilidades
84 | 365

2685 adulto *adj* adult, grown-up
- el desarrollo es completo en todas las hembras adultas
85 | 419

2686 municipal *adj* municipal, town
- el consejo municipal convocó a una reunión urgente
79 | 709

2687 demostración *nf* demonstration
- vení, mi hija; dales una pequeña demostración de tu poder
86 | 236

2688 fundamentalmente *adv* fundamentally, basically
- esa herencia viene ligada fundamentalmente al cristianismo
78 | 978 +o -f

Nationalities and place adjectives

Regions or cities

castellano 1660 Castilian

latino 1862 Latino

latinoamericano 3971 Latin American

andaluz 4591 Andalusian

madrileño 5035 from Madrid

sevillano 6659 from Sevilla

hispanoamericano 7671 Latin American
[WORDS 1 – 8000]

Hispanic

español 285 Spanish

argentino 1626 Argentinian

chileno 3164 Chilean

mexicano 3892 Mexican

cubano 3905 Cuban

peruano 4359 Peruvian

colombiano 4695 Colombian

boliviano 6065 Bolivian

venezolano 6288 Venezuelan

paraguayo 7352 Paraguayan

uruguayo 7784 Uruguayan

nicaragüense 13119 Nicaraguan

panameño 13462 Panamanian

dominicano 13987 Dominican

puertorriqueño 14336 Puerto Rican

guatemalteco 14763 Guatemalan

salvadoreño 17359 El Salvadorian

costarricense 26479 Costa Rican

hondureño 29435 Honduran

Non-Hispanic

inglés 608 English

francés 646 French

italiano 953 Italian

alemán 963 German

europeo 1092 European

americano 1261 American

chino 1444 Chinese

griego 1467 Greek

romano 1774 Roman

japonés 2169 Japanese

ruso 2307 Russian

árabe 2433 Arab

británico 3265 British

turco 3691 Turkish

portugués 3913 Portuguese

holandés 4206 Dutch

brasileño 4391 Brazilian

suizo 4500 Swiss

sueco 5269 Swedish

belga 5625 Belgian

polaco 5852 Polish

escocés 6187 Scottish

estadounidense 6332 US

irlandés 6543 Irish

canadiense 7174 Canadian

húngaro 7716 Hungarian

danés 7798 Danish

checo 9313 Czech

australiano 10628 Australian

noruego 10654 Norwegian

coreano 11306 Korean
[MOST FREQUENT WORDS]

2689 alegrar *v* to be/make happy
• y se alegró de verlo libre
78 | 484 +o -nf

2690 transportar *v* to transport, carry
• un vehículo que servía para transportar al enfermo
81 | 553

2691 cumplimiento *nm* fulfillment, compliment
• con el objeto de implementar el cumplimiento de la nueva legislación
83 | 461

2692 respaldo *nm* support, backing, back
• perdió el respaldo de Rusia a causa de su neutralidad durante la guerra
84 | 422

2693 superficial *adj* superficial
• no tenía más que un conocimiento superficial del idioma
85 | 435

2694 dieciocho *num* eighteen
• hasta que a los dieciocho años se fue de su hogar
78 | 482 +o

2695 incendio *nm* fire, conflagration
• subió y prendió fuego a una torre, y el incendio destruyó todo
83 | 472

2696 dorado *adj* golden, gold-plated
• y adornos de marfil, bronce dorado y cobre
83 | 737 -o

2697 triunfar *v* to triumph
• donde había triunfado la revolución de los bolcheviques
84 | 358

2698 joya *nf* jewel, treasure
• es una auténtica reliquia y una joya artística
78 | 478

2699 favorito *adj* favorite
• su metal favorito era el oro
83 | 402

2700 cementerio *nm* cemetery, graveyard
• el día de los muertos todos van al cementerio
78 | 499

2701 escolar *adj* school, scholastic
• regresaban el final del curso escolar
81 | 479

2702 publicación *nf* publication
- por una parte, la catalogación y publicación de documentos
- 82 | 601 +o -f

2703 variación *nf* variation
- presentan una gran variación en el tamaño y en el peso
- 81 | 898 +nf

2704 cálido *adj* warm
- un aire cálido y denso de sudor
- 82 | 490

2705 inconsciente *adj* unconscious, thoughtless
- supone el conocimiento innato, e incluso inconsciente
- 83 | 414

2706 promoción *nf* promotion
- tiene por misión la promoción de la salud y la curación de la enfermedad
- 84 | 380

2707 enseguida *adv* immediately, at once
- comprenderá enseguida por qué vengo por el patio
- 78 | 676

2708 mágico *adj* magic, magical
- por medio de ese mágico mundo de imágenes nocturnas
- 82 | 566

2709 sentencia *nf* (legal) sentence, judgment
- el juez confirma una sentencia de culpabilidad
- 79 | 623

2710 amargo *adj* bitter, sour, painful
- su ausencia le había dejado un sabor amargo
- 82 | 467

2711 resolución *nf* resolution
- anunció a sus padres su resolución de hacerse ermitaño
- 81 | 788

2712 afortunadamente *adv* luckily, fortunately
- afortunadamente mi mamá me ayuda mucho
- 80 | 475 +o

2713 coincidencia *nf* coincidence
- una feliz coincidencia hizo que nos encontráramos
- 84 | 364

2714 estímulo *nm* stimulus, encouragement
- un estímulo muy grande en nuestra sociedad es el dinero
- 81 | 615

2715 acoger *v* to welcome, accept
- dispuesto, ansioso por acoger a lo bienvenido
- 82 | 384

2716 filosófico *adj* philosophical
- se unió a un grupo filosófico, esotérico, que cultivaba el desarrollo
- 84 | 672

2717 sembrar *v* to sow, plant
- este caso puede sembrar un precedente jurídico
- 81 | 402

2718 acentuar *v* to accent, stress
- tomar un modelo real y acentuar sus rasgos
- 86 | 451

2719 anteriormente *adv* previously
- pidió perdón por la actitud que había tenido anteriormente
- 81 | 545 +o -f

2720 marino *adj* marine, naval
- los arrecifes de coral, las playas y el hábitat marino
- 79 | 658

2721 barra *nf* bar, rod, rail
- reforzado por el borde superior con una barra metálica
- 78 | 500

2722 entretener *v* to entertain, amuse
- trajo juguetes para entretener al nuevo amiguito
- 79 | 408 -nf

2723 desviar *v* to deviate, divert, change
- nada nos hará desviar del camino
- 87 | 383

2724 retroceder *v* to go back
- quería retroceder a otra época, donde estaba la juventud
- 85 | 462

2725 culto *adj* cultured, educated
- es un hombre culto que ama los libros
- 80 | 413

2726 novia *nf* girlfriend, bride
- Sí, ésa; ya es mi novia; por fin me he declarado a ella
- 76 | 653 -nf

2727 piano *nm* piano
- composición de conciertos para piano y orquesta, cuartetos, canciones
- 76 | 947

2728 pretensión *nf* pretension, claim
- tenía pretensión de que era capaz de todo
- 86 | 402

2729 habla *nf* (el) speech, talking
- Borges estudió muy profundamente el habla de Buenos Aires
- 85 | 295

2730 novio *nm* boyfriend, groom
- su hija tiene novio y se va a casar muy pronto
- 73 | 687 -nf

2731 sonreír *v* to smile
- ella sonrió complaciente, seductora
- 71 | 2022 +f -nf

2732 espectador *nm* spectator, onlooker
- era un espectador escondido, un testigo sin nombre
- 78 | 646

2733 relatar *v* to tell, narrate
- puedes relatar historias graciosamente
- 85 | 331

2734 pensado *adj* thought-out, designed
- tengo pensado otro sistema nuevo que voy a ensayar mañana
- 84 | 234 +o -nf

2735 bota *nf* boot, wineskin
- de ver sus pies, calzados con pesadas botas militares
- 79 | 537

2736 oh *interj* oh
- ¡Oh! sí, soy tuya
- 75 | 755 -nf

2737 pretexto *nm* pretext, excuse
- lo cual era sólo un pretexto para salir otra vez al mar
- 83 | 444

2738 horrible *adj* horrible
- fallecidos recientemente en un horrible y lamentable accidente
- 76 | 626 +o -nf

2739 fiebre *nf* fever, excitement
- una fiebre me hizo arder la cabeza
- 80 | 537

2740 difundir *v* to spread (out)
- el bienestar comenzó a difundirse por todos los rincones
- 84 | 444

2741 lucir *v* to show (off), shine
- lucía un viejo y arruinado traje
- 78 | 536

2742 síntesis *nf* synthesis
- hago una síntesis de la suma de muchas ideas
- 83 | 614 -f

2743 este *nm* East
- es igual en el este como en el oeste
- 79 | 799

2744 nervio *nm* nerve
- los impulsos se transmiten de un nervio a otro
- 81 | 538

2745 científico *nm/f* scientist
- los científicos acometerán importantes investigaciones sobre biología
- 79 | 1077 -f

2746 peculiar *adj* peculiar
- no lograba entender el peculiar humor de Julio
- 86 | 425

2747 ejemplar *adj* exemplary, model
- la fuga es también caso ejemplar de «transfinitud» en música
- 85 | 353

2748 grano *nm* grain, kernel
- se almacenaba el grano de trigo que a diario consumía Madrid
- 82 | 541

2749 recientemente *adv* recently
- como si se conocieran recientemente
- 83 | 531 -f

2750 reservar *v* to reserve, book
- el destino me reservaba sus mejores reveses para esas fechas
- 84 | 320

2751 asistencia *nf* attendance, assistance
- habría reunión familiar y mi asistencia era importante
- 82 | 395 +o -f

2752 sacrificar *v* to sacrifice
- en el estudio tú a veces tienes que sacrificar sábados y domingos
- 87 | 313

2753 puramente *adv* purely, simply
- de fines puramente superficiales
- 83 | 309

2754 sonrisa *nf* smile
- sus dientes blancos y su sonrisa fresca y luminosa
- 74 | 1756 +f -nf

2755 exagerar *v* to exaggerate
- una tendencia natural a exagerar el dramatismo de los sucesos
- 85 | 274

2756 león *nm* lion
- de animales carnívoros, tales como leones y hienas
- 83 | 355

2757 bárbaro *adj* savage, horrible
- ¡qué bárbaro! exclamaron a una sola voz
- 81 | 373

2758 aceptación *nf* acceptance, approval
- uno se contenta con la simple aceptación del destino
- 84 | 507 -f

2759 labio *nm* lip
- el labio estaba perforado de tanto morderse
- 71 | 1954 -o +f

2760 visitante *nc* visitor
- era como si la casa se hubiera llenado de visitantes
- 80 | 442

2761 autónomo *adj* autonomous
- y luego el niño ya autónomo, ya libre, parado sobre sus dos pies
- 79 | 1149 +o -f

2762 sonoro *adj* loud, resounding
- dijeron en voz alta y sonora que produjo una resonancia de muchos
- 81 | 524

2763 traslado *nm* transfer
- para hacer el traslado de un sitio a otro
- 85 | 284

2764 residir *v* to reside, live (in)
- la soberanía nacional reside en el pueblo español
- 83 | 503

2765 tentación *nf* temptation
- no resistí la tentación de tentarle con una tequila
- 80 | 457

2766 porvenir *nm* future, time to come
- la incertidumbre de un porvenir que no se puede predecir
- 82 | 337

2767 promover *v* to promote
- pudieron promover una mayor asistencia de público
- 81 | 674 -f

2768 atracción *nf* attraction
- la atracción mutua los llevó a darse el primer beso
84 | 345

2769 jurídico *adj* legal, juridical
- para instituir un cuerpo legislativo y jurídico más formal
78 | 1482 +o -f

2770 reparar *v* to repair, restore
- trabajar el doble para reparar los daños
83 | 393

2771 ilustre *adj* renowned, illustrious
- Platón, siguiendo a su ilustre maestro Sócrates
80 | 356

2772 corona *nf* crown
- colocaba la corona de laurel a los emperadores romanos
80 | 412

2773 administrar *v* to administer, manage
- sus hijos sabían administrar el negocio
86 | 357

2774 docena *nf* dozen
- la docena de huevos que se come en el almuerzo
83 | 434

2775 ahorrar *v* to save (money, time)
- todos viajan en avión, para ahorrar horas
82 | 350

2776 perfección *nf* perfection
- advertimos la perfección técnica de la pintora
86 | 406

2777 humedad *nf* humidity
- sus altas temperaturas, su incómoda humedad y sus escasas lluvias
74 | 691

2778 cosecha *nf* harvest, crop
- había hecho en el jardín una abundante cosecha de flores
80 | 454

2779 enterrar *v* to bury
- lo enterró profundamente bajo las raíces de un lapacho
80 | 491

2780 desesperación *nf* desperation, exasperation
- era una desesperación no poder darles la solución justa
80 | 487

2781 curva *nf* curve
- lo hacen siguiendo una trayectoria curva y no en línea recta
78 | 578

2782 contraer *v* to contract, shrink, abbreviate
- los padres les impedían contraer matrimonio
83 | 356

2783 blando *adj* soft, limp, gentle
- era un lecho nada de blando y nada de cómodo
81 | 480

2784 estable *adj* stable, steady
- pueden edificar una relación estable, basada en el amor
84 | 523 -f

2785 ciertamente *adv* certainly, indeed
- y si había otra persona, ciertamente no era López
79 | 630

2786 dormido *adj* asleep, sleeping
- arrulló al niño dormido en la cama pequeña
76 | 881 -nf

2787 amo *nm* master, boss (m)
- esta pasión desigual entre el amo y el esclavo
81 | 454

2788 reflexionar *v* to reflect, consider on
- he podido reflexionar sobre el concepto moral
79 | 451

2789 humo *nm* smoke
- inhala el humo del cigarrillo que ya le quema los dedos
77 | 853

2790 realización *nf* fulfillment, realization
- Los sueños son la realización de deseos insatisfechos
83 | 610 -f

2791 cuartel *nm* quarters, barracks
- me trasladé al cuartel de policía
80 | 483

2792 tránsito *nm* traffic, transit
- no había tránsito de vehículos en ningún sentido
84 | 374

2793 dieciséis *num* sixteen
- tenía entonces dieciséis años y ninguna experiencia del mundo
77 | 369 +o

2794 énfasis *nm* emphasis
- han querido poner énfasis en sólo uno de los aspectos del narcotráfico
83 | 405

2795 tímido *adj* timid, shy, half-hearted
- soy muy tímido y no me atrevo a abordarla por la calle
81 | 396

2796 empresario *nm* manager, entrepreneur
- la confianza del empresario en cubrir parcelas de mercado a corto plazo
78 | 779

2797 tuyo *pron* yours (sg/+fam)
- es tuyo, te lo cedo
73 | 806 +o -nf

2798 saco *nm* sack, bag, plunder
- ¿hay algo que pese más que un saco de papas?
77 | 527

2799 vasto *adj* vast, immense, huge
- vi un vasto silencio caer sobre la tierra
81 | 522 -o

2800 cruz *nf* cross, burden
- llevó la cruz del Dios hecho Hombre
76 | 579

2801 frustrado *adj* frustrated
- esa generación se quedó frustrada, comenzó a buscar espacios
83 | 297

2802 pausa *nf* pause
- hizo una larga pausa, esperando la respuesta
74 | 790 -nf

2803 comprometido *adj* committed, engaged
- y ella te habrá dicho que está comprometida conmigo
84 | 341

2804 libremente *adv* freely
- podamos elegir libremente a nuestros representantes
86 | 308

2805 vicio *nm* vice, bad habit, defect
- el fumar es el único vicio que me queda
81 | 382

2806 impuesto *nm* tax
- el estereotipo es que los socialistas suben los impuestos
81 | 680

2807 consiguiente *adj* consequent; por consiguiente: consequently
- es mucho más agresiva y, por consiguiente, más peligrosa
79 | 477

2808 arquitecto *nm/f* architect
- la «dimensión humana» conseguida por el arquitecto para el nuevo museo
77 | 646 +o

2809 cruce *nm* crossing, intersection
- somos un estado que está en el cruce de intereses geoestratégicos
83 | 376

2810 centrar *v* to center, focus, base (on)
- todo se centraba alrededor de la novela
80 | 572 -f

2811 convivencia *nf* coexistence, living together
- el hogar es un elemento de convivencia de hombre y mujer
79 | 557

2812 cable *nm* cable, wiring
- se han instalado redes de cable para transmitir la señal televisiva
79 | 439

2813 aburrido *adj* boring, bored
- sin futuro, sin diversión, aburrida, con reglas para todo
77 | 418 -nf

2814 bondad *nf* goodness, kindness
- el cariño de su alma apasionada, llena de bondad y dulzura
83 | 325

2815 experimento *nm* experiment
- hizo el experimento con partículas físicas
82 | 583 -f

2816 recto *adj* right, straight, honest
- I. tomó una regla de ángulo recto de madera
82 | 357

2817 crónica *nf* account, chronicle
- inventó una crónica de la vida de Magdalena bastante creíble
83 | 350

2818 seguida *adv* en seguida: right away, at once
- me casé y bueno, ya empecé en seguida a tener hijos
73 | 757 -nf

2819 originar *v* to give rise (to), cause
- los fantasmas que origina son fenómenos ópticos
81 | 634

2820 socialista *adj* socialist
- se convirtió en el primer ministro socialista del Reino Unido
75 | 1585 +o -f

2821 ahogar *v* to drown, choke, flood
- desea ahogar sus penas con el alcohol
79 | 450

2822 espléndido *adj* splendid, generous
- el interior espléndido, exquisito; es una verdadera joya del arte
80 | 366

2823 esforzar *v* to make an effort, exert oneself
- se esforzaba pero no podía avanzar más allá
83 | 376

2824 dictadura *nf* dictatorship
- denunciaron al gobierno de Castro como una dictadura totalitaria
81 | 554

2825 eficacia *nf* efficiency, effectiveness
- existen métodos para medir la eficacia de este instrumento
79 | 623

2826 detectar *v* to detect
- también pudimos detectar problemas con las curas
80 | 734

2827 vapor *nm* vapor, steam
- el baño comenzó a llenarse de vapor
77 | 686

2828 bebida *nf* drink, beverage
- los pacientes que consumen más de una bebida alcohólica por día
79 | 406

2829 autorizar *v* to authorize, legalize
- se niega a autorizar la boda de su hijo
84 | 303

2830 charla *nf* talk, chat
- la imaginó con sus preguntas, su charla incesante
79 | 354 +o -nf

2831 gestión *nf* management, step, negotiation
- hay deficiencias en la gestión de la economía
78 | 756 -f

2832 afrontar *v* to face, confront
- los hombres deben afrontar las consecuencias de sus actos
83 | 395

2833 existente *adj* existing
- acumulaba el 80% del oro existente en el mundo
81 | 707 +nf

Adjectives with *Ser/estar*

Spanish has two words that express the concept [to be]: *ser* and *estar*. *Ser* is used to refer to the norm (*Juan siempre ha sido flaco* "John has always been skinny)", while *estar* refers to a change from the norm (*Juan ha comido mucho, y ya está gordo* "John has eaten a lot, and now he's fat)". Because some adjectives naturally express the norm and others naturally express a more temporary departure from the norm, they tend to occur more with one or the other of these two verbs.

The following lists show the most common adjectives that always occur with either *ser* or *estar*, as well as those that alternate. In the latter case, we see those that occur with *estar* between 20 and 70 percent of the time, and the figures show [$_{\% \, estar}$ Spanish $_{word\#}$ English)

All with ser	All with estar	Combination
único 181 unique	**dispuesto** 690 willing	0.21 **rojo** 533 red
importante 207 important	**sentado** 1231 seated	0.21 **firme** 1570 firm, steady
posible 225 possible	**convencido** 1294 convinced	0.26 **viejo** 281 old
general 227 general	**acostumbrado** 1595 accus- tomed	0.26 **libre** 413 free, vacant
anterior 370 previous	**contento** 1642 happy	0.30 **activo** 1328 active
capaz 411 capable	**preocupado** 1677 worried	0.31 **completo** 458 complete
común 438 common	**satisfecho** 1735 satisfied	0.37 **vivo** 453 living, alive
contrario 460 contrary	**compuesto** 2063 comprised	0.42 **sano** 1394 healthy
real 462 real	**previsto** 2087 foreseen	0.44 **ciego** 1481 blind
enorme 471 enormous	**cansado** 2148 tired	0.46 **frío** 907 cold
nacional 507 national	**parado** 2245 stopped	0.46 **aburrido** 2814 boring, bored
conocido 540 (well) known	**prohibido** 2258 prohibited	0.52 **oscuro** 888 dark
suficiente 547 sufficient	**resuelto** 2429 resolved	0.52 **fijo** 1061 fixed
absoluto 574 absolute	**escondido** 2547 hidden	0.52 **triste** 1314 sad
rápido 652 fast	**dormido** 2787 asleep	0.56 **limpio** 1397 clean
popular 709 popular	**agotado** 2862 used up	0.60 **claro** 259 clear
famoso 713 famous	**ligado** 2927 joined	0.66 **limitado** 1867 limited
preciso 739 necessary	**vinculado** 3182 connected	0.73 **seco** 1178 dry
amplio 763 wide	**disponible** 3263 available	0.78 **definido** 2044 definite

2834 **cartera** *nf* wallet, satchel
• había olvidado la cartera y no tenía dinero para el taxi
76 | 463

2835 **inclinado** *adj* inclined, slanting
• inclinado hacia abajo con un ángulo de unos 45°
83 | 321

2836 **restar** *v* to subtract, minimize
• sabía sumar, restar, multiplicar y adivinaba el futuro
82 | 404

2837 **circulación** *nf* circulation, traffic
• una de las avenidas en que hay mayor circulación de microbuses
81 | 488 -f

2838 **denuncia** *nf* accusation
• no han dudado en presentar denuncia contra el presidente del gobierno
79 | 535

2839 **concretar** *v* to materialize, fulfill
• en ningún momento han sabido concretar sus peligrosos avances
80 | 399

2840 **picar** *v* to bite, sting, itch
• preguntándose qué bicho la picaba
78 | 358 -nf

2841 **tormenta** *nf* storm
• el calor tardío y el cielo plomizo amenazan tormenta
80 | 484

2842 metálico *adj* metallic
- percibía el frío metálico de un revólver
77 | 621

2843 foco *nm* focus
- constituyen - por así decirlo - el foco de atracción principal
83 | 345

2844 residencia *nf* residence
- el Buckingham Palace es la residencia de la reina en Londres
79 | 446

2845 espectacular *adj* spectacular
- íntimo restaurante con espectacular vista al mar
82 | 475

2846 jurar *v* to swear, take an oath
- le juro que soy estudiante, mire mi credencial
76 | 681 -nf

2847 rezar *v* to pray, recite
- era costumbre rezar el rosario después del paseo
77 | 744

2848 cuero *nm* leather, skin
- pequeñas piezas de cuero, plástico, madera, caucho o metal
76 | 612

2849 misterioso *adj* mysterious
- que el arte tenga algo misterioso dentro de su verdadera esencia
78 | 714

2850 hierba *nf* herb, grass, weed
- hervía alguna hierba medicinal que agriaba el aire
77 | 492

2851 obrero *adj* working class
- cuatro secciones: obrera, campesina, popular y militar
81 | 510

2852 administrativo *adj* administrative
- es la capital y el centro político y administrativo de Italia
76 | 975 +o -f

2853 manzana *nf* apple, (city) block
- una importante cosecha de mandarinas, melones y manzanas
79 | 363

2854 singular *adj* single, singular
- la puso muy contenta la singular visita de Sosa
80 | 496

2855 pedazo *nm* piece, bit
- le da un pedazo de pan
75 | 757 -nf

2856 sabiduría *nf* wisdom, knowledge
- admiro la sabiduría de todos esos filósofos, que saben tantas cosas
83 | 373

2857 inducir *v* to lead to
- esto induce la síntesis de todos los componentes del virus
85 | 398

2858 cigarrillo *nm* cigarette
- se sentaba, fumando cigarrillo tras cigarrillo
73 | 881 -nf

2859 encantar *v* to be very pleasing to
- qué pieza tan linda, me encanta tu casa
72 | 662 +o -nf

2860 crudo *adj* raw, crude, natural
- ¡qué buen aspecto! // Un poco crudo. // Mejor, más natural
80 | 372

2861 agotado *adj* tired, used up, sold out
- los franceses, agotados, también firmaron la paz
82 | 284

2862 deportivo *adj* sports, sporty
- oigo el bramido cercano de un coche deportivo
78 | 651

2863 magnitud *nf* magnitude, extent
- salieron de sus casas, para ver toda la magnitud del desastre
80 | 557

2864 químico *adj* chemical
- estos productos químicos emiten burbujas de gas
76 | 1179 -f

2865 botón *nm* button
- se prendió el último botón de la camisa blanca
78 | 465

2866 teórico *adj* theoretical
- una formación muy teórica, muy académica, muy general
79 | 636 +o -f

2867 igualdad *nf* equality
- plantean igualdad y no discriminación del pueblo cubano
80 | 564 -f

2868 privar *v* to deprive (of)
- le priva al hombre de su libertad
84 | 267

2869 deducir *v* to deduce, infer
- no debe ser tan complicado deducir cuánto cuesta eso
82 | 375

2870 redactar *v* to edit, write, compose
- piensa redactar el título de la obra
85 | 315

2871 noción *nf* notion, idea
- ha perdido la noción de que tal vez la unión hace la fuerza
78 | 486

2872 planear *v* to plan
- Enrique murió mientras planeaba una cruzada a Tierra Santa
85 | 269

2873 abrazar *v* to hug, embrace
- la abrazó fuerte y la besó
77 | 721

2874 tolerar *v* to tolerate, put up with
- no toleraba sus injusticias
84 | 287

2875 semilla *nf* seed
- cada una de esas leyendas contiene una semilla de verdad
79 | 553

2876 avenida *nf* avenue
- la YMCA está en la avenida l6, esquina cinco, entre cuatro y cinco
75 | 615 -nf

2877 descartar *v* to discard, reject, rule out
- lee una declaración oficial para descartar dudas
83 | 385

2878 diablo *nm* devil
- ni Dios ni el Diablo le escucharon
76 | 618 -nf

2879 sujetar *v* to fasten, attach, hold
- un pegamento para sujetar objetos metálicos
79 | 406

2880 hueco *nm* hole, cavity
- entonces se buscó un hueco entre las piedras o debajo de ellas
77 | 502

2881 colaborador *nm* collaborator
- con ayuda de un colaborador de lengua rusa
82 | 384 -f

2882 capricho *nm* caprice, whim
- no creáis que esto lo hacemos por mero capricho
83 | 366

2883 ciudadano *adj* community, citizen
- el deterioro creciente de la seguridad ciudadana
76 | 493 +o

2884 prudente *adj* sensible, prudent
- no era prudente esa pregunta ahora // ¿Por qué no?
84 | 289

2885 guitarra *nf* guitar
- yo soy músico, toco el clarinete y la guitarra
73 | 575 -nf

2886 agencia *nf* agency, branch
- es un empleado de la Agencia de Modelos «Cuerpo Perfecto»
76 | 534 +o -f

2887 rabia *nf* rage
- fue un dolor intenso, solitario, una rabia interna
76 | 641 -nf

2888 telefónico *adj* telephone
- el primer cable telefónico submarino transoceánico del mundo
79 | 409

2889 monumento *nm* monument
- los monumentos sepulcrales imitaron el estilo suntuoso del mausoleo
79 | 374

2890 racional *adj* rational
- no es racional, es una obsesión
81 | 710 -f

2891 previamente *adv* previously
- aunque no esté incluida en forma religiosa previamente establecida
80 | 448

2892 trazar *v* to draw, trace
- el bastón trazó un arco para señalar una dirección
81 | 405

2893 correspondencia *nf* correspondence, connection
- como corresponsal, redacto y dicto correspondencia en inglés
80 | 347

2894 barro *nm* clay, mud
- lo mezclaron con arena y formaron un barro rico en compuestos orgánicos
79 | 597 -o

2895 fuga *nf* flight, escape
- M. soñó de nuevo con la fuga de sus pájaros
80 | 442

2896 presionar *v* to press, pressure
- manipuló los discos y palancas, presionó botones numerados
86 | 332

2897 identificación *nf* identification
- un objetivo relacionado con la identificación de genes
83 | 413

2898 contexto *nm* context
- hay que situarlo en el contexto de la atención global que se presta
78 | 793 -f

2899 sombrero *nm* hat, sombrero
- me daba cuenta del sombrero que llevaba en la cabeza
74 | 892

2900 reiterar *v* to reiterate, repeat
- no se preocupe - reiteró -, estamos para servirla
77 | 625

2901 ayudante *nc* helper, assistant
- al quedarse sin ayudante, tenía que hacerlo todo él solo
82 | 293

2902 indiferente *adj* indifferent
- puede ser que no le guste o . . . sea indiferente
79 | 407

2903 maniobra *nf* maneuver, operation
- no es comprensible que se produzcan unas maniobras militares con fuego real
80 | 479

2904 inesperado *adj* unexpected, unforeseen
- fue tan inesperado que me pareció la imaginación
81 | 505 -o

2905 distraer *v* to distract
- el barullo de vehículos y transeúntes distrae mi atención
79 | 398 -nf

2906 prejuicio *nm* prejudice
- no quiere provocarle un perjuicio contra nosotros
82 | 297

2907 tropezar *v* to trip, stumble
- suben con cuidado las escaleras para no tropezar
77 | 445

2908 recomendación *nf* recommendation
- había tomado en serio la recomendación del médico: ejercicio moderado
82 | 298

2909 francamente *adv* frankly, openly
- ¿no te parece que debiéramos hablar francamente?
79 | 342 +o

2910 diseñar *v* to design, develop
- se han diseñado técnicas que emplean haces de láser
81 | 573 -f

2911 proveer *v* to provide
- un jefe invisible proveía de uniformes y documentos oficiales
83 | 330

2912 seleccionar *v* to select
- voy a seleccionar entre toda mi clientela a cien personas
81 | 334 +o

2913 convivir *v* to coexist
- por su alergia no podía convivir con animales con pelos
82 | 298

2914 instinto *nm* instinct
- yo sentí, con mi instinto femenino, que era sincero
78 | 489

2915 sincero *adj* sincere
- que un sentimiento sea auténtico y sincero
79 | 333

2916 progresar *v* to progress
- para darle oportunidad de progresar porque lugar hay para todos
81 | 285

2917 ideológico *adj* ideological
- el pluralismo ideológico es la esencia de la democracia
81 | 633 +o -f

2918 precaución *nf* caution, forethought
- la precaución le había salvado la vida
82 | 273

2919 robo *nm* theft, robbery
- un ingenioso robo de más de cien millones de pesetas
78 | 332

2920 cabello *nm* hair
- usted tiene el cabello largo y muy bonito
75 | 939

2921 utilidad *nf* usefulness, utility
- ¡lo robarán todo y no será de utilidad para nadie!
80 | 467

2922 queja *nf* complaint
- llegaban a la alcaldía para presentar sus quejas y sus demandas
80 | 361

2923 abundar *v* to be plentiful
- quizás deba abundar con más tiempo y espacio
84 | 356

2924 celo *nm* jealousy, zeal
- está loco sino resentido, me tiene envidia, celos, me detesta
76 | 491

2925 publicidad *nf* advertising, publicity
- ha logrado una de las campañas de publicidad más exitosas
76 | 703 +o -f

2926 ligado *adj* linked, joined
- se había sentido ligado a ella por unos lazos instintivos y secretos
80 | 490 -f +nf

2927 índole *nf* nature, temperament
- eran de índole resignada y sumisa
85 | 287

2928 asimilar *v* to assimilate
- incapaz de asimilar y comprender lo que estaba sucediendo
83 | 234

2929 prolongado *adj* prolonged, lengthy
- antes de saludarse con palabras se dieron un abrazo prolongado
81 | 430

2930 choque *nm* crash, collision
- el choque de meteoritos con las lunas pequeñas del planeta
78 | 339

2931 tecnología *nf* technology
- la creación de efectos especiales con tecnología electrónica
78 | 980 +o -f +nf

2932 tubo *nm* tube, pipe
- encendió un tubo fluorescente que iluminaba el pequeño patio
74 | 569

2933 sordo *adj* deaf, dull
- el despertador soltó su grito sordo bajo la almohada
78 | 458

2934 admirable *adj* admirable
- su admirable vitalidad y su contagiosa alegría de vivir
80 | 307

2935 mercancía *nf* goods, merchandise
- se volvió comerciante para llevar mercancías a lejanos puertos
78 | 410

2936 tronco *nm* trunk, torso
- el árbol crecía, le salían más ramas del tronco joven
78 | 721 -o

2937 culto *nm* worship, cult
- por eso es que el culto a Dionisio estaba tan perseguido
80 | 497

2938 palma *nf* palm tree, palm
- en ocasiones las escribían en hojas de palma
78 | 465

2939 prenda *nf* piece of clothing
- encontró las llaves en alguna prenda de su ropa
78 | 366

2940 coro *nm* choir, chorus
- un tenor que cantaba en el coro con acompañamiento de orquesta
76 | 437

2941 tejer *v* to sew, weave
- aprendió a tejer redes muy confiables
80 | 272

2942 túnel *nm* tunnel
- hay, pues, una luz al final del túnel
79 | 322

2943 cercanía *nf* nearness, proximity
- se sitúa en la cercanía del polo sur
84 | 270

2944 proclamar *v* to proclaim
- en 1810 se proclamó la independencia de Ecuador
79 | 638

2945 cuchillo *nm* knife
- se le cortó el dedo con cuchillo afinado
80 | 538

2946 desprecio *nm* contempt, disdain
- no pude ocultar mi mal humor ni mi desprecio por ese hombre
79 | 383

2947 plástico *nm* plastic
- pueden fabricarse estampando láminas de plástico en un molde
76 | 485

2948 complejo *nm* complex
- Sevilla forma un complejo de civilización y de culturas
82 | 462

2949 plantar *v* to plant
- decidió plantar la idea en su cabeza
79 | 314

2950 naranja *nf* orange (fruit)
- todos los cítricos, incluidas naranjas, limones y toronjas
77 | 385

2951 derrotar *v* to defeat, beat
- pero no lograba derrotar mis dudas
79 | 558

2952 frenar *v* to brake, restrain
- frenó de golpe y la camioneta se detuvo
82 | 397

2953 voluntario *adj* voluntary, volunteer
- fue un exiliado voluntario de su patria
81 | 489

2954 adivinar *v* to guess, solve
- no podía adivinar lo que él iba a hacer
72 | 803

2955 cuota *nf* quota, share, dues
- cambiaron las reglas del «club» y nos bajaron la cuota
79 | 405

2956 mosca *nf* fly (insect)
- en boca cerrada no entran moscas
79 | 481 -o

2957 judicial *adj* judicial
- la citación judicial significaba mero cumplimiento de trámites
75 | 876

2958 pescar *v* to fish
- se iría al río a pescar truchas
77 | 364

2959 doctrina *nf* doctrine, teachings
- los teólogos musulmanes conocían la doctrina de la teología cristiana
79 | 990

2960 reservado *adj* reserved, booked
- era un hombre muy reservado con sus planes
82 | 364

2961 laguna *nf* lagoon
- por un total de 77 canales en el interior de la laguna
80 | 326

2962 distinción *nf* distinction
- vestía con elegancia y distinción, siempre lo de última moda
82 | 421

2963 tribu *nf* tribe
- la unidad social celta era la tribu
79 | 502

2964 refugio *nm* shelter, refuge
- al mediodía obligaba a buscar refugio a la sombra
80 | 434 -o

2965 tragar *v* to swallow
- no come; traga y bebe como un cerdo
76 | 636 -nf

2966 legítimo *adj* legitimate
- dijo que jamás iba a abandonar a su legítimo esposo
79 | 558

2967 flotar *v* to float, flutter
- la hacen muy ligera, lo suficiente para flotar en el agua
78 | 617

2968 convencional *adj* conventional
- quiso que todo fuera convencional y en el viejo estilo
81 | 431

2969 sacudir *v* to shake, jolt
- un fuerte temblor lo hizo sacudir
77 | 754 -o

2970 gigantesco *adj* giant, gigantic
- un brazo poderoso, enorme, gigantesco, hercúleo, me arrebata
79 | 442

2971 cena *nf* dinner
- voy a poner la mesa para la cena
70 | 640 -nf

2972 incertidumbre *nf* uncertainty
- no es posible vivir en el equívoco, en la incertidumbre de no saber quién soy
81 | 321

2973 tierno *adj* tender, soft
- duro y tierno, serio y tarambana, demócrata y feudal
76 | 468

2974 ligeramente *adv* slightly, lightly
- habla con acento ligeramente extranjero
77 | 383

Adjectives of emotion (sentir + ADJ) top 65 words

The following are the most common adjectives that occur in the context *sentir (se)* + ADJ (*se sentía emocionado, de sentirse frustrados*). Each entry shows the following information: [*# with sentir* Spanish WORD# English]. For example, the first entry shows that word *feliz* "happy" (word # 956 in our list) occurs 101 times as the word following *sentir* (se).

Positive

101 **feliz** 956 happy

97 **orgulloso** 2388 proud

82 **satisfecho** 1735 satisfied

49 **atraído** 5803 attracted

33 **capaz** 411 capable

32 **contento** 1642 contented

28 **cómodo** 1627 comfortable

24 **cierto** 123 sure

22 **halagado** 10529 flattered

22 **libre** 413 free

20 **vivo** 453 alive

16 **honrado** 4428 honored

14 **tranquilo** 1144 calm

14 **superior** 535 better

13 **seguro** 1118 safe

9 **popular** 709 popular

7 **emocionado** 5379 excited

7 **animado** 3163 excited

Neutral

21 **inclinado** 2835 inclined

21 **responsable** 955 responsible

12 **conmovido** 7061 touched

12 **sorprendido** 3120 surprised

10 **raro** 849 strange

9 **inseguro** 4529 unsure

9 **rodeado** 1801 surrounded

8 **comprometido** 2803 committed

7 **aislado** 1533 isolated

Semi-negative

50 **cansado** 2147 tired

30 **obligado** 1255 obliged

29 **incapaz** 1733 incapable

Negative

85 **solo** 160 lonely

49 **culpable** 2211 guilty

40 **incómodo** 2535 uncomfortable

26 **humillado** 5763 humiliated

22 **molesto** 3371 annoyed

21 **amenazado** 4350 threatened

19 **avergonzado** 6482 embarrassed

19 **extraño** 551 strange

18 **ofendido** 6578 offended

18 **triste** 1314 sad

18 **perdido** 931 lost

18 **enfermo** 698 ill

17 **defraudado** 9948 disappointed

17 **aliviado** 7426 relieved

15 **frustrado** 2801 frustrated

13 **acosado** 6447 harassed

13 **débil** 1284 weak

12 **tentado** 9349 tempted

10 **deprimido** 5516 depressed

10 **traicionado** 20082 betrayed

8 **aturdido** 7222 bewildered

8 **decepcionado** 6904 let down

8 **turbado** 11533 upset

8 **desconcertado** 4808 disconcerted

8 **atrapado** 4234 trapped

8 **inquieto** 2986 restless

8 **abandonado** 2298 abandoned

8 **sucio** 1994 dirty

7 **desorientado** 5348 disoriented

7 **desolado** 5804 devastated

7 **desamparado** 6566 forsaken

7 **cohibido** 11001 self-conscious

7 **agredido** 15339 attacked

7 **estafado** 17265 cheated

7 **invadido** 7623 assailed

2975 aéreo *adj* aerial, air
- una política de transporte marítimo y aéreo
77 | 725

2976 suprimir *v* to suppress, delete
- adoptó medidas contundentes para suprimir la violencia
81 | 362 -f

2977 ahorro *nm* saving, thrift
- les resultaría acumular esos ahorros y comprarse una vivienda
80 | 553

2978 sobrar *v* to be too much, left over
- no nos quería cobrar porque le sobraba plata
75 | 466 -nf

2979 brotar *v* to sprout
- había visto brotar y crecer cada una de sus plantas
77 | 517

2980 prisión *nf* prison, imprisonment
- no pudo escaparse de la prisión burocrática
78 | 414

2981 investigador *nm/f* researcher, investigator
• casi ningún investigador apuesta ya por la monoterapia contra el sida
76 | 736 -f

2982 técnico *nm/f* technician
• por el trabajo de los técnicos que dan asistencia técnica a los campesinos
76 | 526 +o -f

2983 paraíso *nm* paradise
• es decir, la utopía de establecer un paraíso en la tierra
79 | 349

2984 automático *adj* automatic
• antes de ser pulverizados por el sistema automático de seguridad
78 | 356

2985 postre *nmf* dessert; a la postre: in the end
• hay un postre de helados de fresas
81 | 285

2986 inquieto *adj* restless, anxious
• pero en el fondo me siento inquieto, incómodo
77 | 385

2987 helado *adj* iced, freezing, icy
• azotada por la lluvia y golpeada por el helado viento del sur
72 | 498 -nf

2988 plástico *adj* plastic
• pero su complejidad será plástica, cromática, texturológica
79 | 378

2989 alimentación *nf* feeding, food
• su alimentación es además pobre en ácidos grasos saturados
78 | 522 +o -f

2990 miel *nf* honey
• las abejas que almacenan miel y polen para consumo de los adultos
76 | 458

2991 vulgar *adj* vulgar, common, banal
• en nuestro amor no hubo nada vulgar o material
78 | 357

2992 desafío *nm* challenge, provocation
• se burlaban de él como un desafío personal
82 | 394

2993 aeropuerto *nm* airport
• prohibió el aterrizaje del Concorde en el aeropuerto Kennedy
74 | 449

2994 valorar *v* to value
• este estúpido no valora su riqueza
80 | 450 -f

2995 diferenciar *v* to differentiate, distinguish
• hay que diferenciar muy bien el chiste del chisme
80 | 366 -f

2996 abrigo *nm* overcoat, shelter
• hacía bastante frío y ella olvidó ponerse el abrigo
76 | 405

2997 hábil *adj* skillful, clever
• especialista muy listo, muy hábil, muy capacitado
82 | 261

2998 veinticuatro *num* twenty-four
• se quedan abiertas las veinticuatro horas
77 | 279 +o -nf

2999 sello *nm* stamp, seal
• de arrojar la carta en algún buzón sin sello ni estampillas
75 | 399

3000 campana *nf* bell
• sonó la campana para ir a comer
76 | 411

3001 destacado *adj* outstanding, leading
• una de las más destacadas figuras de la ópera actual
79 | 737 -f +nf

3002 encendido *adj* turned on, burning
• o voy apagar el equipo, o lo voy a dejar encendido
77 | 587

3003 incidente *nm* incident
• surge un incidente, así de momento, que no estaba planeado
82 | 349

3004 fragmento *nm* fragment, passage
• se descubrió un pequeño fragmento de meteorito en el Pacífico
78 | 469

3005 plano *adj* flat, plain, even, level
• eran cincelados en grandes losas planas de piedra
79 | 379

3006 compensar *v* to compensate, make up for
• nada podrá compensar mi culpa
80 | 352

3007 obligatorio *adj* obligatory, compulsory
• respeto el uso obligatorio del cinturón de seguridad
78 | 417

3008 asignar *v* to assign, allocate
• la notación algebraica asigna a cada casilla una letra y un número
80 | 372

3009 contemporáneo *adj* contemporary
• en el mundo contemporáneo los problemas son globales
77 | 655

3010 suscitar *v* to arouse, provoke
• la pintura siempre suscitaba una respuesta en ella
81 | 384

3011 finalizar *v* to end, finalize
• faltaban como treinta minutos para finalizar el partido
80 | 496

3012 reforzar *v* to reinforce, strengthen
• decidió reforzar la seguridad con sendas puertas férreas
82 | 386

3013 mina *nf* mine
- parece la entrada a una mina de carbón
77 | 505

3014 restaurante *nm* restaurant
- vamos a cenar en un restaurante del Centro
75 | 426

3015 porcentaje *nm* percentage
- en óptimas condiciones, es un porcentaje del 98,85 % de seguridad
78 | 657 +o -f +nf

3016 conductor *nm/f* driver, conductor
- yo defendí al chofer, al conductor del vehículo
76 | 518

3017 contigo *pron* with you
- ¿viene contigo mi papá?
73 | 596 -nf

3018 evolucionar *v* to evolve, develop
- «Homo sapiens» evolucionó hace 500.000 años
80 | 498 +o -f

3019 magia *nf* magic
- demuestra, como en un juego de magia, la necesidad de lo misterioso
77 | 380

3020 presidir *v* to preside over
- el sacerdote iba a presidir una ceremonia especial
80 | 340

3021 comedor *nm* dining room
- quite la mesa, recoja el comedor y friegue los platos
74 | 627

3022 seriedad *nf* seriousness
- una imagen de seriedad, una imagen de prestigio, una imagen de firmeza
81 | 331

3023 gallina *nf* hen, coward
- podían comer pato, faisán, paloma, ganso, gallina y perdices
74 | 487

3024 espada *nf* sword
- ese hombre murió con la espada en la mano
77 | 433

3025 discreto *adj* discreet, tactful
- debíamos ser discretas y nunca tener contacto con los clientes
78 | 397

3026 excelencia *nf* excellence
- para mí el conjunto por excelencia son los Beatles, me gustan muchísimo
82 | 294

3027 agitar *v* to shake, move
- el viento agita sus hojas
79 | 593 -o

3028 amoroso *adj* loving, affectionate
- la languidez temblorosa del primer encuentro amoroso
79 | 433

3029 músculo *nm* muscle
- consiste en tensionar los músculos de tu cuerpo, para relajarlos después
74 | 972 -o

3030 optimista *adj* optimistic
- tenía una visión optimista del universo
80 | 264 +o

3031 persecución *nf* pursuit, persecution
- hemos sufrido persecución por la justicia y pérdida de la libertad
81 | 390

3032 imperio *nm* empire, fortune
- leen de la grandeza del Imperio Romano
78 | 568

3033 casco *nm* helmet
- el policía va protegido con un casco y con un escudo
75 | 533

3034 pelea *nf* fight, quarrel
- entre nosotros hay esa pelea, ese desorden, esas envidias, esos rencores
76 | 393 -nf

3035 retorno *nm* return
- es una nueva Inquisición, el retorno a la peor barbarie
79 | 360

3036 oler *v* to smell
- a oler aquel perfume rancio y femenino
69 | 976 +f -nf

3037 aludir *v* to allude to
- el número nueve también alude al embarazo de María
78 | 335

3038 vera *nf* de veras: really, for real
- ¡ah, de veras! Sí, espantoso; claro
72 | 497 -nf

3039 delgado *adj* thin, skinny
- su cuerpo era delgado pero bien proporcionado
77 | 652 -o

3040 latín *nm* Latin
- conocía solamente las lenguas clásicas -latín y griego -
76 | 390

3041 resumir *v* to summarize
- siento no poder resumir los detalles técnicos
80 | 334

3042 rutina *nf* routine
- el hecho de variar de actividad y de salir de la rutina
75 | 433 -nf

3043 tenso *adj* tight, tense
- la piel quedaba tensa como cuero
79 | 343

3044 mejora *nf* improvement
- es una mejora considerable en su nivel de vida
78 | 491 -f

3045 domicilio *nm* residence, address
- fue arrestado en su domicilio de la calle Suárez 75
77 | 306

3046 porquería *nf* filth, junk
- si hubiera podido arrancar esa porquería de mi cabeza
57 | 214 +f -nf

3047 burlar *v* to mock
- se burló de su secreto amor; lo avergonzó ante sus amigos
76 | 441

3048 susto *nm* fright, scare
- el miedo y el susto la habían puesto rígida
73 | 387 -nf

3049 encajar *v* to insert, fit well
- hacía encajar la mentira en un mundo convencionalizado
81 | 223

3050 nadar *v* to swim
- ese chico no sabía nadar bien y casi se ahogó
76 | 338

3051 amanecer *nm* daybreak, dawn
- volvamos al salón, quiero bailar hasta el amanecer
76 | 565

3052 célula *nf* cell (biology)
- cada célula humana contiene cuarenta y seis cromosomas
70 | 1929

3053 acelerar *v* to accelerate, speed (up)
- sentí el corazón acelerar sus latidos y adelanté el paso
80 | 459

3054 crítico *nm* critic
- los críticos la pueden juzgar como una obra extraordinaria
76 | 523

3055 inspiración *nf* inspiration, inhalation
- el amor era la inspiración de poetas
80 | 376 -o

3056 ladrillo *nm* brick
- se trataba de una moderna construcción de ladrillo rojo
76 | 417

3057 proyección *nf* projection, screening
- la proyección que hacemos, lo que creemos que va a resultar
80 | 386

3058 desplegar *v* to unfold, deploy
- el ataque contra la URSS se desplegó desde el océano Glacial Ártico
82 | 331

3059 desembocar *v* to flow, lead into
- en un gran delta antes de desembocar en el mar del Norte
85 | 319

3060 lana *nf* wool
- en diciembre hacía frío y había que vestirse de lana
78 | 371

3061 indirecto *adj* indirect
- tiene objetivo de beneficio directo e indirecto
80 | 348

3062 infierno *nm* hell, inferno
- se supone que los pecadores malos van al infierno
75 | 503

3063 aliviar *v* to lighten, relieve, comfort
- todo inútil: no le pudo aliviar siquiera el sufrimiento
81 | 321

3064 acero *nm* steel
- es como si este hombre heroico fuera de acero
77 | 544

3065 ejecutivo *adj* executive
- una parte de la primera Comisión Ejecutiva bipartita
79 | 512 -f

3066 cazar *v* to hunt
- ¿Cazar elefantes en el África fue parte de la aventura?
76 | 381

3067 ojalá *adv* I hope that
- ojalá que así sea
75 | 447 +o -nf

3068 aplaudir *v* to clap, applaud
- comenzaron a aplaudir y a decir «¡Viva España!»
76 | 319 -nf

3069 preso *nm* prisoner
- el juez dice que se llevará a los presos a la Prisión de Badajoz
74 | 493

3070 billete *nm* ticket, bill, note
- compré un billete para dar otra vuelta en el tren
72 | 479

3071 motivar *v* to motivate, cause
- lo que motivó su protesta
80 | 298 +o -f

3072 descuidar *v* to neglect
- enseñan bastante el francés, pero descuidan el español
82 | 225

3073 referente *adj* concerning
- contiene todos los datos referentes al abonado y su servicio
79 | 351 -f

3074 tontería *nf* stupidity, stupid thing
- donde la ignorancia es felicidad, es tontería ser juicioso
74 | 412 +o -nf

3075 cauce *nm* (river) bed, ditch
- el río siempre irá por ese cauce, por ese valle
80 | 322

3076 ignorancia *nf* ignorance
- mi ignorancia del inglés no me permitía preguntar
77 | 361

3077 acostar *v* to put/go to bed
- vete luego a acostar para que mañana te levantes temprano
73 | 824 +f -nf

3078 encanto *nm* charm, spell
- representó el encanto y la elegancia de esos viejos edificios
76 | 429

3079 propiamente *adv* exactly, properly
- le resultaba propiamente cosa de locos
78 | 427 +o -f

3080 sed *nf* thirst
- tengo mucha sed y no me vendría mal un vasito de cerveza
76 | 399

3081 escudo *nm* shield, coat of arms
- espadas, lanzas, puntas de flechas, escudos, azuelas y hachas
75 | 354

3082 muñeca *nf* doll, wrist
- tiene una muñeca que es bien bonita, que es otra Barbie
70 | 655

3083 dotado *adj* endowed, gifted
- eres un hombre dotado de aptitudes nada desdeñables
77 | 448 +nf

3084 conectar *v* to connect, plug in
- lo sintonizó, y conectó el auricular
78 | 334

3085 rango *nm* rank, range
- los Estatutos tienen un rango jerárquico superior
79 | 405

3086 invento *nm* invention
- Edison anunció en 1877 el invento del fonógrafo
78 | 332

3087 arder *v* to burn, glow
- con un beso que todavía me arde en la boca
75 | 502

3088 recinto *nm* grounds, precincts
- dentro de su recinto circular, con sus paseos, lago, ría, y canales
79 | 360

3089 tinta *nf* ink
- con una pluma fina y la misma tinta negra, escribió su nombre
78 | 337

3090 garganta *nf* throat, gorge
- tiene la garganta muy seca; un caramelo lo aliviará
76 | 721

3091 viajero *nm* traveler, passenger
- es una guía turística para viajeros de fin de semana
75 | 468

3092 asesino *nm* killer, assassin
- el asesino posee ahora el relato de la muerte de su víctima
76 | 409

3093 rito *nm* rite, ritual
- el rito de las iglesias orientales ha utilizado diversas lenguas vernáculas
76 | 470

3094 atractivo *nm* attraction, charm
- la selección puede favorecer el atractivo sexual por su propio bien
81 | 261

3095 callado *adj* quiet, reserved
- se quedó callado, no me contestó nada
73 | 489 +f -nf

3096 frustración *nf* frustration
- me queda la frustración de nunca haber sido Campeón del Mundo
78 | 300

3097 flexible *adj* flexible
- por encima de 20 °C se vuelve blando, flexible y translúcido
79 | 302

3098 cemento *nm* cement, concrete
- otros tipos de cemento se endurecen al reaccionar con el oxígeno
79 | 241

3099 catástrofe *nf* catastrophe
- esa tremenda catástrofe cultural que fue la Guerra Grande
81 | 324

3100 dulce *nm* candy, sweets
- antes de enfermarse era así de gorda; los dulces le encantaban
74 | 432 -nf

3101 recuperación *nf* recovery, recuperation
- su milagrosa recuperación después de largas enfermedades
78 | 543 -f

3102 localizar *v* to locate, find, localize
- para localizar el lugar del misterioso encuentro
77 | 383

3103 mediano *adj* average, medium, ordinary
- aplicando acciones concretas de corto, mediano y largo plazo
77 | 354

3104 almuerzo *nm* lunch
- después a las doce un almuerzo muy bueno, con jugo o fruta 69 | 518 -nf

3105 pacífico *adj* peaceful
- es un tipo pacífico y razonable
78 | 370

3106 uña *nf* nail, fingernail, toenail
- me afilo las uñas, me lustro los dientes, me perfumo el aliento
73 | 600

3107 contradictorio *adj* contradictory
- las dos cuestiones son totalmente contradictorias
81 | 279

3108 excepto *prep* except (for)
- no sabía nadie, excepto ella
77 | 454

3109 herir *v* to wound, hurt
- puedo de nuevo matar y robar, herir o estafar a alguien
76 | 375

3110 costo *nm* price, cost, expense
- el costo de la vivienda social en Colombia es altísimo
71 | 1004 +o -f

Adjectives – differences across registers

The following lists show the adjectives that occur with a much higher frequency than would be expected in either the spoken, fiction, or non-fiction registers. In each case, the word is in the top 10 percent of words for that register, in terms of its relative frequency to the other two registers.

Spoken	Fiction	Non-fiction
ese 32 that	**callado** 3096 quiet	**existente** 2834 existing
mucho 45 many, much	**quieto** 3155 quiet, still	**ligado** 2927 linked
mi 49 my	**pálido** 3162 pale	**destacado** 3002 outstanding
bueno 115 good	**rubio** 3270 blonde	**dotado** 3084 endowed
importante 207 important	**silencioso** 3375 silent	**electrónico** 3150 electronic
claro 259 clear	**despacio** 3399 slow	**geográfico** 3195 geographical
bastante 270 rather, quite a bit	**espeso** 3538 thick	**temporal** 3226 temporary
social 280 social	**tibio** 3591 lukewarm	**procedente** 3261 coming (from)
difícil 314 difficult	**asustado** 3634 scared	**disponible** 3263 available
tu 349 your (sg/+fam)	**flaco** 3674 thin	**británico** 3266 British
económico 426 economic	**tendido** 3728 hung	**laboral** 3269 labor
supuesto 511 por s.: of course	**desierto** 3783 deserted	**financiero** 3290 financial
profesional 640 professional	**apretado** 3807 tight	**simbólico** 3350 symbolic
normal 664 normal	**áspero** 3855 rough	**clave** 3446 key
cuánto 723 how much?	**furioso** 3940 furious	**restante** 3483 remaining
interesante 762 interesting	**temeroso** 3953 fearful	**regional** 3485 regional
determinado 927 determined	**despierto** 3959 awake	**anual** 3509 annual
feliz 956 happy	**diminuto** 4026 diminutive	**creativo** 3552 creative
fundamental 1086 fundamental	**celeste** 4027 sky-blue	**sistemático** 3568 systematic
tranquilo 1144 calm	**cariñoso** 4034 affectionate	**dominante** 3584 dominant
tremendo 1198 tremendous	**hundido** 4056 sunken	**agrícola** 3612 agricultural
lógico 1214 logical	**sereno** 4067 calm	**dicho** 3645 aforementioned
auténtico 1223 authentic	**maldito** 4089 damned	**biológico** 3675 biological
americano 1261 American	**inmóvil** 4094 immovable	**progresivo** 3686 progressive
cultural 1277 cultural	**agradecido** 4124 grateful	**funcional** 3712 functional

Comments

As might be expected, the adjectives from fiction texts tend to provide information on physical appearance, personality, and emotions. Adjectives in non-fiction texts tend to refer to more properties of more abstract nouns. The adjectives in spoken texts that are more common vis-à-vis the other registers tend to express very basic notions (*ese* "that", *mucho* "much/many").

3111 manifiesto *nm* poner de manifiesto: to show
- pone de manifiesto una cosa que es clara
79 | 493 +nf

3112 mortal *adj* mortal, lethal, deadly
- por practicar la vendetta, una enemistad mortal entre familias
75 | 365

3113 repetición *nf* repetition
- son una repetición de todo pero no es creación
78 | 347

3114 patrimonio *nm* patrimony, inheritance
- ¡patrimonio nacional, tesoro artístico, joya imperecedera!
79 | 374

3115 solemne *adj* solemn
- luego fue rezada una solemne misa en la iglesia
78 | 314

3116 estatua *nf* statue
- Miguel Ángel esculpió una estatua de David
74 | 475

3117 decadencia *nf* decline, decay
- y luego el desorden de los espíritus; la decadencia de la moral cívica
80 | 322

3118 mudo *adj* mute, silent
- me paraliza y me deja mudo en su presencia
75 | 598

3119 precipitar *v* to plunge, hurl, rush
- se precipitó al océano Pacífico unas horas después de su lanzamiento
77 | 457 -o

3120 sorprendido *adj* surprised
- estaba sorprendido de su amabilidad y confianza
77 | 334

3121 excluir *v* to exclude, reject
- mas el perdón no siempre excluye castigos ejemplares
79 | 431

3122 enfermero *nm/f* nurse
- tal vez allí encuentre algún médico o enfermero español
70 | 542 +o -nf

3123 psicológico *adj* psychological
- el niño tenía muy pocos estímulos psicológicos y sensoriales
78 | 618 -f

3124 adorar *v* to worship, adore
- el rezar es una forma de adorar a los dioses
76 | 288 -nf

3125 aficionado *nm* fan, devotee
- se ha convertido en la «niña bonita» de los aficionados a la ópera
76 | 437

3126 preferible *adj* preferable
- ¿no es preferible aliarse con él?
78 | 235 +o

3127 célebre *adj* famous, renowned
- organizaba todos los años un célebre concurso de cuentos
78 | 360

3128 agujero *nm* hole, opening
- había un agujero en la capa de ozono, situado sobre el antártico
71 | 589

3129 beneficiar *v* to benefit
- el aire marino benefició la salud de mi hermano
78 | 426 +o -f

3130 arroz *nm* rice
- en Japón el arroz constituye la base de la alimentación
73 | 389

3131 valiente *adj* brave, courageous, bold
- la gente valiente supera el miedo que siente
76 | 359 -nf

3132 delicioso *adj* delicious, delightful, charming
- prepararon un nuevo plato delicioso
75 | 319 -nf

3133 potente *adj* potent, powerful
- es un auto potente con una velocidad impresionante
79 | 345

3134 cerveza *nf* beer, ale
- mientras bebía una cerveza en la mesa de mi amigo
70 | 552

3135 escasez *nf* scarcity, shortage
- por una alimentación inadecuada, por una escasez de fibras en la dieta
81 | 253

3136 ministerio *nm* ministry
- es un libro aprobado por el Ministerio de Educación
76 | 374 +o

3137 vuestro *adj* your (pl/+fam)
- yo os haré mi pueblo y seré vuestro Dios (Éx. 6,7)
68 | 704

3138 notorio *adj* notorious, noticeable
- relaciones extraconyugales ilícitas con escándalo público notorio
80 | 273

3139 transición *nf* transition
- un momento de transición política en que los actores políticos cambian
79 | 551 -f +nf

3140 sexto *adj* sixth
- comprendía desde el primer grado hasta sexto grado
78 | 274 +o

3141 despreciar *v* to despise, scorn
- las mujeres feas no tienen derecho a despreciar a los hombres
78 | 311

3142 negativa *nf* negative, denial
- la negativa, la duda, la espera, la tentación
82 | 258

3143 falda *nf* skirt
- con la falda a la altura de las rodillas
76 | 571

3144 improvisar *v* to improvise
- se pusieron a improvisar frente al micrófono
77 | 323

3145 emerger *v* to emerge, surface
- desde el fondo del pasillo, empezó a emerger de pronto
81 | 330 -o

3146 clavar *v* to nail
- va a clavar su estandarte en lo alto de nuestra trinchera
74 | 773 -o +f

3147 cantante *nc* singer
- los cantantes estuvieron espléndidos y la orquesta también
74 | 424

3148 constancia *nf* perseverance
- seguiremos con constancia hasta que lo logremos
81 | 258

3149 electrónico *adj* electronic
- lo había recibido por correo electrónico y por teléfono
77 | 636 -f +nf

3150 anillo *nm* (finger) ring
- lleva un solo anillo de plata vieja en el índice
75 | 562 -o

3151 balance *nm* outcome, balance
- en la semifinal considero que el balance puede terminar siendo positivo
79 | 425 -f

3152 entendimiento *nm* understanding
- Hegel afirmó haber encontrado un entendimiento racional de la humanidad
78 | 382

3153 volcar *v* to turn/knock over, empty
- volcó el contenido del tacho de comida en la tierra
77 | 300

3154 quieto *adj* still, motionless, calm
- está dormido, quieto y callado
71 | 645 +f -nf

3155 transcurso *nm* passing, course, lapse
- dos personajes que el transcurso del tiempo ha convertido en uno solo
79 | 289

3156 barrer *v* sweep, clean out
- agarra una escoba chiquita y se pone a barrer
78 | 258

3157 desayuno *nm* breakfast
- esta mañana quiere el desayuno en la cama
71 | 405 -nf

3158 alfombra *nf* rug, carpet, mat
- despliega la alfombra sobre el suelo
75 | 417

3159 historiador *nm/f* historian
- el historiador es un científico social
76 | 414

3160 rogar *v* to implore, pray, ask
- quisiera rogarle que nos preste su valiosa ayuda
72 | 571 -nf

3161 pálido *adj* pale, ghastly, faded
- un hombre pálido, un misterioso ángel de sombra
73 | 687 +f

3162 programar *v* to plan, program
- vamos muy bien en los tiempos que nos hemos programado
78 | 306 -f

3163 animado *adj* excited, lively
- ese rostro estaba animado de una pasión feroz
79 | 277

3164 chileno *adj* Chilean
- tomas un argentino, un chileno y un colombiano, un venezolano . . .
65 | 1222

3165 ficción *nf* fiction
- ¿hay diferencias entre la ficción y la realidad?
77 | 371

3166 ensayar *v* to test
- ya tengo pensado otro sistema nuevo que voy a ensayar mañana
76 | 284

3167 materno *adj* maternal
- utilizó los apellidos paterno y materno para firmar sus obras
78 | 279

3168 jugador *nm* player, gambler
- pero los jugadores de rugby no se dan por vencidos
65 | 1666

3169 cartel *nm* poster
- M. señala el cartel de «No entrar»
76 | 319

3170 desconfianza *nf* distrust
- la inseguridad, la desconfianza, la duda, el miedo
80 | 247

3171 respiración *nf* respiration, breath
- ¿qué hace Clara? Su respiración es rítmica. ¿Dormirá?
75 | 578 -o

3172 votar *v* to vote
- habla de la voluntad para ir a votar en las elecciones
72 | 1113 +o -f

3173 caña *nf* cane, reed
- como la caña del bambú que crece siempre hacia arriba
72 | 560

3174 aislar *v* to isolate, insulate
- mantendrá la política de aislar económicamente a Cuba
79 | 289

3175 soltero *adj* single, not married
- cuando era soltero le gustaba salir con chicas
76 | 405

3176 prisionero *nm* prisoner
- los prisioneros son conducidos a prisión en rígido desfile
74 | 477

3177 turista *nc* tourist
- me hospedé como un turista en un pequeño hotel de la playa
73 | 388 +o

3178 abundancia *nf* abundance
- hablan de prosperidad, de abundancia, de reconstrucción
80 | 275

3179 rodar *v* to roll, run, scatter
- las lágrimas siguieron rodando sobre sus mejillas
73 | 490

3180 asistente *nc* assistant
- aquí no hay un director principal y tres asistentes; aquí todos somos lo mismo
77 | 285

3181 vinculado *adj* connected
- se sentía vinculado a los cuatro amigos por un mismo cariño
80 | 442 -f

3182 queso *nm* cheese
- las industrias lácteas, la producción de queso y otros productos
69 | 557

3183 arriesgar *v* to risk, venture
- decidido a arriesgar todo con tal de salvar a mi amada
77 | 284

3184 indicio *nm* indication, sign
- ninguna puerta abierta, ningún sonido, ningún indicio de vida
80 | 315

3185 colgado *adj* hanging
- provenía del crucifijo colgado de la cabecera
72 | 463 -nf

3186 bautizar *v* to baptize, christen
- su misión es decir misa, bautizar a los muchachos
77 | 300

3187 cerro *nm* hill
- el Partenón está erigido en una especie de pequeño cerro, una pequeña montaña
68 | 670 -nf

3188 desatar *v* to untie, unleash, spark off
- quiere desatar lo que Dios ha unido
78 | 341

3189 alentar *v* to encourage
- era capaz de inspirar y alentar una ambición de grandeza
81 | 305

3190 descargar *v* to unleash, unload
- se calló porque no tenía sentido descargar su furia
75 | 324

3191 galería *nf* gallery, balcony
- asistimos a la galería del teatro municipal
76 | 521

3192 engaño *nm* deceit, falsehood, hoax
- esa infernal maquinaria de la mentira, del engaño y de la desinformación
79 | 297

3193 enamorar *v* to fall in love
- jamás me imaginé que me iba a enamorar tanto de un hombre
72 | 417 -nf

3194 geográfico *adj* geographical
- está ubicada en el centro geográfico de la región
78 | 513 -f +nf

3195 continuidad *nf* continuity
- la realidad del instante ancla en la continuidad del tiempo
79 | 412 +nf

3196 receta *nf* recipe, prescription
- voy a leer esa receta para el pastel de papa
77 | 338

3197 conveniencia *nf* convenience, usefulness
- a veces modifican sus reglas sólo por conveniencia
84 | 247

3198 reemplazar *v* to replace
- y afirmaba que nada podía reemplazar al verdadero charol
77 | 567 -o +nf

3199 carencia *nf* lack, shortage
- hay falta de interés político y carencia de idealismo
81 | 325

3200 cerdo *nm* pig, sow, slob
- acompañan diversos platos de pollos, gallinas, cerdos y cordero
72 | 387

3201 soplar *v* to blow (wind)
- quince días de soplar un viento norte asfixiante
75 | 408

3202 frágil *adj* fragile, weak
- la fuerza de la tormenta no respetó el frágil refugio del poncho
77 | 347

3203 empeño *nm* insistence, determination
- el maestro ponía especial empeño en que sus alumnos leyeran
78 | 270

3204 agresión *nf* aggression, attack
- ante la nueva agresión japonesa contra China en el siguiente año
80 | 382

3205 fortaleza *nf* fortress, strength
- el sitio la convirtió en una fortaleza impenetrable
78 | 383

3206 seriamente *adv* seriously
- voy a hablar seriamente con ella
81 | 241

3207 balcón *nm* balcony
- la señora se subió al balcón y trató de matarse
70 | 548 -nf

Verbs of movement (go from A to B) Top 40 words # 1 – 8000

ir 30 to go

(pasar) 67 to pass

salir 111 to go out

entrar 179 to enter

caer 245 to fall

correr 332 to run

mover 402 to move, incite

subir 443 to go up, on

andar 536 to walk

bajar 569 to come down

avanzar 618 to advance

viajar 790 to travel

conducir 868 to lead, drive

manejar 916 to drive, handle

caminar 919 to walk

saltar 1071 to jump, leap

marchar 1203 to go, walk, march

trasladar 1219 to move, transfer

volar 1376 to fly

apartar 1505 to move away, separate

huir 1574 to flee, run away (from)

descender 1645 to descend

desplazar 1771 to move, shift, replace

circular 1822 to circulate, go around, flow

pasear 1985 to go for a walk

tropezar 2907 to trip, stumble

nadar 3050 to swim

acelerar 3053 to accelerate, speed (up)

rodar 3179 to roll, run, scatter

navegar 3375 to navigate, sail

explorar 3595 to explore

deslizar 3651 to slide, glide, slip

trepar 4116 to climb

transitar 4821 to roam, go by

irrumpir 4994 to burst in, raid

vagar 5320 to wander (about)

resbalar 5490 to slip, slide

rondar 5975 to hover, patrol

deambular 6483 to roam, wander

brincar 7761 to leap

revolotear 7814 to flutter, hover

3208 observador *nm* observer
- pero hay una realidad que cualquier observador conoce
- 80 | 483

3209 ridículo *adj* ridiculous, absurd
- a veces corremos el riesgo de meternos en algo ridículo
- 72 | 346 -nf

3210 renta *nf* income
- un contrato, garantizándole una renta de 4000 francos mensuales
- 73 | 663 -f

3211 justificación *nf* justification
- carece de justificación, carece de explicación, carece de fundamento
- 78 | 306

3212 enfrentamiento *nm* confrontation
- se produce a través de un enfrentamiento con el enemigo más próximo
- 77 | 579

3213 junta *nf* meeting, conference, seam
- el jefe había convocado a una junta con sus hombres de confianza
- 76 | 278 +o

3214 irregular *adj* irregular
- un recorrido irregular, con curvas periódicas en sus trayectorias
- 81 | 280

3215 trayectoria *nf* trajectory, path
- desde el triunfo, la trayectoria larguísima, hasta la retirada en plenitud
- 76 | 475 -f +nf

3216 genial *adj* brilliant, inspired
- maravilloso, genial, ¡GENIAAAL! - exclamaba
- 77 | 255

3217 indiferencia *nf* indifference
- C. la miró con la indiferencia superior de veterano
- 78 | 411 -o

3218 taza *nf* cup, bowl
- vino a ofrecerme una taza de té
- 72 | 407 -nf

3219 vínculo *nm* tie, bond, link
- los vínculos étnicos entre ambos pueblos son fuertes
- 79 | 388

3220 cuaderno *nm* notebook, workbook
- después me pasó el cuaderno de registros y firmé en él
- 70 | 511 +f -nf

3221 gracioso *adj* funny, charming, amusing
- era gracioso porque les gustaba oírme y se reían
- 71 | 353 -nf

3222 regir *v* to rule, govern, manage
- los padres deben regir los pormenores de su familia
- 79 | 444 +nf

3223 intermedio *adj* interim, intermediate
- plantea un enorme rango de soluciones intermedias
- 75 | 484 -f

3224 bañar *v* to bathe, take a bath
- si hoy me pudiera bañar en el mar, sabría nadar
75 | 450 -nf

3225 temporal *adj* temporary
- que esto sea una etapa puramente temporal y transitoria
79 | 472 +nf

3226 rozar *v* to touch (lightly)
- sentí sus brazos colgarse del aire y rozar mi pelo
76 | 396

3227 pánico *nm* panic
- con pánico lo busqué, por supuesto, ¡no estaba!
77 | 297

3228 distinguido *adj* distinguished
- andaba con una señora de aspecto bien distinguido
77 | 281

3229 cañón *nm* canyon, cannon
- de morterazos de cañón y de bombardeos de aviación
74 | 429

3230 dudoso *adj* doubtful, dubious
- de las ventas inciertas y transacciones dudosas
79 | 278

3231 pollo *nm* chicken
- en Cuba se usa mucho la sopa de pollo, y la sopa de res
74 | 338

3232 lamentable *adj* regrettable
- ha existido una lamentable confusión
74 | 318

3233 trascendencia *nf* transcendent nature, significance
- su trascendencia artística es indudable
79 | 275 -f

3234 remitir *v* to remit
- ha de remitir información al Congreso
78 | 358

3235 interminable *adj* endless, interminable
- la cola interminable me puso de mal humor
76 | 548 -o

3236 corrupción *nf* corruption
- generan la televisión y el cine y la corrupción en general
76 | 607

3237 confesión *nf* confession, admission
- no era indispensable promesa, ni confesión de amor
75 | 351

3238 corbata *nf* tie, sash
- la vestimenta no es su fuerte: camisa y corbata no armonizan entre sí
72 | 410 -nf

3239 macho *nm* male, manliness
- permitiría escoger a los machos entre un gran número de hembras
71 | 488

3240 disolver *v* to dissolve
- la cosa se disolvió en agua
75 | 380

3241 secuencia *nf* sequence
- para la determinación de la secuencia de DNA del genoma del hombre
74 | 712 +nf

3242 cáncer *nm* cancer
- temen morir de un cáncer o de un tumor cerebral
72 | 727

3243 velar *v* to watch over
- como padre, yo velaba por sus vidas
77 | 276

3244 archivo *nm* archive, file, filing cabinet
- el perverso documento se conserva en el Archivo Nacional
73 | 368

3245 habitualmente *adv* habitually
- ¿cuál es la técnica que utilizas habitualmente para escribir?
77 | 320

3246 trámite *nm* procedure, step, requirement
- se han cometido irregularidades en el trámite del enjuiciamiento penal
74 | 357 +o

3247 tranquilamente *adv* calmly, peacefully
- dejándola fumar tranquilamente en la oscuridad
70 | 271 +o -nf

3248 innecesario *adj* unnecessary
- para evitar todo sufrimiento innecesario a los tripulantes
79 | 237

3249 raya *nf* line, ray, stripe
- una raya de sangre le cruzaba la cara
74 | 372

3250 televisor *nm* television set
- el televisor funciona, pero nadie mira hacia la pantalla
73 | 312

3251 estabilidad *nf* stability
- está perdiendo estabilidad del lado izquierdo
75 | 751 -f +nf

3252 grandeza *nf* greatness, size
- el orgullo, la grandeza y el poder, todo llega a fenecer
76 | 277

3253 prisa *nf* hurry
- no tiene más que su apuro, su prisa y su urgencia
69 | 687 +f -nf

3254 persistir *v* to persist
- cómo persiste esa historia, y es una buena historia
82 | 258 -o

3255 temblar *v* to tremble, shake
- un tremendo impacto que hizo temblar la tierra 67 | 891 +f -nf

3256 verbal *adj* verbal, oral
- para comunicarse en forma verbal o escrita
76 | 336

3257 matemática *nf* mathematics
- utilizan las matemáticas o la estadística para analizar los datos
73 | 420

3258 demonio *nm* demon, devil
- el Mal no es el demonio enemigo, la antítesis de Dios y del Bien
72 | 452

3259 intacto *adj* intact
- el dinero llegó intacto a su destino
78 | 307 -o

3260 procedente *adj* coming (from)
- llega hoy a Madrid procedente de Los Angeles
74 | 631 +nf

3261 cenar *v* to dine
- aquella noche, después de cenar salimos a dar un paseo
70 | 467 -nf

3262 disponible *adj* available
- leía mucho porque tenía mucho tiempo disponible
75 | 414 -f +nf

3263 tornar *v* to transform, turn
- el preciso momento en que se iba a tornar más interesante
74 | 458 -o

3264 encantado *adj* pleased, delighted
- M. quedó encantada con los regalos recibidos
74 | 287 +o -nf

3265 británico *adj* British
- el imperio británico envió sus soldados a conquistar
69 | 1758 -f +nf

3266 manga *nf* sleeve
- limpió la boca con la manga de la blusa
74 | 359

3267 perjudicar *v* to endanger
- una dosis mínima de maldad, que no perjudica a nadie
78 | 275 +o -f

3268 laboral *adj* labor, industry
- agravará el conflicto laboral con huelga indefinida
75 | 571 -f +nf

3269 rubio *adj* blonde, fair
- probablemente un turista blanco y rubio de por allá
70 | 721 +f

3270 prevenir *v* to avoid, prevent
- la rotación de cultivos previene que los parásitos se establezcan
76 | 339

3271 seda *nf* silk
- su amplia blusa de seda flotando en el aire
75 | 595

3272 envidia *nf* envy
- no podía dejar de sentir envidia al ver la suerte de su prima
71 | 437

3273 emergencia *nf* emergency
- usted no es una emergencia; el doctor quiere que vuelva mañana
77 | 359

3274 enamorado *adj* in love
- una mujer de modesta belleza, de la que no estaba enamorado
73 | 530 -nf

3275 grasa *nf* grease, fat
- así como un pedazo de grasa se extiende sobre la sartén caldeada
67 | 630

3276 culminar *v* to culminate, accomplish
- el colapso del sistema feudal culminó con la derrota del clan Taira
78 | 397 +nf

3277 alcalde *nm* mayor
- el alcalde del pueblo, quien, de buena gana, los casó
67 | 566

3278 insuficiente *adj* insufficient
- pensaría que consideraba insuficiente el pago
77 | 324

3279 sostenido *adj* sustained, steady
- de la pausa sostenida, de su inesperada caída agonizante
78 | 292

3280 congreso *nm* congress
- el congreso de la Confederación Argentina no ratificó el tratado
71 | 475 +o -f

3281 espantoso *adj* frightening, dreadful
- mi temor, mi vergüenza, mi espantoso miedo de ser como ella
71 | 353 -nf

3282 aplauso *nm* applause, praise, acclaim
- recibió el aplauso y la admiración de la gente
72 | 365

3283 prima *nf* female cousin, down payment
- visitan una prima y unas parientas
70 | 380 -nf

3284 ansiedad *nf* anxiety
- el sentimiento de separación genera una gran ansiedad
75 | 550 -o

3285 dirigente *nc* leader, director, manager
- el administrador municipal es un vehemente dirigente político
73 | 1187 -f

3286 ascenso *nm* promotion, climb
- fue un ascenso en mi carrera, y era lo que yo quería
77 | 315

3287 finalidad *nf* purpose, aim
- con la finalidad de llegar al mayor número de lectores posible
75 | 363

3288 preceder *v* to precede
- la reflexión debe preceder a la acción
79 | 288 -o

3289 financiero *adj* financial
- un apoyo financiero de 25 millones de dólares
74 | 1115 -f +nf

3290 nostalgia *nf* nostalgia, homesickness
- muchos años después recordaba con nostalgia el día que mi madre me besó
72 | 476

3291 mención *nf* mention
- merecen mención especial dos causas relacionadas
80 | 233

3292 afición *nf* fondness, interest
- bien conocían la afición que David tenía por las mujeres hermosas
71 | 391

3293 colonial *adj* colonial
- el mantenimiento de su Imperio colonial trasatlántico
72 | 536

3294 lástima *nf* shame, pity
- no, no eran. // ¡Qué lástima! Pensé que ya estaban aquí
70 | 580 +f -nf

3295 teatral *adj* theatrical
- llenas de vigor teatral y esplendores orquestales
71 | 495

3296 lápiz *nm* pencil
- cogió lápiz y papel y fue apuntando
75 | 281

3297 vertical *adj* vertical, upright
- una tubería vertical llena de agua de 5 m de altura
78 | 346

3298 nido *nm* nest
- como el cuco que cría a sus polluelos en nido ajeno
74 | 340

3299 gratuito *adj* free, arbitrary, gratuitous
- la enseñanza primaria era gratuita y obligatoria
74 | 312

3300 difícilmente *adv* with difficulty
- todas estas condiciones difícilmente pueden ser satisfechas
76 | 293

3301 orquesta *nf* orchestra, dance band
- es director musical de la orquesta Philharmonia
70 | 591

3302 conexión *nf* connection, relationship
- en estrecha conexión con otros países no-alineados
76 | 398 -f +nf

3303 alternar *v* to alternate
- podíamos alternar las botas: un día él y otro día yo
76 | 239

3304 vegetal *adj* plant, vegetable
- estudio de la vida prehistórica animal y vegetal
70 | 557

3305 usado *adj* worn out, old, used
- tiritando y arrugada como un pañuelo usado
74 | 337

3306 vigor *nm* force, strength, vigor
- todo ello coincidirá con la entrada en vigor de esta ley
78 | 343

3307 salario *nm* salary, wages
- en aumentar el salario mínimo de los trabajadores
74 | 916 -f +nf

3308 acertar *v* to get right
- ¿cree usted que R. acertó o se equivocó?
73 | 367

3309 filo *nm* (cutting) edge
- coloca el filo del cuchillo en la redondez herida y presiona fuerte
74 | 361

3310 ambicioso *adj* ambitious, greedy
- un proyecto más ambicioso que el suyo
79 | 251

3311 policial *adj* police
- suministro de agua, protección policial, servicio de bomberos
73 | 442

3312 poético *adj* poetic
- a hablar en un idioma cada vez más culto y poético
72 | 573

3313 batir *v* to beat (object)
- se puso a batir con fuerza los huevos
74 | 341

3314 maíz *nm* corn, maize
- el cultivo del maíz se convirtió en el alimento principal en Mesoamérica
74 | 492

3315 desgraciadamente *adv* unfortunately
- pero desgraciadamente estaba equivocado
74 | 456 +o -f

3316 satisfactorio *adj* satisfactory
- al final llegan a un desenlace satisfactorio para todos
78 | 313

3317 autonomía *nf* autonomy, range
- el no tenía aún autonomía ni capacidad de decisión
75 | 754 -f +nf

3318 vago *adj* vague
- ofrece sonrisas y vagas promesas de amor
73 | 388

3319 estúpido *adj* stupid, idiotic
- cosas tan estúpidas, cosas que no tenían ningún sentido
71 | 471 -nf

3320 demorar *v* to delay, take time
- demoró un día entero en decidirse
71 | 332

3321 ama *nc* housekeeper, housewife
- la labor de ser madre, esposa y ama de casa
70 | 314 -nf

3322 beso *nm* kiss
- tenía en su mejilla un beso de otra mujer
66 | 788 +f -nf

3323 cintura *nf* waist
- una blusita entallada con un vuelito en la cintura y después la falda
73 | 515 +f -nf

3324 automáticamente *adv* automatically
- que permitía controlar automáticamente la velocidad
77 | 221

3325 pauta *nf* guideline, rule, standard
- no es una pauta rígida, como en Administración de Personal
77 | 384 -f +nf

3326 honesto *adj* honest
- el médico había sido muy honesto, revelándole la verdad
76 | 259

3327 recepción *nf* reception, waiting-room
- no le hacen caso, que sea una recepción, una fiesta, nada
77 | 232

3328 bala *nf* bullet, shot
- la bala de pistola no es muy efectiva de lejos
71 | 445

3329 suicidio *nm* suicide
- estaba hundido en una depresión cercana al suicidio
76 | 282

3330 placa *nf* plaque, plate, badge
- «profesor de estado» como decía la placa de bronce en la puerta
69 | 539

3331 calmar *v* to calm, soothe, relieve
- para calmar su agitación se fue vistiendo sin prisa
72 | 368 +f -nf

3332 brusco *adj* brusque, abrupt, sudden
- le dio la espalda con un brusco movimiento
76 | 325 -o

3333 asesinato *nm* murder, assassination
- el asesinato de atletas israelíes durante los Juegos Olímpicos de 1972
75 | 482

3334 mentalidad *nf* mindset, mind
- es una creencia según la mentalidad de cada uno, ¿verdad?
75 | 308 +o -f

3335 jerarquía *nf* hierarchy, rank
- no sólo figura mi nombre y apellido, sino mi jerarquía en la fábrica
77 | 319

3336 duración *nf* duration, length
- el programa tiene duración de media hora
77 | 410 +nf

3337 hallazgo *nm* finding, discovery
- hizo el extraño hallazgo de una pala escondida
77 | 363

3338 proximidad *nf* proximity
- volvió a sentarse, un tanto alarmado por la proximidad de la serpiente
76 | 344 -o

3339 estadística *nf* statistic
- todavía no existen estadísticas fiables de la incidencia del suicidio
76 | 333 +o -f

3340 presumir *v* to boast, show off, suppose
- te gusta presumir de ser hombre fuerte
74 | 283

3341 trescientos *num* three hundred
- estaba a trescientos kilómetros
72 | 272 +o -nf

3342 iluminado *adj* illuminated
- el lugar estaba iluminado por una luz clara
74 | 460 -o

3343 castillo *nm* castle
- mientras que los nobles y sus criados vivían en castillos
73 | 354

3344 traducción *nf* translation
- es una traducción al inglés de una versión latina
72 | 433 -f

3345 diversión *nf* fun, entertainment
- tienen otra clase de diversiones que es ir a esquiar a la playa
77 | 283

3346 introducción *nf* introduction
- se ha debatido sobre la ley de introducción del euro
77 | 403 -f

3347 lámpara *nf* lamp
- se ha encendido una diminuta lámpara en la noche ciega
71 | 531

3348 dicho *nm* saying, proverb
- persiste el dicho de que «cada mosca tiene su sombra»
76 | 201

3349 simbólico *adj* symbolic
- ¿debía interpretarse en un sentido simbólico o literal?
76 | 377 +nf

3350 fluir *v* to flow
- un estrecho canal en el que el agua fluye con gran rapidez
75 | 392 -o

3351 heroico *adj* heroic
- es un profesional valiente, audaz y heroico
74 | 349

3352 asesinar *v* to murder, assassinate
- dame fuerzas y audacia para asesinar a mis enemigos
74 | 399

3353 audiencia *nf* audience, hearing
- agradeció los aplausos de la audiencia
74 | 347

3354 pasajero *nm* passenger
- viajo como pasajero de un tren de cargo
73 | 403

Verbs of communication Top words # 1 – 10,000

decir 28 to tell, say

hablar 92 to speak, talk

contar 155 to tell, count

explicar 316 to explain

proponer 500 to propose

expresar 660 to express

anunciar 730 to announce, advertise

comentar 742 to comment on

discutir 859 to argue, discuss

mencionar 905 to mention, cite

pronunciar 944 to pronounce

afirmar 978 to declare, assent

aclarar 1133 to clarify, clear up

declarar 1136 to declare, testify

nombrar 1147 to name, appoint

reclamar 1507 to demand, require

gritar 1597 to shout

criticar 1849 to criticize, gossip

protestar 2288 to protest, object

conversar 2507 to converse

rezar 2847 to pray

rogar 3160 to pray, ask, implore

recitar 3594 to recite

charlar 3671 to chat, talk

alegar 3836 to allege

articular 4101 to articulate

invocar 4252 to invoke

dialogar 4883 to confer, talk

murmurar 5372 to murmur

exclamar 5522 to exclaim

clamar 5660 to cry, clamor

susurrar 6352 to whisper

suplicar 6354 to plead, beg

chillar 6921 to shriek, scream

orar 7384 to pray

gruñir 7824 to grunt, grumble

aullar 7955 to howl, yell

enunciar 8073 to enunciate

mascullar 9401 to mutter, grumble

implorar 9767 to implore, beg

platicar 9862 to chat, converse

cuchichear 9883 to whisper, mutter

vociferar 9944 to proclaim, blare

3355 décimo *adj* tenth
- un regalo de una amiga en su décimo aniversario de boda
77 | 239 +o -f

3356 costado *nm* side, flank
- entraba por una pequeña puerta a un costado del edificio
71 | 667 -o +f

3357 otoño *nm* autumn
- pasaré aquí la primavera y el verano y regresaré en el otoño
76 | 410

3358 feria *nf* fair, festival
- se dirigía a la feria que todos los domingos se realizaba en el pueblo
72 | 311

3359 exilio *nm* exile
- se hace más de medio millón de cubanos en el exilio
72 | 366

3360 indudablemente *adv* doubtless, undoubtedly
- estoy loca; indudablemente ¡lo estoy!
71 | 368 +o

3361 preservar *v* to preserve
- hay que preservar el español de los antepasados
81 | 327

3362 portador *nm* bearer, carrier
- era el portador de buenas noticias
77 | 276

3363 obispo *nm* bishop
- el papa tiene muchos títulos: obispo de Roma, vicario de Cristo . . .
71 | 534

3364 disimular *v* to disguise, hide, pretend
- lo hice muy despacio, para disimular mi inquietud
71 | 441 +f

3365 quemado *adj* burned, burnt
- un penetrante olor a carne quemada inundó el aire
74 | 253 -nf

3366 perfeccionar *v* to perfect
- llegan a perfeccionar en forma casi sobrehumana su instrumento
78 | 282

3367 vano *adj* vain, useless
- toda mi vida habrá sido vana y sin sentido
74 | 473 -o

3368 apertura *nf* opening, beginning
- desde el comienzo, desde la primera apertura de aquél libro
75 | 498 +nf

3369 ideología *nf* ideology
- el confucianismo llegó a ser la ideología oficial del estado chino
72 | 596 +o -f

3370 casero *adj* homemade
- los viejos gastaban su jubilación en buena comida casera y vino
75 | 209

3371 molesto *adj* annoyed, bothered, upset
• estaba molesto, enojado consigo mismo
76 | 247

3372 cocinar *v* to cook
• sabía hacer de todo, limpiar, cocinar, coser, todo
72 | 318

3373 auxiliar *adj* auxiliary, ancillary
• facilita los desplazamientos del personal auxiliar
76 | 214

3374 silencioso *adj* quiet, silent
• todo quedó silencioso y sombrío
72 | 769 -o +f

3375 navegar *v* to navigate, sail
• buscan vientos para poder navegar a toda vela
73 | 308

3376 cazador *nm/f* hunter
• el animal acosado huye y el cazador lo asesina
74 | 328

3377 seguro *nm* insurance
• no va a pagar ni el Seguro de Invalidez y Vida, ni el Seguro de Salud
72 | 302

3378 ingenio *nm* ingenuity, talent, wit
• tengo el cerebro vacío; el ingenio no llega hasta arriba
77 | 274

3379 hembra *nf* female, woman
• las especies como los chimpancés cuyas hembras son más promiscuas
71 | 547

3380 bando *nm* faction, side
• políticamente no pertenecían al mismo bando rebelde
74 | 327

3381 nativo *adj* native
• tantas leguas de mi barrio nativo y lejos de mis hermanos
70 | 527

3382 dormitorio *nm* bedroom, dormitory
• para esconderse debajo de una cama en otro dormitorio
67 | 785 +f -nf

3383 plenitud *nf* fullness, abundance
• todos vigorosos, en plenitud de la vida
77 | 268

3384 aceptable *adj* acceptable, suitable
• en busca de una solución aceptable para ambas partes
78 | 248

3385 coraje *nm* courage, toughness
• ataquemos con coraje el campo enemigo
74 | 351

3386 plomo *nm* lead, bullet
• el impacto de un proyectil de plomo podía destruir la armadura
71 | 378

3387 descendiente *nc* descendant
• es una típica descendiente de árabes: tiene una tez olivácea
76 | 298

3388 rotundo *adj* categorical
• abre los brazos en un rotundo gesto de rechazo
75 | 270

3389 república *nf* republic
• el presidente de la República francesa François Mitterrand
72 | 512

3390 sierra *nf* mountain range, saw
• atravesaron la sierra buscando una salida al mar
71 | 360

3391 aplastar *v* to flatten, crush, smash
• al verlo aplastar con la bota una de las velas
75 | 323

3392 guante *nm* glove
• jamás nadie vio sus manos, cubiertas por guante negro
72 | 323

3393 cartón *nm* cardboard, carton, sketch
• los migrantes del campo tienen casitas de cartón y lata
73 | 251

3394 repentino *adj* sudden
• su repentina cólera provocó la hostilidad de los soldados
75 | 403 -o

3395 ansioso *adj* anxious, eager
• me dejó con cierto nerviosismo y ligeramente ansioso
75 | 368 -o

3396 subrayar *v* to underline, highlight, emphasize
• quiero subrayar lo que requiere énfasis
74 | 411 +nf

3397 adolescencia *nf* adolescence
• en la infancia, en la adolescencia o en la adultez
75 | 359

3398 despacio *adj* slow, slowly
• se retira despacio hasta identificarse con la oscuridad
71 | 480 +f -nf

3399 innumerable *adj* innumerable, countless
• es innumerable la cantidad de cosas
75 | 272 -o

3400 complicación *nf* complication
• se debió a posteriores complicaciones, en todo caso imprevisibles
75 | 231

3401 insoportable *adj* unbearable, intolerable
• experimentó una insoportable sensación de angustia
72 | 380 -nf

3402 taxi *nm* taxi, cab
• toma un taxi y le dice: «Lléveme al hospital Rawson»
68 | 433 -nf

3403 porción *nf* part, portion, share
• una porción de la Iglesia que se llama diócesis
76 | 285

3404 timbre *nm* doorbell, bell, seal, stamp
- tocó el timbre y esperó; nadie contestaba
70 | 395

3405 monstruo *nm* monster, monstrosity
- hicieron máscaras imitando horrendos y morbosos monstruos
71 | 368

3406 bebé *nm* baby
- el bebé nació sano y robusto
70 | 398

3407 trayecto *nm* trajectory, course, path
- ¿cuál ha sido su trayecto hasta llegar a director?
75 | 310

3408 globo *nm* balloon, globe
- falta más fuego para que el globo se infle mejor
74 | 342

3409 celebración *nf* celebration
- la llegada de la primavera era una celebración especial
75 | 341

3410 quehacer *nm* task, job, chore
- los quehaceres domésticos: cocinando, lavando . . .
74 | 267

3411 electoral *adj* electoral
- la campaña electoral se encontraba en su apogeo
67 | 2091 +o -f

3412 obsesión *nf* mania, obsession
- envilecido por la obsesión maniática de publicar
71 | 320

3413 bronce *nm* bronze
- puedo leer un letrero en una columna de bronce
72 | 598 -o

3414 formidable *adj* formidable, tremendous
- el hombre era muy formidable y de mucha influencia
74 | 269

3415 licencia *nf* license, permission
- ¿usted no sabe que sin licencia no puede vender?
77 | 261

3416 motivación *nf* motivation
- la principal motivación que tiene es la venganza
76 | 294 +o -f

3417 noventa *num* ninety
- tendría cerca de noventa años de edad
71 | 414 +o -f

3418 anoche *adv* last night
- puedo asegurarles que soy, desde anoche, indestructible
67 | 418 -nf

3419 depresión *nf* depression, slump
- tan particular depresión de tristeza, tanto dolor de tiempo presente
72 | 387

3420 pulmón *nm* lung
- el pulmón herido me impedía respirar profundamente
68 | 433

3421 apoderar *v* to take power
- un abatimiento profundo se apoderó de nosotros y nos entregamos
74 | 335

3422 debatir *v* to debate, discuss
- argumenté con ganas de debatir la tesis
78 | 348

3423 reponer *v* to replace, restore
- la muchacha reponía mercaderías en los espacios vacíos
75 | 320

3424 fibra *nf* fiber, grain
- la fibra óptica se compone de un delicado filamento de cristal
70 | 603

3425 disputar *v* to dispute, contest
- la elección se va a disputar entre profesionales
73 | 421

3426 quinientos *num* five hundred
- uno de quinientos y otro de mil
68 | 323 +o -nf

3427 petróleo *nm* oil, petroleum
- gases licuados, petróleo y gas natural
74 | 741 -f

3428 sucesivamente *adv* successively, step by step
- el primer hijo tenía el número uno, y así sucesivamente
76 | 199

3429 permanencia *nf* permanence, tenure
- la permanencia de conflictos bélicos en el mundo árabe
78 | 317 +nf

3430 vos *pron* you (subj-sg/+fam)
- vos sos bueno, Gordo
58 | 3143 +f -nf

3431 miércoles *nm* Wednesday
- vendría solamente los lunes, los miércoles y los viernes
68 | 382 +o -nf

3432 horno *nm* oven, furnace
- el horno de barro sobre estacas perdía su calor acumulado
70 | 439

3433 logro *nm* success, achievement
- son grandes ejemplos de los logros artísticos de aquella dinastía
77 | 411 +nf

3434 vientre *nm* womb, belly
- vi a un feto chuparse el dedo dentro del vientre de la madre
68 | 725 +f

3435 petición *nf* request, petition
- A. estuvo indecisa en aceptar su petición de matrimonio
74 | 430

3436 civil *nc* civilian
- es por eso que hay diferencias entre los civiles y militares
75 | 270

3437 reparto *nm* distribution, delivery
- se debe hacer otro reparto más equitativo
77 | 273

3438 advertencia *nf* warning, notice
- en tono de advertencia: eso sí, tenga cuidado; no vuelva a perderlas
77 | 263

3439 arrebatar *v* to snatch, grab
- ella se enojó y le arrebató la flor
76 | 323

3440 previsión *nf* forecast, precaution
- mapas climatológicos de los centros de previsión meteorológica
76 | 337

3441 miserable *adj* wretched, miserable
- ¡era un ser miserable, un repugnante gusano!
69 | 409

3442 grato *adj* agreeable, pleasant
- sería muy grato para mí, si usted quisiera cenar conmigo
73 | 278

3443 mandato *nm* mandate, order, command
- fueron obedientes al mandato del jefe
74 | 572 +nf

3444 odiar *v* to hate
- odiaba a los liberales; los persiguió
70 | 610 +f

3445 clave *adj* key
- la palabra clave, por favor - pidió
76 | 349 +nf

3446 diecisiete *num* seventeen
- cuando se quería casar con ella, ella tenía diecisiete años
71 | 330 +o -nf

3447 timidez *nf* shyness, timidity
- no siento timidez alguna, soy otra persona, sin inhibiciones
56 | 172 +f -nf

3448 toque *nm* touch, ringing, warning
- en blanco y negro con un sugerente y dirigido toque de color
69 | 381 +f

3449 máscara *nf* mask
- la cara torcida en una máscara de horror, la carne pintada
70 | 426

3450 venganza *nf* revenge, vengeance
- ¿eso es justicia o . . . venganza?
72 | 376

3451 barba *nf* beard
- disfrazado con una peluca, un bigote y una barba, para no ser reconocido
69 | 590 +f

3452 alarma *nf* alarm
- el timbre de alarma no me preocupó demasiado
73 | 293

3453 insinuar *v* to insinuate, hint
- nadie me pidió ni insinuó que abordara tema alguno
74 | 357

3454 aliento *nm* breath, courage, spirit
- ¿podrían haber dado un nuevo aliento de vida a este texto magnífico
71 | 587 +f

3455 pureza *nf* purity, chastity
- del honor, la dignidad y la pureza de nuestros atletas
76 | 264

3456 fallecer *v* to pass away (to die)
- lamentablemente, falleció de un ataque al corazón
72 | 335

3457 comedia *nf* comedy, play, pretense
- escritas por maestros del drama o de la comedia
69 | 533

3458 aldea *nf* small village
- Macondo era entonces una aldea de veinte casas
72 | 339

3459 enérgico *adj* energetic, vigorous
- le hacía callar con un gesto enérgico
76 | 278

3460 eludir *v* to evade, avoid, elude
- el gobernador no puede eludir la gravísima responsabilidad
76 | 250

3461 párrafo *nm* paragraph
- leí el párrafo que el rabino me indicó
78 | 327

3462 permanentemente *adv* permanently
- vivíamos permanentemente al borde de la catástrofe
75 | 278 -f

3463 brillo *nm* shine, twinkling, sparkle
- es como si tuviera el brillo de los ojos extinguido
73 | 578 -o +f

3464 ocasionar *v* to occasion, bring about
- una malformación epidérmica ocasionando el adelgazamiento de la piel
76 | 270

3465 rastro *nm* track, sign, flea market
- la viuda desapareció un día sin dejar más rastro que un papelito
75 | 361 -o

3466 concretamente *adv* specifically, exactly
- ninguno sabía concretamente en qué consistía la acción
73 | 488 +o -f

3467 ignorante *adj* ignorant
- no terminó la escuela; es ignorante, inculto, analfabeto
74 | 220 -nf

3468 adorno *nm* decoration, adornment
- sobre la mesa del comedor estaba como adorno la estrella de David
72 | 302

3469 curiosamente *adv* strangely, funnily enough
- pero, curiosamente, no se mencionó en absoluto dicho mensaje
74 | 272

3470 lógicamente *adv* logically
- yo, lógicamente, en ese momento no entendí nada
69 | 494 +o -f

3471 mono *nm* monkey
- ante el ancestro de los grandes monos africanos: chimpancé y gorila
74 | 413

3472 razonamiento *nm* reasoning
- no existía un razonamiento capaz de disuadirle
77 | 278

3473 ilustrado *adj* learned, illustrated
- se crió entre libros, oyendo a personas ilustradas
74 | 237

3474 pastor *nm/f* shepherd, pastor
- yo trabajaba de pastor con un rebaño pequeño
74 | 294

3475 tramo *nm* section, stretch, plot
- fue el tramo de 2 kilómetros entre Dos Bocas y San Lorenzo
75 | 436

3476 reto *nm* challenge, defiance
- su fama de duelista, su aire altanero de reto y desdén
72 | 330 +o

3477 altísimo *adj* very high, tall
- han ido evolucionando y ahora el nivel ya es altísimo
73 | 212

3478 estupendo *adj* marvelous, stupendous
- ha sido una noche estupenda, gracias por todo
66 | 395 +o -nf

3479 pesadilla *nf* nightmare
- una mala pesadilla; sólo fue un mal sueño
71 | 427 +f

3480 centenar *nm* hundred
- centenares de ojos miraban y otras tantas voces gritaban
74 | 394 -o +nf

3481 molestia *nf* bother, nuisance, trouble
- póngase cómodo // Si no es molestia; gracias
73 | 267

3482 restante *adj* remaining
- los restantes reinos eran derivados suyos
75 | 424 -o +nf

3483 paja *nf* straw, thatching
- ocupaba una casita de paja y adobe
71 | 400

3484 regional *adj* regional
- de los gobiernos estatales, regionales y locales
71 | 1115 -f +nf

3485 cómico *adj* comic
- combinando lo culto y lo popular, lo cómico y lo serio
69 | 306

3486 concesión *nf* awarding, concession
- con la concesión de los Juegos de Invierno del año 2002 a Salt Lake City
76 | 408 +nf

3487 tardío *adj* late, belated
- no se conocen ciudades del período tardío de esta cultura
76 | 279

3488 nudo *nm* knot
- le cierra al cuello el nudo de la soga
72 | 332

3489 retomar *v* to retake, restart
- intenté retomar la lectura, pero no lo logré
72 | 261

3490 martes *nm* Tuesday
- todos los martes y jueves voy a mi terapia con el psicoanalista
68 | 406

3491 utilización *nf* use, utilization
- sobre la utilización de los enormes medios con los que se ha dotado
73 | 671 -f +nf

3492 tapa *nf* cover, lid
- abrió la tapa de una pequeña caja de cartón
73 | 337

3493 traición *nf* treason, betrayal
- ella sabía que su traición sería imperdonable
73 | 329

3494 asentar *v* to settle, establish, locate
- se asentaron en estos valles en el siglo XVIII
77 | 274 -o +nf

3495 pesca *nf* fishing
- la alcaldía prohibió la pesca de carpa y el uso recreativo del lago
71 | 404

3496 malestar *nm* discomfort, unease, unrest
- sentí un inexplicable malestar y volví más cansada que otras veces
78 | 239

3497 rata *nf* rat
- el gato es apreciado como cazador de ratones y ratas
68 | 444

3498 puntual *adj* punctual
- la oficialidad es muy puntual y no podían hacerlos esperar
74 | 218

3499 defensor *nm* defender
- practicaba la abogacía y era defensor de pobres y esclavos
73 | 373 +nf

3500 auxilio *nm* help, aid, assistance
- es un grito sofocado pidiendo auxilio para sus hijos
72 | 329

Use of the "reflexive marker" *se*

Spanish [*se*] has a wide range of uses, including the true reflexive (*Juan se mató* "John killed himself"), replacing other objects (*Juan se levantó* "John got up" vs. *Juan lo levantó* "John picked him up"), use with verbs of movement (*Juan se cayó* "John fell down"), lexicalized se (*Juan se jactaba* "John was boasting"), impersonal (*se vive bien en México* "one lives well in Mexico"), passive (*se vendieron tres coches* "three cars were sold"), and other suppression of subjects (*se hundió el barco* "the boat sank" vs. *los piratas hundieron el barco* "the pirates sank the boat"), among others. In nearly all cases, *se* "focuses" in on a particular participant, to the suppression or exclusion of others. Mastering the range of uses of se often presents a real problem for language learners.

The following lists provide an overview of which verbs occur with *se*. The first list contains the most frequent verbs that occur with *se* in 100 percent of the cases, and nearly all of these are outside of the "top 5,000" list. The second list is limited to just those verbs in the top 5,000 list that have the highest percentage of occurrence with *se*. To round out the discussion, the final list shows those verbs that never occur with *se*, beginning with the most frequent.

All se

(explanation: number of cases with se)

[Top 15 verbs]

fotografiar 137 to have a picture taken

aliar 106 to become allied with

obstinar 93 to persist in

empecinar 77 to become stubborn

exceptuar 71 to be excluded

sobreponer 71 to prevail

fugar 61 to flee

avenir 55 to agree to

santiguar 51 to cross oneself

legalizar 46 to be legalized

jactar 46 to brag

eslabonar 45 to be linked together

turnar 45 to take turns

columpiar 44 to seesaw

preciar 42 to be appraised

High percentage with se

(explanation % se Spanish WORD # English)

[Top 25 verbs]

0.99 **apoderar** 3421 to take power

0.97 **quejar** 1530 to complain

0.96 **refugiar** 3603 to take refuge

0.96 **percatar** 4826 to become aware

0.95 **arrepentir** 3528 to regret

0.92 **extinguir** 3616 to extinguish

0.92 **adentrar** 4721 to get inside

0.92 **atrever** 1276 to dare

0.91 **enterar** 1543 to find out

0.90 **esforzar** 2823 to exert oneself

0.90 **empeñar** 1998 to struggle for

0.89 **basar** 1430 to base on

0.88 **resignar** 4878 to resign

0.87 **desenvolver** 3740 to prosper

0.87 **referir** 409 to refer (to)

0.87 **deslizar** 3651 to slip

0.86 **interponer** 4229 to get in the way

0.85 **internar** 4899 to penetrate

0.85 **burlar** 3047 to mock

0.84 **acostar** 3077 to go to bed

0.84 **derrumbar** 3544 to knock down

0.84 **aproximar** 2070 to come near

0.84 **equivocar** 1457 to be wrong

0.83 **inscribir** 3993 to register

0.83 **colar** 4237 to slip in

No se

existir 177 to exist

surgir 553 to arise

consistir 688 to consist of

durar 812 to last

permanecer 821 to remain

transcurrir 1579 to take place

constar 1655 to comprise

colaborar 1943 to collaborate

provenir 1958 to come from

protestar 2288 to protest

estallar 2401 to explode

residir 2764 to reside

derrotar 2951 to defeat

sobrar 2978 to be left over

brotar 2979 to sprout

3501 estrechar *v* to tighten, make closer
- para estrechar la comunicación y mantener contactos frecuentes
75 | 276

3502 traspasar *v* to go beyond, cross over
- su capacidad para traspasar fronteras y transmitir una imagen positiva
75 | 271

3503 cobre *nm* copper
- de la mezcla de cobre y estaño se obtenía bronce
68 | 423

3504 imaginario *adj* imaginary
- para llorar por fingidas desventuras de seres imaginarios
73 | 290

3505 brutal *adj* brutal, savage
- le aplicó un golpe brutal por debajo de las costillas
72 | 312

3506 disperso *adj* spread out
- su Imperio estaba disperso desde el punto de vista estratégico
75 | 226

3507 ingenuo *adj* naive, ingenuous
- después de tantos años, ya no tiene derecho a ser ingenuo
71 | 274

3508 anual *adj* annual, yearly
- tiene un presupuesto anual de cien millones de pesetas
70 | 790 -f +nf

3509 intuición *nf* intuition
- soy su madre y la intuición de las madres no falla
75 | 266

3510 invención *nf* invention, contrivance
- era pura invención; no tenía ningún fundamento real
75 | 324 -o

3511 asimismo *adv* as well, also, moreover
- puedo asimismo guiarte en tus actividades inmediatas
72 | 855 -o +nf

3512 vena *nf* vein
- la lesión de una vena produce un flujo continuo de sangre roja oscura
69 | 385

3513 freno *nm* brake
- ocasionalmente se escucha un ruido de frenos o de sirenas fuera
76 | 227

3514 costoso *adj* costly, expensive
- se ha puesto en marcha todo este vasto y costoso operativo
75 | 262

3515 repleto *adj* full, overcrowded
- un estante repleto de pesados libros
70 | 323

3516 consumar *v* to complete, carry out
- se ha consumado un delito contra el Patrimonio Histórico
75 | 265

3517 asaltar *v* to assault
- nuevamente, lo asaltó la idea de estar perdiendo la razón
74 | 263

3518 interrupción *nf* interruption
- se superponían sin interrupción y traspasaban sin ninguna dificultad
74 | 247

3519 condena *nf* sentence (in prison), penalty
- no está satisfecho simplemente con la condena del homicidio
73 | 296

3520 inocencia *nf* innocence
- en su inocencia no podían evaluar la gravedad de la situación
71 | 354

3521 relieve *nm* relief; poner de relieve: to emphasize
- permite poner de relieve la importancia de un monumento histórico
73 | 473 +nf

3522 semejanza *nf* similarity, likeness
- se conservó una semejanza fiel con el original
74 | 275

3523 cumbre *nf* summit, top
- se reunirán para participar en una cumbre con un tema único: el VIH
70 | 371

3524 diariamente *adv* daily
- uno lo confronta diariamente con la secretaria
71 | 238

3525 colmo *nm* climax; para colmo: to top it all
- te habías robado a su nena y para colmo la preñaste
71 | 326 -nf

3526 asombroso *adj* amazing
- ¿hay algo que este asombroso artista no sea capaz de hacer?
75 | 258

3527 administrador *nm/f* administrator, manager
- se contrata los servicios de un administrador profesional
72 | 258

3528 arrepentir *v* to repent, regret
- había que arrepentirse de las malas acciones
71 | 227 -nf

3529 decreto *nm* decree, order
- la Universidad fue creada por un decreto público
72 | 475 -f +nf

3530 exigente *adj* demanding, urgent
- se muestra cada vez más difícil, exigente y desidiosa
74 | 204

3531 ironía *nf* irony
- el comentario fue hecho con ironía y falsa admiración
74 | 320

3532 felicitar *v* to congratulate
- te felicito y nos enorgullecemos por tus triunfos
70 | 284 +o -nf

3533 seña *nf* sign, mark, seal
- le hace señas para que se acerque a su auto
71 | 365 +f

3534 ritual *nm* ritual, rite
- la organización episcopal y ritual de la Iglesia anglicana es la misma
76 | 290 -o

3535 apto *adj* appropriate, fit, able
- algo sutil, flexible, apto para modelar sonidos
75 | 263

3536 incierto *adj* uncertain
- ¿era su destino tan incierto como el mío?
75 | 281

3537 espeso *adj* thick, dense, stiff
- hasta un líquido tan espeso que apenas fluye
73 | 554 -o +f

3538 presenciar *v* to be present at, witness
- entraron para presenciar la ceremonia
70 | 296

3539 escritorio *nm* desk, bureau
- para mantener el escritorio de la oficina limpio
68 | 492 +f -nf

3540 solicitud *nf* request, application
- hice solicitud para los dos y logré plaza en los dos
71 | 269

3541 víspera *nf* eve
- una noche, la víspera de su partida, volvió a su alcoba
74 | 321

3542 insecto *nm* insect
- las ranas se alimentan principalmente de insectos, gusanos, y arañas
67 | 609 -o

3543 ridículo *nm* ridicule
- las que estén excedidas de peso, me luce un poco ridículo ponerse la moda así
69 | 288 -nf

3544 derrumbar *v* to knock down, demolish
- hicimos todo lo posible por derrumbar a L. de su pedestal
75 | 229

3545 ira *nf* rage, wrath
- R. tembló de ira ante la baja traición
71 | 368 -o

3546 ceniza *nf* ash
- sacudiendo la ceniza de su cigarro sobre el fogón
72 | 450 -o +f

3547 apasionado *adj* passionate
- finalmente ellos terminaron con un abrazo apasionado
72 | 251

3548 monja *nf* nun
- la monja reza devotamente sus oraciones y besa el crucifijo
63 | 441 -nf

3549 abstracto *adj* abstract
- figura clave del expresionismo abstracto norteamericano
70 | 412

3550 parto *nm* birth
- la crónica de una maternidad sin parto y de un amor sin sexo
70 | 254

3551 creativo *adj* creative
- ¿o es porque sos creativo, sensible, y artístico?
76 | 293 -f +nf

3552 autoritario *adj* authoritarian
- han querido implantar el control autoritario de la natalidad
75 | 247

3553 excesivamente *adv* excessively
- estaba excesivamente nervioso e inquieto
72 | 225

3554 circuito *nm* circuit, circumference, track
- una cámara de circuito cerrado de televisión
70 | 546 +nf

3555 subterráneo *adj* underground
- creo sentir el temblor subterráneo que precede al terremoto
72 | 318

3556 oveja *nf* sheep, ewe
- se ganó el título de «oveja negra» durante la adolescencia
71 | 298

3557 dueña *nf* landlady, owner (f)
- la dueña del teatro era una mujer muy bien vestida
69 | 353 +f -nf

3558 dañar *v* to damage
- el cigarrillo te va a dañar los pulmones
74 | 246

3559 ubicación *nf* position, location
- conocía las diferencias de ubicación de los lugares
76 | 270

3560 feroz *adj* ferocious, fierce
- animalitos de feroz aspecto y acción rápida
73 | 253

3561 hacienda *nf* ranch
- desde el corral de la hacienda llegaban diluidas voces de gansos
66 | 402

3562 antigüedad *nf* antiquity, seniority
- la planta fue empleada desde la antigüedad para curar heridas
72 | 432

3563 puño *nm* fist, handle, cuff
- él sintió el puño de Dolores escondido en su costado
70 | 462 +f

3564 excusa *nf* excuse
- tendría que inventar una buena excusa para justificar su inasistencia
71 | 300

3565 asombrar *v* to amaze, astound
- se asombró de la furiosa reacción
73 | 280

3566 trama *nf* plot, theme
- esa unidad compleja: esquema, sistema, coherencia, trama, lógica de vida
73 | 277

3567 sistemático *adj* systematic
- era sistemático e incluso resultaba monótono
76 | 369 -f +nf

3568 inclusive *adv* including, even
- hay para todos los gustos, inclusive motivos infantiles
61 | 714 +o -nf

3569 alteración *nf* alteration, change
- la manipulación de los genes humanos con alteración del genotipo
70 | 562 +nf

3570 sumo *adj* utmost, highest
- con sumo gusto les atenderé la próxima semana
73 | 245

3571 eficiente *adj* efficient
- un sistema más eficiente y equitativo
75 | 288

3572 invisible *adj* invisible
- lo esencial y divino es invisible a los ojos
68 | 575 -o

3573 acusación *nf* accusation, charge
- F. se defendió de las acusaciones hacia su gestión
73 | 373

3574 sinceramente *adv* sincerely
- yo . . . sinceramente, me preocupa que ustedes no sepan
70 | 269 +o -nf

3575 salvación *nf* salvation, rescue
- el gurú será la salvación de los discípulos
71 | 336 -o

3576 rebelde *adj* rebel
- tiene un hijo rebelde y se resiste a obedecer
73 | 254

3577 fundador *nm* founder
- Colón fue el fundador de la primera colonia europea en América
72 | 359 -f +nf

3578 oscilar *v* oscillate
- oscilaba según los ciclos económicos
75 | 358 -o +nf

3579 privilegiado *adj* privileged
- le conceden un lugar privilegiado en el panorama internacional
78 | 246

3580 recobrar *v* to recover, regain
- hemos querido recobrar una época de tranquilidad y silencio
77 | 276 -o

3581 original *nm* original
- ¿son los originales? // No, fue la editada por mi abuelo
72 | 254

3582 maquinaria *nf* machinery
- lo fabricamos con maquinaria automática
75 | 328 -f +nf

3583 dominante *adj* dominant, prevailing
- se transformó en la forma del budismo dominante en el Tíbet
74 | 486 -f +nf

3584 vaciar *v* to empty, pour out
- ella lo toma de a sorbitos hasta vaciar su copa
74 | 230

3585 tortura *nf* torture
- fuertemente dramáticas; escenas de sangre y tortura
70 | 285

3586 humano *nm* human
- todos los humanos descienden de una sola mujer
74 | 329 -f

3587 insistencia *nf* insistence, persistence
- ¿qué mensaje es ese que con tanta insistencia quería comunicarme?
77 | 296 -o

3588 morder *v* to bite
- el cirujano se mordió el labio inferior
68 | 519 +f

3589 atrapar *v* to trap, catch
- el fuego los atrapó adentro
73 | 355 -o

3590 tibio *adj* lukewarm
- dándole un tibio beso en la frente
71 | 488 -o +f

3591 amanecer *v* to dawn, get light
- el día amaneció casi nublado y en la mañana hizo frío
70 | 365 +f -nf

3592 sospechoso *adj* suspicious
- notó que un individuo sospechoso se paseaba entre las tumbas
73 | 288

3593 sobrino *nm* nephew
- no sabía que tenías un sobrino y tres primos
71 | 334 -nf

3594 recitar *v* to recite
- recita cuidadosamente las reglas
73 | 289

3595 explorar *v* to explore
- la ilusión de explorar espacios desconocidos
75 | 322 -o

3596 fabuloso *adj* fabulous, fantastic
- pensando en lo que compraría con su fabuloso tesoro
68 | 298 +o -nf

3597 embarcar *v* to embark, load
- faltaba una hora para embarcar en el avión
73 | 228

3598 aguardar *v* to wait for, await
- te resignaste a aguardar que pasara la lluvia
64 | 609 +f

3599 apunte *nm* note, annotation
- y los apuntes los tomáis en clase
70 | 254

3600 antepasado *nm* ancestor
- el cruce de los Neandertal con los antepasados directos del hombre
72 | 332

3601 antemano *adv* beforehand, in advance
- la decisión estaba tomada de antemano
73 | 235

3602 **parir** v to give birth
• su función era nada más que la de parir hijos
68 | 326 -nf

3603 **refugiar** v to take shelter, give refuge
• salió buscando refugiarse en la soledad de la llanura
72 | 283 -o

3604 **sillón** nm armchair, seat
• se sienta en el sillón junto a la estufa
66 | 694 +f -nf

3605 **denso** adj heavy, dense, thick
• el mar frente a mi ventana, el aire denso del trópico
74 | 421 -o

3606 **colectivo** nm collective, group
• entre los grupos políticos y los colectivos profesionales
67 | 365

3607 **dieta** nf diet
• tengo una infección en el hígado y debo hacer dieta
68 | 462

3608 **teniente** nm lieutenant, deputy mayor
• está de uniforme el teniente Ramírez
65 | 494

3609 **polo** nm pole, polo, polo shirt
• hay puro hielo en el polo antártico
71 | 356

3610 **verificar** v to verify
• sacó su boleto para verificar el número de su butaca
71 | 274

3611 **agrícola** adj agricultural, farming
• los elementos vitales: tierra vegetal o agrícola, agua, aire…
72 | 951 -f +nf

3612 **abismo** nm abyss, large gap
• empiezan a cerrar el abismo que separa a los países ricos de los pobres
70 | 316

3613 **algodón** nm cotton
• un camisón barato de algodón con una mancha oscura
70 | 344

3614 **harina** nf flour
• tortilla de harina con grasa
70 | 325

3615 **exactitud** nf accuracy
• nunca se supo con exactitud la causa o el motivo
76 | 252

3616 **extinguir** v to extinguish, put out
• una civilización cuyo mundo se extinguió después de una explosión
74 | 238

3617 **provecho** nm benefit, use
• buscaban la forma de sacar provecho de la situación
75 | 204

3618 **mensual** adj monthly
• con frecuencia variable (semanal, mensual, y anual)
70 | 275 +o

3619 **agradar** v to please
• podría estudiar piano, ya que me agrada la música
72 | 269 -nf

3620 **sobrepasar** v excel, out perform
• sobrepasaban los límites impuestos por puertas o ventanas
74 | 234 +nf

3621 **prudencia** nf prudence, moderation
• la prudencia le ordenaba no pensar así
75 | 241

3622 **insulto** nm insult
• por el mal trato, el insulto, una mala palabra, un gesto
72 | 275

3623 **narrar** v to narrate, tell
• esas palabras pueden narrar una historia
71 | 273

3624 **flujo** nm flow, tide, discharge
• de alcanzar un flujo de agua de 20 metros por segundo
72 | 492 +nf

3625 **aguja** nf needle, spire, stylus
• me había clavado una aguja, así que pensé que era sangre
74 | 336 -o

3626 **planteamiento** nm proposal, exposition
• no me da miedo convivir con alguien, sino el planteamiento de tener hijos
72 | 548 +o -f +nf

3627 **simultáneamente** adv simultaneously
• dado que varias syntagmas operan simultáneamente en una célula
73 | 366 +nf

3628 **florecer** v to flower, bloom, flourish
• ahorita van a florecer las petunias
75 | 358 -o

3629 **torpe** adj clumsy, awkward, slow
• vengativa, torpe conmigo, completamente idiota
71 | 363 -o

3630 **cortina** nf curtain, screen
• las paredes necesitan pintura, las cortinas están desteñidas
66 | 512 +f -nf

3631 **acarrear** v to bring up, entail
• no hay razones para acarrear vicios del pasado
75 | 198 -o

3632 **liso** adj smooth, flat, straight
• de pelo rubio, casi blanco, liso, lacio
71 | 333

3633 **asustado** adj scared, frightened
• ¿tiene miedo? // Un poquito asustado, sí. // No sea cobarde
65 | 466 +f -nf

3634 **profundizar** v to deepen, analyze in depth
• para pensar más y profundizar los temas
72 | 288 +o -f

3635 **apostar** v to wager, bet
• a él nunca le gustó apostar en las carreras
68 | 408

3636 propicio *adj* appropriate, suitable
- parecía ser el momento propicio para hacerlo
76 | 255

3637 reproducción *nf* reproduction
- el nido es tan esencial para la reproducción de las aves
70 | 487 +nf

3638 expansión *nf* expansion, spreading
- sobre todo en períodos de expansión económica
72 | 939 -f +nf

3639 umbral *nm* threshold, outset
- estuvo un momento en el umbral de la entrada de aquel lugar
69 | 332 -o

3640 alusión *nf* allusion, hint
- hacía alusión a las supersticiones del viejo paisano
73 | 244

3641 descenso *nm* decline, descent, lowering
- el principal agente de descenso de la población es la muerte
73 | 405 -o +nf

3642 clasificar *v* to classify, sort, file
- no podemos clasificar esta obra ni como novela corta, ni como cuento
73 | 415 -f +nf

3643 recortar *v* to trim, cut off, clip
- logró recortar un trozo de la túnica
74 | 221

3644 dicho *adj* aforementioned, said
- a organizar su espacio interno en función de dicho sistema
69 | 490 +nf

3645 ambiguo *adj* ambiguous
- mi arte no es de palabras; no es ambiguo; no representa nada
72 | 243

3646 océano *nm* ocean
- abarcaba desde el océano Atlántico hasta el río Mississippi
69 | 575 -o +nf

3647 proposición *nf* proposition
- la proposición de que a los menores se le aplicara la misma ley
71 | 380

3648 absurdo *nm* absurdity, nonsense
- es absurdo pretender que todo sea perfecto
73 | 231

3649 parada *nf* (transportation) stop
- lo encontré frente a la parada de colectivos de la plaza Pereira
70 | 241

3650 encantador *adj* charming
- era un hombre maravilloso, encantador, una mente abierta
70 | 224 -nf

3651 deslizar *v* to slide, glide, slip
- el hielo les hizo deslizar hacia atrás
72 | 587 -o +f

3652 estirar *v* to stretch, strain
- iba a caminar un poco más, estirar las piernas
68 | 433 +f

3653 respetuoso *adj* respectful
- todos nos miraban en un silencio respetuoso
71 | 305

3654 africano *adj* African
- la exportación de animales salvajes de las junglas africanas
72 | 435

3655 titular *nm* headline, holder
- tomé el periódico y leí los titulares
70 | 572 -f

3656 calendario *nm* calendar
- buscó un calendario del año siguiente, 1918, y marcó un día
71 | 343

3657 interlocutor *nm* participant in a dialog
- parecía discutir con un interlocutor invisible
71 | 289

3658 abusar *v* to abuse
- los hábitos dietéticos en los que se abusa del chocolate y los dulces
74 | 196

3659 complementar *v* to complement, supplement
- son la pareja perfecta, que se complementan
75 | 233 -f

3660 disgusto *nm* disgust, annoyance
- mamá rechazaba con disgusto la macabra propuesta
68 | 281 +f -nf

3661 conservación *nf* conservation
- el estudio y la buena conservación de los monumentos
71 | 571 -f +nf

3662 revivir *v* to revive
- revivió en su memoria la imagen de su abuelo anciano
75 | 211

3663 elaboración *nf* production
- la carne que se emplea en su elaboración es de pésima calidad
73 | 538 -f +nf

3664 conmover *v* to move, affect
- la oportunidad de conmoverse hasta las lágrimas
69 | 289

3665 correo *nm* mail, post (office)
- lo primero que hizo J. fue mandar por correo esta invitación
69 | 269

3666 circo *nm* circus
- el rey del circo es el payaso
66 | 377

3667 adversario *nm* adversary
- atacando al adversario en su punto débil
73 | 322

3668 cubierta *nf* covering, top, lid
- un agujero en la cubierta del huevo permite la fusión celular
69 | 335

Preterit/imperfect Top 50 words # 1 – 8000

Unlike English, Spanish has a morphological distinction between two "simple" past tenses. The preterit indicates completed actions (*María se fue* "Mary left", *Jorge lo compró* "George bought it"), while the imperfect refers to an internal point in the action (*Susana miraba* [impf] *la tele cuando lo vio* [pret] "Susan was watching TV when she saw him") or habitual actions in the past (*siempre íbamos a la playa* "we always used to go to the beach").

The meaning of the verb is also important. Some verbs refer to actions that naturally have a clear, sudden endpoint ("to close, die, fall") while others refer more to actions or states without clear endpoints ("to believe, to know, to have") or that refer to naturally repeated actions ("to breathe, to beat [a heart]"). The following lists show which verbs most commonly occur in the preterit, in the imperfect, and which are evenly distributed between the two.

Highly preterit (explanation: % preterit Spanish WORD# English)	**Highly imperfect** (explanation: % imperfect Spanish WORD# English)	**Approximately half preterit, half imperfect** (explanation: % imperfect Spanish WORD # English)
1.00 **fracasar** 2278 to fail	1.00 **soler** 487 to be accustomed to	0.59 **ir** to go 30
1.00 **contratar** 2419 to contract	1.00 **depender** 673 to depend on	0.58 **creer** to believe 91
1.00 **enriquecer** 2682 to enrich	1.00 **constar** 1655 to comprise	0.60 **hablar** to speak 92
1.00 **extinguir** 3617 to extinguish	1.00 **desconocer** 1662 to not know	0.50 **llevar** to carry 93
1.00 **mudar** 3689 to move	1.00 **vigilar** 2248 to watch over	0.49 **seguir** to follow 97
1.00 **concretar** 2840 to materialize, fulfill	1.00 **garantizar** 2346 to guarantee	0.54 **llamar** to (be) name(d) 104
1.00 **redactar** 2871 to edit	1.00 **charlar** 3672 to chat	0.51 **venir** to come 105
1.00 **reiterar** 2901 to reiterate	1.00 **equivaler** 3676 to be equivalent	0.55 **conocer** to know (someone or place) 124
1.00 **diseñar** 2911 to design	1.00 **adorar** 3125 to worship	0.48 **sentir** to feel 131
1.00 **asesinar** 3353 to murder	1.00 **latir** 4380 to beat (heart)	0.43 **mirar** to look at 142
1.00 **emigrar** 3851 to emigrate	1.00 **flotar** 2968 to float	0.44 **contar** to tell, count 155
1.00 **embarcar** 3598 to load	1.00 **fluir** 3351 to flow	0.51 **buscar** to look for 173
1.00 **adherir** 4891 to attach	1.00 **filtrar** 3782 to filter	0.55 **entender** to understand 203
0.99 **entrar** 179 to enter	1.00 **reposar** 4633 to rest	0.54 **recordar** to remind 215
0.97 **conquistar** 2359 to conquer	1.00 **ostentar** 4255 to show off	0.44 **permitir** to allow 220
0.96 **derrotar** 2952 to defeat	1.00 **reinar** 4055 to reign	0.49 **servir** to serve 226
0.94 **heredar** 2556 to inherit	1.00 **sudar** 4620 to sweat	0.43 **mantener** to maintain 234
0.94 **bautizar** 3187 to baptize	0.97 **contrastar** 3735 to contrast with	0.50 **resultar** to turn out 238
0.94 **fundar** 1117 to found	0.95 **complacer** 3824 to satisfy	0.40 **leer** to read 244
0.94 **decidir** 381 to decide	0.94 **presidir** 3021 to preside over	0.47 **formar** to form 287
0.93 **consolidar** 4377 to consolidate	0.94 **albergar** 3823 to harbor	0.40 **traer** to bring 289
0.93 **modificar** 1759 to modify	0.93 **haber** 11 to have (+Ved)	0.44 **suponer** to suppose 305
0.93 **perfeccionar** 3367 to perfect	0.93 **lucir** 2742 to shine	0.42 **tocar** to touch, play 325
0.93 **reanudar** 3687 to resume	0.93 **adornar** 4180 to adorn	0.50 **correr** to run 332
0.93 **reponer** 3424 to replace	0.92 **poseer** 1005 to possess	0.43 **utilizar** to use 338

3669 aniversario *nm* anniversary
- el 25 aniversario de la primera pisada en la Luna
71 | 238

3670 franja *nf* strip, stripe, fringe
- apenas separadas por una franja de tierra verde
72 | 272 +nf

3671 charlar *v* to chat, talk
- buscan un café para charlar, después un bar para seguir hablando
68 | 273 -nf

3672 pila *nf* (baptismal) font, battery, heap
- pone los dedos en la pila de agua bendita
68 | 295

3673 flaco *adj* thin, frail
- ese perro está flaco, ese perro está muriéndose del hambre
68 | 404 +f -nf

3674 biológico *adj* biological
- pobre víctima de algún error genético, biológico o celular
70 | 778 -f +nf

3675 equivaler *v* to be equivalent, tantamount (to)
- desarmar a un hombre casi equivalía a castrarlo
74 | 312 +nf

3676 fomentar *v* to foster, promote, encourage
- con el afán de fomentar la cooperación entre las naciones
73 | 347 -f +nf

3677 goma *nf* rubber
- una pelota de goma, rebotando, va a detenerse a sus pies
68 | 289

3678 enormemente *adv* enormously
- la ejecución técnica del proyecto es enormemente complicada
73 | 222 +o -f

3679 ancho *nm* width
- tendrá 8,5 metros de ancho por catorce metros de alto
72 | 251

3680 emocional *adj* emotional
- pueden originar estrés emocional y vergüenza
70 | 406

3681 diplomático *adj* diplomatic
- generó un conflicto político, diplomático y económico
71 | 348

3682 uva *nf* grape
- los cítricos, mangos, dátiles, higos y uvas
70 | 270

3683 ética *nf* ethics
- su fanatismo por la moral, la ética y la perfección
73 | 352 -f

3684 inscripción *nf* inscription, registration
- una inscripción en escritura jeroglífica, demótica y griega
77 | 231

3685 progresivo *adj* progressive
- vemos un cambio progresivo con el tiempo
74 | 370 -o +nf

3686 reanudar *v* to renew, resume
- rehusó aceptar el veredicto y trató de reanudar la batalla
76 | 275 -o

3687 adquisición *nf* acquisition
- la primera adquisición fue un televisor más grande
74 | 281 -f

3688 mudar *v* to move, change
- aguantó el criticismo sin mudar de expresión
67 | 348 -nf

3689 glorioso *adj* glorious
- culmina un momento glorioso de nuestro pasado
72 | 269

3690 sentir *nm* feeling
- es una expresión personal de un sentir personal de él
72 | 244

3691 turco *adj* Turkish
- se refiere al constante peligro turco, vencido en Lepanto
71 | 428

3692 prescindir *v* to do without
- la Compañía ha resuelto prescindir de sus servicios
73 | 255

3693 renuncia *nf* resignation, renunciation
- ya hubo una renuncia de un secretario de gobernación
72 | 352

3694 préstamo *nm* loan, borrowing
- el préstamo de 50 millones de pesos que otorgó el Banco de Exportaciones
73 | 280

3695 poblado *adj* populated
- es la parte más poblada del país
75 | 271

3696 besar *v* to kiss
- la besa en las mejillas
63 | 1030 +f -nf

3697 impreso *adj* printed
- los medios de comunicación impresos son muy importantes
75 | 233 -o

3698 dedicación *nf* dedication, devotion
- yo lo hacía con una fe y una dedicación religiosa
74 | 206

3699 instituto *nm* institute
- en colaboración con el Instituto Getty de Estados Unidos
71 | 361 +o -f

3700 paloma *nf* dove
- quisiera ser como una paloma: blanca, suave, pacífica, tierna
70 | 435

3701 resaltar *v* to emphasize
• hay que resaltar el valor de estos pilotos
73 | 301

3702 devoción *nf* devotion
• San Francisco era objeto de la especial devoción de doña R.
71 | 249

3703 inverso *adj* inverse, opposite
• va contra la corriente en un sentido inverso al sentido mayoritario
73 | 333

3704 intercambiar *v* to exchange
• no me molestaría intercambiar papeles
73 | 227

3705 consolar *v* to console
• la consolaba la presencia de alguien a su lado
67 | 368 +f -nf

3706 descomponer *v* to decompose, break down
• debe ser posible descomponer la complejidad biológica
74 | 215

3707 enfocar *v* to focus
• permite enfocar una imagen sobre la película
72 | 200

3708 espina *nf* thorn, spine
• no hay rosas sin espinas
71 | 241

3709 aprobación *nf* approval, consent
• no quería hacer nada que no contase con la aprobación de su padre
75 | 467

3710 fachada *nf* front of a building
• está pintada la escena en la fachada de la casa
70 | 388 -o

3711 funcional *adj* functional
• triunfó por la simplicidad funcional de su diseño, de tipo mínimo
74 | 391 +o -f +nf

3712 jugo *nm* juice
• nunca he desayunado; bueno, jugo de naranja eso sí tomaba
64 | 319 -nf

3713 traicionar *v* to betray
• traicionó a todos los que la habían ayudado en el pasado
72 | 247

3714 discípulo *nm* disciple
• ¿eres discípulo de una figura religiosa?
73 | 356

3715 coronel *nm* colonel
• un régimen del coronel Muammar al-Gaddafi
67 | 920 -o

3716 orgánico *adj* organic
• es un estilo orgánico derivado de formas naturales
70 | 808 -f +nf

3717 modificación *nf* modification, alteration
• proponen una modificación de la ley
70 | 722 +o -f +nf

3718 acumulación *nf* accumulation
• el problema de la acumulación de residuos en el medio ambiente
70 | 628 +nf

3719 comparable *adj* comparable
• la producción china de acero es comparable a la de Gran Bretaña
73 | 237 +nf

3720 mantenimiento *nm* maintenance, sustenance
• el mantenimiento de un extenso sistema de defensa aérea
71 | 417 -f +nf

3721 marginal *adj* marginal, minor
• en esa zona marginal en la que nadie ha estado
72 | 266

3722 pardo *adj* brown, dark, dim
• el oso pardo se encuentra en las sierras
68 | 334

3723 cabecera *nf* head, header
• impidió demoler algo de la cabecera de la iglesia basilical
71 | 270

3724 revelación *nf* revelation
• la revelación de Dios: sabiduría y amor, gracia y misericordia
71 | 337 -o

3725 peseta *nf* peseta (money)
• lo mismo hicieron con la peseta española y la lira italiana
53 | 1812 +o -f

3726 cuna *nf* cradle, birth, lineage
• cesaron las canciones de cuna que las madres dedicaban a los críos
70 | 221

3727 tendido *adj* spread, hung, laid (out)
• estaba tendida sobre una toalla y tomaba el sol en la playa
66 | 544 -o +f

3728 horizontal *adj* horizontal
• dos movimientos, uno horizontal, y otro vertical
68 | 370

3729 ácido *nm* acid
• le corroía el alma quemándole como ácido nítrico
67 | 680

3730 incapacidad *nf* inability, incompetence
• imposible por nuestra incapacidad de recordar los detalles
74 | 259

3731 villa *nf* village, town
• el propio atleta se instala en la villa olímpica
70 | 279

3732 lecho *nm* (river) bed, couch
• es el lecho donde yo fui concebido, donde yo nací
70 | 442 -o +f

3733 alquiler *nm* rent, rental
• para pagar el alquiler del piso en que vive
69 | 217

3734 contrastar *v* to contrast
- su simplicidad estilística contrasta con su complejidad psicológica
74 | 243 -o +nf

3735 redacción *nf* editing, wording, essay
- la redacción de un manuscrito científico
69 | 379

3736 ficha *nf* index card, chip, token
- o clasificando fichas de plástico en casillero de acero
68 | 218 +o -nf

3737 penoso *adj* painful, laborious
- su trabajo había sido como un penoso sacrificio
72 | 246

3738 inseguridad *nf* insecurity
- su comportamiento reflejaba la inseguridad y desconfianza
70 | 277

3739 coma *nmf* comma (f), coma (m)
- a la derecha de la coma representan los lugares de las décimas (1/10)
71 | 187 +o

3740 desenvolver *v* to clear up, unwrap
- si yo pudiera desenvolver mis pensamientos y desahogarme
71 | 204

3741 agricultura *nf* agriculture, farming
- la industria, el comercio, la agricultura, la ganadería, la pesca
72 | 591 -f +nf

3742 naturalidad *nf* ease, spontaneity
- su espontaneidad y naturalidad lo hacen ver como una persona de convicciones
71 | 213

3743 serenidad *nf* serenity, calm
- esto nos da serenidad y paz y nos da alegría y optimismo
72 | 261

3744 preferido *adj* preferred, favorite
- el campo es nuestro lugar preferido
72 | 243

3745 pistola *nf* gun, pistol
- la mata a tiros de pistola
65 | 442 +f

3746 interrogar *v* to question, interrogate
- comienzo a interrogar a todos los criminales
70 | 347 +f

3747 insignificante *adj* insignificant
- por este servicio cobramos un insignificante dos por ciento
71 | 236

3748 subsistir *v* to subsist, survive
- algo de alimentos para subsistir
72 | 234

3749 diputado *nm* deputy, member
- para ser diputado hay que ser político
66 | 848 -f

3750 literalmente *adv* literally
- hasta ser borrados literalmente del mapa
74 | 179

3751 duelo *nm* grief, affliction
- decidió hacer su duelo y enfrentar su dolor
69 | 270

3752 revolver *v* to stir, mix, scramble
- quisiera revolver una gran olla puesta sobre el fuego
68 | 323 +f -nf

3753 frecuentemente *adv* frequently, often
- suelo pensar frecuentemente en mi familia
73 | 268

3754 retornar *v* to return, give back
- día tras día retornaba al mismo sitio, esperando encontrarla
74 | 249 -o

3755 comandante *nm* commander, commanding officer
- el Comandante era un ex teniente, expulsado del Ejército
66 | 428

3756 preso *adj* imprisoned, confined
- podría estar preso en un calabozo extraño
72 | 274

3757 ópera *nf* opera
- sin ser ni una ópera ni una comedia musical
62 | 618

3758 réplica *nf* answer, retort, copy
- el tono de su voz no admitía réplica
72 | 316 -o

3759 fuertemente *adv* strongly
- se identifica usted fuertemente con algunos artistas visuales
72 | 287 +nf

3760 global *adj* global, overall
- constituyen una nueva visión global de nuestro planeta Tierra
68 | 697 +o -f +nf

3761 alquilar *v* to rent, hire
- la búsqueda de algún departamento o chalet para alquilar
65 | 268

3762 pulso *nm* pulse, pulsation
- tiembla; la piel se le amorata; su pulso se acelera
68 | 297

3763 radicar *v* to lie, be situated
- ahí radica el mal de la sociedad
72 | 248 -f

3764 explotación *nf* exploitation, cultivation
- lamentamos la explotación del hombre por otro
69 | 576 -f +nf

3765 bestia *nf* beast, brute
- ¡suélteme, mala bestia!
71 | 378 -o +f

3766 mojar *v* to make wet, dampen
- se lava la cara sintiéndose mejor; moja también sus cabellos
66 | 294 +f -nf

3767 abrazo *nm* hug, embrace
- le dieron un abrazo estrecho y apretado, efusivo, y cariñoso
66 | 394 +f -nf

3768 asalto *nm* assault, robbery
- se ha acentuado esta situación de delincuente, de asalto, de robos
71 | 346 -o

3769 reposo *nm* rest, peace
- no necesitaba ningún médico, sólo reposo y descanso
74 | 315 -o

3770 lámina *nf* sheet (of metal)
- y prensar las hojas entre láminas de metal o de cartón liso
67 | 303

3771 pasta *nf* pasta, dough
- no puedo comer toda la pasta pegajosa de mi plato
66 | 304

3772 derribar *v* to knock down, overthrow
- un golpe lo derribó por el suelo, desvanecido
72 | 234 -o

3773 oral *adj* oral
- un diálogo oral entre dos personas de distintas lenguas
72 | 308 -f

3774 polémica *nf* polemics, argument
- opté por ignorarlo para no iniciar polémica alguna con mis compañeros
71 | 378 +o -f +nf

3775 parcial *adj* partial, biased
- para decidir la exclusión total o parcial
73 | 324 -f +nf

3776 chocolate *nm* chocolate
- me enseñó a sopear galletas marías en chocolate caliente
66 | 316

3777 generosidad *nf* generosity
- un hombre de generosidad ilimitada, que ayudaba a todo el que podía
69 | 239

3778 masivo *adj* mass, massive
- los temores empresarios por el ingreso masivo de productos baratos
72 | 444 -f +nf

3779 sobresalir *v* to stand out, excel
- están decididos a sobresalir y a vivir bien
73 | 272 -o

3780 realismo *nm* realism
- fíjate que no es . . . escepticismo sino realismo
68 | 447

3781 filtrar *v* to seep, filter
- la luz que se filtraba por la ventanita desde el pasillo
73 | 221

3782 desierto *adj* deserted, desolate
- y que se hallen solitarios y en lugar desierto
69 | 320 +f

3783 acorde *nm* agreement, accord
- el solsticio de verano es un acorde del ritmo cósmico
71 | 330 -o

3784 sugerencia *nf* suggestion
- habíamos recibido la sugerencia, el deseo, incluso la petición directa
74 | 229

3785 cumpleaños *nm* birthday
- un cumpleaños le regalan a uno un libro, muy bueno
64 | 318 -nf

3786 ronda *nf* round
- serví una ronda de whisky y los miré
69 | 311

3787 movilizar *v* to mobilize
- embarcaron el banano y movilizaron los trenes
73 | 242

3788 capilla *nf* chapel
- hacen abrir la capilla para rezar novenas
66 | 328

3789 enteramente *adv* completely, entirely
- la enciclopedia estaba dedicada enteramente a la aeronáutica
67 | 321

3790 apelar *v* to call upon, appeal to
- se ha resignado y ahora apela a la técnica del avestruz
72 | 213

3791 expediente *nm* dossier, proceedings
- hay un informe jurídico, que revisa el expediente, firmado por él
65 | 481

3792 tolerancia *nf* tolerance
- es difícil tener tolerancia con esos individuos
73 | 267

3793 entusiasmar *v* to fill with enthusiasm, excite
- la idea de irme a Madrid me entusiasma
65 | 246 +o -nf

3794 educativo *adj* educational
- el trabajo educativo se desarrolla por un profesor individual
66 | 871 +o -f +nf

3795 sopa *nf* soup
- la arrojó sobre una olla gigante de sopa de pollo hirviendo
64 | 356 +f -nf

3796 rival *nc* rival
- su primer rival no tardó en lanzar un grito de combate
70 | 454 +nf

3797 ternura *nf* tenderness
- hemos llorado, nos hemos llenado de ternura y de compasión
64 | 565 +f

3798 variante *nf* variant, difference
- tampoco comprende las variantes dialectales e idiomáticas
71 | 360 +nf

3799 coser *v* to sew
- veía a su madre coser los vestuarios
70 | 304 +f -nf

Subjunctive triggers

Spanish has two "moods" of the verb. As opposed to the indicative, the Spanish subjunctive (now moribund in English) refers to events or states whose reality is either negated or uncertain. Examples would be *quiero que lo compre* "I want him to buy it", *dudo que lo compre* "I doubt that he'll buy it", or *busco alguien que lo compre* "I'm looking for someone who buys it". In all cases, it is uncertain whether someone actually buys it, and the verb *comprar* "to buy" is in the subjunctive.

In addition to some conjunctions and adverbs (*para que* "so that", *antes (de) que* "before", etc.), certain classes of verbs and adjectives tend to serve as "triggers" for the subjunctive. These include verbs of doubt, desire, force, and emotional reaction, as well as adjectives expressing opinion, as opposed to fact. The following two lists show the most common triggers for the subjunctive, where the subjunctive occurs in the three word frame [trigger + *que* + subjunctive verb]. In all case, the data refers to [# as trigger Spanish WORD# English]. For example, the first entry shows that *querer* "to want", which is word # 57 in our list, is a trigger for the subjunctive in 591 cases.

Verbs: [desire/emotional reaction]

591 **querer** 57 want

323 **esperar** 163 hope

101 **gustar** 353 to be pleasing

57 **temer** 1387 fear

56 **importar** 464 matter

101 **preferir** 541 prefer

43 **desear** 515 desire

[possibility/doubt]

497 **creer** 91 believe

119 **parecer** 81 seem

117 **poder** 27 may be

79 **pensar** 106 think

57 **suponer** 305 suppose

35 **saber** 46 know

[force]

351 **decir** 28 say

247 **pedir** 204 ask

168 **hacer** 25 make

131 **dejar** 94 let

91 **permitir** 220 allow

69 **evitar** 446 prevent

65 **impedir** 751 prevent

50 **conseguir** 222 achieve

37 **proponer** 500 propose

33 **exigir** 630 demand

29 **ordenar** 1167 order

Adjectives

118 **posible** 225 possible

54 **necesario** 322 necessary

46 **probable** 1840 probable

37 **mejor** 121 better

22 **difícil** 314 difficult

21 **imposible** 592 impossible

20 **bueno** 115 good

20 **importante** 207 important

19 **preciso** 739 necessary

17 **conveniente** 1970 convenient

15 **natural** 414 natural

14 **lógico** 1214 logical

13 **justo** 1834 fair

12 **raro** 849 strange

9 **imprescindible** 2617 essential

8 **inútil** 1564 useless

8 **preferible** 3126 preferable

5 **extraño** 551 strange

5 **fácil** 514 easy

5 **indispensable** 1949 essential

5 **normal** 664 normal

4 **cierto** 123 sure

4 **común** 438 common

4 **habitual** 1403 customary

3800 molde *nm* mold, cast, pattern
- el molde es una cavidad que tiene la forma exacta del barco
- 66 | 274

3801 vigente *adj* in force, valid
- la ley está más vigente que nunca
- 71 | 429 -f +nf

3802 espectro *nm* ghost, specter
- en la casa había fantasmas o acaso un solo espectro más temible
- 69 | 418 -o +nf

3803 saludable *adj* healthy, wholesome
- l., un hombre fuerte y saludable, de pronto enfermó de gravedad
- 72 | 224

3804 recorte *nm* clipping, cutting, trimming
- cuadros, retratos, recortes, carteles, libros, fotografías
- 71 | 229

3805 reglamento *nm* regulations, rules
- otros mecanismos del Reglamento del Congreso de los Diputados
- 70 | 306

3806 apretado *adj* tight, jammed
- hablaba con un cigarrillo apretado entre los labios
- 68 | 399 +f

3807 vitalidad *nf* vitality, health
- su admirable vitalidad y su contagiosa alegría de vivir
- 73 | 189

3808 cuidadosamente *adv* carefully
- me acerqué cuidadosamente para verla mejor
71 | 313 -o

3809 adaptación *nf* adaptation
- la adaptación y traducción de las obras originales al gallego
69 | 519 -f +nf

3810 etiqueta *nf* label, etiquette
- la etiqueta tiene instrucciones de uso y mantenimiento
68 | 225

3811 obviamente *adv* obviously
- nos daban a entender, obviamente, que también éramos sucios
67 | 374 +o -f

3812 muralla *nf* city wall
- la Gran Muralla china o las diversas murallas fronterizas
66 | 314

3813 desaparecido *adj* missing
- desaparecido entero; ni rastro quedó por ningún lado
70 | 237

3814 represión *nf* repression
- la represión, la prohibición, el desmedido control
72 | 272

3815 reducción *nf* reduction
- una verdadera reducción de la oferta y demanda de drogas ilegales
71 | 640 -f +nf

3816 difusión *nf* spread, diffusion
- la difusión de la cultura clásica desde su centro en Roma
71 | 534 -f +nf

3817 pésimo *adj* dreadful, awful
- las trataban muy mal, las trataban pésimo; y eso me dolía mucho
68 | 199 +o -nf

3818 encargo *nm* job, order, errand
- Miguel Ángel emprendió el encargo de hacer las tumbas de los Medici
69 | 271

3819 madurar *v* to mature, ripen
- me falta madurar, me falta adquirir técnicas
70 | 221

3820 almorzar *v* to have lunch
- era la hora de almorzar una comida ligera
63 | 319 +f -nf

3821 oeste *nm* West
- con el pionerismo norteamericano sobre el Oeste
68 | 515 +nf

3822 albergar *v* to lodge, harbor
- la capacidad para albergar cuatrocientos cuarenta vehículos
74 | 272 -o +nf

3823 complacer *v* to please, satisfy
- me complace creer que me brindó su paternal afecto
66 | 283 -nf

3824 pescador *nm/f* fisherman
- Cristo buscó a 12 pescadores que no sabían leer ni escribir
71 | 296

3825 diagnóstico *nm* diagnosis
- el diagnóstico de meningitis la dejó tranquila
67 | 407

3826 cuadra *nf* (city) block
- el auto estaba estacionado a dos cuadras de la casa
63 | 501 +f -nf

3827 remover *v* to remove
- comenzó a remover escombros buscando muertos
72 | 252 -o

3828 pecar *v* to sin
- un hombre que no pecaba por exceso ni por defecto
67 | 239 -nf

3829 rienda *nf* rein, restraint
- la caza le permita dar rienda suelta a cierta agresividad latente
71 | 257

3830 crueldad *nf* cruelty, harshness
- nos golpea con crueldad, sin consideración
74 | 197

3831 acontecer *v* to happen, come about
- dicha circunstancia puede acontecer bajo diversas situaciones
68 | 262

3832 ansia *nf* (el) anxiety, anguish
- imaginaba con ansia el día en que podría salir de su actual prisión
69 | 288

3833 cúpula *nf* cupola, dome
- la cúpula del capitolio de Washington es más alta
68 | 282

3834 desbordar *v* to overflow, spill over
- vi en sus ojos cuajarse una lágrima, que desbordó solitaria
73 | 239 -o

3835 llama *nf* flame, llama
- a veces salía de repente una llama que hasta nos quemaba el pelo
71 | 362 -o +f

3836 alegar *v* to plead, argue
- lo privaron del derecho de alegar ante los Tribunales
70 | 220

3837 vegetación *nf* vegetation
- la vegetación era vasta, inclusiva de las más diversas y exóticas plantas
63 | 382

3838 lema *nm* motto, slogan
- cuyo lema era: «A Dios rogando y con el mazo dando»
71 | 200

3839 encarar *v* to front, confront
- sin saber ya cómo encarar el asunto
67 | 296

3840 bote *nm* boat, container
- los tira en el bote para llevarlos al mar
  65 | 307

3841 solar *adj* solar
- los efectos de la luz solar sobre la densa niebla
  68 | 784 -o +nf

3842 inevitablemente *adv* inevitably
- lo que inevitablemente te arrastra a la envidia, ese pecado tan sutil
  72 | 213 +nf

3843 perfume *nm* perfume
- me llegó el olor del perfume
  66 | 536 +f

3844 central *nf* headquarters
- muy distantes de la central de la compañía que los comercializa
  69 | 526 -f +nf

3845 egoísta *adj* selfish
- fui egoísta, sólo pensé en los míos
  69 | 199

3846 pertenencia *nf* membership, property
- la pertenencia a un grupo, a un club, a un partido, a una empresa
  71 | 220

3847 exótico *adj* exotic
- lo compraste a un traficante de animales exóticos
  70 | 248

3848 tranquilizar *v* to calm down
- nada se va a tranquilizar, ni va a haber calma
  67 | 355 +f

3849 casita *nf* cottage
- su casa, una casita cómoda, pero modesta
  64 | 298 -nf

3850 emigrar *v* to emigrate
- finalmente decidimos emigrar a España
  72 | 245

3851 alianza *nf* alliance
- una alianza entre todas las fuerzas políticas
  71 | 1128 +nf

3852 físicamente *adv* physically
- el niño está físicamente relajado y dispuesto a escuchar
  73 | 176

3853 fascinante *adj* fascinating
- inesperado, imprevisible, intenso y fascinante
  70 | 211

3854 áspero *adj* rough, coarse, harsh
- pregonaba el gitano con áspero acento
  70 | 285 -o +f

3855 desechar *v* to discard
- no debemos desechar ninguna posibilidad
  73 | 162

3856 ratón *nm* mouse, rat
- teníamos aquí en Disneylandia el Ratón Mickey
  64 | 327

3857 hazaña *nf* deed, heroic feat
- la hija del héroe cuenta hazañas increíbles
  68 | 248

3858 dureza *nf* hardness, toughness
- sentí la dureza fría del metal temblar en mi frente
  70 | 262 -o

3859 sábana *nf* (bed) sheet
- mi cuerpo reposó exhausto sobre la sábana limpia
  65 | 546 +f -nf

3860 revisión *nf* checking revision
- para el mantenimiento y revisión de líneas transmisoras eléctricas
  72 | 304 +o -f

3861 retirada *nf* retreat, withdrawal
- el imperialismo europeo, ya en retirada
  67 | 302

3862 básicamente *adv* basically
- estaban pensando básicamente en la modernización del sector
  70 | 386 +o -f +nf

3863 aroma *nm* aroma
- percibió en el aire un aroma de tabaco habano
  66 | 501 -o +f

3864 optimismo *nm* optimism
- sus talentos múltiples justifican su optimismo
  70 | 248

3865 mate *nm* mate (beverage)
- siempre tomo el mate bebido
  61 | 567 +f -nf

3866 lujoso *adj* luxurious
- esta casa moderna, lujosa, y sin duda única en el mundo
  69 | 236

3867 evento *nm* event
- durante muchos años, el principal evento olímpico fue el pentatlón
  67 | 365

3868 físico *nm/f* physicist
- los físicos emplean también reactores de fisión o aceleradores
  72 | 521 +nf

3869 estrenar *v* to use for the first time, debut
- tenía un traje nuevo que iba a estrenar en un banquete
  66 | 267

3870 pasto *nm* grass, pasture
- ella caminaba descalza sobre el pasto e iba regando sus plantas
  65 | 314

3871 hostil *adj* hostile, unfriendly
- tuvieron una mirada hostil y un agrio murmullo de censura
  74 | 252 -o +nf

3872 gallo *nm* rooster
- el primer canto de los gallos al amanecer
  64 | 447 +f -nf

3873 tropical *adj* tropical
- las frutas tropicales incluyen plátanos, mangos, y dátiles
  69 | 310

3874 rendimiento *nm* yield, output, efficiency
- para mejorar el rendimiento de las plantaciones agrícolas
67 | 470 -f +nf

3875 lentitud *nf* slowness
- en forma de humo que se difunde con lentitud
73 | 239 -o

3876 aula *nf (el)* classroom
- pueden enseñarse en el aula lectura, escritura, aritmética
68 | 255

3877 incitar *v* to incite
- el desvelo irritante le incitó a beber un poco de alcohol
70 | 179

3878 franco *adj* open, frank, outspoken
- fue atento a sus deseos, generoso y franco, y de buen humor
70 | 244

3879 inédito *adj* unpublished
- la edición está inédita prácticamente toda
70 | 199

3880 uniforme *adj* uniform
- de edificios de igual altura y uniforme arquitectura
72 | 213

3881 himno *nm* hymn, anthem
- entona el Himno Nacional con voz de barítono
68 | 258

3882 sindicato *nm* trade union
- crearon partidos políticos y sindicatos de trabajadores
66 | 541 -f

3883 mariposa *nf* butterfly, wing nut
- la cría de bellas mariposas tropicales
66 | 417 +f

3884 propiciar *v* to favor, foster, aid
- estaríamos propiciando el divorcio, aunque creyéramos criticarlo
72 | 331 -f +nf

3885 fidelidad *nf* faithfulness, accuracy
- no recuerdo con fidelidad los detalles
70 | 282 -o

3886 retraso *nm* delay
- no llegan aunque dan las once; treinta minutos de retraso
67 | 272

3887 desplazamiento *nm* movement, removal
- el desplazamiento desde un punto a otro
70 | 363 +nf

3888 cuestionar *v* to question
- surgió un deseo de reexaminar y cuestionar las ideas
70 | 305 -f

3889 integrante *adj* integral, part of a group
- quería ser parte integrante de nuestro universo
70 | 347 -f +nf

3890 lingüístico *adj* linguistic
- el estudio del cambio lingüístico y la clasificación de las lenguas
65 | 599 +o -f +nf

3891 compatriota *nc* fellow countryman
- te gusta que tus compatriotas te apoyen como paraguayos
70 | 217

3892 mexicano *adj* Mexican
- recibe su nombre del actual estado mexicano de Veracruz
64 | 1503 -f +nf

3893 fundir *v* to melt, cast, smelt
- los chinos fueron los primeros en fundir el hierro
69 | 248 -o

3894 localidad *nf* town, locality
- una localidad situada al otro lado de la frontera
64 | 454 +nf

3895 reprimir *v* to repress
- no pudo reprimir sus ganas de llorar
72 | 229

3896 autorizado *adj* authorized
- el individuo está autorizado para ejercer los derechos políticos
74 | 204

3897 leal *adj* loyal, faithful
- quería vivir con un marido leal
70 | 237

3898 lobo *nm* wolf
- era un hereje, un anarquista, un lobo con piel de oveja
66 | 326 -o

3899 asamblea *nf* assembly
- esto será objeto de una discusión en la Asamblea Nacional
66 | 359 -f

3900 pañuelo *nm* handkerchief, shawl
- mientras se cubrían la boca con un pañuelo y comenzaban a llorar
63 | 493 +f -nf

3901 meditar *v* to meditate, ponder
- se retira a meditar a solas
68 | 277 +f

3902 temblor *nm* tremor, shudder, shiver
- el cuerpo se le llenaba de violentos temblores
64 | 411 +f

3903 gira *nf* tour
- el Presidente tuvo que posponer una gira muy importante a Estados Unidos
69 | 251

3904 manto *nm* cloak
- te cubrí con mi manto y me senté a llorar contigo
68 | 292 -o

3905 cubano *adj* Cuban
- yo aproveché para encender un buen tabaco cubano
60 | 884 +o -f

3906 asombro *nm* amazement, astonishment
- el grito se le murió en la garganta y quedó muda de asombro
65 | 456 -o +f

3907 gobernador *nm* governor
- hablan el presidente y el gobernador al público
65 | 955 +nf

3908 amplitud *nf* breadth, extent, range
- toda la profundidad y la amplitud adquiridas por su espíritu agudo
72 | 241

3909 carbón *nm* coal, charcoal
- parece la entrada a una mina de carbón o a una cueva de tesoros
70 | 478 -o

3910 campamento *nm* camp, camping
- pero instalar la carpa en un campamento nos resulta insoportable
63 | 378

3911 sangriento *adj* bloody
- de sofocar aquella imagen en el pantano sangriento de la guerra
71 | 219

3912 matemático *adj* mathematical
- un coprocesador matemático para acelerar ciertas operaciones
69 | 389 -f +nf

3913 portugués *adj* Portuguese
- para que Portugal abandonase Goa y el resto de la India portuguesa
64 | 385

3914 intensamente *adv* intensely
- me miraba intensamente a los ojos
72 | 229

3915 suavemente *adv* softly
- y lo mecía suavemente para que no fuese a llorar
66 | 398 -o +f

3916 excursión *nf* excursion
- participaban en una excursión para observar aves migratorias
69 | 239

3917 predicar *v* to preach
- voy a predicar el Evangelio
68 | 211

3918 encarnar *v* to embody
- las muchas formas del mal en que se encarna el demonio
70 | 203

3919 lamentablemente *adv* regrettably
- lamentablemente, mis dificultades idiomáticas me . . . limitan
68 | 267 +o

3920 tomate *nm* tomato
- las fuentes vegetales son brécol, tomates, espinacas, col, pimientos
67 | 212

3921 negociar *v* to negotiate, deal (with/in)
- me dedico a negociar nulidades matrimoniales
68 | 430 -f

3922 cinturón *nm* belt
- mi padre se quitó el cinturón y me pegó una zurra grande
69 | 277 -o

3923 estático *adj* static, motionless
- todo permanecía igual, estático
68 | 247

3924 antaño *adv* in days gone by, last year
- está pintada con el característico rojo colonial de antaño
70 | 228

3925 bulto *nm* bulk, shape
- examinaron cuanto bulto, ropa o jergón hallaron; no encontraron nada
66 | 376 +f -nf

3926 adónde *adv* to where?
- si pudiera hacer otro viaje ¿Adónde iría?
61 | 421 +f -nf

3927 vocabulario *nm* vocabulary
- usando las mejores palabras de un vocabulario no muy amplio
68 | 223

3928 especulación *nf* speculation, conjecture
- este año se caracterizó por la especulación y la incertidumbre
73 | 254 +nf

3929 manual *nm* manual, handbook
- el libro se titula «Manual de Instrucciones para Vivir»
69 | 203

3930 representativo *adj* representative
- fue reconocido como el único gobierno representativo de China
71 | 353 -f +nf

3931 honrar *v* to honor
- tenemos que honrar a nuestros héroes
72 | 163

3932 disparo *nm* shot, discharge
- suena un disparo. // ¡Cuidado, tiene una pistola!
65 | 311 -o

3933 desencadenar *v* to unleash, unchain
- se desencadenó una tormenta de truenos y relámpagos
72 | 366 -o +nf

3934 residuo *nm* residue, waste
- iba pisando residuos de cemento en los mosaicos
69 | 279 -o

3935 vanidad *nf* vanity, conceit
- no digo esto por vanidad o por jactancia
65 | 232

3936 ofender *v* to offend
- se ofendió como si la hubiera insultado
66 | 262 -nf

3937 renovación *nf* renewal, renovation
- significaron una cierta renovación de la moral de la Iglesia
69 | 321 -f +nf

3938 enfriar *v* to cool
- se le va a enfriar el café con leche
70 | 237

3939 furioso *adj* furious
- se irguió furioso, ofendido y cobarde
62 | 390 +f -nf

3940 estudioso *adj* studious
- él había sido el estudioso, el dedicado, el inteligente
71 | 266 -f +nf

3941 ilustrar *v* to illustrate
- dedicado a ilustrar sus sueños con grandes pinturas murales
71 | 267 +nf

3942 ratificar *v* to ratify
- el congreso no ratificó el tratado de límites
69 | 318

3943 peste *nf* plague, pestilence, pest
- incluso la terrible aparición de la peste negra, del siglo XIV
69 | 213 -o

3944 expedición *nf* expedition
- Perry dirigió una expedición naval en la bahía de Edo
67 | 360

3945 destrozar *v* to rip/break into pieces
- las ramas agudas que le destrozaban las ropas
66 | 224 -nf

3946 vasco *adj* Basque
- incorporando La Rioja y las tierras vascas occidentales
58 | 841 -f

3947 simular *v* to pretend, simulate
- siempre, leyendo, o simulando leer
69 | 248 -o

3948 complementario *adj* additional, complementary
- le concedí un tiempo extra, complementario
71 | 297 -f +nf

3949 mecánica *nf* mechanics, mechanism
- los fenómenos podían explicarse mediante la mecánica de Newton
67 | 433

3950 electricidad *nf* electricity
- sucesivamente, me cortaron el gas, la electricidad y el agua
69 | 363 -f +nf

3951 insólito *adj* unusual, uncommon
- pensaba que algo insólito estaba ocurriendo en ese lugar
66 | 355 -o

3952 temeroso *adj* fearful
- es un hombre temeroso, acobardado
67 | 280 +f

3953 extraordinariamente *adv* extraordinarily
- apareció una mujer extraordinariamente hermosa
68 | 206 -f

3954 ascensor *nm* elevator
- cerré la puerta y bajé en el ascensor
64 | 425

3955 bicicleta *nf* bicycle
- una chica pasa en bicicleta por la ruta
66 | 249

3956 consagrado *adj* dedicated, consecrated
- estudia mucho, es muy consagrado, es muy serio
71 | 185

3957 aporte *nm* contribution
- la humanidad espera nuestro aporte a la civilización y a la cultura
64 | 396

3958 despierto *adj* awake
- en la mañana escuchamos al bebé bien despierto
66 | 261 +f -nf

3959 beca *nf* scholarship, grant
- obtuvo una beca para acudir al seminario
68 | 297 +o

3960 consentir *v* to consent to, pamper
- no voy a consentir que un idiota arruine mis planes
67 | 224

3961 trigo *nm* wheat
- el pan: masa de trigo que, fermentado y cocido, le gusta comer
68 | 339

3962 paralizar *v* to paralyze
- dispuesto a paralizar impulsos, y reducir energías
71 | 181

3963 disipar *v* to dissipate, disperse
- unos meses después, se disipó toda duda sobre el futuro
71 | 214 -o

3964 incrementar *v* to increase
- en poco tiempo incrementó la producción de hielo
67 | 772 -f +nf

3965 plataforma *nf* platform, springboard
- el operador de cámara maneja la plataforma móvil que sujeta la cámara
68 | 355

3966 maestra *nf* teacher (f)
- ella era la maestra de kínder del pueblo
61 | 326 +o -nf

3967 clínica *nf* clinic
- las clínicas lejanas, los especialistas, las onerosas medicinas
65 | 338 +o -f

3968 heredero *nm* heir, heiress
- el único y universal legítimo heredero de su hermana fallecida
66 | 277

3969 embarazada *adj* pregnant
- quedó embarazada del único hijo verdaderamente deseado
65 | 207 -nf

3970 estadio *nm* stadium
- para edificar un monumental estadio de fútbol
69 | 370 -f +nf

3971 latinoamericano *adj* Latin American
- situación común a todo el cine latinoamericano y español
63 | 516 +o -f

Verbs – differences across registers

The following lists show the verbs that occur with a much higher frequency than would be expected in either the spoken, fiction, or non-fiction registers. In each case, the word is in the top 10 percent of words for that register, in terms of its relative frequency to the other two registers.

Spoken	Fiction	Non-fiction
Ser 8 to be	**sonreír** 2732 to smile	**reemplazar** 3199 to replace
estar 17 to be	**oler** 3037 to smell	**regir** 3223 to rule
tener 18 to have	**acostar** 3078 to put/go to bed	**culminar** 3277 to culminate
decir 28 to tell, say	**clavar** 3147 to nail	**subrayar** 3397 to highlight
ir 30 to go	**temblar** 3256 to shake	**asentar** 3495 to settle
ver 37 to see	**calmar** 3332 to calm	**oscilar** 3579 to oscillate
saber 46 to know (a fact)	**disimular** 3365 to pretend	**sobrepasar** 3621 to excel
querer 57 to want, love	**odiar** 3445 to hate	**clasificar** 3643 to sort
creer 91 to believe	**morder** 3589 to bite	**equivaler** 3676 to be equivalent
hablar 92 to talk	**amanecer** 3592 to dawn	**fomentar** 3677 to promote
venir 105 to come	**aguardar** 3599 to await	**contrastar** 3735 to contrast with
mirar 142 to look at	**deslizar** 3652 to slide	**albergar** 3823 to harbor
trabajar 183 to work	**estirar** 3653 to stretch	**propiciar** 3885 to foster
entender 203 to understand	**besar** 3697 to kiss	**desencadenar** 3934 to unleash
oír 263 to hear	**consolar** 3706 to console	**ilustrar** 3942 to illustrate
tocar 325 to touch	**interrogar** 3747 to interrogate	**incrementar** 3965 to increase
estudiar 328 to study	**revolver** 3753 to stir, mix	**dotar** 3999 to endow
gustar 353 to be pleasing to	**mojar** 3767 to dampen	**perdurar** 4086 to endure
valer 387 to be worth	**coser** 3800 to sew	**debilitar** 4113 to weaken
fijar 407 to fix, set	**almorzar** 3821 to have lunch	**igualar** 4115 to equate
dedicar 415 to dedicate	**tranquilizar** 3849 to calm down	**regular** 4132 to regulate
comprar 437 to buy	**meditar** 3902 to meditate	**argumentar** 4140 to argue
interesar 448 to interest	**reprochar** 3983 to reproach	**agravar** 4227 to aggravate
imaginar 486 to imagine	**alumbrar** 3986 to illuminate	**configurar** 4258 to configure
enseñar 524 to teach	**reventar** 4010 to burst	**prevalecer** 4266 to prevail

Comments

The words from the spoken register represent some of the most common verbs in Spanish. This is because verbs are in general more common in conversation, which tends to express feelings and opinions more than presenting information about objects and processes. The verbs from fiction texts tend to express concrete actions, whereas those in non-fiction tend to express relationships between more abstract concepts.

3972 tecnológico *adj* technological
- una nueva iniciativa en desarrollo tecnológico
69 | 564 -f +nf

3973 desfile *nm* parade, line, formation
- me gusta ver el desfile de los caballos desde el parque
69 | 268 -o

3974 buque *nm* ship, vessel, hull
- para detectar submarinos y buques enemigos
65 | 517 -o

3975 parentesco *nm* kinship
- de una relación de parentesco, de la paternidad o de la maternidad
68 | 189

3976 fallo *nm* mistake, blunder, fault
- para que todo salga bien, sin fallos
68 | 318 -f

3977 rebeldía *nf* rebelliousness, defiance
- hay una inmensa rebeldía contra todo lo que pueda ser autoridad
66 | 231

3978 desigual *adj* unequal, uneven, irregular
- pero el camino es desigual y escabroso
73 | 206 -o +nf

3979 corrección *nf* correction, amendment
- me había hablado con corrección, pero con firmeza
70 | 230

3980 chispa *nf* spark
- se le encendió una chispa en los ojos
68 | 219 +f

3981 virgen *nf* virgin
- quiero que mi hija se case virgen, con un traje blanco
66 | 235 +f -nf

3982 reprochar *v* to reproach
- J. me va a reprochar el haber sido un desgraciado
66 | 254 +f

3983 supervivencia *nf* survival
- para posibilitar la supervivencia de los animales que todavía están vivos
70 | 348 +nf

3984 caridad *nf* charity
- dan dinero al cura para obras de caridad a los pobres
67 | 232

3985 alumbrar *v* to light, illuminate
- llevaban velas para alumbrar el camino
70 | 217 +f

3986 comunión *nf* communion
- en la misa tomó primera comunión
68 | 209

3987 embajador *nm/f* ambassador
- es nuestro embajador en las Naciones Unidas
66 | 328

3988 tercio *nm* third
- el Oceano Pacífico abarca más de un tercio de la superficie de la Tierra
67 | 364 -f +nf

3989 iluminación *nf* illumination, lighting
- se van las luces y sólo queda la iluminación de velas
69 | 224

3990 censura *nf* censorship, criticism
- estableció la censura de los medios de comunicación
67 | 304

3991 disputa *nf* dispute, argument, quarrel
- refleja tensiones por la disputa de la candidatura presidencial
72 | 304 -o +nf

3992 esplendor *nm* splendor
- era un mundo refinado, de gran esplendor, con joyas y candelabros
67 | 266 -o

3993 inscribir *v* to register, record
- Moisés debió inscribir en sus tablas los diez mandamientos
69 | 234

3994 perjuicio *nm* damage, loss
- el perjuicio es irreparable para los escolares
68 | 270 -f +nf

3995 medalla *nf* medal, medallion
- andaba con medalla de plata en el pecho
60 | 352

3996 lealtad *nf* loyalty, faithfulness
- un sentido de gratitud y lealtad a la autoridad pontificia
69 | 243

3997 divorcio *nm* divorce
- el matrimonio y el divorcio son consideraciones graves
65 | 243 +o

3998 dotar *v* to endow, bestow
- su cobertura lo dotaba de un halo prodigioso
72 | 221 +nf

3999 enfoque *nm* focus, approach
- es un enfoque muy científico sobre la historia
68 | 473 +o -f +nf

4000 civilizado *adj* civilized
- hay otro medio más civilizado de resolver este conflicto
68 | 222

4001 firmeza *nf* firmness
- la firmeza de su carácter; su dureza a la hora de dejarla
71 | 250 -o

4002 indudable *adj* unquestionable
- alcanzó un indudable desarrollo económico y social
70 | 200

4003 colina *nf* hill, slope
- el jeep trepaba la colina sin dificultad
69 | 298 -o

4004 parcela *nf* piece of property
- les dejaba trabajar una parcela de tierra buena
66 | 247

4005 jaula *nf* cage, crate, playpen
- hoy revolotea en la jaula vacía de la jirafa
65 | 304 +f -nf

4006 ajuste *nm* adjustment, settlement
- se requiere un drástico programa de ajuste fiscal
68 | 582 -f +nf

4007 lateral *adj* side, lateral
- con fachada lateral siguiendo la dirección de la calle
64 | 312

4008 entierro *nm* burial
- voy a un entierro, que se ha muerto el abuelo
67 | 285 +f

4009 reventar *v* to burst, puncture
- estuvo a punto de reventarse de presiones interiores
63 | 346 +f -nf

4010 servidor *nm/f* servant
- él no era más que servidor de esos poderosos
68 | 278 -nf

4011 superioridad *nf* superiority
- me estiman mucho por mi superioridad intelectual y mi elevado nivel mental
71 | 286 -o +nf

4012 turismo *nm* tourism
- Mallorca, una de las mecas del turismo europeo
67 | 336 +o -f

4013 barbaridad *nf* atrocity
- estás todo sangrado y rotoso; ¡qué barbaridad!
62 | 263 +o -nf

4014 rollo *nm* roll, coil
- A. se metió un rollo de páginas en los bolsillos
64 | 267

4015 arbitrario *adj* arbitrary
- el dictador lleva un poder arbitrario y brutal
72 | 207 +nf

4016 triángulo *nm* triangle
- un triángulo mágico arte-vida-verdad
66 | 210

4017 aislamiento *nm* isolation
- lucharon por romper el aislamiento de Cuba
70 | 249 +nf

4018 alivio *nm* relief, unburdening
- era un alivio verse y encontrarlo ahí tan sereno
67 | 371 -o +f

4019 entrenamiento *nm* training
- un intenso entrenamiento para alcanzar el punto deseado
68 | 314 -f

4020 truco *nm* trick, ruse
- un milagro sólo es un truco de magia
63 | 253

4021 respetable *adj* respectable
- lo tratan como un hombre respetable y maduro
69 | 177

4022 disparate *nm* nonsense, blunder
- quiere entrarse de monja // ¿De monja? ¡Qué disparate!
66 | 219 -nf

4023 cocinero *nm/f* cook
- un cocinero debe probar todos los sabores
66 | 246 +f -nf

4024 aburrir *v* to bore, tire
- el único problema es aburrirse de esperar que vengan
64 | 213 +f -nf

4025 diminuto *adj* diminutive, tiny, minute
- una anciana regaba concienzudamente su diminuto jardín
64 | 396 -o +f

4026 celeste *adj* heavenly, sky-blue
- la constelación celeste, donde aparece la estrella
65 | 443 -o +f

4027 fotógrafo *nm/f* photographer
- el fotógrafo enfocaba su cámara desde distintos ángulos
64 | 294

4028 imposición *nf* imposition
- la unción de los enfermos por la imposición de manos
71 | 191

4029 diluir *v* to dilute, weaken
- la tinta se diluye en el agua
69 | 200

4030 convincente *adj* convincing
- el hombre tenía un acento tan convincente
70 | 180

4031 consuelo *nm* comfort, consolation
- le murmuraba que Dios tiene un consuelo para cada dolor
65 | 320 +f

4032 periodístico *adj* journalistic
- me contaba detalles de la investigación periodística
67 | 297 -f

4033 cariñoso *adj* affectionate
- como una gata cariñosa que pide una caricia
64 | 264 +f -nf

4034 transmisión *nf* broadcast, transmission
- constituye otro medio de transmisión de señales a grandes distancias
68 | 413 -f +nf

4035 titular *v* to title, call
- iba a titular mi cuento «El salto cualitativo»
68 | 198

4036 sendero *nm* (foot) path
- un sendero de piedra conduce a la residencia
65 | 338 -o +f

4037 frecuentar *v* to frequent, visit
- comienza a frecuentar la bohemia parisina
68 | 175

4038 desacuerdo *nm* disagreement
- se declaró ayer en desacuerdo con la posición expresada
71 | 169

4039 academia *nf* academy
- estudiamos en la academia
65 | 257 +o

4040 acertado *adj* correct, accurate
- en ambas decisiones, estuvo acertado
71 | 155

4041 catedral *nf* cathedral
- te corrés a la Catedral y la dejás delante del altar
64 | 431

4042 mediocre *adj* mediocre
- no eres un ser mediocre, eres una gran artista
66 | 193

4043 vanguardia *nf* vanguard, forefront
- hablé de la vanguardia con los artistas jóvenes
65 | 300

4044 desafiar *v* to defy, stand up to
- la osadía de desafiar ante testigos la autoridad
69 | 221 -o

4045 agitado *adj* agitated, irritated
- inestable, caprichoso, agitado por celos y recelos
67 | 244

4046 precario *adj* precarious
- sonríe plácidamente ante lo precario de su situación
71 | 194

4047 sanitario *adj* health, sanitary, clean
- libre de impurezas de acuerdo con el certificado sanitario
63 | 581 +o -f

4048 comprensible *adj* understandable
- que sea clara, comprensible, fácil, significativa
70 | 162

4049 cuidadoso *adj* careful, cautious
- bien peinado y afeitado; muy cuidadoso de su persona
72 | 214

4050 despojar *v* to deprive, rob
- para despojar al cadáver de sus joyas
69 | 222 -o

4051 embarazo *nm* pregnancy
- el número nueve alude a los nueve meses de embarazo de María
63 | 293

4052 imposibilidad *nf* impossibility
- reconocieron la imposibilidad de ponerse de acuerdo
69 | 232

4053 irracional *adj* irrational
- la delicia irracional de la tentación y el riesgo de la caída
71 | 197 -o

4054 reinar *v* to reign, prevail
- en Marulanda reinaba la anarquía y el desenfreno
70 | 230 -o

4055 hundido *adj* buried, sunken
- con el rostro hundido entre las manos
65 | 286 +f -nf

4056 reportaje *nm* news report
- era el reportaje de una conocida periodista
63 | 212 +o

4057 tambor *nm* drum
- para la percusión se utilizaban tambores pequeños y las campanillas
65 | 370 -o +f

4058 fundación *nf* foundation
- propuso la inmediata fundación de otro club con el mismo nombre
69 | 295 -f +nf

4059 transparencia *nf* transparency, slide
- disminuye la radiación solar y la transparencia del aire
70 | 288

4060 elegancia *nf* elegance, style
- aquella joven de belleza y de elegancia rara
68 | 259 -o

4061 criminal *nc* criminal
- ¿le parece justo tratarlo como a un criminal común?
70 | 168

4062 elogio *nm* praise, eulogy, compliment
- por su genio en el arte era digna de elogio
67 | 197

4063 manta *nf* blanket
- les enrollaba la manta o el poncho alrededor del cuello
67 | 323 -o +f

4064 dinámico *adj* dynamic
- un mundo efervescente, dinámico, rico en posibilidades
69 | 333 -f +nf

4065 hervir *v* to boil
- el agua hierve sin fuego
66 | 289 -o +f

4066 sereno *adj* serene, calm
- tras la tormenta, ya está muy sereno
66 | 242 +f

4067 retirado *adj* retired, remote, secluded
- jefes militares retirados y algunos en servicio activo
69 | 159

4068 alerta *nf* alert
- los programas de prevención y alerta funcionaron
69 | 197

4069 sinceridad *nf* sincerity
- quizás usted dude de la sinceridad de mis deseos
66 | 190

4070 cátedra *nf* academic chair
- trabajando en la cátedra de Teoría Literaria en la universidad
68 | 225 -f

4071 refinado *adj* refined
- me pareció el lugar más refinado y elegante del mundo
68 | 254 -o

4072 repertorio *nm* repertoire, list, index
- la abuela, dueña de un rico repertorio de leyendas y de mitos
62 | 274

4073 plancha *nf* (electric) iron, plate, sheet
- una manchita que después, con la plancha caliente, ensucia toda la ropa
64 | 251

4074 terraza *nf* terrace, balcony
- estaba en esa terraza suspendida que miraba al mar
64 | 369 +f

4075 gala *nf* gala (performance/dinner)
- será una gala a beneficio de la institución
67 | 216

4076 era *nf* era, age
- se vivía una era de paz y de progreso
68 | 340 +nf

4077 arranque *nm* start, outburst, kick-start
- la batería, el alternador, el motor de arranque, el sistema de luces
72 | 153

4078 patada *nf* kick, punt
- le da una patada en el trasero
61 | 324 +f -nf

4079 disculpar *v* to excuse
- no puedo disculpar una falta tan grande
63 | 280 +f -nf

4080 lapso *nm* lapse
- desde 1966, con un lapso intermedio de pocos años
66 | 306

4081 sudor *nm* sweat, perspiration
- gruesas gotas de sudor corren por su cuerpo
61 | 619 -o +f -nf

4082 apetito *nm* appetite
- era un hombre de mucho comer, de mucho apetito
64 | 269

4083 íntimamente *adv* intimately
- estos dos aspectos están íntimamente vinculados en nuestra ley
70 | 162

4084 indicación *nf* indication
- ésta fue la primera indicación del tamaño de nuestra galaxia
67 | 232

4085 perdurar *v* to last, live on, endure
- perduró durante muchos siglos
71 | 214 +nf

4086 aliado *nm* ally
- cuando los aliados desembarcaron en Normandía en junio de 1944
65 | 450 +nf

4087 presidencia *nf* presidency
- en 1958, Jruschov obtuvo la presidencia del gobierno
65 | 535 -f

4088 maldito *adj* damned, wretched
- el calor de este maldito país es sin igual
63 | 448 -o +f

4089 consejero *nm/f* advisor, counselor
- agradezco al consejero por su información útil
67 | 308

4090 inundar *v* to flood, inundate
- una melodía alegre inunda la sala
69 | 254 -o +f

4091 consigna *nf* watchword, motto, slogan
- la consigna mosquetera: «Todos para uno, uno para todos»
68 | 239

4092 cortesía *nf* courtesy
- él había tenido la cortesía de venir a despedirse muy temprano
67 | 233

4093 inmóvil *adj* immovable, motionless
- el está ahí, quieto, inmóvil
66 | 589 -o +f

4094 atributo *nm* attribute, quality
- la razón, la intuición, y la fantasía son atributos del cerebro
66 | 222

4095 furia *nf* fury, rage
- ¡no estás obligado a nada!, dijo con furia inexplicable
62 | 432 -o +f

4096 grosero *adj* crude, rude, crass
- C. era el ejemplar del hombre grosero e irrespetuoso
67 | 191 -nf

4097 catalán *adj* Catalan
- tenían un marcado acento catalán al hablar
60 | 467

4098 estatura *nf* stature, height
- mujer, blanca, 34 años, 1,70 de estatura, 59 kilogramos
64 | 280 -o +f

4099 vejez *nf* old age
- quería vivir hasta la vejez con un marido leal
67 | 281 +f

4100 terremoto *nm* earthquake
- todo vibra porque un terremoto mueve ese sitio de la tierra
65 | 312

4101 articular *v* to articulate
- tan asombrado como yo, no supo articular palabra
66 | 216

4102 tira *nf* strip, strap
- (Toma las tijeras) Con una tira de papel pegada atrás (Corta la tira)
65 | 189

4103 emisor *nm* transmitter, emitter
- lo detectamos por el sonido del emisor de radio que le ponemos
64 | 427 +nf

4104 relevante *adj* relevant, significant
- hay otro hecho aun más significativo, relevante y aún no afrontado
68 | 392 -f +nf

4105 integridad *nf* integrity
- siempre hemos admirado mucho tu integridad y tu valentía
72 | 204

Adverbs – differences across registers

The following lists show the adverbs that occur with a much higher frequency than would be expected in either the spoken, fiction, or non-fiction registers. In each case, the word is in the top 10 percent of adverbs for that register, in terms of its relative frequency to the other two registers.

Spoken

no 10 no

ya 36 already, still

muy 42 very

sí 70 yes

bien 73 well

entonces 76 so, then

ahora 85 now

cómo 126 how?

aquí 129 here

además 159 also, as well

hoy 164 today

ahí 189 there

todavía 211 still, yet

incluso 294 including

solamente 336 only

bueno 337 well…

realmente 416 really

dónde 421 where?

claro 482 of course

precisamente 580 precisely

simplemente 591 simply

totalmente 662 totally

perfectamente 850 perfectly

peor 866 worse

exactamente 977 exactly

Fiction

suavemente 3916 softly

adónde 3927 to where?

adonde 4276 to where

bruscamente 4407 sharply

largamente 4889 for a long time

mentalmente 4933 mentally

Non-fiction

asimismo 3512 moreover

simultáneamente 3628 simultaneously

fuertemente 3760 strongly

inevitablemente 3843 inevitably

básicamente 3863 basically

independientemente 4136 independently

ampliamente 4264 widely

radicalmente 4465 radically

específicamente 4493 specifically

extremadamente 4495 extremely

oficialmente 4546 officially

esencialmente 4608 essentially

tradicionalmente 4658 traditionally

económicamente 4779 economically

parcialmente 4895 partially

inicialmente 4921 initially

4106 autorización *nf* authorization
- se penaliza la reproducción sin la autorización de la mujer
- 73 | 221 -f

4107 audaz *adj* audacious, bold
- posee aire entre audaz y adolescente
- 69 | 217 -o

4108 seminario *nm* seminar, seminary
- hicieron unos cursos aquí, en el seminario de estudios teológicos
- 64 | 235 +o

4109 marea *nf* wave, tide, ebb
- se me sube la sangre en una marea de ira
- 65 | 243

4110 resentimiento *nm* resentment
- albergaba un resentimiento por la pérdida de grandes áreas geográficas
- 66 | 201

4111 delincuente *nc* delinquent
- hay delincuentes que se escudan en la institución policial
- 63 | 359

4112 debilitar *v* to weaken, debilitate
- contribuyen a debilitar el sistema inmunológico
- 72 | 225 -o +nf

4113 fingir *v* to feign, pretend
- era capaz de engañar y fingir inocencia
- 61 | 507 -o +f

4114 igualar *v* to equate, equalize
- donde se igualan o equivalen las texturas
- 71 | 176 +nf

4115 disfrazado *adj* disguised
- parecía disfrazado, muy diferente a las fotos
- 67 | 202

4116 trepar *v* to climb
- es necesario trepar tres o cuatro metros de empinada escalera
- 63 | 362 -o +f

4117 mutuamente *adv* mutually, each other
- nos recordaremos mutuamente con cariño
- 72 | 169

4118 correctamente *adv* correctly
- uno puede hablar el español bien, correctamente, sin tener que cecear
68 | 192

4119 ágil *adj* agile
- con un ágil movimiento, R. esquiva una estocada
67 | 214 -o

4120 atrasado *adj* behind, slow
- el alumno sale más atrasado que cuando entró
67 | 170 -nf

4121 esqueleto *nm* skeleton, framework
- detrás del esqueleto de un edificio en construcción
63 | 301 -o

4122 indignación *nf* indignation
- el rechazo y la enorme indignación que produjeron sus asesinatos
68 | 229 -o

4123 agradecido *adj* grateful, thankful
- estaba muy agradecido de tener trabajo
67 | 205 +f -nf

4124 adicional *adj* additional
- además de esto hay un ingrediente adicional
69 | 430 -f +nf

4125 escultura *nf* sculpture, carving
- posando al lado de un escultura de Cupido apuntando con su arco
63 | 663

4126 condicionado *adj* conditioned
- Pávlov, autor de la teoría del reflejo condicionado
68 | 255 -f +nf

4127 infinidad *nf* infinity, countless
- Buda ha tomado esta apariencia humana infinidad de veces
71 | 143

4128 pilar *nm* pillar, column
- la observaba detrás de un pilar de madera del corredor
68 | 235

4129 óptimo *adj* optimum
- el momento óptimo para animar a un público
68 | 222 -f

4130 súbito *adj* sudden
- un relámpago súbito ilumina la escena
67 | 416 -o +f

4131 regular *v* to regulate, adjust
- necesita someterse a las leyes que regulan la vida espontánea
70 | 372 -f +nf

4132 vosotros *pron* you (subj-pl/+fam)
- pero vosotros, sois más inteligentes
58 | 461 -nf

4133 rematar *v* to finish off, finish up
- era el momento de rematar el final
67 | 217 -o +f

4134 incomprensible *adj* incomprehensible
- que se convirtiera en un juego irracional, incomprensible
67 | 209 -o +f

4135 independientemente *adv* independently
- cada uno había aprendido a vivir independientemente
69 | 336 +o -f +nf

4136 percepción *nf* perception
- allí M. tuvo una nueva percepción de la calidad de vida
66 | 422 -f +nf

4137 minoría *nf* minority
- la Unión de Sudáfrica, dominada por una minoría blanca
67 | 358 +o -f +nf

4138 deterioro *nm* deterioration, damage
- ha provocado el deterioro de los frescos que decoran las tumbas
67 | 289 +nf

4139 argumentar *v* to argue, deduce
- en los foros de discusión pueden argumentar las propias opiniones
70 | 264 -o +nf

4140 guapo *adj* handsome, beautiful
- una muchacha muy bonita . . . muy guapa por cierto
59 | 337 -nf

4141 sanción *nf* sanction, approval, penalty
- los mecanismos punitivos (la aplicación de las sanciones)
66 | 389 -f

4142 poblar *v* to populate, inhabit
- determinaron a poblar los territorios vírgenes
68 | 233 -o

4143 contradecir *v* to contradict, be inconsistent
- ¿no contradice eso la lógica simple?
70 | 168

4144 inmerso *adj* engrossed, immersed
- caminaba ensimismado, absorto, inmerso en su mundo interior
69 | 216 +nf

4145 manipular *v* to manipulate, handle
- se puso a manipular la cerradura de la puerta
68 | 227

4146 maleta *nf* suitcase, case
- entra en ese momento con una maleta llena de ropa
60 | 309 +o -nf

4147 faena *nf* task, job, performance
- la faena era más sencilla: limpiar los interiores de la casa
63 | 258

4148 regar *v* to water, irrigate
- de usar la manguera para regar el césped
64 | 219 -nf

4149 evocar *v* to evoke, recall
- su rostro evoca alguna imagen
67 | 383 -o +f

4150 serpiente *nf* snake
- otros reptiles eran las serpientes y los lagartos
64 | 401 -o +f

4151 proveniente *adj* coming from
- la entrada de plata en Europa proveniente del Nuevo Mundo
69 | 313 -o +nf

4152 primordial *adj* fundamental, primary
• cumplen la misión primordial para la que nacieron
69 | 217 -f +nf

4153 agitación *nf* agitation, excitement
• su agitación nerviosa iba en aumento
67 | 219 -o

4154 prosperar *v* to prosper, thrive
• el comerciante prosperó y amasó una fortuna
71 | 183

4155 ganancia *nf* gain, profit
• la cuenta de pérdidas y ganancias muestra el resultado de la actividad
66 | 463

4156 genético *adj* genetic
• señalaba un marcador genético para la enfermedad de Huntington
61 | 875 -f +nf

4157 pino *nm* pine (tree)
• los árboles más frecuentes son el alerce, el pino, y el abeto
63 | 284

4158 arrasar *v* to raze, ravage
• se cortó, se derribó, se arrasó con todo
70 | 152

4159 rebajar *v* to discount
• el reloj se le había rebajado hasta quince pesos
70 | 162

4160 entrevistar *v* to interview
• pude entrevistar para ABC a Segovia
66 | 200 +o

4161 infeliz *adj* unhappy, unfortunate
• era una ciudad infeliz, con tremendos conflictos políticos
62 | 309 +f -nf

4162 compacto *adj* compact, dense
• la obra incluye un vídeo y un disco compacto
67 | 207

4163 llanto *nm* crying, weeping
• oyeron el llanto de un bebé
61 | 584 +f -nf

4164 ida *nf* departure, first half of a trip
• quitando el viaje, ¿un día de ida y otro de vuelta, no?
66 | 173

4165 criminal *adj* criminal
• adoptó un código criminal especial para controlar la situación
67 | 206

4166 coherente *adj* coherent, connected
• no se le presentaba todavía como sucesión coherente y ordenada
68 | 268 +nf

4167 falla *nf* flaw, failure
• a pesar de sus fallas, a pesar de las limitaciones
66 | 275 +o -f

4168 contribución *nf* contribution
• había tenido una contribución importante a la ciencia médica
68 | 327 -f +nf

4169 burla *nf* mockery, joke, trick
• la hacemos objeto de una burla injuriosa
63 | 308 -o +f

4170 seguidor *nm* follower, supporter, fan
• Mencio, uno de los principales seguidores de Confucio
66 | 479 -f +nf

4171 estratégico *adj* strategic
• yo aguardaba, como dije, en mi posición estratégica
69 | 375 +nf

4172 perla *nf* pearl
• la emperatriz luce perlas, rubíes y esmeraldas
64 | 249

4173 ético *adj* ethical
• discutieron muy poco sobre el aspecto ético de la cuestión
65 | 421 -f +nf

4174 integración *nf* integration
• la aeronáutica acelera el ciclo de integración global
66 | 530 +o -f +nf

4175 enterado *adj* aware of
• no sé; tú, como músico, estás más enterado de esto
66 | 205 +o +f -nf

4176 siesta *nf* siesta, afternoon nap
• dormía una siesta hasta las cuatro
62 | 522 -o +f -nf

4177 replicar *v* to reply
• ¡no tenemos estatutos! - le replicó don José
66 | 406 -o +f

4178 incipiente *adj* incipient, beginning
• se está desarrollando una incipiente infraestructura turística
71 | 160

4179 adornar *v* to adorn, to decorate
• unas rosas rojas adornan la mesa
69 | 219 -o +f

4180 alternativo *adj* alternating, alternative
• unos períodos alternativos de tensión y distensión
69 | 359 -f +nf

4181 expresivo *adj* expressive
• su rostro expresivo reflejaba una tristeza infinita
67 | 282

4182 bigote *nm* mustache
• aquel bien cuidado bigote que se desparramaba sobre sus labios
62 | 467 -o +f

4183 concurrir *v* to coincide, concur, meet
• en las visicitudes que en estos momentos concurren en mi persona
64 | 255

4184 niñez *nf* childhood, infancy
• ¿cómo era la vida durante tu niñez? // ¡Muy linda!
62 | 281 -nf

4185 leña *nf* firewood
- me propongo cortar mucha leña y quemar mucho carbón
65 | 229 -o +f

4186 atardecer *nm* evening, dusk
- la luz tenue, enrojecida, de un atardecer de pueblo
63 | 421 -o +f

4187 restaurar *v* to restore, reinstate
- intentaban restaurar a Bonaparte en el trono
68 | 216

4188 retrasar *v* to delay, fall behind
- me han retrasado dos semanas sobre la fecha de cobro
66 | 196

4189 estatal *adj* state, government-owned
- se privatizó la empresa estatal de teléfonos
64 | 917 +o -f +nf

4190 interrogante *nc* question, interrogator
- el gran interrogante ahora es qué va a pasar en esa investigación
68 | 205

4191 palpar *v* to feel, touch, fondle
- para palpar la flacidez de mi carne
64 | 289 +f -nf

4192 perpetuo *adj* continual, perpetual
- el perpetuo tictac del reloj de péndulo
66 | 282 -o

4193 lente *nmf* lens, [pl] glasses
- le instaló un lente óptica para conseguir una imagen más clara
63 | 280

4194 compás *nm* rhythm, time, compass
- los ruidos de la casa y allá afuera, el compás de la lluvia
64 | 375 -o +f

4195 estéril *adj* sterile, barren
- la mujer es frígida y estéril o indiferente
67 | 207 -o

4196 llanura *nf* plain, prairie, plainness
- la llanura china está rodeada de montañas por el norte y el oeste
61 | 436 -o +f

4197 collar *nm* collar, necklace
- se compra un collar que se echa al cuello
65 | 269 +f

4198 veneno *nm* poison, venom
- el veneno de la cobra asiática es muy tóxico
62 | 268

4199 mármol *nm* marble
- la escultura romana, especialmente los sarcófagos de mármol
66 | 383 -o +f

4200 biografía *nf* biography
- me atreví a escribir esta biografía del héroe
65 | 250

4201 latente *adj* latent
- andaba con un deseo de venganza latente
70 | 158

4202 rebelión *nf* rebellion
- la rebelión de Espartaco contra la esclavitud de los romanos
66 | 302 -o

4203 hígado *nm* liver
- en una cirrosis hepática o en un cáncer de hígado
62 | 283

4204 ladrón *nm* thief
- el ladrón fue conducido a la inspección de policía
60 | 350 +f -nf

4205 aparentar *v* to give the appearance
- vestido de hombre para aparentar serlo
66 | 172

4206 holandés *adj* Dutch
- conservador jefe de pintura flamenca y holandesa
66 | 376 +nf

4207 tablero *nm* board, panel
- ese inmenso tablero de ajedrez
64 | 210

4208 enterrado *adj* buried
- se halla enterrado por otros sedimentos acumulados
67 | 194 +f

4209 imitación *nf* imitation
- para hacer este tipo de libros, a imitación de Estados Unidos
69 | 219

4210 adelanto *nm* advance, progress
- la consideran un gran adelanto en la exploración del espacio
66 | 186

4211 celoso *adj* jealous
- se volvió muy celoso de su suerte
63 | 232 -nf

4212 oscurecer *v* to get dark
- temprano oscureció porque estaba nublado
67 | 223 -o +f

4213 constitucional *adj* constitutional
- la separación constitucional entre Iglesia y Estado
62 | 1032 +o -f +nf

4214 intervalo *nm* interval, gap
- se repiten entre breves intervalos de silencio
63 | 273

4215 trago *nm* swig, drink
- se bebió de un solo trago toda la cerveza
62 | 407 +f -nf

4216 fracción *nf* fraction
- en la primera fracción de segundo después del Big Bang
65 | 317

4217 convento *nm* convent, monastery
- se fueron al convento a buscar unas monjitas
60 | 273 -nf

4218 arroyo *nm* brook, stream, gutter
- cerca de un arroyo que pasa entre los árboles
62 | 494 -o +f

New words since the 1800s

The following lists show the most common nouns, verbs, adjectives, and adverbs that occur in the 1900s, but which do not occur in the 1800s portion of the Corpus del Español (www.corpusdelespanol.org).

Nouns

televisión 1078 television

sector 1096 sector

dólar 1878 dollar

foto 2054 photo

impacto 2390 impact

líder 2427 leader

fútbol 2513 soccer

aeropuerto 2993 airport

enfrentamiento 3212 confrontation

televisor 3250 television set

exilio 3359 exile

motivación 3416 motivation

sugerencia 3784 suggestion

enfoque 3999 focus

emisor 4103 transmitter

computadora 4253 computer

encuesta 4281 survey

grabación 4476 recording

autopista 4523 freeway, motorway

micrófono 4834 microphone

ganador 4855 winner

cabina 4882 cockpit

pionero 4980 pioneer

discriminación 5099 discrimination

interferencia 5266 interference

vivencia 5423 (life) experience

campeonato 5443 championship

culminación 5480 culmination

gol 5507 goal (sports)

maquillaje 5541 makeup

Verbs

liberar 1363 to liberate

desplazar 1771 to move, shift

centrar 2810 to center, focus

detectar 2826 to detect

presionar 2896 to pressure

frenar 2952 to brake

conectar 3084 to connect

emerger 3145 to emerge

programar 3162 to program, plan

culminar 3276 to culminate

intercambiar 3704 to exchange

incrementar 3964 to increase

entrevistar 4160 to interview

configurar 4257 configure

intuir 4368 to sense

expandir 4495 to expand

alertar 4503 to alert, warn

joder 4535 to f**k

financiar 4615 to finance

entrenar 4670 to train

impartir 4736 to impart

percatar 4826 to be beware

irrumpir 4994 to burst in

antojar 5100 to crave, take a fancy to

aflorar 5260 to crop out

postular 5774 to postulate

involucrar 5877 to involve

interferir 5917 to interfere

desproveer 6026 to deprive

gestar 6036 to breed

Adjectives

similar 1325 similar

básico 2295 basic

espectacular 2845 spectacular

deportivo 2862 sports

electrónico 3149 electronic

laboral 3268 labor

creativo 3551 creative

global 3760 global

masivo 3778 mass(ive)

latinoamericano 3971 Latin American

inmerso 4144 engrossed

genético 4156 genetic

estatal 4189 state

publicitario 4297 advertising

comunitario 4416 community

espacial 4424 space

soviético 4438 Soviet

sofisticado 4546 sophisticated

institucional 4595 institutional

irreversible 4847 irreversible

carente 4907 lacking

estructural 5018 structural

rentable 5048 profitable

ambiental 5060 environmental

nuclear 5075 nuclear

apasionante 5145 thrilling

conflictivo 5324 conflicting

obsesivo 5332 obsessive

operativo 5482 operative

ecológico 5498 ecological

Adverbs

obviamente 3811 obviously

básicamente 3862 basically

supuestamente 4262 supposedly

inicialmente 4920 initially

internacionalmente 9341 internationally

culturalmente 9811 culturally

mayoritariamente 9955 generally

esporádicamente 9969 sporadically

nítidamente 9976 neatly

sexualmente 10947 sexually

presuntamente 11772 presumedly

biológicamente 11863 biologically

4219 circular *adj* circular
- un espacio circular con un techo que es como una rueda
67 | 270 -o

4220 enlace *nm* link, connection, bond
- C. y J. contrajeron enlace matrimonial
66 | 231

4221 torcer *v* to twist, bend, distort
- le torció el brazo y logró que soltara la pistola
65 | 252 +f

4222 derramar *v* to shed, pour out
- no iba a derramar su sangre por su patria
66 | 303 -o +f

4223 diccionario *nm* dictionary
- en el diccionario encontré una extraña palabra
63 | 216

4224 reflejado *adj* reflected
- se manifiesta en lo finito y está reflejado en la encarnación
66 | 193 -o

4225 afueras *nf* outskirts, suburbs
- hasta las colinas que rodean las afueras de la ciudad
67 | 170

4226 agravar *v* to aggravate
- el dolor de la derrota agravó todos los males físicos
71 | 207 +nf

4227 ceja *nf* eyebrow, brow
- el pelo sin peinarse, y cejas pobladas bajo una frente estrecha
61 | 391 +f -nf

4228 detallado *adj* detailed, thorough
- es un informe bien preciso y detallado
71 | 234 +nf

4229 interponer *v* to interpose, intervene
- se interpuso con ardor entre la G. y los mozos
70 | 181

4230 topar *v* to run into, bump into
- se topó con M. en la sala de su casa
64 | 222 -o +f

4231 constitución *nf* constitution
- los derechos que la Constitución establece para nuestros ciudadanos
63 | 451 -f +nf

4232 enlazar *v* to link, connect
- enlaza mis piernas entre las suyas y somos un solo cuerpo
68 | 158

4233 clasificación *nf* classification
- ordenadas según el sistema de clasificación norteamericano
65 | 472 -f +nf

4234 atrapado *adj* trapped
- el temor de que un trabajador en una mina esté atrapado
66 | 252 -o

4235 lío *nm* mess, problem, bad situation
- ¡ay!, otra cosa, el carné de conducir es un lío . . . ¡Uy!, ¡qué problema!
61 | 331 +f -nf

4236 sede *nf* headquarters, seat
- cinco asociaciones, dos con sede en Madrid
64 | 486 -f +nf

4237 colar *v* to slip in [se]
- para colarse dentro del cuarto por la ventana abierta
62 | 244 +f -nf

4238 altamente *adv* highly
- le encargará de dirigir la limpieza del combustible altamente radiactivo
66 | 255

4239 litro *nm* liter
- exigía litro exacto para las medidas líquidas
63 | 259

4240 bandeja *nf* tray
- entra A. con una bandeja llena de queso
63 | 285 -o +f

4241 aproximación *nf* approximation
- lo artificial es un camino para una aproximación a lo natural
67 | 285 +nf

4242 liviano *adj* light, frivolous
- era liviana, grácil, firme y elástica como potrilla mora
65 | 257 +f -nf

4243 entusiasmado *adj* enthused, excited
- ¡compañero Miguelí! - exclamó, entusiasmado
64 | 173 +f -nf

4244 trapo *nm* rag, cloth
- soy peor que un trapo de cocina, peor que los algodones sucios
63 | 405 -o +f -nf

4245 conocedor *nm* expert, judge, connoisseur
- un hombre muy lector, gran conocedor de los grandes autores
67 | 150

4246 encaminar *v* to head for, guide
- se levantó y se encaminó al encuentro de la puerta
67 | 238 -o

4247 altar *nm* altar
- el sitio que en una basílica se reserva para el altar mayor
62 | 404 -o +f

4248 acierto *nm* good aim, guess, hit
- todavía era capaz de analizar con acierto
66 | 228

4249 piloto *nm/f* pilot, driver
- él quería ser piloto de Líneas Aéreas Paraguayas
60 | 377

4250 susceptible *adj* susceptible
- sumamente susceptible a las influencias del entorno musical
68 | 188

4251 inolvidable *adj* unforgettable
- esa inolvidable sensación de sus besos que todavía conservaba
64 | 199

4252 invocar *v* to invoke
- invocaba los nombres de líderes muertos
68 | 192 -o

4253 computadora *nf* computer
- el diseño asistido por ordenador o computadora (CAD/CAM)
- 59 | 361

4254 ostentar *v* to flaunt, show off
- Madrid ostenta el título de Capital Cultural de Europa
- 69 | 183 -o

4255 alambre *nm* wire
- por una pieza de alambre de acero inoxidable
- 62 | 270 +f

4256 mango *nm* handle, mango
- una pala muy rara, estrecha y larga con un mango de un metro
- 61 | 250 +f -nf

4257 configurar *v* to make up, comprise
- muchos rasgos configuran esta patología política
- 68 | 281 +nf

4258 rosario *nm* rosary, beads, string
- muchas veces rezábamos también el rosario con ella
- 62 | 297 +f

4259 reconstrucción *nf* reconstruction
- busqué materiales para la reconstrucción de mi casa
- 68 | 301 -f +nf

4260 parroquia *nf* parish
- iban a la misa de los domingos, en la parroquia del lugar
- 63 | 220

4261 ruidoso *adj* noisy
- se escuchan ruidoso tumulto, gritos y gente en desbandada
- 67 | 194 -o +f

4262 supuestamente *adv* supposedly, allegedly
- esa sensibilidad que supuestamente tiene que tener la gente . . .
- 69 | 235

4263 ampliamente *adv* widely
- hoy, sin embargo, su teoría es ampliamente aceptada
- 71 | 296 -f +nf

4264 gigante *adj* gigantic
- una torta gigante de doscientos kilos
- 66 | 225 -o

4265 prevalecer *v* to prevail
- quiero rendir homenaje a los que hacen prevalecer la razón
- 71 | 264 +nf

4266 comprador *nm* buyer
- felicito al comprador por su excelente adquisición
- 65 | 213

4267 piedad *nf* pity, mercy
- para castigar sin piedad al enemigo
- 64 | 324 -o +f

4268 semanal *adj* weekly
- editadas normalmente con una periodicidad diaria o semanal
- 66 | 184 -f

4269 clandestino *adj* undercover, clandestine
- obligó al encargado a transmitir un video clandestino
- 66 | 183

4270 defensivo *adj* defensive
- para el desarrollo de un sistema defensivo de misiles antibalísticos
- 65 | 310 -o +nf

4271 manual *adj* manual
- para mantener un grado elevado de destreza manual y mental
- 66 | 193

4272 engendrar *v* to engender, beget
- piensan que vas a engendrar un niño
- 63 | 230

4273 contagiar *v* to infect, infest
- un gato infectado puede contagiar la enfermedad a otros
- 64 | 190

4274 niebla *nf* fog
- con la oscuridad y con la niebla no podíamos verlos
- 61 | 362 -o +f

4275 adonde *adv* to where
- el lugar adonde hemos llegado es la cocina
- 63 | 197 +f -nf

4276 consagrar *v* to consecrate, establish
- se prometió consagrar su vida a la virtud
- 66 | 227

4277 mixto *adj* mixed, co-ed
- estaban poblados por un grupo étnico mixto denominado siro-hitita
- 68 | 310 -o -f +nf

4278 verbo *nm* verb
- no distingue el sujeto del predicado, un verbo de un adjetivo
- 58 | 362

4279 cadera *nf* hip
- en la caída se había dado un golpe en la cadera
- 61 | 483 -o +f

4280 procesión *nf* procession
- ya no soporta el tráfico y tal procesión de coches
- 64 | 273 -o +f

4281 encuesta *nf* poll, survey, inquiry
- según los resultados de la encuesta, realizada en 35 ciudades
- 61 | 577 +o -f

4282 cría *nf* breeding, raising
- con la cría de animales salvajes en rebaños
- 59 | 318

4283 narración *nf* narration, account
- era una narración, un relato
- 60 | 338

4284 ramo *nm* bunch (of flowers), branch
- le regalé un ramo de rosas blancas
- 63 | 197 -nf

4285 penal *adj* penal
- reformó el derecho penal o criminal
- 63 | 388 +o -f

4286 traidor *nm* traitor
- incluyen la muerte del traidor de Jesús, Judas Iscariote
63 | 262 +f

4287 catálogo *nm* catalog
- se publicó un catálogo de cursos escolares
66 | 199

4288 protector *nm* protector, defender
- las Casas los defendió muchísimo y se llamaba protector de los indios
72 | 169 -o +nf

4289 amparo *nm* protection, shelter
- es mejor que busque el amparo de mi habitación
68 | 228

4290 farmacia *nf* pharmacy, drugstore
- compran en la farmacia los medicamentos recetados
58 | 334

4291 cima *nf* summit, peak, top
- uno se debe sentir así cuando llega a la cima de una montaña
68 | 264 -o +nf

4292 riñón *nm* kidney
- le quitaron el riñón nuevo, le hicieron diálisis
62 | 212

4293 pintoresco *adj* picturesque
- atravesaron en pintoresco grupo las calles pueblerinas
67 | 193

4294 finca *nf* property, estate
- reservó para sí, como finca privada, los terrenos al sur
61 | 273 +o

4295 calificación *nf* evaluation, qualification
- respecto a la calificación de sus años de servicio
65 | 193 +o

4296 caudal *nm* volume, abundance
- la presa de Asuán ha reducido el caudal del Nilo
65 | 229

4297 publicitario *adj* advertising
- vio el anuncio publicitario de un medicamento
60 | 359 +o -f

4298 trastorno *nm* confusion, trouble, upheaval
- además de la depresión neurótica y otros trastornos ansiosos
63 | 381 -f +nf

4299 ceñir *v* to adhere to, fit tightly
- ni ceñirse exclusivamente al arte musical del pasado
66 | 173 -o

4300 jovencito *nm* young person
- sería ir con Pedro, un jovencito de unos 19 años
61 | 196 +f -nf

4301 incorporación *nf* inclusion, incorporation
- la incorporación de España a la Comunidad Europea
68 | 296 -f +nf

4302 corral *nm* corral, yard
- la docena de gallinas que criaba en el corral de su casa
66 | 254 -o

4303 fatiga *nf* fatigue
- para aliviarla de la fatiga de su mucho batallar
67 | 287 -o +f

4304 virgen *adj* virgin
- la contaminación de sus ríos y ecosistemas vírgenes
66 | 165

4305 bruja *nf* witch, hag
- había una bruja que se montaba en una escoba, todas esas leyendas
61 | 251 +f -nf

4306 exploración *nf* exploration
- apoyaban la exploración de lugares remotos
65 | 260

4307 matrimonial *adj* matrimonial
- para que respetaran el modelo matrimonial monógamo
64 | 177

4308 equivalente *adj* equivalent
- el 1 de abril, día equivalente a los Santos Inocentes
70 | 265 -f +nf

4309 ilustración *nf* illustration
- libros de cuentos con hermosas ilustraciones
65 | 203 +nf

4310 cómplice *nc* accomplice
- a quien acusó de ser cómplice del terrorismo internacional
66 | 259 +f -nf

4311 melodía *nf* melody
- evocada por la música, la melodía infinita del amor dulce y triste
62 | 447 -o +f

4312 productor *nm* producer
- entre los principales productores de vino del mundo
68 | 732 +o -f +nf

4313 deseable *adj* desirable
- lo lógico, lo esperable, lo deseable es que . . .
69 | 185 -f +nf

4314 constatar *v* to prove, verify
- logró constatar que nunca antes había estado en ese lugar
63 | 249

4315 portero *nm/f* porter, doorkeeper, goalkeeper
- el portero lo acompañó hasta el ascensor
56 | 338 -nf

4316 conejo *nm* rabbit
- con los ojos rojos y saltones como de conejo
60 | 258

4317 pasivo *adj* passive
- el hombre se hizo a un lado, pasivo, sonriente, tenso
66 | 297 +nf

4318 densidad *nf* density, thickness
- Usted casi puede tocar la densidad del aire con la tensión
65 | 530 -f +nf

4319 dispersar *v* to disperse, scatter, spread
- la energía dispersa en el espacio
  66 | 185 -o

4320 apuesta *nf* wager, bet
- como si hubiesen hecho una apuesta para ver quién tardaba más en liarlo
  63 | 225

4321 nacionalidad *nf* nationality
- nacida de doble nacionalidad: francesa y estadounidense
  63 | 260 +o -f

4322 llamativo *adj* striking
- allí quedaba un solitario y llamativo ejemplar
  67 | 183

4323 vacilar *v* to vacillate, hesitate
- parecían detenerse y vacilar, para después seguir de nuevo
  64 | 320 -o +f

4324 mozo *nm* waiter, youth, bellboy
- el mozo nos trajo un vaso y una botella
  58 | 642 +f -nf

4325 capturar *v* to capture
- tienen una boca enorme para capturar a los insectos voladores
  65 | 237

4326 cuerno *nm* horn, antler
- es un cuerno de rinoceronte
  64 | 259 -o +f

4327 remediar *v* to heal, cure
- ningún milagro podía remediar la tiniebla de sus ojos
  65 | 160

4328 fiar *v* to vouch for, confide, trust
- muy poco se fiaba de la gente de cuna
  62 | 180

4329 desfilar *v* to march, parade
- los vieron desfilar, cada uno con una lanza al hombro
  63 | 199

4330 talla *nf* size (of clothing), stature
- de la talla cuarenta y dos - cuarenta y cuatro
  65 | 257

4331 justificado *adj* justifiable, justified
- según el culpable fue un crimen justificado
  67 | 164

4332 comisario *nm* commissioner, delegate
- el comisario ordenó que se le tomase vivo
  56 | 615

4333 fotográfico *adj* photographic
- una calidad que puede llegar al realismo fotográfico
  62 | 239

4334 acercamiento *nm* approach, approximation
- el acercamiento humanista a la teología y a las Escrituras
  66 | 249

4335 desordenado *adj* messy, confused
- la sala se encontraba desordenada, con una silla tumbada
  65 | 164

4336 gráfico *adj* graphic, explicit
- nunca conocí síntesis más gráfica y más breve de la vida
  66 | 261 -f +nf

4337 reaparecer *v* to reappear
- después reapareció el sargento
  68 | 207 -o

4338 revuelto *adj* confused, messed up
- vamos a la recámara, donde todo está revuelto y en desorden
  62 | 223 +f -nf

4339 contorno *nm* outline, perimeter, edge
- miraban el irregular contorno de las nubes
  66 | 363 -o +f

4340 egoísmo *nm* selfishness
- probablemente sí hay egoísmo, pero hay también celo profesional
  62 | 222

4341 bordo *nm* a bordo: on board
- mi familia viajaba a España a bordo de grandes trasatlánticos
  61 | 299

4342 compensación *nf* compensation
- ninguna compensación alcanzarán nuestros esfuerzos
  67 | 209

4343 prohibición *nf* prohibition
- violando la prohibición estricta de su médico
  67 | 274 +nf

4344 obrar *v* to work, act
- decidió obrar con la eficiencia de un funcionario
  60 | 246

4345 expreso *adj* express, explicit
- que excluyan de forma expresa la utilización de las minas
  70 | 212 +nf

4346 coronar *v* to crown, top
- se hizo coronar emperador por el papa Juan XII
  67 | 194 -o

4347 liquidar *v* to liquidate, sell (off)
- deseoso de liquidar viejas cuentas
  64 | 203

4348 laberinto *nm* maze, labyrinth
- se perdió en el laberinto de callejas
  67 | 356 -o +f

4349 erótico *adj* erotic
- no, un poema sexual; ni erótico ni pornográfico
  63 | 283 -o

4350 amenazado *adj* threatened
- los pantanos de turba son otro ecosistema amenazado
  67 | 221 -o +nf

4351 inminente *aj* imminent
- el bolchevique creía inminente la extensión de la revolución soviética
  66 | 221 -o

4352 eternidad *nf* eternity
- me pareció que pasó una eternidad hasta que abrió la puerta
62 | 315 -o +f

4353 repasar *v* to review, revise
- el magistrado volvió a repasar sus notas
62 | 223 +f -nf

4354 pastilla *nf* pill, capsule
- tomó una pastilla blanca pequeña y se la puso debajo de la lengua
61 | 215

4355 mierda *nf* shit, crap, excrement
- ¡Mierda! Se me han acabado las municiones. ¡Me rindo!
56 | 590 +f -nf

4356 contienda *nf* contest, dispute
- la guerra se tomaba como una contienda personal
67 | 345 -o +nf

4357 imperial *adj* imperial, imperialist
- el arte de la Roma republicana y el de la Roma imperial
63 | 528 -o +nf

4358 inexplicable *adj* unexplainable
- intenta también explicar, conceptualizar, lo inexplicable
64 | 224 -o +f

4359 peruano *adj* Peruvian
- la cerámica maya, la moche y la peruana de Nazca
59 | 334

4360 experimental *adj* experimental
- es imprescindible la comprobación experimental de los cálculos
63 | 438 -f +nf

4361 chorro *nm* stream, jet, spurt
- nos bañó un chorro de espuma
60 | 283 -o +f

4362 opaco *adj* dull, opaque, heavy
- una nube enorme le envolvió con su peso opaco de silencio
63 | 242 +f

4363 clavo *nm* nail, tack, peg
- en la pared, un clavo que sujeta una corona descolorida de plástico
64 | 253 -o +f

4364 sequía *nf* drought
- su preocupación por la falta de agua y por la sequía que afecta al país
64 | 195

4365 dinámica *nf* dynamics
- la propia creación y dinámica de la estructura del Universo
64 | 429 +o -f +nf

4366 ocio *nm* leisure (time)
- en sus momentos de ocio, los dedicó a pasear
62 | 233

4367 normalidad *nf* normality
- después de la crisis todo volvió a la normalidad
64 | 235

4368 intuir *v* to sense
- debes aprender a observar, a intuir
63 | 267 -o +f

4369 resonancia *nf* resonance, repercussion
- ¡qué agradable resonancia tenían esas dos palabras!
67 | 188 -o

4370 devorar *v* to devour, consume
- para devorar enormes trozos de pan remojados
62 | 336 -o +f

4371 efímero *adj* ephemeral, short-lived
- lo perdurable y lo efímero, los aciertos y los errores
66 | 159

4372 chaqueta *nf* jacket
- me quité la chaqueta porque tenía calor
61 | 342 -o +f

4373 aferrar *v* to grasp, clutch
- quiso aferrar el puñal con ambas manos para arrancarlo
65 | 258 -o +f

4374 invertido *adj* reversed, inverted
- en realidad, uno constituía una imagen invertida del otro
68 | 156

4375 asco *nm* disgust
- decían obscenidades que le daban miedo y asco 58 | 343 +f -nf

4376 consolidar *v* to consolidate
- le permitió consolidar su posición en una vida tranquila
63 | 475 -f +nf

4377 apresurar *v* to hurry up, speed up
- N. apresuró su marcha sin distracciones
65 | 313 -o +f

4378 pleito *nm* litigation, suit, dispute
- los inquisidores podían entablar pleito contra cualquier persona sospechosa
63 | 182

4379 latir *v* to beat (heart)
- mi corazón se puso a latir rápidamente
63 | 257 -o +f

4380 sencillez *nf* simplicity
- sabe enfocar con jubilosa sencillez esos temas de la vida elemental
66 | 168

4381 transitorio *adj* transitory
- el período transitorio de una sociedad agrícola a una industrial
69 | 225 +nf

4382 estupidez *nf* stupidity, stupid thing
- supongamos que esa momia soy yo. // ¡Qué estupidez! Te reconozco enseguida
63 | 210 +f -nf

4383 mojado *adj* wet
- se veía desnudo bajo el camisón mojado
59 | 373 +f -nf

4384 descalzo *adj* barefoot
- solían andar descalzos y hasta sin camisa
62 | 308 +f -nf

4385 orientado *adj* positioned, guided
- Stonehenge está orientado según el solsticio de verano
65 | 279 -f +nf

4386 senador *nm/f* senator
- los diputados y los senadores eran nombrados por el Ejecutivo
60 | 554

4387 rencor *nm* grudge, spite
- ¿no me guardas ningún rencor? // ¡Qué cosas te habrán contado de mí!
61 | 354 +f

4388 presidencial *adj* presidential
- obtuvo la nominación presidencial por el Partido Demócrata
62 | 641 -f

4389 apurar *v* to speed up, hurry up
- cuando él se dio cuenta de que lo perseguía apuró el paso
62 | 306 +f -nf

4390 insultar *v* to insult, berate
- el ciudadano acaba de insultar a la autoridad
63 | 188 -nf

4391 brasileño *adj* Brazilian
- he terminado en la ciudad brasileña de Manaos
59 | 403

4392 sustentar *v* to maintain, support
- las bases sobre las que se sustenta el ejercicio del poder político
71 | 219 +nf

4393 probabilidad *nf* probability
- veo una probabilidad del 95 por ciento de que sea así
65 | 292 +nf

4394 minucioso *adj* meticulous, thorough
- solicitó un minucioso análisis del crimen
68 | 188 -o

4395 rústico *adj* rustic, rural
- la puerta de madera espesa y rústica de la casa de adobe
65 | 172 -nf

4396 gobernante *nc* ruler, leader
- la cumbre entre los gobernantes de China y EE.UU.
65 | 450 -f +nf

4397 merced *nf* favor, mercy
- la población civil estaría a merced de sus atacantes
63 | 223

4398 acariciar *v* to stroke, fondle, caress
- al acariciar con los dedos el frío del metal
58 | 848 -o +f -nf

4399 tonelada *nf* ton
- puede llegar hasta 30 toneladas de azúcar por hectárea
64 | 525 -f +nf

4400 rebelde *nc* rebel, insurgent
- su uso de la fuerza contra los rebeldes antisoviéticos en Hungría
63 | 207

4401 anhelo *nm* longing, yearning
- existía una profunda intimidad con Dios y un anhelo por acceder a Él
64 | 213

4402 princesa *nf* princess
- murió en accidente automovilístico la princesa Diana de Gales
66 | 199 -o

4403 decididamente *adv* decidedly, decisively
- ahora ¿esto es lo que realmente sucede? Decididamente, no
66 | 163

4404 embajada *nf* embassy
- fuimos a la embajada para pedir una visa
61 | 221

4405 apagado *adj* turned off
- ¿porqué tienes la luz apagada?
63 | 246 -o +f

4406 bruscamente *adv* quickly, sharply
- el conductor cierra bruscamente la puerta
66 | 271 -o +f

4407 vincular *v* to connect, link, bind
- hay celos profesionales que se vinculan a la envidia
66 | 225 -f

4408 amargura *nf* bitterness, sorrow
- ¡qué tristeza, qué amargura tan grande!
63 | 270 +f

4409 fortalecer *v* to fortify
- los reyes tomaron medidas para fortalecer su autoridad
69 | 342 +nf

4410 validez *nf* validity
- su validez es lo que da constancia a su presencia
67 | 233 -f +nf

4411 tacto *nm* sense of touch, feel
- cuya piel se ha vuelto, al tacto del agua, transparente y tersa
61 | 246

4412 codo *nm* elbow
- dobla los brazos por el codo y levanta cien kilos
62 | 311 -o +f

4413 vibrar *v* to vibrate, tremble
- la música y el estrépito hacían vibrar los vidrios
63 | 273 -o +f

4414 calzar *v* to wear (shoes)
- vestía mis mejores prendas, calzaba zapatos lustrosos
63 | 222 +f -nf

4415 chimenea *nf* chimney, fireplace
- vio el fuego de la chimenea de casa
62 | 305 -o +f

4416 comunitario *adj* of the community
- la existencia individual y comunitaria de las personas
63 | 302 -f +nf

4417 explícito *adj* explicit
- N. era bien explícito; nunca dejaba un cabo suelto
68 | 259 +nf

4418 silvestre *adj* wild
- permiten la existencia de numerosas especies de fauna silvestre
60 | 228

4419 evaluar *v* to evaluate, assess
- que sea capaz de evaluar cuál es el probable efecto
62 | 411 -f +nf

4420 emocionar *v* to move, make, get excited
- me emociona hasta las lágrimas
61 | 172 -nf

4421 editar *v* to edit, publish, release
- mismísimo Plaza y Janés le editó un poemario de lujo
64 | 192 -f

4422 abanico *nm* range, (handheld) fan
- de ampliar el abanico de posibilidades
63 | 214

4423 fiscal *adj* fiscal, treasury
- para armonizar nuestra legislación fiscal y administrativa
60 | 649 -f

4424 espacial *adj* spatial, space
- era la única estación espacial en funcionamiento
62 | 513 -f +nf

4425 violentamente *adv* violently
- el individuo fue echado violentamente del bar
63 | 159

4426 medieval *adj* medieval
- entrelazaba la vida de un personaje medieval con el mundo actual
63 | 455 +nf

4427 camiseta *nf* T-shirt
- viste pantalón vaquero y camiseta
62 | 204

4428 honrado *adj* honest, respectable
- el sujeto laborioso, honrado, respetuoso de los buenos modales
64 | 205 -nf

4429 veloz *adj* fast, quick
- desarrolló un método veloz y rápido para encontrar genes
63 | 251 -o +f

4430 corteza *nf* bark, crust, rind, peel
- veo las viejas cicatrices en la corteza de los árboles
63 | 479 -o

4431 sumergir *v* to submerge, plunge
- para sumergir el submarino introducen agua en los tanques
64 | 260 -o +f

4432 cordillera *nf* mountain range
- en las cumbres de la cordillera todavía quedaba nieve
61 | 443 -o

Word length (Zipf's Law)

Zipf's Law refers to the natural tendency for common words in the language (e.g. "time", "get", "good") to be shorter than less common words (e.g. "reverberation", "industrialize", "mechanistic"). The following table shows this to hold true for Spanish. For example, there are about 5.4 million words in the 20 million word corpus that have two letters. This decreases to 1.3 million tokens of eight letter words, and just about 74,000 tokens of fourteen letter words. The table also lists the number of distinct word forms ("types") and the most common words for each word length.

No. of letters	Tokens (Occurrences)	Types (Forms)	Most common words
1	1,251,320	122	y, a, o
2	5,397,498	818	de, el, la
3	2,801,740	4,539	que, los, las
4	1,652,305	9,710	para, como, pero
5	2,045,998	17,283	había, sobre, entre
6	1,673,851	25,153	porque, cuando, tiempo
7	1,588,419	33,168	también, después, siempre
8	1,264,961	36,167	entonces, mientras, nosotros
9	886,606	36,231	cualquier, situación, problemas
10	631,500	32,152	importante, presidente, desarrollo
11	382,424	23,479	universidad, condiciones, importantes
12	212,806	15,980	precisamente, conocimiento, organización
13	132,865	10,428	internacional, especialmente, investigación
14	73,758	6,508	administración, circunstancias, comportamiento
15+	63,391	9,591	características, responsabilidad, aproximadamente

4433 monótono *adj* monotonous
- llora y llora, un llanto monótono y cansado
65 | 196 +f

4434 longitud *nf* length, longitude
- los marineros se fijaron en su latitud y longitud
60 | 702 -o +nf

4435 espantar *v* to scare, frighten
- los cascabeles se utilizaban para espantar a los malos espíritus
62 | 283 +f -nf

4436 imprevisto *adj* unforeseen, unexpected
- viene un accidente imprevisto y doloroso
64 | 187 +f

4437 psicología *nf* psychology
- a explorar la psicología, la mentalidad de ese hombre
62 | 410 -f +nf

4438 soviético *adj* Soviet
- la intervención del Ejército soviético en Afganistán
57 | 1271 -f +nf

4439 potencial *adj* potential
- para desactivar conflictos potenciales
66 | 370 -f +nf

4440 ambulante *adj* traveling
- era vendedor ambulante de parafina y de velas de sebo
62 | 157

4441 agrupar *v* to (put in) group
- los pingüinos se agrupan en 8 especies y 6 géneros
66 | 315 -f +nf

4442 exageración *nf* exaggeration
- eso es una exageración, la verdad es que aquí está
65 | 137

4443 apreciación *nf* appreciation, assessment
- por lo menos eso creía en mi forma de apreciación infantil:
64 | 180

4444 perverso *adj* perverse, wicked
- tiene un corazón perverso y no comprende el amor
63 | 208 -o

4445 estallido *nm* crash, outbreak, explosion
- escuchó el estallido del vidrio sobre la baldosa
65 | 249 -o +nf

4446 ardiente *adj* passionate, ardent
- crearon algo jocundo, jaranero, erótico y ardiente
63 | 370 -o +f

4447 talón *nm* heel, check, coupon, stub
- el talón del pie se le trabó en el estribo al descabalgar
63 | 214 +f

4448 atener *v* to abide by, comply with
- debían atenerse a las consecuencias
67 | 158

4449 colchón *nm* mattress
- le ofrecemos una cama en el suelo y un colchón sin lana
59 | 237 +f -nf

4450 tenue *adj* tenuous, flimsy
- la tenue llama del farol se extinguió
65 | 235 -o.+f

4451 tinte *nm* tint, dye
- está impregnada con tinte amarillo y otra con magenta
65 | 171

4452 indiscutible *adj* indisputable, unquestionable
- goza de un indiscutible prestigio
68 | 191 +nf

4453 imprenta *nf* printing house
- la imprenta nacional imprimía textos y cartillas
63 | 218

4454 bastón *nm* (walking) cane
- un viejo con bastón que se nos acercó lentamente
61 | 215 +f

4455 sombrío *adj* shady, dark, dismal
- se asomó a la ventana mirando el enorme y sombrío patio
66 | 353 -o +f

4456 humillación *nf* humiliation
- tanta miseria, tanta abyección, tanta humillación del ser humano
64 | 226 -o +f

4457 trance *nm* trance, fix, enrapture
- eran sus ojos los que la mantenían en trance
64 | 240 -o +f

4458 volante *nm* steering wheel
- avanza al volante su poderoso Buick 57
62 | 213 +f

4459 adolescente *adj* adolescent
- alucinados por ese apetito adolescente que todo lo devora
62 | 242

4460 encabezar *v* to head, lead (off)
- el cuento que encabeza la selección
67 | 276 +nf

4461 rosado *adj* pink, rosy
- el cielo había cambiado de color tornándose entre rosado y violeta
59 | 310 +f -nf

4462 amistoso *adj* friendly
- la calificación de amistoso, hostil o indiferente
66 | 176 -o

4463 noble *nc* nobleman, noble
- los nobles y sus criados vivían en castillos
62 | 225 -o

4464 radicalmente *adv* radically
- y modificó radicalmente su actitud
69 | 204 -f +nf

4465 reclamo *nm* claim, complaint, protest
- preferí no responder, ni darle importancia al reclamo de mi madre
65 | 287 -o

4466 asesor *nm/f* adviser, consultant
- el dirigente de la CIA y el principal asesor del presidente
65 | 250 -f

4467 perteneciente *adj* pertaining, belonging
- es un poeta perteneciente a una joven generación
65 | 257 -o +nf

4468 novelista *nc* novelist
- Unamuno fue, además de ensayista, novelista y poeta
57 | 384

4469 herido *nm* wounded (person)
- los heridos murieron como moscas
62 | 256 -o

4470 necesitado *adj* poor, needy
- un país pobre, necesitado de tantas cosas
64 | 162

4471 indefinido *adj* vague, indefinite
- hizo un movimiento indefinido con la cabeza
67 | 160 -o

4472 solidario *adj* united, jointly shared
- el espíritu solidario y de hermandad se fue perdiendo
64 | 196

4473 paralizado *adj* paralyzed
- se quedó tieso como una estatua, paralizado por el terror
63 | 186

4474 grueso *nm* bulk, mass
- el grueso de la colección está formado por las obras realistas
66 | 172 -o

4475 chupar *v* to suck
- le dio de chupar unos pedacitos de caña de azúcar
60 | 268 +f -nf

4476 grabación *nf* recording
- una nueva grabación de los «cinco conciertos» de Beethoven
59 | 325 +o -f

4477 frasco *nm* bottle, jar, flask
- se le volcó un frasco diminuto de extracto
57 | 312 -o +f

4478 inquietante *adj* disquieting
- si nos atrevemos a descubrir el inquietante secreto
64 | 225 -o

4479 visual *adj* visual
- su combinación de drama, música y arte visual
64 | 311 +nf

4480 verdura *nf* vegetables, greenery
- un plato donde encuentras verduras, fruta y también carne
62 | 235

4481 violación *nf* violation, rape
- la violación de la intimidad de los ciudadanos por el espionaje
67 | 279

4482 innovación *nf* innovation
- el cañón presentó la última innovación en tecnología de 35 milímetros
67 | 326 -f +nf

4483 tertulia *nf* get-together, meeting of friends
- a la tertulia, a conversar y a tomar tragos
62 | 245

4484 carcajada *nf* hearty laughter, guffaw
- soltó una gran carcajada y enseñó sus grandes dientes
57 | 523 -o +f -nf

4485 cancha *nf* playing field, court
- para construir una cancha de fútbol de proporciones apreciables
56 | 305

4486 republicano *adj* republican
- no saben del sistema democrático ni del republicano
57 | 566

4487 destruido *adj* destroyed
- han quedado destruidas poblaciones enteras de peces
66 | 171 +nf

4488 aburrimiento *nm* boredom
- hay un ambiente de hastío, de cansancio y aburrimiento
61 | 203 +f

4489 trabajador *adj* hardworking
- unas son muy cumplidas, son muy trabajadoras
65 | 223 -f

4490 inquietar *v* to make uneasy, disturb
- el poder de inquietar al más escéptico
63 | 227 +f -nf

4491 grandioso *adj* magnificent, grandiose
- es grandioso el poder de una sola palabra
65 | 135

4492 específicamente *adv* specifically
- adaptado específicamente a las personas con discapacidades
67 | 329 +o -f +nf

4493 exportación *nf* export, exportation
- por la importación de lana y la exportación de hilo y telas
63 | 636 -f +nf

4494 extremadamente *adv* extremely
- creo que España es un país extremadamente emocional
67 | 289 +nf

4495 expandir *v* to expand
- el proyecto de expandir la capacidad
64 | 338 -o +nf

4496 predecir *v* to predict
- no era difícil predecir el futuro inmediato
64 | 250 +nf

4497 dichoso *adj* fortunate, happy
- estoy hecha polvo con la dichosa misa de Mozart
60 | 215 +f -nf

4498 condicionar *v* to condition, determine
- lo económico no debe condicionar los valores culturales
67 | 255 -f +nf

4499 agrario *adj* agrarian, agricultural
- que pasara de ser un estado agrario a un estado industrializado
60 | 578 -f +nf

4500 suizo *adj* Swiss
- el paisaje suizo de los Alpes
64 | 292 -f +nf

4501 presunto *adj* alleged, presumed
- se creyó inocente por el presunto pecado de la mujer
62 | 292

4502 tranvía *nm* trolley, tram, streetcar
- treparon al tranvía en la estación de los ferrocarriles
58 | 360 +f -nf

4503 alertar *v* to alert, warn
- retumbaron las campanas para alertar al poblado
65 | 191 -o +f

4504 cordón *nm* cord, yarn, braid
- se trata de perforar el cordón umbilical del bebé
61 | 265 -o +f

4505 prioridad *nf* priority
- anotaba temas para cuentos, en orden de prioridad
65 | 343 +o -f +nf

4506 modalidad *nf* mode, manner
- el Tai Chi Chuan es una modalidad de las artes marciales chinas
67 | 410 -f +nf

4507 desenlace *nm* outcome, result
- ¿cómo ve usted el desenlace de ese problema?
63 | 257 -o

4508 bailarín *nm/f* dancer
- salió de puntillas como un bailarín
57 | 419 -o

4509 artefacto *nm* artifact, device
- van a abrir un museo con artefactos indígenas
61 | 194

4510 trono *nm* throne
- el trono de España pasó a la Casa de Borbón
62 | 299 -o

4511 adjetivo *nm* adjective
- ha perdido el neutro en los nombres y los adjetivos
63 | 182

4512 gama *nf* range, musical scale
- pueden producir una gama de tonos
64 | 245 -f +nf

4513 enfermar *v* to become ill
- porque seenfermó de artritis en su forma más agresiva
62 | 174 -nf

4514 gabinete *nm* cabinet, den, office
- entraron a un gabinete lleno de libros
59 | 371

4515 indagar *v* to investigate
- ir hasta lo profundo para indagar las causas
63 | 193

4516 vertiginoso *adj* dizzying
- el vertiginoso crecimiento de los índices de natalidad
63 | 179 -o

4517 decente *adj* respectable, decent
- No, no, no, una niña decente no duerme fuera de su casa
59 | 323 +f -nf

4518 congelado *adj* frozen
- entre la superficie recién congelada y el subyacente permafrost
62 | 185

4519 peón *nm* unskilled laborer, field hand
- muchos son mestizos, muy humildes; son peones
60 | 372 -o

4520 triple *adj* triple
- la respuesta es triple: institucional, social y cultural
64 | 200 +nf

4521 inspector *nm/f* inspector
- apareció un inspector municipal que quiso cobrar impuestos
56 | 353

4522 órbita *nf* orbit, socket, field
- los satélites situados en órbita a una altura de 36.000 kilómetros
63 | 548 -o +nf

4523 autopista *nf* freeway, motorway
- empieza una carretera que no es propiamente autopista
62 | 188

4524 prosa *nf* prose
- es una colección de textos en prosa y en verso
60 | 343

4525 paréntesis *nm* parenthesis, digression
- entre paréntesis quiero decir que lo único que hago es colaborar
62 | 182

4526 fabricación *nf* manufacture, production
- el material podría ser empleado para la fabricación de armamento nuclear
62 | 435 -f +nf

4527 lesión *nf* injury, wound, harm
- trataba de desinfectar la lesión con un algodón chorreando alcohol
58 | 429 +o -f +nf

4528 mejilla *nf* cheek
- le dio un sonoro beso en la mejilla
56 | 729 -o +f -nf

4529 inseguro *adj* unsure, unsafe
- me sentí inmaduro, inseguro, torpe, infantil
61 | 180 +f -nf

4530 muelle *nm* wharf, dock
- prefiriendo contar los barcos que pasan por el muelle
61 | 240 -o

4531 velo *nm* veil
- varias mujeres caminaban con un velo negro sobre la cara
62 | 284 -o +f

4532 decoración *nf* decoration
- con sus flores y su decoración para la fiesta
60 | 353

4533 rancho *nm* ranch, farm
- por el cuarto que servía de dormitorio en el rancho campesino
54 | 545 +f -nf

4534 exceder *v* to excel, exceed
- cuyos límites exceden los del continente
68 | 177 -nf

4535 joder *v* to f**k, screw (around/up)
- -¡Joder! ¡Pues no es eso complicado!
52 | 437 +f -nf

4536 irónico *adj* ironic, mocking
- deja escurrir un comentario irónico de cierto humor maligno
61 | 198

4537 alarmar *v* to alarm
- otro grave accidente alarmó al mundo
61 | 156

4538 negociación *nf* negotiation
- el gobierno ha emprendido una negociación directa con el MRTA
60 | 930 -f +nf

4539 euforia *nf* euphoria, elation
- todo fomentaba la euforia y el optimismo del hombre de letras
64 | 145

4540 convencimiento *nm* convincing
- las diligencias necesarias para adquirir el convencimiento de la verdad
64 | 157

4541 asombrado *adj* amazed, bewildered
- pero estoy así asombrado de que nos haya salido tan bien
63 | 223 +f -nf

4542 rascar *v* to scratch, scrape
- yo le rascaba la espalda con las uñas de los pies
54 | 244 +f -nf

4543 desconcierto *nm* disorder, chaos
- habrá un desconcierto y una confusión general
66 | 189 -o +f

4544 economista *nm/f* economist
- el economista que trabajaba en el Banco Central
65 | 310 +o -f +nf

4545 oficialmente *adv* officially
- el museo será reinaugurado oficialmente en fechas próximas
64 | 257 -f +nf

4546 sofisticado *adj* sophisticated
- han desarrollado también modelos estadísticos muy sofisticados
64 | 225 -f +nf

4547 sobra *nf* excess, surplus, leftover
- ¡hay agua de sobra! ¿Quieres un poco?
60 | 210 +f -nf

4548 enredar *v* to entangle, ensnare
- se enredó en torno a vagas conjeturas
61 | 240 +f -nf

4549 ingenioso *adj* ingenious, clever
- mediante un ingenioso sistema de escorrentías solapadas
65 | 160

4550 tasa *nf* rate, fee, levy
- la tasa de mortalidad era más alta que la tasa de nacimientos
57 | 1389 -f +nf

4551 balanza *nf* balance, (measuring) scale
- sabía poner en la balanza las virtudes y los vicios
66 | 213 +nf

4552 factura *nf* invoice, bill
- a calcular alguna vez cuánto sube la factura telefónica mensual
63 | 200

4553 hormiga *nf* ant
- los animales sociales, como las abejas y las hormigas
57 | 309 -o +f

4554 vulnerable *adj* vulnerable
- con el vino soy muy vulnerable y capaz de hacer locuras
65 | 174

4555 oso *nm* bear
- se proveen de osos polares, zorros, liebres y pájaros árticos
62 | 306 -o

4556 trazo *nm* line, stroke
- haciendo dibujos de trazo grueso con forma de espirales
64 | 167 -o

4557 geométrico *adj* geometric
- su diseño geométrico de zarcillos, cuadrados y octágonos
63 | 253 +nf

4558 suspirar *v* to sigh
- se sentó serio y pensativo, suspiró largamente
56 | 478 +f -nf

4559 gusano *nm* worm, caterpillar
- la mariposa del gusano de seda es originaria de China
59 | 271 -o +f

4560 bendito *adj* blessed
- ¡ay, bendito sea Dios, que encontré a mi hija!
60 | 231 +f -nf

4561 conferir *v* to confer
- y eso les confiere poderes sobrenaturales
66 | 221 -o +nf

4562 manía *nf* obsession, mania
- I. tenía la manía de hacerlo todo perfectamente
58 | 260 +f

4563 disculpa *nf* apology, excuse
- sinceramente le pido disculpas y lo lamento
60 | 220 +f -nf

4564 trascendente *adj* transcendent
- para trasladarnos al mundo de la belleza trascendente y divina
  63 | 217

4565 alarmante *adj* alarming
- comprobaron una alarmante polución en varios establecimientos
  64 | 159

4566 pequeñito *adj* very small, tiny
- tiene un niño, muy pequeñito de ocho, nueve meses
  59 | 200 +o -nf

4567 predominar *v* to predominate
- donde predomina el discurso lírico
  63 | 311 -f +nf

4568 metáfora *nf* metaphor
- como la metáfora, el símbolo o las referencias a determinados objetos
  63 | 240

4569 penetración *nf* penetration, insight
- permite una mayor penetración de rayos ultravioleta
  66 | 179 +nf

4570 pasajero *adj* fleeting, transitory
- temo que el sueño pasajero nunca vuelva más
  65 | 169 -o

4571 whisky *nm* whisky
- el viajero se toma el whisky de un sólo trago
  59 | 334 +f -nf

4572 turístico *adj* tourist
- Andalucía, un destacado destino turístico
  60 | 243 +o -f

4573 despejar *v* to clear (up)
- un fiero rayo despejó las nubes bajas
  65 | 174 -o

4574 delirio *nm* delirium, nonsense
- fue el resultado deldelirio de su fiebre amarilla
  62 | 266 -o +f

4575 impecable *adj* impeccable, faultless
- un gusto impecable y un extraordinario discernimiento
  62 | 201 -o +f

4576 soberbio *adj* proud, arrogant
- la justicia al pobre o al rico, al humilde o al soberbio
  64 | 185 -o +f

4577 librería *nf* bookstore
- este libro lo adquirimos en una librería
  58 | 227

4578 documentación *nf* documentation
- permitió acumular una documentación de gran interés para los historiadores
  59 | 249 +o -f

4579 sonriente *adj* smiling
- una carita sonriente, como el rostro de un angelito
  60 | 340 -o +f

4580 decena *nf* ten (of something)
- con una decena de muertos y centenares de heridos
  66 | 249 -o +nf

4581 nulo *adj* void, null
- debió ser declarado nulo por el Poder Ejecutivo
  63 | 191 +nf

4582 tigre *nm* tiger
- era cazador de tigres, leones y otros animales salvajes
  61 | 255 -o +f

4583 premiar *v* to award
- todo el barrio le premió con una ovación
  62 | 158

4584 implacable *adj* relentless, implacable
- la tiranía implacable pesaba sobre el país
  65 | 285 -o +f

4585 senda *nf* path, lane
- la senda marcada es el único camino
  65 | 198 -o +f

4586 temperamento *nm* temperament, personality
- bueno, yo - por temperamento - soy optimista
  63 | 201

4587 brevemente *adv* briefly
- voy a explicar brevemente nuestra posición
  60 | 194

4588 desayunar *v* to have breakfast
- luego decidió entrar a desayunar en un café
  61 | 193 +f -nf

4589 productivo *adj* productive, profitable
- nuestro olivar es menos productivo que el de otras zonas
  65 | 619 -f +nf

4590 dicha *nf* fortune, happiness, luck
- la dicha de poseer una esposa tan bella y honesta
  61 | 177

4591 andaluz *adj* Andalusian
- las provincias andaluzas - Málaga, Granada, Córdoba...
  54 | 447

4592 acta *nf* (el) (meeting) proceedings, minutes
- parecían actas de reuniones del Partido
  62 | 195

4593 cera *nf* wax
- la luz de las dos velas de cera que había encendido sobre la mesa
  64 | 245 -o +f

4594 tanque *nm* tank, large container
- las tuberías y tanques de refinerías de petróleo
  57 | 222

4595 institucional *adj* institutional
- han contado con un apoyo institucional generoso
  62 | 632 -f +nf

4596 vigoroso *adj* vigorous, strong
- es parte de la vitalidad de un partido vigoroso como el nuestro
  63 | 203 -o

4597 batería *nf* battery, gun deck
- un golpe; dos golpes; una batería completa de golpes
  59 | 212

4598 crema *nf* cream
- 1/2 taza de crema de leche, 2 cucharadas de manteca
61 | 234

4599 atroz *adj* atrocious
- el dolor atroz de la guerra, que hiciera brotar tantas lágrimas
60 | 216 +f

4600 entretenimiento *nm* entertainment
- eran utilizados como entretenimiento; bufones; para hacer reír
62 | 208

4601 pala *nf* shovel
- con la pala cavo la tierra; con la tierra cubro a mi madre
61 | 180

4602 servidumbre *nf* staff of servants, servitude
- la servidumbre levantó la mesa
60 | 242 -o

4603 resucitar *v* to resuscitate
- no me puedo pasar la vida tratando de resucitar a una muerta
66 | 191 -o +f

4604 psicólogo *nm/f* psychologist
- el psicólogo ayuda a los pacientes a comprender mejor sus problemas
59 | 329 -f

4605 sabroso *adj* delicious, tasty
- él ha convertido simple agua en sabroso vino
61 | 222 -nf

4606 actriz *nf* actress
- veíamos a la actriz actuando junto al actor
58 | 304

4607 esencialmente *adv* essentially
- creen que la naturaleza humana es esencialmente buena
64 | 291 -f +nf

4608 larguísimo *adj* very long
- fueron muy duros, fueron años de un larguísimo insomnio
62 | 136

4609 simultáneo *adj* simultaneous
- que permitían el acceso simultáneo de muchos usuarios
65 | 255 -o +nf

4610 burro *nm* donkey
- estar harto de trabajar como un burro bajo presiones constantes
60 | 269 +f -nf

4611 procedencia *nf* origin, source
- su esposa es de procedencia española
65 | 170

4612 fiscal *nc* district attorney, prosecutor
- fue acusado del crimen y un fiscal lo llamó a juicio
61 | 288

4613 trascendental *adj* far-reaching, transcendental
- tomaron decisiones de trascendental importancia
65 | 146 +nf

4614 colorado *adj* red, colored
- entró de repente Gómez y me puse colorado como tomate
59 | 329 +f -nf

4615 financiar *v* to finance
- ¿cómo va a financiar su campaña?
65 | 334 +o -f +nf

4616 participante *nm* participant
- lógico, con la presencia de casi 3 000 participantes
61 | 241 -f +nf

4617 rescate *nm* rescue, ransom
- la búsqueda y el rescate de personas perdidas
64 | 241

4618 apuro *nm* trouble, predicament
- hay personas que, en un momento de apuro, no saben buscar una farmacia
58 | 276 +f -nf

4619 sudar *v* to sweat
- sudaba gotas calientes que le producían escalofríos
58 | 265 +f -nf

4620 prestigioso *adj* prestigious
- se fue a estudiar en un prestigioso conservatorio londinense
62 | 222 +nf

4621 cautela *nf* caution
- miró al perro con cautela; permanecía tranquilo viéndolo
63 | 166 -o +f

4622 crónico *adj* chronic
- la debilidad militar se convirtió en un problema crónico
62 | 199

4623 táctica *nf* tactics, strategy
- la idea de la lucha armada, la estrategia y táctica a seguir
64 | 198

4624 descuido *nm* neglect, oversight
- sospechaba que al menor descuido perdería el equilibrio
61 | 228 +f -nf

4625 bíblico *adj* biblical
- el papa respondió citando el precedente bíblico de David
60 | 270

4626 matanza *nf* slaughter, carnage
- por la matanza de los judíos europeos a manos de los nazis
61 | 190

4627 perturbar *v* to perturb, upset
- el enclaustramiento empezó a perturbar mi concentración
63 | 201 -o

4628 paterno *adj* paternal
- sus dos abuelos, el paterno y el materno, fueron sacerdotes
64 | 189 -o

4629 escrito *nm* manuscript, writing
- informándose de todos los escritos y estudiando hasta la última letra
61 | 314 +nf

4630 pinta *nf* appearance, look, aspect
- ¿lo ves aquí? ¡Hombre! ¿Qué pinta de deportista tiene?
- 57 | 181 -nf

4631 envidiar *v* to envy
- les admiraba, les envidiaba, les codiciaba
- 59 | 179 +f -nf

4632 reposar *v* to rest, lie down
- no busques más, niña mía, reposa en paz sin temor
- 61 | 254 -o +f

4633 acelerado *adj* accelerated, quick
- demostró frenar el proceso acelerado de metástasis
- 67 | 161 -o +nf

4634 árido *adj* arid, dry
- el Sahara es la zona desértica más grande y más árida del mundo
- 63 | 165

4635 caprichoso *adj* capricious, whimsical
- evitan este tratamiento caprichoso poco práctico
- 62 | 224 -o +f

4636 minúsculo *adj* minute, insignificant
- estaba concentrada en un punto minúsculo, menor que un átomo
- 61 | 273 -o +f

4637 caldo *nm* broth, soup
- metió el cucharón en el caldo hirviente del menudo
- 64 | 213 -o

4638 agonía *nf* agony, grief
- debe hacerse para acabar con tanta miseria, agonía y dolor
- 64 | 251 -o +f

4639 deteriorar *v* to deteriorate
- sin deteriorar la salud de los pacientes
- 65 | 179 +nf

4640 tregua *nf* truce, rest
- su mundo duro era sin tregua ni perdón
- 65 | 239 -o +f

4641 vestuario *nm* wardrobe, changing room
- la encargan diseñar el vestuario y el escenario de una ópera
- 60 | 219

4642 desesperar *v* to despair, lose hope
- no hay que desesperarse: puede estar peor
- 61 | 138 +f -nf

4643 bodega *nf* cellar, pantry, warehouse
- bajaré a la bodega; es hora de ocuparse del vino
- 60 | 188

4644 antena *nf* antenna
- detectaron unas interferencias en una antena de comunicaciones
- 56 | 291

4645 ligar *v* to tie, link, bind
- el lazo que ligaba a A. se fue estrechando
- 61 | 183

4646 maldad *nf* evil, wickedness
- la maldad de Satanás no concluyó ahí
- 61 | 228 -o +f

4647 obediencia *nf* obedience
- se le juraba obediencia al dogma católico
- 61 | 210 -o +f

4648 ocurrencia *nf* idea, witty remark
- se congratuló por la absurda ocurrencia que había tenido el día anterior
- 60 | 242 +f

4649 abiertamente *adv* openly
- puede hablarme abiertamente sobre su vida
- 65 | 167

4650 complemento *nm* complement, supplement
- la escultura fue un importante complemento de la arquitectura
- 63 | 222 +o -f +nf

4651 editor *nm/f* editor, publisher
- en la reunión con los editores de periódicos de Canadá
- 59 | 254

4652 periodismo *nm* journalism
- entré al diario de reportero y sigo en el periodismo
- 56 | 288 +o -f

4653 piscina *nf* swimming pool
- nadaba en la piscina del patio
- 57 | 172

4654 provincial *adj* provincial
- dependen de la administración federal, provincial y municipal
- 56 | 550 -f +nf

4655 mediar *v* to mediate
- España también comenzó a mediar en los conflictos centroamericanos
- 66 | 187

4656 endurecer *v* harden, make hard
- el misterio que endureció sus arterias y pudrió sus carnes
- 63 | 163 +f

4657 tradicionalmente *adv* traditionally
- en trabajos que, tradicionalmente, han sido desempeñados por los hombres
- 66 | 248 +o -f +nf

4658 inyección *nf* shot, injection
- el Doctor B. le había dado inyecciones de morfina
- 61 | 181

4659 ilegal *adj* illegal
- una ley que declaraba ilegal el comercio de esclavos con África
- 63 | 262 -f +nf

4660 reproche *nm* reproach, criticism
- con el ceño fruncido, dio gesto de reproche y evidente enojo
- 60 | 254 -o +f

4661 consistencia *nf* consistency
- sin perder la consistencia y la capacidad de convicción
- 63 | 179

4662 nobleza *nf* nobility, uprightness
- la nobleza no se hereda, señor; la crean nuestros actos
- 59 | 323

4663 terrestre *adj* earthly, of the earth
- los efectos de nuestra estrella sobre el clima terrestre
58 | 832 -f +nf

4664 impotencia *nf* impotence
- se notaba la amarga impotencia del vencido
61 | 228 -o

4665 vislumbrar *v* to glimpse
- apenas se podía vislumbrar la ventanilla entre banderas
63 | 209 -o

4666 cordial *adj* cordial, friendly
- me ha gustado mantener una actitud cordial con todo el mundo
62 | 126 -nf

4667 hostilidad *nf* hostility, enmity
- lo recibieron amistosamente sin hostilidad y con gestos amistosos
63 | 240 -o +nf

4668 angustiado *adj* anguished, distressed
- pero estoy angustiada porque no sé dónde ir
58 | 175 -nf

4669 medicamento *nm* medicine, drug
- de tomar todos esos medicamentos que el doctor me recetó
56 | 509

4670 entrenar *v* to train
- se presentó a entrenar con el equipo
58 | 221 +o

4671 piadoso *adj* devout, pious, merciful
- el sacerdote se ve tan piadoso y comprensivo
58 | 200 +f -nf

4672 corporal *adj* of the body, corporal
- su temperatura corporal depende de la temperatura ambiental
62 | 331 +nf

4673 conspiración *nf* conspiracy
- tuvo que confesarle esa conspiración para matarlo
62 | 277 -o

4674 ilimitado *adj* unlimited
- no existen recursos ilimitados para combatir la pobreza
66 | 150 +nf

4675 detención *nf* detention, arrest
- y la posterior detención de sospechosos y delincuentes
62 | 230 +nf

4676 autobús *nm* bus
- a coger el autobús para que nos llevara al centro
54 | 334

4677 firmemente *adv* firmly
- yo estaba firmemente decidido a votarla a favor
68 | 149 -o

4678 esporádico *adj* sporadic
- sobre todo, los casos esporádicos, sin antecedentes familiares
65 | 132

4679 destreza *nf* skill
- ¿ganaba más por acaso, que por destreza en sus negocios?
62 | 173 -o

4680 razonar *v* to reason (out), think
- vuelva a razonar con la lucidez de antes
62 | 176

4681 entrañas *nf* insides, bowels
- para contemplar al descubierto las entrañas del inmenso edificio
61 | 283 -o +f

4682 gratitud *nf* gratitude
- le doy mi gratitud por su generosidad
60 | 182 +f -nf

4683 rectificar *v* to rectify, straighten (out)
- «No tan naive, hijita», rectificó de inmediato la señora
64 | 158

4684 melancólico *adj* melancholy
- encierra un espíritu poético, melancólico, sentimental
63 | 278 -o +f

4685 editorial *nmf* publisher (f), editorial article (m)
- este será publicado por la editorial Oxford University Press
57 | 225 -f

4686 móvil *adj* mobile
- los ejecutivos disponen de coche, teléfono móvil, chalet . . .
65 | 218 +nf

4687 bicho *nm* bug, creature
- no había nada aparte de mosquitos y bichos perjudiciales
57 | 293 +f -nf

4688 martillo *nm* hammer
- es un martillo muy pesado de hierro y madera
58 | 176

4689 robusto *adj* strong, robust, sturdy
- por ese joven de cuerpo robusto y musculoso de atleta
59 | 255 -o +f

4690 cooperación *nf* cooperation
- abre el camino a nuevas formas de cooperación intereuropeas
65 | 347 -f +nf

4691 elevación *nf* rise, elevation, increase
- el precio de ese producto sufrió una elevación del 35 por ciento
66 | 177 +nf

4692 atentado *nm* (terrorist) attack, offense
- está perpetrando un atentado contra los intereses de los consumidores
60 | 315

4693 puñado *nm* fistful, small group
- coge un puñado de tierra y se lo lleva a la boca
58 | 208 -o +f

4694 llano *adj* flat, level, plain
- se encuentra la poco elevada y llana meseta patagónica
60 | 172

4695 colombiano *adj* Colombian
- en los ríos que parecen mares de la frontera colombiana
55 | 362 +o -f

4696 sirena *nf* siren, mermaid
- a lo lejos truena la sirena de un barco
58 | 229 +f -nf

4697 espuma *nf* foam, lather
- las olas acaban en espuma al morir en la playa
57 | 263 -o +f

4698 cirujano *nm/f* surgeon
- un internista, un pediatra, un cirujano, un ginecólogo y dentista
57 | 238

4699 angustioso *adj* distressing
- sentí un angustioso vacío en el estómago
61 | 176 +f

4700 vereda *nf* path, sidewalk
- no había árboles cerca y la vereda corría justo junto a la barranca
57 | 372 +f -nf

4701 excitar *v* to excite
- ninguno de los platos logró excitar su ahuyentado apetito
61 | 234 -o +f

4702 reivindicación *nf* claim, demand, redemption
- ésta es una reivindicación, una exigencia, un acto de justicia
63 | 230 -f +nf

4703 infección *nf* infection
- la infección degeneró en gangrena
55 | 395

4704 chiquillo *nm* kid, youngster
- más contento que un chiquillo con juguete nuevo
52 | 426 +f -nf

4705 distracción *nf* distraction, amusement
- cualquier ruido, cualquier distracción puede ser mortal
60 | 154 -nf

4706 enumerar *v* to enumerate, count
- se ponía a enumerar las 45 Corporaciones Nacionales
67 | 121 +nf

4707 estadístico *adj* statistical
- no hubo colinealidad alguna en el análisis estadístico
60 | 320 +o -f

4708 ingrediente *nm* ingredient
- torta de papas: Ingredientes: kilo de espinacas, limpias, lavadas . . .
66 | 179 +nf

4709 posar *v* to rest, pose, land
- dulcemente le posó las manos en los hombros
61 | 322 -o +f

4710 maligno *adj* evil, malignant
- desalmado, sádico, maligno, racista, incapaz de la menor decencia
58 | 235 -o +f

4711 irritar *v* to irritate
- una enorme capacidad para irritar a las autoridades
60 | 190 +f

4712 pugna *nf* battle, struggle
- se trata de la pugna por el poder político de un estado
63 | 162

4713 comprensivo *adj* understanding
- me enseñó a ser comprensivo, tolerante y leal
62 | 146

4714 hueco *adj* hollow
- ambos derivados del latín cavea,
('sitio hueco ' o 'cueva')
61 | 193

4715 torta *nf* cake
- la torta de chocolate con nueces
58 | 191 +f -nf

4716 intérprete *nc* performer, interpreter
- ella es soprano e intérprete de guitarra
59 | 283 -f +nf

4717 araña *nf* spider
- esta red de mentiras que tejiste como una araña
60 | 245 -o +f

4718 facción *nf* (face) feature, faction
- la palidez ha afilado sus facciones
61 | 317 -o +f

4719 elocuente *adj* eloquent
- no estaba elocuente; contestaba con voz desconocida
65 | 139 -o

4720 tumbar *v* to knock over, cast down
- B. se tumbó al suelo echando espuma
60 | 228 +f -nf

4721 adentrar *v* to penetrate, go inside
- se adentró en las profundidades de sí misma
60 | 210 -o

4722 diplomático *nm/f* diplomat
- el presidente, los ministros y los diplomáticos extranjeros
60 | 159

4723 exhibición *nf* exhibition, showing
- visitamos a la exhibición de arte fotográfico
60 | 211

4724 relajar *v* to relax
- das un masaje que relaja todo el cuerpo
60 | 160

4725 escaparate *nm* showcase, display window
- se detuvo, miró el escaparate de las antigüedades
59 | 179

4726 afín *adj* related, similar
- con versiones siempre afines a la versión del Vaticano
65 | 139 +nf

4727 sargento *nm* sergeant
- con las insignias de sargento, ganadas a fuerza de coraje
51 | 714 +f -nf

4728 recrear *v* to recreate, amuse
- la intención era recrear el poder que tenía el drama
61 | 177 -o +nf

4729 usual *adj* normal, usual
- algo muy usual y muy habitual entre los hombres
63 | 164

4730 estética *nf* aesthetics
- incorpora el psicoanálisis a la estética musical y la mitología
61 | 202 -f

4731 caballería *nf* cavalry, knighthood
- teniendo 8000 hombres de caballería admirablemente montados
59 | 279 -o

4732 padrino *nm* godparent, sponsor
- cuando yo canté misa, él fue mi padrino, me dio algunos consejos
55 | 290 -nf

4733 diversidad *nf* diversity, variety
- contiene una gran diversidad de personas, culturas y lenguas
64 | 359 -f +nf

4734 banquete *nm* banquet, feast
- organizarían la ceremonia religiosa y el banquete de bodas
61 | 172 +f

4735 bancario *adj* bank, banking
- más comúnmente utilizados en el mundo bancario y financiero
61 | 366 +nf

4736 impartir *v* to impart, administer
- vengo en calidad de sacerdote a impartir la bendición
62 | 176 +o -f

4737 andar *nm* walk, gait, pace
- para oír pisadas duras en la acera, o el andar de las patrullas
63 | 288 -o +f

4738 gigante *nc* giant
- tienen gran variedad de tamaños, desde gigantes a enanas
62 | 217 -o

4739 afortunado *adj* fortunate
- he sido muy afortunado; he tenido una vida maravillosamente rica
61 | 168

4740 pabellón *nm* pavilion, sports hall
- una coproducción de la Expo y el Pabellón de España
59 | 186

4741 abeja *nf* bee
- hay insectos como abejas, avispas, moscas, mariposas, y polillas
60 | 277 -o

4742 asentir *v* to assent, agree
- ¿te gusta? Volvía a asentir la niña, sin palabras
57 | 352 -o +f -nf

4743 espontáneamente *adv* spontaneously
- y que se endurece espontáneamente en contacto con el aire
62 | 160

4744 informativo *adj* informative
- de actuar como medio informativo al margen de la noticia oficial
59 | 329 -f +nf

4745 violín *nm* violin
- cayó encima de su violín, un hermosísimo Stradivarius
57 | 286

4746 astro *nm* star
- los movimientos de otros astros y planetas
61 | 173

4747 dictador *nm* dictator
- bajo la dirección del dictador Francisco Franco
60 | 191

4748 roce *nm* brush, graze
- sintiendo el roce inmenso y atemorizante de sus enormes dedos
60 | 185 -o +f

4749 prolongación *nf* extension
- este estilo fue una prolongación del arte románica
63 | 163 -o

4750 cráneo *nm* skull, cranium
- de colocarle los electrodos en el cráneo, la frente y la mejilla
61 | 273 -o

4751 aflojar *v* to loosen
- eso sirvió para aflojar mis tensiones
60 | 216 +f -nf

4752 hola *interj* hello, hi
- se acercó a saludar. - Hola, Mercedes, le dijo
54 | 480 +o +f -nf

4753 importado *adj* imported
- cuando el automóvil importado es un modelo producido localmente
61 | 177

4754 íntegro *adj* whole, entire, honest
- la prensa no ha publicado el texto íntegro de sus palabras
64 | 135

4755 agradecimiento *nm* gratitude, gratefulness
- quiero rendirle tributo de agradecimiento al hombre que me salvó la vida
61 | 163

4756 extra *adj* extra
- se intercala un mes extra cada tres años
61 | 151

4757 audacia *nf* boldness, audacity
- el hombre se jactó de su audacia y su suerte
62 | 160 -o

4758 cólera *nmf* rage (f), cholera (m)
- grandes progresos en erradicar el cólera, la viruela y la malaria
60 | 248 -o

4759 resignación *nf* resignation, acceptance
- estoy dispuesta a aceptarla con resignación, sin oponer resistencia
60 | 203 -o +f

4760 legislación *nf* legislation
- el gobierno de Francia aprobó la primera legislación sobre medioambiente
61 | 550 +o -f +nf

4761 recíproco *adj* reciprocal
- ha sido una actitud de respeto recíproco
62 | 172

4762 caramelo *nm* piece of candy, caramel
- es un caramelo dulce que se chupa
60 | 210 -o +f

4763 pólvora *nf* gunpowder, powder
- ellos atacan con pólvora, nosotros nos defenderemos con hierro
61 | 183 -o

4764 rol *nm* role
- qué opinas sobre esta división de trabajo y tu rol en un hogar
56 | 313 -f

4765 fértil *adj* fertile, rich
- un fértil sedimento que dio abundantes frutos
66 | 195 +nf

4766 ensuciar *v* to get dirty
- entonces se ensucia de lodo
58 | 155 +f -nf

4767 largar *v* to let go, start out
- autoriza a la tropa a largarse detrás de unos avestruces
56 | 336 +f -nf

4768 acomodado *adj* well-to-do, suitable
- las familias más acomodadas tenían pozos cavados a pala y pico
62 | 132

4769 idiota *nc* idiot, dunce
- me llamó inútil, me llamó idiota, me llamó imbécil
55 | 225 +f -nf

4770 bahía *nf* bay
- la playa formaba parte de una hermosa bahía
58 | 286 -o

4771 latitud *nf* latitude
- la latitud se mide hasta 90° N y hasta 90° S
61 | 254 +nf

4772 buey *nm* ox
- tiradas por lentos bueyes de colas pendulares
62 | 278 -o +f

4773 vaivén *nm* swinging, rocking
- el vaivén del mar marcaba el pulso de las horas
62 | 198 -o +f

4774 equivocación *nf* mistake, misconception
- yo era el culpable de esta equivocación profunda y terrible
61 | 153

4775 comunismo *nm* communism
- la Rusia que surge de las cenizas del comunismo
58 | 273 -f

4776 partícula *nf* particle
- la colisión de las partículas de rayos cósmicos con los átomos
57 | 842 -o +nf

4777 intermedio *nm* means, interval
- han venido a nuestras manos por intermedio de los campesinos
60 | 138

4778 económicamente *adv* economically
- para socorrer económicamente a los necesitados de su entorno
63 | 216 +o -f +nf

4779 limosna *nf* alms, charity
- pidiendo limosna en la calle
58 | 167 +f -nf

4780 equivalente *nm* equivalent
- 28 millones de barriles de petróleo es el equivalente de 70 kg. de deuterio
65 | 221 -f +nf

4781 flecha *nf* arrow, dart
- son seminómadas y emplean la lanza, el arco, la flecha para la cacería
61 | 208 -o +f

4782 soberano *adj* sovereign, self-assured
- Perú es un país soberano y tiene derecho a sus propias leyes
63 | 213

4783 presentir *v* to sense in advance
- pues al instante presintió que algo andaba mal
57 | 297 -o +f -nf

4784 desilusión *nf* disappointment, letdown
- no me entendían nada, ni yo les entendía nada. ¡Qué desilusión!
60 | 141

4785 insertar *v* to insert, put in
- buscaba huecos donde insertar palabras que tuviesen sentido
64 | 161 +nf

4786 pato *nm* duck
- las aves acuáticas, incluídos los patos y los gansos
56 | 207

4787 guerrero *adj* warrior, warlike
- los hombres de la clase guerrera estaban muy orgullosos de la lucha
64 | 178 -o

4788 grieta *nf* crack, opening, slit
- por la grieta del suelo se filtraba la luz de la planta baja
57 | 208

4789 jinete *nm* rider, horseman
- el jinete cae de un caballo desbocado
58 | 302 -o +f

4790 involuntario *adj* involuntary
- le chicoteó en una convulsión involuntaria
59 | 178 -o

4791 discurrir *v* to flow, pass, roam
- veía discurrir los días con una angustia creciente
62 | 215 -o

4792 inexistente *adj* non-existent
- la libertad era algo inexistente o reservado a grupos privilegiados
64 | 156 -o +nf

4793 subjetivo *adj* subjective
- desde el subjetivo punto de vista del buen gusto
60 | 343 +o -f +nf

4794 agricultor *nm/f* farmer
- comenzó como una sociedad rural de agricultores independientes
61 | 324 +nf

4795 garra *nf* claw, fang
- una mano que más bien parecía una garra de águila
62 | 180 -o +f

4796 engordar *v* to fatten, get fat
- un alimento especial para engordar animales
59 | 155 -nf

4797 soporte *nm* support, endorsement
- el mismo apoyo y el mismo soporte económico
61 | 290 -f +nf

4798 concurrencia *nf* coming together, participation
- no puede haber paz sin la concurrencia de las partes
60 | 172

4799 pirámide *nf* pyramid
- construyeron las pirámides y otras estructuras monumentales
57 | 222 -f

4800 aventurar *v* to venture, risk
- la primera vez que me aventuraba solo por los caminos
66 | 134

4801 neutro *adj* neutral
- estas partículas pueden ser neutras, positivas o negativas
60 | 164

4802 demandar *v* to claim, sue
- las mujeres salen a las calles para demandar nuevos derechos
64 | 240 -f +nf

4803 fósforo *nm* match, match stick
- enciende un fósforo y quema la carta
54 | 239

4804 profeta *nm* prophet
- Mahoma (c. 570–632), principal profeta del Islam
59 | 287 +nf

4805 renacer *v* to be reborn, reappear
- sintió renacer en su pecho el antiguo cariño
61 | 160

4806 restablecer *v* to reestablish, restore
- para restablecer las relaciones con el Vaticano
63 | 255 -o +nf

4807 muslo *nm* thigh
- el culotte, o pantalones ajustados al muslo que llegan hasta casi la rodilla
58 | 450 -o +f

4808 desconcertado *adj* disoriented, disconcerted
- ¿cómo se siente? - Desconcertado, defraudado, abatido, roto
60 | 226 -o +f

4809 retiro *nm* withdrawal, retreat
- el retiro espiritual me ayudará a recuperar
61 | 161

4810 comando *nm* command, order
- la creación de un sistema de comando militar
57 | 242

4811 sobrevenir *v* to occur, befall, strike
- puede sobrevenir la muerte
63 | 193 -o +f

4812 emisión *nf* broadcast, emission
- las emisiones de radio eran para las noticias urgentes
61 | 570 -f +nf

4813 rebasar *v* to exceed, pass over
- el volcán no tardaría en rebasar su orilla
64 | 182 -o

4814 tenor *nm* a tenor de: in accordance with
- era imprescindible, a tenor de las nuevas circunstancias
60 | 195

4815 recompensa *nf* reward, recompense
- ordenaron su captura vivo o muerto con una recompensa por su cabeza
63 | 141

4816 complicidad *nf* involvement, complicity
- la confidencia estableció una especie de complicidad entre nosotros
62 | 235 -o +f

4817 recelo *nm* mistrust, suspicion
- le rodeaba un halo negro de recelo y de murmuraciones
61 | 171 -o

4818 vibración *nf* vibration
- el sonido se produce por la vibración de una cuerda
58 | 258 -o +f

4819 restricción *nf* restriction
- mediante la regulación y restricción de su comercio
63 | 436 -f +nf

4820 acatar *v* to comply with, abide by
- decide acatar las decisiones del Ministro
62 | 137

4821 transitar *v* to roam, go by
- empezaría a transitar los caminos de la historia
60 | 193

4822 vara *nf* rod, stick
- les golpea con una vara larga
58 | 208 -o +f

4823 clientela *nf* customers, clients
- escuchaba la charla de los dependientes con la clientela en la tienda
59 | 168

4824 soberanía *nf* sovereignty
- proporcionaban a Panamá la soberanía sobre la Zona del Canal
60 | 408 +nf

4825 impreciso *adj* imprecise
- ese mundo de límites imprecisos y mutantes
62 | 180 -o +f

4826 percatar *v* to inform, become aware
- al percatarse de nuestra intención de entrar
61 | 195 +f

4827 frialdad *nf* coldness, indifference
- en la casa hay apatía, abandono, frialdad
59 | 159 +f

4828 encomendar *v* to commend, entrust
- se encomendó a la Divina Providencia
60 | 141

4829 inspección *nf* inspection
- una ola de inspecciones, confiscaciones, arrestos y detenciones
61 | 207

4830 inicial *nf* initial (letters)
- un artículo periodístico firmado con las iniciales D.M.
61 | 152

4831 seducir *v* to seduce, tempt
- me quiere seducir con promesas de éxtasis
57 | 207 -o +f

4832 incidencia *nf* ocurrence, impact
- se produce un aumento en la incidencia del cáncer de tiroides;
57 | 379 -f +nf

4833 retroceso *nm* movement backwards
- no hay ni avance ni retroceso
64 | 154 +nf

4834 micrófono *nm* microphone
- el micrófono de carbono amplifica la energía sonora
54 | 210 +o -f

4835 previsible *adj* foreseeable
- siendo la principal fuente de petróleo en el futuro previsible
61 | 185 -o

4836 ventanilla *nf* (vehicle) window
- la carita pegada a la ventanilla del tren
55 | 303 +f -nf

4837 frontal *adj* frontal
- para ofrecer un punto de vista frontal y otro lateral
64 | 170 -o +nf

4838 extinción *nf* extinction
- provocaron la extinción de los dinosaurios
61 | 229 -f +nf

4839 infinito *nm* infinite, infinity
- y la lista podría ir hasta el infinito
58 | 188 -o

4840 campeón *nm* champion
- como deportista fue campeón sudamericano de baloncesto
51 | 456

4841 incidir *v* to influence, affect
- su actitud podía incidir sobre otros ánimos
60 | 265 -f +nf

4842 monstruoso *adj* monstrous
- mi viciosa mente me suscitó algo monstruoso y grotesco
59 | 176 +f

4843 persistente *adj* persistent
- sus oídos, lastimados por un silbido persistente, comenzaban a doler
64 | 154 -o +nf

4844 oxígeno *nm* oxygen
- la necesidad de respirar oxígeno en los organismos aerobios
56 | 505 -f +nf

4845 rigidez *nf* rigidity
- las propiedades de la madera son dureza, rigidez y densidad
63 | 183 -o +nf

4846 educado *adj* educated
- ¡patán, mal educado, descortés, desagradecido
59 | 127 -nf

4847 irreversible *adj* irreversible
- estarían a merced de una degradación irreversible e incontrolada
63 | 169 +nf

4848 despedida *nf* goodbye, farewell
- fue triste la despedida en el aeropuerto, cuando iba a Israel
57 | 219 +f -nf

4849 vengar *v* to take revenge, avenge
- trataba de vengarse de quien le había robado la mamá
56 | 183

4850 encaje *nm* lace
- tenemos un tapete de encaje, precioso, en blanco
59 | 280 -o +f -nf

4851 estropear *v* to ruin, mess up
- me estropean la pintura o me roban la antena
57 | 159 -nf

4852 repercusión *nf* repercussion, impact
- la decisión tuvo una enorme repercusión en el exterior
64 | 219 -f +nf

4853 prematuro *adj* premature
- entiendo que es un poco prematuro, pero la pregunta vale
63 | 156 -o

4854 fascinar *v* to fascinate
- me fascina descubrir las intimidades del ser humano
58 | 209

4855 ganador *nm* winner
- Ernest Hemingway, ganador del Premio Nobel (1954)
58 | 297

4856 emperador *nm* emperor
- durante el reinado del emperador romano Constantino I el Grande
56 | 722 -o +nf

4857 cometa *nmf* comet (m), kite (f)
- el cometa Halley regresa al Sistema Solar cada 75 años
58 | 275

4858 precedente *nm* precedent
- es un avance sin precedentes en la historia del país
63 | 300 -f +nf

4859 rudo *adj* rude, crude, coarse
- tienen que ser abruptos, y hay veces era hasta rudos
58 | 190 -o +f

4860 cerebral *adj* cerebral
- el hemisferio cerebral izquierdo regula el lenguaje
- 57 | 483 +nf

4861 mosaico *nm* mosaic
- el país era un mosaico de provincias, razas y culturas diversas
- 58 | 182

4862 significación *nf* meaning, significance
- puede dar una significación más trascendente a los contenidos
- 58 | 299 -f

4863 contestación *nf* answer
- esta es una pregunta de difícil contestación
- 59 | 138 +o

4864 pedagógico *adj* pedagogical, teaching
- cree en el valor pedagógico de la literatura infantil
- 57 | 258 +o -f

4865 asilo *nm* asylum, shelter
- ¡te costará caro dar asilo a un esclavo fugitivo!
- 61 | 124

4866 incremento *nm* increase, raise
- sólo se trataba de un incremento del 0.37% el primer año
- 60 | 975 -f +nf

4867 incurrir *v* to incur, fall into
- acabaron de incurrir en desgracia
- 62 | 171

4868 lomo *nm* back, loin, spine
- viaja a lomo de burro
- 58 | 263 -o +f

4869 tentar *v* to tempt, entice
- es pecado muy grave tentar a la muerte
- 57 | 207 -o +f

4870 navegación *nf* navigation, shipping
- desarrollaron una canoa de navegación muy rápida
- 56 | 344 +nf

4871 edificación *nf* construction, building
- el diseño y la edificación de estructuras militares
- 61 | 168

4872 abstracción *nf* abstraction
- había tendido puentes entre surrealismo y abstracción
- 58 | 203

4873 veintidós *num* twenty-two
- yo tenía veintiún, no veintidós años
- 60 | 169 +o

4874 grotesco *adj* grotesque, ridiculous
- para reflejar también el desencanto, la violencia y lo grotesco
- 57 | 229 -o +f

4875 duramente *adv* harshly, severely
- los opositores criticaban duramente su política interna
- 62 | 135

4876 sumido *adj* sunken, drowned
- el país está sumido en una ola de disturbios
- 59 | 218 -o +f

4877 públicamente *adv* publicly, in public
- a muchos de ellos se les ha apoyado públicamente
- 58 | 263

4878 resignar *v* to resign, relinquish
- el procurador general debiera resignar públicamente el cargo
- 60 | 207 -o +f

4879 mortal *nc* mortal
- se consideraba que los dioses actuaban como los mortales
- 60 | 146 -o +f

4880 siniestro *adj* sinister
- sus sospechas se confirmarían un siniestro martes por la tarde
- 57 | 250 -o +f

4881 místico *adj* mystical
- hombre místico, meditativo, oscuro y profundo
- 56 | 231 -o

4882 cabina *nf* cabin, cockpit
- lo vio sentado en la cabina de la camioneta
- 55 | 207 +f

4883 dialogar *v* to confer, talk
- nosotros tendremos ocasión de dialogar sin que nos escuchen
- 59 | 255 -nf

4884 exento *adj* exempt, free
- hasta el amor no está exento de las mil dificultades
- 62 | 209 -o +nf

4885 guerrero *nm/f* warrior, soldier
- los asesinos y los guerreros sólo pueden morir en la guerra
- 60 | 229 -o

4886 acera *nf* sidewalk
- esperaba en la acera a que pasara el tráfico
- 53 | 427 +f -nf

4887 clínico *adj* clinical
- de publicar los resultados de un amplio ensayo clínico
- 55 | 506 +o -f

4888 largamente *adv* for a long time, at length
- es un tema que hemos conversado largamente varias veces
- 60 | 204 -o +f

4889 callejero *adj* of the street
- un perro callejero se rebusca en los basureros de la vecindad
- 61 | 189 -o

4890 adherir *v* to adhere, attach
- se adherían formalmente al programa
- 62 | 177 -o +nf

4891 voluntariamente *adv* voluntarily
- ¿será cierto que haya gente que desaparece voluntariamente? ¡No lo creo!
- 59 | 147

4892 centavo *nm* cent
- con un poquito de crema que le costaba cinco centavos
- 57 | 238 +o -nf

4893 molino *nm* mill, windmill
- una de las máquinas más importantes de la época medieval fue el molino
60 | 172

4894 parcialmente *adv* partially
- esta toxicidad puede bloquearse parcialmente con lactosa
64 | 241 -f +nf

4895 decepción *nf* disappointment, disenchantment
- la mayor decepción y derrota que sufrió en toda su carrera
59 | 152

4896 alojar *v* to host, accommodate
- no podían alojar a tantos delincuentes
61 | 179 -o

4897 debidamente *adv* properly, duly
- es indispensable que conteste debidamente todos los cuestionarios
60 | 167

4898 ente *nm* entity, being, firm
- el Instituto Cervantes es un ente público
60 | 245 -f +nf

4899 internar *v* to confine
- después se nos internó en campos de concentración
59 | 200 -o +f

4900 mismísimo *adj* very same
- canta y guitarrea rock and roll como el mismísimo Elvis
58 | 165 +f

4901 contundente *adj* decisive, blunt, forceful
- y derrotarlos de forma rápida y contundente
59 | 189

4902 inundación *nf* flood, deluge
- la inundación anual del río Nilo
61 | 228 +nf

4903 diligencia *nf* diligence
- lo atendía con una cariñosa diligencia
59 | 188 -o

4904 viceversa *adv* vice versa
- Natalia era su consuelo y viceversa
58 | 147

4905 séptimo *adj* seventh
- la India es el séptimo país más extenso del mundo
61 | 144

4906 complejidad *nf* complexity
- los medios y técnicas utilizados son de gran complejidad
60 | 360 -f +nf

4907 carente *adj* lacking, devoid
- es un problema de la sociedad, que está carente de dirección
62 | 166 -o +nf

4908 nítido *adj* clear, clean, neat
- es apenas audible, pero pronto se vuelve más nítido y claro
60 | 183 -o

4909 imponente *adj* impressive, magnificent
- el sol se presentó imponente y luminoso
62 | 152 -o +f

4910 vecindad *nf* nearness, vicinity
- el fenómeno geopolítico de la vecindad con los Estados Unidos
58 | 175

4911 secular *adj* secular, lay
- y transformando el tema sacro en una historia secular
60 | 221 -o +nf

4912 cabra *nf* goat
- la domesticación de animales, como vacas, ovejas, cabras y cerdos
59 | 231 -o

4913 olfato *nm* sense of smell
- con su fino olfato detectó el olor
60 | 187

4914 denominación *nf* name, denomination
- el territorio conocido históricamente bajo la denominación de Países Bajos
61 | 333 -f +nf

4915 bordear *v* to border
- en dirección noroeste, a través o bordeando Francia y Alemania
61 | 208 -o +f

4916 envergadura *nf* breadth, expanse
- todas palidecen ante la envergadura y la magnitud de su proyecto
63 | 158 +nf

4917 admirador *nm* admirer
- soy un ferviente admirador de ese héroe que usted llama mítico
60 | 138

4918 instruir *v* to instruct
- fomenta la educación intelectual e instruye en la investigación científica
60 | 130

4919 rebaño *nm* herd, flock
- trabajaba de pastor con un rebaño pequeño
60 | 160 -o

4920 inicialmente *adv* initially
- sería inicialmente un proyecto piloto en cuatro o cinco países
61 | 265 -f +nf

4921 vegetal *nm* plant, vegetable
- la principal característica de los vegetales es su capacidad fotosintética
55 | 321 +nf

4922 inseparable *adj* inseparable
- C. era el compañero inseparable de Facundo
60 | 140 -o +nf

4923 fiera *nf* (wild) beast
- deambula de un lado a otro como fiera enjaulada
59 | 251 -o +f -nf

4924 verter *v* to pour, spill, shed
- se suele verter agua sobre la imagen de Buda
61 | 162 -o

4925 desmentir *v* to contradict
- una amable afabilidad que desmiente la seria expresión
62 | 160 -o

4926 inestable *adj* unstable, unsteady
• el neutrón es inestable como partícula aislada
62 | 151 -o +nf

4927 olla *nf* pot, kettle
• la arrojó sobre una olla gigante de sopa de pollo hirviendo
55 | 209 +f -nf

4928 terriblemente *adv* terribly
• esta pesadilla es terriblemente realista
58 | 137 +o -nf

4929 coco *nm* coconut
• en el coco, la cáscara dura exterior es el pericarpio
58 | 178 -nf

4930 sótano *nm* basement
• en un estacionamiento en el sótano de un edificio
55 | 224 +f -nf

4931 agresividad *nf* aggressiveness
• somos seres ajenos a la violencia y a la agresividad que nos rodea
59 | 142

4932 mentalmente *adv* mentally
• ya tenía mentalmente escrita la primera carta
56 | 185 +f -nf

4933 adhesión *nf* adherence
• la observación cuidadosa y la adhesión estricta a las reglas de la lógica
66 | 233 -o +nf

4934 convención *nf* convention, assembly
• los delegados de la convención nacional de su partido
58 | 299 +nf

4935 paraje *nm* place, spot
• los restos en un paraje que es famoso por su arqueología
58 | 229 -o +f

4936 frívolo *adj* trivial, frivolous
• lo que estáis contemplando no es un frívolo baile de máscaras
58 | 139

4937 cohete *nm* rocket
• el Skylab fue lanzado con el cohete Saturno 5
54 | 356 -o

4938 prodigioso *adj* prodigious, famous
• él fue el mago prodigioso que convirtió el desierto en jardín
61 | 194 -o +f

4939 almohada *nf* pillow
• una almohada en la que reposas tu cuello y tu cabeza
53 | 303 +f -nf

4940 eficiencia *nf* efficiency
• para aumentar la eficiencia y reducir los gastos de mantenimiento
59 | 244 +nf

4941 laborioso *adj* laborious, industrious
• es más laborioso restaurar que construir
59 | 152

4942 eclesiástico *adj* ecclesiastical
• desterró a los sacerdotes y otro personal eclesiástico
58 | 225

4943 confundido *adj* confused
• bueno, estoy confundido ahora, no sé; no, es que ahora estoy . . .
56 | 177 +f -nf

4944 tejado *nm* roof, housetop
• escuchamos la lluvia caer sobre el tejado
55 | 239

4945 elefante *nm* elephant
• algunos mamíferos tropicales, como los gorilas, elefantes, y tapires
56 | 216

4946 descifrar *v* to decipher
• para descifrar un fragmento escrito en caracteres cuneiformes
61 | 206 -o +f

4947 navaja *nf* razor, blade, navaja
• tomó la navaja de afeitar y se cortó el cuello
57 | 209 -o +f

4948 maldición *nf* damnation, curse
• los pronunciamientos de maldición y salvación eterna
58 | 174 -o +f -nf

4949 marinero *nm/f* sailor
• los marineros podían salir del barco utilizando una maroma
59 | 216 -o +f

4950 bachillerato *nm* high school diploma
• terminé el bachillerato en la universidad, en Estudios Hispánicos
55 | 321 +o

4951 marrón *adj* brown
• de color casi marrón, daba la impresión de ser madera
55 | 228 -o +f

4952 entablar *v* to start, establish
• para hacer nuevas amistades y entablar conversaciones interesantes
61 | 125

4953 desequilibrio *nm* imbalance, unsteadiness
• el creciente desequilibrio de las cuentas fiscales
60 | 256 -f +nf

4954 sintético *adj* synthetic
• una gran variedad de productos de algodón y fibras sintéticas
62 | 251 -f +nf

4955 bélico *adj* warlike
• fue un activo defensor de la intervención bélica de su país
59 | 267 -f +nf

4956 combinado *adj* combined
• hablan a favor de las ventajas que el tratamiento combinado
62 | 170 -o +nf

4957 desperdicio *nm* waste, refuse, garbage
• bolsas llenas de basuras, de desperdicios
59 | 150 +f

4958 propagar *v* to propagate, spread
- decidió enviar expediciones para propagar el movimiento revolucionario
58 | 158 +nf

4959 ampliación *nf* enlargement, extension
- la ampliación de los horizontes del conocimiento científico
61 | 265 -f +nf

4960 recipiente *nm* container, recipient, tank
- se utilizaba habitualmente para los recipientes de comida y bebida
55 | 249 -o

4961 parlamentario *adj* parliamentary
- la Constitución establecía un sistema parlamentario bicameral
53 | 1279 +o -f +nf

4962 trasero *adj* behind, back
- flanqueada por dos corredores laterales y uno trasero
60 | 253 -o +f

4963 despliegue *nm* deployment, display
- era un despliegue de fuerzas para aplastar el amotinamiento
60 | 162 +nf

4964 libra *nf* pound (money/weight)
- su estimación es de 1,2 – 1,6 millones de libras (240-320 millones de pesetas)
57 | 176

4965 incursión *nf* invasion, incursion
- una incursión de tropas estadounidenses en territorio de México
60 | 171

4966 irreal *adj* unreal
- una sensación de ligereza un tanto irreal
59 | 151 +f

4967 toalla *nf* towel
- viene con el pelo mojado y se seca con la toalla
57 | 241 +f -nf

4968 tenis *nm* tennis
- lo jugábamos con raqueta de tenis
51 | 244 +o

4969 perfilar *v* to outline, shape
- el tema no se perfila en blanco y negro
60 | 166

4970 entusiasta *adj* enthusiastic
- un aplauso prolongado, entusiasta, recibió al mago
61 | 111

4971 descarga *nf* unloading, discharge
- disponen de muelles para la carga y descarga de los buques
55 | 224 -o

4972 patriótico *adj* patriotic
- iban cantando un himno patriótico
58 | 173

4973 higiene *nf* hygiene
- a través de consejos psicológicos, sanidad, higiene, y nutrición
56 | 173

4974 decaer *v* to decay, wane
- juntos vieron prosperar y decaer la familia
60 | 146 +nf

4975 cuenca *nf* socket, basin, bowl
- tratando de reinsertar un ojo en la cuenca vacía de una muñeca
59 | 315 -o +nf

4976 aplastado *adj* crushed, flattened
- simboliza el pecado aplastado bajo el pie de santos
57 | 179 -o +f

4977 cal *nf* lime, whitewash
- como todos los templos allá son recubiertos de cal blanco
59 | 182 -o +f

4978 rítmico *adj* rhythmic
- mantenían el constante swing rítmico característico del jazz
56 | 229 -o

4979 disfrazar *v* to disguise, hide, conceal
- se le hacía imposible disfrazar su enorme embarazo
56 | 159 +f -nf

4980 pionero *nm* pioneer
- puede considerarse uno de los pioneros de la arquitectura mexicana
60 | 210 -f +nf

4981 volcán *nm* volcano
- provocando erupciones en volcanes como el Etna y el Vesubio
53 | 303

4982 puta *nf* whore, prostitute
- ¿acaso soy una puta para que me goce todo el mundo?
51 | 450 +f -nf

4983 hispano *adj* Hispanic
- los calificativos 'hispano' o 'blanco' obedecen a definiciones sociales
59 | 180 -f +nf

4984 diamante *nm* diamond
- las minas de diamantes de Sudáfrica
53 | 266

4985 constructivo *adj* constructive
- bueno o malo, positivo o negativo, constructivo o destructivo
60 | 243 +o -f +nf

4986 delicadeza *nf* gentleness, tenderness
- lo observa con ternura, cubriéndolo con delicadeza con unas pieles
57 | 184 -o +f

4987 ocasional *adj* occasional, random
- daban lugar a ocasionales manifestaciones del malestar civil
61 | 157 -o +nf

4988 expulsión *nf* expulsion, ejection
- desde la expulsión de judíos y moriscos en 1492
58 | 196 +nf

4989 enigma *nm* enigma, mystery
- la tragedia del Hindenburg o el enigma de Tutankamón
58 | 174 -o +f

4990 monumental *adj* monumental
- allí, enfrente, está la monumental iglesia de Nuestra Señora
58 | 229 +nf

4991 hectárea *nf* hectare
- una extensión de doscientas hectáreas en el centro de un valle
59 | 434 -f +nf

4992 accesible *adj* accessible
- para conservar y hacer accesible una obra de arte
63 | 151 -f +nf

4993 inmigrante *nc* immigrant
- para los inmigrantes que llegan a nuestras poblaciones fronterizas
56 | 199 +nf

4994 irrumpir *v* to burst in, raid
- con violencia irrumpieron en la iglesia
61 | 185 -o +f

4995 prevención *nf* prevention, warning
- el control y de prevención de problemas cardiovasculares
57 | 253 -f +nf

4996 cerco *nm* fence, circle, ring
- cuatro días después los soviéticos cerraron el cerco sobre Berlín
58 | 197 -o +f

4997 penumbra *nf* semidarkness, twilight
- el cuarto queda en penumbra con una sola luz
57 | 575 -o +f

4998 jugada *nf* move, play
- una jugada que puede ser decisiva en el partido
52 | 243

4999 estampa *nf* print, engraving, illustration
- la reliquia de Jerusalén pegada a la estampa que trajo de Tierra Santa
58 | 251 -o +f

5000 cueva *nf* cave
- es una pequeña cueva rodeada de inmensas rocas
58 | 210 -o +f

Alphabetical index

headword, *part of speech,* English equivalent, **rank frequency (501, 502...)**

A

a *prep* to, at 5

abajo *adv* down, below, downward 631

abandonado *adj* abandoned 2298

abandonar *v* to abandon, leave (a place) 638

abandono *nm* abandonment, desertion 2524

abanico *nm* range, (handheld) fan 4422

abarcar *v* to encompass, comprise 2163

abeja *nf* bee 4741

abiertamente *adv* openly 4649

abierto *adj* open, unlocked 439

abismo *nm* abyss, large gap 3612

abogado *nm/f* lawyer 1680

abordar *v* to board, get in/on 2273

abrazar *v* to hug, embrace 2873

abrazo *nm* hug, embrace 3767

abrigo *nm* overcoat, shelter 2996

abril *nm* April 1922

abrir *v* to open 252

absolutamente *adv* absolutely, completely 1181

absoluto *adj* absolute 574

absorber *v* to absorb, soak up 2056

abstracción *nf* abstraction 4872

abstracto *adj* abstract 3549

absurdo *adj* absurd 2010

absurdo *nm* absurdity, nonsense 3648

abuela *nf* grandmother 2408

abuelo *nm* grandfather 1740

abundancia *nf* abundance 3178

abundante *adj* abundant, plentiful 2316

abundar *v* to be plentiful 2923

aburrido *adj* boring, bored 2813

aburrimiento *nm* boredom 4488

aburrir *v* to bore, tire 4024

abusar *v* to abuse 3658

abuso *nm* abuse, misuse 2605

acá *adv* here, around here 2230

acabar *v* acabar de V: to have just Ved; finish 266

academia *nf* academy 4039

académico *adj* academic 2399

acariciar *v* to stroke, fondle, caress 4398

acarrear *v* to bring up, entail 3631

acaso *adv* by chance, maybe 1072

acatar *v* to comply with, abide by 4820

acceder *v* to consent, agree, accede 2130

accesible *adj* accessible 4992

acceso *nm* access, entry 1315

accidente *nm* accident, irregularity 1098

acción *nf* action, act, deed 405

aceite *nm* oil 2076

acelerado *adj* accelerated, quick 4633

acelerar *v* to accelerate, speed (up) 3053

acento *nm* accent, stress 2610

acentuar *v* to accent, stress 2718

aceptable *adj* acceptable, suitable 3384

aceptación *nf* acceptance, approval 2758

aceptar *v* to accept 296

acera *nf* sidewalk 4886

acerca *adv* about, concerning 1288

acercamiento *nm* approach, approximation 4334

acercar *v* to come near 410

acero *nm* steel 3064

acertado *adj* correct, accurate 4040

acertar *v* to get right 3308

ácido *nm* acid 3729

acierto *nm* good aim, guess, hit 4248

aclarar *v* to clarify, clear up 1133

acoger *v* to welcome, accept 2715

acomodado *adj* well-to-do, suitable 4768

acomodar *v* to be/make comfortable 2196

acompañar *v* to accompany 512

aconsejar *v* to advise, counsel 1828

acontecer *v* to happen, come about 3831

acontecimiento *nm* event, happening 1125

acordar *v* to remember, remind 595

acorde *nm* agreement, accord 3783

acostar *v* to put/go to bed 3077

acostumbrado *adj* accustomed 1595

acostumbrar *v* to be accustomed to 1628

acta *nf* (el) (meeting) proceedings, minutes 4592

actitud *nf* attitude 644

actividad *nf* activity, action 393

activo *adj* active 1328

acto *nm* act, action 572

actor *nm* actor 1705

actriz *nf* actress 4606

actuación *nf* performance, acting 1924

actual *adj* current 676

actualidad *nf* present (time) 2046

actualmente *adv* now, at present 2362

actuar *v* to act 576

acudir *v* to attend, go to, frequent 1044

acuerdo *nm* accord; de acuerdo: in agreement 313

acumulación *nf* accumulation 3718

acumular *v* to accumulate, amass 1301

acusación *nf* accusation, charge 3573

acusar *v* to accuse 1524

adaptación *nf* adaptation 3809

adaptar *v* to adapt 2087

adecuado *adj* adequate, suitable 948

adelantar *v* to move forward 1777

adelante *adv* forward, further 516

adelanto *nm* advance, progress 4210

además *adv* also, as well, besides 159

adentrar *v* to penetrate, go inside 4721

adentro *adv* inside 2084

adherir *v* to adhere, attach 4890

adhesión *nf* adherence 4933

adicional *adj* additional 4124

adiós *nm* goodbye 2557

adivinar *v* to guess, solve 2954

adjetivo *nm* adjective 4511

administración *nf* administration 2055

administrador *nm/f* administrator, manager 3527

administrar *v* to administer, manage 2773

administrativo *adj* administrative 2852

admirable *adj* admirable 2934

admiración *nf* admiration 2448

admirador *nm* admirer 4917

admirar *v* to admire 1682

admitir *v* to admit 985

adolescencia *nf* adolescence 3397

adolescente *nc* adolescent 2645

adolescente *adj* adolescent 4459

adonde *adv* to where 4275

adónde *adv* to where? 3926

adoptar *v* to adopt 1267

adorar *v* to worship, adore 3124

adornar *v* to adorn, to decorate 4179

adorno *nm* decoration, adornment 3468

adquirir *v* to acquire, get 603

adquisición *nf* acquisition 3687

adulto *nm* adult, grown-up 2200

adulto *adj* adult, grown-up 2685

adversario *nm* adversary 3667

advertencia *nf* warning, notice 3438

advertir *v* to notice, warn 887

aéreo *adj* aerial, air 2975

aeropuerto *nm* airport 2993

afán *nm* eagerness, zeal, effort 2152

afectar *v* to affect 991

afecto *nm* affection, fondness 2132

aferrar *v* to grasp, clutch 4373

afición *nf* fondness, interest 3292

aficionado *nm* fan, devotee 3125

afín *adj* related, similar 4726

afirmación *nf* statement, assertion 2357

afirmar *v* to assert, affirm 978

aflojar *v* to loosen 4751

afortunadamente *adv* luckily, fortunately 2712

afortunado *adj* fortunate 4739

africano *adj* African 3654

afrontar *v* to face, confront 2832

afuera *adv* outside 1858

afueras *nf* outskirts, suburbs 4225

agarrar *v* to grasp, catch 2074

agencia *nf* agency, branch 2886

agente *nc* agent 1806

ágil *adj* agile 4119

agitación *nf* agitation, excitement 4153

agitado *adj* agitated, irritated 4045

agitar *v* to shake, move 3027

agonía *nf* agony, grief 4638

agosto *nm* August 1244

agotado *adj* tired, used up, sold out 2861

agotar *v* to exhaust, wear out, run out 1919

agradable *adj* nice, pleasant 1724

agradar *v* to please 3619

agradecer *v* to thank for 1681

agradecido *aj* grateful, thankful 4123

agradecimiento *nm* gratitude, gratefulness 4755

agrario *adj* agrarian, agricultural 4499

agravar *v* to aggravate 4226

agregar *v* to add, gather 1708

agresión *nf* aggression, attack 3204

agresividad *nf* aggressiveness 4931

agresivo *adj* aggressive 2242

agrícola *adj* agricultural, farming 3611

agricultor *nm/f* farmer 4794

agricultura *nf* agriculture, farming 3741

agrupar *v* to (put in) group 4441

agua *nf* (el) water 194

aguantar *v* to endure, put up with 1895

aguardar *v* to wait for, await 3598

agudo *adj* sharp, acute 2180

aguja *nf* needle, spire, stylus 3625

agujero *nm* hole, opening 3128

ah *interj* oh 1489

ahí *adv* there 189

ahogar *v* to drown, choke, flood 2821

ahora *adv* now 85

ahorrar *v* to save (money, time) 2775

ahorro *nm* saving, thrift 2977

aire *nm* air, wind, appearance 374

aislado *adj* isolated 1533

aislamiento *nm* isolation 4017

aislar *v* to isolate, insulate 3174

ajeno *adj* not belonging to, detached 1175

ajustar *v* to adjust, tighten 1545

ajuste *nm* adjustment, settlement 4006

ala *nf* (el) wing, flank 2260

alambre *nm* wire 4255

alargar *v* to enlarge, elongate 2649

alarma *nf* alarm 3452

alarmante *adj* alarming 4565

alarmar *v* to alarm 4537

albergar *v* to lodge, harbor 3822

alcalde *nm* mayor 3277

alcance *nm* reach, scope 1083

alcanzar *v* to reach, catch up with 329

alcohol *nm* alcohol 2421

aldea *nf* small village 3458

alegar *v* to plead, argue 3836

alegrar *v* to be/make happy 2689

alegre *adj* happy, lively, cheerful 2304

alegría *nf* joy, happiness 1429

alejado *adj* remote, distant, aloof 1894

alejar *v* to move away 1196

alemán *adj* German 963

alentar *v* to encourage 3189

alerta *nf* alert 4068

alertar *v* to alert, warn 4503

alfombra *nf* rug, carpet mat 3158

algo *pron* something, somewhat 101

algodón *nm* cotton 3613

alguien *pron* somebody, someone, anyone 480

alguno *adj* some, someone (pron) 50

aliado *nm* ally 4086

alianza *nf* alliance 3851

aliento *nm* breath, courage, spirit 3454

alimentación *nf* feeding, food 2989

alimentar *v* to feed, support 1609

alimento *nm* food, nourishment 1143

aliviar *v* to lighten, relieve, comfort 3063

alivio *nm* relief, unburdening 4018

allá *adv* there, over there 324

allí *adv* there, over there 167

alma *nf* (el) soul 984

almacén *nm* warehouse, store 2455

almohada *nf* pillow 4939

almorzar *v* to have lunch 3820

almuerzo *nm* lunch 3104

alojar *v* to host, accommodate 4896

alquilar *v* to rent, hire 3761

alquiler *nm* rent, rental 3733

alrededor *adv* about, around, round 556

alrededor *nm* surrounding area, vicinity 1617

altamente *adv* highly 4238

altar *nm* altar 4247

alteración *nf* alteration, change 3569

alterar *v* to alter, modify 1809

alternar *v* to alternate 3303

alternativa *nf* alternative 1800

alternativo *adj* alternating, alternative 4180

altísimo *adj* very high, tall 3477

alto *adj* tall, high 185

altura *nf* height, altitude 578

aludir *v* to allude to 3037

alumbrar *v* to light, illuminate 3985

alumno *nm* student, pupil 969

alusión *nf* allusion, hint 3640

alzar *v* to lift, raise 2511

ama *nc* housekeeper, housewife 3321

amable *adj* kind, nice, friendly 2409

amanecer *nm* daybreak, dawn 3051

amanecer *v* to dawn, get light 3591

amante *nc* lover 1893

amar *v* to love 1486

amargo *adj* bitter, sour, painful 2710

amargura *nf* bitterness, sorrow 4408

amarillo *adj* yellow 1586

ambición *nf* ambition 2440

ambicioso *adj* ambitious, greedy 3310

ambiente *nm* environment, atmosphere 683

ambiguo *adj* ambiguous 3645

ámbito *nm* sphere, space 1547

ambos *adj* both 488

ambulante *adj* traveling 4440

amenaza *nf* threat 2229

amenazado *adj* threatened 4350

amenazar *v* to threaten 2239

americano *adj* American 1261

amiga *nf* friend (f) 1817

amigo *nm* friend 262

amistad *nf* friendship 1232

amistoso *adj* friendly 4462

amo *nm* master, boss (m) 2787

amor *nm* love 423

amoroso *adj* loving, affectionate 3028

amparo *nm* protection, shelter 4289

ampliación *nf* enlargement, extension 4959

ampliamente *adv* widely 4263

ampliar *v* to enlarge, increase, expand 1931

amplio *adj* wide, ample, broad 763

amplitud *nf* breadth, extent, range 3908

añadir *v* to add 1369

análisis *nm* analysis 1148

analizar *v* to analyze 1048

ancho *adj* wide 1720

ancho *nm* width 3679

anciano *adj* elderly, aged 1912

andaluz *adj* Andalusian 4591

andar *v* to walk, function 536

andar *nm* walk, gait, pace 4737

anécdota *nf* anecdote 2028

ángel *nm* angel 2248

ángulo *nm* angle 2389

angustia *nf* anguish, distress 1957

angustiado *adj* anguished, distressed 4668

angustioso *adj* distressing 4699

anhelo *nm* longing, yearning 4401

anillo *nm* (finger) ring 3150

animado *adj* excited, lively 3163

animal *nm* animal 497

animar *v* to cheer up 1354

ánimo *nm* zest, spirit, heart 1240

aniversario *nm* anniversary 3669

año *nm* year 55

anoche *adv* last night 3418

anónimo *adj* anonymous 2499

anotar *v* to annotate, jot, note 2570

ansia *nf* (el) anxiety, anguish 3832

ansiedad *nf* anxiety 3284

ansioso *adj* anxious eager 3395

antaño *adv* in days gone by, last year 3924

ante *prep* before, in the presence of 236

antecedente *nm* antecedent 2567

antemano *adv* beforehand, in advance 3601

antena *nf* antenna 4644

antepasado *nm* ancestor 3600

anterior *adj* previous, preceding 370

anteriormente *adv* previously 2719

antes *adv* before 114

anticipar *v* to anticipate, advance 2366

antigüedad *nf* antiquity, seniority 3562

antiguo *adj* old, ancient, former 348

anual *adj* annual, yearly 3508

anular *v* to annul, cancel 2637

anunciar *v* to announce, advertise 730

anuncio *nm* advertisement, announcement 2114

apagado *adj* turned off 4405

apagar *v* to turn off, extinguish 2104

aparato *nm* apparatus, device 1168

aparecer *v* to appear 221

aparentar *v* to give the appearance 4205

aparente *adj* apparent 2659

aparentemente *adv* apparently 1853

aparición *nf* appearance, apparition 1854

apariencia *nf* appearance, aspect 1863

apartar *v* to move away, separate 1505

aparte *adv* apart, aside, separately 1313

apasionado *adj* passionate 3547

apelar *v* to call upon, appeal to 3790

apellido *nm* last name 2167

apenas *adv* hardly, barely 587

apertura *nf* opening, beginning 3368

apetito *nm* appetite 4082

aplastado *adj* crushed, flattened 4976

aplastar *v* to flatten, crush, smash 3391

aplaudir *v* to clap, applaud 3068

aplauso *nm* applause, praise, acclaim 3282

aplicación *nf* application 2263

aplicado *adj* applied 1827

aplicar *v* to apply 650

apoderar *v* to take power 3421

aportar *v* to provide, contribute 1738

aporte *nm* contribution 3957

apostar *v* to wager, bet 3635

apoyar *v* to support, lean on 616

apoyo *nm* support, backing 830

apreciación *nf* appreciation, assessment 4443

apreciar *v* to appreciate 1483

aprender *v* to learn 422

aprendizaje *nm* learning, apprenticeship 2675

apresurar *v* to hurry up, speed up 4377

apretado *adj* tight, jammed 3806

apretar *v* to squeeze, tighten, compress 2404

aprobación *nf* approval, consent 3709

aprobar *v* to pass (test), approve 1443

apropiado *adj* appropriate 2422

aprovechar *v* to take advantage of 612

aproximación *nf* approximation 4241

aproximadamente *adv* approximately 2256

aproximar *v* to come near, closer 2070

apto *adj* appropriate, fit, able 3535

apuesta *nf* wager, bet 4320

apuntar *v* to point, note, aim 1361

apunte *nm* note, annotation 3599

apurar *v* to speed up, hurry up 4389

apuro *nm* trouble, predicament 4618

aquel *adj* that (over there) 107

aquél *pron* that one over there (m) 1390

aquello *pron* that over there (n) 814

aquí *adv* here 129

árabe *adj* Arab 2433

araña *nf* spider 4717

arbitrario *adj* arbitrary 4015

árbol *nm* tree 833

archivo *nm* archive, file, filing cabinet 3244

arco *nm* arch, arc, bow 2412

arder *v* to burn, glow 3087

ardiente *adj* passionate, ardent 4446

área *nf* (el) area, zone 1602

arena *nf* sand 1635

argentino *adj* Argentine 1626

argumentar *v* to argue, deduce 4139

argumento *nm* argument, plot 1279

árido *adj* arid, dry 4634

arma *nf* (el) weapon 832

armado *adj* armed 1639

armar *v* to arm, put together 2627

armonía *nf* harmony 2529

aroma *nm* aroma 3863

arquitecto *nm/f* architect 2808

arquitectura *nf* architecture 2516

arrancar *v* to start (machine), uproot 1268

arranque *nm* start, outburst, kick-start 4077

arrasar *v* to raze, ravage 4158

arrastrar *v* to drag, pull 1134

arrebatar *v* to snatch, grab 3439

arreglar *v* to fix, arrange 1351

arreglo *nm* arrangement 2607

arrepentir *v* to repent, regret 3528

arriba *adv* up above 544

arriesgar *v* to risk, venture 3183

arrojar *v* to throw, fling 1846

arroyo *nm* brook, stream, gutter 4218

arroz *nm* rice 3130

arte *nm* art, skill 567

artefacto *nm* artifact, device 4509

articular *v* to articulate 4101

artículo *nm* article, product, item 819

artificial *adj* artificial 2018

artista *nc* artist, performer 928

artístico *adj* artistic 1598

asaltar *v* to assault 3517

asalto *nm* assault, robbery 3768

asamblea *nf* assembly 3899

ascender *v* to ascend, be promoted 1909

ascenso *nm* promotion, climb 3286

ascensor *nm* elevator 3954

asco *nm* disgust 4375

asegurar *v* to assure, secure, insure 542

asentar *v* to settle, establish, locate 3494

asentir *v* to assent, agree 4742

asesinar *v* to murder, assassinate 3352

asesinato *nm* murder, assassination 3333

asesino *nm* killer, assassin 3092

asesor *nm/f* adviser, consultant 4466

así *adv* like that 59

asiento *nm* seat, chair 2061

asignar *v* to assign, allocate 3008

asilo *nm* asylum, shelter 4865

asimilar *v* to assimilate 2928

asimismo *adv* as well, also, moreover 3511

asistencia *nf* attendance, assistance 2751

asistente *nc* assistant 3180

asistir *v* to attend 822

asociación *nf* association 2123

asociar *v* to associate with 1661

asomar *v* to appear, show, stick (out) 2383

asombrado *adj* amazed, bewildered 4541

asombrar *v* to amaze, astound 3565

asombro *nm* amazement, astonishment 3906

asombroso *adj* amazing 3526

aspecto *nm* aspect, appearance 385

áspero *adj* rough, coarse, harsh 3854

aspiración *nf* ambition, aspiration 2589

aspirar *v* to aspire, want 1552

astro *nm* star 4746

asumir *v* to assume, take on 1132

asunto *nm* matter, issue, affair 518

asustado *adj* scared, frightened 3633

asustar *v* to frighten, scare 2565

atacar *v* to attack 1393

ataque *nm* attack, raid 1157

atar *v* to tie (up) 2153
atardecer *nm* evening, dusk 4186
atención *nf* attention 441
atender *v* to serve, attend to 697
atener *v* to abide by, comply with 4448
atentado *nm* (terrorist) attack, offense 4692
atento *adj* attentive, polite 2532
atmósfera *nf* atmosphere, environment 2003
atracción *nf* attraction 2768
atractivo *adj* attractive 2131
atractivo *nm* attraction, charm 3094
atraer *v* to attract 1293
atrapado *adj* trapped 4234
atrapar *v* to trap, catch 3589
atrás *adv* back, behind, ago 483
atrasado *adj* behind, slow 4120
atravesar *v* to cross 937
atrever *v* to dare 1276
atribuir *v* to attribute 1539
atributo *nm* attribute, quality 4094
atroz *adj* atrocious 4599
audacia *nf* boldness, audacity 4757
audaz *adj* audacious, bold 4107
audiencia *nf* audience, hearing 3353
aula *nf* (el) classroom 3876
aumentar *v* to increase 633
aumento *nm* increase, rise 1873
aun *adv* even (though), still 843
aún *adv* still, yet 282
aunque *conj* although, even though 117
ausencia *nf* absence 1321
ausente *adj* absent 2562
auténtico *adj* authentic 1223
auto *nm* auto, car 2259
autobús *nm* bus 4676
automáticamente *adv* automatically 3324
automático *adj* automatic 2984
automóvil *nm* automobile 1578
autonomía *nf* autonomy, range 3317
autónomo *adj* autonomous 2761
autopista *nf* freeway, motorway 4523
autor *nm/f* writer, author 538
autoridad *nf* authority 718
autoritario *adj* authoritarian 3552
autorización *nf* authorization 4106
autorizado *adj* authorized 3896
autorizar *v* to authorize, legalize 2829
auxiliar *adj* auxiliary, ancillary 3373
auxilio *nm* help, aid, assistance 3500

avance *nm* advance, progress 1565
avanzado *adj* advanced 1856
avanzar *v* to advance, progress 618
ave *nm* bird 2207
avenida *nf* avenue 2876
aventura *nf* adventure 1366
aventurar *v* to venture, risk 4800
averiguar *v* to investigate, find out 1983
avión *nm* plane, airplane, aircraft 1283
avisar *v* to inform, announce 2268
aviso *nm* warning 2611
ay *interj* oh no! oh my! 2337
ayer *adv* yesterday 1112
ayuda *nf* help, aid 594
ayudante *nc* helper, assistant 2901
ayudar *v* to help 345
azar *nm* random, chance, hazard 2400
azúcar *nm* sugar 2033
azul *adj* blue 904

B

bachillerato *nm* high school diploma 4950
bahía *nf* bay 4770
bailar *v* to dance 2071
bailarín *nm/f* dancer 4508
baile *nm* dance, ball 2222
bajar *v* to come down, let down 569
bajo *prep* under, underneath 214
bajo *adj* short, low 412
bala *nf* bullet, shot 3328
balance *nm* outcome, balance 3151
balanza *nf* balance, (measuring) scale 4551
balcón *nm* balcony 3207
bañar *v* to bathe, take a bath 3224
bancario *adj* bank, banking 4735
banco *nm* (financial) bank, bench 881
banda *nf* (musical) band, sash 2025
bandeja *nf* tray 4240
bandera *nf* flag 2021
bando *nm* faction, side 3380
baño *nm* bathroom, bath, swim 1789
banquete *nm* banquet, feast 4734
bar *nm* (snack) bar, café 2359
barato *adj* inexpensive 1470
barba *nf* beard 3451
barbaridad *nf* atrocity 4013
bárbaro *adj* savage, horrible 2757
barco *nm* boat, ship 1164
barra *nf* bar, rod, rail 2721

barrer *v* sweep, clean out 3156

barrera *nf* barrier, obstacle 2568

barrio *nm* neighborhood, district 1146

barro *nm* clay, mud 2894

basar *v* to base on, base upon 1430

base *nf* base, basis 498

básicamente *adv* basically 3862

básico *adj* basic, essential 2295

bastante *adj* rather, fairly, quite a bit (adv) 270

bastar *v* to be sufficient 899

bastón *nm* (walking) cane 4454

basura *nf* garbage, rubbish 2594

batalla *nf* battle 1091

batería *nf* battery, gun deck 4597

batir *v* to beat (object) 3313

bautizar *v* to baptize, christen 3186

bebé *nm* baby 3406

beber *v* to drink 1476

bebida *nf* drink, beverage 2828

beca *nf* scholarship, grant 3959

bélico *adj* warlike 4955

belleza *nf* beauty 1472

bello *adj* beautiful, fine 1338

bendito *adj* blessed 4560

beneficiar *v* to benefit 3129

beneficio *nm* benefit, profit 1142

besar *v* to kiss 3696

beso *nm* kiss 3322

bestia *nf* beast, brute 3765

bíblico *adj* biblical 4625

biblioteca *nf* library 1825

bicho *nm* bug, creature 4687

bicicleta *nf* bicycle 3955

bien *adv* well 73

bien *nm* goods, property, benefit 667

bienestar *nm* wellbeing, welfare 2335

bigote *nm* mustache 4182

billete *nm* ticket, bill, note 3070

biografía *nf* biography 4200

biológico *adj* biological 3674

blanco *adj* white 250

blando *adj* soft, limp, gentle 2783

bloque *nm* block 2480

boca *nf* mouth, entrance, opening 635

boda *nf* marriage, wedding 2677

bodega *nf* cellar, pantry, warehouse 4643

bola *nf* ball, sphere 2639

bolsa *nf* bag, purse, stock exchange 1915

bolsillo *nm* pocket 2121

bomba *nf* bomb, explosion, pump 1562

bondad *nf* goodness, kindness 2814

bonito *adj* pretty, nice 1707

borde *nm* edge 1763

bordear *v* to border 4915

bordo *nm* a bordo: on board 4341

borrar *v* to erase 1890

bosque *nm* forest 1506

bota *nf* boot, wineskin 2735

bote *nm* boat, container 3840

botella *nf* bottle, flask 2161

botón *nm* button 2865

brasileño *adj* Brazilian 4391

bravo *adj* fierce, angry 2572

brazo *nm* arm 620

breve *adj* brief, short 1153

brevemente *adv* briefly 4587

brillante *adj* brilliant, shiny, sparkling 1342

brillar *v* to shine, twinkle, be outstanding 2558

brillo *nm* shine, twinkling, sparkle 3463

brindar *v* to offer 2170

británico *adj* British 3265

broma *nf* joke 2482

bronce *nm* bronze 3413

brotar *v* to sprout 2979

bruja *nf* witch, hag 4305

bruscamente *adv* quickly, sharply 4406

brusco *adj* brusque, abrupt, sudden 3332

brutal *adj* brutal, savage 3505

bruto *adj* brutal, coarse, clumsy 2642

bueno *adj* good 115

bueno *adv* well... 337

buey *nm* ox 4772

bulto *nm* bulk, shape 3925

buque *nm* ship, vessel, hull 3974

burla *nf* mockery, joke, trick 4169

burlar *v* to mock 3047

burro *nm* donkey 4610

busca *nf* search, hunt 1441

buscar *v* to look for 173

búsqueda *nf* search 1727

C

caballería *nf* cavalry, knighthood 4731

caballero *nm* gentleman, knight 1885

caballo *nm* horse 780

cabecera *nf* head, header 3723

cabello *nm* hair 2920

caber *v* to fit (into) 695

cabeza *nf* head (part of body) 298

cabina *nf* cabin, cockpit 4882

cable *nm* cable, wiring 2812

cabo *nm* end, bit; llevar a c.: to carry out 477

cabra *nf* goat 4912

cada *adj* each, every 96

cadáver *nm* corpse, body 2165

cadena *nf* chain 1236

cadera *nf* hip 4279

caer *v* to fall 245

café *nm* coffee, café 1250

caída *nf* fall, drop, falling 1659

caído *adj* fallen 2168

caja *nf* bank, box, safe 1258

cajón *nm* drawer 2620

cal *nf* lime, whitewash 4977

calcular *v* to calculate, figure out 1155

cálculo *nm* calculation, calculus 1897

caldo *nm* broth, soup 4637

calendario *nm* calendar 3656

calentar *v* to warm, heat 2531

calidad *nf* quality 772

cálido *adj* warm 2704

caliente *adj* hot, warm, spirited 1793

calificación *nf* evaluation, qualification 4295

calificar *v* to grade, rate, qualify 2279

callado *adj* quiet, reserved 3095

callar *v* to be/make quiet 2245

calle *nf* street 248

callejero *adj* of the street 4889

calma *nf* calm, lull 2202

calmar *v* to calm, soothe, relieve 3331

calor *nm* heat, warmth 989

calzar *v* to wear (shoes) 4414

cama *nf* bed (furniture) 1185

cámara *nf* camera, chamber 1172

cambiar *v* to change 246

cambio *nm* change 186

caminar *v* to walk 919

camino *nm* road, route, path 319

camión *nm* truck, van, tanker 2503

camisa *nf* shirt 2443

camiseta *nf* T-shirt 4427

campamento *nm* camp, camping 3910

campana *nf* bell 3000

campaña *nf* campaign 1362

campeón *nm* champion 4840

campesino *adj* rural 1815

campo *nm* field, country 295

caña *nf* cane, reed 3173

canal *nm* channel, canal 1804

cáncer *nm* cancer 3242

cancha *nf* playing field, court 4485

canción *nf* song 1459

candidato *nm* candidate 2149

cañón *nm* canyon, cannon 3229

cansado *adj* tired, tiresome 2147

cansancio *nm* tiredness, weariness 2544

cansar *v* to tire, annoy 2552

cantante *nc* singer 3147

cantar *v* to sing 1124

cantidad *nf* quantity, amount 404

canto *nm* singing, chant 1778

caos *nm* chaos 2419

capa *nf* layer, coat 1496

capacidad *nf* capacity 675

capaz *adj* capable, able 411

capilla *nf* chapel 3788

capital *nmf* capital; city (f), money (m) 651

capitán *nm* captain, chief 2370

capítulo *nm* chapter 1450

capricho *nm* caprice, whim 2882

caprichoso *adj* capricious, whimsical 4635

captar *v* to capture, attract 1996

capturar *v* to capture 4325

cara *nf* face, expression 356

carácter *nm* personality, nature 530

característica *nf* characteristic, aspect 1266

característico *adj* characteristic 2090

caracterizar *v* to characterize, portray 2476

caramelo *nm* piece of candy, caramel 4762

carbón *nm* coal, charcoal 3909

carcajada *nf* hearty laughter, guffaw 4484

cárcel *nf* jail, prison 1991

carecer *v* to be without 1633

carencia *nf* lack, shortage 3199

carente *adj* lacking, devoid 4907

carga *nf* load, charge, cargo 1031

cargar *v* to load (up), carry 748

cargo *nm* position, charge, fee 791

caridad *nf* charity 3984

cariño *nm* love, affection 2246

cariñoso *adj* affectionate 4033

carne *nf* meat, flesh 787

caro *adj* expensive, difficult, dear 1876

carrera *nf* career, course, race 485

carretera *nf* highway, road 1818

carro *nm* car, cart 1871

carta *nf* letter, (playing) card **586**

cartel *nm* poster **3169**

cartera *nf* wallet, satchel **2834**

cartón *nm* cardboard, carton, sketch **3393**

casa *nf* house **116**

casado *adj* married **1830**

casar *v* to marry **1105**

casco *nm* helmet **3033**

casero *adj* homemade **3370**

casi *adv* almost, nearly **146**

casita *nf* cottage **3849**

caso *nm* case, occasion **130**

castellano *adj* Castilian, Spanish **1660**

castigar *v* to punish **2274**

castigo *nm* punishment, penalty **1867**

castillo *nm* castle **3343**

casualidad *nf* chance, coincidence **2190**

catalán *adj* Catalan **4097**

catálogo *nm* catalog **4287**

catástrofe *nf* catastrophe **3099**

cátedra *nf* academic chair **4070**

catedral *nf* cathedral **4041**

categoría *nf* category **1280**

católico *adj* Catholic **2137**

catorce *num* fourteen **2278**

cauce *nm* (river) bed, ditch **3075**

caudal *nm* volume, abundance **4296**

causa *nf* cause **546**

causar *v* to cause, bring about **1007**

cautela *nf* caution **4621**

caza *nf* hunting (game) **2451**

cazador *nm/f* hunter **3376**

cazar *v* to hunt **3066**

ceder *v* to give way, yield **1289**

ceja *nf* eyebrow, brow **4227**

celebración *nf* celebration **3409**

celebrar *v* to celebrate **1059**

célebre *adj* famous, renowned **3127**

celeste *adj* heavenly, sky-blue **4026**

celo *nm* jealousy, zeal **2924**

celoso *adj* jealous **4211**

célula *nf* cell (biology) **3052**

cementerio *nm* cemetery, graveyard **2700**

cemento *nm* cement, concrete **3098**

cena *nf* dinner **2971**

cenar *v* to dine **3261**

ceñir *v* to adhere to, fit tightly **4299**

ceniza *nf* ash **3546**

censura *nf* censorship, criticism **3990**

centavo *nm* cent **4892**

centenar *nm* hundred **3480**

centímetro *nm* centimeter **2329**

central *adj* central **1062**

central *nf* headquarters **3844**

centrar *v* to center, focus, base (on) **2810**

centro *nm* center, middle, downtown **339**

cera *nf* wax **4593**

cerca *adv* close, near **391**

cercanía *nf* nearness, proximity **2943**

cercano *adj* near **942**

cerco *nm* fence, circle, ring **4996**

cerdo *nm* pig, sow, slob **3200**

cerebral *adj* cerebral **4860**

cerebro *nm* brain **1734**

ceremonia *nf* ceremony **2111**

cero *num* zero, naught, nil **2284**

cerrado *adj* closed **680**

cerrar *v* to close **454**

cerro *nm* hill **3187**

certeza *nf* certainty **2663**

cerveza *nf* beer, ale **3134**

cesar *v* to cease, stop **2227**

chaqueta *nf* jacket **4372**

charla *nf* talk, chat **2830**

charlar *v* to chat, talk **3671**

chica *nf* girl, female **1907**

chico *nm* boy **1079**

chileno *adj* Chilean **3164**

chimenea *nf* chimney, fireplace **4415**

chino *adj* Chinese **1444**

chiquillo *nm* kid, youngster **4704**

chispa *nf* spark **3980**

chiste *nm* joke, funny story **2674**

chocar *v* to crash into, collide with **1883**

chocolate *nm* chocolate **3776**

choque *nm* crash, collision **2930**

chorro *nm* stream, jet, spurt **4361**

chupar *v* to suck **4475**

ciclo *nm* cycle **2225**

ciego *adj* blind **1481**

cielo *nm* sky, heaven, ceiling **932**

ciencia *nf* science, knowledge **775**

científico *adj* scientific **1634**

científico *nm/f* scientist **2745**

ciento *num* hundred **300**

cierre *nm* zipper, closing **2481**

ciertamente *adv* certainly, indeed **2785**

cierto *adj* certain, sure, true **123**

cifra *nf* figure, number, amount 1540

cigarrillo *nm* cigarette 2858

cima *nf* summit, peak, top 4291

cinco *num* five 231

cincuenta *num* fifty 782

cine *nm* cinema, US movie theater 1159

cinta *nf* tape, ribbon, film, strip 1916

cintura *nf* waist 3323

cinturón *nm* belt 3922

circo *nm* circus 3666

circuito *nm* circuit, circumference, track 3554

circulación *nf* circulation, traffic 2837

circular *v* to circulate, go around, flow 1822

circular *adj* circular 4219

círculo *nm* circle, club 1222

circunstancia *nf* circumstance 704

cirujano *nm/f* surgeon 4698

cita *nf* appointment, date, quotation 2045

citar *v* to cite, quote 1077

ciudad *nf* city 197

ciudadano *nm* citizen 1787

ciudadano *adj* community, citizen 2883

civil *adj* civil 774

civil *nc* civilian 3436

civilización *nf* civilization 2057

civilizado *adj* civilized 4000

clandestino *adj* undercover, clandestine 4269

claramente *adv* clearly 1477

claridad *nf* clearness, clarity 1630

claro *adj* clear 259

claro *adv* of course, clearly 482

clase *nf* kind, class, order 288

clásico *adj* classic 1329

clasificación *nf* classification 4233

clasificar *v* to classify, sort, file 3642

clavar *v* to nail 3146

clave *nf* key 1903

clave *adj* key 3445

clavo *nm* nail, tack, peg 4363

cliente *nc* client, customer 1550

clientela *nf* customers, clients 4823

clima *nm* climate 1576

clínica *nf* clinic 3967

clínico *adj* clinical 4887

club *nm* club, society 2429

cobrar *v* to charge (money) 1013

cobre *nm* copper 3503

coche *nm* car, carriage 1131

cocina *nf* kitchen 1673

cocinar *v* to cook 3372

cocinero *nm/f* cook 4023

coco *nm* coconut 4929

código *nm* code 2078

codo *nm* elbow 4412

coger *v* to hold, take, catch 1896

coherente *adj* coherent, connected 4166

cohete *nm* rocket 4937

coincidencia *nf* coincidence 2713

coincidir *v* to coincide, agree 920

cola *nf* line, queue, tail 1589

colaboración *nf* collaboration 2387

colaborador *nm* collaborator 2881

colaborar *v* to collaborate, work together 1943

colar *v* to slip in [se] 4237

colchón *nm* mattress 4449

colección *nf* collection 1906

colectivo *adj* collective, joint 1728

colectivo *nm* collective, group 3606

colega *nc* colleague 2094

colegio *nm* (high) school, college 1073

cólera *nmf* rage (f), cholera (m) 4758

colgado *adj* hanging 3185

colgar *v* to hang (up) 2049

colina *nf* hill, slope 4003

collar *nm* collar, necklace 4197

colmo *nm* climax; para colmo: to top it all 3525

colocar *v* to place, position 562

colombiano *adj* Colombian 4695

colonia *nf* colony, cologne 2420

colonial *adj* colonial 3293

color *nm* color 359

colorado *adj* red, colored 4614

columna *nf* column, spine 1406

coma *nmf* comma (f), coma (m) 3739

comandante *nm* commander, commanding officer 3755

comando *nm* command, order 4810

combate *nm* combat, battle, fight 2494

combatir *v* to fight against 1726

combinación *nf* combination 2164

combinado *adj* combined 4956

combinar *v* to combine 2348

comedia *nf* comedy, play, pretense 3457

comedor *nm* dining room 3021

comentar *v* to comment on 742

comentario *nm* remark, comment 1030

comenzar *v* to begin, start 223

comer *v* to eat 389

comercial *adj* commercial, shopping **1253**

comerciante *nc* merchant, businessman **2442**

comercio *nm* commerce, trade **1522**

cometa *nmf* comet (m), kite (f) **4857**

cometer *v* to commit **1213**

cómico *adj* comic **3485**

comida *nf* food, meal **873**

comienzo *nm* start, beginning **1162**

comisario *nm* commissioner, delegate **4332**

comisión *nf* commission, committee **2155**

como *conj* like, as **16**

cómo *adv* how? **126**

comodidad *nf* comfort, convenience **2296**

cómodo *adj* comfortable, convenient **1627**

compacto *adj* compact, dense **4162**

compañera *nf* female companion **2346**

compañero *nm* companion, classmate **693**

compañía *nf* company **798**

comparable *adj* comparable **3719**

comparación *nf* comparison **1772**

comparar *v* to compare **1058**

compartir *v* to share **681**

compás *nm* rhythm, time, compass **4194**

compatriota *nc* fellow countryman **3891**

compensación *nf* compensation **4342**

compensar *v* to compensate, make up for **3006**

competencia *nf* competition, contest **1529**

competir *v* to compete **2486**

complacer *v* to please, satisfy **3823**

complejidad *nf* complexity **4906**

complejo *adj* complex, complicated **1278**

complejo *nm* complex **2948**

complementar *v* to complement, supplement **3659**

complementario *adj* additional, complementary **3948**

complemento *nm* complement, supplement **4650**

completamente *adv* completely **869**

completar *v* to complete **1718**

completo *adj* complete **458**

complicación *nf* complication **3400**

complicado *adj* complicated, complex **1368**

complicar *v* to complicate, make difficult **1911**

cómplice *nc* accomplice **4310**

complicidad *nf* involvement, complicity **4816**

componente *nm* component, ingredient **2656**

componer *v* to compose, be part of **1336**

comportamiento *nm* behavior, conduct **1343**

comportar *v* to behave **2294**

composición *nf* composition, make-up, essay **1898**

compra *nf* shopping, buy, purchase **1374**

comprador *nm* buyer **4266**

comprar *v* to buy **437**

comprender *v* to understand **306**

comprensible *adj* understandable **4048**

comprensión *nf* understanding **1732**

comprensivo *adj* understanding **4713**

comprobar *v* to verify, prove **852**

comprometer *v* to compromise **2069**

comprometido *adj* committed, engaged **2803**

compromiso *nm* compromise, engagement **1029**

compuesto *adj* composite, mixed **2062**

computadora *nf* computer **4253**

común *adj* common **438**

comunicación *nf* communication **659**

comunicar *v* to communicate **952**

comunidad *nf* community **1130**

comunión *nf* communion **3986**

comunismo *nm* communism **4775**

comunista *adj* Communist **2315**

comunitario *adj* of the community **4416**

con *prep* with **13**

concebir *v* to conceive, understand **1518**

conceder *v* to grant, concede **1331**

concentración *nf* concentration, gathering **1670**

concentrar *v* to concentrate **1233**

concepción *nf* conception **2232**

concepto *nm* concept **997**

concesión *nf* awarding, concession **3486**

conciencia *nf* conscience, consciousness **696**

concierto *nm* concert, concerto **2435**

concluir *v* to conclude, finish **1221**

conclusión *nf* conclusion, end **1138**

concretamente *adv* specifically, exactly **3466**

concretar *v* to materialize, fulfill **2839**

concreto *adj* concrete, real **909**

concurrencia *nf* coming together, participation **4798**

concurrir *v* to coincide, concur, meet **4183**

concurso *nm* competition, gathering **2628**

condena *nf* sentence (in prison), penalty **3519**

condenar *v* to convict, condemn **1323**

condición *nf* condition **341**

condicionado *adj* conditioned **4126**

condicionar *v* to condition, determine **4498**

conducir *v* to lead, drive **868**

conducta *nf* conduct, behavior **1388**

conductor *nm/f* driver, conductor **3016**

conectar *v* to connect, plug in **3084**

conejo *nm* rabbit **4316**

conexión *nf* connection, relationship 3302

conferencia *nf* conference, lecture 2171

conferir *v* to confer 4561

confesar *v* to confess, admit 1972

confesión *nf* confession, admission 3237

confianza *nf* confidence, trust 947

confiar *v* to trust, confide 1423

configurar *v* to make up, comprise 4257

confirmar *v* to confirm 1435

conflicto *nm* conflict 1282

conformar *v* to conform 1156

conforme *adj* in agreement 1572

confundido *adj* confused 4943

confundir *v* to confuse 1149

confusión *nf* confusion 1706

confuso *adj* confused, mixed up 2634

congelado *adj* frozen 4518

congreso *nm* congress 3280

conjunto *nm* group, set 721

conmigo *pron* with me 1845

conmover *v* to move, affect 3664

conocedor *nm* expert, judge, connoisseur 4245

conocer *v* to know (someone or place) 124

conocido *adj* known, well-known 540

conocimiento *nm* knowledge 434

conquista *nf* conquest 2650

conquistar *v* to conquer, win (over) 2358

consagrado *adj* dedicated, consecrated 3956

consagrar *v* to consecrate, establish 4276

consciente *adj* conscious, aware 1416

consecuencia *nf* consequence 570

conseguir *v* to get, acquire, obtain 222

consejero *nm/f* advisor, counselor 4089

consejo *nm* advice, council, counsel 1188

consentir *v* to consent to, pamper 3960

conservación *nf* conservation 3661

conservador *adj* conservative 2613

conservar *v* to conserve, preserve 670

considerable *adj* considerable 2283

consideración *nf* consideration, regard 1335

considerar *v* to consider 261

consigna *nf* watchword, motto, slogan 4091

consiguiente *adj* consequent; por consiguiente: consequently 2807

consistencia *nf* consistency 4661

consistir *v* to consist of 688

consolar *v* to console 3705

consolidar *v* to consolidate 4376

conspiración *nf* conspiracy 4673

constancia *nf* perseverance 3148

constante *adj* constant 1034

constantemente *adv* constantly 1868

constar *v* to consist of, comprise 1655

constatar *v* to prove, verify 4314

constitución *nf* constitution 4231

constitucional *adj* constitutional 4213

constituir *v* to constitute, consist of 689

construcción *nf* construction 794

constructivo *adj* constructive 4985

construir *v* to construct, build 525

consuelo *nm* comfort, consolation 4031

consulta *nf* consultation, advice 2194

consultar *v* to consult 1587

consumar *v* to complete, carry out 3516

consumir *v* to consume, take in 1326

consumo *nm* consumption 2136

contacto *nm* contact 648

contagiar *v* to infect, infest 4273

contar *v* to tell, count 155

contemplar *v* to contemplate 807

contemporáneo *adj* contemporary 3009

contener *v* to contain 829

contenido *nm* contents, content 1038

contento *adj* happy, content 1642

contestación *nf* answer 4863

contestar *v* to answer, reply 764

contexto *nm* context 2898

contienda *nf* contest, dispute 4356

contigo *pron* with you 3017

continente *nm* continent 1831

continuación *nf* continuation, follow-up 1921

continuamente *adv* continuously 2585

continuar *v* to continue 403

continuidad *nf* continuity 3195

continuo *adj* continuous 1502

contorno *nm* outline, perimeter, edge 4339

contra *prep* against, opposite 172

contradecir *v* to contradict, be inconsistent 4143

contradicción *nf* contradiction 2073

contradictorio *adj* contradictory 3107

contraer *v* to contract, shrink, abbreviate 2782

contrario *adj* contrary, opposite 460

contrastar *v* to contrast 3734

contraste *nm* contrast 2251

contratar *v* to hire, contract 2418

contrato *nm* contract, agreement 1989

contribución *nf* contribution 4168

contribuir *v* to contribute 1183

control *nm* control 889

controlar *v* to control 1070

contundente *adj* decisive, blunt, forceful 4901

convencer *v* to convince, persuade 1169

convencido *adj* convinced, persuaded 1294

convencimiento *nm* convincing 4540

convención *nf* convention, assembly 4934

convencional *adj* conventional 2968

conveniencia *nf* convenience, usefulness 3197

conveniente *adj* convenient 1970

convenir *v* to be agreeable, be convenient 964

convento *nm* convent, monastery 4217

conversación *nf* conversation 892

conversar *v* to converse, talk 2507

convertir *v* to convert, change, become 271

convicción *nf* conviction 2339

convincente *adj* convincing 4030

convivencia *nf* coexistence, living together 2811

convivir *v* to coexist 2913

convocar *v* to convene, summon 2599

cooperación *nf* cooperation 4690

copa *nf* cup, glass, top (tree) 2267

copia *nf* copy 2098

copiar *v* to copy 2402

coraje *nm* courage, toughness 3385

corazón *nm* heart, core 649

corbata *nf* tie, sash 3238

cordial *adj* cordial, friendly 4666

cordillera *nf* mountain range 4432

cordón *nm* cord, yarn, braid 4504

coro *nm* choir, chorus 2940

corona *nf* crown 2772

coronar *v* to crown, top 4346

coronel *nm* colonel 3715

corporal *adj* of the body, corporal 4672

corral *nm* corral, yard 4302

corrección *nf* correction, amendment 3979

correctamente *adv* correctly 4118

correcto *adj* correct, suitable 1234

corredor *nm/f* broker, corridor, runner 2591

corregir *v* to correct, rectify 1585

correo *nm* mail, post (office) 3665

correr *v* to run 332

correspondencia *nf* correspondence, connection 2893

corresponder *v* to correspond with 599

correspondiente *adj* corresponding 1461

corriente *nf* current, flow 838

corriente *adj* current, common 1709

corrupción *nf* corruption 3236

cortar *v* to cut 597

corte *nmf* court (f), cut (m) 1041

cortesía *nf* courtesy 4092

corteza *nf* bark, crust, rind, peel 4430

cortina *nf* curtain, screen 3630

corto *adj* short, brief 537

cosa *nf* thing 78

cosecha *nf* harvest, crop 2778

coser *v* to sew 3799

costa *nf* coast 1126

costado *nm* side, flank 3356

costar *v* to cost, be hard 626

costo *nm* price, cost, expense 3110

costoso *adj* costly, expensive 3514

costumbre *nf* habit, custom, usage 700

cotidiano *adj* daily 1434

cráneo *nm* skull, cranium 4750

creación *nf* creation 1173

creador *nm* creator 2393

crear *v* to create 251

creativo *adj* creative 3551

crecer *v* to grow, increase 552

creciente *adj* growing, increasing 2484

crecimiento *nm* growth, increase 1902

crédito *nm* credit, reputation 1799

creencia *nf* belief 2236

creer *v* to believe, think 91

crema *nf* cream 4598

cría *nf* breeding, raising 4282

criar *v* to bring up, rear 1962

criatura *nf* creature, child 2235

crimen *nm* crime, murder 1783

criminal *nc* criminal 4061

criminal *adj* criminal 4165

crisis *nf* crisis 1085

cristal *nm* glass, crystal, window 2026

cristiano *adj* Christian 1114

criterio *nm* criterion 1292

crítica *nf* criticism, critique 1344

criticar *v* to criticize 1849

crítico *adj* critical 1656

crítico *nm* critic 3054

crónica *nf* account, chronicle 2817

crónico *adj* chronic 4622

cruce *nm* crossing, intersection 2809

crudo *adj* raw, crude, natural 2860

cruel *adj* cruel, harsh 2453

crueldad *nf* cruelty, harshness 3830

cruz *nf* cross, burden **2800**
cruzar *v* to cross **726**
cuaderno *nm* notebook, workbook **3220**
cuadra *nf* (city) block **3826**
cuadrado *adj* square **2198**
cuadro *nm* painting, picture **779**
cual *pron* which, who, whom **153**
cuál *pron* which? **395**
cualidad *nf* quality, attribute **1997**
cualquier *adj* any, anyone (pron) **149**
cuando *conj* when **40**
cuando *adv* when **1803**
cuándo *adv* when? **1199**
cuanto *adj* en cuanto a: in terms of, regarding **213**
cuánto *adj* how much? **723**
cuarenta *num* forty **943**
cuartel *nm* quarters, barracks **2791**
cuarto *nm* room, chamber **655**
cuarto *adj* fourth **897**
cuatro *num* four **188**
cubano *adj* Cuban **3905**
cubierta *nf* covering, top, lid **3668**
cubierto *adj* covered **1646**
cubrir *v* to cover **691**
cuchillo *nm* knife **2945**
cuello *nm* neck, collar **1920**
cuenca *nf* socket, basin, bowl **4975**
cuenta *nf* bill, account **170**
cuento *nm* story, tale **1357**
cuerda *nf* cord, rope **2193**
cuerno *nm* horn, antler **4326**
cuero *nm* leather, skin **2848**
cuerpo *nm* body **232**
cuestión *nf* question, matter **398**
cuestionar *v* to question **3888**
cueva *nf* cave **5000**
cuidado *nm* care, carefulness **754**
cuidadosamente *av* carefully **3808**
cuidadoso *adj* careful, cautious **4049**
cuidar *v* to take care of **846**
culminar *v* to culminate, accomplish **3276**
culpa *nf* blame, fault **1053**
culpable *adj* guilty **2211**
cultivar *v* to cultivate, produce **1936**
cultivo *nm* cultivation, crop **2333**
culto *adj* cultured, educated **2725**
culto *nm* worship, cult **2937**
cultura *nf* culture **521**
cultural *adj* cultural **1277**

cumbre *nf* summit, top **3523**
cumpleaños *nm* birthday **3785**
cumplimiento *nm* fulfillment, compliment **2691**
cumplir *v* to fulfill **363**
cuna *nf* cradle, birth, lineage **3726**
cuota *nf* quota, share, dues **2955**
cúpula *nf* cupola, dome **3833**
cura *nmf* priest (m), cure (f) **2103**
curar *v* to cure **2097**
curiosamente *adv* strangely, funnily enough **3469**
curiosidad *nf* curiosity, quaintness **1857**
curioso *adj* curious, strange **1084**
curso *nm* course, direction **610**
curva *nf* curve **2781**
cuyo *adj* whose **264**

D

dado *adj* given **968**
dama *nf* lady, dame **2159**
dañar *v* to damage **3558**
daño *nm* harm, injury, damage **1045**
danza *nf* dance **2434**
dar *v* to give **39**
dato *nm* data, fact **513**
de *prep* of, from **2**
debajo *adv* underneath, below **820**
debate *nm* debate **2261**
debatir *v* to debate, discuss **3422**
deber *v* should, ought to; to owe **75**
deber *nm* duty, obligation **1588**
debidamente *adv* properly, duly **4897**
debido *adj* debido a: due to **981**
débil *adj* weak **1284**
debilidad *nf* weakness **2439**
debilitar *v* to weaken, debilitate **4112**
década *nf* decade **2127**
decadencia *nf* decline, decay **3117**
decaer *v* to decay, wane **4974**
decena *nf* ten (of something) **4580**
decente *adj* respectable, decent **4517**
decepción *nf* disappointment, disenchantment **4895**
decididamente *adv* decidedly, decisively **4403**
decidido *adj* determined, resolute **1988**
decidir *v* to decide **381**
décimo *adj* tenth **3355**
decir *v* to tell, say **28**
decisión *nf* decision **549**
decisivo *adj* decisive, conclusive **2638**
declaración *nf* declaration, statement **1746**

declarar v to declare, testify 1136

decoración nf decoration 4532

decreto nm decree, order 3529

dedicación nf dedication, devotion 3698

dedicar v to dedicate, devote 415

dedo nm finger, toe, digit 1248

deducir v to deduce, infer 2869

defecto nm defect 1497

defender v to defend, protect 665

defensa nf defense, plea 815

defensivo adj defensive 4270

defensor nm defender 3499

definición nf definition 1676

definido adj definite 2043

definir v to define 974

definitivamente adv definitely, finally 1358

definitivo adj definitive, conclusive 803

dejar v to let, leave 94

delante adv (in) front (of), ahead 885

delgado adj thin, skinny 3039

delicadeza nf gentleness, tenderness 4986

delicado adj delicate 1380

delicioso adj delicious, delightful, charming 3132

delincuente nc delinquent 4111

delirio nm delirium, nonsense 4574

delito nm crime, offense 2219

demanda nf petition, request, demand 1950

demandar v to claim, sue 4802

demás adj the rest, others 312

demasiado adj too much, too many 335

democracia nf democracy 2576

democrático adj democratic 2271

demonio nm demon, devil 3258

demorar v to delay, take time 3320

demostración nf demonstration 2687

demostrar v to show, demonstrate 501

denominación nf name, denomination 4914

denominar v to call, name 1869

densidad nf density, thickness 4318

denso adj heavy, dense, thick 3605

dentro adv inside 174

denuncia nf accusation 2838

denunciar v to denounce 2332

departamento nm department, apartment 1462

dependencia nf dependence, dependency 2575

depender v to depend on 673

deporte nm sport 2019

deportivo adj sports, sporty 2862

depositar v to deposit, place, store 1995

depósito nm deposit, sediment 2664

depresión nf depression, slump 3419

derecha nf right, right hand 1035

derecho nm right, justice, law 427

derecho adj right, straight 912

derivar v to derive, come (from) 1739

derramar v to shed, pour out 4222

derribar v to knock down, overthrow 3772

derrota nf defeat, loss 2601

derrotar v to defeat, beat 2951

derrumbar v to knock down, demolish 3544

desacuerdo nm disagreement 4038

desafiar v to defy, stand up to 4044

desafío nm challenge, provocation 2992

desagradable adj unpleasant 2237

desaparecer v to disappear, vanish 528

desaparecido adj missing 3813

desaparición nf disappearance 2470

desarrollado adj developed, grown 2369

desarrollar v to develop 491

desarrollo nm development 685

desastre nm disaster 1953

desatar v to untie, unleash, spark off 3188

desayunar v to have breakfast 4588

desayuno nm breakfast 3157

desbordar v to overflow, spill over 3834

descalzo adj barefoot 4384

descansar v to rest 1257

descanso nm rest, interval, break 1930

descarga nf unloading, discharge 4971

descargar v to unleash, unload 3190

descartar v to discard, reject, rule out 2877

descender v to descend 1645

descendiente nc descendant 3387

descenso nm decline, descent, lowering 3641

descifrar v to decipher 4946

descomponer v to decompose, break down 3706

desconcertado adj disoriented, disconcerted 4808

desconcierto nm disorder, chaos 4543

desconfianza nf distrust 3170

desconocer v to not know, not recognize 1662

desconocido adj unknown 1302

describir v to describe 1151

descripción nf description 2550

descubrimiento nm discovery 1622

descubrir v to discover 369

descuidar v to neglect 3072

descuido nm neglect, oversight 4624

desde prep from, since 61

deseable *adj* desirable 4313

desear *v* to want, desire, wish for 515

desechar *v* to discard 3855

desembocar *v* to flow, lead into 3059

desempeñar *v* to carry out, fulfill 2100

desencadenar *v* to unleash, unchain 3933

desenlace *nm* outcome, result 4507

desenvolver *v* to clear up, unwrap 3740

deseo *nm* desire, wish 579

desequilibrio *nm* imbalance, unsteadiness 4953

desesperación *nf* desperation, exasperation 2780

desesperado *adj* desperate, hopeless 2156

desesperar *v* to despair, lose hope 4642

desfilar *v* to march, parade 4329

desfile *nm* parade, line, formation 3973

desgracia *nf* misfortune, bad luck 1584

desgraciadamente *adv* unfortunately 3315

deshacer *v* to undo, destroy, take apart 2324

desierto *nm* desert 2431

desierto *adj* deserted, desolate 3782

designar *v* to designate 2479

desigual *adj* unequal, uneven, irregular 3978

desilusión *nf* disappointment, letdown 4784

deslizar *v* to slide, glide, slip 3651

desmentir *v* to contradict 4925

desnudo *adj* nude, naked 2008

desorden *nm* disorder, mess 2374

desordenado *adj* messy, confused 4335

despacho *nm* office, study 2487

despacio *adj* slow, slowly 3398

despedida *nf* goodbye, farewell 4848

despedir *v* to say goodbye (to), dismiss 1940

despejar *v* to clear (up) 4573

desperdicio *nm* waste, refuse, garbage 4957

despertar *v* to wake (up), arouse 734

despierto *adj* awake 3958

desplazamiento *nm* movement, removal 3887

desplazar *v* to replace, move, shift 1771

desplegar *v* to unfold, deploy 3058

despliegue *nm* deployment, display 4963

despojar *v* to deprive, rob 4050

despreciar *v* to despise, scorn 3141

desprecio *nm* contempt, disdain 2946

desprender *v* to detach, release, remove 1819

después *adv* after 87

destacado *adj* outstanding, leading 3001

destacar *v* to emphasize, stand out 941

destinar *v* to assign, appoint 1057

destino *nm* destination, destiny 844

destreza *nf* skill 4679

destrozar *v* to rip/break into pieces 3945

destrucción *nf* destruction 2301

destruido *adj* destroyed 4487

destruir *v* to destroy, ruin 1207

desviar *v* to deviate, divert, change 2723

detallado *adj* detailed, thorough 4228

detalle *nm* detail 784

detectar *v* to detect 2826

detención *nf* detention, arrest 4675

detener *v* to stop, detain 490

deteriorar *v* to deteriorate 4639

deterioro *nm* deterioration, damage 4138

determinación *nf* determination 2640

determinado *adj* determined, fixed 927

determinar *v* to determine, decide 1009

detrás *adv* behind 701

deuda *nf* debt 2139

devoción *nf* devotion 3702

devolver *v* to return, give back 1003

devorar *v* to devour, consume 4370

día *nm* day 71

diablo *nm* devil 2878

diagnóstico *nm* diagnosis 3825

dialogar *v* to confer, talk 4883

diálogo *nm* dialogue, conversation 1251

diamante *nm* diamond 4984

diariamente *adv* daily 3524

diario *nm* newspaper 903

diario *adj* daily 979

dibujar *v* to draw, sketch 2317

dibujo *nm* drawing, sketch 1692

diccionario *nm* dictionary 4223

dicha *nf* fortune, happiness, luck 4590

dicho *nm* saying, proverb 3348

dicho *adj* aforementioned, said 3644

dichoso *adj* fortunate, happy 4497

diciembre *nm* December 1341

dictador *nm* dictator 4747

dictadura *nf* dictatorship 2824

dictar *v* to dictate, announce 1881

dieciocho *num* eighteen 2694

dieciséis *num* sixteen 2793

diecisiete *num* seventeen 3446

diente *nm* tooth, cog 1859

dieta *nf* diet 3607

diez *num* ten 346

diferencia *nf* difference 400

diferenciar *v* to differentiate, distinguish 2995

diferente *adj* different, separate 365

difícil *adj* difficult, hard 314

difícilmente *adv* with difficulty 3300

dificultad *nf* difficulty, obstacle 741

difundir *v* to spread (out) 2740

difusión *nf* spread, diffusion 3816

dignidad *nf* dignity 2092

digno *adj* worthy 1561

diligencia *nf* diligence 4903

diluir *v* to dilute, weaken 4029

dimensión *nf* dimension, size 1549

diminuto *adj* diminutive, tiny, minute 4025

dinámica *nf* dynamics 4365

dinámico *adj* dynamic 4064

dinero *nm* money 291

dios *nm* god, divinity 274

diplomático *adj* diplomatic 3681

diplomático *nm/f* diplomat 4722

diputado *nm* deputy, member 3749

dirección *nf* direction, address 636

directamente *adv* directly, straight away 936

directo *adj* direct, straight 733

director *nm/f* director, manager, principal 816

dirigente *nc* leader, director, manager 3285

dirigir *v* to direct, manage 331

disciplina *nf* discipline, subject 1401

discípulo *nm* disciple 3714

disco *nm* disc, disk, record 1948

discreto *adj* discreet, tactful 3025

disculpa *nf* apology, excuse 4563

disculpar *v* to excuse 4079

discurrir *v* to flow, pass, roam 4791

discurso *nm* lecture, discourse, talk 1254

discusión *nf* discussion, argument 1055

discutir *v* to argue, discuss 859

diseñar *v* to design, develop 2910

diseño *nm* design 2013

disfrazado *adj* disguised 4115

disfrazar *v* to disguise, hide, conceal 4979

disfrutar *v* to enjoy 1269

disgusto *nm* disgust, annoyance 3660

disimular *v* to disguise, hide, pretend 3364

disipar *v* to dissipate, disperse 3963

disminuir *v* to decrease, diminish 1982

disolver *v* to dissolve 3240

disparar *v* to shoot (at) 2141

disparate *nm* nonsense, blunder 4022

disparo *nm* shot, discharge 3932

dispersar *v* to disperse, scatter, spread 4319

disperso *adj* spread out 3506

disponer *v* to have means, dispose 658

disponible *adj* available 3262

disposición *nf* disposal, disposition 1398

dispuesto *adj* willing, ready 690

disputa *nf* dispute, argument, quarrel 3991

disputar *v* to dispute, contest 3425

distancia *nf* distance 678

distante *adj* distant, far, remote 2351

distinción *nf* distinction 2962

distinguido *adj* distinguished 3228

distinguir *v* to distinguish 945

distinto *adj* distinct, different 254

distracción *nf* distraction, amusement 4705

distraer *v* to distract 2905

distribución *nf* distribution 2299

distribuir *v* to distribute, deliver 1503

diversidad *nf* diversity, variety 4733

diversión *nf* fun, entertainment 3345

diverso *adj* different, several, diverse 740

divertido *adj* funny, amusing 2553

divertir *v* to amuse, entertain 2356

dividir *v* to divide 1015

divino *adj* divine 1888

división *nf* division 1992

divorcio *nm* divorce 3997

doblar *v* to bend, turn 1981

doble *adj* double 1002

doble *nm* double 2354

doce *num* twelve 823

docena *nf* dozen 2774

doctor *nm/f* doctor 778

doctrina *nf* doctrine, teachings 2959

documentación *nf* documentation 4578

documento *nm* document 1076

dólar *nm* dollar 1878

doler *v* to hurt 2037

dolor *nm* pain, ache, sorrow 705

doloroso *adj* painful 2080

doméstico *adj* domestic 1960

domicilio *nm* residence, address 3045

dominante *adj* dominant, prevailing 3583

dominar *v* to dominate, master 926

domingo *nm* Sunday 1121

dominio *nm* power, control 1619

don *nm* courtesy title (m), Mr., gift 303

doña *nf* courtesy title (f), Mrs. 2410

donde *conj* where 84

dónde *adv* where? 421

dorado *adj* golden, gold-plated **2696**

dormido *adj* asleep, sleeping **2786**

dormir *v* to sleep **857**

dormitorio *nm* bedroom, dormitory **3382**

dos *num* two **56**

doscientos *num* two hundred **2344**

dosis *nf* dose **2609**

dotado *adj* endowed, gifted **3083**

dotar *v* to endow, bestow **3998**

drama *nm* drama **2350**

dramático *adj* dramatic **2011**

droga *nf* drug **2371**

duda *nf* doubt **399**

dudar *v* to (have) doubt **1252**

dudoso *adj* doubtful, dubious **3230**

duelo *nm* grief, affliction **3751**

dueña *nf* landlady, owner (f) **3557**

dueño *nm* owner, landlord (m) **1093**

dulce *adj* sweet **1882**

dulce *nm* candy, sweets **3100**

duración *nf* duration, length **3336**

duramente *adv* harshly, severely **4875**

durante *adv* during, for (time) **148**

durar *v* to last **812**

dureza *nf* hardness, toughness **3858**

duro *adj* hard **615**

duro *nm* duro (money) **2083**

E

echar *v* to throw, cast **455**

eclesiástico *adj* ecclesiastical **4942**

eco *nm* echo, response **2042**

economía *nf* economy, economics, thriftiness **1504**

económicamente *adv* economically **4778**

económico *adj* economic **426**

economista *nm/f* economist **4544**

edad *nf* age **350**

edición *nf* edition, publication **2195**

edificación *nf* construction, building **4871**

edificio *nm* building **717**

editar *v* to edit, publish, release **4421**

editor *nm/f* editor, publisher **4651**

editorial *nmf* publisher (f), editorial article (m) **4685**

educación *nf* education **845**

educado *adj* educated **4846**

educar *v* to educate **2068**

educativo *adj* educational **3794**

efectivamente *adv* in fact, actually, indeed **1604**

efectivo *adj* effective **1820**

efecto *nm* effect **418**

efectuar *v* to carry out, cause to happen **2523**

eficacia *nf* efficiency, effectiveness **2825**

eficaz *adj* effective **1976**

eficiencia *nf* efficiency **4940**

eficiente *adj* efficient **3571**

efímero *adj* ephemeral, short-lived **4371**

egoísmo *nm* selfishness **4340**

egoísta *adj* selfish **3845**

eh *interj* eh **2520**

eje *nm* axis, shaft, crux **2521**

ejecución *nf* performance, execution **2415**

ejecutar *v* to execute, carry out **2285**

ejecutivo *adj* executive **3065**

ejemplar *nm* copy, issue **2101**

ejemplar *adj* exemplary, model **2747**

ejemplo *nm* example **162**

ejercer *v* to practice, exercise **1004**

ejercicio *nm* exercise, practice **1242**

ejército *nm* army **1218**

el, la *art* the **1**

él *pron* he, [ellos] them (m) **41**

elaboración *nf* production **3663**

elaborar *v* to make, develop **1592**

elección *nf* election, choice **827**

electoral *adj* electoral **3411**

electricidad *nf* electricity **3950**

eléctrico *adj* electric **1333**

electrónico *adj* electronic **3149**

elefante *nm* elephant **4945**

elegancia *nf* elegance, style **4060**

elegante *adj* elegant, smart, stylish **1918**

elegir *v* to choose, elect **494**

elemental *adj* elemental, basic **1901**

elemento *nm* element **607**

elevación *nf* rise, elevation, increase **4691**

elevado *adj* elevated, high, lofty **1512**

elevar *v* to elevate, raise **1123**

eliminar *v* to eliminate, exclude **1612**

ella *pron* she, [ellas] them (f) **69**

ello *pron* it (subj-n) **343**

elocuente *adj* eloquent **4719**

elogio *nm* praise, eulogy, compliment **4062**

eludir *v* to evade, avoid, elude **3460**

embajada *nf* embassy **4404**

embajador *nm/f* ambassador **3987**

embarazada *adj* pregnant **3969**

embarazo *nm* pregnancy **4051**

embarcar *v* to embark, load **3597**

embargo *nm* sin embargo: nevertheless 180

emergencia *nf* emergency 3273

emerger *v* to emerge, surface 3145

emigrar *v* to emigrate 3850

emisión *nf* broadcast, emission 4812

emisor *nm* transmitter, emitter 4103

emitir *v* to emit, give (off) 1811

emoción *nf* emotion, excitement 1577

emocional *adj* emotional 3680

emocionar *v* to move, make/get excited 4420

empeñar *v* [se] to insist on 1998

empeño *nm* insistence, determination 3203

emperador *nm* emperor 4856

empezar *v* to begin, start 161

empleado *nm* employee 1104

emplear *v* to employ 962

empleo *nm* work, job, occupation 1436

emprender *v* to undertake, embark on 2365

empresa *nf* firm, company, venture 517

empresario *nm* manager, entrepreneur 2796

empujar *v* to push, shove 1877

en *prep* in, on 6

enamorado *adj* in love 3274

enamorar *v* to fall in love 3193

encabezar *v* to head, lead (off) 4460

encajar *v* to insert, fit well 3049

encaje *nm* lace 4850

encaminar *v* to head for, guide 4246

encantado *adj* pleased, delighted 3264

encantador *adj* charming 3650

encantar *v* to be very pleasing to 2859

encanto *nm* charm, spell 3078

encarar *v* to front, confront 3839

encargado *adj* in charge of 1479

encargar *v* to entrust, [se] take charge of 1054

encargo *nm* job, order, errand 3818

encarnar *v* to embody 3918

encender *v* to turn on 2133

encendido *adj* turned on, burning 3002

encerrado *adj* locked (up) 2376

encerrar *v* to shut (in) 1861

encima *adv* above, on top, in addition 436

encomendar *v* to commend, entrust 4828

encontrar *v* to find 100

encuentro *nm* meeting, game, skirmish 836

encuesta *nf* poll, survey, inquiry 4281

endurecer *v* harden, make hard 4656

enemigo *nm* enemy 1024

energía *nf* energy, power 946

enérgico *adj* energetic, vigorous 3459

enero *nm* January 1449

énfasis *nm* emphasis 2794

enfermar *v* to become ill 4513

enfermedad *nf* illness, sickness 666

enfermero *nm/f* nurse 3122

enfermo *adj* ill, sick 698

enfocar *v* to focus 3707

enfoque *nm* focus, approach 3999

enfrentamiento *nm* confrontation 3212

enfrentar *v* to confront, face 862

enfrente *adv* in front (of) 2541

enfriar *v* to cool 3938

engañar *v* to trick, deceive 1917

engaño *nm* deceit, falsehood, hoax 3192

engendrar *v* to engender, beget 4272

engordar *v* to fatten, get fat 4796

enigma *nm* enigma, mystery 4989

enlace *nm* link, connection, bond 4220

enlazar *v* to link, connect 4232

enorme *adj* enormous, vast 471

enormemente *adv* enormously 3678

enredar *v* to entangle, ensnare 4548

enriquecer *v* to enrich 2681

ensayar *v* to test 3166

ensayo *nm* essay, rehearsal 1835

enseguida *adv* immediately, at once 2707

enseñanza *nf* teaching, instruction 1751

enseñar *v* to teach, show 524

ensuciar *v* to get dirty 4766

entablar *v* to start, establish 4952

ente *nm* entity, being, firm 4898

entender *v* to understand 203

entendido *adj* understood 1852

entendimiento *nm* understanding 3152

enterado *adj* aware of 4175

enteramente *adv* completely, entirely 3789

enterar *v* to find out [se] 1543

entero *adj* entire, whole, complete 760

enterrado *adj* buried 4208

enterrar *v* to bury 2779

entidad *nf* entity 2660

entierro *nm* burial 4008

entonces *adv* so, then 76

entorno *nm* environment, surroundings 2614

entrada *nf* entrance, admission ticket 647

entrañas *nf* insides, bowels 4681

entrar *v* to enter 179

entre *prep* between, among 58

entrega *nf* delivery 2182

entregar *v* to deliver 558

entrenamiento *nm* training 4019

entrenar *v* to train 4670

entretener *v* to entertain, amuse 2722

entretenimiento *nm* entertainment 4600

entrevista *nf* interview, meeting 1419

entrevistar *v* to interview 4160

entusiasmado *adj* enthused, excited 4243

entusiasmar *v* to fill with enthusiasm, excite 3793

entusiasmo *nm* enthusiasm 1765

entusiasta *adj* enthusiastic 4970

enumerar *v* to enumerate, count 4706

envergadura *nf* breadth, expanse 4916

enviar *v* to send 842

envidia *nf* envy 3272

envidiar *v* to envy 4631

envolver *v* to wrap 2363

envuelto *adj* wrapped 2473

episodio *nm* episode, incident 2355

época *nf* time, age, period 358

equilibrar *v* to balance 2382

equilibrio *nm* balance 1487

equipo *nm* team, equipment, outfit 737

equivalente *adj* equivalent 4308

equivalente *nm* equivalent 4780

equivaler *v* to be equivalent, tantamount (to) 3675

equivocación *nf* mistake, misconception 4774

equivocado *adj* mistaken, wrong 2353

equivocar *v* to be wrong 1457

era *nf* era, age 4076

erótico *adj* erotic 4349

error *nm* error, mistake 738

escala *nf* scale, ladder, rank 1542

escalera *nf* stairs, ladder 2595

escándalo *nm* scandal 2093

escapar *v* to escape 757

escaparate *nm* showcase, display window 4725

escasez *nf* scarcity, shortage 3135

escaso *adj* scarce, very little 1110

escena *nf* scene, stage, setting 1139

escenario *nm* stage, setting, scene 1638

esclavo *nm* slave 2377

escoger *v* to choose 2048

escolar *adj* school, scholastic 2701

esconder *v* to hide, conceal 1802

escondido *adj* hidden 2546

escribir *v* to write 187

escrito *nm* manuscript, writing 4629

escritor *nm/f* writer 1011

escritorio *nm* desk, bureau 3539

escritura *nf* writing, scripture 2432

escuchar *v* to listen to 360

escudo *nm* shield, coat of arms 3081

escuela *nf* school 532

escultura *nf* sculpture, carving 4125

ese *adj* that (m) [*esa* (f)] 32

ése *pron* that one (m), [*ésa* (f)] 855

esencia *nf* essence 1672

esencial *adj* essential 1573

esencialmente *adv* essentially 4607

esfera *nf* sphere, globe 2514

esforzar *v* to make an effort, exert oneself 2823

esfuerzo *nm* effort, endeavor 444

eso *pron* that (n) 63

espacial *adj* spatial, space 4424

espacio *nm* space, room 474

espada *nf* sword 3024

espalda *nf* back (body) 1499

español *adj* Spanish 285

espantar *v* to scare, frighten 4435

espantoso *adj* frightening, dreadful 3281

especial *adj* special 364

especialidad *nf* specialty, specialized field 2517

especialista *nc* specialist 1886

especializar *v* to specialize, major in 2474

especialmente *adv* especially 684

especie *nf* kind, sort, species 388

específicamente *adv* specifically 4492

específico *adj* specific 2372

espectacular *adj* spectacular 2845

espectáculo *nm* spectacle, show 1420

espectador *nm* spectator, onlooker 2732

espectro *nm* ghost, specter 3802

especulación *nf* speculation, conjecture 3928

espejo *nm* mirror, reflection 1730

espera *nf* wait 1525

esperanza *nf* hope 805

esperar *v* to wait, hope (for), expect 163

espeso *adj* thick, dense, stiff 3537

espina *nf* thorn, spine 3708

espíritu *nm* spirit, ghost 731

espiritual *adj* spiritual 1865

espléndido *adj* splendid, generous 2822

esplendor *nm* splendor 3992

espontáneamente *adv* spontaneously 4743

espontáneo *adj* spontaneous 2172

esporádico *adj* sporadic 4678

esposa *nf* wife 951

esposo *nm* husband, spouse 2676

espuma *nf* foam, lather 4697

esqueleto *nm* skeleton, framework 4121

esquema *nm* outline, diagram, plan 2466

esquina *nf* corner 1926

estabilidad *nf* stability 3251

estable *adj* stable, steady 2784

establecer *v* to establish 565

establecido *adj* established 1515

establecimiento *nm* establishment 2289

estación *nf* station, season 1275

estadio *nm* stadium 3970

estadística *nf* statistic 3339

estadístico *adj* statistical 4707

estado *nm* state, condition, status 351

estallar *v* to break out, explode, start 2401

estallido *nm* crash, outbreak, explosion 4445

estampa *nf* print, engraving, illustration 4999

estancia *nf* stay, stance, ranch 2364

estar *v* to be (location, change from norm) 17

estatal *adj* state, government-owned 4189

estático *adj* static, motionless 3923

estatua *nf* statue 3116

estatura *nf* stature, height 4098

este *adj* this (m) [esta (f)] 29

este *n* East 2743

éste *pron* this one (m), [ésta (f)] 168

estéril *adj* sterile, barren 4195

estética *nf* aesthetics 4730

estético *adj* esthetic 2569

estilo *nm* style 707

estimar *v* to estimate, hold in esteem 1433

estimular *v* to stimulate, encourage 2662

estímulo *nm* stimulus, encouragement 2714

estirar *v* to stretch, strain 3652

esto *pron* this (n) 110

estómago *nm* stomach 2636

estrategia *nf* strategy 2505

estratégico *adj* strategic 4171

estrechar *v* to tighten, make closer 3501

estrecho *adj* narrow 1686

estrella *nf* star 1194

estrenar *v* to use for the first time, debut 3869

estrictamente *adv* strictly 2587

estricto *adj* strict, rigorous 2079

estropear *v* to ruin, mess up 4851

estructura *nf* structure 1141

estudiante *nc* student 1019

estudiar *v* to study 328

estudio *nm* study, learning 321

estudioso *adj* studious 3940

estupendo *adj* marvelous, stupendous 3478

estupidez *nf* stupidity, stupid thing 4382

estúpido *adj* stupid, idiotic 3319

etapa *nf* stage, period 921

etcétera *n* etcetera 2154

eternidad *nf* eternity 4352

eterno *adj* eternal 1872

ética *nf* ethics 3683

ético *adj* ethical 4173

etiqueta *nf* label, etiquette 3810

euforia *nf* euphoria, elation 4539

europeo *adj* European 1092

evaluar *v* to evaluate, assess 4419

evento *nm* event 3867

evidencia *nf* evidence, certainty 2091

evidente *adj* evident, obvious 1051

evidentemente *adv* evidently, obviously 1766

evitar *v* to avoid, prevent 446

evocar *v* to evoke, recall 4149

evolución *nf* evolution, development 1754

evolucionar *v* to evolve, develop 3018

exactamente *adv* exactly 977

exactitud *nf* accuracy 3615

exacto *adj* exact, faithful, true 879

exageración *nf* exaggeration 4442

exagerado *adj* exaggerated 2603

exagerar *v* to exaggerate 2755

examen *nm* examination, exam 1286

examinar *v* to examine, inspect 1780

exceder *v* to excel, exceed 4534

excelencia *nf* excellence 3026

excelente *adj* excellent 1273

excepción *nf* exception 1319

excepcional *adj* exceptional, unusual 2392

excepto *prep* except (for) 3108

excesivamente *adv* excessively 3553

excesivo *adj* excessive 1607

exceso *nm* excess 1495

excitar *v* to excite 4701

excluir *v* to exclude, reject 3121

exclusivamente *adv* exclusively 1769

exclusivo *adj* exclusive 2253

excursión *nf* excursion 3916

excusa *nf* excuse 3564

exento *adj* exempt, free 4884

exhibición *nf* exhibition, showing 4723

exhibir *v* to exhibit, show off 2122

exigencia *nf* requirement, demand 1711

exigente *adj* demanding, urgent 3530

exigir *v* to demand 630

exilio *nm* exile 3359

existencia *nf* existence, life 840

existente *adj* existing 2833

existir *v* to exist 177

éxito *nm* success 714

exótico *adj* exotic 3847

expandir *v* to expand 4495

expansión *nf* expansion, spreading 3638

expectativa *nf* expectation, hope, prospect 2456

expedición *nf* expedition 3944

expediente *nm* dossier, proceedings 3791

experiencia *nf* experience 361

experimental *adj* experimental 4360

experimentar *v* to experience, experiment 1484

experimento *nm* experiment 2815

experto *nm* expert 1452

explicación *nf* explanation 818

explicar *v* to explain 316

explícito *adj* explicit 4417

exploración *nf* exploration 4306

explorar *v* to explore 3595

explosión *nf* explosion 2175

explotación *nf* exploitation, cultivation 3764

explotar *v* to explode, exploit 1938

exponer *v* to expound, expose 773

exportación *nf* export, exportation 4493

exposición *nf* exhibition, display 1689

expresar *v* to express 660

expresión *nf* expression 555

expresivo *adj* expressive 4181

expreso *adj* express, explicit 4345

expulsar *v* to expel, throw out 2110

expulsión *nf* expulsion, ejection 4988

exquisito *adj* exquisite, superb 2592

extender *v* to extend, spread 851

extensión *nf* extension, area, expanse 2082

extenso *adj* extensive, large 2306

exterior *adj* exterior, outside 1163

exterior *nm* exterior, outside 1795

externo *adj* external, outward 2047

extinción *nf* extinction 4838

extinguir *v* to extinguish, put out 3616

extra *adj* extra 4756

extraer *v* to extract, take out 2102

extrañar *v* to miss, long for 2564

extranjero *adj* foreign, alien 1042

extranjero *nm* foreigner 1171

extraño *adj* strange, foreign 551

extraordinariamente *adv* extraordinarily 3953

extraordinario *adj* extraordinary, exceptional 860

extremadamente *adv* extremely 4494

extremo *nm* edge, border, end 1036

extremo *adj* extreme 1571

F

fábrica *nf* factory, manufacture 1498

fabricación *nf* manufacture, production 4526

fabricar *v* to manufacture 1408

fabuloso *adj* fabulous, fantastic 3596

facción *nf* (face) feature, faction 4718

fachada *nf* front of a building 3710

fácil *adj* easy 514

facilidad *nf* ease, facility 1108

facilitar *v* to facilitate 1381

fácilmente *adv* easily 1629

factor *nm* factor, cause, influence 1925

factura *nf* invoice, bill 4552

facultad *nf* faculty, ability 1383

faena *nf* task, job, performance 4147

falda *nf* skirt 3143

falla *nf* flaw, failure 4167

fallar *v* to fail, miss 1664

fallecer *v* to pass away (to die) 3456

fallo *nm* mistake, blunder, fault 3976

falso *adj* false 1140

falta *nf* lack, shortage 344

faltar *v* to be lacking 510

fama *nf* reputation, fame 1967

familia *nf* family 201

familiar *adj* familiar, of the family 744

familiar *nm* relative 1934

famoso *adj* famous, well-known 713

fantasía *nf* fantasy, fancy 2050

fantasma *nm* ghost, phantom 2449

fantástico *adj* fantastic, unreal 2360

farmacia *nf* pharmacy, drugstore 4290

fascinante *adj* fascinating 3853

fascinar *v* to fascinate 4854

fase *nf* phase, stage 2310

fatal *adj* fateful, deadly, awful 2539

fatiga *nf* fatigue 4303

favor *nm* favor, benefit 468

favorable *adj* favorable, suitable 2204

favorecer *v* to favor, help 2044

favorito *adj* favorite 2699
fe *nf* faith 1060
febrero *nm* February 1722
fecha *nf* date, day 749
felicidad *nf* happiness 1892
felicitar *v* to congratulate 3532
feliz *adj* happy, fortunate 956
femenino *adj* feminine, female 1345
fenómeno *nm* phenomenon 966
feo *adj* ugly, nasty, rude 2381
feria *nf* fair, festival 3358
feroz *adj* ferocious, fierce 3560
ferrocarril *nm* railway 2537
fértil *adj* fertile, rich 4765
fiar *v* to vouch for, confide, trust 4328
fibra *nf* fiber, grain 3424
ficción *nf* fiction 3165
ficha *nf* index card, chip, token 3736
fidelidad *nf* faithfulness, accuracy 3885
fiebre *nf* fever, excitement 2739
fiel *adj* faithful, loyal 1913
fiera *nf* (wild) beast 4923
fiesta *nf* party, feast 988
figura *nf* figure 495
figurar *v* to appear, represent, figure (in) 1227
fijar *v* to set, fix, [se] notice 407
fijo *adj* fixed, steady 1061
fila *nf* line, row, file 1647
filo *nm* (cutting) edge 3309
filosofía *nf* philosophy 1808
filosófico *adj* philosophical 2716
filósofo *nm* philosopher 2653
filtrar *v* to seep, filter 3781
fin *nm* end 156
final *nmf* al final: finally, in the end 307
final *adj* final 771
finalidad *nf* purpose, aim 3287
finalizar *v* to end, finalize 3011
finalmente *adv* finally, at last 728
financiar *v* to finance 4615
financiero *adj* financial 3289
finca *nf* property, estate 4294
fingir *v* to feign, pretend 4113
fino *adj* fine, delicate 1348
firma *nf* company, signature, signing 1567
firmar *v* to sign 870
firme *adj* firm, steady 1570
firmemente *adv* firmly 4677
firmeza *nf* firmness 4001

fiscal *adj* fiscal, treasury 4423
fiscal *nc* district attorney, prosecutor 4612
físicamente *adv* physically 3852
físico *adj* physical 643
físico *nm/f* physicist 3868
flaco *adj* thin, frail 3673
flecha *nf* arrow, dart 4781
flexible *adj* flexible 3097
flor *nf* flower 950
florecer *v* to flower, bloom, flourish 3628
flotar *v* to float, flutter 2967
fluir *v* to flow 3350
flujo *nm* flow, tide, discharge 3624
foco *nm* focus 2843
fomentar *v* to foster, promote, encourage 3676
fondo *nm* bottom, end 318
forma *nf* form, shape, way 113
formación *nf* formation, education 938
formal *adj* formal, polite 2036
formar *v* to form 287
formidable *adj* formidable, tremendous 3414
fórmula *nf* formula 1546
formular *v* to formulate 2462
fortalecer *v* to fortify 4409
fortaleza *nf* fortress, strength 3205
fortuna *nf* fortune, fate 1782
forzar *v* to force 1959
fósforo *nm* match, match stick 4803
foto *nf* photo, picture 2054
fotografía *nf* photograph 1385
fotográfico *adj* photographic 4333
fotógrafo *nm/f* photographer 4027
fracasar *v* to fail, to be unsuccessful 2277
fracaso *nm* failure, collapse 1451
fracción *nf* fraction 4216
frágil *adj* fragile, weak 3202
fragmento *nm* fragment, passage 3004
francamente *adv* frankly, openly 2909
francés *adj* French 646
franco *adj* open, frank, outspoken 3878
franja *nf* strip, stripe, fringe 3670
frasco *nm* bottle, jar, flask 4477
frase *nf* phrase 809
frecuencia *nf* frequency 1137
frecuentar *v* to frequent, visit 4037
frecuente *adj* frequent 1693
frecuentemente *adv* frequently, often 3753
frenar *v* to brake, restrain 2952
freno *nm* brake 3513

frente *nmf* al frente: facing; frente a: across from 260

fresco *adj* cool, healthy, fresh 2124

fresco *nm* freshness, coolness 2679

frialdad *nf* coldness, indifference 4827

frío *adj* cold 907

frío *nm* cold 1120

frívolo *adj* trivial, frivolous 4936

frontal *adj* frontal 4837

frontera *nf* border, frontier 1150

frustración *nf* frustration 3096

frustrado *adj* frustrated 2801

fruta *nf* fruit 1701

fruto *nm* fruit, result 1490

fuego *nm* fire, gunfire 1346

fuente *nf* source; fountain 801

fuera *adv* out, outside, away 451

fuerte *adj* strong 1010

fuertemente *adv* strongly 3759

fuerza *nf* strength, force, power 255

fuga *nf* flight, escape 2895

fumar *v* to smoke 2472

función *nf* function, meeting 543

funcional *adj* functional 3711

funcionamiento *nm* functioning, operation 2258

funcionar *v* to work, function 692

funcionario *nm* civil servant 1653

fundación *nf* foundation 4058

fundador *nm* founder 3577

fundamental *adj* fundamental 1086

fundamentalmente *adv* fundamentally, basically 2688

fundamento *nm* foundation, ground 2597

fundar *v* to found, base 1117

fundir *v* to melt, cast, smelt 3893

furia *nf* fury, rage 4095

furioso *adj* furious 3939

fútbol *nm* soccer 2513

futuro *nm* future 623

futuro *adj* future 1300

G

gabinete *nm* cabinet, den, office 4514

gala *nf* gala (performance/dinner) 4075

galería *nf* gallery, balcony 3191

gallina *nf* hen, coward 3023

gallo *nm* rooster 3872

gama *nf* range, musical scale 4512

gana *nf* desire 1177

ganado *nm* livestock, cattle 2425

ganador *nm* winner 4855

ganancia *nf* gain, profit 4155

ganar *v* to win, earn 286

garantía *nf* guarantee, warranty 2106

garantizar *v* to guarantee 2345

garganta *nf* throat, gorge 3090

garra *nf* claw, fang 4795

gas *nm* gas 2144

gastar *v* to spend (money) 1526

gasto *nm* expense, expenditure 1249

gato *nm* cat 1412

generación *nf* generation 906

general *adj* general 227

general *nm* general 1400

generalizar *v* to generalize, popularize 2621

generalmente *adv* generally, usually 1463

generar *v* to generate 2157

género *nm* sort, gender, genre 1501

generosidad *nf* generosity 3777

generoso *adj* generous 2398

genético *adj* genetic 4156

genial *adj* brilliant, inspired 3216

genio *nm* genius, disposition 2654

gente *nf* people 158

geografía *nf* geography 2670

geográfico *adj* geographical 3194

geométrico *adj* geometric 4557

gestión *nf* management, step, negotiation 2831

gesto *nm* gesture 1065

gigante *adj* gigantic 4264

gigante *nc* giant 4738

gigantesco *adj* giant, gigantic 2970

gira *nf* tour 3903

girar *v* to rotate, revolve 1371

giro *nm* turn, draft, expression 2465

global *adj* global, overall 3760

globo *nm* balloon, globe 3408

gloria *nf* glory, fame 2146

glorioso *adj* glorious 3689

gobernador *nm* governor 3907

gobernante *nc* ruler, leader 4396

gobernar *v* to govern 2322

gobierno *nm* government 476

golpe *nm* hit, strike, punch 657

golpear *v* to hit, strike 1904

goma *nf* rubber 3677

gordo *adj* fat, thick 2217

gota *nf* drop 2619

gozar *v* to enjoy 1304

grabación *nf* recording 4476

grabar *v* to record, engrave 1448

gracia *nf* (pl) thank you; grace, favor 272

gracioso *adj* funny, charming, amusing 3221

grado *nm* degree, grade 756

gráfico *adj* graphic, explicit 4336

grande *adj* large, great, big 62

grandeza *nf* greatness, size 3252

grandioso *adj* magnificent, grandiose 4491

grano *nm* grain, kernel 2748

grasa *nf* grease, fat 3275

gratitud *nf* gratitude 4682

grato *adj* agreeable, pleasant 3442

gratuito *adj* free, arbitrary, gratuitous 3299

grave *adj* serious, solemn 548

gravedad *nf* seriousness, gravity 2596

griego *adj* Greek 1467

grieta *nf* crack, opening, slit 4788

gris *adj* gray, gloomy 2290

gritar *v* to shout 1597

grito *nm* cry, shout, scream 1671

grosero *adj* crude, rude, crass 4096

grotesco *adj* grotesque, ridiculous 4874

grueso *adj* thick 2262

grueso *nm* bulk, mass 4474

grupo *nm* group 216

guante *nm* glove 3392

guapo *adj* handsome, beautiful 4140

guardar *v* to keep, save 566

guardia *nc* guard, watch, lookout 1842

guerra *nf* war, warfare 377

guerrero *adj* warrior, warlike 4787

guerrero *nm/f* warrior, soldier 4885

guía *nc* guide, leader 2318

guiar *v* to guide, lead, steer 2522

guitarra *nf* guitar 2885

gusano *nm* worm, caterpillar 4559

gustar *v* to be pleasing to 353

gusto *nm* pleasure, taste, preference 593

H

haber *v* to have (+Ved) 11

hábil *adj* skillful, clever 2997

habilidad *nf* ability, skill, talent 1582

habitación *nf* room, bedroom, habitat 1610

habitante *nm* inhabitant 1287

habitar *v* to inhabit 2624

hábito *nm* habit 1596

habitual *adj* usual, habitual, customary 1403

habitualmente *adv* habitually 3245

habla *nf* (el) speech, talking 2729

hablar *v* to speak, talk 92

hacer *v* to do, make 25

hacia *prep* toward, towards 125

hacienda *nf* ranch 3561

hallar *v* to find (out) 1166

hallazgo *nm* finding, discovery 3337

hambre *nf* (el) hunger, starvation 1204

harina *nf* flour 3614

harto *adj* fed up with 2600

hasta *prep* until, up to, even (adv) 54

hazaña *nf* deed, heroic feat 3857

hecho *nm* fact, happening 235

hectárea *nf* hectare 4991

helado *adj* iced, freezing, icy 2987

hembra *nf* female, woman 3379

heredar *v* to inherit 2555

heredero *nm* heir, heiress 3968

herencia *nf* inheritance, legacy 2016

herida *nf* wound, injury 2460

herido *adj* wounded, injured 2647

herido *nm* wounded (person) 4469

herir *v* to wound, hurt 3109

hermana *nf* sister 1256

hermano *nm* brother, [pl] siblings 539

hermoso *adj* beautiful, lovely 1224

héroe *nm* hero 2186

heroico *adj* heroic 3351

herramienta *nf* tool 2498

hervir *v* to boil 4065

hielo *nm* ice 2321

hierba *nf* herb, grass, weed 2850

hierro *nm* iron 1716

hígado *nm* liver 4203

higiene *nf* hygiene 4973

hija *nf* daughter 715

hijo *nm* son, [pl] children 166

hilo *nm* thread, yarn, wire 1851

himno *nm* hymn, anthem 3881

hipótesis *nf* hypothesis 2461

hispano *adj* Hispanic 4983

historia *nf* history, story 192

historiador *nm/f* historian 3159

histórico *adj* historical 980

hogar *nm* home, hearth 992

hoja *nf* sheet, leaf 1000

hola *interj* hello, hi 4752

holandés *adj* Dutch 4206

hombre *nm* man, mankind, husband 80

hombro *nm* shoulder 1927

homenaje *nm* homage, tribute 2396

hondo *adj* deep 2549

honesto *adj* honest 3326

honor *nm* honor, honesty 1211

honrado *adj* honest, respectable 4428

honrar *v* to honor 3931

hora *nf* hour, time (specific) 143

horario *nm* schedule, timetable 2095

horizontal *adj* horizontal 3728

horizonte *nm* horizon 2140

hormiga *nf* ant 4553

horno *nm* oven, furnace 3432

horrible *adj* horrible 2738

horror *nm* horror, atrocity 2334

hospital *nm* hospital 1298

hostil *adj* hostile, unfriendly 3871

hostilidad *nf* hostility, enmity 4667

hotel *nm* hotel 1643

hoy *adv* today, nowadays 164

hueco *nm* hole, cavity 2880

hueco *adj* hollow 4714

huelga *nf* strike, protest 2604

huella *nf* trace, track, footstep 2099

hueso *nm* bone 1695

huevo *nm* egg 1900

huir *v* to flee, run away 1574

humanidad *nf* humanity, mankind 1566

humano *adj* human 218

humano *nm* human 3586

humedad *nf* humidity 2777

húmedo *adj* humid, damp 2665

humilde *adj* humble, modest 2367

humillación *nf* humiliation 4456

humo *nm* smoke 2789

humor *nm* mood, humor 1889

hundido *adj* buried, sunken 4055

hundir *v* to sink, submerge 1850

I

ida *nf* departure, first half of a trip 4164

idea *nf* idea 193

ideal *nm* ideal, goal 1702

ideal *adj* ideal 1717

idéntico *adj* identical 2085

identidad *nf* identity 1583

identificación *nf* identification 2897

identificar *v* to identify 986

ideología *nf* ideology 3369

ideológico *adj* ideological 2917

idioma *nm* (specific) language 1027

idiota *nc* idiot, dunce 4769

iglesia *nf* church 1111

ignorancia *nf* ignorance 3076

ignorante *adj* ignorant 3467

ignorar *v* to be unaware 1247

igual *adj* equal, same (as) 239

igualar *v* to equate, equalize 4114

igualdad *nf* equality 2867

igualmente *adv* equally 1431

ilegal *adj* illegal 4659

ilimitado *adj* unlimited 4674

iluminación *nf* illumination, lighting 3989

iluminado *adj* illuminated 3342

iluminar *v* to illuminate, light up 2515

ilusión *nf* illusion, hope, dream 1372

ilustración *nf* illustration 4309

ilustrado *adj* learned, illustrated 3473

ilustrar *v* to illustrate 3941

ilustre *adj* renowned, illustrious 2771

imagen *nf* image, picture 484

imaginación *nf* imagination, fantasy 1838

imaginar *v* to imagine 486

imaginario *adj* imaginary 3504

imitación *nf* imitation 4209

imitar *v* to imitate, copy, mimic 2063

impacto *nm* impact 2390

impartir *v* to impart, administer 4736

impecable *adj* impeccable, faultless 4575

impedir *v* to prevent, hinder 751

imperial *adj* imperial, imperialist 4357

imperio *nm* empire, fortune 3032

implacable *adj* relentless, implacable 4584

implicar *v* to implicate, imply 1788

imponente *adj* impressive, magnificent 4909

imponer *v* to impose, enforce 641

importado *adj* imported 4753

importancia *nf* importance 429

importante *adj* important 207

importar *v* to matter, import 464

imposibilidad *nf* impossibility 4052

imposible *adj* impossible 592

imposición *nf* imposition 4028

impotencia *nf* impotence 4664

impreciso *adj* imprecise 4825

imprenta *nf* printing house 4453

imprescindible *adj* essential, indispensable 2617

impresión *nf* impression, printing 874

impresionante *adj* impressive, astonishing 2320

impresionar *v* to impress 2292

impreso *adj* printed 3697

imprevisto *adj* unforeseen, unexpected 4436

imprimir *v* to print 2502

improvisar *v* to improvise 3144

impuesto *nm* tax 2806

impulsar *v* to push, promote, drive 1875

impulso *nm* impulse, momentum 1520

inaugurar *v* to inaugurate, start 2403

incapacidad *nf* inability, incompetence 3730

incapaz *adj* incapable 1733

incendio *nm* fire, conflagration 2695

incertidumbre *nf* uncertainty 2972

incidencia *nf* ocurrence, impact 4832

incidente *nm* incident 3003

incidir *v* to influence, affect 4841

incierto *adj* uncertain 3536

incipiente *adj* incipient, beginning 4178

incitar *v* to incite 3877

inclinación *nf* slope, incline, tendency 2035

inclinado *adj* inclined, slanting 2835

inclinar *v* to bow, tilt, incline 1814

incluir *v* to include 720

inclusive *adv* including, even 3568

incluso *adv* including, even (adv) 294

incómodo *adj* uncomfortable 2535

incomprensible *adj* incomprehensible 4134

inconsciente *adj* unconscious, thoughtless 2705

inconveniente *nm* inconvenience, drawback 2151

incorporación *nf* inclusion, incorporation 4301

incorporar *v* to incorporate, include 1087

increíble *adj* incredible, unbelievable 1669

incrementar *v* to increase 3964

incremento *nm* increase, raise 4866

incurrir *v* to incur, fall into 4867

incursión *nf* invasion, incursion 4965

indagar *v* to investigate 4515

indefinido *adj* vague, indefinite 4471

independencia *nf* independence 1767

independiente *adj* independent, self-sufficient 1291

independientemente *adv* independently 4135

indicación *nf* indication 4084

indicar *v* to indicate 479

índice *nm* index, forefinger 2000

indicio *nm* indication, sign 3184

indiferencia *nf* indifference 3217

indiferente *adj* indifferent 2902

indígena *adj* indigenous, native 2302

indignación *nf* indignation 4122

indio *nm* Indian 1411

indirecto *adj* indirect 3061

indiscutible *adj* indisputable, unquestionable 4452

indispensable *adj* indispensable, essential 1949

individual *adj* individual 1482

individuo *nm* individual, person 1037

índole *nf* nature, temperament 2927

inducir *v* to lead to 2857

indudable *adj* unquestionable 4002

indudablemente *adv* doubtless, undoubtedly 3360

industria *nf* industry, factory 1884

industrial *adj* industrial 2005

inédito *adj* unpublished 3879

inesperado *adj* unexpected, unforeseen 2904

inestable *adj* unstable, unsteady 4926

inevitable *adj* inevitable, unavoidable 1694

inevitablemente *adv* inevitably 3842

inexistente *adj* non-existent 4792

inexplicable *adj* unexplainable 4358

infancia *nf* infancy, childhood 1928

infantil *adj* of children, childlike, infantile 1186

infección *nf* infection 4703

infeliz *adj* unhappy, unfortunate 4161

inferior *adj* lower, inferior 1350

infierno *nm* hell, inferno 3062

infinidad *nf* infinity, countless 4127

infinito *adj* infinite 2215

infinito *nm* infinite, infinity 4839

influencia *nf* influence 1102

influir *v* to (have) influence 2022

información *nf* information 682

informar *v* to inform 835

informativo *adj* informative 4744

informe *nm* report 1548

ingeniero *nm/f* engineer 1761

ingenio *nm* ingenuity, talent, wit 3378

ingenioso *adj* ingenious, clever 4549

ingenuo *adj* naive, ingenuous 3507

inglés *adj* English 608

ingrediente *nm* ingredient 4708

ingresar *v* to join, deposit, admit 1791

ingreso *nm* entrance, admission, income 1690

inicial *adj* initial 1879

inicial *nf* initial (letters) 4830

inicialmente *adv* initially 4920

iniciar *v* to initiate, start 568

iniciativa *nf* initiative 1668

inicio *nm* beginning, start 2512

injusticia *nf* injustice 2554

injusto *adj* unfair, unjust 2378

inmediatamente *adv* immediately 882

inmediato *adj* immediate 724

inmenso *adj* immense, vast, huge 1074

inmerso *adj* engrossed, immersed 4144

inmigrante *nc* immigrant 4993

inminente *adj* imminent 4351

inmóvil *adj* immovable, motionless 4093

innecesario *adj* unnecessary 3248

innovación *nf* innovation 4482

innumerable *adj* innumerable, countless 3399

inocencia *nf* innocence 3520

inocente *adj* innocent, naïve 2538

inolvidable *adj* unforgettable 4251

inquietante *adj* disquieting 4478

inquietar *v* to make uneasy, disturb 4490

inquieto *adj* restless, anxious 2986

inquietud *nf* restlessness, anxiety 1453

inscribir *v* to register, record 3993

inscripción *nf* inscription, registration 3684

insecto *nm* insect 3542

inseguridad *nf* insecurity 3738

inseguro *adj* unsure, unsafe 4529

inseparable *adj* inseparable 4922

insertar *v* to insert, put in 4785

insignificante *adj* insignificant 3747

insinuar *v* to insinuate, hint 3453

insistencia *nf* insistence, persistence 3587

insistir *v* to insist on 699

insólito *adj* unusual, uncommon 3951

insoportable *adj* unbearable, intolerable 3401

inspección *nf* inspection 4829

inspector *nm/f* inspector 4521

inspiración *nf* inspiration, inhalation 3055

inspirar *v* to inspire, inhale 2072

instalación *nf* installation, facilities 2395

instalar *v* to install 958

instancia *nf* instance 2495

instante *nm* instant, moment 1215

instinto *nm* instinct 2914

institución *nf* institution 1115

institucional *adj* institutional 4595

instituto *nm* institute 3699

instrucción *nf* instruction 1611

instruir *v* to instruct 4918

instrumento *nm* instrument 813

insuficiente *adj* insufficient 3278

insultar *v* to insult, berate 4390

insulto *nm* insult 3622

intacto *adj* intact 3259

integración *nf* integration 4174

integrante *adj* integral, part of a group 3889

integrar *v* to integrate, fit in 1439

integridad *nf* integrity 4105

íntegro *adj* whole, entire, honest 4754

intelectual *adj* intellectual 1103

inteligencia *nf* intelligence 1375

inteligente *adj* intelligent 1447

intención *nf* intention 876

intensamente *adv* intensely 3914

intensidad *nf* intensity, force 2174

intenso *adj* intense, acute 1119

intentar *v* to try, attempt 376

intento *nm* attempt, try 1012

intercambiar *v* to exchange 3704

intercambio *nm* exchange, interchange 2490

interés *nm* interest 308

interesado *adj* (self-) interested 1605

interesante *adj* interesting 762

interesar *v* to interest 448

interior *nm* interior, inside 614

interior *adj* interior, inside 1263

interlocutor *nm* participant in a dialog 3657

intermedio *adj* interim, intermediate 3223

intermedio *nm* means, interval 4777

interminable *adj* endless, interminable 3235

internacional *adj* international 1189

internar *v* to confine 4899

interno *adj* internal 783

interponer *v* to interpose, intervene 4229

interpretación *nf* interpretation, interpreting 1468

interpretar *v* to interpret 983

intérprete *nc* performer, interpreter 4716

interrogante *nc* question, interrogator 4190

interrogar *v* to question, interrogate 3746

interrumpir *v* to interrupt 1405

interrupción *nf* interruption 3518

intervalo *nm* interval, gap 4214

intervención *nf* intervention 1615

intervenir *v* to intervene 847

íntimamente *adv* intimately 4083

intimidad *nf* private life, intimacy 2540

íntimo *adj* close, intimate 1684

introducción *nf* introduction 3346

introducir *v* to introduce, bring in 949

intuición *nf* intuition 3509

intuir *v* to sense 4368

inundación *nf* flood, deluge 4902

inundar *v* to flood, inundate 4090

inútil *adj* useless 1564

invadir *v* to invade, overcome 1764

invasión *nf* invasion 2573

invención *nf* invention, contrivance 3510

inventar *v* to invent, make up 1018

invento *nm* invention 3086

inversión *nf* investment, outlay 2458

inverso *adj* inverse, opposite 3703

invertido *adj* reversed, inverted 4374

invertir *v* to invest 1945

investigación *nf* investigation 890

investigador *nm/f* researcher, investigator 2981

investigar *v* to investigate 1749

invierno *nm* winter 1340

invisible *adj* invisible 3572

invitación *nf* invitation 2300

invitado *nm* guest 2583

invitar *v* to invite 954

invocar *v* to invoke 4252

involuntario *adj* involuntary 4790

inyección *nf* shot, injection 4658

ir *v* to go 30

ira *nf* rage, wrath 3545

ironía *nf* irony 3531

irónico *adj* ironic, mocking 4536

irracional *adj* irrational 4053

irreal *adj* unreal 4966

irregular *adj* irregular 3214

irreversible *adj* irreversible 4847

irritar *v* to irritate 4711

irrumpir *v* to burst in, raid 4994

isla *nf* island 1229

italiano *adj* Italian 953

izquierda *nf* left 940

izquierdo *adj* left (opposite of right) 1703

J

jamás *adv* never 788

japonés *adj* Japanese 2169

jardín *nm* garden 1837

jaula *nf* cage, crate, playpen 4005

jefe *nm/f* leader, boss, manager 761

jerarquía *nf* hierarchy, rank 3335

jinete *nm* rider, horseman 4789

joder *v* to f**k, screw (around/up) 4535

jornada *nf* (working) day, shift 2007

joven *adj* young 442

joven *nc* teenager, young person 581

jovencito *nm* young person 4300

joya *nf* jewel, treasure 2698

judicial *adj* judicial 2957

judío *adj* Jewish 2319

juego *nm* game, play, sport 371

jueves *nm* Thursday 2606

juez *nc* judge 1259

jugada *nf* move, play 4998

jugador *nm* player, gambler 3168

jugar *v* to play (sport/game) 355

jugo *nm* juice 3712

juguete *nm* toy 2672

juicio *nm* judgment 795

julio *nm* July 1559

junio *nm* June 2349

junta *nf* meeting, conference, seam 3213

juntar *v* to bring together 2280

junto *adv* together with, next to 378

junto *adj* together 729

jurar *v* to swear, take an oath 2846

jurídico *adj* legal, juridical 2769

justamente *adv* just, exactly 1485

justicia *nf* justice, fairness 1290

justificación *nf* justification 3211

justificado *adj* justifiable, justified 4331

justificar *v* to justify, excuse 1308

justo *adv* just 915

justo *adj* fair, just 1834

juvenil *adj* young, juvenile 2561

juventud *nf* youth 1311

juzgar *v* to judge 1396

K

kilo *nm* kilogram 2648

kilómetro *nm* kilometer 1297

L

la *pron* [3rd person] (dir obj-f) 33

laberinto *nm* maze, labyrinth 4348

labio *nm* lip 2759

labor *nf* labor, work, task 930

laboral *adj* labor, industry 3268

laboratorio *nm* laboratory 2264

laborioso *adj* laborious, industrious 4941

lado *nm* side 165

ladrillo *nm* brick 3056

ladrón *nm* thief 4204

lago *nm* lake 2680

lágrima *nf* tear, teardrop 2386

laguna *nf* lagoon 2961

lamentable *adj* regrettable 3232

lamentablemente *adv* regrettably 3919

lamentar *v* to regret 2509

lámina *nf* sheet (of metal) 3770

lámpara *nf* lamp 3347

lana *nf* wool 3060

lanzar *v* to throw, launch 611

lápiz *nm* pencil 3296

lapso *nm* lapse 4080

largamente *adv* for a long time, at length 4888

largar *v* to let go, start out 4767

largo *adj* long 175

largo *nm* a lo largo: throughout; length 1640

larguísimo *adj* very long 4608

lástima *nf* shame, pity 3294

lata *nf* (tin) can 2493

latente *adj* latent 4201

lateral *adj* side, lateral 4007

latín *nm* Latin 3040

latino *adj* Latin 1862

latinoamericano *adj* Latin American 3971

latir *v* to beat (heart) 4379

latitud *nf* latitude 4771

lavar *v* to wash 1762

lazo *nm* bow, knot, tie, lasso 2612

le *pron* [3rd person] (indir obj) 19

leal *adj* loyal, faithful 3897

lealtad *nf* loyalty, faithfulness 3996

lección *nf* lesson 1977

leche *nf* milk 1334

lecho *nm* (river) bed, couch 3732

lector *nm* reader, lecturer 1810

lectura *nf* reading 839

leer *v* to read 244

legal *adj* legal 2017

legislación *nf* legislation 4760

legítimo *adj* legitimate 2966

lejano *adj* distant 1152

lejos *adv* far (away, off) 469

lema *nm* motto, slogan 3838

leña *nf* firewood 4185

lengua *nf* language, tongue, strip (of land) 596

lenguaje *nm* language, speech 841

lentamente *adv* slowly 1975

lente *nmf* lens, [pl] glasses 4193

lentitud *nf* slowness 3875

lento *adj* slow 1128

león *nm* lion 2756

lesión *nf* injury, wound, harm 4527

letra *nf* letter, handwriting, lyrics 865

levantar *v* to raise, lift 372

leve *adj* slight, trifling, light 2671

ley *nf* law, bill, rule 384

leyenda *nf* legend 2031

liberación *nf* liberation 2361

liberal *adj* liberal 2014

liberar *v* to free, liberate 1363

libertad *nf* freedom, liberty 435

libra *nf* pound (money/weight) 4964

librar *v* to liberate, set free 2556

libre *adj* free, vacant 413

libremente *adv* freely 2804

librería *nf* bookstore 4577

libro *nm* book 253

licencia *nf* license, permission 3415

líder *nc* leader 2427

ligado *adj* linked, joined 2926

ligar *v* to tie, link, bind 4645

ligeramente *adv* slightly, lightly 2974

ligero *adj* light (in weight), slight 1696

limitación *nf* limitation 2581

limitado *adj* limited 1866

limitar *v* to limit 1021

límite *nm* limit 934

limosna *nf* alms, charity 4779

limpiar *v* to clean 1537

limpieza *nf* cleanliness, purity 2447

limpio *adj* clean 1397

lindo *adj* pretty, nice, lovely 2582

línea *nf* line, course 473

lingüístico *adj* linguistic 3890

lío *nm* mess, problem, bad situation 4235

liquidar *v* to liquidate, sell (off) 4347

líquido *nm* liquid 2438

liso *adj* smooth, flat, straight 3632

lista *nf* list, roster, roll 1049

listo *adj* ready, clever, smart 1456

literalmente *adv* literally 3750

literario *adj* literary 1494

literatura *nf* literature 1090

litro *nm* liter 4239

liviano *adj* light, frivolous 4242

llama *nf* flame, llama 3835

llamada *nf* call, knock 1022

llamado *nm* call, calling 1510

llamar *v* to call, name 104

llamativo *adj* striking 4322

llano *adj* flat, level, plain 4694

llanto *nm* crying, weeping 4163

llanura *nf* plain, prairie, plainness 4196

llave *nf* key, faucet, wrench 2150

llegada *nf* arrival 1616

llegar *v* to arrive 66

llenar *v* to fill 925

lleno *adj* full, filled 508

llevar *v* to take, carry 93

llorar *v* to cry 1466

llover *v* to rain 2053

lluvia *nf* rain 1217

lo *art* the (+ neuter) 20

lo *pron* [3rd person] (dir obj-m) 21

lobo *nm* wolf 3898

local *adj* local 1516

local *nm* place, quarters 1880

localidad *nf* town, locality 3894

localizar *v* to locate, find, localize 3102

loco *adj* crazy, insane 1377

locura *nf* madness, insanity 2441

lógica *nf* logic 2015

lógicamente *adv* logically 3470

lógico *adj* logical 1214

lograr *v* to achieve, get, manage 311

logro *nm* success, achievement 3433

lomo *nm* back, loin, spine 4868

longitud *nf* length, longitude 4434

lucha *nf* fight, struggle, wrestle 758

luchar *v* to fight, wrestle 1026

lucir *v* to show (off), shine 2741

luego *adv* later, afterwards 132

lugar *nm* place, position 135

lujo *nm* luxury 1614

lujoso *adj* luxurious 3866

luminoso *adj* bright, luminous 2651

luna *nf* moon 2394

lunes *nm* Monday 2187

luz *nf* light 256

M

macho *nm* male, manliness 3239

madera *nf* wood 987

madre *nf* mother 278

madrugada *nf* dawn, daybreak 2241

madurar *v* to mature, ripen 3819

madurez *nf* maturity, ripeness 2684

maduro *adj* mature, ripe 2578

maestra *nf* teacher (f) 3966

maestro *nm* teacher (m), master 961

maestro *adj* master 1469

magia *nf* magic 3019

mágico *adj* magic, magical 2708

magnífico *adj* magnificent, splendid 1812

magnitud *nf* magnitude, extent 2863

maíz *nm* corn, maize 3314

mal *adv* badly 301

mal *nm* evil 1580

maldad *nf* evil, wickedness 4646

maldición *nf* damnation, curse 4948

maldito *adj* damned, wretched 4088

malestar *nm* discomfort, unease, unrest 3496

maleta *nf* suitcase, case 4146

maligno *adj* evil, malignant 4710

malo *adj* bad 275

mamá *nf* mom 2286

mañana *nf* morning, tomorrow 401

mañana *adv* tomorrow 1235

mancha *nf* stain, spot 2491

mandar *v* to send, order 529

mandato *nm* mandate, order, command 3443

mando *nm* command, authority 2125

manejar *v* to drive, handle 916

manejo *nm* handling, management 2385

manera *nf* way, manner 152

manga *nf* sleeve 3266

mango *nm* handle, mango 4256

manía *nf* obsession, mania 4562

manifestación *nf* protest, manifestation 1551

manifestar *v* to express, show 1069

manifiesto *nm* poner de manifiesto: to show 3111

maniobra *nf* maneuver, operation 2903

manipular *v* to manipulate, handle 4145

mano *nf* hand 150

manta *nf* blanket 4063

mantener *v* to keep, maintain 234

mantenimiento *nm* maintenance, sustenance 3720

manto *nm* cloak 3904

manual *nm* manual, handbook 3929

manual *adj* manual 4271

manzana *nf* apple, (city) block 2853

mapa *nm* map 2185

máquina *nf* machine 806

maquinaria *nf* machinery 3582

mar *nmf* sea 645

maravilla *nf* wonder, marvel 2023

maravilloso *adj* wonderful, marvelous 1743

marca *nf* mark, brand, trademark 1370

marcar *v* to mark, note, dial 677

marcha *nf* march, progress 785

marchar *v* to go, leave, march 1203

marco *nm* frame, mark, setting 1316

marea *nf* wave, tide, ebb 4109

margen *nmf* edge, margin, border, brink 1413

marginal *adj* marginal, minor 3721

marido *nm* husband 1032

marinero *nm/f* sailor 4949

marino *adj* marine, naval 2720

mariposa *nf* butterfly, wing nut 3883

mármol *nm* marble 4199

marrón *adj* brown 4951

martes *nm* Tuesday 3490

martillo *nm* hammer 4688

marzo *nm* March 2002

mas *conj* but, however 777

más *adj* more 24

masa *nf* mass, dough, bulk, crowd 935

máscara *nf* mask 3449

masculino *adj* masculine, manly, male 2142

masivo *adj* mass, massive 3778

matanza *nf* slaughter, carnage 4626

matar *v* to kill 557

mate *nm* mate (beverage) 3865

matemática *nf* mathematics 3257

matemático *adj* mathematical 3912

materia *nf* matter, subject 668

material *nm* material, element 656

material *adj* material 1414

materno *adj* maternal 3167

matiz *nm* shade, tint, nuance 2291

matrimonial *adj* matrimonial 4307

matrimonio *nm* marriage, married couple 1109

máximo *adj* maximum 1089

máximo *nm* maximum 2308

mayo *nm* May 1422

mayor *adj* larger, older, main 138

mayoría *nf* majority 531

me *pron* me (obj) 35

mecánica *nf* mechanics, mechanism 3949

mecánico *adj* mechanical 1973

mecanismo *nm* mechanism 1599

medalla *nf* medal, medallion 3995

media *nf* average; a m.: halfways 2342

mediado *adj* mid, middle 2566

mediano *adj* average, medium, ordinary 3103

mediante *prep* by means of 896

mediar *v* to mediate 4655

medicamento *nm* medicine, drug 4669

medicina *nf* medicine 1725

médico *nm/f* doctor 564

médico *adj* medical 1170

medida *nf* measure; a medida que: to the extent 333

medieval *adj* medieval 4426

medio *nm* means, middle; por medio: through 171

medio *adj* half, middle 208

mediocre *adj* mediocre 4042

mediodía *nm* noon, midday 2618

medir *v* to measure 929

meditar *v* to meditate, ponder 3901

mejilla *nf* cheek 4528

mejor *adj* best, better (adv) 121

mejora *nf* improvement 3044

mejorar *v* to improve, get better 960

melancólico *adj* melancholy 4684

melodía *nf* melody 4311

memoria *nf* memory 605

mención *nf* mention 3291

mencionar *v* to mention, cite 905

menor *adj* younger, youngest 334

menos *adj* less, fewer 98

mensaje *nm* message 1047

mensual *adj* monthly 3618

mental *adj* mental 1674

mentalidad *nf* mindset, mind 3334

mentalmente *adv* mentally 4932

mente *nf* mind 993

mentir *v* to (tell a) lie 2416

mentira *nf* lie 1768

menudo *adv* a menudo: often 1944

mercado *nm* market 609

mercancía *nf* goods, merchandise 2935

merced *nf* favor, mercy 4397

merecer *v* to deserve, be worthy (of) 716

mérito *nm* worth, merit 1935

mero *adj* mere 2060

mes *nm* month 210

mesa *nf* table, board 461

meta *nf* goal, aim, purpose 2293

metáfora *nf* metaphor 4568

metal *nm* metal 2075

metálico *adj* metallic 2842

meter *v* to put (into) 573

método *nm* method 1129

metro *nm* meter, subway 563

mexicano *adj* Mexican 3892

mezcla *nf* mixture, blend 1606

mezclado *adj* mixed 2579

mezclar *v* to mix 1500

mi *adj* my 49

mí *pron* me (obj prep) 357

micrófono *nm* microphone 4834

miedo *nm* fear 450

miel *nf* honey 2990

miembro *nm* member, limb 732

mientras *conj* while, whereas, as long as 154

miércoles *nm* Wednesday 3431

mierda *nf* shit, crap, excrement 4355

mil *num* thousand 217

milagro *nm* miracle 2181

militar *adj* military 856

militar *nm* soldier, military person 1697

millón *num* million, fortune 523

mina *nf* mine 3013

mínimo *adj* minimum 990

mínimo *nm* minimum 2343

ministerio *nm* ministry 3136

ministro *nm/f* (government) secretary, minister 1519

minoría *nf* minority 4137

minucioso *adj* meticulous, thorough 4394

minúsculo *adj* minute, insignificant 4636

minuto *nm* minute 459

mío *pron* mine 872

mirada *nf* gaze, look 1197

mirar *v* to look, watch 142

misa *nf* (religious) mass 2510

miserable *adj* wretched, miserable 3441

miseria *nf* misery, wretchedness 1963

misión *nf* mission, task 1432

mismísimo *adj* very same 4900

mismo *adj* same 51

misterio *nm* mystery 2223

misterioso *adj* mysterious 2849

místico *adj* mystical 4881

mitad *nf* half, middle 625

mito *nm* myth 2467

mixto *adj* mixed, co-ed 4277

moda *nf* fashion, form 1180

modalidad *nf* mode, manner 4506

modelo *nc* model, pattern 747

moderno *adj* modern 671

modesto *adj* modest, humble 2024

modificación *nf* modification, alteration 3717

modificar *v* to modify 1758

modo *nm* way, manner 198

mojado *adj* wet 4383

mojar *v* to make wet, dampen 3766

molde *nm* mold, cast, pattern 3800

molestar *v* to bother, disturb, upset 1272

molestia *nf* bother, nuisance, trouble 3481

molesto *adj* annoyed, bothered, upset 3371

molino *nm* mill, windmill 4893

momento *nm* moment, time 108

moneda *nf* coins, currency 1107

monja *nf* nun 3548

mono *nm* monkey 3471

monótono *adj* monotonous 4433

monstruo *nm* monster, monstrosity 3405

monstruoso *adj* monstrous 4842

montaña *nf* mountain 1212

montar *v* to ride, mount, assemble 998

monte *nm* mountain 1844

montón *nm* lot of, heap, pile 1946

monumental *adj* monumental 4990

monumento *nm* monument 2889

moral *adj* moral 1082

moral *nf* morals, ethics 1756

morder *v* to bite 3588

moreno *adj* dark, brown 2303

morir *v* to die 293

mortal *adj* mortal, lethal, deadly 3112

mortal *nc* mortal 4879

mosaico *nm* mosaic 4861

mosca *nf* fly (insect) 2956

mostrar *v* to show 392

motivación *nf* motivation 3416

motivar *v* to motivate, cause 3071

motivo *nm* motive, cause 504

motor *nm* engine, motor 1698

mover *v* to move, incite 402

móvil *adj* mobile 4686

movilizar *v* to mobilize 3787

movimiento *nm* movement 362

mozo *nm* waiter, youth, bellboy 4324

muchacha *nf* girl 2506

muchacho *nm* boy 1687

muchísimo *adj* great many, great amount 1305

mucho *adj* much, many, a lot (adv) 45

mudar *v* to move, change 3688

mudo *adj* mute, silent 3118

mueble *nm* (piece of) furniture 1952

muelle *nm* wharf, dock 4530

muerte *nf* death 424

muerto *adj* dead 687

muerto *nm* dead person 2032

muestra *nf* proof, sample, sign 1594

mujer *nf* woman, wife 127

múltiple *adj* multiple, many 1556

multiplicar *v* to multiply 2034

multitud *nf* multitude 2424

mundial *adj* worldwide 1951

mundo *nm* world 118

muñeca *nf* doll, wrist 3082

municipal *adj* municipal, town 2686

muralla *nf* city wall 3812

muro *nm* (outer) wall, rampart 1942

músculo *nm* muscle 3029

museo *nm* museum 2525

música *nf* music 550

musical *adj* musical 1752

músico *nm/f* musician 2518

muslo *nm* thigh 4807

mutuamente *adv* mutually, each other 4117

mutuo *adj* mutual 2326

muy *adv* very, really 42

N

nacer *v* to be born 330

nacimiento *nm* birth, origin 1339

nación *nf* nation 1891

nacional *adj* national 507

nacionalidad *nf* nationality 4321

nada *pron* nothing, (not) at all 95

nadar *v* to swim 3050

nadie *pron* nobody, anybody 233

naranja *nf* orange (fruit) 2950

nariz *nf* nose 2119

narración *nf* narration, account 4283

narrar *v* to narrate, tell 3623

nativo *adj* native 3381

natural *adj* natural 414

naturaleza *nf* nature, character 674

naturalidad *nf* ease, spontaneity 3742

naturalmente *adv* naturally 1523

navaja *nf* razor, blade, navaja 4947

nave *nf* spacecraft, ship 2542

navegación *nf* navigation, shipping 4870

navegar *v* to navigate, sail 3375

necesariamente *adv* necessarily 2282

necesario *adj* necessary 322

necesidad *nf* necessity, need 340

necesitado *adj* poor, needy 4470

necesitar *v* to need 229

negar *v* to deny, refuse 617

negativa *nf* negative, denial 3142

negativo *adj* negative, pessimistic 1631

negociación *nf* negotiation 4538

negociar *v* to negotiate, deal (with/in) 3921

negocio *nm* business, transaction 864

negro *adj* black 317

nervio *nm* nerve 2744

nervioso *adj* nervous, uptight 1410

neutro *adj* neutral 4801

ni *conj* not even, neither, nor 64

nido *nm* nest 3298

niebla *nf* fog 4274

nieto *nm* grandchild 2615

nieve *nf* snow 2423

niña *nf* child, young girl 1052

niñez *nf* childhood, infancy 4184

ninguno *adj* no, none, nobody (pron) 144

niño *nm* child, little boy 178

nítido *adj* clear, clean, neat 4908

nivel *nm* level 475

no *adv* no 10

noble *adj* noble 2545

noble *nc* nobleman, noble 4463

nobleza *nf* nobility, uprightness 4662

noche *nf* night, evening 196

noción *nf* notion, idea 2871

nocturno *adj* nocturnal, evening 1979

nombrar *v* to name, appoint 1147

nombre *nm* name, noun 199

norma *nf* standard, pattern, norm 1349

normal *adj* normal, usual, regular 664

normalidad *nf* normality 4367

normalmente *adv* normally 2212

norte *nm* north 895

norteamericano *adj* North American 1246

nos *pron* us (obj) 65

nosotros *pron* we (subj) 191

nostalgia *nf* nostalgia, homesickness 3290

nota *nf* note, grade 853

notable *adj* outstanding, noteworthy 1475

notar *v* to notice 571

noticia *nf* news 703

notorio *adj* notorious, noticeable 3138

novedad *nf* latest news, newness 1864

novela *nf* novel 1080

novelista *nc* novelist 4468

noventa *num* ninety 3417

novia *nf* girlfriend, bride 2726

noviembre *nm* November 2148

novio *nm* boyfriend, groom 2730

nube *nf* cloud 1961

núcleo *nm* nucleus, core 2238

nudo *nm* knot 3488

nuestro *adj* our 82

nuevamente *adv* anew, again 1454

nueve *num* nine 786

nuevo *adj* new 99

nulo *adj* void, null 4581

número *nm* number 315

numeroso *adj* numerous 1101

nunca *adv* never, ever 151

O

o *conj* or 26

obedecer *v* to obey 1513

obediencia *nf* obedience 4647

obispo *nm* bishop 3363

objetivo *nm* objective 1210

objetivo *adj* objective, impartial 2027

objeto *nm* object, thing 419

obligación *nf* obligation 1040

obligado *adj* obliged, required 1255

obligar *v* to obligate, force 642

obligatorio *adj* obligatory, compulsory 3007

obra *nf* work, book, deed 206

obrar *v* to work, act 4344

obrero *nm/f* worker, laborer 2243

obrero *adj* working class 2851

observación *nf* observation 1535

observador *nm* observer 3208

observar *v* to observe 478

obsesión *nf* mania, obsession 3412

obstáculo *nm* obstacle 2588

obstante *adj* no + obstante: nevertheless 1679

obtener *v* to obtain 466

obviamente *adv* obviously 3811

obvio *adj* obvious 2586

ocasión *nf* opportunity, occasion 463

ocasional *adj* occasional, random 4987

ocasionar *v* to occasion, bring about 3464

occidental *adj* occidental, western 2323

océano *nm* ocean 3646

ochenta *num* eighty 2120

ocho *num* eight 492

ocio *nm* leisure (time) 4366

octubre *nm* October 1688

ocultar *v* to hide 1541

oculto *adj* hidden, occult 2039

ocupación *nf* occupation, use 2059

ocupado *adj* busy, occupied 1601

ocupar *v* to occupy, use 397

ocurrencia *nf* idea, witty remark 4648

ocurrir *v* to happen, occur 200

odiar *v* to hate 3444

odio *nm* hatred 2177

oeste *nm* West 3821

ofender *v* to offend 3936

oferta *nf* offer, bid, supply 2205

oficial *adj* official, authorized 1099

oficial *nc* official, officer 1781

oficialmente *adv* officially 4545

oficina *nf* office 1113

oficio *nm* job, occupation, function 1644

ofrecer *v* to offer, present 368

oh *interj* oh 2736

oído *nm* hearing, ear 1969

oír *v* to hear 263

ojalá *adv* I hope that 3067

ojo *nm* eye 247

ola *nf* wave, billow 2406

oler *v* to smell 3036

olfato *nm* sense of smell 4913

olla *nf* pot, kettle 4927

olor *nm* smell, odor, fragrance 1986

olvidar *v* to forget 383

olvido *nm* forgetfulness, omission 2504

once *num* eleven 1455

onda *nf* wave, ripple 2160

opaco *adj* dull, opaque, heavy 4362

opción *nf* option, choice 2305

ópera *nf* opera 3757

operación *nf* operation 848

operar *v* to operate 1424

opinar *v* to think, be of the opinion 1209

opinión *nf* opinion, view 632

oponer *v* to oppose 1225

oportunidad *nf* opportunity, chance 624

oportuno *adj* opportune, timely 1937

oposición *nf* opposition 1699

optar *v* to choose, opt for 2384

optimismo *nm* optimism 3864

optimista *adj* optimistic 3030

óptimo *adj* optimum 4129

opuesto *adj* opposite, contrary 1785

oración *nf* prayer 2543

oral *adj* oral 3773

órbita *nf* orbit, socket, field 4522

orden *nmf* order; sequence (m), religious (f) 302

ordenado *adj* organized, clean 2417

ordenar *v* to put in order, organize 1167

ordinario *adj* vulgar, ordinary 2478

oreja *nf* ear 2407

orgánico *adj* organic 3716

organismo *nm* organization, organism, (human) body 1458

organización *nf* organization 1243

organizado *adj* organized 2058

organizar *v* to organize 825

órgano *nm* organ 1563

orgullo *nm* pride 2006

orgulloso *adj* proud, arrogant 2388

orientación *nf* orientation, direction 2683

orientado *adj* positioned, guided 4385

oriental *adj* eastern, oriental 1955

orientar *v* guide, show the way 2250

oriente *nm* East 2413

origen *nm* origin, cause 606

original *adj* original 1191

original *nm* original 3581

originar *v* to give rise (to), cause 2819

orilla *nf* shore, edge 2096

oro *nm* gold 914

orquesta *nf* orchestra, dance band 3301

os *pron* you (obj-pl/+fam) 1373

oscilar *v* oscillate 3578

oscurecer *v* to get dark 4212

oscuridad *nf* darkness 2468

oscuro *adj* dark, obscure 888

oso *nm* bear 4555

ostentar *v* to flaunt, show off 4254

otoño *nm* autumn 3357

otorgar *v* to give, grant, award 2224

otro *adj* other, another 31

oveja *nf* sheep, ewe 3556

oxígeno *nm* oxygen 4844

P

pabellón *nm* pavilion, sports hall 4740

paciencia *nf* patience 2336

paciente *nc* patient 1511

pacífico *adj* peaceful 3105

pacto *nm* pact, agreement 2530

padecer *v* to suffer 1590

padre *nm* father 182

padrino *nm* godparent, sponsor 4732

pagar *v* to pay 342

página *nf* page 1135

pago *nm* payment 1807

país *nm* country 133

paisaje *nm* landscape 1508

paja *nf* straw, thatching 3483

pájaro *nm* bird 1824

pala *nf* shovel 4601

palabra *nf* word 176

palacio *nm* palace 1968

pálido *adj* pale, ghastly, faded 3161

palma *nf* palm tree, palm 2938

palo *nm* stick, pole 2012

paloma *nf* dove 3700

palpar *v* to feel, touch, fondle 4191

pan *nm* bread 1392

pánico *nm* panic 3227

panorama *nm* panorama, landscape 2500

pantalla *nf* screen, monitor 2330

pantalón *nm* pants, trousers 2489

pañuelo *nm* handkerchief, shawl 3900

papa *nmf* Pope (m), potato (f) 2669

papá *nm* dad 2281

papel *nm* paper, role, part 277

paquete *nm* package, packet 2166

par *nmf* pair, couple (m); a la par: at same time 768

para *prep* for, to, in order to 15

parada *nf* (transportation) stop 3649

parado *adj* stopped, standing 2244

paraíso *nm* paradise 2983

paraje *nm* place, spot 4935

paralelo *adj* parallel 2477

paralizado *adj* paralyzed 4473

paralizar *v* to paralyze 3962

parar *v* to stop (moving) 1001

parcela *nf* piece of property 4004

parcial *adj* partial, biased 3775

parcialmente *adv* partially 4894

pardo *adj* brown, dark, dim 3722

parecer *v* to seem, look like 81

parecer *nm* opinion, looks 1933

parecido *adj* similar 837

pared *nf* (interior) wall 736

pareja *nf* couple, pair 901

parentesco *nm* kinship 3975

paréntesis *nm* parenthesis, digression 4525

pariente *nc* relative 2297

parir *v* to give birth 3602

parlamentario *adj* parliamentary 4961

parque *nm* park 1760

párrafo *nm* paragraph 3461

parroquia *nf* parish 4260

parte *nf* part, portion 86

participación *nf* participation, involvement 1438

participante *nm* participant 4616

participar *v* to participate 750

partícula *nf* particle 4776

particular *adj* particular, peculiar 854

particular *nm* particular, detail, individual 1260

particularmente *adv* particularly, personally 2652

partida *nf* game, match, departure 1165

partidario *nm* supporter, partisan 2436

partido *nm* party, group, (sports) match 425

partir *v* to divide, leave; a partir de: starting 290

parto *nm* birth 3550

pasado *adj* past, last 445

pasado *nm* past 902

pasaje *nm* fare, passage, lane 2446

pasajero *nm* passenger 3354

pasajero *adj* fleeting, transitory 4570

pasar *v* to pass, spend (time) 67

pasear *v* to go for a walk, ride 1985

paseo *nm* walk, ride 2209

pasillo *nm* hall, corridor 2666

pasión *nf* passion, desire 1445

pasivo *adj* passive 4317

paso *nm* step, pace 267

pasta *nf* pasta, dough 3771

pastilla *nf* pill, capsule 4354

pasto *nm* grass, pasture 3870

pastor *nm/f* shepherd, pastor 3474

pata *nf* leg, paw 2052

patada *nf* kick, punt 4078

paterno *adj* paternal 4628

patio *nm* courtyard, playground, yard 1700

pato *nm* duck 4786

patria *nf* native land, fatherland 2135

patrimonio *nm* patrimony, inheritance 3114

patriótico *adj* patriotic 4972

patrón *nm* employer, landlord, patron saint 1648

pausa *nf* pause 2802

pauta *nf* guideline, rule, standard 3325

paz *nf* peace 702

pecado *nm* sin 2551

pecar *v* to sin 3828

pecho *nm* chest, breast 1649

peculiar *adj* peculiar 2746

pedagógico *adj* pedagogical, teaching 4864

pedazo *nm* piece, bit 2855

pedir *v* to ask for, request 204

pegar *v* to hit, stick (on) 1395

pelea *nf* fight, quarrel 3034

pelear *v* to fight, struggle 1823

película *nf* movie, film 826

peligro *nm* danger, menace 913

peligroso *adj* dangerous 1127

pelo *nm* hair 1056

pelota *nf* ball 2445

pena *nf* trouble; valer la pena: be of worth 575

penal *adj* penal 4285

pendiente *adj* aware of, pending 1296

penetración *nf* penetration, insight 4569

penetrar *v* to penetrate, come in 1531

penoso *adj* painful, laborious 3737

pensado *adj* thought-out, designed 2734

pensamiento *nm* thought, thinking 789

pensar *v* to think 106

pensión *nf* boarding house 2469

penumbra *nf* semidarkness, twilight 4997

peón *nm* unskilled laborer, field hand 4519

peor *adv* worse 866

peor *adj* worse, worst 1965

pequeñito *adj* very small, tiny 4566

pequeño *adj* little, small, young 184

percatar *v* to inform, become aware 4826

percepción *nf* perception 4136

percibir *v* to perceive, notice 1575

perder *v* to lose, miss 190

pérdida *nf* loss 1417

perdido *adj* lost 931

perdón *nm* forgiveness, pardon 2240

perdonar *v* to forgive, excuse 1678

perdurar *v* to last, live on, endure 4085

perfección *nf* perfection 2776

perfeccionar *v* to perfect 3366

perfectamente *adv* perfectly 850

perfecto *adj* perfect 810

perfil *nm* profile, outline 2108

perfilar *v* to outline, shape 4969

perfume *nm* perfume 3843

periódico *nm* newspaper, periodical 765

periodismo *nm* journalism 4652

periodista *nc* journalist 1464

periodístico *adj* journalistic 4032

período *nm* period, time 1440

perjudicar *v* to endanger 3267

perjuicio *nm* damage, loss 3994

perla *nf* pearl 4172

permanecer *v* to stay, remain 821

permanencia *nf* permanence, tenure 3429

permanente *adj* permanent 1239

permanentemente *adv* permanently 3462

permiso *nm* permission, permit 1753

permitir *v* to allow, permit 220

pero *conj* but, yet, except 23

perpetuo *adj* continual, perpetual 4192

perro *nm* dog 939

persecución *nf* pursuit, persecution 3031

perseguir *v* to persecute, pursue, chase 1094

persistente *adj* persistent 4843

persistir *v* to persist 3254

persona *nf* person 137

personaje *nm* character (e.g. movie) 712

personal *adj* personal 590

personal *nm* personnel, staff, staffing 1404

personalidad *nf* personality, celebrity 1421

personalmente *adv* personally 1964

perspectiva *nf* perspective 1066

pertenecer *v* to belong 654

perteneciente *adj* pertaining, belonging 4467

pertenencia *nf* membership, property 3846

perturbar *v* to perturb, upset 4627

peruano *adj* Peruvian 4359

perverso *adj* perverse, wicked 4444

pesadilla *nf* nightmare 3479

pesado *adj* heavy, boring, tiresome 1367

pesar *nm* sorrow; a pesar de: in spite of 366

pesar *v* to weigh 770

pesca *nf* fishing 3495

pescado *nm* fish 2584

pescador *nm/f* fisherman 3824

pescar *v* to fish 2958

peseta *nf* peseta (money) 3725

pésimo *adj* dreadful, awful 3817

peso *nm* peso (money), weight, load 417

peste *nf* plague, pestilence, pest 3943

petición *nf* request, petition 3435

petróleo *nm* oil, petroleum 3427

pez *nm* (alive) fish 2426

piadoso *adj* devout, pious, merciful 4671

piano *nm* piano 2727

picar *v* to bite, sting, itch 2840

pico *nm* y pico: and a bit; beak, peak 1553

pie *nm* foot, base 386

piedad *nf* pity, mercy 4267

piedra *nf* stone, rock 719

piel *nf* skin, hide, fur 884

pierna *nf* leg 1201

pieza *nf* piece, part 639

pila *nf* (baptismal) font, battery, heap 3672

pilar *nm* pillar, column 4128

piloto *nm/f* pilot, driver 4249

pino *nm* pine (tree) 4157

pinta *nf* appearance, look, aspect 4630

pintado *adj* painted 2347

pintar *v* to paint 1158

pintor *nm/f* painter 2218

pintoresco *adj* picturesque 4293

pintura *nf* painting, paint 1097

pionero *nm* pioneer 4980

pirámide *nf* pyramid 4799

pisar *v* to step on 2667

piscina *nf* swimming pool 4653

piso *nm* floor, story 797

pista *nf* clue, track, trace 2065

pistola *nf* gun, pistol 3745

placa *nf* plaque, plate, badge 3330

placer *nm* pleasure 1205

plan *nm* plan 598

plancha *nf* (electric) iron, plate, sheet 4073

planear *v* to plan 2872

planeta *nm* planet 2004

plano *nm* plane, map, level 875

plano *adj* flat, plain, even, level 3005

planta *nf* plant, floor 711

plantar *v* to plant 2949

planteamiento *nm* proposal, exposition 3626

plantear *v* to propose, present 910

plástico *nm* plastic 2947

plástico *adj* plastic 2988

plata *nf* silver, money 1281

plataforma *nf* platform, springboard 3965

plato *nm* plate, dish 1836

playa *nf* beach, seaside 1713

plaza *nf* square, marketplace 1020

plazo *nm* deadline, installment 1295

pleito *nm* litigation, suit, dispute 4378

plenamente *adv* fully 2340

plenitud *nf* fullness, abundance 3383

pleno *adj* complete, full 679

plomo *nm* lead, bullet 3386

pluma *nf* pen, feather 2444

población *nf* population 900

poblado *adj* populated 3695

poblar *v* to populate, inhabit 4142

pobre *adj* poor 373

pobreza *nf* poverty, lack, scarcity 1874

poco *adj* little, few, a little bit (adv) 74

poder *v* to be able to; can 27

poder *nm* power 428

poderoso *adj* powerful 1560

poema *nm* poem 1855

poesía *nf* poetry, poem 1841

poeta *nc* poet 1262

poético *adj* poetic 3312

polémica *nf* polemics, argument 3774

policía *nc* police, police force, police officer 1017

policial *adj* police 3311

política *nf* politics, policy 506

político *adj* political 284

político *nm/f* politician 1237

pollo *nm* chicken 3231

polo *nm* pole, polo, polo shirt 3609

polvo *nm* dust, powder 1971

pólvora *nf* gunpowder, powder 4763

poner *v* to put (on), get (+adj) 77

popular *adj* popular 709

poquito *adj* little bit 2463

por *prep* by, for, through 12

porcentaje *nm* percentage 3015

porción *nf* part, portion, share 3403

porque *conj* because 38

porquería *nf* filth, junk 3046

portador *nm* bearer, carrier 3362

portar *v* to behave [se], carry 2254

portero *nm/f* porter, doorkeeper, goalkeeper 4315

portugués *adj* Portuguese 3913

porvenir *nm* future, time to come 2766

posar *v* to rest, pose, land 4709

poseer *v* to possess, own 1005

posesión *nf* possession 2158

posibilidad *nf* possibility 367

posible *adj* possible 225

posiblemente *adv* possibly 1980

posición *nf* position 503

positivo *adj* positive 1356

posterior *adj* rear, backside 1399

posteriormente *adv* afterwards 2430

postre *nmf* dessert; a la postre: in the end 2985

postura *nf* posture, position, attitude 1636

potencia *nf* power, potential 1779

potencial *adj* potential 4439

potente *adj* potent, powerful 3133

pozo *nm* well, shaft 2625

práctica *nf* practice, skill 933

prácticamente *adv* practically 1106

practicar *v* to practice 1303

práctico *adj* practical, skillful 1270

precario *adj* precarious 4046

precaución *nf* caution, forethought 2918

precedente *nm* precedent 4858

preceder *v* to precede 3288

precio *nm* price, cost, value 708

precioso *adj* beautiful, precious 1839

precipitar *v* to plunge, hurl, rush 3119

precisamente *adv* precisely 580

precisar *v* to do exactly, specify 1923

precisión *nf* precision 1847

preciso *adj* precise, necessary 739

predecir *v* to predict 4496

predicar *v* to preach 3917

predominar *v* to predominate 4567

preferencia *nf* preference 2623

preferible *adj* preferable 3126

preferido *adj* preferred, favorite 3744

preferir *v* to prefer 541

pregunta *nf* question 481

preguntar *v* to ask (a question) 323

prejuicio *nm* prejudice 2906

prematuro *adj* premature 4853

premiar *v* to award 4583

premio *nm* prize, reward 1337

prenda *nf* piece of clothing 2939

prender *v* to turn on, apprehend 2454

prensa *nf* press 1318

preocupación *nf* worry, concern 995

preocupado *adj* worried, concerned 1677

preocupar *v* to worry 766

preparación *nf* preparation, training 2128

preparado *adj* prepared 1067

preparar *v* to prepare 499

presa *nf* dam, prisoner (f) 2635

prescindir *v* to do without 3692

presencia *nf* presence, appearance 519

presenciar *v* to be present at, witness 3538

presentación *nf* presentation, introduction 1990

presentar *v* to introduce, present 249

presente *nm* present 802

presente *adj* present, current 1088

presentir *v* to sense in advance 4783

preservar *v* to preserve 3361

presidencia *nf* presidency 4087

presidencial *adj* presidential 4388

presidente *nm* president 831

presidir *v* to preside over 3020

presión *nf* pressure 967

presionar *v* to press, pressure 2896

preso *nm* prisoner 3069

preso *adj* imprisoned, confined 3756

prestado *adj* borrowed, lent 2682

préstamo *nm* loan, borrowing 3694

prestar *v* to lend 767

prestigio *nm* prestige 1908

prestigioso *adj* prestigious 4620

presumir *v* to boast, show off, suppose 3340

presunto *adj* alleged, presumed 4501

presupuesto *nm* budget 2630

pretender *v* to attempt 584

pretensión *nf* pretension, claim 2728

pretexto *nm* pretext, excuse 2737

prevalecer *v* to prevail 4265

prevención *nf* prevention, warning 4995

prevenir *v* to avoid, prevent 3270

prever *v* to foresee, anticipate, forecast 2105

previamente *adv* previously 2891

previo *adj* previous 1437

previsible *adj* foreseeable 4835

previsión *nf* forecast, precaution 3440

previsto *adj* foreseen, planned 2086

prima *nf* female cousin, down payment 3283

primario *adj* primary 1715

primavera *nf* spring, spring-like 2325

primero *adj* first 60

primitivo *adj* primitive 2038

primo *nm* cousin 1860

primordial *adj* fundamental, primary 4152

princesa *nf* princess 4402

principal *adj* main, principal 496

principalmente *adv* principally, mainly 2226

príncipe *nm* prince 2616

principio *nm* beginning, principle 237

prioridad *nf* priority 4505

prisa *nf* hurry 3253

prisión *nf* prison, imprisonment 2980

prisionero *nm* prisoner 3176

privado *adj* private 706

privar *v* to deprive (of) 2868

privilegiado *adj* privileged 3579

privilegio *nm* privilege 1843

probabilidad *nf* probability 4393

probable *adj* probable 1840

probablemente *adv* probably 971

probar *v* to test, prove, try 911

problema *nm* problem 169

procedencia *nf* origin, source 4611

procedente *adj* coming (from) 3260

proceder *v* to proceed, start 1322

procedimiento *nm* procedure, proceedings 1544

procesión *nf* procession 4280

proceso *nm* process, procedure 452

proclamar *v* to proclaim 2944

procurar *v* to try, seek 1100

prodigioso *adj* prodigious, famous 4938

producción *nf* production 1721

producir *v* to produce, cause 195

productivo *adj* productive, profitable 4589

producto *nm* product 589

productor *nm* producer 4312

profesión *nf* profession, occupation 1206

profesional *adj* professional 640

profesor *nm/f* professor, teacher 621

profeta *nm* prophet 4804

profundamente *adv* profoundly, deeply 1365

profundidad *nf* depth, profundity 1330

profundizar *v* to deepen, analyze in depth 3634

profundo *adj* deep, profound 489

programa *nm* program, plan 467

programar *v* to plan, program 3162

progresar *v* to progress 2916

progresivo *adj* progressive 3685

progreso *nm* progress 1591

prohibición *nf* prohibition 4343

prohibido *adj* prohibited 2257

prohibir *v* to prohibit, forbid 1741

prolongación *nf* extension 4749

prolongado *adj* prolonged, lengthy 2929

prolongar *v* to extend, prolong 2077

promesa *nf* promise 2051

prometer *v* to promise 1641

promoción *nf* promotion 2706

promover *v* to promote 2767

pronto *adv* soon, quick 396

pronunciar *v* to pronounce 944

propaganda *nf* advertising, propaganda 2508

propagar *v* to propagate, spread 4958

propiamente *adv* exactly, properly 3079

propiciar *v* to favor, foster, aid 3884

propicio *adj* appropriate, suitable 3636

propiedad *nf* property 588

propietario *nm* owner 2526

propio *adj* own, proper, typical 140

proponer *v* to propose 500

proporción *nf* proportion 2109

proporcionar *v* to supply 1742

proposición *nf* proposition 3647

propósito *nm* intention, purpose 752

propuesta *nf* proposal, proposition 2173

prosa *nf* prose 4524

proseguir *v* to continue, carry on 2534

prosperar *v* to prosper, thrive 4154

protagonista *nc* protagonist, main character 2536

protección *nf* protection 1652

protector *nm* protector, defender 4288

proteger *v* to protect 1006

protesta *nf* objection, protest 2134

protestar *v* to protest, object 2288

provecho *nm* benefit, use 3617

proveer *v* to provide 2911

proveniente *adj* coming from 4151

provenir *v* to come from, be from 1958

provincia *nf* province, region 1624

provincial *adj* provincial 4654

provocar *v* to cause, provoke 663

proximidad *nf* proximity 3338

próximo *adj* next 440

proyección *nf* projection, screening 3057

proyectar *v* to project 1471

proyecto *nm* project, plan 604

prudencia *nf* prudence, moderation 3621

prudente *adj* sensible, prudent 2884

prueba *nf* proof, trial, test 505

psicología *nf* psychology 4437

psicológico *adj* psychological 3123

psicólogo *nm/f* psychologist 4604

publicación *nf* publication 2702

públicamente *adv* publicly, in public 4877

publicar *v* to publish 743

publicidad *nf* advertising, publicity 2925

publicitario *adj* advertising 4297

público *adj* public 465

público *nm* public, audience 769

pueblo *nm* people, village 241

puente *nm* bridge 1353

puerta *nf* door 354

puerto *nm* port, harbor 1364

pues *conj* then, well then 103

puesto *nm* job, place, position 755

pugna *nf* battle, struggle 4712

pulmón *nm* lung 3420

pulso *nm* pulse, pulsation 3762

puñado *nm* fistful, small group 4693

puño *nm* fist, handle, cuff 3563

punta *nf* tip, point 1427

punto *nm* point, dot, period 147

puntual *adj* punctual 3498

puramente *adv* purely, simply 2753

pureza *nf* purity, chastity 3455

puro *adj* pure, clean 637

puta *nf* whore, prostitute 4982

Q

que *conj* that, which 3

qué *pron* what?, which?, how (+ adj)! 47

quebrar *v* to break, bend, weaken 2375

quedar *v* to remain, stay 89

quehacer *nm* task, job, chore 3410

queja *nf* complaint 2922

quejar *v* to complain 1530

quemado *adj* burned, burnt 3365

quemar *v* to burn 1509

querer *v* to want, love 57

querido *adj* dear, beloved 2009

queso *nm* cheese 3182

quien *pron* who, whom 141

quién *pron* who?, whom? 292

quieto *adj* still, motionless, calm 3154

químico *adj* chemical 2864

quince *num* fifteen 1033

quinientos *num* five hundred 3426

quinto *adj* fifth 1179

quitar *v* to remove, take away 669

quizás *adv* perhaps, maybe 297

R

rabia *nf* rage 2887

racional *adj* rational 2890

radical *adj* radical 1987

radicalmente *adv* radically 4464

radicar *v* to lie, be situated 3763

radio *nmf* radio; set (m), communication (f) 824

raíz *nf* root 1028

rama *nf* branch, bough, limb 1160

ramo *nm* bunch (of flowers), branch 4284

rancho *nm* ranch, farm 4533

rango *nm* rank, range 3085

rápidamente *adv* rapidly, quickly 1008

rapidez *nf* speed, velocity 1899

rápido *adj* quick, fast 652

raro *adj* strange, rare, scarce 849

rascar *v* to scratch, scrape 4542

rasgo *nm* feature, trait 1355

rastro *nm* track, sign, flea market 3465

rata *nf* rat 3497

ratificar *v* to ratify 3942

rato *nm* moment, while, time 1478

ratón *nm* mouse, rat 3856

raya *nf* line, ray, stripe 3249

rayo *nm* ray, beam, lightning 2197

raza *nf* race, lineage 1620

razón *nf* reason; tener razón: to be right 212

razonable *adj* reasonable 2405

razonamiento *nm* reasoning 3472

razonar *v* to reason (out), think 4680

reacción *nf* reaction 1122

reaccionar *v* to react 1521

real *adj* royal, real, authentic 462

realidad *nf* reality, actuality 202

realismo *nm* realism 3780

realista *adj* realistic 2678

realización *nf* fulfillment, realization 2790

realizar *v* to fulfill, carry out 299

realmente *adv* really, actually, in fact 416

reanudar *v* to renew, resume 3686

reaparecer *v* to reappear 4337

rebajar *v* to discount 4159

rebaño *nm* herd, flock 4919

rebasar *v* to exceed, pass over 4813

rebelde *adj* rebel 3576

rebelde *nc* rebel, insurgent 4400

rebeldía *nf* rebelliousness, defiance 3977

rebelión *nf* rebellion 4202

recelo *nm* mistrust, suspicion 4817

recepción *nf* reception, waiting-room 3327

receta *nf* recipe, prescription 3196

rechazar *v* to reject 1182

rechazo *nm* rejection, refusal 2275

recibir *v* to receive 205

recién *adv* recently, just 863

reciente *adj* recent 1332

recientemente *adv* recently 2749

recinto *nm* grounds, precincts 3088

recipiente *nm* container, recipient, tank 4960

recíproco *adj* reciprocal 4761

recitar *v* to recite 3594

reclamar *v* to demand, require 1507

reclamo *nm* claim, complaint, protest 4465

recobrar *v* to recover, regain 3580

recoger *v* to pick up 634

recomendación *nf* recommendation 2908

recomendar *v* to recommend 1581

recompensa *nf* reward, recompense 4815

reconocer *v* to recognize, admit 327

reconocimiento *nm* recognition, acknowledgment 1794

reconstrucción *nf* reconstruction 4259

reconstruir *v* to reconstruct 2328

recordar *v* to remember, remind 215

recorrer *v* to travel, cover (distance) 808

recorrido *nm* journey, itinerary, route 2231

recortar *v* to trim, cut off, clip 3643

recorte *nm* clipping, cutting, trimming 3804

recrear *v* to recreate, amuse 4728

rectificar *v* to rectify, straighten (out) 4683

recto *adj* right, straight, honest 2816

recuerdo *nm* memory, keepsake 628

recuperación *nf* recovery, recuperation 3101

recuperar *v* to recuperate, recover 965

recurrir *v* to resort to 1555

recurso *nm* resource, recourse, means 735

red *nf* network, net, system 1658

redacción *nf* editing, wording, essay 3735

redactar *v* to edit, write, compose 2870

redondo *adj* round 1757

reducción *nf* reduction 3815

reducido *adj* reduced, limited 1736

reducir *v* to reduce 996

reemplazar *v* to replace 3198

referencia *nf* reference, allusion 1063

referente *adj* concerning 3073

referir *v* to refer (to) 409

refinado *adj* refined 4071

reflejado *adj* reflected 4224

reflejar *v* to reflect 1176

reflejo *nm* reflection 1675

reflexión *nf* reflection 1826

reflexionar *v* to reflect, consider on 2788

reforma *nf* reform, improvement 2641

reforzar *v* to reinforce, strengthen 3012

refugiar *v* to take shelter, give refuge 3603

refugio *nm* shelter, refuge 2964

regalar *v* to give (as a gift) 1528

regalo *nm* gift, present 2067

regar *v* to water, irrigate 4148

régimen *nm* regime, diet 1426

región *nf* region 1050

regional *adj* regional 3484

regir *v* to rule, govern, manage 3222

registrar *v* to register, record 1536

registro *nm* register, record 2214

regla *nf* rule, ruler, regulation 1014

reglamento *nm* regulations, rules 3805

regresar *v* to return (to a place) 799

regreso *nm* return 1557

regular *adj* regular 1956

regular *v* to regulate, adjust 4131

reina *nf* queen 2020

reinar *v* to reign, prevail 4054

reino *nm* kingdom, reign 2255

reír *v* to laugh (at) 1493

reiterar *v* to reiterate, repeat 2900

reivindicación *nf* claim, demand, redemption 4702

relación *nf* relationship, relation 230

relacionado *adj* related, regarding 1402

relacionar *v* to relate 1745

relajar *v* to relax 4724

relatar *v* to tell, narrate 2733

relativamente *adv* relatively 2519

relativo *adj* relative 1747

relato *nm* tale, story 2221

relevante *adj* relevant, significant 4104

relieve *nm* relief; poner de relieve: to emphasize 3521

religión *nf* religion 1460

religioso *adj* religious 886

reloj *nm* clock, watch 1685

rematar *v* to finish off, finish up 4133

remediar *v* to heal, cure 4327

remedio *nm* alternative, cure, solution 1379

remitir *v* to remit 3234

remontar *v* to go back to (time) 2580

remoto *adj* remote, far-off 2313

remover *v* to remove 3827

renacer *v* to be reborn, reappear 4805

rencor *nm* grudge, spite 4387

rendimiento *nm* yield, output, efficiency 3874

rendir *v* [se] to give in; to render 1534

renovación *nf* renewal, renovation 3937

renovar *v* to renew, renovate 2269

renta *nf* income 3210

renuncia *nf* resignation, renunciation 3693

renunciar *v* to give up, renounce 1621

reparar *v* to repair, restore 2770

repartir *v* to divide, deliver, distribute 1161

reparto *nm* distribution, delivery 3437

repasar *v* to review, revise 4353

repente *adv* de + repente: suddenly 2183

repentino *adj* sudden 3394

repercusión *nf* repercussion, impact 4852

repertorio *nm* repertoire, list, index 4072

repetición *nf* repetition 3113

repetido *adj* repeated 2471

repetir *v* to repeat 382

repleto *adj* full, overcrowded 3515

réplica *nf* answer, retort, copy 3758

replicar *v* to reply 4177

reponer *v* to replace, restore 3423

reportaje *nm* news report 4056

reposar *v* to rest, lie down 4632

reposo *nm* rest, peace 3769

representación *nf* representation 1425

representante *nc* representative 1491

representar *v* to represent 527

representativo *adj* representative 3930

represión *nf* repression 3814

reprimir *v* to repress 3895

reprochar *v* to reproach 3982

reproche *nm* reproach, criticism 4660

reproducción *nf* reproduction 3637

reproducir *v* to reproduce, repeat 1654

república *nf* republic 3389

republicano *adj* republican 4486

requerir *v* to require 1081

requisito *nm* prerequisite, requirement 2644

resaltar *v* to emphasize 3701

rescatar *v* to rescue, save 2559

rescate *nm* rescue, ransom 4617

resentimiento *nm* resentment 4110

reserva *nf* reservation, reserve 1527

reservado *adj* reserved, booked 2960

reservar *v* to reserve, book 2750

residencia *nf* residence 2844

residir *v* to reside, live (in) 2764

residuo *nm* residue, waste 3934

resignación *nf* resignation, acceptance 4759

resignar *v* to resign, relinquish 4878

resistencia *nf* resistance, opposition 1415

resistir *v* to resist, endure 1312

resolución *nf* resolution 2711

resolver *v* to resolve, settle, work out 622

resonancia *nf* resonance, repercussion 4369

respaldo *nm* support, backing, back 2692

respectivo *adj* respective 1797

respecto *nm* respect, con respecto a: with regards to 433

respetable *adj* respectable 4021

respetar *v* to respect **880**

respeto *nm* respect, regard **894**

respetuoso *adj* respectful **3653**

respiración *nf* respiration, breath **3171**

respirar *v* to breathe **1792**

responder *v* to answer, respond **456**

responsabilidad *nf* responsibility **781**

responsable *adj* responsible **955**

respuesta *nf* answer, reply **472**

restablecer *v* to reestablish, restore **4806**

restante *adj* remaining **3482**

restar *v* to subtract, minimize **2836**

restaurante *nm* restaurant **3014**

restaurar *v* to restore, reinstate **4187**

resto *nm* rest, remainder, leftover **447**

restricción *nf* restriction **4819**

resucitar *v* to resuscitate **4603**

resuelto *adj* resolved, determined **2428**

resultado *nm* result, outcome **379**

resultar *v* to result, turn out **238**

resumen *nm* summary **2593**

resumir *v* to summarize **3041**

retener *v* to keep, retain **2452**

retirada *nf* retreat, withdrawal **3861**

retirado *aj* retired, remote, secluded **4067**

retirar *v* to take away, retire **817**

retiro *nm* withdrawal, retreat **4809**

reto *nm* challenge, defiance **3476**

retomar *v* to retake, restart **3489**

retornar *v* to return, give back **3754**

retorno *nm* return **3035**

retrasar *v* to delay, fall behind **4188**

retraso *nm* delay **3886**

retrato *nm* portrait, photograph **2492**

retroceder *v* to go back **2724**

retroceso *nm* movement backwards **4833**

reunión *nf* meeting, reunion **746**

reunir *v* to gather, meet, collect **509**

revelación *nf* revelation **3724**

revelar *v* to reveal, disclose **1691**

reventar *v* to burst, puncture **4009**

revés *nm* al revés: backwards, upside down, inside out **1993**

revisar *v* to check, revise, inspect **1632**

revisión *nf* checking revision **3860**

revista *nf* magazine, journal **804**

revivir *v* to revive **3662**

revolución *nf* revolution **957**

revolucionario *adj* revolutionary **1947**

revolver *v* to stir, mix, scramble **3752**

revuelto *adj* confused, messed up **4338**

rey *nm* king **1238**

rezar *v* to pray, recite **2847**

rico *adj* rich, tasty **627**

ridículo *adj* ridiculous, absurd **3209**

ridículo *nm* ridicule **3543**

rienda *nf* rein, restraint **3829**

riesgo *nm* risk **1016**

rigidez *nf* rigidity **4845**

rígido *adj* rigid, stiff, firm **2411**

rigor *nm* harshness, rigor **2249**

riguroso *adj* rigorous, severe **2528**

rincón *nm* corner, nook **2118**

riñón *nm* kidney **4292**

río *nm* river **559**

riqueza *nf* riches, wealth **1474**

risa *nf* laugh, chuckle **2192**

rítmico *adj* rhythmic **4978**

ritmo *nm* rhythm **877**

rito *nm* rite, ritual **3093**

ritual *nm* ritual, rite **3534**

rival *nc* rival **3796**

robar *v* to rob, steal **1492**

robo *nm* theft, robbery **2919**

robusto *adj* strong, robust, sturdy **4689**

roca *nf* rock **2497**

roce *nm* brush, graze **4748**

rodar *v* to roll, run, scatter **3179**

rodeado *adj* surrounded **1801**

rodear *v* to surround **1174**

rodilla *nf* knee **2208**

rogar *v* to implore, pray, ask **3160**

rojo *adj* red **533**

rol *nm* role **4764**

rollo *nm* roll, coil **4014**

romano *adj* Roman **1774**

romántico *adj* romantic **2338**

romper *v* to break **601**

ronda *nf* round **3786**

ropa *nf* clothes, clothing **1285**

rosa *nf* rose **1978**

rosado *adj* pink, rosy **4461**

rosario *nm* rosary, beads, string **4258**

rostro *nm* face, countenance **2040**

roto *adj* broken, torn **1914**

rotundo *adj* categorical **3388**

rozar *v* to touch (lightly) **3226**

rubio *adj* blonde, fair **3269**

rudo *adj* rude, crude, coarse 4859

rueda *nf* wheel 1352

ruido *nm* noise 1184

ruidoso *adj* noisy 4261

ruina *nf* ruin, collapse 2397

rumbo *nm* direction, course, bearing 2414

rumor *nm* rumor, murmur 2626

ruptura *nf* break-up, rupture 2457

rural *adj* rural, country 2631

ruso *adj* Russian 2307

rústico *adj* rustic, rural 4395

ruta *nf* route 2113

rutina *nf* routine 3042

S

sábado *nm* Saturday 1816

sábana *nf* (bed) sheet 3859

saber *v* to know (a fact), find out 46

saber *nm* knowledge 1625

sabiduría *nf* wisdom, knowledge 2856

sabio *adj* wise, learned 1790

sabor *nm* taste, flavor, sensation 2126

sabroso *adj* delicious, tasty 4605

sacar *v* to take out 228

sacerdote *nm* priest 1974

saco *nm* sack, bag, plunder 2798

sacrificar *v* to sacrifice 2752

sacrificio *nm* sacrifice 1848

sacudir *v* to shake, jolt 2969

sagrado *adj* sacred 1775

sal *nf* salt 2608

sala *nf* room, hall 811

salario *nm* salary, wages 3307

salida *nf* exit, escape, outcome 694

salir *v* to leave, go out 111

salón *nm* hall, room 1637

saltar *v* to jump, leap, hop 1071

salto *nm* jump, hop, skip 1391

salud *nf* health 973

saludable *adj* healthy, wholesome 3803

saludar *v* to greet, say hello 1744

saludo *nm* greeting 2661

salvación *nf* salvation, rescue 3575

salvaje *adj* wild, savage, uncultivated 2001

salvar *v* to save, rescue 753

salvo *adv* except (for), but 924

sanción *nf* sanction, approval, penalty 4141

sangre *nf* blood 613

sangriento *adj* bloody 3911

sanitario *adj* health, sanitary, clean 4047

sano *adj* healthy, wholesome 1394

santa *nf* saint (f) 793

santo *nm* saint (m) 258

sargento *nm* sergeant 4727

satisfacción *nf* satisfaction 1299

satisfacer *v* to satisfy 1517

satisfactorio *adj* satisfactory 3316

satisfecho *adj* satisfied 1735

se *pron* ["reflexive" marker] 9

secar *v* to dry 2496

sección *nf* section, cut 1910

seco *adj* dry, arid 1178

secretario *nm/f* secretary 1245

secreto *adj* secret 1731

secreto *nm* secret 1954

sector *nm* sector, area, section 1096

secuencia *nf* sequence 3241

secular *adj* secular, lay 4911

secundario *adj* secondary 2213

sed *nf* thirst 3080

seda *nf* silk 3271

sede *nf* headquarters, seat 4236

seducir *v* to seduce, tempt 4831

seguida *adv* en seguida: right away, at once 2818

seguido *adj* in a row, successive 1465

seguidor *nm* follower, supporter, fan 4170

seguir *v* to follow, keep on 97

según *prep* according to 257

segundo *adj* second 243

segundo *nm* second 577

seguramente *adv* surely, securely 994

seguridad *nf* security, safety 560

seguro *adj* safe, sure, secure 1118

seguro *nm* insurance 3377

seis *num* six 375

selección *nf* selection, choice 2533

seleccionar *v* to select 2912

sello *nm* stamp, seal 2999

selva *nf* forest, jungle 2138

semana *nf* week 304

semanal *adj* weekly 4268

sembrar *v* to sow, plant 2717

semejante *adj* similar, such, alike 1039

semejanza *nf* similarity, likeness 3522

semilla *nf* seed 2875

seminario *nm* seminar, seminary 4108

seña *nf* sign, mark, seal 3533

senador *nm/f* senator 4386

señal *nf* sign, mark, token 1360
señalar *v* to point (out), signal 493
sencillamente *adv* simply 2352
sencillez *nf* simplicity 4380
sencillo *adj* simple, plain, easy 922
senda *nf* path, lane 4585
sendero *nm* (foot) path 4036
seno *nm* breast, bosom, cavity 1776
señor *nm* sir, Mr., lord 240
señora *nf* Mrs., lady, madam 976
señorita *nf* young woman 2622
sensación *nf* sensation, feeling 1023
sensibilidad *nf* sensitivity 1554
sensible *adj* sensitive, sentient 2030
sentado *adj* seated 1231
sentar *v* to sit (down), seat 710
sentencia *nf* (legal) sentence, judgment 2709
sentido *nm* sense, feeling 265
sentimental *adj* sentimental 2646
sentimiento *nm* feeling, sentiment 867
sentir *v* to feel, regret 131
sentir *nm* feeling 3690
separación *nf* separation 2041
separado *adj* separate 1208
separar *v* to separate 792
septiembre *nm* September 2574
séptimo *adj* seventh 4905
sequía *nf* drought 4364
ser *v* to be (norm) 8
ser *nm* being 352
serenidad *nf* serenity, calm 3743
sereno *adj* serene, calm 4066
seriamente *adv* seriously 3206
serie *nf* series 522
seriedad *nf* seriousness 3022
serio *adj* serious 545
serpiente *nf* snake 4150
servicio *nm* service, helpfulness 390
servidor *nm/f* servant 4010
servidumbre *nf* staff of servants, servitude 4602
servir *v* to serve 226
sesenta *num* sixty 1306
sesión *nf* session, meeting 1683
setenta *num* seventy 1773
severo *adj* severe 1832
sexo *nm* sex 1667
sexto *adj* sixth 3140
sexual *adj* sexual 1796
si *conj* if, whether 34

sí *adv* yes 70
siempre *adv* always, forever 90
sierra *nf* mountain range, saw 3390
siesta *nf* siesta, afternoon nap 4176
siete *num* seven 470
siglo *nm* century, age 273
significación *nf* meaning, significance 4862
significado *nm* meaning 1966
significar *v* to mean 502
significativo *adj* significant, meaningful 1939
signo *nm* sign, mark, symbol 1359
siguiente *adj* following, next 309
silencio *nm* silence 923
silencioso *adj* quiet, silent 3374
silla *nf* chair, seat 1307
sillón *nm* armchair, seat 3604
silvestre *adj* wild 4418
simbólico *adj* symbolic 3349
símbolo *nm* symbol 1723
similar *adj* similar 1325
simpatía *nf* sympathy, affinity 2327
simpático *adj* nice, likeable, friendly 2590
simple *adj* simple, mere, simple-minded 661
simplemente *adv* simply, just 591
simular *v* to pretend, simulate 3947
simultáneamente *adv* simultaneously 3627
simultáneo *adj* simultaneous 4609
sin *prep* without 43
sinceramente *adv* sincerely 3574
sinceridad *nf* sincerity 4069
sincero *adj* sincere 2915
sindicato *nm* trade union 3882
singular *adj* single, singular 2854
siniestro *adj* sinister 4880
sino *conj* but, except, rather 109
síntesis *nf* synthesis 2742
sintético *adj* synthetic 4954
síntoma *nm* symptom 2228
siquiera *adv* even (if) 602
sirena *nf* siren, mermaid 4696
sistema *nm* system 430
sistemático *adj* systematic 3567
sitio *nm* place, space 672
situación *nf* situation 268
situado *adj* situated, located 1798
situar *v* to situate, place, locate 2089
soberanía *nf* sovereignty 4824
soberano *adj* sovereign, self-assured 4782
soberbio *adj* proud, arrogant 4576

sobra *nf* excess, surplus, leftover 4547

sobrar *v* to be too much, left over 2978

sobre *prep* on top of, over, about 48

sobrepasar *v* excel, out perform 3620

sobresalir *v* to stand out, excel 3779

sobrevenir *v* to occur, befall, strike 4811

sobrevivir *v* to survive, outlive 1999

sobrino *nm* nephew 3593

social *adj* social 280

socialista *adj* socialist 2820

sociedad *nf* society 408

socio *nm* member, partner 2314

sofisticado *adj* sophisticated 4546

sol *nm* sun 686

solamente *adv* only 336

solar *adj* solar 3841

soldado *nm/f* soldier 1568

soledad *nf* loneliness, solitude 2116

solemne *adj* solemn 3115

soler *v* to be accustomed to 487

solicitar *v* to solicit, request 1384

solicitud *nf* request, application 3540

solidaridad *nf* solidarity, togetherness 2668

solidario *adj* united, jointly shared 4472

sólido *adj* solid, strong 1569

solitario *adj* solitary, lonely 2064

solo *adj* lonely, alone 160

solo *adv* only, just 102

soltar *v* to release, loosen, let out 2272

soltero *adj* single, not married 3175

solución *nf* solution, answer 871

solucionar *v* to solve, settle 2184

sombra *nf* shade, shadow 1324

sombrero *nm* hat, sombrero 2899

sombrío *adj* shady, dark, dismal 4455

someter *v* to subject 1116

sonar *v* to sound, ring 1068

soñar *v* to dream 1593

sonido *nm* sound 1192

sonoro *adj* loud, resounding 2762

sonreír *v* to smile 2731

sonriente *adj* smiling 4579

sonrisa *nf* smile 2754

sopa *nf* soup 3795

soplar *v* to blow (wind) 3201

soportar *v* to endure, stand (something) 1310

soporte *nm* support, endorsement 4797

sordo *adj* deaf, dull 2933

sorprendente *adj* surprising, astonishing 2203

sorprender *v* to surprise 1320

sorprendido *adj* surprised 3120

sorpresa *nf* surprise 1264

sospecha *nf* suspicion 2602

sospechar *v* to suspect, suppose 1984

sospechoso *adj* suspicious 3592

sostener *v* to support, hold up 883

sostenido *adj* sustained, steady 3279

sótano *nm* basement 4930

soviético *adj* Soviet 4438

su *adj* his/her/their/your (-fam) 14

suave *adj* soft, gentle, mild 1784

suavemente *adv* softly 3915

subir *v* to go up 443

súbito *adj* sudden 4130

subjetivo *adj* subjective 4793

subrayar *v* to underline, highlight, emphasize 3396

subsistir *v* to subsist, survive 3748

subterráneo *adj* underground 3555

suceder *v* to happen 406

sucesión *nf* succession, series 2655

sucesivamente *adv* successively, step by step 3428

sucesivo *adj* successive, following 2379

suceso *nm* event, incident 2563

sucio *adj* dirty, filthy, underhanded 1994

sudar *v* to sweat 4619

sudor *nm* sweat, perspiration 4081

sueldo *nm* salary, pay 1770

suelo *nm* ground, floor 432

suelto *adj* loose 1941

sueño *nm* dream, sleep 583

suerte *nf* luck, fortune 725

suficiente *adj* sufficient, enough 547

suficientemente *adv* enough 1805

sufrimiento *nm* suffering 2658

sufrir *v* to suffer, undergo 457

sugerencia *nf* suggestion 3784

sugerir *v* to suggest, hint at 1327

suicidio *nm* suicide 3329

suizo *adj* Swiss 4500

sujetar *v* to fasten, attach, hold 2879

sujeto *nm* subject, individual 1748

sujeto *adj* fastened, subject to 1759

suma *nf* sum, amount, summary 1271

sumamente *adv* extremely, highly 2380

sumar *v* to add up, amount to 1608

sumergir *v* to submerge, plunge 4431

sumido *adj* sunken, drowned 4876

sumo *adj* utmost, highest 3570

superar *v* to overcome, surpass 975

superficial *adj* superficial 2693

superficie *nf* surface, area 1442

superior *adj* superior, upper 535

superioridad *nf* superiority 4011

supervivencia *nf* survival 3983

suponer *v* to suppose, assume 305

supremo *adj* supreme 2633

suprimir *v* to suppress, delete 2976

supuestamente *adv* supposedly, allegedly 4262

supuesto *adj* supposed; por supuesto: of course 511

sur *nm* south 1064

surgir *v* to appear, spring (forth) 553

susceptible *adj* susceptible 4250

suscitar *v* to arouse, provoke 3010

suspender *v* to suspend, hang, fail 1929

suspirar *v* to sigh 4558

sustancia *nf* substance, essence 2598

sustentar *v* to maintain, support 4392

sustituir *v* to substitute, replace 1786

susto *nm* fright, scare 3048

sutil *adj* subtle 2577

suyo *pron* his, hers, yours (-fam), theirs 520

T

tabaco *nm* tobacco, cigarette, cigar 2560

tabla *nf* chart, board, table, plank 1833

tablero *nm* board, panel 4207

táctica *nf* tactics, strategy 4623

tacto *nm* sense of touch, feel 4411

tal *adj* such (a) 120

talento *nm* talent, skill 2143

talla *nf* size (of clothing), stature 4330

taller *nm* workshop, shop 2373

talón *nm* heel, check, coupon, stub 4447

tamaño *nm* size, dimension 776

también *adv* also 53

tambor *nm* drum 4057

tampoco *adv* neither, nor, either 279

tan *adv* such, as, too, so 83

tanque *nm* tank, large container 4594

tanto *adj* so much, so many 79

tapa *nf* cover, lid 3492

tapar *v* to cover, wrap 2129

tardar *v* to delay, take long 959

tarde *nf* afternoon, evening 242

tarde *adv* late 1046

tardío *adj* late, belated 3487

tarea *nf* task, job 585

tarjeta *nf* card 2309

tasa *nf* rate, fee, levy 4550

taxi *nm* taxi, cab 3402

taza *nf* cup, bowl 3218

te *pron* you (obj/+fam) 136

té *nm* tea 2145

teatral *adj* theatrical 3295

teatro *nm* theater, drama 861

techo *nm* roof 1386

técnica *nf* technique, skill 1187

técnico *adj* technical 1480

técnico *nm/f* technician 2982

tecnología *nf* technology 2931

tecnológico *adj* technological 3972

tejado *nm* roof, housetop 4944

tejer *v* to sew, weave 2941

tejido *nm* fabric, tissue 2547

tela *nf* cloth, fabric 1719

telefónico *adj* telephone 2888

teléfono *nm* phone, telephone 999

televisión *nf* TV, television 1078

televisor *nm* television set 3250

tema *nm* theme, subject, topic 283

temblar *v* to tremble, shake 3255

temblor *nm* tremor, shudder, shiver 3902

temer *v* to fear 1387

temeroso *adj* fearful 3952

temor *nm* fear 1154

temperamento *nm* temperament, personality 4586

temperatura *nf* temperature 1558

templo *nm* temple, church 2437

temporada *nf* season, period, time 1887

temporal *adj* temporary 3225

temprano *adj* early 1200

tendencia *nf* tendency, style 1347

tender *v* to tend to, lay out 727

tendido *adj* spread, hung, laid (out) 3727

tener *v* to have 18

teniente *nm* lieutenant, deputy mayor 3608

tenis *nm* tennis 4968

tenor *nm* a tenor de: in accordance with 4814

tensión *nf* tension, stress, strain 1514

tenso *adj* tight, tense 3043

tentación *nf* temptation 2765

tentar *v* to tempt, entice 4869

tenue *adj* tenuous, flimsy 4450

teoría *nf* theory 970

teórico *adj* theoretical 2866

tercero *adj* third 394

tercio *nm* third 3988

terminar *v* to finish, end 219

término *nm* term (language), end 561

ternura *nf* tenderness 3797

terraza *nf* terrace, balcony 4074

terremoto *nm* earthquake 4100

terreno *nm* ground, earth, terrain 796

terrestre *adj* earthly, of the earth 4663

terrible *adj* terrible 1228

terriblemente *adv* terribly 4928

territorio *nm* territory 1382

terror *nm* terror, horror 2189

tertulia *nf* get-together, meeting of friends 4483

tesis *nf* thesis, exposition 2117

tesoro *nm* treasure, thesaurus 2629

testigo *nm* witness 1618

testimonio *nm* testimony, evidence 2066

texto *nm* text 800

ti *pron* you (obj prep-sg/+fam) 1704

tía *nf* aunt 2199

tibio *adj* lukewarm 3590

tiempo *nm* time (general), weather 68

tienda *nf* shop, store, tent 1650

tierno *adj* tender, soft 2973

tierra *nf* earth, land, ground 276

tigre *nm* tiger 4582

timbre *nm* doorbell, bell, seal, stamp 3404

timidez *nf* shyness, timidity 3447

tímido *adj* timid, shy, half-hearted 2795

tinta *nf* ink 3089

tinte *nm* tint, dye 4451

tío *nm* uncle, guy 1755

típico *adj* typical 1651

tipo *nm* type, kind 157

tira *nf* strip, strap 4102

tirar *v* to throw, pull 759

tiro *nm* throw, shot 1737

titular *nm* headline, holder 3655

titular *v* to title, call 4035

título *nm* title, heading 653

toalla *nf* towel 4967

tocar *v* to touch, play (instrument) 325

todavía *adv* still, yet 211

todo *adj* all, every 22

tolerancia *nf* tolerance 3792

tolerar *v* to tolerate, put up with 2874

tomar *v* to take, drink 122

tomate *nm* tomato 3920

tonelada *nf* ton 4399

tono *nm* tone 972

tontería *nf* stupidity, stupid thing 3074

tonto *adj* stupid, dumb 2191

topar *v* to run into, bump into 4230

toque *nm* touch, ringing, warning 3448

torcer *v* to twist, bend, distort 4221

tormenta *nf* storm 2841

tornar *v* to transform, turn 3263

torno *nm* en torno a: about, regarding 1230

toro *nm* bull 2331

torpe *adj* clumsy, awkward, slow 3629

torre *nf* tower 2162

torta *nf* cake 4715

tortura *nf* torture 3585

total *adj* total, entire 629

total *nm* (sum) total 1043

totalidad *nf* whole, totality 2276

totalmente *adv* totally, completely 662

trabajador *nm/f* worker, laborer 1714

trabajador *adj* hardworking 4489

trabajar *v* to work 183

trabajo *nm* work, job, effort 145

tradición *nf* tradition 898

tradicional *adj* traditional 1309

tradicionalmente *adv* traditionally 4657

traducción *nf* translation 3344

traducir *v* to translate 1603

traer *v* to bring, carry 289

tráfico *nm* traffic, trade 2188

tragar *v* to swallow 2965

tragedia *nf* tragedy 1905

trágico *adj* tragic 2501

trago *nm* swig, drink 4215

traición *nf* treason, betrayal 3493

traicionar *v* to betray 3713

traidor *nm* traitor 4286

traje *nm* suit, dress, costume 1710

trama *nf* plot, theme 3566

trámite *nm* procedure, step, requirement 3246

tramo *nm* section, stretch, plot 3475

trampa *nf* trick, trap; hacer trampa: to cheat 2548

trance *nm* trance, fix, enrapture 4457

tranquilamente *adv* calmly, peacefully 3247

tranquilidad *nf* tranquility, peace 1729

tranquilizar *v* to calm down 3848

tranquilo *adj* calm, tranquil, relaxed 1144

transcurrir *v* to occur, take place 1579

transcurso *nm* passing, course, lapse 3155

transformación *nf* transformation 2450

transformar *v* to transform, change **891**

transición *nf* transition **3139**

transitar *v* to roam, go by **4821**

tránsito *nm* traffic, transit **2792**

transitorio *adj* transitory **4381**

transmisión *nf* broadcast, transmission **4034**

transmitir *v* to transmit, broadcast **1202**

transparencia *nf* transparency, slide **4059**

transparente *adj* transparent, clear **2657**

transportar *v* to transport, carry **2690**

transporte *nm* transportation, transport **1657**

tranvía *nm* trolley, tram, streetcar **4502**

trapo *nm* rag, cloth **4244**

tras *prep* after, behind **534**

trascendencia *nf* transcendent nature, significance **3233**

trascendental *adj* far-reaching, transcendental **4613**

trascendente *adj* transcendent **4564**

trasero *adj* behind, back **4962**

trasladar *v* to move, transfer **1219**

traslado *nm* transfer **2763**

traspasar *v* to go beyond, cross over **3502**

trastorno *nm* confusion, trouble, upheaval **4298**

tratado *nm* treaty, treatise **2270**

tratamiento *nm* treatment, processing **1418**

tratar *v* to try, treat, deal with **134**

trato *nm* treatment, manner, agreement **1241**

través *adv* a través: across, over, through **347**

trayecto *nm* trajectory, course, path **3407**

trayectoria *nf* trajectory, path **3215**

trazar *v* to draw, trace **2892**

trazo *nm* line, stroke **4556**

trece *num* thirteen **2115**

tregua *nf* truce, rest **4640**

treinta *num* thirty **722**

tremendo *adj* tremendous, dreadful, huge **1198**

tren *nm* train, convoy **1220**

trepar *v* to climb **4116**

tres *num* three **119**

trescientos *num* three hundred **3341**

triángulo *nm* triangle **4016**

tribu *nf* tribe **2963**

tribunal *nm* court **2571**

trigo *nm* wheat **3961**

triple *adj* triple **4520**

triste *adj* sad, unhappy **1314**

tristeza *nf* sadness **2233**

triunfar *v* to triumph **2697**

triunfo *nm* triumph, victory **1813**

tronco *nm* trunk, torso **2936**

trono *nm* throne **4510**

tropa *nf* troops, forces **2312**

tropezar *v* to trip, stumble **2907**

tropical *adj* tropical **3873**

trozo *nm* piece, chunk **2527**

truco *nm* trick, ruse **4020**

tu *adj* your (sg/+fam) **349**

tú *pron* you (subj-sg/+fam) **554**

tubo *nm* tube, pipe **2932**

tumba *nf* tomb, grave **2485**

tumbar *v* to knock over, cast down **4720**

túnel *nm* tunnel **2942**

turco *adj* Turkish **3691**

turismo *nm* tourism **4012**

turista *nc* tourist **3177**

turístico *adj* tourist **4572**

turno *nm* turn, shift; en turno a: around **2252**

tuyo *pron* yours (sg/+fam) **2797**

U

ubicación *nf* position, location **3559**

ubicar *v* to find, locate **1750**

últimamente *adv* lately, recently **2475**

último *adj* last, final **139**

umbral *nm* threshold, outset **3639**

un *art* a, an **7**

uña *nf* nail, fingernail, toenail **3106**

únicamente *adv* only **1409**

único *adj* only, unique, sole **181**

unidad *nf* unit, unity **1025**

unido *adj* united **858**

uniforme *nm* uniform **2341**

uniforme *adj* uniform **3880**

unión *nf* union **2081**

unir *v* to unite, join (together) **918**

universal *adj* universal **1488**

universidad *nf* university, college **1473**

universitario *adj* university **2029**

universo *nm* universe **2179**

uno *num* one **72**

urbano *adj* urban, city, urbane **2176**

urgencia *nf* urgency **2391**

urgente *adj* urgent **2265**

usado *adj* worn out, old, used **3305**

usar *v* to use **380**

uso *nm* use **619**

usted *pron* you (subj/-fam) **269**

usual *adj* normal, usual **4729**

útil *adj* useful 1195

utilidad *nf* usefulness, utility 2921

utilización *nf* use, utilization 3491

utilizar *v* to use, utilize 338

uva *nf* grape 3682

V

vaca *nf* cow 2234

vacaciones *nf* vacation 1623

vaciar *v* to empty, pour out 3584

vacilar *v* to vacillate, hesitate 4323

vacío *adj* empty, vacant 1532

vacío *nm* emptiness, void 1538

vago *adj* vague 3318

vaivén *nm* swinging, rocking 4773

valer *v* to be worth, cost 387

validez *nf* validity 4410

válido *adj* valid 2216

valiente *adj* brave, courageous, bold 3131

valioso *adj* valuable, precious 2178

valle *nm* valley 1663

valor *nm* value, worth 326

valorar *v* to value 2994

vanguardia *nf* vanguard, forefront 4043

vanidad *nf* vanity, conceit 3935

vano *adj* vain, useless 3367

vapor *nm* vapor, steam 2827

vara *nf* rod, stick 4822

variación *nf* variation 2703

variado *adj* varied, mixed 2464

variante *nf* variant, difference 3798

variar *v* to change, vary 2210

variedad *nf* variety 2368

varios *adj* several, various 224

varón *nm* male, man 2088

vasco *adj* Basque 3946

vaso *nm* (drinking) glass, vase 2107

vasto *adj* vast, immense, huge 2799

vecindad *nf* nearness, vicinity 4910

vecino *nm* neighbor 1095

vecino *adj* nearby, neighboring 1666

vegetación *nf* vegetation 3837

vegetal *adj* plant, vegetable 3304

vegetal *nm* plant, vegetable 4921

vehículo *nm* vehicle, car 1446

veinte *num* twenty 582

veinticinco *num* twenty-five 2311

veinticuatro *num* twenty-four 2998

veintidós *num* twenty-two 4873

vejez *nf* old age 4099

vela *nf* candle, sail, vigil 2287

velar *v* to watch over 3243

velo *nm* veil 4531

velocidad *nf* speed, velocity 1145

veloz *adj* fast, quick 4429

vena *nf* vein 3512

vencer *v* to overcome, conquer 1193

vendedor *nm/f* salesperson 2266

vender *v* to sell 526

veneno *nm* poison, venom 4198

venganza *nf* revenge, vengeance 3450

vengar *v* to take revenge, avenge 4849

venir *v* to come 105

venta *nf* sale 1075

ventaja *nf* advantage, benefit 1226

ventana *nf* window 1265

ventanilla *nf* (vehicle) window 4836

ver *v* to see 37

vera *nf* de veras: really, for real 3038

verano *nm* summer 893

verbal *adj* verbal, oral 3256

verbo *nm* verb 4278

verdad *nf* truth 209

verdaderamente *adv* truly 1407

verdadero *adj* true, real 420

verde *adj* green 878

verdura *nf* vegetables, greenery 4480

vereda *nf* path, sidewalk 4700

vergüenza *nf* embarrassment 2206

verificar *v* to verify 3610

versión *nf* version, account 1613

verso *nm* verse, poem 2643

verter *v* to pour, spill, shed 4924

vertical *adj* vertical, upright 3297

vertiginoso *adj* dizzying 4516

vestido *adj* dressed 1870

vestido *nm* dress 2220

vestir *v* to wear, dress 1317

vestuario *nm* wardrobe, changing room 4641

vez *nf* time (specific occurrence) 44

vía *nf* por vía: by means; road, way 982

viajar *v* to travel 790

viaje *nm* travel, trip 431

viajero *nm* traveler, passenger 3091

vibración *nf* vibration 4818

vibrar *v* to vibrate, tremble 4413

viceversa *adv* vice versa 4904

vicio *nm* vice, bad habit, defect 2805

víctima *nf* victim, casualty 1712
victoria *nf* victory, triumph 1821
vida *nf* life 88
vidrio *nm* glass, pane 2112
viejo *adj* old, aged 281
viento *nm* wind, scent 1216
vientre *nm* womb, belly 3434
viernes *nm* Friday 2483
vigente *adj* in force, valid 3801
vigilancia *nf* surveillance, vigilance 2632
vigilar *v* to watch over, guard 2247
vigor *nm* force, strength, vigor 3306
vigoroso *adj* vigorous, strong 4596
villa *nf* village, town 3731
vinculado *adj* connected 3181
vincular *v* to connect, link, bind 4407
vínculo *nm* tie, bond, link 3219
vino *nm* wine 917
violación *nf* violation, rape 4481
violar *v* to violate, trespass, rape 2673
violencia *nf* violence 1190
violentamente *adv* violently 4425
violento *adj* violent 1389
violín *nm* violin 4745
virgen *nf* virgin 3981
virgen *adj* virgin 4304
virtud *nf* virtue, quality 1378
visible *adj* visible 2459
visión *nf* vision 908
visita *nf* visit, visitor, guest 828
visitante *nc* visitor 2760
visitar *v* to visit 834
vislumbrar *v* to glimpse 4665
víspera *nf* eve 3541
vista *nf* view, sight 310
visual *adj* visual 4479
vital *adj* vital, lively, essential 1428
vitalidad *nf* vitality, health 3807

viuda *nf* widow 2488
vivienda *nf* housing, dwelling 1600
vivir *v* to live 128
vivo *adj* alive, bright 453
vocabulario *nm* vocabulary 3927
vocación *nf* vocation, calling 1829
volante *nm* steering wheel 4458
volar *v* to fly 1376
volcán *nm* volcano 4981
volcar *v* to turn/knock over, empty 3153
volumen *nm* volume 1274
voluntad *nf* will, willpower, intention 745
voluntariamente *adv* voluntarily 4891
voluntario *adj* voluntary, volunteer 2953
volver *v* to return, to V again 112
vos *pron* you (subj-sg/+fam) 3430
vosotros *pron* you (subj-pl/+fam) 4132
votar *v* to vote 3172
voto *nm* vote 2201
voz *nf* voice 320
vuelo *nm* flight 1665
vuelta *nf* return, turn 600
vuestro *adj* your (pl/+fam) 3137
vulgar *adj* vulgar, common, banal 2991
vulnerable *adj* vulnerable 4554

W

whisky *nm* whisky 4571

Y

y *conj* and 4
ya *adv* already, still 36
yo *pron* I (subj) 52

Z

zapato *nm* shoe 1932
zona *nf* area, zone 449

Part of speech index

rank frequency (501, 502...), **headword,** English equivalent

Function words

Article

1 **el, la** the

7 **un** a, an

Conjunction

3 **que** that, which

4 **y** and

16 **como** like, as

23 **pero** but, yet, except

26 **o** or

34 **si** if, whether

38 **porque** because

40 **cuando** when

64 **ni** not even, neither, nor

84 **donde** where

103 **pues** then, well then

109 **sino** but, except, rather

117 **aunque** although, even though

154 **mientras** while, whereas, as long as

777 **mas** but, however

Interjection

1489 **ah** oh

2337 **ay** oh no!, oh my!

2520 **eh** eh

2736 **oh** oh

4752 **hola** hello, hi

Number

56 **dos** two

72 **uno** one

119 **tres** three

188 **cuatro** four

217 **mil** thousand

231 **cinco** five

300 **ciento** hundred

346 **diez** ten

375 **seis** six

470 **siete** seven

492 **ocho** eight

523 **millón** million, fortune

582 **veinte** twenty

722 **treinta** thirty

782 **cincuenta** fifty

786 **nueve** nine

823 **doce** twelve

943 **cuarenta** forty

1033 **quince** fifteen

1306 **sesenta** sixty

1455 **once** eleven

1773 **setenta** seventy

2115 **trece** thirteen

2120 **ochenta** eighty

2278 **catorce** fourteen

2284 **cero** zero, naught, nil

2311 **veinticinco** twenty-five

2344 **doscientos** two hundred

2694 **dieciocho** eighteen

2793 **dieciséis** sixteen

2998 **veinticuatro** twenty-four

3341 **trescientos** three hundred

3417 **noventa** ninety

3426 **quinientos** five hundred

3446 **diecisiete** seventeen

4873 **veintidós** twenty-two

Preposition

2 **de** of, from

5 **a** to, at

6 **en** in, on

12 **por** by, for, through

13 **con** with

15 **para** for, to, in order to

43 **sin** without

48 **sobre** on top of, over, about

54 **hasta** until, up to, even (ADV)

58 **entre** between, among

61 **desde** from, since

125 **hacia** toward, towards

172 **contra** against, opposite

214 **bajo** under, underneath

236 **ante** before, in the presence of

257 **según** according to
534 **tras** after, behind
896 **mediante** by means of
3108 **excepto** except (for)

Pronoun

9 **se** ["reflexive" marker]
19 **le** [3rd person] (indir obj)
21 **lo** [3rd person] (dir obj-m)
33 **la** [3rd person] (dir obj-f)
35 **me** me (obj)
41 **él** he, [ellos] them (m)
47 **qué** what?, which?, how (+ ADJ)!
52 **yo** I (subj)
63 **eso** that (n)
65 **nos** us (obj)
69 **ella** she, [ellas] them (f)
95 **nada** nothing, (not) at all
101 **algo** something, somewhat
110 **esto** this (n)
136 **te** you (obj/+fam)
141 **quien** who, whom
153 **cual** which, who, whom
168 **éste** this one (m), [ésta (f)]
191 **nosotros** we (subj)
233 **nadie** nobody, anybody
269 **usted** you (subj/-fam)
292 **quién** who?, whom?
343 **ello** it (subj-n)
357 **mí** me (obj prep)
395 **cuál** which?
480 **alguien** somebody, someone, anyone
520 **suyo** his, hers, yours (-fam), theirs
554 **tú** you (subj-sg/+fam)
814 **aquello** that over there (n)
855 **ése** that one (m), [ésa (f)]
872 **mío** mine
1373 **os** you (obj-pl/+fam)
1390 **aquél** that one over there (m)
1704 **ti** you (obj prep-sg/+fam)
1845 **conmigo** with me
2797 **tuyo** yours (sg/+fam)
3017 **contigo** with you
3430 **vos** you (subj-sg/+fam)
4132 **vosotros** you (subj-pl/+fam)

Lexical words

Adjective

14 **su** his/her/their/your (-fam)
20 **lo** the (+ neuter)
22 **todo** all, every
24 **más** more
29 **este** this (m) [esta (f)]
31 **otro** other, another
32 **ese** that (m) [esa (f)]
45 **mucho** much, many, a lot (ADV)
49 **mi** my
50 **alguno** some, someone (PRON)
51 **mismo** same
60 **primero** first
62 **grande** large, great, big
74 **poco** little, few, a little bit (ADV)
79 **tanto** so much, so many
82 **nuestro** our
96 **cada** each, every
98 **menos** less, fewer
99 **nuevo** new
107 **aquel** that (over there)
115 **bueno** good
120 **tal** such (a)
121 **mejor** best, better (ADV)
123 **cierto** certain, sure, true
138 **mayor** larger, older, main
139 **último** last, final
140 **propio** own, proper, typical
144 **ninguno** no, none, nobody (PRON)
149 **cualquier** any, anyone (PRON)
160 **solo** lonely, alone
175 **largo** long
181 **único** only, unique, sole
184 **pequeño** little, small, young
185 **alto** tall, high
207 **importante** important
208 **medio** half, middle
213 **cuanto** en cuanto a: in terms of, regarding
218 **humano** human
224 **varios** several, various
225 **posible** possible
227 **general** general
239 **igual** equal, same (as)
243 **segundo** second
250 **blanco** white
254 **distinto** distinct, different
259 **claro** clear

264	**cuyo** whose	545	**serio** serious
270	**bastante** rather, fairly, quite a bit (ADV)	547	**suficiente** sufficient, enough
275	**malo** bad	548	**grave** serious, solemn
280	**social** social	551	**extraño** strange, foreign
281	**viejo** old, aged	574	**absoluto** absolute
284	**político** political	590	**personal** personal
285	**español** Spanish	592	**imposible** impossible
309	**siguiente** following, next	608	**inglés** English
312	**demás** the rest, others	615	**duro** hard
314	**difícil** difficult, hard	627	**rico** rich, tasty
317	**negro** black	629	**total** total, entire
322	**necesario** necessary	637	**puro** pure, clean
334	**menor** younger, youngest	640	**profesional** professional
335	**demasiado** too much, too many	643	**físico** physical
348	**antiguo** old, ancient, former	646	**francés** French
349	**tu** your (sg/+fam)	652	**rápido** quick, fast
364	**especial** special	661	**simple** simple, mere, simple-minded
365	**diferente** different, separate	664	**normal** normal, usual, regular
370	**anterior** previous, preceding	671	**moderno** modern
373	**pobre** poor	676	**actual** current
394	**tercero** third	679	**pleno** complete, full
411	**capaz** capable, able	680	**cerrado** closed
412	**bajo** short, low	687	**muerto** dead
413	**libre** free, vacant	690	**dispuesto** willing, ready
414	**natural** natural	698	**enfermo** ill, sick
420	**verdadero** true, real	706	**privado** private
426	**económico** economic	709	**popular** popular
438	**común** common	713	**famoso** famous, well-known
439	**abierto** open, unlocked	723	**cuánto** how much?
440	**próximo** next	724	**inmediato** immediate
442	**joven** young	729	**junto** together
445	**pasado** past, last	733	**directo** direct, straight
453	**vivo** alive, bright	739	**preciso** precise, necessary
458	**completo** complete	740	**diverso** different, several, diverse
460	**contrario** contrary, opposite	744	**familiar** familiar, of the family
462	**real** royal, real, authentic	760	**entero** entire, whole, complete
465	**público** public	762	**interesante** interesting
471	**enorme** enormous, vast	763	**amplio** wide, ample, broad
488	**ambos** both	771	**final** final
489	**profundo** deep, profound	774	**civil** civil
496	**principal** main, principal	783	**interno** internal
507	**nacional** national	803	**definitivo** definitive, conclusive
508	**lleno** full, filled	810	**perfecto** perfect
511	**supuesto** supposed; por supuesto: of course	837	**parecido** similar
514	**fácil** easy	849	**raro** strange, rare, scarce
533	**rojo** red	854	**particular** particular, peculiar
535	**superior** superior, upper	856	**militar** military
537	**corto** short, brief	858	**unido** united
540	**conocido** known, well-known	860	**extraordinario** extraordinary, exceptional

878 **verde** green
879 **exacto** exact, faithful, true
886 **religioso** religious
888 **oscuro** dark, obscure
897 **cuarto** fourth
904 **azul** blue
907 **frío** cold
909 **concreto** concrete, real
912 **derecho** right, straight
922 **sencillo** simple, plain, easy
927 **determinado** determined, fixed
931 **perdido** lost
942 **cercano** near
948 **adecuado** adequate, suitable
953 **italiano** Italian
955 **responsable** responsible
956 **feliz** happy, fortunate
963 **alemán** German
968 **dado** given
979 **diario** daily
980 **histórico** historical
981 **debido** debido a: due to
990 **mínimo** minimum
1002 **doble** double
1010 **fuerte** strong
1034 **constante** constant
1039 **semejante** similar, such, alike
1042 **extranjero** foreign, alien
1051 **evidente** evident, obvious
1061 **fijo** fixed, steady
1062 **central** central
1067 **preparado** prepared
1074 **inmenso** immense, vast, huge
1082 **moral** moral
1084 **curioso** curious, strange
1086 **fundamental** fundamental
1088 **presente** present, current
1089 **máximo** maximum
1092 **europeo** European
1099 **oficial** official, authorized
1101 **numeroso** numerous
1103 **intelectual** intellectual
1110 **escaso** scarce, very little
1114 **cristiano** Christian
1118 **seguro** safe, sure, secure
1119 **intenso** intense, acute
1127 **peligroso** dangerous
1128 **lento** slow
1140 **falso** false

1144 **tranquilo** calm, tranquil, relaxed
1152 **lejano** distant
1153 **breve** brief, short
1163 **exterior** exterior, outside
1170 **médico** medical
1175 **ajeno** not belonging to, detached
1178 **seco** dry, arid
1179 **quinto** fifth
1186 **infantil** of children, childlike, infantile
1189 **internacional** international
1191 **original** original
1195 **útil** useful
1198 **tremendo** tremendous, dreadful, huge
1200 **temprano** early
1208 **separado** separate
1214 **lógico** logical
1223 **auténtico** authentic
1224 **hermoso** beautiful, lovely
1228 **terrible** terrible
1231 **sentado** seated
1234 **correcto** correct, suitable
1239 **permanente** permanent
1246 **norteamericano** North American
1253 **comercial** commercial, shopping
1255 **obligado** obliged, required
1261 **americano** American
1263 **interior** interior, inside
1270 **práctico** practical, skillful
1273 **excelente** excellent
1277 **cultural** cultural
1278 **complejo** complex, complicated
1284 **débil** weak
1291 **independiente** independent, self-sufficient
1294 **convencido** convinced, persuaded
1296 **pendiente** aware of, pending
1300 **futuro** future
1302 **desconocido** unknown
1305 **muchísimo** great many, great amount
1309 **tradicional** traditional
1314 **triste** sad, unhappy
1325 **similar** similar
1328 **activo** active
1329 **clásico** classic
1332 **reciente** recent
1333 **eléctrico** electric
1338 **bello** beautiful, fine
1342 **brillante** brilliant, shiny, sparkling
1345 **femenino** feminine, female
1348 **fino** fine, delicate

1350 **inferior** lower, inferior

1356 **positivo** positive

1367 **pesado** heavy, boring, tiresome

1368 **complicado** complicated, complex

1377 **loco** crazy, insane

1380 **delicado** delicate

1389 **violento** violent

1394 **sano** healthy, wholesome

1397 **limpio** clean

1399 **posterior** rear, backside

1402 **relacionado** related, regarding

1403 **habitual** usual, habitual, customary

1410 **nervioso** nervous, uptight

1414 **material** material

1416 **consciente** conscious, aware

1428 **vital** vital, lively, essential

1434 **cotidiano** daily

1437 **previo** previous

1444 **chino** Chinese

1447 **inteligente** intelligent

1456 **listo** ready, clever, smart

1461 **correspondiente** corresponding

1465 **seguido** in a row, successive

1467 **griego** Greek

1469 **maestro** master

1470 **barato** inexpensive

1475 **notable** outstanding, noteworthy

1479 **encargado** in charge of

1480 **técnico** technical

1481 **ciego** blind

1482 **individual** individual

1488 **universal** universal

1494 **literario** literary

1502 **continuo** continuous

1512 **elevado** elevated, high, lofty

1515 **establecido** established

1516 **local** local

1532 **vacío** empty, vacant

1533 **aislado** isolated

1556 **múltiple** multiple, many

1560 **poderoso** powerful

1561 **digno** worthy

1564 **inútil** useless

1569 **sólido** solid, strong

1570 **firme** firm, steady

1571 **extremo** extreme

1572 **conforme** in agreement

1573 **esencial** essential

1586 **amarillo** yellow

1595 **acostumbrado** accustomed

1598 **artístico** artistic

1601 **ocupado** busy, occupied

1605 **interesado** (self-) interested

1607 **excesivo** excessive

1626 **argentino** Argentine

1627 **cómodo** comfortable, convenient

1631 **negativo** negative, pessimistic

1634 **científico** scientific

1639 **armado** armed

1642 **contento** happy, content

1646 **cubierto** covered

1651 **típico** typical

1656 **crítico** critical

1660 **castellano** Castilian, Spanish

1666 **vecino** nearby, neighboring

1669 **increíble** incredible, unbelievable

1674 **mental** mental

1677 **preocupado** worried, concerned

1679 **obstante** no + obstante: nevertheless

1684 **íntimo** close, intimate

1686 **estrecho** narrow

1693 **frecuente** frequent

1694 **inevitable** inevitable, unavoidable

1696 **ligero** light (in weight), slight

1703 **izquierdo** left (opposite of right)

1707 **bonito** pretty, nice

1709 **corriente** current, common

1715 **primario** primary

1717 **ideal** ideal

1720 **ancho** wide

1724 **agradable** nice, pleasant

1728 **colectivo** collective, joint

1731 **secreto** secret

1733 **incapaz** incapable

1735 **satisfecho** satisfied

1736 **reducido** reduced, limited

1743 **maravilloso** wonderful, marvelous

1747 **relativo** relative

1752 **musical** musical

1757 **redondo** round

1759 **sujeto** fastened, subject to

1774 **romano** Roman

1775 **sagrado** sacred

1784 **suave** soft, gentle, mild

1785 **opuesto** opposite, contrary

1790 **sabio** wise, learned

1793 **caliente** hot, warm, spirited

1796 **sexual** sexual

1797	**respectivo** respective	2009	**querido** dear, beloved
1798	**situado** situated, located	2010	**absurdo** absurd
1801	**rodeado** surrounded	2011	**dramático** dramatic
1812	**magnífico** magnificent, splendid	2014	**liberal** liberal
1815	**campesino** rural	2017	**legal** legal
1820	**efectivo** effective	2018	**artificial** artificial
1827	**aplicado** applied	2024	**modesto** modest, humble
1830	**casado** married	2027	**objetivo** objective, impartial
1832	**severo** severe	2029	**universitario** university
1834	**justo** fair, just	2030	**sensible** sensitive, sentient
1839	**precioso** beautiful, precious	2036	**formal** formal, polite
1840	**probable** probable	2038	**primitivo** primitive
1852	**entendido** understood	2039	**oculto** hidden, occult
1856	**avanzado** advanced	2043	**definido** definite
1862	**latino** Latin	2047	**externo** external, outward
1865	**espiritual** spiritual	2058	**organizado** organized
1866	**limitado** limited	2060	**mero** mere
1870	**vestido** dressed	2062	**compuesto** composite, mixed
1872	**eterno** eternal	2064	**solitario** solitary, lonely
1876	**caro** expensive, difficult, dear	2079	**estricto** strict, rigorous
1879	**inicial** initial	2080	**doloroso** painful
1882	**dulce** sweet	2085	**idéntico** identical
1888	**divino** divine	2086	**previsto** foreseen, planned
1894	**alejado** remote, distant, aloof	2090	**característico** characteristic
1901	**elemental** elemental, basic	2124	**fresco** cool, healthy, fresh
1912	**anciano** elderly, aged	2131	**atractivo** attractive
1913	**fiel** faithful, loyal	2137	**católico** Catholic
1914	**roto** broken, torn	2142	**masculino** masculine, manly, male
1918	**elegante** elegant, smart, stylish	2147	**cansado** tired, tiresome
1937	**oportuno** opportune, timely	2156	**desesperado** desperate, hopeless
1939	**significativo** significant, meaningful	2168	**caído** fallen
1941	**suelto** loose	2169	**japonés** Japanese
1947	**revolucionario** revolutionary	2172	**espontáneo** spontaneous
1949	**indispensable** indispensable, essential	2176	**urbano** urban, city, urbane
1951	**mundial** worldwide	2178	**valioso** valuable, precious
1955	**oriental** eastern, oriental	2180	**agudo** sharp, acute
1956	**regular** regular	2191	**tonto** stupid, dumb
1960	**doméstico** domestic	2198	**cuadrado** square
1965	**peor** worse, worst	2203	**sorprendente** surprising, astonishing
1970	**conveniente** convenient	2204	**favorable** favorable, suitable
1973	**mecánico** mechanical	2211	**culpable** guilty
1976	**eficaz** effective	2213	**secundario** secondary
1979	**nocturno** nocturnal, evening	2215	**infinito** infinite
1987	**radical** radical	2216	**válido** valid
1988	**decidido** determined, resolute	2217	**gordo** fat, thick
1994	**sucio** dirty, filthy, underhanded	2237	**desagradable** unpleasant
2001	**salvaje** wild, savage, uncultivated	2242	**agresivo** aggressive
2005	**industrial** industrial	2244	**parado** stopped, standing
2008	**desnudo** nude, naked	2253	**exclusivo** exclusive

2257 **prohibido** prohibited	2477 **paralelo** parallel
2262 **grueso** thick	2478 **ordinario** vulgar, ordinary
2265 **urgente** urgent	2484 **creciente** growing, increasing
2271 **democrático** democratic	2499 **anónimo** anonymous
2283 **considerable** considerable	2501 **trágico** tragic
2290 **gris** gray, gloomy	2528 **riguroso** rigorous, severe
2295 **básico** basic, essential	2532 **atento** attentive, polite
2298 **abandonado** abandoned	2535 **incómodo** uncomfortable
2302 **indígena** indigenous, native	2538 **inocente** innocent, naïve
2303 **moreno** dark, brown	2539 **fatal** fateful, deadly, awful
2304 **alegre** happy, lively, cheerful	2545 **noble** noble
2306 **extenso** extensive, large	2546 **escondido** hidden
2307 **ruso** Russian	2549 **hondo** deep
2313 **remoto** remote, far-off	2553 **divertido** funny, amusing
2315 **comunista** Communist	2561 **juvenil** young, juvenile
2316 **abundante** abundant, plentiful	2562 **ausente** absent
2319 **judío** Jewish	2566 **mediado** mid, middle
2320 **impresionante** impressive, astonishing	2569 **estético** esthetic
2323 **occidental** occidental, western	2572 **bravo** fierce, angry
2326 **mutuo** mutual	2577 **sutil** subtle
2338 **romántico** romantic	2578 **maduro** mature, ripe
2347 **pintado** painted	2579 **mezclado** mixed
2351 **distante** distant, far, remote	2582 **lindo** pretty, nice, lovely
2353 **equivocado** mistaken, wrong	2586 **obvio** obvious
2360 **fantástico** fantastic, unreal	2590 **simpático** nice, likeable, friendly
2367 **humilde** humble, modest	2592 **exquisito** exquisite, superb
2369 **desarrollado** developed, grown	2600 **harto** fed up with
2372 **específico** specific	2603 **exagerado** exaggerated
2376 **encerrado** locked (up)	2613 **conservador** conservative
2378 **injusto** unfair, unjust	2617 **imprescindible** essential, indispensable
2379 **sucesivo** successive, following	2631 **rural** rural, country
2381 **feo** ugly, nasty, rude	2633 **supremo** supreme
2388 **orgulloso** proud, arrogant	2634 **confuso** confused, mixed up
2392 **excepcional** exceptional, unusual	2638 **decisivo** decisive, conclusive
2398 **generoso** generous	2642 **bruto** brutal, coarse, clumsy
2399 **académico** academic	2646 **sentimental** sentimental
2405 **razonable** reasonable	2647 **herido** wounded, injured
2409 **amable** kind, nice, friendly	2651 **luminoso** bright, luminous
2411 **rígido** rigid, stiff, firm	2657 **transparente** transparent, clear
2417 **ordenado** organized, clean	2659 **aparente** apparent
2422 **apropiado** appropriate	2665 **húmedo** humid, damp
2428 **resuelto** resolved, determined	2671 **leve** slight, trifling, light
2433 **árabe** Arab	2678 **realista** realistic
2453 **cruel** cruel, harsh	2682 **prestado** borrowed, lent
2459 **visible** visible	2685 **adulto** adult, grown-up
2463 **poquito** little bit	2686 **municipal** municipal, town
2464 **variado** varied, mixed	2693 **superficial** superficial
2471 **repetido** repeated	2696 **dorado** golden, gold-plated
2473 **envuelto** wrapped	2699 **favorito** favorite

2701	**escolar** school, scholastic	2917	**ideológico** ideological
2704	**cálido** warm	2926	**ligado** linked, joined
2705	**inconsciente** unconscious, thoughtless	2929	**prolongado** prolonged, lengthy
2708	**mágico** magic, magical	2933	**sordo** deaf, dull
2710	**amargo** bitter, sour, painful	2934	**admirable** admirable
2716	**filosófico** philosophical	2953	**voluntario** voluntary, volunteer
2720	**marino** marine, naval	2957	**judicial** judicial
2725	**culto** cultured, educated	2960	**reservado** reserved, booked
2734	**pensado** thought-out, designed	2966	**legítimo** legitimate
2738	**horrible** horrible	2968	**convencional** conventional
2746	**peculiar** peculiar	2970	**gigantesco** giant, gigantic
2747	**ejemplar** exemplary, model	2973	**tierno** tender, soft
2757	**bárbaro** savage, horrible	2975	**aéreo** aerial, air
2761	**autónomo** autonomous	2984	**automático** automatic
2762	**sonoro** loud, resounding	2986	**inquieto** restless, anxious
2769	**jurídico** legal, juridical	2987	**helado** iced, freezing, icy
2771	**ilustre** renowned, illustrious	2988	**plástico** plastic
2783	**blando** soft, limp, gentle	2991	**vulgar** vulgar, common, banal
2784	**estable** stable, steady	2997	**hábil** skillful, clever
2786	**dormido** asleep, sleeping	3001	**destacado** outstanding, leading
2795	**tímido** timid, shy, half-hearted	3002	**encendido** turned on, burning
2799	**vasto** vast, immense, huge	3005	**plano** flat, plain, even, level
2801	**frustrado** frustrated	3007	**obligatorio** obligatory, compulsory
2803	**comprometido** committed, engaged	3009	**contemporáneo** contemporary
2807	**consiguiente** por consiguiente: consequently	3025	**discreto** discreet, tactful
2813	**aburrido** boring, bored	3028	**amoroso** loving, affectionate
2816	**recto** right, straight, honest	3030	**optimista** optimistic
2820	**socialista** socialist	3039	**delgado** thin, skinny
2822	**espléndido** splendid, generous	3043	**tenso** tight, tense
2833	**existente** existing	3061	**indirecto** indirect
2835	**inclinado** inclined, slanting	3065	**ejecutivo** executive
2842	**metálico** metallic	3073	**referente** concerning
2845	**espectacular** spectacular	3083	**dotado** endowed, gifted
2849	**misterioso** mysterious	3095	**callado** quiet, reserved
2851	**obrero** working class	3097	**flexible** flexible
2852	**administrativo** administrative	3103	**mediano** average, medium, ordinary
2854	**singular** single, singular	3105	**pacífico** peaceful
2860	**crudo** raw, crude, natural	3107	**contradictorio** contradictory
2861	**agotado** tired, used up, sold out	3112	**mortal** mortal, lethal, deadly
2862	**deportivo** sports, sporty	3115	**solemne** solemn
2864	**químico** chemical	3118	**mudo** mute, silent
2866	**teórico** theoretical	3120	**sorprendido** surprised
2883	**ciudadano** community, citizen	3123	**psicológico** psychological
2884	**prudente** sensible, prudent	3126	**preferible** preferable
2888	**telefónico** telephone	3127	**célebre** famous, renowned
2890	**racional** rational	3131	**valiente** brave, courageous, bold
2902	**indiferente** indifferent	3132	**delicioso** delicious, delightful, charming
2904	**inesperado** unexpected, unforeseen	3133	**potente** potent, powerful
2915	**sincero** sincere	3137	**vuestro** your (pl/+fam)

3138 **notorio** notorious, noticeable

3140 **sexto** sixth

3149 **electrónico** electronic

3154 **quieto** still, motionless, calm

3161 **pálido** pale, ghastly, faded

3163 **animado** excited, lively

3164 **chileno** Chilean

3167 **materno** maternal

3175 **soltero** single, not married

3181 **vinculado** connected

3185 **colgado** hanging

3194 **geográfico** geographical

3202 **frágil** fragile, weak

3209 **ridículo** ridiculous, absurd

3214 **irregular** irregular

3216 **genial** brilliant, inspired

3221 **gracioso** funny, charming, amusing

3223 **intermedio** interim, intermediate

3225 **temporal** temporary

3228 **distinguido** distinguished

3230 **dudoso** doubtful, dubious

3232 **lamentable** regrettable

3235 **interminable** endless, interminable

3248 **innecesario** unnecessary

3256 **verbal** verbal, oral

3259 **intacto** intact

3260 **procedente** coming (from)

3262 **disponible** available

3264 **encantado** pleased, delighted

3265 **británico** British

3268 **laboral** labor, industry

3269 **rubio** blonde, fair

3274 **enamorado** in love

3278 **insuficiente** insufficient

3279 **sostenido** sustained, steady

3281 **espantoso** frightening, dreadful

3289 **financiero** financial

3293 **colonial** colonial

3295 **teatral** theatrical

3297 **vertical** vertical, upright

3299 **gratuito** free, arbitrary, gratuitous

3304 **vegetal** plant, vegetable

3305 **usado** worn out, old, used

3310 **ambicioso** ambitious, greedy

3311 **policial** police

3312 **poético** poetic

3316 **satisfactorio** satisfactory

3318 **vago** vague

3319 **estúpido** stupid, idiotic

3326 **honesto** honest

3332 **brusco** brusque, abrupt, sudden

3342 **iluminado** illuminated

3349 **simbólico** symbolic

3351 **heroico** heroic

3355 **décimo** tenth

3365 **quemado** burned, burnt

3367 **vano** vain, useless

3370 **casero** homemade

3371 **molesto** annoyed, bothered, upset

3373 **auxiliar** auxiliary, ancillary

3374 **silencioso** quiet, silent

3381 **nativo** native

3384 **aceptable** acceptable, suitable

3388 **rotundo** categorical

3394 **repentino** sudden

3395 **ansioso** anxious, eager

3398 **despacio** slow, slowly

3399 **innumerable** innumerable, countless

3401 **insoportable** unbearable, intolerable

3411 **electoral** electoral

3414 **formidable** formidable, tremendous

3441 **miserable** wretched, miserable

3442 **grato** agreeable, pleasant

3445 **clave** key

3459 **enérgico** energetic, vigorous

3467 **ignorante** ignorant

3473 **ilustrado** learned, illustrated

3477 **altísimo** very high, tall

3478 **estupendo** marvelous, stupendous

3482 **restante** remaining

3484 **regional** regional

3485 **cómico** comic

3487 **tardío** late, belated

3498 **puntual** punctual

3504 **imaginario** imaginary

3505 **brutal** brutal, savage

3506 **disperso** spread out

3507 **ingenuo** naive, ingenuous

3508 **anual** annual, yearly

3514 **costoso** costly, expensive

3515 **repleto** full, overcrowded

3526 **asombroso** amazing

3530 **exigente** demanding, urgent

3535 **apto** appropriate, fit, able

3536 **incierto** uncertain

3537 **espeso** thick, dense, stiff

3547 **apasionado** passionate

3549 **abstracto** abstract

3551	**creativo** creative	3775	**parcial** partial, biased
3552	**autoritario** authoritarian	3778	**masivo** mass, massive
3555	**subterráneo** underground	3782	**desierto** deserted, desolate
3560	**feroz** ferocious, fierce	3794	**educativo** educational
3567	**sistemático** systematic	3801	**vigente** in force, valid
3570	**sumo** utmost, highest	3803	**saludable** healthy, wholesome
3571	**eficiente** efficient	3806	**apretado** tight, jammed
3572	**invisible** invisible	3813	**desaparecido** missing
3576	**rebelde** rebel	3817	**pésimo** dreadful, awful
3579	**privilegiado** privileged	3841	**solar** solar
3583	**dominante** dominant, prevailing	3845	**egoísta** selfish
3590	**tibio** lukewarm	3847	**exótico** exotic
3592	**sospechoso** suspicious	3853	**fascinante** fascinating
3596	**fabuloso** fabulous, fantastic	3854	**áspero** rough, coarse, harsh
3605	**denso** heavy, dense, thick	3866	**lujoso** luxurious
3611	**agrícola** agricultural, farming	3871	**hostil** hostile, unfriendly
3618	**mensual** monthly	3873	**tropical** tropical
3629	**torpe** clumsy, awkward, slow	3878	**franco** open, frank, outspoken
3632	**liso** smooth, flat, straight	3879	**inédito** unpublished
3633	**asustado** scared, frightened	3880	**uniforme** uniform
3636	**propicio** appropriate, suitable	3889	**integrante** integral, part of a group
3644	**dicho** aforementioned, said	3890	**lingüístico** linguistic
3645	**ambiguo** ambiguous	3892	**mexicano** Mexican
3650	**encantador** charming	3896	**autorizado** authorized
3653	**respetuoso** respectful	3897	**leal** loyal, faithful
3654	**africano** African	3905	**cubano** Cuban
3673	**flaco** thin, frail	3911	**sangriento** bloody
3674	**biológico** biological	3912	**matemático** mathematical
3680	**emocional** emotional	3913	**portugués** Portuguese
3681	**diplomático** diplomatic	3923	**estático** static, motionless
3685	**progresivo** progressive	3930	**representativo** representative
3689	**glorioso** glorious	3939	**furioso** furious
3691	**turco** Turkish	3940	**estudioso** studious
3695	**poblado** populated	3946	**vasco** Basque
3697	**impreso** printed	3948	**complementario** additional, complementary
3703	**inverso** inverse, opposite	3951	**insólito** unusual, uncommon
3711	**funcional** functional	3952	**temeroso** fearful
3716	**orgánico** organic	3956	**consagrado** dedicated, consecrated
3719	**comparable** comparable	3958	**despierto** awake
3721	**marginal** marginal, minor	3969	**embarazada** pregnant
3722	**pardo** brown, dark, dim	3971	**latinoamericano** Latin American
3727	**tendido** spread, hung, laid (out)	3972	**tecnológico** technological
3728	**horizontal** horizontal	3978	**desigual** unequal, uneven, irregular
3737	**penoso** painful, laborious	4000	**civilizado** civilized
3744	**preferido** preferred, favorite	4002	**indudable** unquestionable
3747	**insignificante** insignificant	4007	**lateral** side, lateral
3756	**preso** imprisoned, confined	4015	**arbitrario** arbitrary
3760	**global** global, overall	4021	**respetable** respectable
3773	**oral** oral	4025	**diminuto** diminutive, tiny, minute

4026 **celeste** heavenly, sky-blue

4030 **convincente** convincing

4032 **periodístico** journalistic

4033 **cariñoso** affectionate

4040 **acertado** correct, accurate

4042 **mediocre** mediocre

4045 **agitado** agitated, irritated

4046 **precario** precarious

4047 **sanitario** health, sanitary, clean

4048 **comprensible** understandable

4049 **cuidadoso** careful, cautious

4053 **irracional** irrational

4055 **hundido** buried, sunken

4064 **dinámico** dynamic

4066 **sereno** serene, calm

4067 **retirado** retired, remote, secluded

4071 **refinado** refined

4088 **maldito** damned, wretched

4093 **inmóvil** immovable, motionless

4096 **grosero** crude, rude, crass

4097 **catalán** Catalan

4104 **relevante** relevant, significant

4107 **audaz** audacious, bold

4115 **disfrazado** disguised

4119 **ágil** agile

4120 **atrasado** behind, slow

4123 **agradecido** grateful, thankful

4124 **adicional** additional

4126 **condicionado** conditioned

4129 **óptimo** optimum

4130 **súbito** sudden

4134 **incomprensible** incomprehensible

4140 **guapo** handsome, beautiful

4144 **inmerso** engrossed, immersed

4151 **proveniente** coming from

4152 **primordial** fundamental, primary

4156 **genético** genetic

4161 **infeliz** unhappy, unfortunate

4162 **compacto** compact, dense

4165 **criminal** criminal

4166 **coherente** coherent, connected

4171 **estratégico** strategic

4173 **ético** ethical

4175 **enterado** aware of

4178 **incipiente** incipient, beginning

4180 **alternativo** alternating, alternative

4181 **expresivo** expressive

4189 **estatal** state, government-owned

4192 **perpetuo** continual, perpetual

4195 **estéril** sterile, barren

4201 **latente** latent

4206 **holandés** Dutch

4208 **enterrado** buried

4211 **celoso** jealous

4213 **constitucional** constitutional

4219 **circular** circular

4224 **reflejado** reflected

4228 **detallado** detailed, thorough

4234 **atrapado** trapped

4242 **liviano** light, frivolous

4243 **entusiasmado** enthused, excited

4250 **susceptible** susceptible

4251 **inolvidable** unforgettable

4261 **ruidoso** noisy

4264 **gigante** gigantic

4268 **semanal** weekly

4269 **clandestino** undercover, clandestine

4270 **defensivo** defensive

4271 **manual** manual

4277 **mixto** mixed, co-ed

4285 **penal** penal

4293 **pintoresco** picturesque

4297 **publicitario** advertising

4304 **virgen** virgin

4307 **matrimonial** matrimonial

4308 **equivalente** equivalent

4313 **deseable** desirable

4317 **pasivo** passive

4322 **llamativo** striking

4331 **justificado** justifiable, justified

4333 **fotográfico** photographic

4335 **desordenado** messy, confused

4336 **gráfico** graphic, explicit

4338 **revuelto** confused, messed up

4345 **expreso** express, explicit

4349 **erótico** erotic

4350 **amenazado** threatened

4351 **inminente** imminent

4357 **imperial** imperial, imperialist

4358 **inexplicable** unexplainable

4359 **peruano** Peruvian

4360 **experimental** experimental

4362 **opaco** dull, opaque, heavy

4371 **efímero** ephemeral, short-lived

4374 **invertido** reversed, inverted

4381 **transitorio** transitory

4383 **mojado** wet

4384 **descalzo** barefoot

4385 **orientado** positioned, guided
4388 **presidencial** presidential
4391 **brasileño** Brazilian
4394 **minucioso** meticulous, thorough
4395 **rústico** rustic, rural
4405 **apagado** turned off
4416 **comunitario** of the community
4417 **explícito** explicit
4418 **silvestre** wild
4423 **fiscal** fiscal, treasury
4424 **espacial** spatial, space
4426 **medieval** medieval
4428 **honrado** honest, respectable
4429 **veloz** fast, quick
4433 **monótono** monotonous
4436 **imprevisto** unforeseen, unexpected
4438 **soviético** Soviet
4439 **potencial** potential
4440 **ambulante** traveling
4444 **perverso** perverse, wicked
4446 **ardiente** passionate, ardent
4450 **tenue** tenuous, flimsy
4452 **indiscutible** indisputable, unquestionable
4455 **sombrío** shady, dark, dismal
4459 **adolescente** adolescent
4461 **rosado** pink, rosy
4462 **amistoso** friendly
4467 **perteneciente** pertaining, belonging
4470 **necesitado** poor, needy
4471 **indefinido** vague, indefinite
4472 **solidario** united, jointly shared
4473 **paralizado** paralyzed
4478 **inquietante** disquieting
4479 **visual** visual
4486 **republicano** republican
4487 **destruido** destroyed
4489 **trabajador** hardworking
4491 **grandioso** magnificent, grandiose
4497 **dichoso** fortunate, happy
4499 **agrario** agrarian, agricultural
4500 **suizo** Swiss
4501 **presunto** alleged, presumed
4516 **vertiginoso** dizzying
4517 **decente** respectable, decent
4518 **congelado** frozen
4520 **triple** triple
4529 **inseguro** unsure, unsafe
4536 **irónico** ironic, mocking
4541 **asombrado** amazed, bewildered

4546 **sofisticado** sophisticated
4549 **ingenioso** ingenious, clever
4554 **vulnerable** vulnerable
4557 **geométrico** geometric
4560 **bendito** blessed
4564 **trascendente** transcendent
4565 **alarmante** alarming
4566 **pequeñito** very small, tiny
4570 **pasajero** fleeting, transitory
4572 **turístico** tourist
4575 **impecable** impeccable, faultless
4576 **soberbio** proud, arrogant
4579 **sonriente** smiling
4581 **nulo** void, null
4584 **implacable** relentless, implacable
4589 **productivo** productive, profitable
4591 **andaluz** Andalusian
4595 **institucional** institutional
4596 **vigoroso** vigorous, strong
4599 **atroz** atrocious
4605 **sabroso** delicious, tasty
4608 **larguísimo** very long
4609 **simultáneo** simultaneous
4613 **trascendental** far-reaching, transcendental
4614 **colorado** red, colored
4620 **prestigioso** prestigious
4622 **crónico** chronic
4625 **bíblico** biblical
4628 **paterno** paternal
4633 **acelerado** accelerated, quick
4634 **árido** arid, dry
4635 **caprichoso** capricious, whimsical
4636 **minúsculo** minute, insignificant
4654 **provincial** provincial
4659 **ilegal** illegal
4663 **terrestre** earthly, of the earth
4666 **cordial** cordial, friendly
4668 **angustiado** anguished, distressed
4671 **piadoso** devout, pious, merciful
4672 **corporal** of the body, corporal
4674 **ilimitado** unlimited
4678 **esporádico** sporadic
4684 **melancólico** melancholy
4686 **móvil** mobile
4689 **robusto** strong, robust, sturdy
4694 **llano** flat, level, plain
4695 **colombiano** Colombian
4699 **angustioso** distressing
4707 **estadístico** statistical

4710 **maligno** evil, malignant

4713 **comprensivo** understanding

4714 **hueco** hollow

4719 **elocuente** eloquent

4726 **afín** related, similar

4729 **usual** normal, usual

4735 **bancario** bank, banking

4739 **afortunado** fortunate

4744 **informativo** informative

4753 **importado** imported

4754 **íntegro** whole, entire, honest

4756 **extra** extra

4761 **recíproco** reciprocal

4765 **fértil** fertile, rich

4768 **acomodado** well-to-do, suitable

4782 **soberano** sovereign, self-assured

4787 **guerrero** warrior, warlike

4790 **involuntario** involuntary

4792 **inexistente** non-existent

4793 **subjetivo** subjective

4801 **neutro** neutral

4808 **desconcertado** disoriented, disconcerted

4825 **impreciso** imprecise

4835 **previsible** foreseeable

4837 **frontal** frontal

4842 **monstruoso** monstrous

4843 **persistente** persistent

4846 **educado** educated

4847 **irreversible** irreversible

4853 **prematuro** premature

4859 **rudo** rude, crude, coarse

4860 **cerebral** cerebral

4864 **pedagógico** pedagogical, teaching

4874 **grotesco** grotesque, ridiculous

4876 **sumido** sunken, drowned

4880 **siniestro** sinister

4881 **místico** mystical

4884 **exento** exempt, free

4887 **clínico** clinical

4889 **callejero** of the street

4900 **mismísimo** very same

4901 **contundente** decisive, blunt, forceful

4905 **séptimo** seventh

4907 **carente** lacking, devoid

4908 **nítido** clear, clean, neat

4909 **imponente** impressive, magnificent

4911 **secular** secular, lay

4922 **inseparable** inseparable

4926 **inestable** unstable, unsteady

4936 **frívolo** trivial, frivolous

4938 **prodigioso** prodigious, famous

4941 **laborioso** laborious, industrious

4942 **eclesiástico** ecclesiastical

4943 **confundido** confused

4951 **marrón** brown

4954 **sintético** synthetic

4955 **bélico** warlike

4956 **combinado** combined

4961 **parlamentario** parliamentary

4962 **trasero** behind, back

4966 **irreal** unreal

4970 **entusiasta** enthusiastic

4972 **patriótico** patriotic

4976 **aplastado** crushed, flattened

4978 **rítmico** rhythmic

4983 **hispano** Hispanic

4985 **constructivo** constructive

4987 **ocasional** occasional, random

4990 **monumental** monumental

4992 **accesible** accesible

Adverb

10 **no** no

36 **ya** already, still

42 **muy** very, really

53 **también** also

59 **así** like that

70 **sí** yes

73 **bien** well

76 **entonces** so, then

83 **tan** such, as, too, so

85 **ahora** now

87 **después** after

90 **siempre** always, forever

102 **sólo** only, just

114 **antes** before

126 **cómo** how?

129 **aquí** here

132 **luego** later, afterwards

146 **casi** almost, nearly

148 **durante** during, for (time)

151 **nunca** never, ever

159 **además** also, as well, besides

164 **hoy** today, nowadays

167 **allí** there, over there

174 **dentro** inside

189 **ahí** there

211 **todavía** still, yet

279 **tampoco** neither, nor, either

282 **aún** still, yet

294 **incluso** including, even (ADV)

297 **quizás** perhaps, maybe

301 **mal** badly

324 **allá** there, over there

336 **solamente** only

337 **bueno** well…

347 **través** a través: across, over, through

378 **junto** together with, next to

391 **cerca** close, near

396 **pronto** soon, quick

416 **realmente** really, actually, in fact

421 **dónde** where?

436 **encima** above, on top, in addition

451 **fuera** out, outside, away

469 **lejos** far (away, off)

482 **claro** of course, clearly

483 **atrás** back, behind, ago

516 **adelante** forward, further

544 **arriba** up, above

556 **alrededor** about, around, round

580 **precisamente** precisely

587 **apenas** hardly, barely

591 **simplemente** simply, just

602 **siquiera** even (if)

631 **abajo** down, below, downward

662 **totalmente** totally, completely

684 **especialmente** especially

701 **detrás** behind

728 **finalmente** finally, at last

788 **jamás** never

820 **debajo** underneath, below

843 **aun** even (though), still

850 **perfectamente** perfectly

863 **recién** recently, just

866 **peor** worse

869 **completamente** completely

882 **inmediatamente** immediately

885 **delante** (in) front (of), ahead

915 **justo** just

924 **salvo** except (for), but

936 **directamente** directly, straight away

971 **probablemente** probably

977 **exactamente** exactly

994 **seguramente** surely, securely

1008 **rápidamente** rapidly, quickly

1046 **tarde** late

1072 **acaso** by chance, maybe

1106 **prácticamente** practically

1112 **ayer** yesterday

1181 **absolutamente** absolutely, completely

1199 **cuándo** when?

1235 **mañana** tomorrow

1288 **acerca** about, concerning

1313 **aparte** apart, aside, separately

1358 **definitivamente** definitely, finally

1365 **profundamente** profoundly, deeply

1407 **verdaderamente** truly

1409 **únicamente** only

1431 **igualmente** equally

1454 **nuevamente** anew, again

1463 **generalmente** generally, usually

1477 **claramente** clearly

1485 **justamente** just, exactly

1523 **naturalmente** naturally

1604 **efectivamente** in fact, actually, indeed

1629 **fácilmente** easily

1766 **evidentemente** evidently, obviously

1769 **exclusivamente** exclusively

1803 **cuando** when

1805 **suficientemente** enough

1853 **aparentemente** apparently

1858 **afuera** outside

1868 **constantemente** constantly

1944 **menudo** a menudo: often

1964 **personalmente** personally

1975 **lentamente** slowly

1980 **posiblemente** possibly

2084 **adentro** inside

2183 **repente** de + repente: suddenly

2212 **normalmente** normally

2226 **principalmente** principally, mainly

2230 **acá** here, around here

2256 **aproximadamente** approximately

2282 **necesariamente** necessarily

2340 **plenamente** fully

2352 **sencillamente** simply

2362 **actualmente** now, at present

2380 **sumamente** extremely, highly

2430 **posteriormente** afterwards

2475 **últimamente** lately, recently

2519 **relativamente** relatively

2541 **enfrente** in front (of)

2585 **continuamente** continuously

2587 **estrictamente** strictly

2652 **particularmente** particularly, personally

2688 **fundamentalmente** fundamentally

2707 **enseguida** immediately, at once

2712 **afortunadamente** luckily, fortunately

2719 **anteriormente** previously

2749 **recientemente** recently

2753 **puramente** purely, simply

2785 **ciertamente** certainly, indeed

2804 **libremente** freely

2818 **seguida** en seguida: right away, at once

2891 **previamente** previously

2909 **francamente** frankly, openly

2974 **ligeramente** slightly, lightly

3067 **ojalá** I hope that

3079 **propiamente** exactly, properly

3206 **seriamente** seriously

3245 **habitualmente** habitually

3247 **tranquilamente** calmly, peacefully

3300 **difícilmente** with difficulty

3315 **desgraciadamente** unfortunately

3324 **automáticamente** automatically

3360 **indudablemente** doubtless, undoubtedly

3418 **anoche** last night

3428 **sucesivamente** successively, step by step

3462 **permanentemente** permanently

3466 **concretamente** specifically, exactly

3469 **curiosamente** strangely, funnily enough

3470 **lógicamente** logically

3511 **asimismo** as well, also, moreover

3524 **diariamente** daily

3553 **excesivamente** excessively

3568 **inclusive** including, even

3574 **sinceramente** sincerely

3601 **antemano** beforehand, in advance

3627 **simultáneamente** simultaneously

3678 **enormemente** enormously

3750 **literalmente** literally

3753 **frecuentemente** frequently, often

3759 **fuertemente** strongly

3789 **enteramente** completely, entirely

3808 **cuidadosamente** carefully

3811 **obviamente** obviously

3842 **inevitablemente** inevitably

3852 **físicamente** physically

3862 **básicamente** basically

3914 **intensamente** intensely

3915 **suavemente** softly

3919 **lamentablemente** regrettably

3924 **antaño** in days gone by, last year

3926 **adónde** to where?

3953 **extraordinariamente** extraordinarily

4083 **íntimamente** intimately

4117 **mutuamente** mutually, each other

4118 **correctamente** correctly

4135 **independientemente** independently

4238 **altamente** highly

4262 **supuestamente** supposedly, allegedly

4263 **ampliamente** widely

4275 **adonde** to where

4403 **decididamente** decidedly, decisively

4406 **bruscamente** quickly, sharply

4425 **violentamente** violently

4464 **radicalmente** radically

4492 **específicamente** specifically

4494 **extremadamente** extremely

4545 **oficialmente** officially

4587 **brevemente** briefly

4607 **esencialmente** essentially

4649 **abiertamente** openly

4657 **tradicionalmente** traditionally

4677 **firmemente** firmly

4743 **espontáneamente** spontaneously

4778 **económicamente** economically

4875 **duramente** harshly, severely

4877 **públicamente** publicly, in public

4888 **largamente** for a long time, at length

4891 **voluntariamente** voluntarily

4894 **parcialmente** partially

4897 **debidamente** properly, duly

4904 **viceversa** vice versa

4920 **inicialmente** initially

4928 **terriblemente** terribly

4932 **mentalmente** mentally

Noun

44 **vez** time (specific occurrence)

55 **año** year

68 **tiempo** time (general), weather

71 **día** day

78 **cosa** thing

80 **hombre** man, mankind, husband

86 **parte** part, portion

88 **vida** life

108 **momento** moment, time

113 **forma** form, shape, way

116 **casa** house

118 **mundo** world

127 **mujer** woman, wife

130 **caso** case, occasion

133 **país** country

135 **lugar** place, position
137 **persona** person
143 **hora** hour, time (specific)
145 **trabajo** work, job, effort
147 **punto** point, dot, period
150 **mano** hand
152 **manera** way, manner
156 **fin** end
157 **tipo** type, kind
158 **gente** people
162 **ejemplo** example
165 **lado** side
166 **hijo** son, [pl] children
169 **problema** problem
170 **cuenta** bill, account
171 **medio** means, middle; pormedio: through
176 **palabra** word
178 **niño** child, little boy
180 **embargo** sin embargo: nevertheless
182 **padre** father
186 **cambio** change
192 **historia** history, story
193 **idea** idea
194 **agua** water
196 **noche** night, evening
197 **ciudad** city
198 **modo** way, manner
199 **nombre** name, noun
201 **familia** family
202 **realidad** reality, actuality
206 **obra** work, book, deed
209 **verdad** truth
210 **mes** month
212 **razón** reason; tener razón: to be right
216 **grupo** group
230 **relación** relationship, relation
232 **cuerpo** body
235 **hecho** fact, happening
237 **principio** beginning, principle
240 **señor** sir, Mr, lord
241 **pueblo** people, village
242 **tarde** afternoon, evening
247 **ojo** eye
248 **calle** street
253 **libro** book
255 **fuerza** strength, force, power
256 **luz** light
258 **santo** saint (m)
260 **frente** al frente facing; frente a: across from

262 **amigo** friend
265 **sentido** sense, feeling
267 **paso** step, pace
268 **situación** situation
272 **gracia** (pl) thank you; grace, favor
273 **siglo** century, age
274 **dios** god, divinity
276 **tierra** earth, land, ground
277 **papel** paper, role, part
278 **madre** mother
283 **tema** theme, subject, topic
288 **clase** kind, class, order
291 **dinero** money
295 **campo** field, country
298 **cabeza** head (part of body)
302 **orden** order; sequence (m), religious (f)
303 **don** courtesy title (m), Mr., gift
304 **semana** week
307 **final** al final: finally, in the end
308 **interés** interest
310 **vista** view, sight
313 **acuerdo** accord; de acuerdo: in agreement
315 **número** number
318 **fondo** bottom, end
319 **camino** road, route, path
320 **voz** voice
321 **estudio** study, learning
326 **valor** value, worth
333 **medida** measure; a medida que: to the extent
339 **centro** center, middle, downtown
340 **necesidad** necessity, need
341 **condición** condition
344 **falta** lack, shortage
350 **edad** age
351 **estado** state, condition, status
352 **ser** being
354 **puerta** door
356 **cara** face, expression
358 **época** time, age, period
359 **color** color
361 **experiencia** experience
362 **movimiento** movement
366 **pesar** sorrow; a pesar de: in spite of
367 **posibilidad** possibility
371 **juego** game, play, sport
374 **aire** air, wind, appearance
377 **guerra** war, warfare
379 **resultado** result, outcome
384 **ley** law, bill, rule

385 **aspecto** aspect, appearance

386 **pie** foot, base

388 **especie** kind, sort, species

390 **servicio** service, helpfulness

393 **actividad** activity, action

398 **cuestión** question, matter

399 **duda** doubt

400 **diferencia** difference

401 **mañana** morning, tomorrow

404 **cantidad** quantity, amount

405 **acción** action, act, deed

408 **sociedad** society

417 **peso** peso (money), weight, load

418 **efecto** effect

419 **objeto** object, thing

423 **amor** love

424 **muerte** death

425 **partido** party, group, (sports) match

427 **derecho** right, justice, law

428 **poder** power

429 **importancia** importance

430 **sistema** system

431 **viaje** travel, trip

432 **suelo** ground, floor

433 **respecto** respect, con respecto a: with regards to

434 **conocimiento** knowledge

435 **libertad** freedom, liberty

441 **atención** attention

444 **esfuerzo** effort, endeavor

447 **resto** rest, remainder, leftover

449 **zona** area, zone

450 **miedo** fear

452 **proceso** process, procedure

459 **minuto** minute

461 **mesa** table, board

463 **ocasión** opportunity, occasion

467 **programa** program, plan

468 **favor** favor, benefit

472 **respuesta** answer, reply

473 **línea** line, course

474 **espacio** space, room

475 **nivel** level

476 **gobierno** government

477 **cabo** end, bit; llevar a cabo: to carry out

481 **pregunta** question

484 **imagen** image, picture

485 **carrera** career, course, race

495 **figura** figure

497 **animal** animal

498 **base** base, basis

503 **posición** position

504 **motivo** motive, cause

505 **prueba** proof, trial, test

506 **política** politics, policy

513 **dato** data, fact

517 **empresa** firm, company, venture

518 **asunto** matter, issue, affair

519 **presencia** presence, appearance

521 **cultura** culture

522 **serie** series

530 **carácter** personality, nature

531 **mayoría** majority

532 **escuela** school

538 **autor** writer, author

539 **hermano** brother, [pl] siblings

543 **función** function, meeting

546 **causa** cause

549 **decisión** decision

550 **música** music

555 **expresión** expression

559 **río** river

560 **seguridad** security, safety

561 **término** term (language), end

563 **metro** meter, subway

564 **médico** doctor

567 **arte** art, skill

570 **consecuencia** consequence

572 **acto** act, action

575 **pena** trouble; valer la pena: be of worth

577 **segundo** second

578 **altura** height, altitude

579 **deseo** desire, wish

581 **joven** teenager, young person

583 **sueño** dream, sleep

585 **tarea** task, job

586 **carta** letter, (playing) card

588 **propiedad** property

589 **producto** product

593 **gusto** pleasure, taste, preference

594 **ayuda** help, aid

596 **lengua** language, tongue, strip (of land)

598 **plan** plan

600 **vuelta** return, turn

604 **proyecto** project, plan

605 **memoria** memory

606 **origen** origin, cause

607 **elemento** element

609 **mercado** market

610 **curso** course, direction

613 **sangre** blood

614 **interior** interior, inside

619 **uso** use

620 **brazo** arm

621 **profesor** professor, teacher

623 **futuro** future

624 **oportunidad** opportunity, chance

625 **mitad** half, middle

628 **recuerdo** memory, keepsake

632 **opinión** opinion, view

635 **boca** mouth, entrance, opening

636 **dirección** direction, address

639 **pieza** piece, part

644 **actitud** attitude

645 **mar** sea

647 **entrada** entrance, admisión ticket

648 **contacto** contact

649 **corazón** heart, core

651 **capital** capital; city (f), money (m)

653 **título** title, heading

655 **cuarto** room, chamber

656 **material** material, element

657 **golpe** hit, strike, punch

659 **comunicación** communication

666 **enfermedad** illness, sickness

667 **bien** goods, property, benefit

668 **materia** matter, subject

672 **sitio** place, space

674 **naturaleza** nature, character

675 **capacidad** capacity

678 **distancia** distance

682 **información** information

683 **ambiente** environment, atmosphere

685 **desarrollo** development

686 **sol** sun

693 **compañero** companion, classmate

694 **salida** exit, escape, outcome

696 **conciencia** conscience, consciousness

700 **costumbre** habit, custom, usage

702 **paz** peace

703 **noticia** news

704 **circunstancia** circumstance

705 **dolor** pain, ache, sorrow

707 **estilo** style

708 **precio** price, cost, value

711 **planta** plant, floor

712 **personaje** character (e.g. movie)

714 **éxito** success

715 **hija** daughter

717 **edificio** building

718 **autoridad** authority

719 **piedra** stone, rock

721 **conjunto** group, set

725 **suerte** luck, fortune

731 **espíritu** spirit, ghost

732 **miembro** member, limb

735 **recurso** resource, recourse, means

736 **pared** (interior) wall

737 **equipo** team, equipment, outfit

738 **error** error, mistake

741 **dificultad** difficulty, obstacle

745 **voluntad** will, willpower, intention

746 **reunión** meeting, reunion

747 **modelo** model, pattern

749 **fecha** date, day

752 **propósito** intention, purpose

754 **cuidado** care, carefulness

755 **puesto** job, place, position

756 **grado** degree, grade

758 **lucha** fight, struggle, wrestle

761 **jefe** leader, boss, manager

765 **periódico** newspaper, periodical

768 **par** pair, couple (m); a la par: at same time

769 **público** public, audience

772 **calidad** quality

775 **ciencia** science, knowledge

776 **tamaño** size, dimension

778 **doctor** doctor

779 **cuadro** painting, picture

780 **caballo** horse

781 **responsabilidad** responsibility

784 **detalle** detail

785 **marcha** march, progress

787 **carne** meat, flesh

789 **pensamiento** thought, thinking

791 **cargo** position, charge, fee

793 **santa** saint (f)

794 **construcción** construction

795 **juicio** judgment

796 **terreno** ground, earth, terrain

797 **piso** floor, storey

798 **compañía** company

800 **texto** text

801 **fuente** source; fountain

802 **presente** present

804 **revista** magazine, journal

805 **esperanza** hope

806 **máquina** machine

809 **frase** phrase

811 **sala** room, hall

813 **instrumento** instrument

815 **defensa** defense, plea

816 **director** director, manager, principal

818 **explicación** explanation

819 **artículo** article, product, item

824 **radio** radio; set (m), communication (f)

826 **película** movie, film

827 **elección** election, choice

828 **visita** visit, visitor, guest

830 **apoyo** support, backing

831 **presidente** president

832 **arma** weapon

833 **árbol** tree

836 **encuentro** meeting, game, skirmish

838 **corriente** current, flow

839 **lectura** reading

840 **existencia** existence, life

841 **lenguaje** language, speech

844 **destino** destination, destiny

845 **educación** education

848 **operación** operation

853 **nota** note, grade

861 **teatro** theater, drama

864 **negocio** business, transaction

865 **letra** letter, handwriting, lyrics

867 **sentimiento** feeling, sentiment

871 **solución** solution, answer

873 **comida** food, meal

874 **impresión** impression, printing

875 **plano** plane, map, level

876 **intención** intention

877 **ritmo** rhythm

881 **banco** (financial) bank, bench

884 **piel** skin, hide, fur

889 **control** control

890 **investigación** investigation

892 **conversación** conversation

893 **verano** summer

894 **respeto** respect, regard

895 **norte** north

898 **tradición** tradition

900 **población** population

901 **pareja** couple, pair

902 **pasado** past

903 **diario** newspaper

906 **generación** generation

908 **visión** vision

913 **peligro** danger, menace

914 **oro** gold

917 **vino** wine

921 **etapa** stage, period

923 **silencio** silence

928 **artista** artist, performer

930 **labor** labor, work, task

932 **cielo** sky, heaven, ceiling

933 **práctica** practice, skill

934 **límite** limit

935 **masa** mass, dough, bulk, crowd

938 **formación** formation, education

939 **perro** dog

940 **izquierda** left

946 **energía** energy, power

947 **confianza** confidence, trust

950 **flor** flower

951 **esposa** wife

957 **revolución** revolution

961 **maestro** teacher (m), master

966 **fenómeno** phenomenon

967 **presión** pressure

969 **alumno** student, pupil

970 **teoría** theory

972 **tono** tone

973 **salud** health

976 **señora** Mrs., lady, madam

982 **vía** por vía: by means; road, way

984 **alma** soul

987 **madera** wood

988 **fiesta** party, feast

989 **calor** heat, warmth

992 **hogar** home, hearth

993 **mente** mind

995 **preocupación** worry, concern

997 **concepto** concept

999 **teléfono** phone, telephone

1000 **hoja** sheet, leaf

1011 **escritor** writer

1012 **intento** attempt, try

1014 **regla** rule, ruler, regulation

1016 **riesgo** risk

1017 **policía** police, police force, police officer

1019 **estudiante** student

1020 **plaza** square, marketplace

1022 **llamada** call, knock

1023 **sensación** sensation, feeling

1024 **enemigo** enemy
1025 **unidad** unit, unity
1027 **idioma** (specific) language
1028 **raíz** root
1029 **compromiso** compromise, engagement
1030 **comentario** remark, comment
1031 **carga** load, charge, cargo
1032 **marido** husband
1035 **derecha** right, right hand
1036 **extremo** edge, border, end
1037 **individuo** individual, person
1038 **contenido** contents, content
1040 **obligación** obligation
1041 **corte** court (f), cut (m)
1043 **total** (sum) total
1045 **daño** harm, injury, damage
1047 **mensaje** message
1049 **lista** list, roster, roll
1050 **región** region
1052 **niña** child, young girl
1053 **culpa** blame, fault
1055 **discusión** discussion, argument
1056 **pelo** hair
1060 **fe** faith
1063 **referencia** reference, allusion
1064 **sur** south
1065 **gesto** gesture
1066 **perspectiva** perspective
1073 **colegio** (high) school, college
1075 **venta** sale
1076 **documento** document
1078 **televisión** TV, television
1079 **chico** boy
1080 **novela** novel
1083 **alcance** reach, scope
1085 **crisis** crisis
1090 **literatura** literature
1091 **batalla** battle
1093 **dueño** owner, landlord (m)
1095 **vecino** neighbor
1096 **sector** sector, area, section
1097 **pintura** painting, paint
1098 **accidente** accident, irregularity
1102 **influencia** influence
1104 **empleado** employee
1107 **moneda** coins, currency
1108 **facilidad** ease, facility
1109 **matrimonio** marriage, married couple
1111 **iglesia** church

1113 **oficina** office
1115 **institución** institution
1120 **frío** cold
1121 **domingo** Sunday
1122 **reacción** reaction
1125 **acontecimiento** event, happening
1126 **costa** coast
1129 **método** method
1130 **comunidad** community
1131 **coche** car, carriage
1135 **página** page
1137 **frecuencia** frequency
1138 **conclusión** conclusion, end
1139 **escena** scene, stage, setting
1141 **estructura** structure
1142 **beneficio** benefit, profit
1143 **alimento** food, nourishment
1145 **velocidad** speed, velocity
1146 **barrio** neighborhood, district
1148 **análisis** analysis
1150 **frontera** border, frontier
1154 **temor** fear
1157 **ataque** attack, raid
1159 **cine** cinema, US movie theater
1160 **rama** branch, bough, limb
1162 **comienzo** start, beginning
1164 **barco** boat, ship
1165 **partida** game, match, departure
1168 **aparato** apparatus, device
1171 **extranjero** foreigner
1172 **cámara** camera, chamber
1173 **creación** creation
1177 **gana** desire
1180 **moda** fashion, form
1184 **ruido** noise
1185 **cama** bed (furniture)
1187 **técnica** technique, skill
1188 **consejo** advice, council, counsel
1190 **violencia** violence
1192 **sonido** sound
1194 **estrella** star
1197 **mirada** gaze, look
1201 **pierna** leg
1204 **hambre** hunger, starvation
1205 **placer** pleasure
1206 **profesión** profession, occupation
1210 **objetivo** objective
1211 **honor** honor, honesty
1212 **montaña** mountain

1215 **instante** instant, moment

1216 **viento** wind, scent

1217 **lluvia** rain

1218 **ejército** army

1220 **tren** train, convoy

1222 **círculo** circle, club

1226 **ventaja** advantage, benefit

1229 **isla** island

1230 **torno** en torno a: about, regarding

1232 **amistad** friendship

1236 **cadena** chain

1237 **político** politician

1238 **rey** king

1240 **ánimo** zest, spirit, heart

1241 **trato** treatment, manner, agreement

1242 **ejercicio** exercise, practice

1243 **organización** organization

1244 **agosto** August

1245 **secretario** secretary

1248 **dedo** finger, toe, digit

1249 **gasto** expense, expenditure

1250 **café** coffee, café

1251 **diálogo** dialogue, conversation

1254 **discurso** lecture, discourse, talk

1256 **hermana** sister

1258 **caja** bank, box, safe

1259 **juez** judge

1260 **particular** particular, detail, individual

1262 **poeta** poet

1264 **sorpresa** surprise

1265 **ventana** window

1266 **característica** characteristic, aspect

1271 **suma** sum, amount, summary

1274 **volumen** volume

1275 **estación** station, season

1279 **argumento** argument, plot

1280 **categoría** category

1281 **plata** silver, money

1282 **conflicto** conflict

1283 **avión** plane, airplane, aircraft

1285 **ropa** clothes, clothing

1286 **examen** examination, exam

1287 **habitante** inhabitant

1290 **justicia** justice, fairness

1292 **criterio** criterion

1295 **plazo** deadline, installment

1297 **kilómetro** kilometer

1298 **hospital** hospital

1299 **satisfacción** satisfaction

1307 **silla** chair, seat

1311 **juventud** youth

1315 **acceso** access, entry

1316 **marco** frame, mark, setting

1318 **prensa** press

1319 **excepción** exception

1321 **ausencia** absence

1324 **sombra** shade, shadow

1330 **profundidad** depth, profundity

1334 **leche** milk

1335 **consideración** consideration, regard

1337 **premio** prize, reward

1339 **nacimiento** birth, origin

1340 **invierno** winter

1341 **diciembre** December

1343 **comportamiento** behavior, conduct

1344 **crítica** criticism, critique

1346 **fuego** fire, gunfire

1347 **tendencia** tendency, style

1349 **norma** standard, pattern, norm

1352 **rueda** wheel

1353 **puente** bridge

1355 **rasgo** feature, trait

1357 **cuento** story, tale

1359 **signo** sign, mark, symbol

1360 **señal** sign, mark, token

1362 **campaña** campaign

1364 **puerto** port, harbor

1366 **aventura** adventure

1370 **marca** mark, brand, trademark

1372 **ilusión** illusion, hope, dream

1374 **compra** shopping, buy, purchase

1375 **inteligencia** intelligence

1378 **virtud** virtue, quality

1379 **remedio** alternative, cure, solution

1382 **territorio** territory

1383 **facultad** faculty, ability

1385 **fotografía** photograph

1386 **techo** roof

1388 **conducta** conduct, behavior

1391 **salto** jump, hop, skip

1392 **pan** bread

1398 **disposición** disposal, disposition

1400 **general** general

1401 **disciplina** discipline, subject

1404 **personal** personnel, staff, staffing

1406 **columna** column, spine

1411 **indio** Indian

1412 **gato** cat

1413 **margen** edge, margin, border, brink
1415 **resistencia** resistance, opposition
1417 **pérdida** loss
1418 **tratamiento** treatment, processing
1419 **entrevista** interview, meeting
1420 **espectáculo** spectacle, show
1421 **personalidad** personality, celebrity
1422 **mayo** May
1425 **representación** representation
1426 **régimen** regime, diet
1427 **punta** tip, point
1429 **alegría** joy, happiness
1432 **misión** mission, task
1436 **empleo** work, job, occupation
1438 **participación** participation, involvement
1440 **período** period, time
1441 **busca** search, hunt
1442 **superficie** surface, area
1445 **pasión** passion, desire
1446 **vehículo** vehicle, car
1449 **enero** January
1450 **capítulo** chapter
1451 **fracaso** failure, collapse
1452 **experto** expert
1453 **inquietud** restlessness, anxiety
1458 **organismo** organization, organism, (human) body
1459 **canción** song
1460 **religión** religion
1462 **departamento** department, apartment
1464 **periodista** journalist
1468 **interpretación** interpretation, interpreting
1472 **belleza** beauty
1473 **universidad** university, college
1474 **riqueza** riches, wealth
1478 **rato** moment, while, time
1487 **equilibrio** balance
1490 **fruto** fruit, result
1491 **representante** representative
1495 **exceso** excess
1496 **capa** layer, coat
1497 **defecto** defect
1498 **fábrica** factory, manufacture
1499 **espalda** back (body)
1501 **género** sort, gender, genre
1504 **economía** economy, economics, thriftiness
1506 **bosque** forest
1508 **paisaje** landscape
1510 **llamado** call, calling
1511 **paciente** patient

1514 **tensión** tension, stress, strain
1519 **ministro** (government) secretary, minister
1520 **impulso** impulse, momentum
1522 **comercio** commerce, trade
1525 **espera** wait
1527 **reserva** reservation, reserve
1529 **competencia** competition, contest
1535 **observación** observation
1538 **vacío** emptiness, void
1540 **cifra** figure, number, amount
1542 **escala** scale, ladder, rank
1544 **procedimiento** procedure, proceedings
1546 **fórmula** formula
1547 **ámbito** sphere, space
1548 **informe** report
1549 **dimensión** dimension, size
1550 **cliente** client, customer
1551 **manifestación** protest, manifestation
1553 **pico** y pico: and a bit; beak, peak
1554 **sensibilidad** sensitivity
1557 **regreso** return
1558 **temperatura** temperature
1559 **julio** July
1562 **bomba** bomb, explosion, pump
1563 **órgano** organ
1565 **avance** advance, progress
1566 **humanidad** humanity, mankind
1567 **firma** company, signature, signing
1568 **soldado** soldier
1576 **clima** climate
1577 **emoción** emotion, excitement
1578 **automóvil** automobile
1580 **mal** evil
1582 **habilidad** ability, skill, talent
1583 **identidad** identity
1584 **desgracia** misfortune, bad luck
1588 **deber** duty, obligation
1589 **cola** line, queue, tail
1591 **progreso** progress
1594 **muestra** proof, sample, sign
1596 **hábito** habit
1599 **mecanismo** mechanism
1600 **vivienda** housing, dwelling
1602 **área** area, zone
1606 **mezcla** mixture, blend
1610 **habitación** room, bedroom, habitat
1611 **instrucción** instruction
1613 **versión** version, account
1614 **lujo** luxury

1615 **intervención** intervention

1616 **llegada** arrival

1617 **alrededor** surrounding area, vicinity

1618 **testigo** witness

1619 **dominio** power, control

1620 **raza** race, lineage

1622 **descubrimiento** discovery

1623 **vacaciones** vacation

1624 **provincia** province, region

1625 **saber** knowledge

1630 **claridad** clearness, clarity

1635 **arena** sand

1636 **postura** posture, position, attitude

1637 **salón** hall, room

1638 **escenario** stage, setting, scene

1640 **largo** a lo largo: throughout; length

1643 **hotel** hotel

1644 **oficio** job, occupation, function

1647 **fila** line, row, file

1648 **patrón** employer, landlord, patron saint

1649 **pecho** chest, breast

1650 **tienda** shop, store, tent

1652 **protección** protection

1653 **funcionario** civil servant

1657 **transporte** transportation, transport

1658 **red** network, net, system

1659 **caída** fall, drop, falling

1663 **valle** valley

1665 **vuelo** flight

1667 **sexo** sex

1668 **iniciativa** initiative

1670 **concentración** concentration, gathering

1671 **grito** cry, shout, scream

1672 **esencia** essence

1673 **cocina** kitchen

1675 **reflejo** reflection

1676 **definición** definition

1680 **abogado** lawyer

1683 **sesión** session, meeting

1685 **reloj** clock, watch

1687 **muchacho** boy

1688 **octubre** October

1689 **exposición** exhibition, display

1690 **ingreso** entrance, admission, income

1692 **dibujo** drawing, sketch

1695 **hueso** bone

1697 **militar** soldier, military person

1698 **motor** engine, motor

1699 **oposición** opposition

1700 **patio** courtyard, playground, yard

1701 **fruta** fruit

1702 **ideal** ideal, goal

1705 **actor** actor

1706 **confusión** confusion

1710 **traje** suit, dress, costume

1711 **exigencia** requirement, demand

1712 **víctima** victim, casualty

1713 **playa** beach, seaside

1714 **trabajador** worker, laborer

1716 **hierro** iron

1719 **tela** cloth, fabric

1721 **producción** production

1722 **febrero** February

1723 **símbolo** symbol

1725 **medicina** medicine

1727 **búsqueda** search

1729 **tranquilidad** tranquility, peace

1730 **espejo** mirror, reflection

1732 **comprensión** understanding

1734 **cerebro** brain

1737 **tiro** throw, shot

1740 **abuelo** grandfather

1746 **declaración** declaration, statement

1748 **sujeto** subject, individual

1751 **enseñanza** teaching, instruction

1753 **permiso** permission, permit

1754 **evolución** evolution, development

1755 **tío** uncle, guy

1756 **moral** morals, ethics

1760 **parque** park

1761 **ingeniero** engineer

1763 **borde** edge

1765 **entusiasmo** enthusiasm

1767 **independencia** independence

1768 **mentira** lie

1770 **sueldo** salary, pay

1772 **comparación** comparison

1776 **seno** breast, bosom, cavity

1778 **canto** singing, chant

1779 **potencia** power, potential

1781 **oficial** official, officer

1782 **fortuna** fortune, fate

1783 **crimen** crime, murder

1787 **ciudadano** citizen

1789 **baño** bathroom, bath, swim

1794 **reconocimiento** recognition

1795 **exterior** exterior, outside

1799 **crédito** credit, reputation

1800	**alternativa** alternative	1897	**cálculo** calculation, calculus
1804	**canal** channel, canal	1898	**composición** composition, make-up, essay
1806	**agente** agent	1899	**rapidez** speed, velocity
1807	**pago** payment	1900	**huevo** egg
1808	**filosofía** philosophy	1902	**crecimiento** growth, increase
1810	**lector** reader, lecturer	1903	**clave** key
1813	**triunfo** triumph, victory	1905	**tragedia** tragedy
1816	**sábado** Saturday	1906	**colección** collection
1817	**amiga** friend (f)	1907	**chica** girl, female
1818	**carretera** highway, road	1908	**prestigio** prestige
1821	**victoria** victory, triumph	1910	**sección** section, cut
1824	**pájaro** bird	1915	**bolsa** bag, purse, stock exchange
1825	**biblioteca** library	1916	**cinta** tape, ribbon, film, strip
1826	**reflexión** reflection	1920	**cuello** neck, collar
1829	**vocación** vocation, calling	1921	**continuación** continuation, follow-up
1831	**continente** continent	1922	**abril** April
1833	**tabla** chart, board, table, plank	1924	**actuación** performance, acting
1835	**ensayo** essay, rehearsal	1925	**factor** factor, cause, influence
1836	**plato** plate, dish	1926	**esquina** corner
1837	**jardín** garden	1927	**hombro** shoulder
1838	**imaginación** imagination, fantasy	1928	**infancia** infancy, childhood
1841	**poesía** poetry, poem	1930	**descanso** rest, interval, break
1842	**guardia** guard, watch, lookout	1932	**zapato** shoe
1843	**privilegio** privilege	1933	**parecer** opinion, looks
1844	**monte** mountain	1934	**familiar** relative
1847	**precisión** precision	1935	**mérito** worth, merit
1848	**sacrificio** sacrifice	1942	**muro** (outer) wall, rampart
1851	**hilo** thread, yarn, wire	1946	**montón** lot of, heap, pile
1854	**aparición** appearance, apparition	1948	**disco** disc, disk, record
1855	**poema** poem	1950	**demanda** petition, request, demand
1857	**curiosidad** curiosity, quaintness	1952	**mueble** (piece of) furniture
1859	**diente** tooth, cog	1953	**desastre** disaster
1860	**primo** cousin	1954	**secreto** secret
1863	**apariencia** appearance, aspect	1957	**angustia** anguish, distress
1864	**novedad** latest news, newness	1961	**nube** cloud
1867	**castigo** punishment, penalty	1963	**miseria** misery, wretchedness
1871	**carro** car, cart	1966	**significado** meaning
1873	**aumento** increase, rise	1967	**fama** reputation, fame
1874	**pobreza** poverty, lack, scarcity	1968	**palacio** palace
1878	**dólar** dollar	1969	**oído** hearing, ear
1880	**local** place, quarters	1971	**polvo** dust, powder
1884	**industria** industry, factory	1974	**sacerdote** priest
1885	**caballero** gentleman, knight	1977	**lección** lesson
1886	**especialista** specialist	1978	**rosa** rose
1887	**temporada** season, period, time	1986	**olor** smell, odor, fragrance
1889	**humor** mood, humor	1989	**contrato** contract, agreement
1891	**nación** nation	1990	**presentación** presentation, introduction
1892	**felicidad** happiness	1991	**cárcel** jail, prison
1893	**amante** lover	1992	**división** division

1993 **revés** al revés: backwards, upside down

1997 **cualidad** quality, attribute

2000 **índice** index, forefinger

2002 **marzo** March

2003 **atmósfera** atmosphere, environment

2004 **planeta** planet

2006 **orgullo** pride

2007 **jornada** (working) day, shift

2012 **palo** stick, pole

2013 **diseño** design

2015 **lógica** logic

2016 **herencia** inheritance, legacy

2019 **deporte** sport

2020 **reina** queen

2021 **bandera** flag

2023 **maravilla** wonder, marvel

2025 **banda** (musical) band, sash

2026 **cristal** glass, crystal, window

2028 **anécdota** anecdote

2031 **leyenda** legend

2032 **muerto** dead person

2033 **azúcar** sugar

2035 **inclinación** slope, incline, tendency

2040 **rostro** face, countenance

2041 **separación** separation

2042 **eco** echo, response

2045 **cita** appointment, date, quotation

2046 **actualidad** present (time)

2050 **fantasía** fantasy, fancy

2051 **promesa** promise

2052 **pata** leg, paw

2054 **foto** photo, picture

2055 **administración** administration

2057 **civilización** civilization

2059 **ocupación** occupation, use

2061 **asiento** seat, chair

2065 **pista** clue, track, trace

2066 **testimonio** testimony, evidence

2067 **regalo** gift, present

2073 **contradicción** contradiction

2075 **metal** metal

2076 **aceite** oil

2078 **código** code

2081 **unión** union

2082 **extensión** extension, area, expanse

2083 **duro** duro (money)

2088 **varón** male, man

2091 **evidencia** evidence, certainty

2092 **dignidad** dignity

2093 **escándalo** scandal

2094 **colega** colleague

2095 **horario** schedule, timetable

2096 **orilla** shore, edge

2098 **copia** copy

2099 **huella** trace, track, footstep

2101 **ejemplar** copy, issue

2103 **cura** priest (m), cure (f)

2106 **garantía** guarantee, warranty

2107 **vaso** (drinking) glass, vase

2108 **perfil** profile, outline

2109 **proporción** proportion

2111 **ceremonia** ceremony

2112 **vidrio** glass, pane

2113 **ruta** route

2114 **anuncio** advertisement, announcement

2116 **soledad** loneliness, solitude

2117 **tesis** thesis, exposition

2118 **rincón** corner, nook

2119 **nariz** nose

2121 **bolsillo** pocket

2123 **asociación** association

2125 **mando** command, authority

2126 **sabor** taste, flavor, sensation

2127 **década** decade

2128 **preparación** preparation, training

2132 **afecto** affection, fondness

2134 **protesta** objection, protest

2135 **patria** native land, fatherland

2136 **consumo** consumption

2138 **selva** forest, jungle

2139 **deuda** debt

2140 **horizonte** horizon

2143 **talento** talent, skill

2144 **gas** gas

2145 **té** tea

2146 **gloria** glory, fame

2148 **noviembre** November

2149 **candidato** candidate

2150 **llave** key, faucet, wrench

2151 **inconveniente** inconvenience, drawback

2152 **afán** eagerness, zeal, effort

2154 **etcétera** etcetera

2155 **comisión** commission, committee

2158 **posesión** possession

2159 **dama** lady, dame

2160 **onda** wave, ripple

2161 **botella** bottle, flask

2162 **torre** tower

2164 **combinación** combination

2165 **cadáver** corpse, body

2166 **paquete** package, packet

2167 **apellido** last name

2171 **conferencia** conference, lecture

2173 **propuesta** proposal, proposition

2174 **intensidad** intensity, force

2175 **explosión** explosion

2177 **odio** hatred

2179 **universo** universe

2181 **milagro** miracle

2182 **entrega** delivery

2185 **mapa** map

2186 **héroe** hero

2187 **lunes** Monday

2188 **tráfico** traffic, trade

2189 **terror** terror, horror

2190 **casualidad** chance, coincidence

2192 **risa** laugh, chuckle

2193 **cuerda** cord, rope

2194 **consulta** consultation, advice

2195 **edición** edition, publication

2197 **rayo** ray, beam, lightning

2199 **tía** aunt

2200 **adulto** adult, grown-up

2201 **voto** vote

2202 **calma** calm, lull

2205 **oferta** offer, bid, supply

2206 **vergüenza** embarrassment

2207 **ave** bird

2208 **rodilla** knee

2209 **paseo** walk, ride

2214 **registro** register, record

2218 **pintor** painter

2219 **delito** crime, offense

2220 **vestido** dress

2221 **relato** tale, story

2222 **baile** dance, ball

2223 **misterio** mystery

2225 **ciclo** cycle

2228 **síntoma** symptom

2229 **amenaza** threat

2231 **recorrido** journey, itinerary, route

2232 **concepción** conception

2233 **tristeza** sadness

2234 **vaca** cow

2235 **criatura** creature, child

2236 **creencia** belief

2238 **núcleo** nucleus, core

2240 **perdón** forgiveness, pardon

2241 **madrugada** dawn, daybreak

2243 **obrero** worker, laborer

2246 **cariño** love, affection

2248 **ángel** angel

2249 **rigor** harshness, rigor

2251 **contraste** contrast

2252 **turno** turn, shift; en turno a: around

2255 **reino** kingdom, reign

2258 **funcionamiento** functioning, operation

2259 **auto** auto, car

2260 **ala** wing, flank

2261 **debate** debate

2263 **aplicación** application

2264 **laboratorio** laboratory

2266 **vendedor** salesperson

2267 **copa** cup, glass, top (tree)

2270 **tratado** treaty, treatise

2275 **rechazo** rejection, refusal

2276 **totalidad** whole, totality

2281 **papá** dad

2286 **mamá** mom

2287 **vela** candle, sail, vigil

2289 **establecimiento** establishment

2291 **matiz** shade, tint, nuance

2293 **meta** goal, aim, purpose

2296 **comodidad** comfort, convenience

2297 **pariente** relative

2299 **distribución** distribution

2300 **invitación** invitation

2301 **destrucción** destruction

2305 **opción** option, choice

2308 **máximo** maximum

2309 **tarjeta** card

2310 **fase** phase, stage

2312 **tropa** troops, forces

2314 **socio** member, partner

2318 **guía** guide, leader

2321 **hielo** ice

2325 **primavera** spring, spring-like

2327 **simpatía** sympathy, affinity

2329 **centímetro** centimeter

2330 **pantalla** screen, monitor

2331 **toro** bull

2333 **cultivo** cultivation, crop

2334 **horror** horror, atrocity

2335 **bienestar** wellbeing, welfare

2336 **paciencia** patience

2339 **convicción** conviction

2341	**uniforme** uniform	2434	**danza** dance
2342	**media** average; a media: halfways	2435	**concierto** concert, concerto
2343	**mínimo** minimum	2436	**partidario** supporter, partisan
2346	**compañera** female companion	2437	**templo** temple, church
2349	**junio** June	2438	**líquido** liquid
2350	**drama** drama	2439	**debilidad** weakness
2354	**doble** double	2440	**ambición** ambition
2355	**episodio** episode, incident	2441	**locura** madness, insanity
2357	**afirmación** statement, assertion	2442	**comerciante** merchant, businessman
2359	**bar** (snack) bar, café	2443	**camisa** shirt
2361	**liberación** liberation	2444	**pluma** pen, feather
2364	**estancia** stay, stance, ranch	2445	**pelota** ball
2368	**variedad** variety	2446	**pasaje** fare, passage, lane
2370	**capitán** captain, chief	2447	**limpieza** cleanliness, purity
2371	**droga** drug	2448	**admiración** admiration
2373	**taller** workshop, shop	2449	**fantasma** ghost, phantom
2374	**desorden** disorder, mess	2450	**transformación** transformation
2377	**esclavo** slave	2451	**caza** hunting (game)
2385	**manejo** handling, management	2455	**almacén** warehouse, store
2386	**lágrima** tear, teardrop	2456	**expectativa** expectation, hope, prospect
2387	**colaboración** collaboration	2457	**ruptura** break-up, rupture
2389	**ángulo** angle	2458	**inversión** investment, outlay
2390	**impacto** impact	2460	**herida** wound, injury
2391	**urgencia** urgency	2461	**hipótesis** hypothesis
2393	**creador** creator	2465	**giro** turn, draft, expression
2394	**luna** moon	2466	**esquema** outline, diagram, plan
2395	**instalación** installation, facilities	2467	**mito** myth
2396	**homenaje** homage, tribute	2468	**oscuridad** darkness
2397	**ruina** ruin, collapse	2469	**pensión** boarding house
2400	**azar** random, chance, hazard	2470	**desaparición** disappearance
2406	**ola** wave, billow	2480	**bloque** block
2407	**oreja** ear	2481	**cierre** zipper, closing
2408	**abuela** grandmother	2482	**broma** joke
2410	**doña** courtesy title (f), Mrs.	2483	**viernes** Friday
2412	**arco** arch, arc, bow	2485	**tumba** tomb, grave
2413	**oriente** East	2487	**despacho** office, study
2414	**rumbo** direction, course, bearing	2488	**viuda** widow
2415	**ejecución** performance, execution	2489	**pantalón** pants, trousers
2419	**caos** chaos	2490	**intercambio** exchange, interchange
2420	**colonia** colony, cologne	2491	**mancha** stain, spot
2421	**alcohol** alcohol	2492	**retrato** portrait, photograph
2423	**nieve** snow	2493	**lata** (tin) can
2424	**multitud** multitude	2494	**combate** combat, battle, fight
2425	**ganado** livestock, cattle	2495	**instancia** instance
2426	**pez** (alive) fish	2497	**roca** rock
2427	**líder** leader	2498	**herramienta** tool
2429	**club** club, society	2500	**panorama** panorama, landscape
2431	**desierto** desert	2503	**camión** truck, van, tanker
2432	**escritura** writing, scripture	2504	**olvido** forgetfulness, omission

2505 **estrategia** strategy

2506 **muchacha** girl

2508 **propaganda** advertising, propaganda

2510 **misa** (religious) mass

2512 **inicio** beginning, start

2513 **fútbol** soccer

2514 **esfera** sphere, globe

2516 **arquitectura** architecture

2517 **especialidad** specialty, specialized field

2518 **músico** musician

2521 **eje** axis, shaft, crux

2524 **abandono** abandonment, desertion

2525 **museo** museum

2526 **propietario** owner

2527 **trozo** piece, chunk

2529 **armonía** harmony

2530 **pacto** pact, agreement

2533 **selección** selection, choice

2536 **protagonista** protagonist, main character

2537 **ferrocarril** railway

2540 **intimidad** private life, intimacy

2542 **nave** spacecraft, ship

2543 **oración** prayer

2544 **cansancio** tiredness, weariness

2547 **tejido** fabric, tissue

2548 **trampa** trick, trap; hacer trampa: to cheat

2550 **descripción** description

2551 **pecado** sin

2554 **injusticia** injustice

2557 **adiós** goodbye

2560 **tabaco** tobacco, cigarette, cigar

2563 **suceso** event, incident

2567 **antecedente** antecedent

2568 **barrera** barrier, obstacle

2571 **tribunal** court

2573 **invasión** invasion

2574 **septiembre** September

2575 **dependencia** dependence, dependency

2576 **democracia** democracy

2581 **limitación** limitation

2583 **invitado** guest

2584 **pescado** fish

2588 **obstáculo** obstacle

2589 **aspiración** ambition, aspiration

2591 **corredor** broker, corridor, runner

2593 **resumen** summary

2594 **basura** garbage, rubbish

2595 **escalera** stairs, ladder

2596 **gravedad** seriousness, gravity

2597 **fundamento** foundation, ground

2598 **sustancia** substance, essence

2601 **derrota** defeat, loss

2602 **sospecha** suspicion

2604 **huelga** strike, protest

2605 **abuso** abuse, misuse

2606 **jueves** Thursday

2607 **arreglo** arrangement

2608 **sal** salt

2609 **dosis** dose

2610 **acento** accent, stress

2611 **aviso** warning

2612 **lazo** bow, knot, tie, lasso

2614 **entorno** environment, surroundings

2615 **nieto** grandchild

2616 **príncipe** prince

2618 **mediodía** noon, midday

2619 **gota** drop

2620 **cajón** drawer

2622 **señorita** young woman

2623 **preferencia** preference

2625 **pozo** well, shaft

2626 **rumor** rumor, murmur

2628 **concurso** competition, gathering

2629 **tesoro** treasure, thesaurus

2630 **presupuesto** budget

2632 **vigilancia** surveillance, vigilance

2635 **presa** dam, prisoner (f)

2636 **estómago** stomach

2639 **bola** ball, sphere

2640 **determinación** determination

2641 **reforma** reform, improvement

2643 **verso** verse, poem

2644 **requisito** prerequisite, requirement

2645 **adolescente** adolescent

2648 **kilo** kilogram

2650 **conquista** conquest

2653 **filósofo** philosopher

2654 **genio** genius, disposition

2655 **sucesión** succession, series

2656 **componente** component, ingredient

2658 **sufrimiento** suffering

2660 **entidad** entity

2661 **saludo** greeting

2663 **certeza** certainty

2664 **depósito** deposit, sediment

2666 **pasillo** hall, corridor

2668 **solidaridad** solidarity, togetherness

2669 **papa** Pope (m), potato (f)

2670 **geografía** geography

2672 **juguete** toy

2674 **chiste** joke, funny story

2675 **aprendizaje** learning, apprenticeship

2676 **esposo** husband, spouse

2677 **boda** marriage, wedding

2679 **fresco** freshness, coolness

2680 **lago** lake

2683 **orientación** orientation, direction

2684 **madurez** maturity, ripeness

2687 **demostración** demonstration

2691 **cumplimiento** fulfillment, compliment

2692 **respaldo** support, backing, back

2695 **incendio** fire, conflagration

2698 **joya** jewel, treasure

2700 **cementerio** cemetery, graveyard

2702 **publicación** publication

2703 **variación** variation

2706 **promoción** promotion

2709 **sentencia** (legal) sentence, judgment

2711 **resolución** resolution

2713 **coincidencia** coincidence

2714 **estímulo** stimulus, encouragement

2721 **barra** bar, rod, rail

2726 **novia** girlfriend, bride

2727 **piano** piano

2728 **pretensión** pretension, claim

2729 **habla** speech, talking

2730 **novio** boyfriend, groom

2732 **espectador** spectator, onlooker

2735 **bota** boot, wineskin

2737 **pretexto** pretext, excuse

2739 **fiebre** fever, excitement

2742 **síntesis** synthesis

2743 **este** East

2744 **nervio** nerve

2745 **científico** scientist

2748 **grano** grain, kernel

2751 **asistencia** attendance, assistance

2754 **sonrisa** smile

2756 **león** lion

2758 **aceptación** acceptance, approval

2759 **labio** lip

2760 **visitante** visitor

2763 **traslado** transfer

2765 **tentación** temptation

2766 **porvenir** future, time to come

2768 **atracción** attraction

2772 **corona** crown

2774 **docena** dozen

2776 **perfección** perfection

2777 **humedad** humidity

2778 **cosecha** harvest, crop

2780 **desesperación** desperation, exasperation

2781 **curva** curve

2787 **amo** master, boss (m)

2789 **humo** smoke

2790 **realización** fulfillment, realization

2791 **cuartel** quarters, barracks

2792 **tránsito** traffic, transit

2794 **énfasis** emphasis

2796 **empresario** manager, entrepreneur

2798 **saco** sack, bag, plunder

2800 **cruz** cross, burden

2802 **pausa** pause

2805 **vicio** vice, bad habit, defect

2806 **impuesto** tax

2808 **arquitecto** architect

2809 **cruce** crossing, intersection

2811 **convivencia** coexistence, living together

2812 **cable** cable, wiring

2814 **bondad** goodness, kindness

2815 **experimento** experiment

2817 **crónica** account, chronicle

2824 **dictadura** dictatorship

2825 **eficacia** efficiency, effectiveness

2827 **vapor** vapor, steam

2828 **bebida** drink, beverage

2830 **charla** talk, chat

2831 **gestión** management, step, negotiation

2834 **cartera** wallet, satchel

2837 **circulación** circulation, traffic

2838 **denuncia** accusation

2841 **tormenta** storm

2843 **foco** focus

2844 **residencia** residence

2848 **cuero** leather, skin

2850 **hierba** herb, grass, weed

2853 **manzana** apple, (city) block

2855 **pedazo** piece, bit

2856 **sabiduría** wisdom, knowledge

2858 **cigarrillo** cigarette

2863 **magnitud** magnitude, extent

2865 **botón** button

2867 **igualdad** equality

2871 **noción** notion, idea

2875 **semilla** seed

2876 **avenida** avenue

2878 **diablo** devil

2880 **hueco** hole, cavity

2881 **colaborador** collaborator

2882 **capricho** caprice, whim

2885 **guitarra** guitar

2886 **agencia** agency, branch

2887 **rabia** rage

2889 **monumento** monument

2893 **correspondencia** correspondence

2894 **barro** clay, mud

2895 **fuga** flight, escape

2897 **identificación** identification

2898 **contexto** context

2899 **sombrero** hat, sombrero

2901 **ayudante** helper, assistant

2903 **maniobra** maneuver, operation

2906 **prejuicio** prejudice

2908 **recomendación** recommendation

2914 **instinto** instinct

2918 **precaución** caution, forethought

2919 **robo** theft, robbery

2920 **cabello** hair

2921 **utilidad** usefulness, utility

2922 **queja** complaint

2924 **celo** jealousy, zeal

2925 **publicidad** advertising, publicity

2927 **índole** nature, temperament

2930 **choque** crash, collision

2931 **tecnología** technology

2932 **tubo** tube, pipe

2935 **mercancía** goods, merchandise

2936 **tronco** trunk, torso

2937 **culto** worship, cult

2938 **palma** palm tree, palm

2939 **prenda** piece of clothing

2940 **coro** choir, chorus

2942 **túnel** tunnel

2943 **cercanía** nearness, proximity

2945 **cuchillo** knife

2946 **desprecio** contempt, disdain

2947 **plástico** plastic

2948 **complejo** complex

2950 **naranja** orange (fruit)

2955 **cuota** quota, share, dues

2956 **mosca** fly (insect)

2959 **doctrina** doctrine, teachings

2961 **laguna** lagoon

2962 **distinción** distinction

2963 **tribu** tribe

2964 **refugio** shelter, refuge

2971 **cena** dinner

2972 **incertidumbre** uncertainty

2977 **ahorro** saving, thrift

2980 **prisión** prison, imprisonment

2981 **investigador** researcher, investigator

2982 **técnico** technician

2983 **paraíso** paradise

2985 **postre** dessert; a la postre: in the end

2989 **alimentación** feeding, food

2990 **miel** honey

2992 **desafío** challenge, provocation

2993 **aeropuerto** airport

2996 **abrigo** overcoat, shelter

2999 **sello** stamp, seal

3000 **campana** bell

3003 **incidente** incident

3004 **fragmento** fragment, passage

3013 **mina** mine

3014 **restaurante** restaurant

3015 **porcentaje** percentage

3016 **conductor** driver, conductor

3019 **magia** magic

3021 **comedor** dining room

3022 **seriedad** seriousness

3023 **gallina** hen, coward

3024 **espada** sword

3026 **excelencia** excellence

3029 **músculo** muscle

3031 **persecución** pursuit, persecution

3032 **imperio** empire, fortune

3033 **casco** helmet

3034 **pelea** fight, quarrel

3035 **retorno** return

3038 **vera** de veras: really, for real

3040 **latín** Latin

3042 **rutina** routine

3044 **mejora** improvement

3045 **domicilio** residence, address

3046 **porquería** filth, junk

3048 **susto** fright, scare

3051 **amanecer** daybreak, dawn

3052 **célula** cell (biology)

3054 **crítico** critic

3055 **inspiración** inspiration, inhalation

3056 **ladrillo** brick

3057 **proyección** projection, screening

3060 **lana** wool

3062 **infierno** hell, inferno

3064 **acero** steel

3069 **preso** prisoner

3070 **billete** ticket, bill, note

3074 **tontería** stupidity, stupid thing

3075 **cauce** (river) bed, ditch

3076 **ignorancia** ignorance

3078 **encanto** charm, spell

3080 **sed** thirst

3081 **escudo** shield, coat of arms

3082 **muñeca** doll, wrist

3085 **rango** rank, range

3086 **invento** invention

3088 **recinto** grounds, precincts

3089 **tinta** ink

3090 **garganta** throat, gorge

3091 **viajero** traveler, passenger

3092 **asesino** killer, assassin

3093 **rito** rite, ritual

3094 **atractivo** attraction, charm

3096 **frustración** frustration

3098 **cemento** cement, concrete

3099 **catástrofe** catastrophe

3100 **dulce** candy, sweets

3101 **recuperación** recovery, recuperation

3104 **almuerzo** lunch

3106 **uña** nail, fingernail, toenail

3110 **costo** price, cost, expense

3111 **manifiesto** poner de manifiesto: to show

3113 **repetición** repetition

3114 **patrimonio** patrimony, inheritance

3116 **estatua** statue

3117 **decadencia** decline, decay

3122 **enfermero** nurse

3125 **aficionado** fan, devotee

3128 **agujero** hole, opening

3130 **arroz** rice

3134 **cerveza** beer, ale

3135 **escasez** scarcity, shortage

3136 **ministerio** ministry

3139 **transición** transition

3142 **negativa** negative, denial

3143 **falda** skirt

3147 **cantante** singer

3148 **constancia** perseverance

3150 **anillo** (finger) ring

3151 **balance** outcome, balance

3152 **entendimiento** understanding

3155 **transcurso** passing, course, lapse

3157 **desayuno** breakfast

3158 **alfombra** rug, carpet, mat

3159 **historiador** historian

3165 **ficción** fiction

3168 **jugador** player, gambler

3169 **cartel** poster

3170 **desconfianza** distrust

3171 **respiración** respiration, breath

3173 **caña** cane, reed

3176 **prisionero** prisoner

3177 **turista** tourist

3178 **abundancia** abundance

3180 **asistente** assistant

3182 **queso** cheese

3184 **indicio** indication, sign

3187 **cerro** hill

3191 **galería** gallery, balcony

3192 **engaño** deceit, falsehood, hoax

3195 **continuidad** continuity

3196 **receta** recipe, prescription

3197 **conveniencia** convenience, usefulness

3199 **carencia** lack, shortage

3200 **cerdo** pig, sow, slob

3203 **empeño** insistence, determination

3204 **agresión** aggression, attack

3205 **fortaleza** fortress, strength

3207 **balcón** balcony

3208 **observador** observer

3210 **renta** income

3211 **justificación** justification

3212 **enfrentamiento** confrontation

3213 **junta** meeting, conference, seam

3215 **trayectoria** trajectory, path

3217 **indiferencia** indifference

3218 **taza** cup, bowl

3219 **vínculo** tie, bond, link

3220 **cuaderno** notebook, workbook

3227 **pánico** panic

3229 **cañón** canyon, cannon

3231 **pollo** chicken

3233 **trascendencia** transcendent nature

3236 **corrupción** corruption

3237 **confesión** confession, admission

3238 **corbata** tie, sash

3239 **macho** male, manliness

3241 **secuencia** sequence

3242 **cáncer** cancer

3244 **archivo** archive, file, filing cabinet

3246 **trámite** procedure, step, requirement

3249 **raya** line, ray, stripe

3250 **televisor** television set
3251 **estabilidad** stability
3252 **grandeza** greatness, size
3253 **prisa** hurry
3257 **matemática** mathematics
3258 **demonio** demon, devil
3266 **manga** sleeve
3271 **seda** silk
3272 **envidia** envy
3273 **emergencia** emergency
3275 **grasa** grease, fat
3277 **alcalde** mayor
3280 **congreso** congress
3282 **aplauso** applause, praise, acclaim
3283 **prima** female cousin, down payment
3284 **ansiedad** anxiety
3285 **dirigente** leader, director, manager
3286 **ascenso** promotion, climb
3287 **finalidad** purpose, aim
3290 **nostalgia** nostalgia, homesickness
3291 **mención** mention
3292 **afición** fondness, interest
3294 **lástima** shame, pity
3296 **lápiz** pencil
3298 **nido** nest
3301 **orquesta** orchestra, dance band
3302 **conexión** connection, relationship
3306 **vigor** force, strength, vigor
3307 **salario** salary, wages
3309 **filo** (cutting) edge
3314 **maíz** corn, maize
3317 **autonomía** autonomy, range
3321 **ama** housekeeper, housewife
3322 **beso** kiss
3323 **cintura** waist
3325 **pauta** guideline, rule, standard
3327 **recepción** reception, waiting-room
3328 **bala** bullet, shot
3329 **suicidio** suicide
3330 **placa** plaque, plate, badge
3333 **asesinato** murder, assassination
3334 **mentalidad** mindset, mind
3335 **jerarquía** hierarchy, rank
3336 **duración** duration, length
3337 **hallazgo** finding, discovery
3338 **proximidad** proximity
3339 **estadística** statistic
3343 **castillo** castle
3344 **traducción** translation

3345 **diversión** fun, entertainment
3346 **introducción** introduction
3347 **lámpara** lamp
3348 **dicho** saying, proverb
3353 **audiencia** audience, hearing
3354 **pasajero** passenger
3356 **costado** side, flank
3357 **otoño** autumn
3358 **feria** fair, festival
3359 **exilio** exile
3362 **portador** bearer, carrier
3363 **obispo** bishop
3368 **apertura** opening, beginning
3369 **ideología** ideology
3376 **cazador** hunter
3377 **seguro** insurance
3378 **ingenio** ingenuity, talent, wit
3379 **hembra** female, woman
3380 **bando** faction, side
3382 **dormitorio** bedroom, dormitory
3383 **plenitud** fullness, abundance
3385 **coraje** courage, toughness
3386 **plomo** lead, bullet
3387 **descendiente** descendant
3389 **república** republic
3390 **sierra** mountain range, saw
3392 **guante** glove
3393 **cartón** cardboard, carton, sketch
3397 **adolescencia** adolescence
3400 **complicación** complication
3402 **taxi** taxi, cab
3403 **porción** part, portion, share
3404 **timbre** doorbell, bell, seal, stamp
3405 **monstruo** monster, monstrosity
3406 **bebé** baby
3407 **trayecto** trajectory, course, path
3408 **globo** balloon, globe
3409 **celebración** celebration
3410 **quehacer** task, job, chore
3412 **obsesión** mania, obsession
3413 **bronce** bronze
3415 **licencia** license, permission
3416 **motivación** motivation
3419 **depresión** depression, slump
3420 **pulmón** lung
3424 **fibra** fiber, grain
3427 **petróleo** oil, petroleum
3429 **permanencia** permanence, tenure
3431 **miércoles** Wednesday

3432 **horno** oven, furnace

3433 **logro** success, achievement

3434 **vientre** womb, belly

3435 **petición** request, petition

3436 **civil** civilian

3437 **reparto** distribution, delivery

3438 **advertencia** warning, notice

3440 **previsión** forecast, precaution

3443 **mandato** mandate, order, command

3447 **timidez** shyness, timidity

3448 **toque** touch, ringing, warning

3449 **máscara** mask

3450 **venganza** revenge, vengeance

3451 **barba** beard

3452 **alarma** alarm

3454 **aliento** breath, courage, spirit

3455 **pureza** purity, chastity

3457 **comedia** comedy, play, pretense

3458 **aldea** small village

3461 **párrafo** paragraph

3463 **brillo** shine, twinkling, sparkle

3465 **rastro** track, sign, flea market

3468 **adorno** decoration, adornment

3471 **mono** monkey

3472 **razonamiento** reasoning

3474 **pastor** shepherd, pastor

3475 **tramo** section, stretch, plot

3476 **reto** challenge, defiance

3479 **pesadilla** nightmare

3480 **centenar** hundred

3481 **molestia** bother, nuisance, trouble

3483 **paja** straw, thatching

3486 **concesión** awarding, concession

3488 **nudo** knot

3490 **martes** Tuesday

3491 **utilización** use, utilization

3492 **tapa** cover, lid

3493 **traición** treason, betrayal

3495 **pesca** fishing

3496 **malestar** discomfort, unease, unrest

3497 **rata** rat

3499 **defensor** defender

3500 **auxilio** help, aid, assistance

3503 **cobre** copper

3509 **intuición** intuition

3510 **invención** invention, contrivance

3512 **vena** vein

3513 **freno** brake

3518 **interrupción** interruption

3519 **condena** sentence (in prison), penalty

3520 **inocencia** innocence

3521 **relieve** relief; poner de relieve: to emphasize

3522 **semejanza** similarity, likeness

3523 **cumbre** summit, top

3525 **colmo** climax; para colmo: to top it all

3527 **administrador** administrator, manager

3529 **decreto** decree, order

3531 **ironía** irony

3533 **seña** sign, mark, seal

3534 **ritual** ritual, rite

3539 **escritorio** desk, bureau

3540 **solicitud** request, application

3541 **víspera** eve

3542 **insecto** insect

3543 **ridículo** ridicule

3545 **ira** rage, wrath

3546 **ceniza** ash

3548 **monja** nun

3550 **parto** birth

3554 **circuito** circuit, circumference, track

3556 **oveja** sheep, ewe

3557 **dueña** landlady, owner (f)

3559 **ubicación** position, location

3561 **hacienda** ranch

3562 **antigüedad** antiquity, seniority

3563 **puño** fist, handle, cuff

3564 **excusa** excuse

3566 **trama** plot, theme

3569 **alteración** alteration, change

3573 **acusación** accusation, charge

3575 **salvación** salvation, rescue

3577 **fundador** founder

3581 **original** original

3582 **maquinaria** machinery

3585 **tortura** torture

3586 **humano** human

3587 **insistencia** insistence, persistence

3593 **sobrino** nephew

3599 **apunte** note, annotation

3600 **antepasado** ancestor

3604 **sillón** armchair, seat

3606 **colectivo** collective, group

3607 **dieta** diet

3608 **teniente** lieutenant, deputy mayor

3609 **polo** pole, polo, polo shirt

3612 **abismo** abyss, large gap

3613 **algodón** cotton

3614 **harina** flour

3615 **exactitud** accuracy

3617 **provecho** benefit, use

3621 **prudencia** prudence, moderation

3622 **insulto** insult

3624 **flujo** flow, tide, discharge

3625 **aguja** needle, spire, stylus

3626 **planteamiento** proposal, exposition

3630 **cortina** curtain, screen

3637 **reproducción** reproduction

3638 **expansión** expansion, spreading

3639 **umbral** threshold, outset

3640 **alusión** allusion, hint

3641 **descenso** decline, descent, lowering

3646 **océano** ocean

3647 **proposición** proposition

3648 **absurdo** absurdity, nonsense

3649 **parada** (transportation) stop

3655 **titular** headline, holder

3656 **calendario** calendar

3657 **interlocutor** participant in a dialog

3660 **disgusto** disgust, annoyance

3661 **conservación** conservation

3663 **elaboración** production

3665 **correo** mail, post (office)

3666 **circo** circus

3667 **adversario** adversary

3668 **cubierta** covering, top, lid

3669 **aniversario** anniversary

3670 **franja** strip, stripe, fringe

3672 **pila** (baptismal) font, battery, heap

3677 **goma** rubber

3679 **ancho** width

3682 **uva** grape

3683 **ética** ethics

3684 **inscripción** inscription, registration

3687 **adquisición** acquisition

3690 **sentir** feeling

3693 **renuncia** resignation, renunciation

3694 **préstamo** loan, borrowing

3698 **dedicación** dedication, devotion

3699 **instituto** institute

3700 **paloma** dove

3702 **devoción** devotion

3708 **espina** thorn, spine

3709 **aprobación** approval, consent

3710 **fachada** front of a building

3712 **jugo** juice

3714 **discípulo** disciple

3715 **coronel** colonel

3717 **modificación** modification, alteration

3718 **acumulación** accumulation

3720 **mantenimiento** maintenance, sustenance

3723 **cabecera** head, header

3724 **revelación** revelation

3725 **peseta** peseta (money)

3726 **cuna** cradle, birth, lineage

3729 **ácido** acid

3730 **incapacidad** inability, incompetence

3731 **villa** village, town

3732 **lecho** (river) bed, couch

3733 **alquiler** rent, rental

3735 **redacción** editing, wording, essay

3736 **ficha** index card, chip, token

3738 **inseguridad** insecurity

3739 **coma** comma (f), coma (m)

3741 **agricultura** agriculture, farming

3742 **naturalidad** ease, spontaneity

3743 **serenidad** serenity, calm

3745 **pistola** gun, pistol

3749 **diputado** deputy, member

3751 **duelo** grief, affliction

3755 **comandante** commanding officer

3757 **ópera** opera

3758 **réplica** answer, retort, copy

3762 **pulso** pulse, pulsation

3764 **explotación** exploitation, cultivation

3765 **bestia** beast, brute

3767 **abrazo** hug, embrace

3768 **asalto** assault, robbery

3769 **reposo** rest, peace

3770 **lámina** sheet (of metal)

3771 **pasta** pasta, dough

3774 **polémica** polemics, argument

3776 **chocolate** chocolate

3777 **generosidad** generosity

3780 **realismo** realism

3783 **acorde** agreement, accord

3784 **sugerencia** suggestion

3785 **cumpleaños** birthday

3786 **ronda** round

3788 **capilla** chapel

3791 **expediente** dossier, proceedings

3792 **tolerancia** tolerance

3795 **sopa** soup

3796 **rival** rival

3797 **ternura** tenderness

3798 **variante** variant, difference

3800 **molde** mold, cast, pattern

3802 **espectro** ghost, specter

3804 **recorte** clipping, cutting, trimming

3805 **reglamento** regulations, rules

3807 **vitalidad** vitality, health

3809 **adaptación** adaptation

3810 **etiqueta** label, etiquette

3812 **muralla** city wall

3814 **represión** repression

3815 **reducción** reduction

3816 **difusión** spread, diffusion

3818 **encargo** job, order, errand

3821 **oeste** West

3824 **pescador** fisherman

3825 **diagnóstico** diagnosis

3826 **cuadra** (city) block

3829 **rienda** rein, restraint

3830 **crueldad** cruelty, harshness

3832 **ansia** anxiety, anguish

3833 **cúpula** cupola, dome

3835 **llama** flame, llama

3837 **vegetación** vegetation

3838 **lema** motto, slogan

3840 **bote** boat, container

3843 **perfume** perfume

3844 **central** headquarters

3846 **pertenencia** membership, property

3849 **casita** cottage

3851 **alianza** alliance

3856 **ratón** mouse, rat

3857 **hazaña** deed, heroic feat

3858 **dureza** hardness, toughness

3859 **sábana** (bed) sheet

3860 **revisión** checking revision

3861 **retirada** retreat, withdrawal

3863 **aroma** aroma

3864 **optimismo** optimism

3865 **mate** mate (beverage)

3867 **evento** event

3868 **físico** physicist

3870 **pasto** grass, pasture

3872 **gallo** rooster

3874 **rendimiento** yield, output, efficiency

3875 **lentitud** slowness

3876 **aula** classroom

3881 **himno** hymn, anthem

3882 **sindicato** trade union

3883 **mariposa** butterfly, wing nut

3885 **fidelidad** faithfulness, accuracy

3886 **retraso** delay

3887 **desplazamiento** movement, removal

3891 **compatriota** fellow countryman

3894 **localidad** town, locality

3898 **lobo** wolf

3899 **asamblea** assembly

3900 **pañuelo** handkerchief, shawl

3902 **temblor** tremor, shudder, shiver

3903 **gira** tour

3904 **manto** cloak

3906 **asombro** amazement, astonishment

3907 **gobernador** governor

3908 **amplitud** breadth, extent, range

3909 **carbón** coal, charcoal

3910 **campamento** camp, camping

3916 **excursión** excursion

3920 **tomate** tomato

3922 **cinturón** belt

3925 **bulto** bulk, shape

3927 **vocabulario** vocabulary

3928 **especulación** speculation, conjecture

3929 **manual** manual, handbook

3932 **disparo** shot, discharge

3934 **residuo** residue, waste

3935 **vanidad** vanity, conceit

3937 **renovación** renewal, renovation

3943 **peste** plague, pestilence, pest

3944 **expedición** expedition

3949 **mecánica** mechanics, mechanism

3950 **electricidad** electricity

3954 **ascensor** elevator

3955 **bicicleta** bicycle

3957 **aporte** contribution

3959 **beca** scholarship, grant

3961 **trigo** wheat

3965 **plataforma** platform, springboard

3966 **maestra** teacher (f)

3967 **clínica** clinic

3968 **heredero** heir, heiress

3970 **estadio** stadium

3973 **desfile** parade, line, formation

3974 **buque** ship, vessel, hull

3975 **parentesco** kinship

3976 **fallo** mistake, blunder, fault

3977 **rebeldía** rebelliousness, defiance

3979 **corrección** correction, amendment

3980 **chispa** spark

3981 **virgen** virgin

3983 **supervivencia** survival

3984 **caridad** charity

3986 **comunión** communion

3987 **embajador** ambassador

3988 **tercio** third

3989 **iluminación** illumination, lighting

3990 **censura** censorship, criticism

3991 **disputa** dispute, argument, quarrel

3992 **esplendor** splendor

3994 **perjuicio** damage, loss

3995 **medalla** medal, medallion

3996 **lealtad** loyalty, faithfulness

3997 **divorcio** divorce

3999 **enfoque** focus, approach

4001 **firmeza** firmness

4003 **colina** hill, slope

4004 **parcela** piece of property

4005 **jaula** cage, crate, playpen

4006 **ajuste** adjustment, settlement

4008 **entierro** burial

4010 **servidor** servant

4011 **superioridad** superiority

4012 **turismo** tourism

4013 **barbaridad** atrocity

4014 **rollo** roll, coil

4016 **triángulo** triangle

4017 **aislamiento** isolation

4018 **alivio** relief, unburdening

4019 **entrenamiento** training

4020 **truco** trick, ruse

4022 **disparate** nonsense, blunder

4023 **cocinero** cook

4027 **fotógrafo** photographer

4028 **imposición** imposition

4031 **consuelo** comfort, consolation

4034 **transmisión** broadcast, transmission

4036 **sendero** (foot) path

4038 **desacuerdo** disagreement

4039 **academia** academy

4041 **catedral** cathedral

4043 **vanguardia** vanguard, forefront

4051 **embarazo** pregnancy

4052 **imposibilidad** impossibility

4056 **reportaje** news report

4057 **tambor** drum

4058 **fundación** foundation

4059 **transparencia** transparency, slide

4060 **elegancia** elegance, style

4061 **criminal** criminal

4062 **elogio** praise, eulogy, compliment

4063 **manta** blanket

4068 **alerta** alert

4069 **sinceridad** sincerity

4070 **cátedra** academic chair

4072 **repertorio** repertoire, list, index

4073 **plancha** (electric) iron, plate, sheet

4074 **terraza** terrace, balcony

4075 **gala** gala (performance/dinner)

4076 **era** era, age

4077 **arranque** start, outburst, kick-start

4078 **patada** kick, punt

4080 **lapso** lapse

4081 **sudor** sweat, perspiration

4082 **apetito** appetite

4084 **indicación** indication

4086 **aliado** ally

4087 **presidencia** presidency

4089 **consejero** advisor, counselor

4091 **consigna** watchword, motto, slogan

4092 **cortesía** courtesy

4094 **atributo** attribute, quality

4095 **furia** fury, rage

4098 **estatura** stature, height

4099 **vejez** old age

4100 **terremoto** earthquake

4102 **tira** strip, strap

4103 **emisor** transmitter, emitter

4105 **integridad** integrity

4106 **autorización** authorization

4108 **seminario** seminar, seminary

4109 **marea** wave, tide, ebb

4110 **resentimiento** resentment

4111 **delincuente** delinquent

4121 **esqueleto** skeleton, framework

4122 **indignación** indignation

4125 **escultura** sculpture, carving

4127 **infinidad** infinity, countless

4128 **pilar** pillar, column

4136 **percepción** perception

4137 **minoría** minority

4138 **deterioro** deterioration, damage

4141 **sanción** sanction, approval, penalty

4146 **maleta** suitcase, case

4147 **faena** task, job, performance

4150 **serpiente** snake

4153 **agitación** agitation, excitement

4155 **ganancia** gain, profit

4157 **pino** pine (tree)

4163 **llanto** crying, weeping

4164 **ida** departure, first half of a trip

4167 **falla** flaw, failure

4168 **contribución** contribution

4169 **burla** mockery, joke, trick

4170 **seguidor** follower, supporter, fan

4172 **perla** pearl

4174 **integración** integration

4176 **siesta** siesta, afternoon nap

4182 **bigote** mustache

4184 **niñez** childhood, infancy

4185 **leña** firewood

4186 **atardecer** evening, dusk

4190 **interrogante** question, interrogator

4193 **lente** lens, [pl] glasses

4194 **compás** rhythm, time, compass

4196 **llanura** plain, prairie, plainness

4197 **collar** collar, necklace

4198 **veneno** poison, venom

4199 **mármol** marble

4200 **biografía** biography

4202 **rebelión** rebellion

4203 **hígado** liver

4204 **ladrón** thief

4207 **tablero** board, panel

4209 **imitación** imitation

4210 **adelanto** advance, progress

4214 **intervalo** interval, gap

4215 **trago** swig, drink

4216 **fracción** fraction

4217 **convento** convent, monastery

4218 **arroyo** brook, stream, gutter

4220 **enlace** link, connection, bond

4223 **diccionario** dictionary

4225 **afueras** outskirts, suburbs

4227 **ceja** eyebrow, brow

4231 **constitución** constitution

4233 **clasificación** classification

4235 **lío** mess, problem, bad situation

4236 **sede** headquarters, seat

4239 **litro** liter

4240 **bandeja** tray

4241 **aproximación** approximation

4244 **trapo** rag, cloth

4245 **conocedor** expert, judge, connoisseur

4247 **altar** altar

4248 **acierto** good aim, guess, hit

4249 **piloto** pilot, driver

4253 **computadora** computer

4255 **alambre** wire

4256 **mango** handle, mango

4258 **rosario** rosary, beads, string

4259 **reconstrucción** reconstruction

4260 **parroquia** parish

4266 **comprador** buyer

4267 **piedad** pity, mercy

4274 **niebla** fog

4278 **verbo** verb

4279 **cadera** hip

4280 **procesión** procession

4281 **encuesta** poll, survey, inquiry

4282 **cría** breeding, raising

4283 **narración** narration, account

4284 **ramo** bunch (of flowers), branch

4286 **traidor** traitor

4287 **catálogo** catalog

4288 **protector** protector, defender

4289 **amparo** protection, shelter

4290 **farmacia** pharmacy, drugstore

4291 **cima** summit, peak, top

4292 **riñón** kidney

4294 **finca** property, estate

4295 **calificación** evaluation, qualification

4296 **caudal** volume, abundance

4298 **trastorno** confusion, trouble, upheaval

4300 **jovencito** young person

4301 **incorporación** inclusion, incorporation

4302 **corral** corral, yard

4303 **fatiga** fatigue

4305 **bruja** witch, hag

4306 **exploración** exploration

4309 **ilustración** illustration

4310 **cómplice** accomplice

4311 **melodía** melody

4312 **productor** producer

4315 **portero** porter, doorkeeper, goalkeeper

4316 **conejo** rabbit

4318 **densidad** density, thickness

4320 **apuesta** wager, bet

4321 **nacionalidad** nationality

4324 **mozo** waiter, youth, bellboy

4326 **cuerno** horn, antler

4330 **talla** size (of clothing), stature

4332 **comisario** commissioner, delegate

4334 **acercamiento** approach, approximation

4339 **contorno** outline, perimeter, edge

4340 **egoísmo** selfishness

4341 **bordo** a bordo: on board

4342 **compensación** compensation

4343 **prohibición** prohibition

4348 **laberinto** maze, labyrinth

4352 **eternidad** eternity

4354 **pastilla** pill, capsule

4355 **mierda** shit, crap, excrement

4356 **contienda** contest, dispute

4361 **chorro** stream, jet, spurt

4363 **clavo** nail, tack, peg

4364 **sequía** drought

4365 **dinámica** dynamics

4366 **ocio** leisure (time)

4367 **normalidad** normality

4369 **resonancia** resonance, repercussion

4372 **chaqueta** jacket

4375 **asco** disgust

4378 **pleito** litigation, suit, dispute

4380 **sencillez** simplicity

4382 **estupidez** stupidity, stupid thing

4386 **senador** senator

4387 **rencor** grudge, spite

4393 **probabilidad** probability

4396 **gobernante** ruler, leader

4397 **merced** favor, mercy

4399 **tonelada** ton

4400 **rebelde** rebel, insurgent

4401 **anhelo** longing, yearning

4402 **princesa** princess

4404 **embajada** embassy

4408 **amargura** bitterness, sorrow

4410 **validez** validity

4411 **tacto** sense of touch, feel

4412 **codo** elbow

4415 **chimenea** chimney, fireplace

4422 **abanico** range, (handheld) fan

4427 **camiseta** T-shirt

4430 **corteza** bark, crust, rind, peel

4432 **cordillera** mountain range

4434 **longitud** length, longitude

4437 **psicología** psychology

4442 **exageración** exaggeration

4443 **apreciación** appreciation, assessment

4445 **estallido** crash, outbreak, explosion

4447 **talón** heel, check, coupon, stub

4449 **colchón** mattress

4451 **tinte** tint, dye

4453 **imprenta** printing house

4454 **bastón** (walking) cane

4456 **humillación** humiliation

4457 **trance** trance, fix, enrapture

4458 **volante** steering wheel

4463 **noble** nobleman, noble

4465 **reclamo** claim, complaint, protest

4466 **asesor** adviser, consultant

4468 **novelista** novelist

4469 **herido** wounded (person)

4474 **grueso** bulk, mass

4476 **grabación** recording

4477 **frasco** bottle, jar, flask

4480 **verdura** vegetables, greenery

4481 **violación** violation, rape

4482 **innovación** innovation

4483 **tertulia** get-together, meeting of friends

4484 **carcajada** hearty laughter, guffaw

4485 **cancha** playing field, court

4488 **aburrimiento** boredom

4493 **exportación** export, exportation

4502 **tranvía** trolley, tram, streetcar

4504 **cordón** cord, yarn, braid

4505 **prioridad** priority

4506 **modalidad** mode, manner

4507 **desenlace** outcome, result

4508 **bailarín** dancer

4509 **artefacto** artifact, device

4510 **trono** throne

4511 **adjetivo** adjective

4512 **gama** range, musical scale

4514 **gabinete** cabinet, den, office

4519 **peón** unskilled laborer, field hand

4521 **inspector** inspector

4522 **órbita** orbit, socket, field

4523 **autopista** freeway, motorway

4524 **prosa** prose

4525 **paréntesis** parenthesis, digression

4526 **fabricación** manufacture, production

4527 **lesión** injury, wound, harm

4528 **mejilla** cheek

4530 **muelle** wharf, dock

4531 **velo** veil

4532 **decoración** decoration

4533 **rancho** ranch, farm

4538 **negociación** negotiation

4539 **euforia** euphoria, elation

4540 **convencimiento** convincing

4543 **desconcierto** disorder, chaos

4544 **economista** economist

4547 **sobra** excess, surplus, leftover

4550 **tasa** rate, fee, levy

4551 **balanza** balance, (measuring) scale

4552 **factura** invoice, bill

4553 **hormiga** ant

4555 **oso** bear

4556 **trazo** line, stroke

4559 **gusano** worm, caterpillar

4562 **manía** obsession, mania

4563 **disculpa** apology, excuse

4568 **metáfora** metaphor

4569 **penetración** penetration, insight

4571 **whisky** whisky

4574 **delirio** delirium, nonsense

4577 **librería** bookstore

4578 **documentación** documentation

4580 **decena** ten (of something)

4582 **tigre** tiger

4585 **senda** path, lane

4586 **temperamento** temperament, personality

4590 **dicha** fortune, happiness, luck

4592 **acta** (meeting) proceedings, minutes

4593 **cera** wax

4594 **tanque** tank, large container

4597 **batería** battery, gun deck

4598 **crema** cream

4600 **entretenimiento** entertainment

4601 **pala** shovel

4602 **servidumbre** staff of servants, servitude

4604 **psicólogo** psychologist

4606 **actriz** actress

4610 **burro** donkey

4611 **procedencia** origin, source

4612 **fiscal** district attorney, prosecutor

4616 **participante** participant

4617 **rescate** rescue, ransom

4618 **apuro** trouble, predicament

4621 **cautela** caution

4623 **táctica** tactics, strategy

4624 **descuido** neglect, oversight

4626 **matanza** slaughter, carnage

4629 **escrito** manuscript, writing

4630 **pinta** appearance, look, aspect

4637 **caldo** broth, soup

4638 **agonía** agony, grief

4640 **tregua** truce, rest

4641 **vestuario** wardrobe, changing room

4643 **bodega** cellar, pantry, warehouse

4644 **antena** antenna

4646 **maldad** evil, wickedness

4647 **obediencia** obedience

4648 **ocurrencia** idea, witty remark

4650 **complemento** complement, supplement

4651 **editor** editor, publisher

4652 **periodismo** journalism

4653 **piscina** swimming pool

4658 **inyección** shot, injection

4660 **reproche** reproach, criticism

4661 **consistencia** consistency

4662 **nobleza** nobility, uprightness

4664 **impotencia** impotence

4667 **hostilidad** hostility, enmity

4669 **medicamento** medicine, drug

4673 **conspiración** conspiracy

4675 **detención** detention, arrest

4676 **autobús** bus

4679 **destreza** skill

4681 **entrañas** insides, bowels

4682 **gratitud** gratitude

4685 **editorial** publisher (f), editorial article (m)

4687 **bicho** bug, creature

4688 **martillo** hammer

4690 **cooperación** cooperation

4691 **elevación** rise, elevation, increase

4692 **atentado** (terrorist) attack, offense

4693 **puñado** fistful, small group

4696 **sirena** siren, mermaid

4697 **espuma** foam, lather

4698 **cirujano** surgeon

4700 **vereda** path, sidewalk

4702 **reivindicación** claim, demand, redemption

4703 **infección** infection

4704 **chiquillo** kid, youngster

4705 **distracción** distraction, amusement

4708 **ingrediente** ingredient

4712 **pugna** battle, struggle

4715 **torta** cake

4716 **intérprete** performer, interpreter

4717 **araña** spider

4718 **facción** (face) feature, faction

4722 **diplomático** diplomat

4723 **exhibición** exhibition, showing

4725 **escaparate** showcase, display window

4727 **sargento** sergeant

4730 **estética** aesthetics

4731 **caballería** cavalry, knighthood

4732 **padrino** godparent, sponsor

4733 **diversidad** diversity, variety

4734 **banquete** banquet, feast

4737 **andar** walk, gait, pace

4738 **gigante** giant

4740 **pabellón** pavilion, sports hall

4741 **abeja** bee

4745 **violín** violin

4746 **astro** star

4747 **dictador** dictator

4748 **roce** brush, graze

4749 **prolongación** extension

4750 **cráneo** skull, cranium

4755 **agradecimiento** gratitude, gratefulness

4757 **audacia** boldness, audacity

4758 **cólera** rage (f), cholera (m)

4759 **resignación** resignation, acceptance

4760 **legislación** legislation

4762 **caramelo** piece of candy, caramel

4763 **pólvora** gunpowder, powder

4764 **rol** role

4769 **idiota** idiot, dunce

4770 **bahía** bay

4771 **latitud** latitude

4772 **buey** ox

4773 **vaivén** swinging, rocking

4774 **equivocación** mistake, misconception

4775 **comunismo** communism

4776 **partícula** particle

4777 **intermedio** means, interval

4779 **limosna** alms, charity

4780 **equivalente** equivalent

4781 **flecha** arrow, dart

4784 **desilusión** disappointment, letdown

4786 **pato** duck

4788 **grieta** crack, opening, slit

4789 **jinete** rider, horseman

4794 **agricultor** farmer

4795 **garra** claw, fang

4797 **soporte** support, endorsement

4798 **concurrencia** coming together

4799 **pirámide** pyramid

4803 **fósforo** match, match stick

4804 **profeta** prophet

4807 **muslo** thigh

4809 **retiro** withdrawal, retreat

4810 **comando** command, order

4812 **emisión** broadcast, emission

4814 **tenor** a tenor de: in accordance with

4815 **recompensa** reward, recompense

4816 **complicidad** involvement, complicity

4817 **recelo** mistrust, suspicion

4818 **vibración** vibration

4819 **restricción** restriction

4822 **vara** rod, stick

4823 **clientela** customers, clients

4824 **soberanía** sovereignty

4827 **frialdad** coldness, indifference

4829 **inspección** inspection

4830 **inicial** initial (letters)

4832 **incidencia** ocurrence, impact

4833 **retroceso** movement backwards

4834 **micrófono** microphone

4836 **ventanilla** (vehicle) window

4838 **extinción** extinction

4839 **infinito** infinite, infinity

4840 **campeón** champion

4844 **oxígeno** oxygen

4845 **rigidez** rigidity

4848 **despedida** goodbye, farewell

4850 **encaje** lace

4852 **repercusión** repercussion, impact

4855 **ganador** winner

4856 **emperador** emperor

4857 **cometa** comet (m), kite (f)

4858 **precedente** precedent

4861 **mosaico** mosaic

4862 **significación** meaning, significance

4863 **contestación** answer

4865 **asilo** asylum, shelter

4866 **incremento** increase, raise

4868 **lomo** back, loin, spine

4870 **navegación** navigation, shipping

4871 **edificación** construction, building

4872 **abstracción** abstraction

4879 **mortal** mortal

4882 **cabina** cabin, cockpit

4885 **guerrero** warrior, soldier

4886 **acera** sidewalk

4892 **centavo** cent

4893 **molino** mill, windmill

4895 **decepción** disappointment

4898 **ente** entity, being, firm

4902 **inundación** flood, deluge

4903 **diligencia** diligence

4906 **complejidad** complexity

4910 **vecindad** nearness, vicinity

4912 **cabra** goat

4913 **olfato** sense of smell

4914 **denominación** name, denomination

4916 **envergadura** breadth, expanse

4917 **admirador** admirer

4919 **rebaño** herd, flock

4921 **vegetal** plant, vegetable

4923 **fiera** (wild) beast

4927 **olla** pot, kettle

4929 **coco** coconut

4930 **sótano** basement

4931 **agresividad** aggressiveness

4933 **adhesión** adherence

4934 **convención** convention, assembly

4935 **paraje** place, spot

4937 **cohete** rocket

4939 **almohada** pillow

4940 **eficiencia** efficiency

4944 **tejado** roof, housetop

4945 **elefante** elephant

4947 **navaja** razor, blade, navaja

4948 **maldición** damnation, curse

4949 **marinero** sailor

4950 **bachillerato** high school diploma

4953 **desequilibrio** imbalance, unsteadiness

4957 **desperdicio** waste, refuse, garbage

4959 **ampliación** enlargement, extension

4960 **recipiente** container, recipient, tank

4963 **despliegue** deployment, display

4964 **libra** pound (money/weight)

4965 **incursión** invasion, incursion

4967 **toalla** towel

4968 **tenis** tennis

4971 **descarga** unloading, discharge

4973 **higiene** hygiene

4975 **cuenca** socket, basin, bowl

4977 **cal** lime, whitewash

4980 **pionero** pioneer

4981 **volcán** volcano

4982 **puta** whore, prostitute

4984 **diamante** diamond

4986 **delicadeza** gentleness, tenderness

4988 **expulsión** expulsion, ejection

4989 **enigma** enigma, mystery

4991 **hectárea** hectare

4993 **inmigrante** immigrant

4995 **prevención** prevention, warning

4996 **cerco** fence, circle, ring

4997 **penumbra** semidarkness, twilight

4998 **jugada** move, play

4999 **estampa** print, engraving, illustration

5000 **cueva** cave

Verb

8 **ser** to be (norm)

11 **haber** to have (+Ved)

17 **estar** to be (location, change from norm)

18 **tener** to have

25 **hacer** to do, make

27 **poder** to be able to; can

28 **decir** to tell, say

30 **ir** to go

37 **ver** to see

39 **dar** to give

46 **saber** to know (a fact), find out

57 **querer** to want, love

66 **llegar** to arrive

67 **pasar** to pass, spend (time)

75 **deber** should, ought to; to owe

77 **poner** to put (on), get (+ADJ)

81 **parecer** to seem, look like

89 **quedar** to remain, stay

91 **creer** to believe, think

92 **hablar** to speak, talk

93 **llevar** to take, carry

94 **dejar** to let, leave

97 **seguir** to follow, keep on

100 **encontrar** to find

104 **llamar** to call, name

105 **venir** to come

106 **pensar** to think

111 **salir** to leave, go out

112 **volver** to return, to V again

122 **tomar** to take, drink

124 **conocer** to know (someone or place)

128 **vivir** to live

131 **sentir** to feel, regret

134 **tratar** to try, treat, deal with

142 **mirar** to look, watch

155 **contar** to tell, count

161 **empezar** to begin, start

163 **esperar** to wait, hope (for), expect

173 **buscar** to look for

177 **existir** to exist

179 **entrar** to enter

183 **trabajar** to work

187 **escribir** to write

190 **perder** to lose, miss

195 **producir** to produce, cause

200 **ocurrir** to happen, occur

203 **entender** to understand

204 **pedir** to ask for, request

205 **recibir** to receive

215 **recordar** to remember, remind

219 **terminar** to finish, end

220	**permitir** to allow, permit		380	**usar** to use
221	**aparecer** to appear		381	**decidir** to decide
222	**conseguir** to get, acquire, obtain		382	**repetir** to repeat
223	**comenzar** to begin, start		383	**olvidar** to forget
226	**servir** to serve		387	**valer** to be worth, cost
228	**sacar** to take out		389	**comer** to eat
229	**necesitar** to need		392	**mostrar** to show
234	**mantener** to keep, maintain		397	**ocupar** to occupy, use
238	**resultar** to result, turn out		402	**mover** to move, incite
244	**leer** to read		403	**continuar** to continue
245	**caer** to fall		406	**suceder** to happen
246	**cambiar** to change		407	**fijar** to set, fix, [se] notice
249	**presentar** to introduce, present		409	**referir** to refer (to)
251	**crear** to create		410	**acercar** to come near
252	**abrir** to open		415	**dedicar** to dedicate, devote
261	**considerar** to consider		422	**aprender** to learn
263	**oír** to hear		437	**comprar** to buy
266	**acabar** acabar de V: to have just Ved; finish		443	**subir** to go up
271	**convertir** to convert, change, become		446	**evitar** to avoid, prevent
286	**ganar** to win, earn		448	**interesar** to interest
287	**formar** to form		454	**cerrar** to close
289	**traer** to bring, carry		455	**echar** to throw, cast
290	**partir** to divide, leave; a partir de: starting		456	**responder** to answer, respond
293	**morir** to die		457	**sufrir** to suffer, undergo
296	**aceptar** to accept		464	**importar** to matter, import
299	**realizar** to fulfill, carry out		466	**obtener** to obtain
305	**suponer** to suppose, assume		478	**observar** to observe
306	**comprender** to understand		479	**indicar** to indicate
311	**lograr** to achieve, get, manage		486	**imaginar** to imagine
316	**explicar** to explain		487	**soler** to be accustomed to
323	**preguntar** to ask (a question)		490	**detener** to stop, detain
325	**tocar** to touch, play (instrument)		491	**desarrollar** to develop
327	**reconocer** to recognize, admit		493	**señalar** to point (out), signal
328	**estudiar** to study		494	**elegir** to choose, elect
329	**alcanzar** to reach, catch up with		499	**preparar** to prepare
330	**nacer** to be born		500	**proponer** to propose
331	**dirigir** to direct, manage		501	**demostrar** to show, demonstrate
332	**correr** to run		502	**significar** to mean
338	**utilizar** to use, utilize		509	**reunir** to gather, meet, collect
342	**pagar** to pay		510	**faltar** to be lacking
345	**ayudar** to help		512	**acompañar** to accompany
353	**gustar** to be pleasing to		515	**desear** to want, desire, wish for
355	**jugar** to play (sport/game)		524	**enseñar** to teach, show
360	**escuchar** to listen to		525	**construir** to construct, build
363	**cumplir** to fulfill		526	**vender** to sell
368	**ofrecer** to offer, present		527	**representar** to represent
369	**descubrir** to discover		528	**desaparecer** to disappear, vanish
372	**levantar** to raise, lift		529	**mandar** to send, order
376	**intentar** to try, attempt		536	**andar** to walk, function

541 **preferir** to prefer

542 **asegurar** to assure, secure, insure

552 **crecer** to grow, increase

553 **surgir** to appear, spring (forth)

557 **matar** to kill

558 **entregar** to deliver

562 **colocar** to place, position

565 **establecer** to establish

566 **guardar** to keep, save

568 **iniciar** to initiate, start

569 **bajar** to come down, let down

571 **notar** to notice

573 **meter** to put (into)

576 **actuar** to act

584 **pretender** to attempt

595 **acordar** to remember, remind

597 **cortar** to cut

599 **corresponder** to correspond with

601 **romper** to break

603 **adquirir** to acquire, get

611 **lanzar** to throw, launch

612 **aprovechar** to take advantage of

616 **apoyar** to support, lean on

617 **negar** to deny, refuse

618 **avanzar** to advance, progress

622 **resolver** to resolve, settle, work out

626 **costar** to cost, be hard

630 **exigir** to demand

633 **aumentar** to increase

634 **recoger** to pick up

638 **abandonar** to abandon, leave (a place)

641 **imponer** to impose, enforce

642 **obligar** to obligate, force

650 **aplicar** to apply

654 **pertenecer** to belong

658 **disponer** to have means, dispose

660 **expresar** to express

663 **provocar** to cause, provoke

665 **defender** to defend, protect

669 **quitar** to remove, take away

670 **conservar** to conserve, preserve

673 **depender** to depend on

677 **marcar** to mark, note, dial

681 **compartir** to share

688 **consistir** to consist of

689 **constituir** to constitute, consist of

691 **cubrir** to cover

692 **funcionar** to work, function

695 **caber** to fit (into)

697 **atender** to serve, attend to

699 **insistir** to insist on

710 **sentar** to sit (down), seat

716 **merecer** to deserve, be worthy (of)

720 **incluir** to include

726 **cruzar** to cross

727 **tender** to tend to, lay out

730 **anunciar** to announce, advertise

734 **despertar** to wake (up), arouse

742 **comentar** to comment on

743 **publicar** to publish

748 **cargar** to load (up), carry

750 **participar** to participate

751 **impedir** to prevent, hinder

753 **salvar** to save, rescue

757 **escapar** to escape

759 **tirar** to throw, pull

764 **contestar** to answer, reply

766 **preocupar** to worry

767 **prestar** to lend

770 **pesar** to weigh

773 **exponer** to expound, expose

790 **viajar** to travel

792 **separar** to separate

799 **regresar** to return (to a place)

807 **contemplar** to contemplate

808 **recorrer** to travel, cover (distance)

812 **durar** to last

817 **retirar** to take away, retire

821 **permanecer** to stay, remain

822 **asistir** to attend

825 **organizar** to organize

829 **contener** to contain

834 **visitar** to visit

835 **informar** to inform

842 **enviar** to send

846 **cuidar** to take care of

847 **intervenir** to intervene

851 **extender** to extend, spread

852 **comprobar** to verify, prove

857 **dormir** to sleep

859 **discutir** to argue, discuss

862 **enfrentar** to confront, face

868 **conducir** to lead, drive

870 **firmar** to sign

880 **respetar** to respect

883 **sostener** to support, hold up

887 **advertir** to notice, warn

891 **transformar** to transform, change

899	**bastar** to be sufficient	1058	**comparar** to compare
905	**mencionar** to mention, cite	1059	**celebrar** to celebrate
910	**plantear** to propose, present	1068	**sonar** to sound, ring
911	**probar** to test, prove, try	1069	**manifestar** to express, show
916	**manejar** to drive, handle	1070	**controlar** to control
918	**unir** to unite, join (together)	1071	**saltar** to jump, leap, hop
919	**caminar** to walk	1077	**citar** to cite, quote
920	**coincidir** to coincide, agree	1081	**requerir** to require
925	**llenar** to fill	1087	**incorporar** to incorporate, include
926	**dominar** to dominate, master	1094	**perseguir** to persecute, pursue, chase
929	**medir** to measure	1100	**procurar** to try, seek
937	**atravesar** to cross	1105	**casar** to marry
941	**destacar** to emphasize, stand out	1116	**someter** to subject
944	**pronunciar** to pronounce	1117	**fundar** to found, base
945	**distinguir** to distinguish	1123	**elevar** to elevate, raise
949	**introducir** to introduce, bring in	1124	**cantar** to sing
952	**comunicar** to communicate	1132	**asumir** to assume, take on
954	**invitar** to invite	1133	**aclarar** to clarify, clear up
958	**instalar** to install	1134	**arrastrar** to drag, pull
959	**tardar** to delay, take long	1136	**declarar** to declare, testify
960	**mejorar** to improve, get better	1147	**nombrar** to name, appoint
962	**emplear** to employ	1149	**confundir** to confuse
964	**convenir** to be agreeable, be convenient	1151	**describir** to describe
965	**recuperar** to recuperate, recover	1155	**calcular** to calculate, figure out
974	**definir** to define	1156	**conformar** to conform
975	**superar** to overcome, surpass	1158	**pintar** to paint
978	**afirmar** to assert, affirm	1161	**repartir** to divide, deliver, distribute
983	**interpretar** to interpret	1166	**hallar** to find (out)
985	**admitir** to admit	1167	**ordenar** to put in order, organize
986	**identificar** to identify	1169	**convencer** to convince, persuade
991	**afectar** to affect	1174	**rodear** to surround
996	**reducir** to reduce	1176	**reflejar** to reflect
998	**montar** to ride, mount, assemble	1182	**rechazar** to reject
1001	**parar** to stop (moving)	1183	**contribuir** to contribute
1003	**devolver** to return, give back	1193	**vencer** to overcome, conquer
1004	**ejercer** to practice, exercise	1196	**alejar** to move away
1005	**poseer** to possess, own	1202	**transmitir** to transmit, broadcast
1006	**proteger** to protect	1203	**marchar** to go, leave, march
1007	**causar** to cause, bring about	1207	**destruir** to destroy, ruin
1009	**determinar** to determine, decide	1209	**opinar** to think, be of the opinion
1013	**cobrar** to charge (money)	1213	**cometer** to commit
1015	**dividir** to divide	1219	**trasladar** to move, transfer
1018	**inventar** to invent, make up	1221	**concluir** to conclude, finish
1021	**limitar** to limit	1225	**oponer** to oppose
1026	**luchar** to fight, wrestle	1227	**figurar** to appear, represent, figure (in)
1044	**acudir** to attend, go to, frequent	1233	**concentrar** to concentrate
1048	**analizar** to analyze	1247	**ignorar** to be unaware
1054	**encargar** to entrust, [se] take charge of	1252	**dudar** to (have) doubt
1057	**destinar** to assign, appoint	1257	**descansar** to rest

1267 **adoptar** to adopt

1268 **arrancar** to start (machine), uproot

1269 **disfrutar** to enjoy

1272 **molestar** to bother, disturb, upset

1276 **atrever** to dare

1289 **ceder** to give way, yield

1293 **atraer** to attract

1301 **acumular** to accumulate, amass

1303 **practicar** to practice

1304 **gozar** to enjoy

1308 **justificar** to justify, excuse

1310 **soportar** to endure, stand (something)

1312 **resistir** to resist, endure

1317 **vestir** to wear, dress

1320 **sorprender** to surprise

1322 **proceder** to proceed, start

1323 **condenar** to convict, condemn

1326 **consumir** to consume, take in

1327 **sugerir** to suggest, hint at

1331 **conceder** to grant, concede

1336 **componer** to compose, be part of

1351 **arreglar** to fix, arrange

1354 **animar** to cheer up

1361 **apuntar** to point, note, aim

1363 **liberar** to free, liberate

1369 **añadir** to add

1371 **girar** to rotate, revolve

1376 **volar** to fly

1381 **facilitar** to facilitate

1384 **solicitar** to solicit, request

1387 **temer** to fear

1393 **atacar** to attack

1395 **pegar** to hit, stick (on)

1396 **juzgar** to judge

1405 **interrumpir** to interrupt

1408 **fabricar** to manufacture

1423 **confiar** to trust, confide

1424 **operar** to operate

1430 **basar** to base on, base upon

1433 **estimar** to estimate, hold in esteem

1435 **confirmar** to confirm

1439 **integrar** to integrate, fit in

1443 **aprobar** to pass (test), approve

1448 **grabar** to record, engrave

1457 **equivocar** to be wrong

1466 **llorar** to cry

1471 **proyectar** to project

1476 **beber** to drink

1483 **apreciar** to appreciate

1484 **experimentar** to experience, experiment

1486 **amar** to love

1492 **robar** to rob, steal

1493 **reír** to laugh (at)

1500 **mezclar** to mix

1503 **distribuir** to distribute, deliver

1505 **apartar** to move away, separate

1507 **reclamar** to demand, require

1509 **quemar** to burn

1513 **obedecer** to obey

1517 **satisfacer** to satisfy

1518 **concebir** to conceive, understand

1521 **reaccionar** to react

1524 **acusar** to accuse

1526 **gastar** to spend (money)

1528 **regalar** to give (as a gift)

1530 **quejar** to complain

1531 **penetrar** to penetrate, come in

1534 **rendir** [se] to give in; to render

1536 **registrar** to register, record

1537 **limpiar** to clean

1539 **atribuir** to attribute

1541 **ocultar** to hide

1543 **enterar** to find out [se]

1545 **ajustar** to adjust, tighten

1552 **aspirar** to aspire, want

1555 **recurrir** to resort to

1574 **huir** to flee, run away

1575 **percibir** to perceive, notice

1579 **transcurrir** to occur, take place

1581 **recomendar** to recommend

1585 **corregir** to correct, rectify

1587 **consultar** to consult

1590 **padecer** to suffer

1592 **elaborar** to make, develop

1593 **soñar** to dream

1597 **gritar** to shout

1603 **traducir** to translate

1608 **sumar** to add up, amount to

1609 **alimentar** to feed, support

1612 **eliminar** to eliminate, exclude

1621 **renunciar** to give up, renounce

1628 **acostumbrar** to be accustomed to

1632 **revisar** to check, revise, inspect

1633 **carecer** to be without

1641 **prometer** to promise

1645 **descender** to descend

1654 **reproducir** to reproduce, repeat

1655 **constar** to consist of, comprise

1661	**asociar** to associate with		1909	**ascender** to ascend, be promoted
1662	**desconocer** to not know, not recognize		1911	**complicar** to complicate, make difficult
1664	**fallar** to fail, miss		1917	**engañar** to trick, deceive
1678	**perdonar** to forgive, excuse		1919	**agotar** to exhaust, wear out, run out
1681	**agradecer** to thank for		1923	**precisar** to do exactly, specify
1682	**admirar** to admire		1929	**suspender** to suspend, hang, fail
1691	**revelar** to reveal, disclose		1931	**ampliar** to enlarge, increase, expand
1708	**agregar** to add, gather		1936	**cultivar** to cultivate, produce
1718	**completar** to complete		1938	**explotar** to explode, exploit
1726	**combatir** to fight against		1940	**despedir** to say goodbye (to), dismiss
1738	**aportar** to provide, contribute		1943	**colaborar** to collaborate, work together
1739	**derivar** to derive, come (from)		1945	**invertir** to invest
1741	**prohibir** to prohibit, forbid		1958	**provenir** to come from, be from
1742	**proporcionar** to supply		1959	**forzar** to force
1744	**saludar** to greet, say hello		1962	**criar** to bring up, rear
1745	**relacionar** to relate		1972	**confesar** to confess, admit
1749	**investigar** to investigate		1981	**doblar** to bend, turn
1750	**ubicar** to find, locate		1982	**disminuir** to decrease, diminish
1758	**modificar** to modify		1983	**averiguar** to investigate, find out
1762	**lavar** to wash		1984	**sospechar** to suspect, suppose
1764	**invadir** to invade, overcome		1985	**pasear** to go for a walk, ride
1771	**desplazar** to replace, move, shift		1995	**depositar** to deposit, place, store
1777	**adelantar** to move forward		1996	**captar** to capture, attract
1780	**examinar** to examine, inspect		1998	**empeñar** [se] to insist on
1786	**sustituir** to substitute, replace		1999	**sobrevivir** to survive, outlive
1788	**implicar** to implicate, imply		2022	**influir** to (have) influence
1791	**ingresar** to join, deposit, admit		2034	**multiplicar** to multiply
1792	**respirar** to breathe		2037	**doler** to hurt
1802	**esconder** to hide, conceal		2044	**favorecer** to favor, help
1809	**alterar** to alter, modify		2048	**escoger** to choose
1811	**emitir** to emit, give (off)		2049	**colgar** to hang (up)
1814	**inclinar** to bow, tilt, incline		2053	**llover** to rain
1819	**desprender** to detach, release, remove		2056	**absorber** to absorb, soak up
1822	**circular** to circulate, go around, flow		2063	**imitar** to imitate, copy, mimic
1823	**pelear** to fight, struggle		2068	**educar** to educate
1828	**aconsejar** to advise, counsel		2069	**comprometer** to compromise
1846	**arrojar** to throw, fling		2070	**aproximar** to come near, closer
1849	**criticar** to criticize		2071	**bailar** to dance
1850	**hundir** to sink, submerge		2072	**inspirar** to inspire, inhale
1861	**encerrar** to shut (in)		2074	**agarrar** to grasp, catch
1869	**denominar** to call, name		2077	**prolongar** to extend, prolong
1875	**impulsar** to push, promote, drive		2087	**adaptar** to adapt
1877	**empujar** to push, shove		2089	**situar** to situate, place, locate
1881	**dictar** to dictate, announce		2097	**curar** to cure
1883	**chocar** to crash into, collide with		2100	**desempeñar** to carry out, fulfill
1890	**borrar** to erase		2102	**extraer** to extract, take out
1895	**aguantar** to endure, put up with		2104	**apagar** to turn off, extinguish
1896	**coger** to hold, take, catch		2105	**prever** to foresee, anticipate, forecast
1904	**golpear** to hit, strike		2110	**expulsar** to expel, throw out

2122 **exhibir** to exhibit, show off

2129 **tapar** to cover, wrap

2130 **acceder** to consent, agree, accede

2133 **encender** to turn on

2141 **disparar** to shoot (at)

2153 **atar** to tie (up)

2157 **generar** to generate

2163 **abarcar** to encompass, comprise

2170 **brindar** to offer

2184 **solucionar** to solve, settle

2196 **acomodar** to be/make comfortable

2210 **variar** to change, vary

2224 **otorgar** to give, grant, award

2227 **cesar** to cease, stop

2239 **amenazar** to threaten

2245 **callar** to be/make quiet

2247 **vigilar** to watch over, guard

2250 **orientar** guide, show the way

2254 **portar** to behave [se], carry

2268 **avisar** to inform, announce

2269 **renovar** to renew, renovate

2272 **soltar** to release, loosen, let out

2273 **abordar** to board, get in/on

2274 **castigar** to punish

2277 **fracasar** to fail, to unsuccessful

2279 **calificar** to grade, rate, qualify

2280 **juntar** to bring together

2285 **ejecutar** to execute, carry out

2288 **protestar** to protest, object

2292 **impresionar** to impress

2294 **comportar** to behave

2317 **dibujar** to draw, sketch

2322 **gobernar** to govern

2324 **deshacer** to undo, destroy, take apart

2328 **reconstruir** to reconstruct

2332 **denunciar** to denounce

2345 **garantizar** to guarantee

2348 **combinar** to combine

2356 **divertir** to amuse, entertain

2358 **conquistar** to conquer, win (over)

2363 **envolver** to wrap

2365 **emprender** to undertake, embark on

2366 **anticipar** to anticipate, advance

2375 **quebrar** to break, bend, weaken

2382 **equilibrar** to balance

2383 **asomar** to appear, show, stick (out)

2384 **optar** to choose, opt for

2401 **estallar** to break out, explode, start

2402 **copiar** to copy

2403 **inaugurar** to inaugurate, start

2404 **apretar** to squeeze, tighten, compress

2416 **mentir** to (tell a) lie

2418 **contratar** to hire, contract

2452 **retener** to keep, retain

2454 **prender** to turn on, apprehend

2462 **formular** to formulate

2472 **fumar** to smoke

2474 **especializar** to specialize, major in

2476 **caracterizar** to characterize, portray

2479 **designar** to designate

2486 **competir** to compete

2496 **secar** to dry

2502 **imprimir** to print

2507 **conversar** to converse, talk

2509 **lamentar** to regret

2511 **alzar** to lift, raise

2515 **iluminar** to illuminate, light up

2522 **guiar** to guide, lead, steer

2523 **efectuar** to carry out, cause to happen

2531 **calentar** to warm, heat

2534 **proseguir** to continue, carry on

2552 **cansar** to tire, annoy

2555 **heredar** to inherit

2556 **librar** to liberate, set free

2558 **brillar** to shine, twinkle, be outstanding

2559 **rescatar** to rescue, save

2564 **extrañar** to miss, long for

2565 **asustar** to frighten, scare

2570 **anotar** to annotate, jot, note

2580 **remontar** to go back to (time)

2599 **convocar** to convene, summon

2621 **generalizar** to generalize, popularize

2624 **habitar** to inhabit

2627 **armar** to arm, put together

2637 **anular** to annul, cancel

2649 **alargar** to enlarge, elongate

2662 **estimular** to stimulate, encourage

2667 **pisar** to step on

2673 **violar** to violate, trespass, rape

2681 **enriquecer** to enrich

2689 **alegrar** to be/make happy

2690 **transportar** to transport, carry

2697 **triunfar** to triumph

2715 **acoger** to welcome, accept

2717 **sembrar** to sow, plant

2718 **acentuar** to accent, stress

2722 **entretener** to entertain, amuse

2723 **desviar** to deviate, divert, change

2724 **retroceder** to go back

2731 **sonreír** to smile

2733 **relatar** to tell, narrate

2740 **difundir** to spread (out)

2741 **lucir** to show (off), shine

2750 **reservar** to reserve, book

2752 **sacrificar** to sacrifice

2755 **exagerar** to exaggerate

2764 **residir** to reside, live (in)

2767 **promover** to promote

2770 **reparar** to repair, restore

2773 **administrar** to administer, manage

2775 **ahorrar** to save (money, time)

2779 **enterrar** to bury

2782 **contraer** to contract, shrink, abbreviate

2788 **reflexionar** to reflect, consider on

2810 **centrar** to center, focus, base (on)

2819 **originar** to give rise (to), cause

2821 **ahogar** to drown, choke, flood

2823 **esforzar** to make an effort, exert oneself

2826 **detectar** to detect

2829 **autorizar** to authorize, legalize

2832 **afrontar** to face, confront

2836 **restar** to subtract, minimize

2839 **concretar** to materialize, fulfill

2840 **picar** to bite, sting, itch

2846 **jurar** to swear, take an oath

2847 **rezar** to pray, recite

2857 **inducir** to lead to

2859 **encantar** to be very pleasing to

2868 **privar** to deprive (of)

2869 **deducir** to deduce, infer

2870 **redactar** to edit, write, compose

2872 **planear** to plan

2873 **abrazar** to hug, embrace

2874 **tolerar** to tolerate, put up with

2877 **descartar** to discard, reject, rule out

2879 **sujetar** to fasten, attach, hold

2892 **trazar** to draw, trace

2896 **presionar** to press, pressure

2900 **reiterar** to reiterate, repeat

2905 **distraer** to distract

2907 **tropezar** to trip, stumble

2910 **diseñar** to design, develop

2911 **proveer** to provide

2912 **seleccionar** to select

2913 **convivir** to coexist

2916 **progresar** to progress

2923 **abundar** to be plentiful

2928 **asimilar** to assimilate

2941 **tejer** to sew, weave

2944 **proclamar** to proclaim

2949 **plantar** to plant

2951 **derrotar** to defeat, beat

2952 **frenar** to brake, restrain

2954 **adivinar** to guess, solve

2958 **pescar** to fish

2965 **tragar** to swallow

2967 **flotar** to float, flutter

2969 **sacudir** to shake, jolt

2976 **suprimir** to suppress, delete

2978 **sobrar** to be too much, left over

2979 **brotar** to sprout

2994 **valorar** to value

2995 **diferenciar** to differentiate, distinguish

3006 **compensar** to compensate, make up for

3008 **asignar** to assign, allocate

3010 **suscitar** to arouse, provoke

3011 **finalizar** to end, finalize

3012 **reforzar** to reinforce, strengthen

3018 **evolucionar** to evolve, develop

3020 **presidir** to preside over

3027 **agitar** to shake, move

3036 **oler** to smell

3037 **aludir** to allude to

3041 **resumir** to summarize

3047 **burlar** to mock

3049 **encajar** to insert, fit well

3050 **nadar** to swim

3053 **acelerar** to accelerate, speed (up)

3058 **desplegar** to unfold, deploy

3059 **desembocar** to flow, lead into

3063 **aliviar** to lighten, relieve, comfort

3066 **cazar** to hunt

3068 **aplaudir** to clap, applaud

3071 **motivar** to motivate, cause

3072 **descuidar** to neglect

3077 **acostar** to put/go to bed

3084 **conectar** to connect, plug in

3087 **arder** to burn, glow

3102 **localizar** to locate, find, localize

3109 **herir** to wound, hurt

3119 **precipitar** to plunge, hurl, rush

3121 **excluir** to exclude, reject

3124 **adorar** to worship, adore

3129 **beneficiar** to benefit

3141 **despreciar** to despise, scorn

3144 **improvisar** to improvise

3145 **emerger** to emerge, surface

3146 **clavar** to nail

3153 **volcar** to turn/knock over, empty

3156 **barrer** sweep, clean out

3160 **rogar** to implore, pray, ask

3162 **programar** to plan, program

3166 **ensayar** to test

3172 **votar** to vote

3174 **aislar** to isolate, insulate

3179 **rodar** to roll, run, scatter

3183 **arriesgar** to risk, venture

3186 **bautizar** to baptize, christen

3188 **desatar** to untie, unleash, spark off

3189 **alentar** to encourage

3190 **descargar** to unleash, unload

3193 **enamorar** to fall in love

3198 **reemplazar** to replace

3201 **soplar** to blow (wind)

3222 **regir** to rule, govern, manage

3224 **bañar** to bathe, take a bath

3226 **rozar** to touch (lightly)

3234 **remitir** to remit

3240 **disolver** to dissolve

3243 **velar** to watch over

3254 **persistir** to persist

3255 **temblar** to tremble, shake

3261 **cenar** to dine

3263 **tornar** to transform, turn

3267 **perjudicar** to endanger

3270 **prevenir** to avoid, prevent

3276 **culminar** to culminate, accomplish

3288 **preceder** to precede

3303 **alternar** to alternate

3308 **acertar** to get right

3313 **batir** to beat (object)

3320 **demorar** to delay, take time

3331 **calmar** to calm, soothe, relieve

3340 **presumir** to boast, show off, suppose

3350 **fluir** to flow

3352 **asesinar** to murder, assassinate

3361 **preservar** to preserve

3364 **disimular** to disguise, hide, pretend

3366 **perfeccionar** to perfect

3372 **cocinar** to cook

3375 **navegar** to navigate, sail

3391 **aplastar** to flatten, crush, smash

3396 **subrayar** to underline, emphasize

3421 **apoderar** to take power

3422 **debatir** to debate, discuss

3423 **reponer** to replace, restore

3425 **disputar** to dispute, contest

3439 **arrebatar** to snatch, grab

3444 **odiar** to hate

3453 **insinuar** to insinuate, hint

3456 **fallecer** to pass away (to die)

3460 **eludir** to evade, avoid, elude

3464 **ocasionar** to occasion, bring about

3489 **retomar** to retake, restart

3494 **asentar** to settle, establish, locate

3501 **estrechar** to tighten, make closer

3502 **traspasar** to go beyond, cross over

3516 **consumar** to complete, carry out

3517 **asaltar** to assault

3528 **arrepentir** to repent, regret

3532 **felicitar** to congratulate

3538 **presenciar** to be present at, witness

3544 **derrumbar** to knock down, demolish

3558 **dañar** to damage

3565 **asombrar** to amaze, astound

3578 **oscilar** oscillate

3580 **recobrar** to recover, regain

3584 **vaciar** to empty, pour out

3588 **morder** to bite

3589 **atrapar** to trap, catch

3591 **amanecer** to dawn, get light

3594 **recitar** to recite

3595 **explorar** to explore

3597 **embarcar** to embark, load

3598 **aguardar** to wait for, await

3602 **parir** to give birth

3603 **refugiar** to take shelter, give refuge

3610 **verificar** to verify

3616 **extinguir** to extinguish, put out

3619 **agradar** to please

3620 **sobrepasar** excel, out perform

3623 **narrar** to narrate, tell

3628 **florecer** to flower, bloom, flourish

3631 **acarrear** to bring up, entail

3634 **profundizar** to deepen, analyze in depth

3635 **apostar** to wager, bet

3642 **clasificar** to classify, sort, file

3643 **recortar** to trim, cut off, clip

3651 **deslizar** to slide, glide, slip

3652 **estirar** to stretch, strain

3658 **abusar** to abuse

3659 **complementar** to complement, supplement

3662 **revivir** to revive

3664 **conmover** to move, affect

3671 **charlar** to chat, talk

3675 **equivaler** to be equivalent, tantamount (to)

3676 **fomentar** to foster, promote, encourage

3686 **reanudar** to renew, resume

3688 **mudar** to move, change

3692 **prescindir** to do without

3696 **besar** to kiss

3701 **resaltar** to emphasize

3704 **intercambiar** to exchange

3705 **consolar** to console

3706 **descomponer** to decompose, break down

3707 **enfocar** to focus

3713 **traicionar** to betray

3734 **contrastar** to contrast

3740 **desenvolver** to clear up, unwrap

3746 **interrogar** to question, interrogate

3748 **subsistir** to subsist, survive

3752 **revolver** to stir, mix, scramble

3754 **retornar** to return, give back

3761 **alquilar** to rent, hire

3763 **radicar** to lie, be situated

3766 **mojar** to make wet, dampen

3772 **derribar** to knock down, overthrow

3779 **sobresalir** to stand out, excel

3781 **filtrar** to seep, filter

3787 **movilizar** to mobilize

3790 **apelar** to call upon, appeal to

3793 **entusiasmar** to fill with enthusiasm, excite

3799 **coser** to sew

3819 **madurar** to mature, ripen

3820 **almorzar** to have lunch

3822 **albergar** to lodge, harbor

3823 **complacer** to please, satisfy

3827 **remover** to remove

3828 **pecar** to sin

3831 **acontecer** to happen, come about

3834 **desbordar** to overflow, spill over

3836 **alegar** to plead, argue

3839 **encarar** to front, confront

3848 **tranquilizar** to calm down

3850 **emigrar** to emigrate

3855 **desechar** to discard

3869 **estrenar** to use for the first time, debut

3877 **incitar** to incite

3884 **propiciar** to favor, foster, aid

3888 **cuestionar** to question

3893 **fundir** to melt, cast, smelt

3895 **reprimir** to repress

3901 **meditar** to meditate, ponder

3917 **predicar** to preach

3918 **encarnar** to embody

3921 **negociar** to negotiate, deal (with/in)

3931 **honrar** to honor

3933 **desencadenar** to unleash, unchain

3936 **ofender** to offend

3938 **enfriar** to cool

3941 **ilustrar** to illustrate

3942 **ratificar** to ratify

3945 **destrozar** to rip/break into pieces

3947 **simular** to pretend, simulate

3960 **consentir** to consent to, pamper

3962 **paralizar** to paralyze

3963 **disipar** to dissipate, disperse

3964 **incrementar** to increase

3982 **reprochar** to reproach

3985 **alumbrar** to light, illuminate

3993 **inscribir** to register, record

3998 **dotar** to endow, bestow

4009 **reventar** to burst, puncture

4024 **aburrir** to bore, tire

4029 **diluir** to dilute, weaken

4035 **titular** to title, call

4037 **frecuentar** to frequent, visit

4044 **desafiar** to defy, stand up to

4050 **despojar** to deprive, rob

4054 **reinar** to reign, prevail

4065 **hervir** to boil

4079 **disculpar** to excuse

4085 **perdurar** to last, live on, endure

4090 **inundar** to flood, inundate

4101 **articular** to articulate

4112 **debilitar** to weaken, debilitate

4113 **fingir** to feign, pretend

4114 **igualar** to equate, equalize

4116 **trepar** to climb

4131 **regular** to regulate, adjust

4133 **rematar** to finish off, finish up

4139 **argumentar** to argue, deduce

4142 **poblar** to populate, inhabit

4143 **contradecir** to contradict, be inconsistent

4145 **manipular** to manipulate, handle

4148 **regar** to water, irrigate

4149 **evocar** to evoke, recall

4154 **prosperar** to prosper, thrive

4158 **arrasar** to raze, ravage

4159 **rebajar** to discount

4160 **entrevistar** to interview

4177 **replicar** to reply

4179 **adornar** to adorn, to decorate

4183 **concurrir** to coincide, concur, meet

4187 **restaurar** to restore, reinstate

4188 **retrasar** to delay, fall behind

4191 **palpar** to feel, touch, fondle

4205 **aparentar** to give the appearance

4212 **oscurecer** to get dark

4221 **torcer** to twist, bend, distort

4222 **derramar** to shed, pour out

4226 **agravar** to aggravate

4229 **interponer** to interpose, intervene

4230 **topar** to run into, bump into

4232 **enlazar** to link, connect

4237 **colar** to slip in [se]

4246 **encaminar** to head for, guide

4252 **invocar** to invoke

4254 **ostentar** to flaunt, show off

4257 **configurar** to make up, comprise

4265 **prevalecer** to prevail

4272 **engendrar** to engender, beget

4273 **contagiar** to infect, infest

4276 **consagrar** to consecrate, establish

4299 **ceñir** to adhere to, fit tightly

4314 **constatar** to prove, verify

4319 **dispersar** to disperse, scatter, spread

4323 **vacilar** to vacillate, hesitate

4325 **capturar** to capture

4327 **remediar** to heal, cure

4328 **fiar** to vouch for, confide, trust

4329 **desfilar** to march, parade

4337 **reaparecer** to reappear

4344 **obrar** to work, act

4346 **coronar** to crown, top

4347 **liquidar** to liquidate, sell (off)

4353 **repasar** to review, revise

4368 **intuir** to sense

4370 **devorar** to devour, consume

4373 **aferrar** to grasp, clutch

4376 **consolidar** to consolidate

4377 **apresurar** to hurry up, speed up

4379 **latir** to beat (heart)

4389 **apurar** to speed up, hurry up

4390 **insultar** to insult, berate

4392 **sustentar** to maintain, support

4398 **acariciar** to stroke, fondle, caress

4407 **vincular** to conenct, link, bind

4409 **fortalecer** to fortify

4413 **vibrar** to vibrate, tremble

4414 **calzar** to wear (shoes)

4419 **evaluar** to evaluate, assess

4420 **emocionar** to move, make/get excited

4421 **editar** to edit, publish, release

4431 **sumergir** to submerge, plunge

4435 **espantar** to scare, frighten

4441 **agrupar** to (put in) group

4448 **atener** to abide by, comply with

4460 **encabezar** to head, lead (off)

4475 **chupar** to suck

4490 **inquietar** to make uneasy, disturb

4495 **expandir** to expand

4496 **predecir** to predict

4498 **condicionar** to condition, determine

4503 **alertar** to alert, warn

4513 **enfermar** to become ill

4515 **indagar** to investigate

4534 **exceder** to excel, exceed

4535 **joder** to f**k, screw (around/up)

4537 **alarmar** to alarm

4542 **rascar** to scratch, scrape

4548 **enredar** to entangle, ensnare

4558 **suspirar** to sigh

4561 **conferir** to confer

4567 **predominar** to predominate

4573 **despejar** to clear (up)

4583 **premiar** to award

4588 **desayunar** to have breakfast

4603 **resucitar** to resuscitate

4615 **financiar** to finance

4619 **sudar** to sweat

4627 **perturbar** to perturb, upset

4631 **envidiar** to envy

4632 **reposar** to rest, lie down

4639 **deteriorar** to deteriorate

4642 **desesperar** to despair, lose hope

4645 **ligar** to tie, link, bind

4655 **mediar** to mediate

4656 **endurecer** harden, make hard

4665 **vislumbrar** to glimpse

4670 **entrenar** to train

4680 **razonar** to reason (out), think

4683 **rectificar** to rectify, straighten (out)

4701 **excitar** to excite

4706 **enumerar** to enumerate, count

4709 **posar** to rest, pose, land

4711 **irritar** to irritate

4720 **tumbar** to knock over, cast down

4721 **adentrar** to penetrate, go inside

4724 **relajar** to relax

4728 **recrear** to recreate, amuse

4736 **impartir** to impart, administer

4742 **asentir** to assent, agree

4751 **aflojar** to loosen

4766 **ensuciar** to get dirty

4767 **largar** to let go, start out

4783 **presentir** to sense in advance

4785 **insertar** to insert, put in

4791 **discurrir** to flow, pass, roam

4796 **engordar** to fatten, get fat

4800 **aventurar** to venture, risk

4802 **demandar** to claim, sue

4805 **renacer** to be reborn, reappear

4806 **restablecer** to reestablish, restore

4811 **sobrevenir** to occur, befall, strike

4813 **rebasar** to exceed, pass over

4820 **acatar** to comply with, abide by

4821 **transitar** to roam, go by

4826 **percatar** to inform, become aware

4828 **encomendar** to commend, entrust

4831 **seducir** to seduce, tempt

4841 **incidir** to influence, affect

4849 **vengar** to take revenge, avenge

4851 **estropear** to ruin, mess up

4854 **fascinar** to fascinate

4867 **incurrir** to incur, fall into

4869 **tentar** to tempt, entice

4878 **resignar** to resign, relinquish

4883 **dialogar** to confer, talk

4890 **adherir** to adhere, attach

4896 **alojar** to host, accommodate

4899 **internar** to confine

4915 **bordear** to border

4918 **instruir** to instruct

4924 **verter** to pour, spill, shed

4925 **desmentir** to contradict

4946 **descifrar** to decipher

4952 **entablar** to start, establish

4958 **propagar** to propagate, spread

4969 **perfilar** to outline, shape

4974 **decaer** to decay, wane

4979 **disfrazar** to disguise, hide, conceal

4994 **irrumpir** to burst in, raid